THE
UNFOLDING TRADITION

Jewish Law After Sinai

About the cover:

The cover image features the central panel from Avner Moriah's mural, "Gathering at Mount Sinai," which is on permanent display at the Jewish Theological Seminary.

The circular frame portrays the Israelites' journey into Egypt and their exodus out. The revelation at the mountain is depicted in the dispersal of the people, moving away from the mountain. Moses' ascents and descents are shown in the various mountains that merge into one large mountain in the background. The juxtaposition of the images raises questions about how we interpret revelation, and inspires us to ask if there was only one revelation at Sinai, or if this was part of a continual interpretive process. That interpretive process determines how we understand the authority and interpretation of Jewish law, which is the central theme of this book.

The artist, Avner Moriah, was born in Jerusalem, where he now lives and works. He holds an MFA from Yale University, and his works have been acquired by the Metropolitan Museum of Art, the Jewish Museum of New York, and the Israel Museum, among others.

THE
UNFOLDING TRADITION

Jewish Law After Sinai

ELLIOT N. DORFF

AVIV PRESS

NEW YORK

Library of Congress Cataloging-in-Publication Data

Dorff, Elliot N.
    The unfolding tradition: Jewish law after Sinai / by Elliot N.
Dorff.
        p. cm.
    Includes bibliographical references and index.
    ISBN 0-916219-29-1 (alk. paper)
    1. Jewish law.   2. Jewish law—Philosophy.   3. Conservative
Judaism.   I. Title.

BM521.D67 2005
296.1'8'0882968342—dc22   2004065982

Published by Aviv Press
An imprint of the Rabbinical Assembly
3080 Broadway, New York, NY 10027

*The author and publisher gratefully acknowledge a generous donation
from Richard M. Wortman, which helped offset the costs of publication.
This gift is in memory of Irwin M. Wortman, a man who had a deep sense
of justice and devoted himself to making the world a better place.*

Cover image by Avner Moriah, center panel from *Gathering at Mount
Sinai*, 2001. Used with permission.

Cover design by Rebecca Neimark

Printed in the United States of America

In honor of Professor Arthur Rosett,

With whom I have taught a course on Jewish law
    at the U.C.L.A. School of Law ever since 1974,

With whom I wrote *A Living Tree: The Roots and
    Growth of Jewish Law,* a book on Jewish law as a
    legal system,

And from whom I have learned to see many
    of the theoretical foundations of Jewish law
    through its comparison to Anglo-American law.

An extraordinary teacher and thinker, and a wonderful
    friend.

Make for yourself a teacher, and acquire a friend.

(Avot 1:6)

Give ear, my people, to my teaching,
    turn your ear to what I say.

I will expound a theme,
    hold forth on the lessons of the past,
    things we have heard and known,
    that our fathers have told us.

We will not withhold them from their children,
    telling the coming generation
    the praises of the LORD and His might,
    and the wonders He performed.

He established a decree in Jacob,
    ordained a teaching in Israel,
    charging our fathers to make them
    known to their children, that a future
    generation might know
    – children yet to be born –
    and in turn tell their children
    that they might put their confidence in God,
    and not forget God's great deeds,
    but observe His commandments . . .

(Psalm 78:1–7)

TABLE OF CONTENTS

Note

The following abbreviations are used in this volume:

M. = Mishnah

T. = Tosefta

B. = Bavli (Babylonian Talmud)

Y. = Yerushalmi (Jerusalem or Palestinian Talmud)

Selections have been reproduced in this volume as they appeared in their original publication; no attempt has been made to standardize transliteration of Hebrew terms in the selections.

PREFACE

TRADITIONAL JUDAISM BELIEVES that Jewish law was revealed to Moses at Sinai, through the transmission of the Torah. Yet in every generation the Torah is given new meanings and applications. While the authority of Jewish law does not diminish, it must be interpreted and applied anew in each generation, making it truly a tradition whose meaning and import unfold from Sinai to our own day. The particular process rabbis use to interpret Jewish law depends critically on their deeper convictions concerning the nature and goals of Judaism, the place of God and human beings in determining the content of Jewish law, the degree to which historical, moral, social, and economic considerations can and should have a role in shaping Jewish law, and the reasons why one should obey Jewish law—or at least pay attention to it—in the first place. All of these larger issues are treated in a person's theory of law.

Some people who specialize in making legal rulings and do that often have never thought about these issues consciously, and, conversely, some legal theorists have rarely, if ever, decided a matter in Jewish law; jurists and philosophers, after all, have different skills and do different things. Those people who combine both activities in their work, however, often find that each benefits the other, for a jurist who has thought deeply about the philosophical underpinnings of the law has a much clearer understanding of the tasks involved and the broader implications of ruling on particular issues, and a philosopher who has crafted legal rulings and had them evaluated by other people has a much better sense of how the law operates in reality and how that should affect one's thinking about the larger context of the law.

Among the thinkers included in this volume, some have done much more legal than philosophical work, and some have done the reverse, but they have all gotten a taste of what the other activity is like. Most of the writers in this volume have learned from the practice of both law and philosophy, and we are all the better for that. Some of this volume's authors have not delved into legal decision-making, but in my judgment they have created a theory of Jewish law that is suggestive and creative, and so I have included them.

It is always easier to describe the ends of a spectrum than the middle of it, and that applies to Jewish law as well. This book will therefore focus most on Conservative theories of Jewish law to afford readers a sense of the range of positions in the middle of the contemporary religious spectrum together with the ways such thinkers justify their positions and apply them to specific circumstances. I then devote a chapter to comparing those on the right and left of the Conservative movement, thereby indicating where the lines of distinction are clear and where they are fuzzy. Finally, I devote a chapter to analyzing the theoretical presumptions underlying some specific decisions of the Conservative movement's Committee on Jewish Law and Standards to provide some examples of how theory affects practice. In focusing on the middle of the spectrum, I will be doing the hard work first, explaining and evaluating theories filled with strong convictions but also many nuances and attempts to balance competing goods. Then I will turn to theories that make bolder and often clearer statements on both the right and the left, indicating the advantages and disadvantages of doing that. I thus hope that readers will gain an appreciation of the stakes in affirming one theory in preference to others as well as the strengths and weaknesses of each one.

To set the stage for the theories I discuss, in chapter 1 I describe what a theory of law is in the first place and why one should care about theories of Jewish law altogether. In chapter 2 I present in summary fashion the biblical and rabbinic roots of all theories of Jewish law.

With those chapters as a foundation, I then turn to an exploration of the theories of law that have been produced within the Conservative movement. Chapter 3 includes readings from some of the early exponents of the Conservative approach to Jewish law—Zacharias Frankel, Solomon Schechter, and Mordecai Kaplan. Chapter 4 addresses Conservative theories of Jewish law produced in the middle of the twentieth century—by Robert Gordis, Jacob Agus, and Abraham Joshua Heschel. The emphasis of this book, though, is on Conservative theories of Jewish law articulated since 1970. These are divided into two chapters (in no special order): chapter 5 includes writings by Edward Feld, Joel Roth, Neil Gillman, Louis Jacobs, and David M. Gordis; and chapter 6 includes articles by Elliot Dorff, Alana Suskin, Raymond Scheindlin, and Gordon Tucker. Two of these—the articles by Alana Suskin and Raymond Scheindlin—were written specifically for this volume and are published here for the first time, and so I would especially like to thank those authors for adding completely new perspectives on Jewish law.

In chapters 3–6, before the excerpt from a given person's writings, I describe his or her theory, often with some comparisons to other theories, and then I present some evaluative points, indicating at least some of the strengths and weaknesses of the theory. Every theory about anything (science, economics, history, morals, religion, etc.) is a human creation, and since no human being is omniscient, every theory is inadequate to some degree. At the same time, for a theory to be significant and worth considering, it must help people at least to some extent to understand the phenomenon in question. That is true for the specific case of theories of Jewish law as well. In particular, let me state at the outset that my own theory definitely has its weaknesses as well as its strengths, and so in my discussion of it I identify at least some of its most important problems as well as the factors that have led me to adopt it.

Things become clearer when one sees them from the vantage point of those who hold other views. Thus chapter 7 includes a discussion of a selection of theorists to the right and the left of the Conservative movement. To the right is Yeshayahu Leibowitz, who is perhaps idiosyncratic by virtue of the fact that he is so Kantian, but yet represents a thoroughly thought-out and mainstream Orthodox view of Jewish law. David Hartman, in contrast, while Orthodox in practice and in affiliation, has written a theory of Jewish law that is sometimes hard to distinguish from some Conservative writers, and so his theory is one that tests the border on the right of the Conservative movement—that is, the line between Orthodox and Conservative approaches to Jewish law. I next turn to the border on the left, where I present and evaluate the four official platform statements that the Reform rabbinate has produced. Then I consider other approaches on the left, in some respects more liberal than that of the Reform rabbinate. Those include Arthur Waskow and Arthur Green. Because this book focuses on Conservative theories in order to grapple with the nuances of the middle of the spectrum, I have not included full readings from each of these theorists, but I do quote amply from their writings to illustrate their positions. Finally, I include an exchange that took place between Eugene Borowitz and me in the pages of the journal *Conservative Judaism,* for it clearly illustrates the issues that divide the approaches to Jewish law of even a traditional Reform Jew like Borowitz from a Conservative one. Hopefully, these comparative remarks will illustrate that Conservative theorists are not just stating the obvious, that, indeed, other intelligent, morally sensitive, and

Jewishly committed people have formulated theories of Jewish law that differ markedly from Conservative ones. Conversely, it will also explain why Conservative thinkers do not affirm the clearer and bolder statements to the right and left but rather choose to live with the ambiguity—but the reality—of the middle. Moreover, this chapter will indicate what some of the critical points of difference are as well as the chief justifications of the various stances.

Finally, in chapter 8, I examine several specific topics that have been addressed by the Conservative movement's Committee on Jewish Law and Standards to test how the responsa adopted by the Committee reflect Conservative theories of Jewish law. The responsa I examine concern Sabbath observance, women as rabbis, women as witnesses, responses to miscarriage, and end-of-life issues. After considering the theoretical underpinnings of those responsa, I turn to one of the ways in which the Conservative movement has provided legal education, namely, through Rabbinic Letters. This final chapter, then, will illustrate the practical results of adopting a Conservative approach to Jewish law.

All of the theorists considered in this volume are rabbis. There is nothing that would prevent someone who is not a rabbi from creating a theory of Jewish law; on the other hand, it is no surpise that rabbis are especially concerned with this issue. After all, they have dedicated themselves to serious Jewish study and service, and so it makes sense that they would be interested in figuring out their own approach to Judaism generally and to Jewish law in particular. I shall follow the usual academic convention of referring to people without their titles, but let me say here that all the people included in this volume (myself excluded, of course) have been rabbis to me in the original and strongest sense of that word. That is, they have truly been my teachers, and I am indebted to all of them.

My experience with legal theory began with some courses on Anglo-American legal theories that I took as part of my doctoral work in philosophy at Columbia University. I wrote my dissertation there on moral theory, but both morals and laws are ways in which a society tries to establish norms, and so it is not surprising that theories about morals and laws, although different in some important respects, have a lot to say to each other.

During the same years I was privileged to be part of the Talmud program of the Rabbinical School of the Jewish Theological Seminary of America, and there I learned over 300 pages of Talmud with many commentaries as well as several methods to interpret those texts. I cannot say that I thought much about theoretical issues at that time, but my Seminary training grounded me in the texts of Jewish law and gave me the tools to explore it further. For that, I am deeply grateful to the members of the Seminary administration and to the lay donors who made it possible for that program to exist, and I especially appreciate the skilled and dedicated teaching of my professors. I would particularly like to thank Professor Israel Francus, who played a pivotal role not only in imparting to me crucial skills of Talmud study, but, even more importantly, ignited my interest in Talmud through his wonderful sense of the holiness, the intellectual ferment, and the sheer joy of that study.

Since 1984 I have been privileged to be a member of the Conservative movement's Committee on Jewish Law and Standards (CJLS), and in that capacity I have written some fifteen responsa on specific issues. With each one, I have had the great benefit of the constructive criticism of my colleagues on the Committee, always given not only with informed, acute, and compassionate reasoning, but also with love. I am deeply indebted to the Rabbinical Assembly and the members of the CJLS for expanding my knowledge of Jewish law and for honing my skills to make legal decisions.

Each year since 1994, I have been teaching a course for rabbinical students at the University of Judaism's Ziegler School of Rabbinic Studies called "Theories of Jewish Law within the Conservative Movement." (I taught that course also at the Jewish Theological Seminary when I was a Visiting Professor of Philosophy there in 1999–2000.) Through their comments in class and their papers, my students have helped me immensely to probe some of the assumptions of various theories of Jewish law and to assess their strengths and weaknesses. Many of my comments about these theories in these pages were stimulated by their questions and observations. The ancient Rabbis were certainly right when they said, "Much have I learned from my teachers, more from my colleagues, and most of all from my students" (Taanit 7a; Makkot 10a).

I would especially like to thank one of my students at the Ziegler School, Hil Margolin—a practicing attorney for several decades before he entered rabbinical school—for his assiduous, careful, and enthusiastic work in scanning the readings into my manuscript and in preparing it for publication. I would also like to thank the wonderful people at the Rabbinical Assembly who made this volume possible, including Rabbi Ira Stone and the Publications Committee that he chairs; Amy Gottlieb, Rabbinical Assembly director of publications, for her unstinting encouragement and wise advice; Michelle Kwitkin-Close, copy-editor *extraordinaire*, who tightened and clarified my English and raised important questions for me to ponder about what I was saying; Annette Muffs Botnick, for her work in preparing the index; Lisa Feld, for her work in obtaining permissions; and James Harris, for his careful work in preparing the manuscript for publication. My expression of gratitude would never even approach completeness without thanking the love of my life, my wife, Marlynn, for her patience in allowing me to devote the time necessary to writing a book like this and for her ideas about what to include in chapter 8, and, ultimately, to God for giving me a wonderful and now growing family—Tammy and her son Zachary Ethan; Michael and Tanya and their daughter, Zoe Elliana; Havi and Adam and their children, Noa Yarden and Ayden Chaya; and Jonathan and Mara and their son, Amiel Shalom. May they increase!

My knowledge of how the issues in legal theory apply specifically to Jewish law has been especially honed through a course I have been team-teaching ever since 1974 at the School of Law of the University of California at Los Angeles (U.C.L.A.) with Professor Arthur Rosett, a professor of law there who specializes in contracts, judicial procedures, and international law. Comparing Jewish to American law—and, truthfully, any comparative law study—immediately raises the deep, philosophical questions about both legal systems and, when one can generalize, about law as a phenomenon in any culture. Why should one obey the law at all? What is the relationship between law and morality? law and religion? law and custom? How does the law change over time and yet retain continuity and authority? What are the limits of the jurisdiction of the law, and why? What happens when there are conflicts in jurisdiction between two or more legal systems? Professor Rosett and I have had the joy of discussing—actually, arguing about!—these matters for thirty years now, and we wrote a book together based on our course, entitled A Living Tree: The Roots and Growth of Jewish Law. In the process of teaching the course and writing the book, I have learned an immense amount about how Jewish law functions as viewed from the vantage point of the American legal system, one that differs from Jewish law in its assumptions about the role and place of law and in the way that it functions, and yet has some remarkable similarities to Jewish law in both respects. Arthur and I have become very close friends over the years, and it is both my honor and my pleasure to dedicate this volume to him in gratitude for all he has taught me and in token of our wonderful and cherished friendship.

ELLIOT N. DORFF
University of Judaism, Los Angeles
May 2005

CHAPTER ONE

Bringing the Topic Down to Earth

THE VERY TOPIC OF THIS BOOK, legal theories in Judaism generally and in Conservative Judaism in particular, probably already makes some people's eyes gloss over.

They rightfully ask: What is Conservative Judaism? What is a legal theory? What is the relationship between them? Why should I care? The purpose of this chapter is to answer those questions, at least in a preliminary way, in an effort to make the topic understandable, interesting, and even important. Quite a tall order!

WHAT IS CONSERVATIVE JUDAISM?

The name "Conservative Judaism" is itself misleading because the word "conservative" is usually used to indicate the opposite of liberal, that is, a position, person, or group that resists change. Most English speakers would associate those labeled "conservative" with particular political, social, and economic positions; and conservative religious groups, like the Southern Baptists and Roman Catholics, are often among the chief supporters of conservative social stances.

As used to describe the "Conservative movement," however, the word has a different meaning. Its founders called it "conservative" because rather than "reform" Judaism, as some Jews in the nineteenth and early twentieth centuries wanted to do (thus creating the Reform movement), the founders of the Conservative movement wanted to "conserve" it. That is, from the very beginnings of Conservative Judaism, the objective was to make traditional Judaism thrive in a modern context. Jews in the United States during the late decades of the nineteenth century and the first thirteen years of the twentieth were divided into reformers and traditionalists, many of the latter Sephardic Jews. It was only in 1913, when Solomon Schechter's efforts to prevent a split in the traditionalist camp failed, that he founded the United Synagogue of America, a name that indicated his aspiration to unite all traditional Jews in America. The Orthodox, however, formed their own organizations, and so the Conservative movement became more clearly defined as *both* traditional and modern. The Preamble to the Constitution of the United Synagogue adopted in 1913 still summarizes well both the traditional and modern perspectives and values that Conservative Judaism stands for:

> The purpose of this organization is as follows:
>
>> The advancement of the cause of Judaism in America and the maintenance of Jewish tradition in its historical continuity,
>> To assert and establish loyalty to the Torah and its historical exposition,
>> To further the observance of the Sabbath and the dietary laws,
>> To preserve in the service the reference to Israel's past and the hopes for Israel's restoration,
>> To maintain the traditional character of the liturgy with Hebrew as the language of prayer,
>> To foster Jewish religious life in the home, as expressed in traditional observances,
>> To encourage the establishment of Jewish religious schools, in the curricula of which the study of Hebrew language and literature shall be given a prominent place, both as the key to the true understanding of Judaism, and as a bond holding together the scattered communities of Israel throughout the world.
>> It shall be the aim of the United Synagogue of America, while not endorsing the innovations introduced by any of its constituent bodies, to embrace all elements essentially loyal to traditional Judaism and in sympathy with the purposes outlined above.

Thus the word used for Conservative Judaism in Israel is *Masorti,* meaning "traditional." I suggested in 1980 that we North American Jews adopt that word as well to describe what we stand for, especially because historically Judaism has not only affirmed certain beliefs and mandated that we behave in a certain way, but has also described a methodology by which the law may and should change over time.[1]

Whatever the name—Conservative, Masorti, or Traditional—the point of this form of Judaism is then to make it a central force in our lives and in the lives of our descendants by balancing and mixing the traditional with the modern. In each case, achieving the proper balance and mixing requires *judgment.* It is always easiest to understand, explain, and have passion for one or the other of the ends of a spectrum, for then one embraces that endpoint consistently, without requiring much thought. It is harder to affirm a middle point on any spectrum, for then one must have the maturity, intelligence, psychological security, and wisdom to exercise judgment and to live with inconsistencies. On the other hand, the great advantage of affirming most middle positions is that most of life's issues fall neither at one extreme nor the other, but somewhere in the middle. So the neatness, clarity, and psychological security that one sacrifices in taking a middle position is often more than made up for by the fact that it reflects the real world and offers insights as to how to live in it. It may be easier and more comfortable to pretend that the world we experience operates in clear categories and then to live our lives that way, with everything either black or white; but ultimately that requires shutting oneself off from the real world, with all its grays, with considerable prices to pay for doing so.

In terms of Jewish law, taking a middle position has meant that the Conservative movement is committed to teach Jewish ritual practices and moral norms to Jews of all ages, encouraging them to abide by those laws in both their private and public lives. It has also meant that from time to time the Conservative movement has adopted changes in Jewish practice, adding some things (e.g., bat mitzvah ceremonies, new rituals for the birth of girls, and new prayers for the modern State of Israel, including a blessing before Hallel on that day and a special paragraph to be included in the Amidah), subtracting others (e.g., making the laws governing children born through incest or adultery effectively null and void, and removing the barriers to women leading Jewish worship), and changing the form of others (e.g., mixed pews for worship, males and females studying together and using the same curriculum, and additions to the *ketubah*, the marriage document, so as to protect the woman's ability to remarry in the case of divorce).

Sometimes changes have come about through a conscious decision, sometimes through popular custom, and sometimes through both. So, for example, the practice of boys and girls (and men and women) sitting together in the same classroom learning the same curriculum has characterized Conservative educational institutions from the earliest years of the movement's existence, but, except in the case of admitting women to rabbinical school, it has never been subjected to legal analysis; it is simply the way the Conservative movement carries out Jewish education. Similarly, mixed seating for worship was legally justified only decades after it had become the all-but-universal Conservative practice.[2] Those are good examples of changes that were spawned by custom. Conversely, the movement has established a Committee on Jewish Law and Standards in North America and a *Va'ad Halakhah* in Israel to subject most legal matters to rabbinic analysis and conscious decisions on everything from the kosher status of cheeses to stem cell research and sexual norms.

In all cases, in order to conserve the tradition, Conservative ideology places the burden of proof squarely on the shoulders of those who want to change Jewish law or practice, rather than on those who want to maintain what has come down to us as our ancestral ways of following God's will. Sometimes, at least in the eyes of most Conservative Jews, that challenge can be met, and hence the changes that the Conservative movement has instituted in, for example, the status of women in worship, family law, and testimony. The burden placed on those who would change Jewish law, however, methodologically actualizes the commitment of the founders and current members of the movement to *conserve* the tradition. Conservative Judaism thus balances a reticence to change with a method for justifying and making it possible on occasion. Moreover, any changes introduced occur within the religious and educational context established by Conservative Judaism to encourage commitment to tradition in the vast majority of its principles and details.

Similarly, with regard to Jewish beliefs, the Conservative movement seeks to be historically authentic. While there certainly are some core Jewish beliefs that have characterized Judaism throughout the ages, there never has been an official creed that has gained the status and authority of defining who is a Jew and who is not. Rather, Jewish identity has been a legal status, defined either by being born to a Jewish woman or by being converted to Judaism in accord with the demands of Jewish law. Thus, very much like American identity, where one can be born in the United States and thus be a citizen even without knowing English or who George Washington was, one can similarly be born to a Jewish woman and thus be Jewish without knowing a thing about Jewish belief or practice. That is not optimal for the community or the individual in either the American or Jewish case, but this feature of both systems demonstrates how much American identity and Jewish identity are defined by law rather than by knowledge, belief, or commitment.

That, of course, does not mean that either America or Judaism is bereft of core convictions. On the contrary, in both cases, one could fairly easily describe the perspectives and values of America's Founding Fathers and of Americans to this day, and one could just as easily describe the core convictions of Judaism. I have, in fact, done that in another place in order to compare and contrast them.[3] The point, though, is that acceptance of a list of beliefs or a specific interpretation of them is not required in order to be either American or Jewish. There are certainly limits in both systems: one could not, for example, say that American convictions support rule by a dictator or that Judaism allows for faith in Jesus as Christ. Within a very broad range, though, Americans and Jews share a joy in arguing about what they believe and how that should be put into effect now.

Among Jews the core beliefs concern God, Torah, and Israel (both the People and the Land), together with corollary beliefs in the importance of family, community, prayer, study, law, morality, caring for others through social action *(gemilut ḥasadim)* and acts of righteousness and charity *(tzedakah)*, and a messianic future. Jews from Judaism's very beginnings to our own time, though, have argued about which beliefs are central and how to interpret them. Conservative Judaism follows that lead by affirming belief in, and commitment to, those core beliefs but affirming as well the health and necessity of ongoing theological discussion and challenge. Thus the only official statement of Conservative belief, *Emet Ve-emunah,* states with regard to God, "One can live fully and authentically as a Jew without having a single satisfactory answer to such doubts [about God]; one cannot, however, live a thoughtful Jewish life without having asked the questions."[4]

For a more thorough description of the philosophy, history, and institutions of Conservative Judaism, see my book *Conservative Judaism: Our Ancestors to Our Descendants.*[5] For purposes of this book, suffice it to say that Conservative Judaism is a historically authentic form of Judaism—I would say *the most* historically authentic form of Judaism—in that it embraces both tradition and modernity and tries in everything it does to blend the two wisely in the many ways that our ancestors did. In doing so, Conservative Judaism seeks to deepen and broaden Jewish life for us now so that the Judaism we pass on to our descendants can be as rich, vibrant, relevant, and moving as the tradition that our ancestors passed down to us.

WHAT IS PHILOSOPHY?

While many American and European Jews know at least something about Conservative Judaism, many Jews have not studied philosophy and the theories it spawns. It is thus precisely here that many readers may worry that the subject of this book will go over their heads. To allay that fear, in this section I will explain first what philosophy is and then, in the next, what a theory of law is. To help with the explanation, see the chart on the next page, which I shall then explain.

Levels of Abstraction in Human Knowledge

	Art	Medicine	Religion	Law
Philosophy	aesthetics	philosophy of medicine, ethics of medicine	philosophy of religion	philosophy of law = legal theory = jurisprudence
Science	art critics	researchers	scholars of religion	scholars of law
Technology	painters	physicians	rabbis, teachers	lawyers, legislators, judges
Phenomena	paints, canvas	vaccinations, drugs, hospitals	rituals, moral norms, beliefs	laws, police cars, courts, prisons

The chart above, as the title indicates, is about levels of abstraction; it is not about levels of importance to society, or even about levels of income. On the contrary, one could easily argue that many technicians (e.g., painters, doctors, rabbis, lawyers) are more important to society than the people who do scholarly research in their fields and even more than those who think about the philosophical underpinnings of what they do.

Salaries, in fact, indicate that that is exactly how society evaluates these activities, for at least some of those technicians (doctors, rabbis, lawyers) earn considerably more than those who do research in medicine, religion, or law and more still than philosophers who consider moral and methodological questions about the practice of medicine, religion, or law. Thus the chart, from bottom to top, simply indicates the progression from the most concrete experiences we have in a given area of life to the most abstract.

In all the various areas of life, we first learn about *phenomena*. So, for example, in the world of art, we first become aware of paints, a canvas, brushes, and so forth. Some of the other phenomena of art include museums, art shows, and books of art. In the area of medicine we encounter vaccinations, drugs, hospitals, white coats, operating rooms, etc. In the area of religion we encounter rituals for the life cycle and seasons of the year, moral norms, lists of beliefs, worship, social action, and often family and community customs and specified times for meeting. In the area of law we experience laws, police cars, courts, prisons and other penalties, and so forth.

On the next level of abstraction we have the technician, the person who knows *how* to wield those tools to create a painting. (The word "technician" comes from the Greek root *techne,* meaning knowledge of how to do something.) Technicians may learn their skills in part by reading books, but that is never enough, for a major component in gaining technical skills is learning from others who know how and then trying to do the task on one's own. In fact, even those who excel in the book-learning related to a profession may fail to become such a professional if they cannot perform the skills necessary; indeed, as a seminary and a law school professor for over three decades now, I can attest that the very best students are not necessarily the best lawyers or rabbis, for the practice of the profession requires many non-intellectual skills. The intellect will tell you *what* is the case but will not tell you *how* to use that information. Those who hope to be professional (or even amateur) painters, for example, can certainly benefit from classes on the techniques of painting and even from books on that subject, but ultimately they must hone their skills by actually painting, preferably under the tutelage of one or more master painters.

That is equally true for professionals who require more book learning, such as doctors, rabbis, and lawyers. That is why so many medical schools, seminaries, and law schools now include clinical training in their curriculum, usually in the last part of the program, and that is why so many of the actual skills of even those professions are only learned on the job. There one learns from people who have had much experience in the field, but even if one is lucky enough to have a good mentor, inevitably one learns also from trial and error. Really good technicians will develop a sixth sense about how to anticipate problems and take steps to avoid them, how to analyze problems when they occur and resolve them, and how to experiment with using new techniques to make their work more effective.

We now move to the next level of abstraction, the level of the science of the subject. The word "science" comes from the Latin *scire* meaning "to know," but at this level it is knowledge *that* something is the case, or, alternatively, knowledge of *what* is the case. One scientist of art is the art critic, who may or may not know how to paint but who does know how to evaluate paintings and how to compare them to other paintings. Typically such people have learned about art history so that they can see a particular painting from the perspective of many other paintings and so that they can know what to look for in determining how a particular painting succeeds or fails in communicating to those who see it (and perhaps moving or inspiring them as well). They will learn, for example, about the use of color, light, texture, shape, size, position, and a host of other elements that characterize a painting. Art critics may see things in a painting that the painter himself or herself did not see, just as literary critics sometimes see things in a text from a perspective that an author had never consciously considered. Conversely, while the painter may have learned the skills to use those elements well, he or she may not be able to evaluate the work of others or see it in the context of the history of art. Painters may gain perspective on their own work and learn how to improve it by learning about art history, but the skills of painting and the skills of evaluating art are ultimately two different—and independent—sets of skills.

The same holds true for the relationship between medical research and the practice of medicine. Those who engage in the practice of medicine certainly need to keep up with the latest in medical research so that their practice may be informed and improved by what researchers have discovered, but medical practitioners do not necessarily (or even usually) carry out the research themselves. Some physicians participate in "clinical research," in which they help drug companies or laboratory researchers test new medicines or techniques, but this role as research scientists is an addition or complement to their primary role as physicians treating patients. When they do that, they find that sometimes these aspects of their work conflict, as, for instance, when their research goals would require that they give a patient a placebo as a comparative test case, but their clinical goals as a physician would demand that they give the patient the most effective therapy available. The ethics of that conflict are sticky, although guidelines have been developed to manage that conflict of interest. In any case, clinical doctors do not usually do research in the area that they practice (except, perhaps, to develop new techniques), while doctors who do pure research (as opposed to clinical research) usually do not also treat patients. None of this means that practicing physicians and researchers cannot learn from each other; on the contrary, they surely can. But they regularly spend their days doing different things. While the practicing doctor treats patients who have (or are seeking to avoid) a given condition, the researcher looks for new ways to prevent or treat diseases, first testing such possibilities on cells, then on animals, and finally on human beings.

Seminary professors and other scholars of religion are the scientists of religion. They do research and write articles and books on the nature of religion, the anthropology, sociology, economics, politics, and texts of religion, comparative religion, and the like. As scientists, they may also write about theology, but I will explain the difference between doing that and working on the next level of abstraction, philosophy of religion, below.

As in art and medicine, scholars of religion may or may not be good at the practical skills of the rabbinate, and, conversely, rabbis may or may not be good at the scholarly pursuits of religious scientists on academic faculties, but people working on each level can certainly learn from each other.

The same remarks hold for law. The lawyer who knows how to win a case involving a personal injury may or may not know how to write an article describing the development of the law of personal injuries or the various options for changing the law and the advantages and disadvantages of various approaches to making and interpreting laws on personal injuries. Conversely, the law professor who knows how to write such an article may or may not have the practical skills and aggressive personality necessary to win a case in court. In fact, the standard joke in law schools is that A students will become law professors, B students will become judges, and C students will earn all the money as lawyers!

Finally, when we take the level of abstraction one step further, we reach the domain of philosophy. Philosophers ask questions about the following areas:

1) *Meaning.* Philosophers will ask what we mean by terms that are critical to carrying out the various functions of life. In art, for example, philosophers will ask what we mean by "beautiful" and "ugly"; in medicine, philosophers will ask what we mean by "health" and "cure"; in religion, philosophers will ask what a given text or person means by "God" or "the gods," "messianic times," "afterlife," "salvation," and the like; and in law, philosophers will ask what we mean by "justice," "authority," and, indeed, by "law" in the first place.

2) *Knowledge and Truth.* Once questions of terminology are settled, philosophers will often proceed to the next question, namely, how we can know whether a given claim is true. Note that there are two aspects to this quest. First, we have the epistemological question—that is, how we can *know* about the truth of anything, including the particular claim that we are now investigating. (This will also depend on what we mean by "truth" in the first place.) Second, we have the factual question, namely, when we measure a given claim against our experience (to take one theory of truth), does it correspond to our experience or not? Or does it do so in some ways but not in others?

So, for example, a philosopher of art who deals with questions of aesthetics will want to know, first, whether beauty is an objective quality or set of qualities (in contrast to a matter of subjective individual taste). If, then, beauty is objective, how do we measure it—both in general and in any case in particular? For the philosopher of medicine and, indeed, for any philosopher of science, the question of truth will be the methods by which physicians (or other scientists) can know whether a given medicine works or a particular theory about Mars is true. That is, what method should they use, and why can they be assured that that method will produce truthful results? In religion, as in aesthetics, the question of truth is more complicated, for one first has to determine the nature of religious truths before one can proceed to the methodological question of determining how one can know such truths and be assured in any given case that one has reached the truth. So, for example, what does it mean to say that God revealed the Torah, and how can we know whether God did or not? Finally, in law, the kind of truth that one seeks is closer to what philosophers call a coherence theory of truth—that is: does a law or judgment fit the body of laws and precedents that make up the legal system, and, if so, is it just? So, for example, if a woman kills her abusive husband, is capital punishment in accord with the law, and if so, is it just?

3) *Morals.* While some philosophers who deal with morals concentrate on the "meta-ethical" questions of the meaning of the terms "good" and "bad," "right" and "wrong," and the standards by which actions should be judged, others deal with concrete moral questions themselves. So, for example, should there be a moral critique of art? What if, for example, a work of art inspires people to hate others or do violence to them, or what if it dishonors something that some people hold as holy (as in the case of an exhibit in the Brooklyn Museum of Art of a painting of Jesus that was executed in dung)? Or is art to be free of moral judgment, lest censorship squelch artistic creativity?

There are many questions of medical ethics, and those questions have become ever more acute as medicine has advanced and made more things possible but not necessarily desirable. So, for example, should researchers destroy embryos in stem cell research in the effort to discover cures for a variety of diseases? Or, in a clinical example, if a person cannot eat independently, under what circumstances should we intubate (put tubes into) that person so as to provide artificial nutrition and hydration? If we do that, under what circumstances may be extubate (pull the tubes out of) the person?

Moral questions about religious practices also exist, on both theoretical and practical levels. Theoretical questions include: Is something good because God says it is? Or does God command something because it is good on other grounds? Practical questions include: Should a religious practice that has been the tradition for generations (for example,

discriminating against women in religious leadership) be changed because we now find it immoral? If so, what kinds of arguments are
needed to support such changes, and how can the continuity and authority of the tradition be maintained even in the process of changing it?

And finally, philosophers will ask moral questions in law. On the
theoretical level, they will ask about the relationship(s) between law and
morality and between law and justice. They will also analyze issues on a
practical level, such as whether a given piece of proposed legislation realizes moral purposes or impedes them.

4) *Comparisons.* The relationship between any phenomenon and morality is just one instance—although probably the most critical one—of a
broader philosophical field of questions that probe the relationship between that given phenomenon and other phenomena. For example,
what is, or should be, the relationship between art and politics? between
art and economics? between art and religion? Similarly, what is, or
should be, the relationship between medicine and politics? between
medicine and economics (especially with regard to the cost and distribution of health care)? between medicine and religion (especially when a
given religion demands that a particular procedure or research project
be done or not done, contrary to the will of the medical practitioners or
researchers involved—e.g., stem cell research or abortions)? With religion itself, philosophers may ask comparative questions of this sort—
namely, what is, or should be, the relationship between religion and art,
politics, medicine, social action, scientific research, etc.? And finally,
with regard to law, philosophers will ask about the relationships between law and society, law and literature, law and economics, etc.

5) *Goals.* Finally, philosophers often ask questions of goals—that is, in a
given area of life, what are we ultimately trying to achieve? So in our
examples, philosophers might ask about the goals of art, medicine, religion, and law. Is art designed simply to please the senses, or to communicate some truths about life, or to rouse people to some activity, or
something else? Is medicine supposed to save lives at all costs, or is it
also supposed to help people die? Moreover, what if we cannot afford,
say, heart transplants for all who need them while still providing pre-
ventive care for everyone in our society who needs that? Does one goal
completely trump the other? If so, which, and why? If not, how do we
balance one goal against the other? Similarly, what are the goals and
functions of religion? Is one goal more important than the others? If so,
which, and what does that mean for the other goals of religion? If not,
how do we balance them? For example, should a synagogue invest most

of its time, effort, and money in "inreach" activities designed to deepen the Jewish knowledge and commitments of those already affiliated, or "outreach" activities designed to pull more Jews in to synagogue life? Or should these concerns be balanced, and, if so, how? Finally, is the goal of the law justice, is it simply social order, or is it something else? Should lawyers strive solely to make money, or should they instead try to see justice done? How does the answer to that question affect the duty of individual attorneys to offer their services free of charge to those who cannot afford the usual fees? Should lawyers in an adversarial system of justice like American law defend a person they know to be guilty?

These, then, are the typical aspects of any given area of life that philosophers treat. One step above philosophy in abstraction is metaphysics, which Aristotle called "the queen of the sciences," because it speaks about the issues that transcend and undergird all aspects of life. Metaphysics, now usually studied in philosophy departments, asks about the nature of objects and forces, potentiality and actuality, being and nothingness, identity (how do you know when you have the same thing, even though it has changed in significant forms?), and the like.

One last comment on the nature of philosophy before I describe theories of law. What distinguishes theologians from philosophers of religion? After all, they ask some of the same questions, such as: What is the meaning of God? What is the goal of prayer? Why should I be moral, and how does that relate, if at all, to religion?

The difference is that a theologian asks and answers such questions from *within* a given tradition—and is, in fact, usually a member of that tradition. Thus the tools that a theologian will use will be the texts, traditions, and methods of the tradition, and his or her audience will be primarily other people who share that tradition. In contrast, philosophers of religion, even those who affirm a given religion, will ask those questions (and others) from *outside* any given tradition, at least as much as possible. That sometimes has meant that philosophers of religion are actually hostile to religion, but that is not necessarily the case: philosophers of religion may be just as sympathetic to, and interested in, the phenomena they study as philosophers of art, medicine, or law are with regard to the phenomena they study. Moreover, one who begins with a perspective hostile to religion is no more likely to be objective and accurate about religion than is someone who is deeply religious.

Finally, some people can function sometimes as theologians and sometimes as philosophers—or at least can attempt to do so. That was true, for example, of Paul Tillich among Protestants and of Abraham Joshua Heschel among Jews. This distinction is not always understood or honored, though, and truthfully sometimes people blur what they are doing. So, for example, Heschel subtitled his book *Man Is Not Alone* as *A Philosophy of Religion* because in that book he was asking philosophical questions, using philosophical arguments, and addressing non-Jews as well as Jews. In contrast, his book *God in Search of Man* he subtitled *A Philosophy of Judaism,* although the latter was really a theology of Judaism because its topic was specifically Judaism and it used primarily Jewish, rather than philosophical, arguments.

This distinction carries over to philosophies (or theories) of law as well. Some who write about Jewish law do so from within the community committed to it, and so they ask about specific aspects of Jewish law, use the methods of Jewish law, and address, at least primarily, Jews. On the other hand, philosophers of Jewish law, even if committed Jews themselves, will often invoke comparisons to other legal systems, thus moving the discussion outside the narrow realm of Judaism. They will use philosophical arguments about how to understand and evaluate aspects of Jewish law, investigating the standard philosophical questions I described above. Finally, in addressing such questions, they will intend to address non-Jews as well as Jews, using Jewish law simply as an example of a religious legal system for purposes of comparison to other religious and non-religious legal systems.

WHAT IS A THEORY OF LAW?

Now that I have explained what philosophy is generally and what philosophy of law is in particular, it is time to describe what goes into a comprehensive philosophy of law. Actually, a comprehensive theology of Jewish law will include many of the same elements, but as explained in the last paragraph, its methods and intended audience will be different. Not all treatments of Jewish law will explicitly discuss all these issues, and then it will be the task of the reader to unearth the assumptions that the author is making in the areas that he or she does not articulate, for often those very assumptions indicate the strengths and weaknesses, as well as the range and limitations, of the theory. So here is what you should look for in understanding and evaluating any theory of law, including any theory of Jewish law:

1. How does the theory understand the nature and status of individual human beings and human communities? For religious theories of law, how does a given theory understand the nature and status of God (or the transcendent element of human experience conceived in some other way)? In addition to these questions asking about individuals, society, and God as they *are* now (the "is" questions), what is its understanding of what human beings and human societies *ought* to strive to become (the "ought" questions)?
2. What is the role of law in society? That is, why have law at all? What are its aims?
3. What is the scope of the law—that is, what topics does it address, and which topics, if any, are beyond its jurisdiction? How does its scope follow from its purposes in any given society?
4. What gives the law authority? (There often are multiple bases for the law's authority.)
5. How shall specific laws be determined, and why should they be determined that way? (For example, should they be determined by majority vote? representatives of the majority? a group of people who qualify in some way other than by vote, such as wealth or education or lineage? a dictator's decree? a judge's ruling?)
6. How does the law maintain continuity and coherence, while at the same time allowing for change?
7. What is the relationship between law and morality, law and religion, law and economics, law and art, and law and custom? How does the legal system handle conflicts of jurisdiction with another legal system?

Theories of law usually refer to a particular system of laws (American law, Jewish law, etc.), with examples drawn from that body of law. Some theories, however, seek to explain law in all its manifestations (e.g., Aquinas). Furthermore, most theories of law seek to explain how the law has functioned in the past as well as how it should function now, but some (e.g., feminist theories) seek to redirect the law in new ways.

COMPARING AMERICAN AND JEWISH LEGAL THEORIES

To make these theoretical questions clearer, I shall briefly compare some of the major features of two systems of law that the reader may know something about—namely, American law and Jewish law. (For more on this, see chapter 1 and appendix B of my book, *To Do the Right and the Good: A Jewish Approach to Modern Social Ethics,* and see my article, "Jewish Law as an Evolving, Religious Legal System," *Hastings Law Journal* 29:6 [July, 1978], pp. 1331–1360.)

1) *The broad view of individuals and communities.* American law is strongly rooted in Enlightenment assumptions, as articulated in the Dec-

laration of Independence: "We hold these truths to be self-evident, that all men are created equal, that they are endowed by their Creator with certain unalienable Rights, that among these are Life, Liberty, and the pursuit of Happiness." The broad view on which contemporary American law is based, then, is that all people are individuals with rights (even though Jefferson probably did not intend to include women, slaves, or even white men lacking property). We are all, in a way, from Missouri, the "Show me" state, for the government has to show me why I should not have any particular right. That is, the burden of proof is on the government to justify depriving me of any rights. Governments do that regularly when they make demands, such as paying taxes, and when they prohibit things, such as robbery, but in every case the government can be challenged in court to prove the necessity of doing so.

That is because, as the Declaration continues, "To secure these rights, Governments are instituted among Men, deriving their just powers from the consent of the governed." Ultimately, "whenever any Form of Government becomes destructive of those ends," and when all efforts to change oppressive laws fail, "it is the Right of the People to alter or to abolish it, and to institute new Government, laying its foundation on such principles and organizing its powers in such form, as to them shall seem most likely to effect their Safety and Happiness." The purpose of law, then, is to secure individuals' rights, and law gets its authority from the willingness of the governed to give up some of their rights (e.g., to all profits they earn) to enable the government to secure the rest of them. In accord with these perceptions of the role and goals of law, the Founding Fathers instituted a representative, majoritarian government with a number of checks and balances and with constitutional guarantees of a list of rights in the first ten amendments to ensure that nobody would have too much power at any one time and that the rights of individuals would be preserved, often even against the will of the majority.

The individual, in this American view, is to be prized and protected because of his or her inherent rights. Every community, then, is voluntary. That is, as an American, I may join or leave any group at any time. This applies even to the United States itself. Gaining American citizenship is hard, but if I am already an American citizen, I can, except if I have committed a crime, leave the country and give up my citizenship any time I want to do so.

Like American law, Jewish law demands that each person be treated with respect, but for a different reason. In American law it is because "[all men] are endowed by their Creator with . . . rights." For Judaism, the reason is instead that all human beings have been created in the image of God. In neither system, though, does this respect for persons mean that everything that a person does is to be applauded or even condoned. Hence there are laws defining what people should and should not do, and penalties are prescribed for violating those laws. Still, even someone condemned to death for committing a capital offense must, according to the Torah, be removed before nightfall from the post on which he or she was hanged, for, as the Torah says, "an impaled body is an affront to (literally, "a curse of") God" (Deuteronomy 21:23). That is, the image of God in each of us must be respected—even with regard to someone who has committed the most egregious of crimes, and even as they are punished for those crimes.

Unlike American communities, which are completely voluntary, the Jewish community is organic. Classical Jewish law defines a Jew as someone who is born to a Jewish woman or reborn, as it were, into Judaism through the rites of conversion. Once a Jew, a person cannot relinquish that status. A Jew who converts to another religion becomes an apostate, such that he or she loses all the rights of being Jewish, including marriage as a Jew to another Jew, burial as a Jew, being counted as part of the prayer quorum *(minyan)*, etc. However, according to Jewish law such a person still bears all the responsibilities of Jewish law. Jewish identity, then, is construed as being part of the Jewish body politic; just as a part of a body cannot on its own decide to leave the rest of it, so too no Jew can sever himself or herself from the Jewish community.

This thick sense of community has widespread legal implications not only with regard to membership and apostasy, but also in a host of other areas, for it makes all Jews liable for each other's welfare: "All of Israel are responsible for one another, *kol yisrael areivim zeh bazeh*" (Shevuot 39a). So, for example, if I see someone drowning or accosted by robbers, I must, according to Jewish law, take steps to save the person while still protecting my own life (B. Sanhedrin 73a). In American law, if I try to help someone in need and unintentionally hurt the person in the process, until recently, when most states passed "Good Samaritan laws," I could actually be sued for any harm done. Conversely, only two states—Wisconsin and Vermont—have any laws whatsoever to oblige me to help someone in distress—and then failing to do so is only a misdemeanor payable by a fine of no more than $100.

2) *The role and goals of law.* American law is also dedicated to noble goals: in the words of the Preamble to the Constitution, it is intended "to form a more perfect Union, establish Justice, insure domestic Tranquility, provide for the common defence, promote the general Welfare, and secure the Blessings of Liberty to ourselves and our Posterity."

These are all the pragmatic goals of a nation constituted of individuals with rights who must give up some of those rights to achieve those goals.

In the central Jewish story, the Exodus from Egypt and the trek to Sinai and to the Promised Land, the people leave Egypt not as individuals but as a group, and it is as a community that they stand at Sinai. While there they receive and accept God's commandments, with not a single right among them. The goal of the law, then, is not to secure rights, as it is in American law, but rather to follow God's will and attain the physical and spiritual rewards for doing so.

That theologically-centered goal embodies in it the ultimate messianic mission of Jewish law to create a world in which swords are beaten into plowshares and in which there is no poverty, a world ruled by the Torah either directly (Isaiah 2:2–4) or indirectly through each person worshiping his or her own god but learning and following the Torah at the same time (Micah 4:1–5). American law does not aspire to change the whole world, ridding it of violence or want, and certainly not to unify the world in covenant with God.

3) *The scope of the law.* The First Amendment to the Constitution specifically bans Congress from making laws "respecting an establishment of religion, or prohibiting the free exercise thereof; or abridging the freedom of speech or of the press; or the right of the people peaceably to assemble, and to petition the Government for a redress of grievances." The remaining nine of the first ten amendments, referred to as the Bill of Rights, further restricts the government from interfering in other rights held by the people, including the Ninth Amendment's sweeping declaration that "the enumeration in the Constitution of certain rights shall not be construed to deny or disparage others retained by the people." In this spirit, the United States Supreme Court has, in recent decades, established a constitutional right to privacy which, among other things, prevents states from prohibiting abortion or from punishing consensual sex in private by adults, whether they be heterosexual or homosexual. The scope of American law is therefore clearly restricted to areas of social interaction, and even there a federal law may be declared unconstitutional if it belongs to the jurisdiction of the states. The social nature of American law is clearly articulated in the purposes of the law enumerated in the Preamble to the Constitution.

Because Jewish law is given by God, it has a much broader scope. It does indeed intend to govern people's social interactions, and hence the Torah contains laws requiring, for example, just weights and measures (Leviticus 19:35–36). It also, though, governs individuals in their private behavior, and so Jewish law not only provides for marriage for those who wish to marry, but actually obliges people to marry, to procreate if they can, and then to educate their children in the Jewish tradition and in a trade. It even contains rules about the position in which one should sleep and how one should tie one's shoes. Americans see these issues—including the more serious issues about marriage, procreation, and private, consensual, adult sex—as private matters in which the state should not interfere; for Jewish law, though, God's care and concern for us leads God to legislate in these areas as well.

4) *The origins and functioning of the law.* In classical Judaism, God is construed as the Author of the laws. This, of course, is very different from a government created by "We, the People of the United States."

In the actual functioning of the law, though, American and Jewish law are not nearly as different from each other as their disparate origins might suggest. That is because in Deuteronomy 17, God authorizes the judges of each generation—later called "rabbis"—to interpret and apply those laws. Some Americans ("strict constructionists") think that "judge-made law" is a violation of the American system because only Congress is supposed to make the laws; judges have authority exclusively to interpret and apply them. Others ("loose constructionists") interpret judicial power more broadly as judges test the constitutionality of laws and overturn some of them on that basis, as in the Supreme Court's decisions about segregation and abortion. In Jewish law, there is no legislative body because Deuteronomy 4:2 and 13:1 prohibit adding to, or subtracting from, the law given to Moses. Therefore, "judge-made law" has become the standard operating principle, as rabbis throughout the ages have used their authority to stretch the law to apply to new circumstances so that it would not become irrelevant and inoperative. Thus even though in theory the Torah is based on God's commandments, in practice human beings acting as judges have had an immense role in determining the contents and shape of the law. American law differs from Jewish law insofar as it depends on legislators, but human beings do exert legal authority in both systems.

In Jewish law, those human beings have not been chosen by majority vote, as legislators (and even many police chiefs and judges) are in American law. Rabbis instead gain their authority through a combination of two factors: (a) ordination, attesting a thorough education in the Jewish tradition and personal commitment to it; and (b) appointment by a community as its rabbi. As a result, even though the authority of rabbis depends crucially on their education and their willingness to model a Jewish life, it depends just as critically on the agreement of Jews to accept the rabbi's interpretations and applications of the Jewish tradition, something not all that far from Jefferson's idea of "consent of the governed."

Furthermore, in both systems—and, truthfully, in any legal system—*the operative law is determined by the interaction between what the authorities say and what the people who are supposed to be governed by the law actually do.* No book of statutes or judicial rulings in and of itself defines the law. Even in American law, where there are active legislatures on federal, state, county, and city levels and where there are police to enforce laws on all those levels, the practice of the people is critical in deciding what is, and what is not, law. Conversely, the practices of the people do not completely define the law: sometimes legal authorities can—and do—uproot accepted practices, or institute new ones.

Specifically, this interaction between law and custom can go in four logically possible directions. I will use American examples first, for those are probably more familiar to most readers. Specifically, then, (a) sometimes law can establish new customs or reinforce old ones. To take a constitutional example, until the presidency of Franklin Delano Roosevelt, the accepted custom was that presidents should not serve for more than two consecutive terms. After he broke that custom, the Twenty-second Amendment to the Constitution was ratified to establish it legally for all future presidencies. More commonly, (b) laws can change or undermine established customs. The most obvious example is the string of Supreme Court decisions, beginning with *Brown vs. Board of Education* in 1954, that not only struck down laws requiring segregation in schooling, restaurants, and other facilities, but also has gradually undermined the de facto segregation of the races in professional and social settings, in movies and television, and even in advertising. Conversely, sometimes (c) custom produces laws. For example, while for years the law required sellers and buyers to engage in a series of legal steps to complete a deal that would be recognized in court, merchants found that much too cumbersome and instead defined agreements in other ways, until ultimately the states had to make the law catch up with commercial custom by passing some form of the Uniform Commercial Code created in 1977. And sometimes (d) custom undermines laws, as it undermined the 55-mile-per-hour speed limit on interstate highways and as it undermined even the constitutional amendment of Prohibition.

If custom acts in all these ways in American law, where there are functioning legislatures and police forces, it acts all the more potently in

Jewish law. That is because Jews are spread all over the world and thus have a wider variety of customs than Americans do, even accounting for regional differences within America. Moreover, the absence of a legislature and a police force enforcing Jewish law makes custom all the more authoritative.

5) *Motivations to obey the law.* And yet, despite these similarities in how the law uses human authorities and custom, the Jewish and American legal systems differ significantly in tone and motivation as a result of their differing origins. American law, created, as it was, by the representatives of the people, must reflect the will of the people in order to remain authoritative. One obeys the law, then, primarily because one has committed oneself to abide by the will of the majority; that is the bargain into which one enters when one lives in a representative democracy. Americans also obey the law for other reasons, including the fact that they usually agree with it, they want an ordered society, they do not want to be punished by the police, and, in some cases, such as submitting to the military draft, because they see obedience as something they are called to do as patriotic Americans (love of country).

As a religious legal system, the motivations to obey Jewish law share in those practical concerns, but go beyond them. The Torah itself and the later books of the Bible suggest a number of reasons as to why we should follow God's commandments, and the Rabbis and medieval and modern Jewish philosophers add to that list.[6] The overriding motivation for obeying Jewish law, though, remains love for God and maintaining the ongoing covenantal relationship between the People Israel and God.

One other motive deserves special attention. Americans expect that the law will conform to moral norms; therefore there can be a moral critique of the law, and Americans have indeed used morality as a way to change the law, as in all of the civil rights legislation. The tricky part of this is that when Americans disagree about what is moral, the government needs to stay out of the matter (as in the case of abortion), as contentious as that has been. Americans expect their law to be moral because they themselves want it to be, even if they, their legislators, and their judges sometimes badly misconstrue what that means—as in the *Dred Scott* decision of the Supreme Court.

In Jewish law, though, the morality of the law is rooted not in a given community's desire that the law be moral, but in God, who is understood to be moral and to demand morality of us. There are, of course, problems with that assumption, not only as a result of the Holocaust but also because of Job and the many like him who have suffered without apparent justification. Indeed, the Bible itself raises questions about God's morality, beginning with Abraham's ringing question, "Shall the Judge of all the earth not do justice?" (Genesis 18:25). That challenge, though, makes sense only if Abraham could presume that God is, in fact, just. Despite some evidence to the contrary, that is indeed the prevailing view in the Bible and in rabbinic literature, as Moses declares: "The Rock!—His deeds are perfect, yea, all His ways are just; a faithful God, never false, true and upright is He" (Deuteronomy 32:4).[7] Therefore, a sense of morality pervades the Jewish legal system to a greater degree than one expects in a set of laws instituted by human beings. This manifests itself in at least two ways: (a) because Jewish law is supposed to be the decree of a morally good God, moral critiques of the law or of judgments rendered under it are clearly admissible and persuasive, much more so than in the American system, where the will of the majority, whether moral or not, governs; and (b) one of the important reasons Jews obey the law is that they understand it to be moral, as it calls on us not only to fulfill the minimal requirements of morality but to aspire to be God-like.

I have drawn this sketch of the differing perspectives of Jewish and American law to indicate the nature of the worldviews embodied in those two differing legal theories—their views of the individual, the community, the scope and goals of the law, the ways in which it should function, and the motivations to obey the law. I have not described either of their views on the many relationships that the law might have to other aspects of human life, but those too might very easily fit into a legal theory. Hopefully this sketch, though, will make it clear that legal theories—even two with which American Jews identify—can differ significantly in how they construe various aspects of law and the individuals and communities it serves.

WHY CARE ABOUT LEGAL THEORIES?

All of this, I am afraid, may still seem abstract—interesting, perhaps, but not practically relevant. While I am certainly one who enjoys intellectual activity for its own sake, in this case the abstract concepts have significant practical import. Why is that?

First, the particular legal theory that you embrace says a lot about you. It bespeaks how you think of yourself, others in your community, humanity as a whole, God, the role of law in life, and even what you ultimately hope for. So pick carefully!

Second, legal theories often have a direct effect on the content of the law. So, for example, Communists, who believe that group welfare must take precedence over individual well-being, have historically established governments with strict surveillance of citizens and tight laws governing their activity. Whether that tactic is the best means to achieve group welfare is arguable, but that has been the pattern in places like China and the former Soviet Union. On the other hand, Americans inherit a perspective that believes that each individual is born with inalienable rights, and so we want as little government as possible, only as much as is necessary to afford security and other social services. Republicans and Democrats differ as to how much government should get involved in the various areas of life, but American law begins with constitutional guarantees to protect individuals from the government. Jews qua Jews will take a stand somewhere in between those extremes, committed as their tradition is to a rich, organic sense of community as well as to the divine image inherent in each individual human being. Such broad theories will produce very different laws governing privacy, legal protections from prosecution, government-mandated education for children, health care decisions, the place and privileges of private business and social services, the role of government, and even the breadth of creative license in the arts.

Third, whatever legal theory you choose to embrace will have an important role in determining what you identify as authoritative law and what not, both for yourself and for others. That is because legal theories speak about questions of authority—why pay attention to the law, why obey it, which laws are binding, which are not, why that is the case, and how those laws that are binding exert their authority. Thus legal theories will do nothing less than tell you what you must do or refrain from doing, even as conditions and practices change, and why.

Fourth, legal theories speak about tradition and change—which laws of the past still have authority, which do not, and which new ones are now binding, as well as the proper procedures by which these decisions should be made. When most *people* in a society change the way they have been doing things, when and how does that get reflected in the law—or should those in charge of the law seek to resist the change and return the people to their former way of doing things? So, for example, if a substantial majority of Jews do not observe the dietary laws, does that mean the they are no longer binding and the law should catch up with current practice, or does that mean that Jewish leaders need to reinforce their efforts to get Jews to keep kosher? Furthermore, by what authority and in what ways may *legal officials* (in contrast to the people governed by the law) change the law? For example, on what grounds and in what way, if any, may the law in the Torah forbidding a child born out of incest or adultery (a *mamzer*) from marrying a Jew for ten generations (Deuteronomy 23:3) be nullified, at least in practice if not in theory? What about the rabbis' understanding of the Torah—even if it is not clear there—as forbidding women from serving as witnesses?[8] What about laws that the rabbis themselves instituted? How one deals with all of these aspects of law and change depends critically on how one understands the nature and authority of the law in the first place as well as the processes by which and circumstances under which it can and cannot change—in other words, on one's theory of law.

In a course on jurisprudence that I took at Columbia Law School, the professor, Harry W. Jones, had a memorable way of describing the three major theories for how American judges should understand their role in interpreting the law. Using baseball slang for how umpires see their job, Jones said, "Some judges would say, 'I call them as they are.' Others would say, 'I calls them as I sees them.' Still others would say, 'They ain't nothin' til I calls them!'" Since Jewish law does not have a legislature, it depends even more heavily on judicial opinions than American law does, and so these varying theories of the role of judges will become all the more important in defining how and when *Jewish* law should change.

In that same course, Jones told us that Benjamin Cardozo, later appointed by President Hoover as a justice of the United States Supreme Court (1932–38), took a year off in the middle of his judicial career, which began in 1913, to study theory of law and to write a book about it, *Nature of the Judicial Process* (1921). Cardozo's decisions after he wrote that book, Jones told us, are markedly better than the ones before that year because his post-sabbatical rulings reflect a clear perception of how any given decision fits into a larger understanding of the role of law and the functioning of judges. Indeed, it was Cardozo who, in his legal decisions and subsequent books, argued for a broad view of the law, including matters of economics, social welfare, and even the relationship between law and literature in legal discussions and rulings.

Fifth and finally, legal theories can motivate people who embrace them to obey the law. That is because legal theories speak also of motivations, of why one should obey the law in the first place. Even in legal systems with full enforcement capabilities, such as American law, adherence to the law on the part of the populace can never be a matter of enforcement alone; assuming an eight-hour work day, one would need three police officers for every citizen as well as police officers to police the other police officers! The system would collapse under its own weight within seconds. The only way a legal system can operate effectively is if the vast majority of people obey the law for other reasons; then the police can enforce it for the few who do not (the real criminals) or the rest of us who sometimes stray in, say, driving too fast. I describe the motivations that the Bible and the Rabbis suggest for abiding by Jewish law elsewhere;[9] but suffice it to say here that theories of law are important also for describing to those bound by the law why, in addition to the fear of being punished, they should uphold the law.

As we begin our study of theories of law in Judaism, then, we will be looking at nothing less than the beating heart of Jewish law, how its blood courses through the body of the Jewish people, changing course from time to time, but always delivering critical nutrients and life itself to the Jewish body and soul. These theories will seek to explain where the law comes from, why it is important and even authoritative, when and how it should change, and what its goals are. They will also describe how Jewish law is related to other parts of the Jewish experience, such as Jewish morals, rituals, history, and theology. The various theorists will have differing views on these matters, but they will all be addressing the core convictions of how Judaism has understood and should now understand God, the world, Jews and non-Jews, the past, present, and future, belief and practice. I hope that, as with Cardozo, studying these theories will enable readers to understand their Jewish commitments better so that they can incorporate Judaism into their decisions and actions in a more informed, reasoned, and sensitive way. Ultimately, I hope that studying these theories will guide readers' actions so that they can live their lives more consciously and authentically in the service of God. In the language of the morning liturgy, may this study motivate us "to understand, to discern, to heed, to learn and to teach, to observe and to fulfill all the words of the teachings of Your Torah with love."

CHAPTER TWO

The Biblical and Rabbinic Roots of Jewish Legal Theories[1]

THE DISCUSSION IN CHAPTER ONE of judges not only interpreting the law, but even changing it, may have surprised some readers. After all, some sections of the Torah make it seem that God gave the law, and no human tinkering—let alone a conscious change of the law—is allowed. That certainly is the explicit meaning of the two passages in Deuteronomy (4:2 and 13:1) in which Jews are told "not to add anything to what I command you or take anything away from it, but keep the commandments of the Lord your God which I enjoin upon you." Moreover, since the laws are given at Mount Sinai in an overpowering event, with thunder, lightning, and earthquakes (Exodus 19), the biblical narrative could easily lead one to think, "Hands off! This is God's law, and don't you dare tamper with it!" The understanding of the origins and functioning of Jewish law that many Jews have is often based on these biblical passages alone.[2]

Judaism, however, is NOT identical with the religion of the Bible. Judaism is based upon the way in which the Rabbis of the Talmud and Midrash defined the contents of the Bible and interpreted it (often in ways that differed from non-religious, Christian, Muslim, and other Jewish understandings of it). Similarly, neither Christianity nor Islam is the religion of their holy scriptures alone, but they are both *traditions* based on those scriptures. Specifically, the early Church Fathers decided that our Bible and a number of other books (their "New Testament") counted as Scripture, and they then interpreted even the books that Jews and Christians share in ways that sometimes agree with, and sometimes disagree with, the ways that the Rabbis interpreted them. So, for example, for Augustine, the Garden of Eden story is proof that all people are born into Original Sin, but the Rabbis understood that story as about the sins of Adam and Eve alone, without any implications for anybody else's moral or theological status. Similarly, Islam is the religion of the Bible as retold by Mohammed in the Koran and then as interpreted by the imams. Consequently, if one wants to have an accurate picture of classical Judaism, and if one wants to get a sense of how Conservative legal theories fit, or fail to fit, the age-old and ongoing Jewish tradition, it is crucial to see how *the Rabbis* understood the authority and functioning of Jewish law.

When we consult biblical and rabbinic sources, we discover some important and surprising things. First of all, the Bible claims that God spoke to Moses and the prophets directly, and it leaves open the possibility of future prophets:

> Adonai your God will raise up for you a prophet from among your own people, like myself [Moses]; him you shall heed. This is just what you asked of Adonai your God at Horeb, on the day of the Assembly, saying, "Let me not hear the voice of Adonai my God any longer or see this wondrous fire any more, lest I die." Whereupon Adonai said to me: "They have done well in speaking thus. I will raise up a prophet for them from among their own people, like yourself: I will put My words in his mouth, and he will speak to them all that I command him; and if anybody fails to heed the words he speaks in My name, I Myself will call him to account. But any prophet who presumes to speak in My name an oracle that I did not command him to utter, or who speaks in the name of other gods—that prophet shall die." And should you ask yourselves, "How can we know that the oracle was not spoken by Adonai?"—if the prophet speaks in the name of Adonai and the oracle does not come true, that oracle was not spoken by Adonai; the prophet has uttered it presumptuously: do not stand in dread of him.
>
> (Deuteronomy 18:15–22)

The Rabbis, however, claimed that God ceased to make the divine will known through prophecy shortly after the destruction of the First Temple:

> When the latter prophets, Haggai, Zechariah, and Malachi died, the Holy Spirit departed from Israel.
>
> (B. Sanhedrin 11a)

> The Holy Blessed One, said: "Twenty-four books [the Hebrew Bible] have I written for you; beware and make no addition to them." For what reason? "Of making many books there is no end" (Ecclesiastes 12:12). He who reads a single verse that is not from the twenty-four is as though he read in "the outside books." Beware of making many books [to add to the Scriptures], for whoever does so will have no portion in the world to come.
>
> (Numbers Rabbah 14:4)

Furthermore, the Rabbis introduced distinctions in the authority of the prophets who had prophesied before the destruction of the First Temple, claiming that Moses' prophecies were most authoritative because his vision was clearest and most inclusive:

> What was the distinction between Moses and the other prophets? The latter looked through nine lenses, whereas Moses looked only through one. They looked through a cloudy lens, but Moses through one that was clear.
>
> (Leviticus Rabbah 1:14)

> Forty-eight prophets and seven prophetesses spoke prophecies for Israel, and they neither deducted from, nor added to, what was written in the Torah, with the exception of the law to read the Book of Esther on the Feast of Purim.
>
> (B. Megillah 14a)

In place of prophecy, the Rabbis greatly expanded the judicial powers that the Torah had created in chapter 17 of Deuteronomy, and they claimed that *their interpretations were the new and only way in which God spoke to humanity:*

> Rabbi Avdimi from Haifa said: Since the day when the Temple was destroyed, the prophetic gift was taken away from the prophets and given to the Sages.—Is then a sage not also a prophet?—What he meant was this: Although it has been taken from the prophets, it has not been taken from the Sages. Amemar said: A sage is even superior to a prophet, as it says, "And a prophet has a heart of wisdom" (Psalm 90:12). Who is (usually) compared with whom? Is not the smaller compared with the greater?
>
> (B. Bava Batra 12a)

They even denied authority to new revelations (that is, new, direct words from God) claimed by members of their own sect, as in this remarkable story:

> We learned elsewhere: If he cut it [the material for an oven] into separate tiles, placing sand between each tile, Rabbi Eliezer declared it pure, but the Sages declared it impure. . . . On that day Rabbi Eliezer brought forward every imaginable argument, but they did not accept them. Said he to them, "If the law agrees with me, let this carob tree prove it!" Thereupon the carob tree was torn a hundred cubits out of its place—others affirm, four hundred cubits. "No proof can be brought from a carob tree," they retorted. Again he said to them, "If the law agrees

with me, let the stream of water prove it." The stream of water then flowed backwards. "No proof can be brought from a stream of water," they rejoined. Again he urged, "If the law agrees with me, let the walls of the schoolhouse prove it," whereupon the walls began to fall. But Rabbi Yehoshua scolded them, saying: "When scholars are engaged in a legal dispute, what right have you to interfere?" Therefore they did not fall in honor of Rabbi Yehoshua, nor did they resume an upright position in honor of Rabbi Eliezer, and they are still standing there inclined. Again he said to them, "If the law agrees with me, let it be proved in Heaven." At that moment a Heavenly Voice cried out, "Why do you dispute with Rabbi Eliezer, seeing that in all matters the law agrees with him!" But Rabbi Yehoshua arose and exclaimed, "It is not in Heaven!" (Deuteronomy 30:12). What did he mean by this? Rabbi Yirmiyah said, "That the Torah had already been given at Mount Sinai; therefore we pay no attention to a Heavenly Voice, because You [God] have long since written in the Torah at Mount Sinai, 'One must follow the majority' (Exodus 23:2)." Rabbi Natan met Elijah [the Prophet] and asked him: "What did the Holy Blessed One do in that hour?" "He laughed with joy," he replied, "and said, 'My children have defeated Me, My children have defeated Me.'"

(B. Bava Metzia 59a–b)[3]

Notice that there is no dispute that the Heavenly Voice is truly from God; that is, everyone agrees that this revelation is authentic. Nevertheless the majority refuses to accept it as legally significant. If that does not make it clear that the rabbinic methodology is significantly different from the biblical one, nothing will! The Rabbis clearly and consciously shifted the operation of the law from the prophets to the judges, from revelation to interpretation.

Why did they do that?

(1) Undoubtedly part of the reason has to do with problems in using revelation. The Bible itself struggles to create a way of distinguishing true prophets from false ones (Deuteronomy 13:2–6; 18:9–22), and Jeremiah, especially, complains of the many false prophets in his time (e.g., Jeremiah 14:14; 23:25, 32; 27:10, 14, 16; 29:23; etc.). The problem of identifying and weeding out false prophets was a continuing problem for the Rabbis—especially in light of the many people in their time roaming the hills of Judea claiming to be prophets (Jesus included). Thus they said:

To what are a prophet and a sage to be compared? To a king who sent his two ambassadors to a state. For one of them he wrote, "If he does not show you my seal and my letter of appointment, do not believe him"; for the other he wrote, "Even if he does not show you my seal and my letter of appointment, believe him without a seal or a letter of appointment." Similarly, in regard to a prophet, it is written, "If he gives you a sign or a portent [believe him]" (Deuteronomy 13:2), but here [in Deuteronomy 17:11, concerning judges] it is written, "You shall act in accordance with the instruction that they give you [even without a sign]."

(Y. Berakhot 1:4)

This is an especially forceful endorsement of rabbinic authority because Deuteronomy 13, which is quoted here, says that even if the prophet gives you a sign or portent and it comes true, you should not believe in the prophet if he tells you to follow another god or disobey God's laws, "for Adonai your God is testing you" (Deuteronomy 13:4). Rabbis, though, are to be followed even without a confirming sign or portent. The following source demonstrates exactly how far this rabbinic authority goes:

"You shall act in . . . accordance with the instruction that they give you. You shall not deviate. . . . to the right or to the left" (Deuteronomy 17:11). Even if they demonstrate that what seems to you to be right is really left, and that what seems to you to be left is really right, listen to [and obey] them.

(Sifrei Deuteronomy, Shoftim, #154)

On the other hand, another strain within the tradition maintains that rabbinic rulings, just like prophetic revelations, are to be judged for the propriety of their content before being obeyed as authoritative law:

"You must not deviate from the verdict that they announce to you either to the right or to the left" (Deuteronomy 17:11). You might think that this means that if they tell you that right is left and left is right, you are to obey them; therefore the Torah tells you, "to the right or to the left," [to indicate that] when they tell you that right is right and left is left [you are to obey them, but not otherwise].

(Y. Horayot 1:1)

(2) Besides the problem of distinguishing between true prophets and false ones, there is yet another problem with prophecy. If you accept it, then the law is always subject to change or complete cancellation at a moment's notice because God could conceivably announce completely new rules through a prophet—or at least a prophet could claim that God had done so. In other words, accepting prophecy spells legal chaos. Consequently the Rabbis in the above story about the oven were well

advised to reject divine intrusions into the lawmaking process and to claim instead that God had had His say once and for all. So part of the reason for substituting interpretation for prophecy is because of the problems inherent in using prophecy—namely, the difficulty of distinguishing true prophets from false ones and the legal chaos that prophecy can cause.

(3) Another part of the reason is that the Rabbis were convinced that the Torah needs interpretation, that nobody could follow God's will on the basis of the Torah alone. There are sects of Christians who are "fundamentalists." They try to make their decisions in life solely on the basis of the Bible. Many Muslims do the same thing with the Koran. There also have been sects of Jews who have tried that, including the Karaites (who were strongest in the ninth and tenth centuries but who still exist today) and, to a lesser degree, the Sadducees. Even though those groups maintain that they are relying solely on their Holy Scriptures, which they take to be the only and authentic word of God, what actually happens is that they are living according to their own particular convictions about what constitutes Scripture and what it means. The Rabbis were much more conscious and honest about the necessity and process of interpreting Scripture to know what it means. They also realized that the text itself is an open, rich one, lending itself to multiple understandings:

> Is not My word like a hammer that breaks a rock?
>
> (Jeremiah 23:29)

> As the hammer causes numerous sparks to flash forth, so is a scriptural verse capable of many interpretations.
>
> (B. Sanhedrin 34a)

> There are seventy faces to the Torah.
>
> (Numbers Rabbah 13:15–16)

> "The words of the wise are as goads. . . . They are given from one shepherd" (Ecclesiastes 12:11). That is, the words of the Torah and the words of the Sages have been given from the same shepherd [Moses]. "And furthermore, my son, be careful: Of making many books there is no end" (Ecclesiastes 12:12) means: More than to the words of the Torah, pay attention to the words of the Scribes. In the same strain it says, "For your beloved ones are better than wine" (Song of Songs 1:2), which means: The words of the beloved ones [the Sages] are better than the wine of the Torah. Why? Because one cannot give a proper

decision from the words of the Torah, since the Torah is shut up [cryptic and therefore ambiguous] and consists entirely of headings. . . . From the words of the Sages, however, one can derive the proper law because they explain the Torah. And the reason that the words of the Sages are compared to goads *(darvonot)* is because they cause understanding to dwell *(medayerin binah)* in people [a play on words].

(Numbers Rabbah 14:4)

(4) Moreover, interpretation is necessary not only because the Torah on its own is ambiguous; it is also necessary if Jewish law is to retain sufficient flexibility:

If the Torah had been given in a fixed form, the situation would have been intolerable. What is the meaning of the oft-recurring phrase, "Adonai *spoke* to Moses"? Moses said before Him, "Sovereign of the Universe! Let me know what the final decision is on each matter of law." He replied, "The majority [of the judges] must be followed: when the majority declares a thing permitted, it is permissible; when the majority declares it forbidden, it is not allowed; so that the Torah may be capable of interpretation with forty-nine points *for* and forty-nine points *against.*"

(Y. Sanhedrin 22a)

In fact, the Rabbis considered new interpretations and expansions of the law not only necessary, but also desirable:

A king had two slaves whom he loved intensely. He gave each one a measure of wheat and a bundle of flax. The intelligent one wove the flax into a cloth and made flour from the wheat, sifted it, ground it, kneaded it, baked it, and set it [the bread] on the table on the cloth he had made before the king returned. The stupid one did not do a thing [with the gifts the king had given him]. After some time the king returned to his house and said to them: "My sons, bring me what I gave you." One brought out the table set with the bread on the tablecloth; the other brought out the wheat in a basket and the bundle of flax with it. What an embarrassment that was! Which do you think was the more beloved? [Similarly] when the Holy Blessed One gave the Torah to Israel, He gave it as wheat from which to make flour and flax from which to make clothing, through the rules of interpretation.

(Seder Eliyahu Zuta, chapter 2)

(5) Finally, human interpretation and application of the law are necessary because God Himself required it in chapter 17 of Deuteronomy. Thus *not* to interpret the law anew in each generation would be to disobey God's law!

No person should say, "I will not observe the precepts of the elders" [i.e., the Oral Law], since they are not of Mosaic authority [literally, contained in the Torah]. For God has said, "No, my child, but whatever they decree for you, you must perform," as it says, "According to the Torah that they [i.e., the elders in days to come] *shall* teach you shall you do" (Deuteronomy 17:11): for even for Me do they [the Rabbis] make decrees, as it says, "when you [i.e., the Rabbis] decree a command, it shall be fulfilled for you" [i.e., by Me, God, a playful interpretation of Job 22:28].

(Pesikta Rabbati, ed. Friedmann, 7b)

That is all well and good, but with all of these interpretations, how is there to be any coherence in the law—any sense that, despite the many different understandings and applications of the law, this is still one reasonably consistent system? And how do the various interpretations of the word of God continue to have divine authority?

Those are hard questions, but the Rabbis faced them squarely. They answered the question of coherence in three ways. First of all, the tradition would remain coherent despite the many variations of opinion because they all derive from God:

Lest a person say, "Since some scholars declare a thing impure and others declare it pure, some pronounce a thing to be forbidden and others pronounce it to be permitted, some disqualify an object while others uphold its fitness, how can I study Torah under such circumstances?" Scripture states, "They are given from one shepherd" (Ecclesiastes 12:11): One God has given them, one leader [Moses] has uttered them at the command of the Lord of all creation, blessed be He, as it says, "And God spoke *all* these words" (Exodus 20:1). You, then, should, on your part, make your ear like a grain receiver and acquire a heart that can understand the words of the scholars who declare a thing impure as well as those who declare it pure, the words of those who declare a thing forbidden as well as those who pronounce it permitted, and the words of those who disqualify an object as well as those who uphold its fitness. Although one scholar offers his view and another offers his, the words of both are all derived from what Moses, the shepherd, received from the One Lord of the Universe.

(Numbers Rabbah 14:4)

In other words, however much the interpretations of various rabbis may vary, they are all interpretations of one document, the Torah, and they will all be cohesive because God, the Author of that document, can be presumed to be consistent. In somewhat the same way, American law is consistent because it all derives from the framework and powers that were established in the Constitution—however much new laws and judicial rulings have changed the substance of American law since then.

Second, the tradition would be cohesive because there is a sense of continuity within the tradition itself. There is a famous story in the Talmud that illustrates this point. When Moses visits the academy of Rabbi Akiva, who lived some 1400 years after him, he does not even understand what Rabbi Akiva is saying, let alone agree with it. Nevertheless Moses is comforted when Rabbi Akiva cites one of the new laws in Moses' name because that indicates that Rabbi Akiva and his contemporaries understood themselves to be part of the ongoing tradition that stretches back to Moses. There is thus a sense of continuity among the people upholding and interpreting the tradition, however much it has changed in form and content:

> Rav Yehudah said in the name of Rav: When Moses ascended on high, he found the Holy Blessed One engaged in affixing crowns to the letters [of the Torah]. Said Moses: "Sovereign of the Universe, who stays Your hand?" [That is, is there anything lacking in the Torah so that additions are necessary?] He answered, "There will arise a man at the end of many generations, Akiva ben Yosef by name, who will expound upon each decorative marking heaps and heaps of laws." "Sovereign of the Universe," said Moses, "permit me to see him." He replied, "Turn around." Moses went and sat down behind eight rows [of Rabbi Akiva's disciples and listened to the discourses on the law]. Not being able to follow their arguments, he was ill at ease. When they came to a certain subject and the student said to the teacher, "From where do you know it?" and the latter replied, "It is a law given to Moses at Sinai," he [Moses] was comforted. Thereupon he returned to the Holy Blessed One, and said, "Sovereign of the Universe, You have such a man and yet You give the Torah by me?!"
>
> (B. Menaḥot 29b)

Incidentally, this story also clearly indicates that the Rabbis realized that there had been changes in the law.

This sense of continuity is dependent, of course, on having people who have studied the Torah sufficiently to carry on its spirit and substance in new settings, and the Rabbis were keenly aware of what happens to the law's coherence when those to whom it is entrusted do not know it thoroughly:

> When the disciples of Shammai and Hillel increased who had not served [that is, studied with] their teachers sufficiently, dissensions increased in Israel and the Torah became like two Torahs.
>
> (B. Sotah 47b)

But they also were convinced that the continuity and consistency that they sensed was real, that the law in its present form, however different from the Torah, was the direct extension of it:

> Moses received the Torah from Sinai and handed it down to Joshua, and Joshua to the elders, and the elders to the prophets, and the prophets handed it down to the men of the Great Assembly.
>
> (M. Avot 1:1)

> At the same time when the Holy Blessed One revealed Himself on Sinai to give the Torah to Israel, He delivered it to Moses in order: Scripture, Mishnah, Talmud, and Aggadah.
>
> (Exodus Rabbah 47:1)

Again, the comparison to American law is instructive. Judges can make really revolutionary decisions, but they correctly feel the need to tie those decisions to already existing laws and precedents in order to preserve a sense of continuity within the American legal system. The Supreme Court's decision in 1954 requiring integration of the public schools is a good example. Segregated schools clearly continued to exist in the United States after the First and Fourteenth Amendments to the Constitution became law in 1791 and 1868 respectively, and the framers of those amendments certainly did not intend to outlaw such schools in passing them. Moreover, the Supreme Court itself specifically upheld the constitutionality of segregated facilities in 1896. Nevertheless, in 1954 the Supreme Court declared segregated schools unconstitutional and based their decision on the First and Fourteenth Amendments in order to preserve a sense of continuity and consistency in the law. Shades of Rabbi Akiva!

Third, Jewish law would retain its coherence because it includes a way of making decisions. All opinions could be aired in discussion, and, in fact, all are to be considered "the words of the living God," but in the end a decision must be made:

> Rabbi Abba stated in the name of Shemuel: For three years there was a dispute between the School of Shammai and the School of Hillel, the former asserting, "The law is in agreement with our views," and the latter contending, "The law is in agreement with our views." Then a Heavenly Voice announced, "The utterances of both are the words of the living God, but the law is in agreement with the rulings of the School of Hillel." Since, however, "both are the words of the living God," why was the School of Hillel entitled to have law fixed in agree-

ment with their rulings? Because they were kindly and modest, they studied their own rulings and those of the School of Shammai, and they were even so humble as to mention the opinions of the School of Shammai before their own.

(B. Eruvin 13b)

There is a famous instance in the Mishnah in which the authority of the President of the Sanhedrin was asserted forcefully when it was called into question. Until the fourth century C.E., there was no fixed Jewish calendar. Instead witnesses would come to the Sanhedrin during the day and testify that they had seen the first sliver of the new moon on the previous night. The President of the Sanhedrin would then declare that day to be the first day of the new month. There were some special rules to make sure that the calendar would never be too much out of step with the movements of the sun and the moon, no matter whether there were witnesses to the new moon or not, but fixing the dates of the calendar did depend to a large extent on the testimony of witnesses. You can imagine how important this was: after all, if the first day of the Hebrew month Tishrei, for example, was declared to be on a Monday, then that day was Rosh Hashanah, no work should be done, special services should be held, and Yom Kippur would be ten days later, on the Tuesday night and Wednesday of the following week. If, on the other hand, the first day of the month were declared to be on Tuesday, then both Rosh Hashanah and Yom Kippur would take place a day later, with all of the special laws of the High Holy Days observed then. With this as a background, you can understand the story in the following mishnah and why it is important:

> On one occasion two witnesses came and said: "We saw the new moon at its expected time [the night after the twenty-ninth day of the previous month], but on the next night it could not be seen" [when it should have been even larger and clearer]. Yet Rabban Gamliel [who was President of the Sanhedrin] accepted them as true witnesses [assuming that they did not see the moon on the next night simply because clouds covered it]. Rabbi Dosa ben Harkinas said, "I maintain that they are false witnesses," and Rabbi Yehoshua ben Hananiah [who was Vice-President of the Sanhedrin] said to him, "I see the strength of your arguments." Rabban Gamliel sent a message to him [Rabbi Yehoshua], saying, "I order you to come to me with your staff and money on the day on which, according to your calculations, Yom Kippur falls."
>
> Rabbi Akiva went and found him [Rabbi Yehoshua] in distress [since he would have to publicly violate the laws of Yom Kippur on the day that he thought to be Yom Kippur]. He [Rabbi Akiva] said to him [Rabbi Yehoshua]: "I can prove [from the Torah] that everything that

Rabban Gamliel has done, he has done [correctly], for the Torah says, 'These are the appointed seasons of Adonai, holy convocations, *which you shall proclaim* in their appointed season' (Leviticus 23:4)." [This means]: Whether they are proclaimed at their proper time or not, I [God] have no other "appointed seasons" but these [which you—that is, the People Israel through its official decision-making body, the Sanhedrin—declare].

He [Rabbi Yehoshua] then went to Rabbi Dosa ben Harkinas [who had agreed with Rabbi Yehoshua that the witnesses were false], and said to him: "If we call into question the decisions of the Court of Rabban Gamliel, we must call into question the decisions of every single court that has existed from the days of Moses to the present day. . . . So he [Rabbi Yehoshua] took his staff and money in his hand and went to Yavneh to Rabban Gamliel on the day on which Yom Kippur fell according to his own calculation. Rabban Gamliel stood up, kissed him on his head, and said to him, "Come in peace, my teacher and my pupil: my teacher in wisdom, and my pupil in that you have accepted my decision."

(M. Rosh Hashanah 2:8–9)

The situation became more complicated when the Sanhedrin ceased to exist and there was no longer a central authority in Judaism, but there are still ways in which decisions are made in Jewish law, thus preserving its continuity. In some places and times, Jewish communities have been sufficiently organized to have a centralized court system for a community or a group of communities. When that is not possible, each community follows the decisions of its local rabbi, its *mara d'atra* ("the teacher [or master] of the place"), and the court that he or she often chairs, for each community is *commanded* to establish a court:

Courts should be established in Israel and outside it, as it says, "Such shall be your law of procedure throughout the generations in *all* your settlements" (Numbers 35:29), from which we learn that the courts must be established in Israel and outside it. So why does the Torah say, "in all the settlements that Adonai your God is giving you" (Deuteronomy 16:18)? To teach you that in Israel you establish courts in every district and city, but outside Israel only in every district.

(T. Sanhedrin 3:5; cf. B. Makkot 7a)

That means, of course, that many different decisions can be made on any given issue in the various places in which Jews live, but even then there is a general rule to coordinate the decisions and give Jewish law coherence. Maimonides summarizes it clearly:

After the Supreme Court [Sanhedrin] ceased to exist, disputes multiplied in Israel: one declaring something "impure," giving a reason for his ruling; another declaring it "pure," giving a reason for his ruling; one forbidding [something], another permitting [it]. In case there is a difference of opinion between two scholars or two courts, one pronouncing "pure" what the other pronounces "impure," one declaring "forbidden" what the other declared to be "permitted," and it is impossible to determine the correct decision—if the controversy is with regard to a scriptural law, the more stringent view is followed; if it is with regard to a rabbinical law, the more lenient view is followed. This principle holds in post-Sanhedrin times, and it determined the law even at the time of the Sanhedrin if the case had not yet reached that tribunal. It governs whether those who hold different views are contemporaries or live at different times.

(Maimonides, Mishneh Torah, *Hilkhot Mamrim* 1:4–5)

Moreover, since Jews have lived under many different conditions in the scattered places in which they have found themselves, it probably is a good thing that the court in each area makes decisions appropriate to its particular setting. Jewish law thereby gains the necessary flexibility to enable it to work in many different times and places. Nevertheless, there is a clear way of making decisions wherever Jews live and that, together with the sense of continuity and the dependence upon one Torah discussed earlier, gives Jewish law coherence and a reasonable degree of consistency.

The second question posed above goes to the very root of the authority of Jewish law: With all of the various interpretations of the law and the new applications of it, how is it in any sense divine? After all, the Rabbis explicitly claimed that it is the *human* judges in each generation that have the authority to make decisions in Jewish law, that God no longer has the right or authority to determine the law even if He wants to (remember the story of the oven above). So, how is Jewish law as the Rabbis interpret it still God's word?

That is a crucial question, and it is important to remember why it arises in the first place. On the one hand, the Rabbis clearly wanted to retain divine authority for Jewish law: there are many reasons to observe it, but the most important one by far—at least as they saw it—is that it is the will of God. On the other hand, the Rabbis had to assert the right of rabbis in each generation to interpret and apply the law for all of the reasons discussed above: the difficulties of using prophecy as a legal guide; the ambiguity of the Torah, especially in regard to how it is to be applied to new situations; the need to retain flexibility in the law in order to enable it to function under new circumstances; and the commandment of God Himself that judges in each generation take on the responsibility of interpreting the law.

There is no simple way of affirming both the divine authority of the law and the right of human beings to interpret it. The Rabbis, in a style typical of them, claimed two opposite things in order to assert the truth of both of them. On the one hand, they maintained that all later developments in the law were already revealed at Sinai:

> What is the meaning of the verse, "And I will give you the tablets of stone, and the law and the commandment, that I have written, so that you may teach them" (Exodus 24:12)? "Tablets of stone" [refers to] the Decalogue; "law" [refers to] the Pentateuch; "commandment" [refers to] the Mishnah; "that I have written" [refers to] the Prophets and Hagiographa [Writings]; "so that you may teach them" [refers to] the Gemara [Talmud]. The verse [thus] teaches that all of those sources were given to Moses on Sinai.
>
> (B. Berakhot 5a)[4]

> Even that which a distinguished student was destined to teach in the presence of his teacher was already said to Moses on Sinai.
>
> (Y. Peah 17a)

Consequently, since all of the interpretations, extensions, and revisions of the law by the rabbis of all generations to come were already revealed at Sinai, they carry God's authority. On the other hand, as we have seen in the sources cited above, the Rabbis were aware that many of their interpretations and laws were new—so new that even Moses could not understand them—and they even held that it is God's desire that the law not be fixed, that the Rabbis instead apply the law anew in each generation. Moreover they claimed that these new interpretations were the form in which God revealed His will to us in post-biblical times. The Rabbis therefore also said this:

> When God revealed His presence to the Israelites, He did not display all His goodness at once, because they could not have borne so much good; for had He revealed His goodness to them at one time they would have died. . . . When Joseph made himself known to his brothers, they were unable to answer him because they were astounded by him (Genesis 45:3). If *God* were to reveal Himself all at once, how much more powerful would be the effect. So He shows Himself little by little.
>
> (Tanḥuma Buber, Devarim, 1a)

Matters that had not been disclosed to Moses were disclosed to Rabbi Akiva and his colleagues.

(Numbers Rabbah 19:6)

How is it possible that everything was revealed at Sinai and yet new things are revealed each day? Actually, it is not as contradictory as it seems. Anyone who has ever read a good story as a child and then again as an adult will know how that can be. We understand the story in one way the first time, but the second time we may see completely new levels of meaning in it. The text is the same, but it can say something new to us because we change as we grow, and we can relate the story to more areas of life and appreciate more of the themes of the story. *Alice in Wonderland,* for example, is not just a funny story about a girl who has a crazy dream. It is also a satire on many different types of people and even includes some interesting problems of logic. Children certainly do not see it that way when they read it (or see the movie) at age seven or eight, but adults appreciate it on these other levels. Similar things apply to the stories in the Bible. Those who read them in childhood and never again have missed a great deal of their meaning. The Bible is *at least* good literature, which must be studied and appreciated again and again throughout life.

Law operates in a similar way. On the one hand, with the exception of the last sixteen amendments, the Constitution of the United States is the same as it was in 1791, when the Bill of Rights was ratified. Its meaning, however, has extended far beyond the intentions of its framers, as judges, lawyers, and scholars have carefully examined its every phrase in applying it to new problems and circumstances. It has even changed meaning a number of times as the Supreme Court reversed itself or greatly narrowed or expanded the application of its previous rulings. *Yet, in an important sense, all of the later developments were already inherent in the original Constitution because they all are derived from the governmental bodies that the Constitution established and the general principles that it enunciated.* The Constitution is understood and applied in many novel ways each year—or, in more theological terms, many new, previously undiscovered meanings and applications are revealed in it as time goes on. But all of the new meanings are dependent upon the Constitution, which established the structure for those interpretations and applications in the first place. That is the sense of continuity that the law enjoys.

The exact same thing is true about Jewish law. On the one hand, every interpretation and application of Jewish law that ever has been, is, or will be was already revealed at Sinai because every one of them comes directly or indirectly from the procedures and principles that the Jewish constitution, the Torah, established. Even the *takkanot* (revisions) that rabbis have enacted over the centuries are based upon the Torah's authorization of judges to act on behalf of Jewish law in every generation. The *takkanot* may represent a change in the content of the law, as their name implies, but they nevertheless are an organic part of Jewish law because they were enacted by its duly authorized interpreters. Similarly, and more importantly, each time that a Jewish court or judge decided to interpret the Torah or Talmud in one way and not another, the meaning of those texts changed. Sometimes the texts were given meanings that they never had had before through this process of *midrash* (interpretation), and sometimes several possible alternative interpretations were precluded by this process.

In any case, expanding or contracting the meaning or application of a given verse in the Torah was possible only because the Torah itself established the ground rules and procedures of Jewish law. In that sense, *every* later development in Jewish law, no matter how far removed in content from the simple meaning of the Torah, was already revealed to Moses at Sinai. On the other hand, in every generation the Torah is given new meanings and applications, and in that sense matters that had not been revealed to Moses were revealed to Rabbi Akiva and his colleagues.

The authority of Jewish law does not diminish, then, as it is applied anew in every generation. It *must* be so interpreted and applied if it is to continue to live, and the Rabbis clearly recognized that. So far we have seen that idea expressed in what the Rabbis *said*, but the evidence is more overwhelming if we consider what the Rabbis actually *did*. Through using the methods of exegesis (interpretation) that they developed (some of which are contained in "The Baraita of Rabbi Yishmael," found in the early part of the daily Shaḥarit service in many prayerbooks), they, at one extreme, made some biblical laws totally inoperative and, at the other extreme, they created whole new bodies of law. For example, the Bible requires capital punishment for a whole variety of offenses, but the Rabbis created court procedures for capital cases that were so demanding that it became virtually impossible to obtain a capital conviction in Jewish law. To give you an idea of what they did, some of the requirements that they instituted are:

1. The culprit for a capital offense must be warned by two witnesses immediately before he or she committed the act that it is unlawful and carries the death penalty. After all, the accused may not have known that the act is il-

legal or is punished so severely, and how can you hold people liable for a penalty as severe as death if they did not know those things?

2. The accused had to respond, "Even so, I am going to do it," for otherwise one cannot be sure that the culprit heard the warning.
3. The defendant had to commit the act within three seconds after hearing the warning because people forget things, and if the culprit forgot the law, we should not hold him or her responsible for a penalty as serious as death.
4. The witnesses may not be related to each other or to the culprit, for relatives may hide or distort the truth on each other's behalf.
5. There must be at least one judge on the court who votes to acquit the defendant, for otherwise the court might be prejudiced against him or her—which, by the way, is the exact opposite of the requirement in American law for a unanimous jury in capital cases.

Some of those requirements—and some of the other things the Rabbis required for a capital conviction—are clearly implausible extensions of principles that are reasonable in a different form, and the Rabbis certainly knew that. They had decided, though, to abolish the death penalty, despite the numerous times the Bible requires it, and they used court procedures to accomplish that. Put another way, they interpreted the death penalty out of existence, and they realized that result and the issues involved fully:

> A court that has killed a person once in a seven-year period is called "a hanging court" [literally, a destructive court]. Rabbi Elazar ben Azariah said, "Even once in seventy years." Rabbi Tarfon and Rabbi Akiva said, "Were we members of the court, no person would ever have been put to death." Rabban Shimon ben Gamliel retorted, "If so, they would have increased shedders of blood [murderers] in Israel."
>
> (M. Makkot 1:10)

On the other hand, while the Rabbis effectually nullified the death penalty, they created a whole structure of Sabbath laws far beyond those in the Bible—to the extent that they themselves said:

> The laws of the Sabbath are like mountains hanging by a hair, for they consist of little Scripture and many laws.
>
> (M. Ḥagigah 1:8)

Thus the Rabbis of the Talmud and Midrash clearly and consciously changed Jewish law as evidenced both by what they said and by what they did, adding a number of laws, dropping some, and changing the form of some.

Two things must be emphasized about this. First of all, they consid-

ered their actions authorized by God because *they*—the Rabbis themselves—were the ones empowered by the Torah to interpret and apply it
in every age. This is similar to American law, wherein the Constitution
establishes some laws as well as provisions for human beings to interpret
and apply those laws. In both systems the interpretations in later generations may vary widely from the original intention of the constitutional
(or biblical) laws—even to the extent of nullifying them—*but the new interpretations carry constitutional authority because they are made by the
bodies established by the Constitution.* This is the reason why lawyers
cite recent court decisions about the Constitution rather than the Constitution itself, and that is also the reason for the geonic rule in Jewish law
that *hilkh'ta kevatra'ei* ("the law is according to the last [that is, the
most recent] authorities"). In both cases, it is the *forms* (institutions) established by the Constitution that determine its meaning, even to the
point of effectively canceling sections of its contents, and it is because the
new rulings issue from the duly authorized bodies that they carry constitutional authority.

Second, and perhaps more importantly, with all of the changes that
the Rabbis instituted, they did *not* think that "anything goes," that they
could play completely fast and loose with the law. On the contrary, for
them it was clearly a matter of "*tradition* and change." In fact, change
in law is only significant if the law is taken seriously in the first place.
Otherwise, the whole legal system is not a matter of practical concern,
and changes in it are irrelevant.

The Rabbis dared to make the changes that they did because they
took the law seriously. They practiced it, honored it, and were deeply
concerned with its continuing authority and viability. For them it was
clear that it is the law that defines Jews as Jews; without it there is no
point to their separate identity:

> "[. . . they rejected My rules and spurned My laws. Yet even then,
> when they are in the land of their enemies,] I will not reject them or
> spurn them [so as to destroy them, annulling my Covenant with
> them]" (Leviticus 26:43–44). All the good gifts that were given them
> were taken from them. And if it had not been for the Book of the
> Torah that was left to them, they would not have differed at all from
> the nations of the world.
>
> (Sifra 112c)

Israel's acceptance of the Torah was the reason that it had a special relationship (covenant) with God:

If it were not for My Torah that you accepted, I should not recognize you, and I should not regard you more than any of the idolatrous nations of the world.

(Exodus Rabbah, *Ki Tissa*, 47:3)

Moreover, obeying the Torah is Israel's gift to God and the world, and through it Israel gains not only worth, but beauty:

God said, "If you read the Torah, you do a kindness, for you help to preserve My world, since if it were not for the Torah, the world would again become 'without form and void'" [as before creation, Genesis 1:2]. . . . The matter is like a king who had a precious stone, and he entrusted it to his friend and said to him, "I pray you, pay attention to it and guard it, as is fitting, for if you lose it, you cannot pay me its worth, and I have no other jewel like it, and so you would sin against yourself and against me; therefore, do your duty by both of us, and guard the jewel as is fitting." So Moses said to the Israelites, "If you keep the Torah, not only upon yourselves do you confer a benefit, but also upon God," as it is said, "And it shall be a benefit for us" (Deuteronomy 6:25).[5]

(Deuteronomy Rabbah, *Nitzavim*, 8:5)

"You are beautiful, my love" (Song of Songs 1:15). "You are beautiful" through the commandments, both positive and negative; beautiful through loving deeds; beautiful in your house with the heave-offerings and the tithes; beautiful in the field by keeping the commands about gleaning, the forgotten sheaf, and the second tithe; beautiful in the laws about mixed seeds, fringes, first fruits, and the fourth-year planting; beautiful in the law of circumcision; beautiful in prayer, in the reading of the Shema, in the law of the *mezuzah* and the phylacteries *(tefillin)*, in the law of the palm-branch *(lulav)* and the citron *(etrog)*; beautiful too, in repentance and in good works; beautiful in this world and beautiful in the world to come.

(Song of Songs Rabbah I, #15, I, on Song of Songs 1:15)

Consequently, the Rabbis say, Jews who do not observe the Law might as well not have been created:

Rabbi Yoḥanan ben Zakkai said: If you have learned much Torah, do not take credit for yourself, for you were created for that purpose.

(M. Avot 2:9)

Rava said: If someone fulfills the Torah not for its own sake [that is, for an ulterior motive], it were better had he or she never been created.

(B. Berakhot 17a)

In sum, then, the Rabbis of the Talmud and Midrash, who were the framers of Judaism and gave it its distinctive cast, held unequivocally that a Jew must observe the Torah's laws. They also held, though, that the Torah was not given once and for all at Sinai but rather must be interpreted and applied anew in each generation. Only if that happens can the Torah continue to be an important concern of Jews, a program for living. The alternative is to let it petrify into a relic of history. Thus it is not so much "tradition and change" as it is *tradition, which mandates and includes change.*

If the Torah is to retain a reasonable degree of consistency, however, it cannot be left to every individual to decide which laws to keep intact, which to change, and how. That must be done together as a community. I discuss more fully the process by which communal decisions in Jewish law are made in the Conservative movement in my book, *Conservative Judaism: Our Ancestors to Our Descendants* (New York: United Synagogue of Conservative Judaism, 1996), pp. 152–192.

We are now ready, though, to consider some of the theories of law created within the Conservative movement, followed by comparisons to theories of movements to the right and left. As we do this, look for each theory's responses to the issues delineated in chapter 1. Look also for the way in which each theory builds on this rabbinic base of taking the Torah very seriously *and therefore* also taking seriously the role of Jews in each generation—laypeople as well as rabbis—to make it live in the modern world.

CHAPTER THREE

Early Statements
of Conservative Legal Theory

A. ZACHARIAS FRANKEL (1801–75)

Zacharias Frankel is generally regarded as the ideological founder of the
Conservative movement in Judaism. After receiving a talmudic education under Bezalel Ronsburg, he studied philosophy, philology, and natural sciences in Budapest (1825–30). He was the first Bohemian rabbi
with a secular, academic education and one of the first to preach in German. He served congregations in Teplitz and Dresden. In 1854, after actively working for the establishment of a traditional but modern
rabbinical school in Breslau, he became its head, a position he held for
twenty-two years, training a generation of rabbis to respond to the challenges of his day.

Those challenges in many ways resemble our own, and then, as
now, they were anything but easy to meet. Rabbis always and everywhere had to confront and try to overcome varying degrees of Jewish
ignorance and superstitions, but until the end of the eighteenth century,
they could always rely on the fact that the non-Jewish government
would see the Jews as a distinct group, to be governed by Jewish authorities. This kind of corporate organizational pattern, in which the
government let the various subgroups within its realm govern themselves so long as they paid taxes to the government and, in some cases,
provided men for the army, began with the Romans and was subsequently used by the Muslims and most Christian rulers as well. It subjected Jews to second-class citizenship, often including restrictions on
where they could live (ghettos) and how they could earn a living, to say
nothing of the persecutions and outright murders that they all too
often endured; but it also provided an external guarantee that Jews
would abide by Jewish law as defined and administered by Jewish authorities.

In the 1760s, however, the German government embraced the Enlightenment principles that had been developed by seventeenth-century philosophers like John Locke, Thomas Hobbes, and Jean-Jacques Rousseau. Those principles were also officially embraced by the United States in its 1776 Declaration of Independence and by France during its Revolution of 1789. Thomas Jefferson's formulation of Enlightenment principles in the Declaration of Independence is a good summary of this new way of thinking: "We hold these truths to be self-evident, that all men are created equal, that they are endowed by their Creator with certain unalienable Rights, that among these are Life, Liberty, and the pursuit of Happiness." People were no longer to be seen as members of a particular group from the moment of their birth, with defined rights and limitations depending upon the religious group and economic class into which they were born; they were rather to be seen as individuals with inherent rights that could not be alienated—that is, taken away—by any government. Individuals themselves could alienate some of their rights, and they regularly did that when they left the "state of nature" to gain the benefits of a society, giving up their rights to kill others, to steal from them, etc., and taking on the responsibilities of paying taxes, serving in the army when necessary, etc. Governments, however, would need to justify any use of their power to deprive people of rights as somehow required to benefit the society. In theory, governments could go a long way in trying to make such arguments, as socialists and communists later did, and to this day the Scandinavian countries, for example, combine a large degree of freedom of thought and expression with a heavy tax burden placed on all citizens to support generous social benefits for all. In all countries governed by Enlightenment principles, however, freedom of expression, assembly, the press, and religion, together with other rights—rights that Americans know as the Bill of Rights—have been assured as an outgrowth of the view that no government could justly deprive individuals of those rights.

In Germany beginning in the 1760s, that meant a new burst of freedom for Jews. At least theoretically—and to varying degrees in fact—they no longer were restricted in what or where they could learn, where they could live, what they could do to earn a living (except for criminal activities, of course), or what religion they might affirm, if any. The first generation living under Enlightenment principles largely continued to practice Judaism but also took advantage of some of the new freedoms. As Moses Mendelssohn, a rabbi, philosopher, and statesman of the time, suggested, one should be a Jew at home and a German in the street. In this, these German Jews were very similar to the first generation of Eastern European Jews who came to America between 1881 and 1923, for in large proportion they too maintained their Jewish practices while trying to eke out a living and become good citizens in this land of new-found freedoms for them.

The second generation of Jews who grew into adulthood in Germany during the first three decades of the nineteenth century (and their counterparts in the United States between roughly 1920 and 1960), though, had another agenda. Many still maintained a connection to their Judaism, if only because they had grown up in a home that took Judaism seriously and because their parents were still alive, but they also wanted to attain success in the modern world governed by Enlightenment principles and laws. That meant engaging in university studies, business, government, and the tasks of daily life with non-Jews. That inevitably raised questions about observance of the Jewish dietary laws, the Sabbath, the High Holy Days, and the Festivals. For some it even raised the possibility—or at least the temptation—to marry a non-Jew.

The third generation of Jews in Germany, who grew into adulthood between 1830 and 1860 (with parallels to adults in the United States from 1960 to 1990), was yet further removed from their Jewish roots. If anything, they took their German (or American) identity for granted; it was their Jewish identity that they needed to figure out. As a result, many assimilated into the general culture, with little knowledge of their Jewish heritage and few, if any, expressions of it. Moreover, intermarriage between Jews and non-Jews increased in the third generation in both settings, both because Jews had become acceptable marriage partners for non-Jews and because assimilated Jews did not see any particularly strong reason to restrict their marital choices to Jews.

It was precisely during this third generation in Germany that Frankel was active. One way he sought to stem the tide of assimilation was to show that contemporary Jews did not have to give up their commitments to modern thought and scholarship in order to affirm Judaism. On the contrary, Jewish scholarship could and should use the very best in the new scholarly techniques applied in similar fields.

For that reason, and probably because he himself was convinced of its necessity, Frankel was among the chief exponents of studying Jewish sources through *a historical approach*. Until Frankel's time, Jews had understood their tradition through the eyes of the Rabbis. So, for example, if you wanted to know what a given biblical verse meant, you would consult the various works of rabbinic interpretation *(midrash)*, the Mishnah and Talmud, and the medieval commentators (such as Rashi) who continued and expanded on those earlier rabbinic materials. True, most Jewish medieval commentators regularly distinguished between what they took to be the direct meaning of the text (the *peshat*) in contrast to the accepted rabbinic understanding of it (the *derash*), and some medieval commentators (especially Ibn Ezra) even hinted at the possibility that the Torah consisted of disparate texts written at different places and times. In the seventeenth century, Benedict (Baruch) Spinoza, in his *Theological-Political Treatise,* suggested outright that the Torah was written by human beings for political purposes, but he was excommunicated by the Jewish community of Amsterdam at the time and his ideas were seen as heretical. Thus it was not until the nineteenth century, in Germany, that Jews integrally involved in the Jewish community began to study the Torah and rabbinic literature historically—that is, applying to one's own tradition the same methods used to study other ancient civilizations. Those methods included cross-cultural studies, linguistic comparisons and analysis, and, in the twentieth century, archeology. In this the Jews were following the lead of nineteenth-century non-Jewish historians, in their new form of historical analysis of all ancient traditions.

For the Jews involved, these methods did not replace the classical and medieval commentaries; the new, historical methods were used *in addition to* those traditional methods of understanding the text. Moreover, the Jews who used these methods certainly did not share the goals of some Protestant scholars like Karl Heinrich Graf and Julius Wellhausen, who, rooted in Hegelian notions of stages of history superceding previous stages, sought to use these methods to undermine the authority of Jewish Scriptures. Specifically, Graf and Wellhausen sought to prove that the Torah consisted of four different documents written in different times by human beings, which would prove that the authority of Judaism never rested on a direct revelation from God. Therefore the "Old Testament" need not be seen as having any more divine authority than the Gospels, which clearly had been written by human beings. On the contrary, the Gospels, in their view, represented a refinement of the Torah's ideas and so should supercede the religion based on the latter—namely, Judaism. Much of their scholarship, minus their supercessionist agenda, was adopted by later biblical scholars, including Jews, but these notions, of course, raise major problems for the ongoing practice of Judaism: suggesting that the Torah was written by human beings at disparate times and places immediately raises the question of why *its* ideas should be believed or commandments should be obeyed, rather than those of any other ancient text.

Frankel tried to appeal to the modern intellectual interests of the young Jews of his age and yet promote a traditional form of Judaism by advocating historical scholarship of Judaism along with traditional practice rooted in that history. Thus, while he participated in the Frankfurt Rabbinical Conference of 1845, which was summoned by the growing Reform movement, he left the conference in anger over the issue of its proposal to abandon Hebrew in favor of the German vernacular for worship. Ironically, classical Jewish law allows that very thing, for according to the Mishnah, a Jew may recite the Shema and the Amidah in any language (a ruling repeated in the codes).[1] Nevertheless, traditional Jewish practice over the ages had been to recite prayers in Hebrew, if at all possible, even though Hebrew had not been the spoken language of the Jewish people since the First Temple was destroyed in 586 B.C.E. Frankel dramatically left the Reform movement over this cultural preference for Hebrew in the liturgy, foreshadowing Conservative Judaism's later interests in not only the beliefs and rituals of Judaism, but its cultural manifestations as well.

In the following article, translated from the lead article in the second volume (1845) of the journal Frankel founded, *Zeitschrift fur judische religiouse Interessen (Journal for Jewish Religious Matters)*, Frankel describes his view of the process and parameters of change in Judaism. "Maintaining the integrity of Judaism simultaneously with progress, this is the essential problem of the present," he wrote in 1845, an apt description of the problem in the twenty-first century as well. Jewish law is based on divine revelation, according to Frankel, and it has two purposes: (1) to achieve the goals explicit in the laws themselves (as, for example, the law requiring honest weights and measures in Leviticus 19:35–36 and Deuteronomy 25:13–16), and (2) to remind man of God to "enable the spiritual and the heavenly within him to gain victory over the earthly and the beastly in his character," as, for example, the laws requiring daily worship. Because Judaism is a religion of action, "neither pure abstract contemplation nor dark mysticism could ever strike root in Judaism." Frankel rejects a Judaism based solely on, and identified by, beliefs, for that would belong only to the theologians when they happen to be thinking about religious matters—in contrast to a religion of action, which belongs to every follower and is always vibrant. He also rejects "dark mysticism," presumably because that has too much of a tendency to retreat into irrationality and narcissism; he wants instead "a rational faith."

This becomes clear when he objects to Orthodoxy and advocates instead "a third party," in between Orthodoxy and Reform, that "has arisen from the first party." Note that from the very beginning Conservative Jewish thinkers have understood their mission to maintain roots in traditional Judaism. That is, Conservative Judaism has always been a reaction to and rejection of the Reform approach in the name of tradition, and this was true already with Frankel, before the name "Conservative" was coined to indicate a movement devoted to conserving the Jewish tradition. Even though this "third party" would eventually also reject Orthodoxy to enable Judaism to adopt aspects of modern thought and practice, its orientation away from the Reform approach of introducing radical changes into Judaism is critical in understanding what would later become a mainstay of Conservative Jewish law—namely, that the burden of proof is always on the one who wants to change the law, rather than on the one who wants to continue what it has been in the past. Had the Conservative movement begun with the opposite orientation—that is, had it grown out of the Reform movement—the burden of proof would instead rest on the one who wants to argue for tradition. This has become evident in the Reform movement's own struggle to become more traditional in the last quarter of the twentieth century, where initiatives on the part of some of its leaders to make Reform Jewish practice more traditional have had to be watered down in order to be adopted to preserve individual autonomy (an important mainstay of the Reform movement). That is, if we begin with the presumption of reforming Judaism to fit it to the times, the burden of proof rests on the one who wants to retain or reintroduce Jewish traditions, despite the fact that moderns do not seem inclined to observe them. Frankel already presages the opposite mode in Conservative Judaism, where tradition rules unless a good argument can be mounted to revise it.

At the same time, Frankel is neither Orthodox nor Orthoprax—that is, he neither believes as the Orthodox do, nor does he advocate abiding by Jewish law as the Orthodox do. He is not an Orthodox believer because he is committed to studying the Torah and rabbinic texts historically and thus to seeing the Torah as written and edited by human beings in specific times and places, rather than by God directly. He is not Orthodox in his practice because he demands that Jewish law is not fulfilled by action alone, that it rather "shall not be empty of spirit and that it shall not become merely mechanical, expressing itself mainly in the form." Orthodox spokesmen, of course, would also ideally want people's intention and consciousness coupled with their observance, their *kavanah* (directionality, intention, consciousness) together with their *keva* (fixed practice), but unlike the Orthodox, Frankel would not be satisfied with actions alone. In this he actually demands more than the Orthodox.

Moreover, Frankel believes that a proper Judaism "holds that we must omit certain unimportant actions which are not inherently connected either with the high ideas or with the religious forms delineated by the revealed laws. We must . . . take into consideration the opposition between faith and conditions of the time." He argues that traditional Judaism itself allows for changes in the law to suit the needs and sensitivities of the time, that "the letter of the law is not decisive, but rather that the spirit must animate the law and raise it to a divine status worthy to become a norm to man who is himself endowed with spirit."

Notice two things here. First, he believes that law must fit the community, and so rabbis need to pay attention, as the Talmud says, to "that which was adopted by the entire community of Israel and was accepted by the people and became part of its life"—that is, its customs. "The people is not altogether mere clay to be molded by the will of theologians and scholars. In religious activities, as in those of ordinary life, it decides for itself. This right was conceded by Judaism to the people." That includes not only giving credence and authority to new practices the people have adopted, but also abrogating traditional practices that the people have abandoned: "When the people allows certain practices to fall into disuse, then the practices cease to exist." Later Conservative thinkers will also pay great attention to the role of custom in fixing the content of the law, and they will have to deal with the question of identifying when the law should remain binding even if the majority of Jews no longer practice it—as, for example, with the Jewish dietary laws in our time. In the closing paragraph of this essay, Frankel already anticipates the critical role of rabbis as educators to "guard the sense of piety of the people and to raise their spirit to the height of the great ideas" inherent in the tradition. So attention to the people's custom will not always mean surrendering to it; sometimes it will mean doing everything possible to change it. Which reaction to popular custom to adopt will be an important, and sometimes a hard, judgment call for rabbis to make.

Second, Frankel perceives changes in the law *not* as mere compromises with current practice, but as ways to animate the law and renew its divine spirit—that is, to keep the law an effective avenue to God and to God's values and ideals. This too will become a common theme in later Conservative thought, as Conservative leaders endeavor to make Judaism nothing less than meaningful service to the Eternal.

On Changes In Judaism*

BY ZACHARIAS FRANKEL

THE PURPOSE OF THE *Zeitschrift* is the reconciliation of belief and life, the assurance of progress within our faith, and the refining and re-generating of Judaism from and through itself. This is the circle in which our effort must move. Anything outside this circle ceases to be Judaism. Those to whom even this circle seems to be extensive, incline to stagnation and oppose the demands of life and its activity. For cen-turies Judaism has engaged in a successful struggle with the world. Through the ages Judaism has shed its light abroad and illumined the way of many nations who even today, whether consciously or uncon-sciously, make use of its enlightenment. Not in vain did Judaism op-pose paganism, materialism, sensuality, and the striving after earthly things. Through many generations Judaism sustained and guarded the sparks of divine spirit, and in helping them to develop, developed it-self. Shall we assume that its power is now exhausted and consumed, that its living high spirit has lost its force? Does the spirit of the age re-ally rise against it with might and strength?

Maintaining the integrity of Judaism simultaneously with progress, this is the essential problem of the present. Can we deny the difficulty of a satisfactory solution? Where is the point where the two apparent contraries can meet? What ought to be our point of departure in the at-tempt to reconcile essential Judaism and progress and what type of op-position may we expect to encounter? How can we assure rest for the soul so that it shall not be torn apart or be numbed by severe doubts while searching for the warm ray of faith, and yet allot to reason its right, and enable it to lend strength and lucidity to the religious feeling which springs from the emotions? The opposing elements which so sel-dom are in balance must be united and this is our task.

In order to find the way for uniting them, we must consider both the starting point and the aim of the movement which seeks this recon-ciliation. Even in advocating social and political change one must think of the starting point and the goal. Usually the former is the situa-tion as it is, while the latter is the situation as it should be. The aim can be arrived at by reflection and definition, but the starting point is rooted in life relations. Both elements must be properly understood and valued in order to determine the chain of activity and thought which will lead from "what is" to "what ought to be." In religious

---

*A translation, in condensed form, of the lead article in the second vol-ume of the *Zeitschrift* (1845), from *Tradition and Change*, Mordecai Waxman, ed. (New York: The Burning Bush Press, 1958), pp. 43–50.

matters there is in addition to the starting point also an inner force which must be reckoned with and added to the mere statement of "what is." To be understood, religion must be lived and deeply felt. And if we want to determine the measure for a discreet progress and change, we must first of all have a clear conception of the point of departure, namely Judaism itself. Judaism is a great historical truth, and its role in world history cannot be minimized either through mistaken interpretation or through prejudiced polemic.

Judaism contains, at its core, the highest teachings about God, His attributes, and doctrines, about the existence of man, his goal in life and the nature of his activity. To the Jew his God is a personal and an extra-mundane Being, and yet One who is within the world; nay more, even One who lives within his heart, for whom the right name is "Father." The beautiful expression of the Bible: "You are children of your eternal God" (Deut. 14:1) was conceived by Judaism in a warm and profound sense. The loving relation between father and children became the essence of the whole complex of its faith and formed the corner and the capstone of its spiritual structure. To this fundamental thought embodied in the Scriptures in brief dry sentences, there is added an oral tradition which breathes warmth and gentleness about the relation between the Jew and his God. This tradition is filled with the awareness of God and in consequence embodies a truth the value of which cannot in any way be lessened or be made light of.

Judaism ties its teachings to divine revelation, which is an expression of the highest will of God. The eternal truths regarding the Godhead and morality flow from this source, and around these there are grouped other laws which are saturated with the same spirit, and in which the high ideas of the nobility of man and his closeness to God find expression. These revealed laws are the guardians of Judaism, the never-slumbering watchmen of the holiest elements within it. They are designed to protect the highest truths, and they have faithfully carried out this mission to the present day. These laws have one of two purposes. Some have the purpose within themselves, though it may not always be clearly evident in each particular law. Thus the dietary laws aim at cultivating restraint of appetite; the sexual laws at inculcating chastity and purity of morals. Other laws which mirror the power of God as the creator have another function—to remind man of God. Through their practice man is enabled to bind himself to the divine and enable the spiritual and the heavenly within him to gain victory over the earthly and the beastly in his character. It is clear that man can apprehend the highest ideas meaningfully, only by means of sense data. Ideas are not always presented or apprehended with clarity. Men cannot rise to lofty complicated ideas at will, and frequently, in the whirl of life, these ideas are entirely lost to the mass of men. Abstraction and mere contemplation are not enough. The soul must have experience of sensation and reverence; the idea must clothe itself in a body, else it is lost to man. To prevent this loss is one of the aims of the precepts. They express recognition of, and reverence for, the divine will; they themselves become spiritualized and carriers of spiritual impulses.

Again, Judaism is a religion which has a direct influence on life's activity. It is a religion of action, demanding the performance of precepts which either directly aim at ennobling man or, by reminding man of the divine, strengthen his feelings of dependence on God. And because of this trait neither pure abstract contemplation nor dark mysticism could ever strike root in Judaism. This, in turn, guaranteed that the lofty religious ideas were maintained in their purity, with the result that even today the divine light shines in Judaism.

By emphasizing religious activity, Judaism is completely tied to life and becomes the property of every individual Jew. A religion of pure ideas belongs primarily to the theologians; the masses who are not adapted to such conceptions concern themselves little with the particulars of such religions because they have little relationship to life. On the other hand, a religion of action is always present, demanding practice in activity and an expression of will, and its demands are reflected in the manifold life of the individual, with the result that the faith becomes the common property of every follower.

Thus we have reached the starting point for the consideration of the current parties in Judaism. The viewpoint of the Orthodox party is clear. It has grown up in pious activity; to it the performance of precepts is inseparable from faith, for to it, the two are closely and inwardly connected. Were it to tear itself away from observance and give up the precepts, then it would find itself estranged from its own self and feel as though plunged into an abyss. Given this viewpoint, the direction and emphasis of the Orthodox party is clear. Where else, save in the combination of faith and meticulous observance of the precepts, can it find that complete satisfaction which it has enjoyed in the heritage of the fathers? When will it reject that which it has so long kept holy and inviolable? No—that is unthinkable.

Against this party there has arisen of late another one (Reform) which finds its aim in the opposite direction. This party sees salvation in overcoming the past, in carrying progress to the limit, in rejecting religious forms and returning merely to the simple original ideas. In fact, we can hardly call it a party in Judaism, though its adherents still bear the name Jew, and are considered as such in social and political life, and do not belong to another faith. They do not, however, belong wholly to Judaism, for by limiting Judaism to some principles of faith, they place themselves partly outside the limits of Judaism.

We will now turn to a third party which has arisen from the first party, and not only stands within the bound of Judaism, but is also filled with real zeal for its preservation and endeavors to hand it over to its descendants and make it the common good of all times.

This party bases itself upon rational faith and recognizes that the task of Judaism is religious action, but it demands that this action shall not be empty of spirit and that it shall not become merely mechanical, expressing itself mainly in the form. It has also reached the view that religious activity, itself, must be brought up to a higher level through giving weight to the many meanings with which it should be endowed.

Furthermore, it holds that we must omit certain unimportant actions which are not inherently connected either with the high ideas or with the religious forms delineated by the revealed laws. We must, it feels, take into consideration the opposition between faith and conditions of the time. True faith, due to its divine nature, is above time, and just as the nobler part of man is not subjected to time, so does faith rise above all time, and the word which issued from the mouth of God is rooted in eternity. But time has a force and might which must be taken account of. There is then created a dualism in which faith and time face each other, and man chooses either to live beyond time or to be subjected to it. It is in this situation that the Jew finds himself today; he cannot escape the influence of the conditions of the time and yet when the demands of faith bring him to opposition with the spirit of the time, it is hoped that he will heed its call—find the power to resist the blandishments of the times. This third party, then, declares that Judaism must be saved for all time. It affirms both the divine value and historical basis of Judaism and, therefore, believes that by introducing some changes it may achieve some agreement with the concepts and conditions of the time.

In order to have a conception of what changes should and can be introduced, we must ask ourselves the question—does Judaism allow any changes in any of its religious forms? Does it consider all of them immutable, or can they be altered? Without entering into the citation of authorities pro and con, we may point out that Judaism does indeed allow changes. The early teachers, by interpretation, changed the literal meaning of the Scriptures; later scholars that of the Mishnah, and the post-Talmudic scholars that of the Talmud. All these interpretations were not intended as idle speculation. They addressed themselves to life activities and imparted different forms to the practice of certain precepts. Thanks to such studies, Judaism achieved stabilization and avoided estrangement from the conditions of the time in various periods. Not in vain was the day declared a festival when the Pharisees overcame the Sadducees and ruled that the Biblical statement "An eye for an eye, a hand for a hand" was not to be taken literally, but was designed merely to indicate that the proper compensation should be imposed for such injury (*Megillat Taanit*, Ch. 4). This was a triumph not because of the humanitarian interpretation that it proposed, but, mainly, because it led to the establishment of the principle that the letter of the law is not decisive, but rather that the spirit must animate the law and raise it to a divine status worthy to become a norm to man who is himself endowed with spirit. The teachers of the oral law supported such interpretations in a number of cases. But on the other hand, they established a rule which was intended as a guardian and protector against undue changes. It reads as follows: That which was adopted by the entire community of Israel and was accepted by the people and became a part of its life, can not be changed by any authority (*Abodah Zarah*, 36).

In this fundamental statement there lies a living truth. Through it there speaks a profound view of Judaism which can serve for all times as a formula for needed changes and can be employed both against destructive reform and against stagnation.

This fundamental statement helps to make clear to us what changes in Judaism are justified and how they can be realized. True, Judaism demands religious activity, but the people is not altogether mere clay to be molded by the will of theologians and scholars. In religious activities, as in those of ordinary life, it decides for itself. This right was conceded by Judaism to the people. At such times as an earlier religious ordinance was not accepted by the entire community of Israel, it was given up. Consequently, when a new ordinance was about to be enacted it was necessary to see whether it would find acceptance by the people. When the people allows certain practices to fall into disuse, then the practices cease to exist. There is in such cases no danger for faith. A people used to activity will not hurt itself and will not destroy its practices. Its own sense of religiosity warns against it. Only those practices from which it is entirely estranged and which yield it no satisfaction will be abandoned and will thus die of themselves. On the whole there is always a great fund of faith and religious activity to afford security against negation and destruction.

We have, then, reached a decisive point in regard to moderate changes, namely, that they must come from the people and that the will of the entire community must decide. Still, this rule alone may accomplish little. The whole community is a heavy unharmonious body, and its will is difficult to recognize. It comes to expression only after many years. We must find a way to carry on such changes in the proper manner, and this can be done by the help of the scholars. Judaism has no priests as representatives of faith, nor does it require special spiritual sanctimoniousness in its spokesmen. The power to represent it is not the share of any one family, nor does it pass from father to son. Knowledge and mastery of the law supply the sanctity, and these can be attained by everybody. In Jewish life, spiritual and intellectual ability ultimately took the place of the former priesthood which, even in early times, was limited in its function primarily to the sacrificial cult. Even in early days, Judaism recognized the will of the people as a great force, and because of this recognition a great religious activity came into being. But this activity, in turn, was translated into a living force by the teachers of the people through the use of original ordinances and through interpretation of the Scriptures. At times these actions of the sages lightened the amount of observance; at times they increased it. That the results of the studies and research of the teachers found acceptance among the people proves, on the one hand, that the teachers knew the character of their time, and, on the other hand, that the people had confidence in them and that they considered them true representatives of their faith.

Should Jewish theologians and scholars of our time succeed in acquiring such a confidence, then they will attain influence with the introduction of whatever changes may be necessary. The will of the community of Israel will then find its representatives, and knowledge will be its proper exercise.

The scholars thus have an important duty in order to make their work effective. It is to guard the sense of piety of the people and to raise their spirit to the height of the great ideas. For this they need the confidence of the people. Opposition to the views of the people, such as some reformers display, is unholy and fruitless. The teacher thereby loses the power to make the essence of faith effective, for in place of that confidence which is the basis in correct relations between teacher and community there comes mistrust and an unwillingness to follow. The truths of faith must be brought nearer to the people so that they may learn to understand the divine content within them and thus come to understand the spiritual nature and inner worth of the forms which embody these truths. Once the people are saturated with an awareness of the essential truths and the forms which embody them, a firm ground will have been established for adhering to Jewish practices. And if the people then cease to practice some unimportant customs and forms of observances, it will not be a matter of great concern. And it will not, as recent changes have, lead some Jews into shock and hopelessness. They will no longer see all such changes as leading to the disappearance of our faith and spelling, as their pusillanimity leads them to believe, the end of the existence of Judaism.

B. SOLOMON SCHECHTER (1847–1915)

Solomon Schechter studied in European seminaries and universities and subsequently taught at Cambridge University. He achieved world-wide scholarly renown for recognizing the importance of the medieval documents discovered by Samson Wertheimer in the *genizah* (store room) of the Cairo synagogue and for organizing the effort and the funding to bring those documents to the British Museum and then, in part, to the library of the Jewish Theological Seminary of America. He served as Chancellor of the Seminary from 1902 to 1915, during which time he managed to reorganize and find funding for the ailing seminary. As a result, that institution is still sometimes called, as it was in his time, "Schechter's Seminary," and many Conservative day schools are part of the Solomon Schechter Day School Association, some even named after him. As the one who revitalized the Seminary and founded the United Synagogue, he is arguably the institutional founder of the Conservative movement.

However, he himself did not see his work in that way, for he repeatedly asserted that he was not creating a new party, but reviving a very old one—namely, traditional Judaism. To underscore this point, he generally referred to the "Conservative tendency" rather than to "the Conservative movement." This—together with the fact that his area of scholarly expertise was rabbinics and not theology or philosophy—may also explain why he nowhere set forth a coherent statement of his own theological views. Nevertheless, his writings bespeak his fundamental commitments and the kind of Judaism he espoused and sought to promote.

That Judaism was strongly rooted in *klal yisrael*—the community of the People Israel, or, as he translated the term, "Catholic Israel." We are used to thinking of the word "Catholic," especially when capitalized, to refer to the Catholic Church, but Schechter was referring to the primary meaning of the word—namely, broad and comprehensive (for example, one could say that a given person has catholic interests). By the term "Catholic Israel," then, Schechter intended to focus attention on the communal aspects of Judaism.

This manifested itself in several ways. One was his Zionism. In 1906, just eight years after the First Zionist Congress met in Basel, Switzerland, Schechter wrote a strong defense of Zionism. While we may take Zionism for granted, living as we do more than fifty years after the founding of the State of Israel, in the early twentieth century Zionism was anything but a foregone conclusion. Many Orthodox Jews objected to Zionism on the grounds that establishing a Jewish state in the homeland would be pushing God's hand, and we should instead piously wait for the Messiah to lead us there. Many Reform Jews also objected to Zionism, but for a different reason: they saw it as a counterproductive expression of Jewish nationalism when the world was, and should be, moving to universalism. To encourage all Jews to live in one place was, in this view, to undermine the ability of Jews to spread God's light to the nations; "the remnant of Israel" instead were, in the words of the biblical prophet Micah, supposed to live "among many nations, as the dew from God and as the rain on the grass" (Micah 5:6). In one of his addresses, Schechter admits that not all people at the Seminary were Zionists, but as early as 1918 (three years after his death) the United Synagogue convention passed a resolution committing itself not only to pray for Zion but also to work for the Zionist enterprise. In any case, Schechter saw reestablishment of a Jewish state in Palestine as "a mighty bulwark against the incessantly assailing forces of assimilation," and toward the end of his life he called Zionism "the most cherished dream I was worthy of having."[2]

Schechter's emphasis on Catholic Israel also led him to seek to create a cross-denominational synagogue movement. By 1885, when the

Reform rabbis adopted their Pittsburgh Platform, it had become clear that Reform Judaism would specifically reject traditional practices such as the dietary laws, and Schechter strongly objected to that form of Judaism. He calls it "spirit without letter," and he describes it as belonging "to the species known to the mystics as 'nude souls,' *neshamot artila'ot,* wandering about in the universe without balance and without consistency."[3] So the synagogues he sought to unite were all those that espoused some form of traditional Judaism. When the Union of Orthodox Hebrew Congregations was founded, though, he had to face the fact that the Orthodox would not join his cross-denominational effort, and so he founded the United Synagogue of America in 1913. Even then, as the name indicates, he hoped that ultimately all traditional synagogues in America would join hands in the new organization, regardless of whatever tendencies they adopted regarding the practice and beliefs of Judaism.

For our purposes in this volume on theories of law, probably the most important implications of Schechter's doctrine of "Catholic Israel" concern the ways it influences our understanding of the nature and operation of Jewish law. In the essay that follows, Schechter describes the fact that a serious historical study of the Jewish tradition reveals that the meaning and practical import of the Torah has always been defined by the oral tradition. That, in turn, was shaped by both the Rabbis in every generation and "the collective conscience of Catholic Israel as embodied in the Universal Synagogue"—that is, the generally accepted views, values, and practices of devoted Jews. This is the "secondary meaning" of which he speaks: the "first meaning" is the plain sense of the Torah itself, but the rabbinic tradition that we inherited did not let the Torah in its direct meaning govern. Instead, what became Jewish law was a function of two things: how the Rabbis interpreted the Torah, and how the Jews practiced it. What the Rabbis said and what the people did were not always in agreement, but, in any case, it was in the discussions and decisions of the Rabbis and in the practices of the people that one finds the "secondary meaning" of the Torah, which in fact sets the parameters of Jewish law. As Schechter puts it, "Another consequence of this conception of Tradition is that it is neither Scripture nor primitive Judaism [that is, Judaism as it was in early times], but general custom which forms the real rule of practice." "Hence," he says in very strong language, "a return to Mosaism would be illegal, pernicious, and indeed impossible"—illegal, because Jewish law interprets the Torah in specific ways and includes many rules not found in the Torah; pernicious, because an attempt to return to the laws of the Torah would reverse thousands of years of tradition and thereby probably undermine allegiance to the Jewish tradition altogether; and impossible, because for better or for worse, Judaism for centuries has not been the religion of the Torah but rather the religion of the Torah *as interpreted by rabbis and practiced by Jews in each generation,* and it is impossible to turn back the clock on that development.

Schechter admits to some nostalgia for a time in which the Torah governed directly. He calls traditional Judaism a kind of "bimet-allism"—that is, a market in which there are two currencies used in commercial transactions—"in which bold speculators in theology try to keep up the market value of an inferior currency by denouncing loudly the bright shining gold which, they would have us believe, is less fitted to circulate in the vulgar use of daily life than the small cash of historical interpretation." In other words, the gold of the Torah, which, after all, is the most precious metal, is being exchanged for the "small cash" of historical interpretation and practice. "Nor can I quite reconcile myself to this alliance of religion with history, which seems to me both unworthy and unnatural." History never ruled just because it describes what is (or what was). Historical developments influenced the Jewish tradition only when rabbis tied them to the concepts, values, and laws of the Torah. So for Schechter, just as Torah does not rule by itself, neither does history. Still, in the end, it is the rabbis' ongoing interpretations of the Torah and the changing practices of Catholic Israel that determine the content of Jewish law.

Notice what this says about the nature of God and human beings and the relationship between them. The Torah is not to be understood in a fundamentalistic way; like the classical Rabbis before him, Schechter affirms that the meaning and the legal import of the Torah must be determined by rabbis and by the customs of devout Jews in each generation. Ultimately, though, the Torah *is* the basis for Jewish practice. Schechter strongly objected to "higher" biblical criticism, which seeks to identify strata in the Torah as coming from different times and places. Against the background of people like Graf and Wellhausen, he calls such studies "Higher Anti-Semitism."[4] Thus for him, the grounding of Jewish law in the Torah gives it a strong basis in God's will and thus divine authority. Even though Schechter is not clear about the nature of revelation—whether God spoke words at Sinai, or whether God inspired the human writers of the Torah—what is clear for him is that the Torah reflects God's will. It is not a document created by human beings alone. At the same time, the meaning and practical import of the Torah has always been, and will continue to be, defined by human beings—rabbis in each generation and the people themselves. Thus God and Jews *together* create the Jewish tradition, including its legal component.

But also notice that at the end of this essay, Schechter asserts that the historical school to which he is committed does not have a theology of its own, but rather consists only of "scientific work"—that is, scholarly analyses of the meanings and development of the tradition, using cross-cultural tools as well as traditional interpretations. But in the last line, Schechter says that he neither hopes nor expects that leaving theological questions aside in the name of getting on with scholarly analysis will suffice for the next generation. For some such scholars, including many on the Seminary's own Talmud faculty, setting theology aside would remain their mode on into the 1970s, but for others, like Mordecai Kaplan, those questions would arise in the very next generation.

Moreover, in evaluating Schechter's approach to Jewish law, one must acknowledge that he is not clear about how the decisions of rabbis and the practices of Catholic Israel are supposed to complement each other. If both rabbis and lay people are involved in determining the law, which, if either, has ultimate authority? If decisions are to be made jointly, how and with what rules of procedure should that occur? However that cooperation happens, it depends on a rabbinate that knows the secular world and is open to modernity and a laity that is educated in the Jewish tradition, both of which are often lacking.

To his credit, though, Schechter has put his finger on a characteristic of Jewish law since the time of Moses—namely, that it is always the product of an interaction between the leaders and the laity. Sometimes leaders do all they can to change communal practice, as Moses and many other biblical figures did repeatedly in trying to fight the masses' love of idolatry; and sometimes, as in the case of Moses' judging of the people before the revelation at Mount Sinai, presumably in accord with their own established commercial practices (Exodus 18), Jewish law originates with the people. Schechter's commitment to tradition and simultaneously to Catholic Israel and its customs captures the tension between the two that has shaped Jewish law from its inception. His theory may not give clear directions for how and why Jewish legal decisions are to be made, and thus those looking for a clear and undisputed way of determining Jewish law will not like his approach; but it does accurately articulate the continuing interaction between Jewish leaders and laity in defining Jewish practice.

Historical Judaism*

SOLOMON SCHECHTER

IN READING THE PROOFS (of this volume) I have been struck by the fact that there is assumed in them a certain conception of the Synagogue which, familiar though it be to the Jewish student, may appear obscure and even strange to the general English reader. For brevity's sake I will call it the High Synagogue, though it does not correspond in all details to what one is acccustomed to understand under the term of High Church. The High Synagogue has a history which is not altogether without its points of interest.

Some years ago when the waves of the Higher Criticism of the Old Testament reached the shores of this country (England), and such questions as the heterogeneous composition of the Pentateuch, the comparatively late date of the Levitical Legislation, and the post-exilic origin of certain Prophecies as well as of the Psalms began to be freely discussed by the press and even in the pulpit, the invidious remark was often made: What will now become of Judaism when its last stronghold, the Law, is being shaken to its very foundations?

Such a remark shows a very superficial acquaintance with the nature of an old historical religion like Judaism, and the richness of the resources it has to fall back upon in cases of emergency.

As a fact, the emergency did not quite surprise Judaism. The alarm signal was given some 150 years ago by an Italian Rabbi, Abiad Sar Shalom Basilea, in his pamphlet *The Faith of the Sages.* The pamphlet is, as the title indicates, of a polemical character, reviewing the work of the Jewish rationalistic schools; and after warming up in his attacks against their heterodox views, Basilea exclaims: "Nature and simple meaning, they are our misfortune." By "nature and simple meaning" Basilea, who wrote in Hebrew, understood what we would call Natural Science and Philology. With the right instinct of faith, Basilea hit on the real sore points. For though he mostly argues against the philosophical systems of Aristotle and his commentators, he felt that it is not speculation that will ever seriously endanger religion. There is hardly any metaphysical system, old or new, which has not in course

*Excerpted from the Introduction to *Studies in Judaism,* First Series (Philadelphia, 1896).

of time been adapted by able dialecticians to the creed which they happened to hold. In our own time we have seen the glorious, though not entirely novel spectacle, of Agnosticism itself becoming the rightful handmaid of Queen Theology. The real danger lies in "nature" (or Natural Science) with its stern demand of law and regularity in all phenomena, and in the "simple meaning" (or Philology) with its inconsiderate insistence on truth. Of the two, the "simple meaning" is the more objectionable. Not only is it very often at variance with Tradition, which has its own code of interpretation, but it is constantly increasing the difficulties raised by science. For if words could only have more than one meaning, there would be no objection to reading the first words of Genesis, "In *a* beginning God *evolved*." The difficulties of science would then be disposed of easily enough. Maimonides, who was as bold an interpreter as he was a deep metaphysician, hinted plainly enough that were he as convinced of the eternity of matter as he was satisfied of the impossibility of any corporeal quality in the Deity, he would feel as little compunction in explaining (figuratively) the contents of the first chapter of Genesis as he did in allegorising the anthropomorphic passages of the Bible. Thus in the end all the difficulties resolve themselves into the one great difficulty of the "simple meaning." The best way to meet this difficulty was found to be to shift the centre of gravity in Judaism and to place it in the secondary meaning, thus making religion independent of philology and all its dangerous consequences.

The shifting work was chiefly done, perhaps not quite consciously, by the historical school which followed upon that of Mendelssohn and his first successors. The historical school, which is still in the ascendant, comprises many of the best Jewish writers who either by their learning or by their ecclesiastical profession as Rabbis and preachers in great communities have acquired some important position among their brethren. The men who have inaugurated this movement were Krochmal (1785–1841), Rapoport (1790–1867), and Zunz (1794–1886).

It is not a mere coincidence that the first representatives of the historical school were also the first Jewish scholars who proved themselves more or less ready to join the modern school of Bible Criticism, and even to contribute their share to it. The first two, Krochmal and Rapoport, early in the second quarter of this century accepted and defended the modern view about a second Isaiah, the post-exilic origin of many Psalms, and the late date of Ecclesiastes; whilst Zunz, who began (in 1832) with denying the authenticity of Ezekiel, concluded his literary career (1873) with a study on the Bible (*Gesammelte Schriften*, i. pp. 217–290), in which he expressed his view "that the Book of Leviticus dates from a later period than the Book of Deuteronomy, later even than Ezekiel, having been composed during the age of the Second Temple, when there already existed a well-established priesthood which superintended the sacrificial worship." But when Revelation or the Written Word is reduced to the level of history, there is no difficulty in elevating history in its aspect of Tradition to the rank of Scripture, for both have then the same human or divine origin (according to the student's predilection for the one or the other adjective), and emanate from the same authority. Tradition becomes thus the means whereby the modern divine seeks to compensate himself for the loss of the Bible, and the theological balance is to the satisfaction of all parties happily readjusted.

Jewish Tradition, or, as it is commonly called, the Oral Law, or, as we may term it (in consideration of its claims to represent an interpretation of the Bible), the Secondary Meaning of the Scriptures, is mainly embodied in the works of the Rabbis and their subsequent followers during the Middle Ages. Hence the zeal and energy with which the historical school applied itself to the Jewish post-biblical literature, not only elucidating its texts by means of new critical editions, dictionaries, and commentaries, but also trying to trace its origins and to pursue its history through its gradual development. To the work of Krochmal in this direction a special essay is devoted in this volume. The labours of Rapoport are more of a biographical and bibliographical nature, being occupied mostly with the minor details in the lives and writings of various famous Jewish Rabbis in the Middle Ages; thus they offer but little opportunity for general theological comment. Of more importance in this respect are the hints thrown out in his various works by Zunz, who was just as emphatic in asserting the claims of Tradition as he was advanced in his views on Bible criticism. Zunz's greatest work is *Die Gottesdienstliche Vorträge*—an awkward title, which in fact means "The History of the Interpretation of the Scriptures as Forming a Part of the Divine Service." Now if a work displaying such wide learning and critical acumen, and written in such an impartial spirit can be said to have a bias, it was towards bridging over the seemingly wide gap between the Written Word (the Scriptures) and the Spoken Word (the Oral Law or Tradition), which was the more deeply felt, as most of Zunz's older contemporaries were men grown up in the habits of thought of the eighteenth century—a century distinguished both for its ignorance of, and its power of ignoring, the teachings of history. Indeed it would seem that ages employed in making history have no time for studying it.

Zunz accomplished the task he set himself, by showing, as already indicated, the late date of certain portions of the Bible, which by setting the early history of Israel in an ideal light betray the moralising tendency of their authors, and are, in fact, little more than a traditional interpretation of older portions of Scripture, adapted to the religious needs of the time. Placing thus the origin of Tradition in the Bible itself, it was a comparatively easy matter for Zunz to prove its further continuity. Prophecy and Interpretation are with him the natural expressions of the religious life of the nation; and though by the loss of Israel's political independence the voice of the prophets gradually died away, the voice of God was still heard. Israel continues to consult God through the medium of the Scriptures, and He answers His people by the mouth of the Scribes, the Sages, the Interpreters of the Law; whilst the liturgy of the Synagogue, springing up at the time when Psalms were still being composed, expands in its later stages through the work of the Poets of the Synagogue into such a rich luxuriance "that it forms in itself a treasure of history, poetry, philosophy; and prophecy and psalms are again revived in the hymnology of the Middle Ages." This is in brief the lesson to be learned from Zunz's *Gottesdienstliche Vorträge* as far as it deals with the significance of Tradition; and it is in the introduction to this work that Zunz expresses himself to the following effect: Indispensable is the free Spoken Word. Mankind has acquired all its ideal treasures only by Word of Mouth, an education continuing through all stages of life. In Israel, too, the Word of Instruction transmitted from mouth to mouth was never silenced.

The historical school has never, to my knowledge, offered to the world a theological programme of its own. By the nature of its task, its labours are mostly conducted in the field of philology and archaeology, and it pays but little attention to pure dogmatic questions. On the whole, its attitude towards religion may be defined as an enlightened Scepticism combined with a staunch conservatism which is not even wholly devoid of a certain mystical touch. As far as we may gather from vague remarks and hints thrown out now and then, its theological position may perhaps be thus defined:—It is not the mere revealed Bible that is of first importance to the Jew, but the Bible as it repeats itself in history, in other words, at it is interpreted by Tradition. The Talmud, that wonderful mine of religious ideas from which it would be just as easy to draw up a manual for the most orthodox as to extract a *vademecum* for the most sceptical, lends some countenance to this view by certain controversial passages—not to be taken seriously—in which "the words of the scribes" are placed almost above the words of the Torah. Since then the interpretation of Scripture or the Secondary Meaning is mainly a product of changing historical influences, it follows that the centre of authority is actually removed from the Bible and placed in some *living body*, which, by reason of its being in touch with the ideal aspirations and the religious needs of the age, is best able to determine the nature of the Secondary Meaning. This living body, however, is not represented by any section of the nation, or any corporate priesthood, or Rabbihood, but by the collective conscience of Catholic Israel as embodied in the Universal Synagogue. The Synagogue "with its long, continuous cry after God for more than twenty-three centuries," with its unremittent activity in teaching and developing the word of God, with its uninterrupted succession of Prophets, Psalmists, Scribes, Assideans, Rabbis, Patriarchs, Interpreters, Elucidators, Eminences, and Teachers, with its glorious record of saints, martyrs, sages, philosophers, scholars, and mystics—this Synagogue, the only true witness to the past, and forming in all ages the sublimest expression of Israel's religious life, must also retain its authority as the sole true guide for the present and the future. And being in communion with this Synagogue, we may also look hopefully for a safe and rational solution of our present theological troubles. For was it not the Synagogue which even in antiquity determined the fate of Scripture? On the one hand, for example, books like Ezekiel, the Song of Songs, and Ecclesiastes were only declared to be Holy Writ in virtue of the interpretation put upon them by the Rabbis: and, on the other hand, it was the veto of the Rabbis which excluded from the canon the works that now pass under the name of Apocrypha. We may, therefore, safely trust that the Synagogue will again assert its divine right in passing judgment upon the Bible when it feels called upon to exercise that holy office. It is "God who has chosen the Torah, and Moses His servant, and Israel His people." But indeed God's choice invariably coincides with the wishes of Israel; He "performeth all things" upon which the councils of Israel, meeting under promise of the Divine presence and communion, have previously agreed. As the Talmud somewhere expresses itself with regard to the Book of Esther, "They have confirmed above what Israel has accepted below."

Another consequence of this conception of Tradition is that it is neither Scripture nor primitive Judaism, but general custom which forms the real rule of practice. Holy Writ as well as history, Zunz tells us, teaches that the law of Moses was never fully and absolutely put in practice. Liberty was always given to the great teachers of every generation to make modifications and innovations in harmony with the spirit of existing institutions. Hence a return to Mosaism would be illegal, pernicious, and indeed impossible. The norm as well as the sanction of Judaism is the practice actually in vogue. Its consecration is the consecration of general use—or, in other words, of Catholic Israel. It was probably with a view to this communion that the later mystics introduced a short prayer to be said before the performance of any religious ceremony, in which, among other things, the speaker professes his readiness to act "in the name of all Israel."

It would be out of place in an introductory essay to pursue any further this interesting subject with its far-reaching consequences upon Jewish life and Jewish thought. But the foregoing remarks may suffice to show that Judaism did not remain quite inactive at the approach of the great religious crisis which our generation has witnessed. Like so many other religious communities, it reviewed its forces, entrenched itself on the field of history, and what it lost of its old devotion to the Bible, it has sought to make up by a renewed reverence for institutions.

In this connection, a mere mention may suffice of the ultra-Orthodox party, led by the late Dr. S. R. Hirsch of Frankfort (1808–1889) whose defiance of reason and criticism even a Ward might have envied, and whose saintliness and sublimity even a Keble might have admired. And, to take an example from the opposite school, we must at least record the name of that devout Jew, Osias Schorr (1816–1895), in whom we have profound learning combined with an uncompromising disposition of mind productive of a typical champion of Radicalism in things religious. These men are, however, representative of two extremes, and their followers constitute mere minorities; the majority is with the historical school.

How long the position of this school will prove tenable is another question. Being brought up in the old Low Synagogue, where, with all attachment to tradition, the Bible was looked upon as the crown and the climax of Judaism, the old Adam still asserts itself in me, and in unguarded moments makes me rebel against this new rival of revelation in the shape of history. At times this now fashionable exaltation of Tradition at the expense of Scripture even impresses me as a sort of religious bimetallism in which bold speculators in theology try to keep up the market value of an inferior currency by denouncing loudly the bright shining gold which, they would have us believe, is less fitted to circulate in the vulgar use of daily life than the small cash of historical interpretation. Nor can I quite reconcile myself to this alliance of religion with history, which seems to be both unworthy and unnatural. The Jew, some writer aptly remarked, was the first and the fiercest Nonconformist of the East, and so Judaism was always a protesting religion. To break the idols, whether of the past or of the present, has always been a sacred mission of Judaism, and has indeed been esteemed by it as a necessary preliminary to the advent of the kingdom of God on earth. One of its daily prayers was and still is: "We therefore hope in Thee, O Lord our God, that we may speedily behold the glory of Thy might, when ... the idols will be cut off, when the world will be perfected under the kingdom of the Almighty." It bowed before truth, but it had never made a covenant with facts only because they were facts. History had to be re-made and to sanctify itself before it found its way into its sacred annals. Nor did Judaism make a virtue of swallowing down institutions. Such institutions as crept into it in course of time had, when the Synagogue was conscious of their claims to form part of religion, to submit to the laborious process of a thorough adaptation to prophetic notions before they were formally sanctioned. But when this process was deemed impossible or impracticable, Judaism boldly denounced the past in such fierce language as the prophets used and as still finds its echo in such passages of the liturgy as "First our ancestors were worshippers of idols and now God has brought us near to His service"; or "But of a truth, we and our ancestors have sinned."

However, it would be unfair to argue any further against a theological system which, as already said, was never avowed distinctly by the historical school—a school, moreover, with which speculation is a matter of minor importance. The main strength of this school lies in its scientific work, for which Judaism will always be under a sense of deep gratitude. And living as we do in an age in which history reigns supreme in all departments of human thought, we may hope that even its theology, as far as it goes, will "do" for us, though I neither hope nor believe that it will do for those who come after us.

<hr/>

C. MORDECAI M. KAPLAN (1881–1983)

Mordecai Kaplan was surely the most influential figure in the development of Conservative ideology from the 1910s to the 1960s, and his influence continues on to our own day. Part of the reason for this was his innovative way of understanding Judaism, to which we shall turn shortly. Another part of his influence derived from his creativity, for he was the first to have a bat mitzvah ceremony for his daughter (in 1922), an early example of his many liturgical experiments and contributions. He was also one of the founders of the Jewish camping movement. His commencement address in 1945 at the Jewish Theological Seminary, reprinted as the last chapter of his book, *The Future of the American Jew,* envisioned a University of Judaism that would combine classical Jewish studies with the study and development of Jewish art, music, dance, and literature, and in the years following he and Simon Greenberg, together with leaders in the Los Angeles community, translated this vision into a reality, establishing it there in 1948. His institutional efforts, though, focused most on creating and running the Jewish Reconstructionist Foundation, which he saw as simply the structure to express and further a particular tendency within Conservative Judaism, but which eventually created a separate Reconstructionist movement, including the Reconstructionist Rabbinical College, the Reconstructionist Rabbinical Association, and the Federation of Reconstructionist Congregations and Fellowships.

Except perhaps for his writings, Kaplan's greatest impact undoubtedly stemmed from his influence on students as a professor at the Jewish Theological Seminary from 1909 to 1963. A challenging teacher deeply interested in what his students thought, he forced more than two generations of future Conservative rabbis and educators to define and defend their own ideas about Judaism, whether they agreed with him or not.

Even though Professor Kaplan had retired by the time I began rabbinical school, I remember a graphic example of this from one occasion on which he had accepted an invitation to address the students of the Rabbinical School at a Rosh Ḥodesh breakfast. The person leading Grace after Meals led us in singing the verses at the end, including the troublesome verse from Psalm 37:25, "I was a lad and have grown old, and I have never seen a righteous person abandoned or his children wanting for bread." After being introduced, Kaplan got up and thundered: "If you don't believe it, don't say it!" That was typical of his complete intolerance for fuzzy religious thinking and his absolute insistence on honesty in affirming religious convictions. Moreover, the sheer energy of the man—manifested also in his service as a congregational rabbi at the Society for the Advancement of Judaism (S.A.J.), a synagogue he founded; presidency of the Rabbinical Assembly (1932–33); and authorship of numerous books and articles—clearly made him someone who simply could not be ignored.

It was, however, undoubtedly his particular way of "reconstructing" Judaism, as he put it, that accounts for the bulk of his influence, for it was that vision of Judaism that drove all of his other work. In essays appearing primarily in *The Menorah Journal* and the *S.A.J. Review* from 1909 to 1933, in his first comprehensive statement of his beliefs, *Judaism as a Civilization* (1934), and subsequently in many books and in ongoing essays in the journal he founded, *The Reconstructionist,* Kaplan asserted that people erred in thinking about Judaism as solely a religion—that is, as beliefs and rituals. Instead, he argued, Judaism consists of an entire civilization, including an attachment to a land (Israel), a language (Hebrew), moral values, law, history, literature, art, music, and dance.

One distinct advantage of understanding Judaism this way is that it explains why people who do not believe in God, practice Jewish rituals, or belong to a synagogue nevertheless can and do identify as Jews: they simply associate themselves with some of the other civilizational aspects of Judaism. This is an aspect of Judaism that Christians and Muslims rarely understand, for people raised in Christian homes who later deny that Jesus is Christ no longer see themselves as Christian, and people born into Islam who no longer believe that the Koran is God's ultimate revelation and Mohammed God's most authoritative prophet no longer consider themselves Muslim. That is because those theological beliefs are built into the very definition of what it means to be a Christian or a Muslim. Jews, however, can deny all of Judaism's religious affirmations (God, the authority of the commandments, etc.) and nevertheless can correctly identify as Jews if they were born to a Jewish woman, even if they know or do nothing more about their Judaism. In fact, some non-religious or even anti-religious Jews can even be leaders of the Jewish community in certain aspects of Jewish life, as, for example, secular Zionists and some non-religious Jews heavily involved with Jewish culture or philanthropy. Kaplan's concept of Judaism as a civilization explains how that is possible.

At the same time, every civilization focuses on specific elements unique to that civilization. Ancient Athens, for example, was known for its philosophy, drama, and architecture. Ancient Rome was famous for its military exploits and for imposing its law on all its conquered territories. Modern British civilization through the early twentieth century was characterized by its sense of fair play ("cricket") and colonialism ("The sun never sets on the British Empire"). American civilization is probably best known for its keen sense of individual rights, its technological know-how, and its materialism.

In the same way, Kaplan asserted, Jewish civilization is a *religious* civilization because the Jewish religion is at its core. Note, for example, that

Israel is *not* the Jewish land because Jews have lived there for most of their history; on the contrary, the majority of the world's Jews lived there only from the time of Joshua until the destruction of the First Temple (c. 1200 B.C.E.–586 B.C.E.), and while a significant percentage of world Jewry now lives there again, the majority still lives outside the Land of Israel. That Israel should be the Jewish land only makes sense in terms of theological claims: that God gave it to us, however one understands that claim. (Kaplan himself, staunch Zionist though he was, would have considerable difficulty with that claim because, as I shall explain below, he did not believe in a personal God who could will or give anything.) Similarly, Hebrew is not the Jewish language because most Jews spoke it for most of Jewish history or do so today; again, except for the period until 586 B.C.E., Jews spoke other languages as their native tongues, and it was only because of the assiduous work of Eliezer Ben Yehudah (1858–1922) and his colleagues in the late nineteenth and early twentieth centuries that Hebrew is again spoken today. Rather, Hebrew survived all these centuries as *the* Jewish language because it is the language of our sacred texts—the Torah, the Mishnah, and, perhaps especially, the prayerbook. Jews eat all kinds of foods, but those foods cannot be identifiably Jewish unless they are kosher; Jews commonly know that "kosher style" foods are in the mode of Eastern European kosher cuisine but are not authentically Jewish, and no meal with pork products or shellfish could be ever be identified as Jewish. Thus while Judaism includes all elements characteristic of civilizations, its core is religious. That is why those Jews who do not participate in or believe in any of the religious parts of Judaism correctly feel that they are identifying with the periphery of Judaism and not its core.

Finally, for Kaplan, Judaism is an *evolving* religious civilization. No part of it, including its religious core, is static; it rather changes over time, adding some things, deleting others, and changing the form of others. This dynamic view of Jewish culture—and of life in general—Kaplan learned from John Dewey, and it undoubtedly fit nicely with Kaplan's own personality.

These parts of Kaplan's philosophy, as we shall see, are not only adopted, but taken for granted by later Conservative thinkers. In fact, while Orthodox and Reform thinkers were much slower to see Judaism as not only religious but also as civilizational, since the establishment of the State of Israel in 1948 they too have adopted this aspect of Kaplan's thought, although often (especially among the Orthodox) without acknowledging the source of this insight about Judaism.

Kaplan's theology, however, has garnered less agreement among Conservative Jews, and even less among Reform and Orthodox Jews.

Specifically, Kaplan maintained that God is not a supernatural Person, as the Bible, Talmud, and most previous Jewish philosophers have asserted; that is, he did not affirm "theism." Kaplan instead believed in "deism," in which God is the creative Force that brought the universe into being and, in Kaplan's form of deism, continues to "make for salvation"—that is, continually spurs nature in general and human beings in particular to actualize their potential for good. This, of course, immediately raises the problem of evil: Is it caused by another force (thus undermining monotheism), or does it come from the absence of God (as Maimonides claimed), or is God limited (as Kaplan's disciples, Harold Kushner and Harold Schulweis have claimed), or is there some other explanation of how evil can exist in a world created by a God pushing everything and everyone in it to actualize their potential for good? It also immediately raises problems for prayer: Can one really pray to a "force"?

For our purposes in this volume, though, the most important question Kaplan's theology raises is how such a view of God affects our understanding of Jewish law. As a force and not a person, God cannot have a will and therefore cannot command anything. Jewish moral laws, which Kaplan thinks are built into nature and therefore are universal, are rooted in God by virtue of the fact that God, the creative Force that formed nature in the first place, made nature as it did. That is, Kaplan is a "natural law" theorist, thinking that just as there are physical laws like gravity inherent in nature, so too there are moral laws incorporated into the very structure of nature. Thus moral laws are enforced to some extent by nature itself (e.g., if we pollute the environment, it becomes unlivable) and to a greater extent by the governments people create to govern their interactions. As a result, in the post-Enlightenment societies in which Jews live, Jewish moral demands are primarily enforced on Jews by the secular law.

In addition, Kaplan suggests that Jewish *moral* laws might be enforced by a comprehensive, "constitutional" Jewish communal organization (a *kehillah*). That is, in one of his many innovative ideas, he suggests an expansion of some of the communal organizations that existed in Europe (e.g., Germany's *Judische Gemeinde*), so that Jews would join the local Jewish community as a whole for a stipulated fee (which could be reduced, if necessary, for given people). The community would then provide the personnel, places, and materials for worship, education, social action, social activities, social services, athletics, Zionist efforts, cultural programs, etc., and members could avail themselves of as many, or as few, of its services as they pleased, free of any further charge. If such a communal structure were to exist, Kaplan says, Jewish moral norms could be enforced by the Jewish community as they had been before the Enlightenment—namely, through excommunication—for then Jews would have a real stake in remaining part of the community. A person threatened with excommunication for defaming someone or stealing from someone would quickly seek to make restitution in order to retain his or her friends and services.

Judaism's ritual laws, however, can never be enforced. Their authority cannot be rooted in God's will because for Kaplan God is a Power moving us to create and maximize the good in ourselves and in the world. As a power, God does not have a will, any more than the winds that move clouds have a will. Moreover, Kaplan astutely observes that modern Jews, even those who do not adopt his theology, generally do not believe that God will punish them if they fail to keep kosher, for example, or reward them if they do. Jewish rituals, then, are instead Jewish "folkways," the practices by which Jews mark life-cycle events, the round of the seasons, and many daily activities like eating, getting up, and going to sleep.

The primary function of Jewish folkways, for Kaplan, is to unite the Jewish people, just as football jerseys mark who is playing on whose team. The jerseys clearly have a practical purpose in enabling everyone to identify the members of the two teams, but they also serve to rouse the spirit of the two teams, for they symbolize the communal life of the two competing groups off the football field as well as on it. To accomplish that purpose of communal identification and spirit, the jerseys may have colors or symbols representing something in the community's life, but they may also have been chosen completely arbitrarily a long time ago just to distinguish one team from another. Jewish rituals may also be arbitrary in some ways, although Jewish tradition tends to invest even those aspects that seem to be arbitrary with retroactive meaning.

A second function of Jewish rituals is to teach theological and moral lessons, and for that some clear connections between the ritual and the lessons it teaches are desirable (and maybe even necessary). Kaplan interprets the Sabbath, for example, as a way to mark the value of creativity by desisting from it one day in seven so that one can better appreciate it. The Sabbath also, for Kaplan, aids our creativity in the week to come, just as an artist has to step back from his painting to see it in context and to plan what to do next.[5] The Sabbath thereby reminds us of the creative nature of God and the moral value of exercising creativity ourselves, and it could only do that if it were on the seventh day, in accord with the Bible's creation story, and if it required us to desist from work. Similarly, through Jewish life-cycle ceremonies the Jewish tradition seeks to articulate and teach its distinctive understanding of the given life passage and its message about what the person involved and the community witnessing the event should learn about life. Thus a bar/bat mitzvah ceremony is not a test of physical endurance, as it is in some cultures, or the occasion of a circumcision or a clitoridectomy, as it is in others to mark the beginning of sexual maturity; it is rather a time in which the youngster demonstrates Jewish learning and dedicates himself or herself to more.

Finally, for Kaplan, rituals serve as "sancta," that is, as ways of bringing us into contact with the holy. Jewish seasonal celebrations, for example, remind us of our ties to nature and its rhythms while simultaneously reconnecting us to Jewish history, community, and values. Thus Passover, to take one such festival, not only recalls the Exodus from Egypt and marks the onset of spring; it also teaches us about God's role in making people free and our need to emulate that divine trait through our own efforts. Kaplan's first liturgical publication, in fact, was *The New Haggadah for the Pesah Seder,* in which he, Ira Eisenstein, and Eugene Kohn, his colleagues at S.A.J. and co-authors, omitted mention of the ten plagues (the historicity of which he thought was scientifically suspect) and he added biblical passages about Moses that did not appear in the original text, so that the seder would highlight not only the divine role in the Exodus and all future acts of liberation but also the human role.

As much as Kaplan believed that any healthy community must and should have such ritual expressions to express its identity and values, in calling Jewish rituals "folkways" he made an important statement about how he perceived Jewish law—namely, not as law at all. In his view, law is restricted to rules that are enforced. In a society like the United States, however, religion is voluntary, and no religious laws are enforced; thus Jewish law is not law, insofar as he construed the meaning of the term. Therefore, even if a comprehensive, Jewish social structure of the type he describes existed, *ritual* rules should not be enforced, according to Kaplan, because that would be counterproductive. Jewish folkways are intended, first and foremost, to help to identify Jews as Jews. If a Jew does not want to use that mode of identification, forcing him or her to do so through the community's power of excommunication would only cause resentment, not loyalty. Currently, without Kaplan's *kehillah* structure, enforcing ritual laws in nations with freedom of religion is not only undesirable, but impossible; but even if such a comprehensive communal organizational structure should exist, ritual rules would be, for Kaplan, not law to be enforced as such.

In the essay below, Kaplan acknowledges the theological and legal diversity within the Conservative movement of his time and argues that any attempt to introduce "uniformity by fiat" would have highly undesirable consequences. Moreover, there are already four important aspects in the Conservative movement's approach to Judaism on which everyone within it agrees, including the centrality of the Land of Israel and religion in Jewish life. When it comes to law, there are three distinct approaches in Judaism—Right, Center, and Left. In describing them, he articulates his own "Left" approach to Jewish law, based on "a humanist conception of the origin, development, and application of the Jewish religion," in which "social practice should be subject to some system of civil law, [but] ritual practice cannot properly be included within the category of law," for law requires "some kind of sanction."

In another essay, chapter 19 of his book *The Future of the American Jew* (1948), he deems it a contribution of the Conservative movement to conceive of Jewish law not as binding because "it was supernaturally revealed," but rather because "it is binding intrinsically, in that it is the expression of the religious spirit of the Jewish people." He is not at all happy that most Jews do not observe Jewish law; on the contrary, he asserts that "no Jew who experiences in his own being anything of his people's will to live should accept with equanimity this defunct state of Jewish law."

It is "self-deluding, compensatory reasoning," though, to maintain that Jewish law is authoritative because God commanded it even if most Jews do not abide by it; that position is not only untrue but harmful, "because it obscures the urgent need of reconstituting Jewish society in order that Jewish law be reinstated." In such a modern context, Jews would be bound by the law of the state, and that would include not only its commercial laws, as Jewish law accepted in the past, but also all of the other aspects of civil law, including its moral and family laws. Kaplan returns to these themes in his essay criticizing Robert Gordis' theory of Jewish law, reprinted below on pages 121–129.

Ritual laws would be determined by the community, and there would have to be some uniformity since a flag, to use Kaplan's example, can only function as the symbol of a group if everyone recognizes the same flag. Still, observing the details of ritual laws as stated in the Shulḥan Arukh and other codes of law would not be required; sufficient uniformity would be attained if Jews practiced just the general outlines of Jewish ritual law. Moreover, Jewish law in both moral and ritual areas would not be developed by reinterpretation alone; legislation would be necessary—in, for example, equalizing the position of women with that of men in Jewish life. Here Kaplan articulates in legal terms the degree of creativity that he thinks modern circumstances require of contemporary rabbis and lay leaders.

Kaplan's approach to Jewish law has challenged virtually every other thinker's understanding of it. Few agree with it completely or even substantially (Reconstructionists constitute only 3% of the 46% of North American Jews who belong to a synagogue—less than 1.5% of the total Jewish population in North America[6]), and many argue vigorously against Kaplan's form of Judaism. Moreover, even though Kaplan probably articulated how most modern Jews understand Jewish law, few lay Jews want to admit to such a theology. Whether they abide by Jewish law or not, they somehow want to believe that God commanded it.

Kaplan's approach to Jewish law, though, simply cannot be ignored, for it amounts to a Copernican Revolution in Jewish legal theory. Instead of God commanding the law in some way, human beings created it, developed it historically, and currently have the power and even the duty to evaluate it and apply it to the needs and sensibilities of the times. Jewish moral laws are not distinctly Jewish; they are universal. Jewish ritual laws are not laws at all: they are "folkways" or communal "usages." And yet Kaplan is not interested in discarding Jewish practices, whether moral or ritual, altogether; on the contrary, he wants, to use his term, to "salvage" as much as possible from the tradition. To do that, however, he thinks that he must "reconstruct" Jewish law to make it fit the voluntaristic societies in which we live.

Clearly there are many grounds for objecting to Kaplan's theory of Jewish law. Those who believe in a personal, supernatural God will dismiss it immediately, for its assumptions about the origins, authority, and application of the law as being completely human are, according to such people, wrong from the outset. Even those who have some sympathy for the human element in shaping Jewish law might see it, as we shall see, as the product of both God and human beings, and they may want a clearly divine element in its making if it is going to be experienced as a distinctly *religious* legal system.

Furthermore, if Jewish moral law is indeed just universal norms, then why does Judaism differ in significant ways from other religions and secular philosophies in its understanding of who we are and who we ought to be, as even Kaplan demonstrates in his long chapter on ethics in *The Future of the American Jew*? And while Kaplan acknowledges that rituals have to be shared by a community if they are going to fulfill their functions, he dismisses the possibility of defining rituals through classical, legal formulations. But then how are they to be determined—by the *kehillah*? But if no *kehillah* yet exists (as is still the case), who has the authority to make changes in the rituals and to invent new ones? And since he emphasizes that we cannot rely exclusively on the legal methodologies of the past, based primarily on evolving interpretations and applications of past precedents, but must rather use legislation to a much larger extent than it had been used until now, has he not severed the methodological ties, as well as many in content, with Jewish law of the past?

But probably the most problematic aspect of Kaplan's theory of Jewish law is his insistence that law can only exist with sanctions; as I indicated in chapter 2 above, for law to shape people's behavior they must obey it for all kinds of reasons other than sanctions or else it will collapse instantaneously. That is, Kaplan, in rejecting Jewish law as law, is using much too narrow an understanding of the nature of law; with a broader and more accurate one, other theorists, as we shall see, continue to see Jewish law as law and use legal reasoning to apply it to modern times despite their open acknowledgment, along with Kaplan, that Jewish law cannot and will not be enforced by governmental authorities in a voluntaristic society.

On the other hand, Kaplan's theory of Judaism in general and of Jewish law in particular would never have had the wide influence it has had if it were not for its many strengths. Understanding Judaism as a civilization has been adopted explicitly by virtually everyone in the Conservative movement and by most in the Reform and Orthodox movements as well, even if the Orthodox, in particular, are reticent to acknowledge their debt to Kaplan in this.

This civilizational focus means that even though Kaplan does not see Jewish moral law as distinctively Jewish or Jewish ritual law as law, he is concerned to teach and nurture Jewish practices—not as law, but as "folkways"—to give people an identity and to teach them the values, history, and hopes of the Jewish tradition. Thus what may look to some like a completely antinomian approach is, on the contrary, a theory that encourages Jewish practice, albeit for primarily communal rather than theological reasons. Because Kaplan places Jewish "usages" completely in human hands, he also provides great leeway and encouragement for creating new Jewish usages (with his daughter's bat mitzvah ceremony as the first of many examples of his own liturgical creativity). Flexibility and creativity are definite advantages of Kaplan's approach.

Moreover, people who practice Jewish rituals based on his theory will never resent those rituals, for they will be doing them voluntarily as a positive affirmation of their own Jewish identity. They are therefore more likely to do them less regularly than those who see them as law, but rarely mechanically and often with considerable attention and meaning. For Kaplan, guilt and fear are definitely *not* the right motives for Jews to obey Jewish ritual laws; his emphasis is distinctly on the positive, attracting people not with vinegar but with honey.

Jewish moral laws now become the particular Jewish expression of universal morals, and thus those who believe in Kaplan's approach would follow them not as a special burden placed by God on Jews to be a chosen people, "a kingdom of priests and a holy nation" (Exodus 19:6), but as far-reaching norms incumbent on all citizens of the world. Because that widens the scope of the community bound by moral rules to include all of humanity, Jews may feel even more obligated to obey them. His idea of a *kehillah* to serve Jews and give Jewish life breadth, depth, and dynamism also, if ever realized, would provide an enforcement mechanism for Jewish morals. Finally, Kaplan's view of Jewish laws as "sancta," as ways we experience and attach ourselves to God, gives his theory of law a distinctively religious cast even as it radically reinterprets who God is and places authority to interpret, apply, and create the corpus of the law squarely in human hands.

With all these strengths, it is no wonder that Kaplan's theory of Jewish law presents minimally an inescapable challenge to those who dislike it and an identifiably Jewish, intelligent, modern, positive, and creative approach to Jewish practice for those who agree with it. Indeed, even those who find themselves unable to adopt Kaplan's theory because of its problems, noted above, often nevertheless borrow from the creativity of Kaplan and his disciples in shaping their own practice of Jewish law. Thus Kaplan's theory has had much wider influence than the numbers of the current Reconstructionist movement would suggest.

*Unity in Diversity in the Conservative Movement**

BY MORDECAI M. KAPLAN

I

The trend in Judaism designated in this country as Conservative is associated with the Jewish Theological Seminary of America and with the two organizations that have emanated from it, the Rabbinical Assembly and the United Synagogue. Conservative Judaism properly

*An address Kaplan delivered on June 22, 1947 at the United Synagogue convention.

traces its origin to Zacharias Frankel, the founder of the movement known as Historical Judaism, who lived a century ago. It has had no less a personality than Solomon Schechter to give it its initial impulse in this country. Nevertheless, both doctrinally and from the standpoint of practical directives, it is still inchoate and amorphous. The Conservative movement has had at its disposal the most creative men in the field of Jewish scholarship and those elements of the Jewish laity which are most active in the fields of congregational and educational endeavor. Despite, or perhaps because of, these advantages, it has been functioning to this day without an acceptable philosophy or program to guide its own adherents or to win new adherents.

Conservatism's lack of a philosophy and program has long been recognized. That did not faze some of the leaders of the Conservative movement. They, in fact, made a virtue of that lack. In the semantics of two or three decades ago, Conservative Judaism boasted of being adjectiveless Judaism. Later it came to be described as middle-of-the-road Judaism. As such, its main attributes, like those which the Medieval philosophers ascribed to God, were negative in character. It was identified as being neither Reform nor Orthodox. As we take stock of the assets of our movement, we cannot honestly say that its indefinable status has contributed to its effectiveness or progress. If we have made any organizational headway, it has been in spite, and not because, of our lack of a philosophy or program.

From the standpoint of bringing order out of the chaos in our inner life as a people, the Conservative movement has been merely marking time. Like so many other activities in Jewish life, it has been propelled less by any inner vitality than by the galvanic kind of energy which any skillful appeal to organizational loyalty can evoke. Organizational loyalty should not, however, serve as a substitute for clear, forthright thought and for the intrinsic enthusiasm which a cause should elicit. When it does so serve, it generates the surface appearance of activity, beneath which stagnation in ideas and creative values reigns undisturbed.

If we want to break the spell which keeps our movement from making any headway except in numbers, we should look for some psychological cause which could have produced that state of self-induced inhibition. We would then discover this situation: Those who belong to the Conservative movement do not happen to be of one mind theologically. They, therefore, labor under the mistaken notion that this diversity constitutes an inner contradiction in the movement, and that in the interests of the movement it should be replaced by unanimity in religious doctrine and regimen.

The truth, however, is that the very attempt to introduce uniformity by fiat must lead to highly undesirable consequences. It is bound to lead to a struggle for power among the various groups within the movement. Any one group which may be in a better position to assert itself than the others will seek to impose its ideas and its will on the others and treat their adherents as second class citizens who should be glad that they are at least tolerated. In the end, this method of dealing with diversity is certain to prove divisive. It may ultimately drive away the strong minority groups, and hold fast within the grip of a deadening uniformity those who remain.

It seems to me that a better and happier solution may be found for the problem created by the existence of diversity within the ranks of the Conservative movement. I venture to submit a plan that would neither ignore nor seek to suppress the existing diversity, but try to channel it in such a way as to render it productive of the most good. Following the advice of our Sages that we should emulate the good in our non-Jewish neighbors, we should take a page out of the experience of the Protestant sects. Though they are divided on what they regard as highly important doctrines and religious practices, they nevertheless manage to cooperate within the frame of some of their most influential organizations and institutions. The Federal Council of the Churches of Christ in America consists of all the major Protestant denominations and many of the lesser ones. The five principal seminaries which train for the ministry, such as the Union Theological Seminary and the Divinity Schools of Chicago, Harvard and Yale Universities and the McCormick Theological Seminary, have from eight to ten denominations represented on their faculties and as many as twenty-two on their student bodies. There is no reason why we Jews who, despite our differences, have much more in common than those Protestant sects, should not be able to work together without trying to suppress our differences.

The only legitimate and fruitful conception of the Conservative movement is one which frankly recognizes the existence of more than one type of approach to the problem of Judaism. These groups should get to know themselves and one another and learn to cooperate in that which they hold in common, recognizing each other's right to foster their respective differences. For the sake of common action in behalf of the Conservative movement, it is necessary for them to become fully aware of what differentiates all of them from other groups, in terms of positive principles and of the many affirmative activities which those principles call for. Following the recognition of what the groups hold in common, each group should draw up a clear and comprehensive statement of its own guiding principles of belief and action. All that I shall attempt to do is to suggest what might constitute the common affirmative denominator, and to describe the actual differences in belief and practice that exist among us today, which it would be fatuous to deny and ruinous to try to suppress.

II

The areas of agreement amongst us are four in number. They are the following: 1) The indispensability of Eretz Yisrael for Jewish life in the Diaspora, 2) The primacy of religion as the expression of collective Jewish life, 3) The maximum possible plenitude of Jewish content, including the use of Hebrew, and 4) The encouragement of the scientific approach in Jewish higher learning.

These areas of agreement are so far-reaching and penetrating in their implications that the term "Conservative," far from being the negative designation which it is generally held to be, includes enough grounds and motives for common action to render the dividing differences of minor account, if not almost nugatory. This becomes evident when we consider what is involved in each of those areas.

1) The assumption that Eretz Yisrael and its rehabilitation as the center of world Jewry is indispensable to Diaspora Jewry is not held by the Conservative party merely as a Zionist or political proposition. It is held as a central element in its conception of Judaism as a way of life. That assumption had no place whatever in the school of thought which was the forerunner of the Conservative movement. Neither Zacharias Frankel, the first head of the Breslau Jewish Theological Seminary, nor Moritz Guedeman, Chief Rabbi of Vienna during the last quarter of the nineteenth century, would have subscribed to it. In fact, the latter was one of the notorious group of "Protest Rabbiner" who prevented the first Zionist Congress from being held in Munich. It is entirely owing to the initiative taken by Solomon Schechter that Eretz Yisrael has come to occupy the place of centrality in the philosophy of the Conservative movement.

Largely under the influence of Ahad Ha-Am, and due to his own deep insight into the sterility of Diaspora Judaism, on the one hand, and the fructifying power of participation in the upbuilding of Eretz Yisrael, on the other, Schechter took the position that such participation is more than a matter of politics; it is a matter of the spiritual well-being of the Jew. He thereby contributed to the Conservative movement its most important affirmation. That affirmation is chiefly responsible for the transfer of the spiritual center of gravity from abstractions about God and man to the concrete reality of the Jewish people. Therein the Conservative movement is worlds apart from either Orthodoxy or Reform, and in a way that does not merely negate their approach, but that evokes many a constructive principle of thought and action.

2) The primacy of religion as the expression of collective Jewish life as the second area of consensus among the adherents of the Conservative movement, is intended to negate the secularist revolution in Judaism. The emphasis on the concrete reality of the Jewish people is liable to bracket the Conservative movement with the secularist revolution. It is therefore important to stress that, for us Jews, mere existence as a people is meaningless. Our collective life as a people must be deliberately cultivated as a means of enabling the individual Jew to achieve his destiny as a human being. The Jewish way of life must help the individual Jew to be and do his best and to experience that sense of at-homeness in the world which only beneficent religion can give. There are wide divergencies of belief among the followers of Conservatism with regard to the origin and nature of the Jewish way of life. But whatever its origin or nature, they agree not only as to its religious function, but that without it the Jewish people would be like a body without a soul.

3) A third area of consensus among the adherents of the Conservative movement is the assumption that Jewish living must not merely be cor-

rect and conform to certain prescribed rules of belief and action. It must also be rich in content and ever creative of new content. This assumption is of particular relevance in the Diaspora under modern conditions. Jewish life has to be lived within the frame of an overpowering and all-embracing non-Jewish civilization which, by its sheer magnitude, tends to crowd out all Jewish interests from the consciousness of the average Jew. It is only with the greatest difficulty that he can manage to prevent those interests from being swamped completely. The temptation is, therefore, great to fall back upon some minimum regimen to satisfy the call of the past and the desire to be loyal to tradition. To yield to that temptation, however, is to allow oneself to be absorbed by the environment, without leaving a trace of Jewish identity.

The only way to meet the strong centrifugal pull of the surrounding life and culture is to intensify the centripetal tendencies of Jewish life. This can be achieved only by following the principle of introducing as much of the content of Jewish living as possible into every nook and cranny that has not as yet been flooded by the environing civilization. To that end we should discover a new use for ritual observances, new occasions for cultivating esthetic expression of Jewish values and emotions, new reasons for introducing the study of the Hebrew language into the high schools and colleges attended by Jewish students, to say nothing of its more intensive and extensive study in Jewish schools and its maximum use in worship.

4) The fourth differential which is common to all groups within the Conservative movement is the encouragement of the scientific approach to Jewish higher learning. None who adheres to this movement is any longer satisfied with the type of study which prevailed in the past, and which is still upheld in the Orthodox *yeshibot*. All non-Jewish learning, by reason of its great prestige and utility, is still regarded by the consistently Orthodox as a powerful rival to Jewish learning. Mathematics and the other exact sciences are perhaps an exception, because of their assumed neutrality, from the standpoint of traditional religion. Such challenges as modern astronomy or geology seem to present to tradition are regarded as capable of being met by means of proper interpretation. But the biological sciences are considered as opening up dangerous vistas for doubt and disbelief. This is true to an even greater degree of the human sciences, namely, psychology, sociology, anthropology and the comparative study of religion. Even if a way be found to study those human sciences so that they cannot do any harm to traditional religion, Orthodoxy strenuously opposes any tendency to apply their methods of research and reasoning to the content of Jewish tradition.

It is quite evident that this restrictive attitude toward the study of the past would have narrowed the scope of Jewish creative thought and effort. We should never have had any part of the Jewish past brought to life by great historians like Isaac Hirsch Weiss, Leopold Zunz, Zacharias Frankel, Heinrich Graetz and Simon Dubnow, if the Orthodox of the school of Samson Raphael Hirsch had had their way. The Historical School in Judaism, which laid the foundation of the scientific study of Judaism, produced very few who identified themselves with the Reform movement. That the overwhelming majority of those whose names belong to the roster of that school of thought were the forerunners of the Conservative movement is no mere coincidence. When the scientific approach to the study of Jewish tradition is motivated by the purpose of finding direction for the future, it has a twofold effect. It steeps one in the abundance of Jewish content, and it gives one a sense of historical development. This twofold effect is most congenial to the Conservative movement. It fosters a feeling of continuity with the past without enslaving one to it.

The foregoing four principles are sufficiently important and inclusive for those who subscribe to them to constitute a distinct party or movement in Jewish life. We may even go further and say that the adherents of the Conservative movement not only subscribe to those four principles, but also recognize them as interdependent and mutually organic.

By an accident of history the Conservative movement has fallen heir to a name which many of its foremost adherents regard as unfortunate, and in a way, misrepresentative of its true character. For the adjective "conservative" generally denotes being fearful of change. The matter of name, however, is not too serious. It is what is put into the name that counts. Nevertheless, we should not permit the movement to be the victim of too many such accidents of history. We should just now be on our guard against that which is liable to prove a most dangerous accident, namely freezing of the status quo of the movement into a fixed and permanent form. That is all too liable to come about if we permit any one school of thought which happens at a given time to be most vocal or most active to speak in the name of our movement as a whole.

Indeed, the conspicuously wholesome feature about our movement has been the fact that it has been possible for a number of distinct schools of thought to arise within it. Now that we can afford to be sure of the common frame within which those schools of thought or distinctive groups may recognize their intrinsic unity, the danger of their going off on their own is virtually over. Hence, it is proper that we should identify such schools of thought and practice as exist among us. So far no formal or authoritative statement of principle has come from any one of the existing schools of thought. Perhaps this discussion will ultimately elicit the long overdue statements on their part. Those statements will have the authority necessary for the effective functioning of our movement. Since the conditions and exigencies of life vary with each individual even within each group or school of thought, any description of the characteristic beliefs and practices of each group cannot be more than a stylized approximation to the actual facts. With this qualification in mind I herewith proceed to give in outline form the philosophies and programs of the three discernible groups or schools of thought in the Conservative movement, which, for purposes of discussion, may be designated respectively as Right, Center and Left.

III

A) The Rightists subscribe to the thirteen principles of the Maimonidean creed. In retaining the principles concerning the personal Messiah and bodily resurrection, they reserve to themselves the right to interpret those principles figuratively. They permit themselves such liberties of belief concerning the authorship of the Torah as an Ibn Ezra, for example, permitted himself. These liberties, of course, are very limited, and intended only for the initiated. On the whole, they accept the traditional belief with regard to the supernatural origin and character of the Torah. They resort to Maimonides' *Moreh Nebukim* for the solution of textual difficulties and contradictions. Their theology coincides almost entirely with that formulated in Joseph Albo's *Ikkarim.*

In the matter of ritual practice, they are guided in the main by the *Shulhan Aruk,* which they regard as authoritative and binding. While they recognize the need for change to meet new conditions of life, they put little faith in any existing rabbinical group as qualified to effect such change. Nothing less than the convening of a Synod recognized by the entire body of the Jewish people would satisfy them as competent to deal with the problem of changing any of the traditional laws.

In their ritual observances they follow strictly the letter of the *Shulhan Aruk.* They are at one with the strictly Orthodox group in the requirement of ritual baths for married women after their menstruation period. They consider the use of the razor for shaving forbidden. In the observance of the dietary laws, they adhere strictly to the prohibition of foods prepared by Gentiles. They would not eat even fish meals in non-kosher eating places. They abide by the prohibition of wine handled by a non-Jew. They would not turn on the electric light on the Sabbath. Some do not even answer the telephone on the Sabbath, ring the door-bells, or use the elevator, particularly one that is self-running.

The fact that many of their own people find it impossible to get along without infringing on the dietary laws and Sabbath observance does not elicit, from this school of thought, the least apology. They maintain that if Jews had really wished to abide by traditional law, they would not find it impossible.

In the prayer-book they would not permit any tampering with the traditional text of any part of the service. They do not accept the Sabbath and Festival Prayerbook published by the Joint Prayer Book Commission of the Rabbinical Assembly and the United Synagogue, because of the changes it has introduced in the petitions for the restoration of the sacrificial cult. The ritual of having the *kohanim* bless the congregation at festival services is strictly adhered to. The practice of praying thrice daily, putting on *tefillin* on week-days, is strictly upheld. They do not, as a rule, permit the seating together of men and women during services. They do not have Confirmation exercises on *Shabuot* because they consider such exercises as an innovation introduced from the Christian religion. They are, as a rule, averse to late Friday night services. In a few instances where they have Friday night gatherings, they take care not to dignify as services the exercises which are then held, including a sermon or lecture.

In marriage laws they refuse to make any compromise whatever in the matter of divorce, *halizah* or a *kohen's* marrying a divorcee, and follow strictly the letter and spirit of the *Shulhan Aruk*. They insist on the presence of ten men at the marriage ceremony and require that the witnesses who sign the *ketubah* be strictly observant of the traditional practices.

B) The Centrist group is, in large measure, the continuation of the school of thought, first articulated by Zacharias Frankel and later transferred to this country by Solomon Schechter. That school of thought has not made a fetish of consistency. "On the whole," says Solomon Schechter, "its attitude toward religion may be defined as an enlightened Skepticism combined with a staunch conservatism which is not devoid of a certain mystical touch." They might be said to hold that, in the basic principles of religion as well as of politics and economics, the human mind has so far proved unable to arrive at satisfactory solutions by means of strict adherence to logic. In fact, all such attempts have often led to tyranny and oppression, besides leaving the original confusions and uncertainties just where they were at first. Life and history have a logic of their own, which we cannot afford to disregard. From the standpoint of tolerance and freedom, better results seem, indeed, to have been achieved by the method of "muddling through" than by the desire to hew strictly to the line of reason.

One thing, however, is certain. The Center group no longer believes in the divine revelation as a historical event but as a theological concept. That difference is far more revolutionary than it sounds. As a historical event, "revelation" or the traditional term *"Torah min ha-Shamayim"* denotes a miracle that was visible and audible at a particular time and place. As a theological concept "revelation" denotes the natural experience of the human mind which reacts to anything as opening up new vistas of meaning and holiness. Despite the "Higher anti-Semitism" which Solomon Schechter rightly discerned in much of the Higher Criticism, he seems to speak with pride of the fact that "the first representatives of the Historical School were also the first Jewish scholars who proved themselves more or less ready to join the modern school of Bible Criticism and even to contribute their share to it." They could not possibly have been so ready to join the modern school of Biblical Criticism if they had believed in the traditional sense of *Torah min ha-Shamayim*, or revelation as an historical event.

The closest that the Historical School has come to defining its theological position is the following statement by Schechter in his introduction to the First Series of Studies in Judaism: "It is not the mere revealed Bible that is of first importance to the Jew, but the Bible as it repeats itself in history, in other words, as it is interpreted by tradition. . . . Since then the interpretation of Scripture or the Secondary Meaning is mainly a product of changing historical influences, it follows that the center of authority is actually removed from the Bible and placed in some *living body*, which by reason of its being in touch with the ideal aspirations and religious needs of the age, is best able to determine the nature of the Secondary Meaning. This living body, however, is not represented by any section of the nation, or any corporate priesthood, or Rabbihood, but by the collective conscience of Catholic Israel as embodied in the Universal Synagogue."

It follows from that statement that only such change as falls within the category of interpretation is possible in Judaism, as Schechter conceived it. Since we Jews do not have any authoritative body, whether corporate priesthood or "rabbihood," analogous to that which the Catholic Church possesses, no amendment or new legislation could acquire the status of revelation.

Traditional Jewish law, however, is regarded by the Center group as itself sufficiently flexible and latitudinarian to permit, within its own frame, whatever indispensable changes the needs of the times call for. The fact that so far little has been achieved by the process of interpretation is charged up to the inertia of those who should have performed the task of interpretation rather than to any obstacle inherent in the tradition itself. Life, however, cannot wait. Thanks to the demands of the times certain changes have taken place in Jewish life, which those of the Center group feel will have to be sanctioned formally, as they are now accepted informally. Among those changes are the following:

There is a marked leniency in the observance of the Sabbath. Those who work on the Sabbath, or engage in business because of economic necessity, need not labor under a sense of sin. Even those who are not under such necessity are not expected to conform to the letter of the *Shulhan Aruk*. From this point on there is no established norm with regard to the details of Sabbath observance. Most turn on the lights, but some do not. Most do not ride, but some do. As many prepare breakfast and reheat their other foods as do not.

Similar leniency obtains in the dietary laws. Though in principle observed, in practice there is a marked departure from the letter of the *Shulhan Aruk*. As many draw the line between home and outside as do not. Most have two sets of dishes, few do not. No one has any scruples about eating fish and milk foods in hotels and restaurants. On Passover, however, there is a close approach to strict conformity to traditional laws concerning *hametz*.

In the matter of ritual purity, there are very few who still adhere to the law requiring the ritual bath. All scruples with regard to men's shaving with a razor are gone.

As far as worship is concerned, the range of differences is rather large. The only departure from tradition common to nearly all congregations of the center group are the mixed pews and the frequent use of English in the prayers. Beyond that, there is no uniformity except with regard to covering the head in the synagogue. Most use no musical instruments, some do. Of those congregations which have mixed choirs very few engage non-Jewish singers. Nearly all have the first *Amidah*, and most have also the additional *Amidah* repeated by the cantor. The only changes in the prayer text affecting doctrine are the recent ones incorporated in the new Sabbath and Festival Prayer Book. Late Friday night services are regarded as entirely proper. In a few instances, even the Torah is read at that time, and on the Friday night before *Shabuot*, Confirmation exercises are held.

In most of the congregations the entire *Sidrah* of the week is read on Sabbath morning, in few, only a portion. Of the latter, most cover the entire contents of the Torah usually in a three years' cycle; very few, however, read each year the same part of the *Sidrah*, which they regard as of most interest. The traditional distinction of *kohen, levi* and Israelite is maintained in nearly all of these congregations.

The practice of having confirmation classes for girls and confirmation exercises on *Shabuot* has become quite general.

There is no uniform standard with regard to the recital of daily prayers, the use of *tefillin* by the men, or their wearing of a *tallit katan*. The same is true of washing before meals and reciting grace. The tendency to observe them is on the wane.

The most troublesome problem is that of the marriage and divorce laws. Most rabbis in this group treat the *ketubah* quite seriously, though they would not insist upon the witnesses being strictly observant of ritual practices. Some, however, treat it perfunctorily, or omit it altogether from the marriage ritual. Very few insist upon the presence of ten men at the marriage ceremony. Some would refuse to sanction the marriage of a divorcee to a *kohen,* but most would not. *Halitzah* is virtually ignored, but with a sense of guilt. Most rabbis in this group refuse to officiate at the wedding of a divorced woman who has not received a Jewish bill of divorce, but they advise the couple to apply to a Reform rabbi; some merely avow their helplessness; a minority over-ride their scruples. For years the entire matter has been the subject of discussion and deliberation by the Rabbinical Assembly, without any practical results.

C) The third group, which might be designated as the Leftist, consists for the most part of those who have been influenced by the Reconstructionist movement. That movement has been on the American-Jewish scene since the appearance of the Reconstructionist magazine in January 1935. Reconstructionism transcends the lines that divide the three synagogue denominations. Its primary aim is to find a basis of an affirmative character for unity among all who want to remain Jews and to raise their children as Jews and to have that unity translated into organic community life. However, it comes with a conception of Judaism and Jewish religion which, when accepted by members of the Conservative movement, necessitates their constituting a third group within that movement.

The two main principles of the Leftists are the following:

a) To be a Jew means to be involved not only in a set of beliefs and practices usually identified as religion, but in the civilization or culture of a people, with all that such involvement implies.

b) The Jewish religion in which the values of that civilization are utilized as a means of individual and collective salvation, though indebted for its unique character to the divine intuitions of its lawgivers, prophets and sages, has been subject to the laws and limitations of the human mind and spirit.

The principle that Judaism is to be reckoned with as a civilization instead of merely as a religion is not inconsistent with the views of either the Rightist or the Centrist group of the Conservative movement. It does not imply any idea or ideal that conflicts with traditional teaching. It is more than anything else a formula for the social strategy best suited to advance Jewish life. Instead of having Jewish life centered around the synagogue, Judaism viewed as a civilization calls for a distribution of authority and influence among the various organizations that carry on Jewish activities. Though the synagogue, by reason of its being the chief vehicle for the articulation of the meaning of Judaism, should normally be the chief mouthpiece of the Jewish people, both inwardly and in relation to the outer world, it should not aspire to be more than *primus inter pares*. This conception of the place of the synagogue in Jewish life should logically be acceptable, regardless of one's theological views concerning Judaism. But it is viewed by the Rightist and Centrist groups as a concession to secularism, for no other reason than that it regards the Jewish people as subject to the same laws of social groupings as are all other peoples.

The main differential of the Leftist group, however, derives mainly from the principle that the Jewish religion has been subject to the laws and limitations of the human mind and spirit. That principle calls for a humanist conception of the origin, development and application of Jewish religion. It is not merely as a theoretic outlook, however, that this conception is stressed, but as suggesting the proper method of approach to all phases of Jewish teaching and preaching, from the most elementary to the most advanced stages of educational activity. It prescribes complete freedom of thought and inquiry, not merely as permissive but as imperative, no matter how deeply rooted the beliefs or traditions. It assumes that only through such freedom is it possible for the individual to arrive at a sense of personal involvement in and responsibility for the religion he professes, and to experience an inward drive to live in conformity with what he professes.

The question of distinctive Jewish practice, accordingly, is answered in the light of the two following principles: In the first place, since to be a Jew is to be a part of the civilization of a people, it must find expression in conformity to some system of law which regulates the social relations which obtain within that people. A people is not a voluntary society. It is a social organism into which one is born, and which can function as such only because those who belong to it abide by a system of law governing its social relationships. The two essential traits of that kind of system of law are, first, the fact that it represents the general will of the people, and secondly, that it is accompanied by some kind of sanction. The sanction need be no more than general disapproval, which may, or may not, culminate in ostracism.

In the second place, the principle, that the Jewish religion is to be viewed as having evolved naturally, gives rise to two corollaries touching Jewish practice. The first is that a distinction should be drawn between social and ritual practice. While social practice should be subject to some system of civil law, ritual practice cannot properly be included within the category of law. In tradition, where all kinds of ordinances, both social and ritual, are assumed to be part of supernaturally revealed Torah, there is warrant for a legalistic approach as well to social practice, for that approach implies implicit obedience and the exercise of sanctions in case of disobedience. Neither of these conditions can be expected to exist any longer in the modern world with regard to ritual practice, primarily as a result of the renunciation of the belief in the supernatural origin of the Jewish religion.

The foregoing does not negate the need of transferring some of the ritual practices to the social area of Jewish life where the concept of law does obtain. Thus, some minimum cessation from work on the Sabbath and festivals, observance of the rite of circumcision and the Jewish validation of marriage should constitute part of Jewish civil law. That would mean that they have to be lived up to as a requirement for being a loyal Jew. But it does not mean that the many detailed rules which are enumerated in the *Shulhan Aruk* as part of their observance would have to fall within the category of law.

Another qualification to be reckoned with, in the case of ritual practices, is that their removal from the category of law does not negate the need of establishing some standards by which the individual might be guided in his desire to achieve through these ritual practices a spiritual kinship with his fellow-Jews. Uniformity of some kind is essential, if religious observances are to serve a purpose of that kind. In case, however, circumstances prevent a Jew from adhering fully to the established norm, he ought to know just how far he may diverge without destroying the sense of spiritual kinship with the rest of his people.

The function of Jewish civil law undergoes a radical transformation, once we reckon with Jewish religion as the product of an historical process. We are no longer limited by the principle that any law which is to be enacted must in no way run counter to the traditional law of our ancestors. As a living people, we have a right to amend and change any law that has come down from the past, now that we no longer accept the assumption that it emanated directly from God. Take, for example, the status of woman in traditional Jewish law. By no manner of interpretation is it possible to interpret the traditional law with regard to that status as one of equality with that of the man. The only feasible remedy is to legislate that the woman be given equal status with the man. That illustrates the only workable approach henceforth to the problem of Jewish civil law.

The Reconstructionist movement, which is Leftist in form, has not been on the scene long enough to evolve a characteristic regimen of ritual observance. What it has to say about Jewish civil law presupposes a strong communal organization. Though an attempt has been made to evolve some theory with regard to ritual observance, as is done in

"Toward a Guide for Ritual Observance," the practical aspect of ritual observance is still in the process of formulation.

It is thus evident that those who associate themselves with the Conservative movement, or are associated with it in the minds of others, are actually divided into three distinct groups or schools of thought. The foregoing is an attempt to describe them in terms of their respective ideologies and practice patterns.

It is by no means assumed that every rabbi or layman who is identified as Conservative at present can, or does, actually belong only to one of the three groups. The very lack of uniformity within each group and the lack, hitherto, of any recognized classification into groups of any kind has bred in most of us a natural resistance to being classified. But these facts should not deter us from proceeding with the process of formulating our points of agreement and of difference. That is the only way to free the Conservative movement from the blight of inactivity and the danger of petrification. Though I have been fair and objective, I may have failed to give a true picture of our present condition. I am more than eager to make good whatever error of omission or commission will be pointed out to me.

How would the approach here suggested work in practice? Whenever we solicit a congregation to join the United Synagogue, we should inform its members of the four basic principles to which they are expected to subscribe in common with all groups or schools of thought within the Conservative movement. As for the rest, they are to be given the choice with which group they prefer to identify themselves. This very method of joining the United Synagogue would provide both occasion and stimulus for the re-education of our men and women in the content of Judaism. It would get them to think about it as they have never done before. They would begin to realize what it means to be Jews.

In the Rabbinical Assembly, the constructive ideas and activities of each group would be granted a hearing. No one group would be more authoritative than the others. The publications of the Rabbinical Assembly would not be in the hands of the one dominant group.

No doubt other specific problems are likely to arise with regard to coordinating the functions of both the Rabbinical Assembly and the United Synagogue in accordance with the plan here proposed. But all these problems can be solved without creating any rift within the movement as a whole, if both the United Synagogue and the Rabbinical Assembly are willing to accept the principle of unity in diversity as an essential characteristic of the Conservative movement.

The basic question which we have to answer forthwith is: Are we willing to accept these differences among us, to live with them and, with the aid of the democratic process, try to resolve all possible conflicts to which they may give rise? Or shall we go on assuming that it is possible for the Conservative movement to evolve some monolithic type of thought and practice? I submit that such an assumption will do neither us nor Jewish life as a whole any good. It will only hinder our efforts in behalf of our people and our faith, and render us uncreative and spiritually sterile in the future, as it did in the past. Driven underground, our differences will only cancel out one another, leaving us completely neutralized. Brought to the surface and granted the normal interchange in the free market of ideas and ideals, our differences will enable each group among us to further in its own way what we all agree on as essential to the future of Judaism. We shall thus all be partners in the great adventure which all of us who have anything to contribute to the revitalization of Jewish life should be permitted to share.

CHAPTER FOUR

Mid-Twentieth-Century Theorists

﷽

A. ROBERT GORDIS (1908–90)

In the late 1940s and the early 1950s, several factors made it imperative to formulate a distinctly Conservative philosophy of law. The Holocaust had just wiped out the eminent rabbinical seminaries of Europe. That meant that American Jews could no longer depend on, and were no longer constrained by, European rabbinic scholarship. On the contrary, American Jewry had suddenly become the largest Jewish community in the world. American rabbis, then, had to take on the responsibility of shaping Judaism in the second half of the twentieth century. Since the vast majority of America's Jews were affiliated with the Conservative movement, that task was especially critical for Conservative rabbis. Boaz Cohen, Robert Gordis, Jacob Agus, Abraham Heschel, and others leaped into the fray in what must have been an immensely exciting and heady time.[1]

Rabbi Robert Gordis was acknowledged by many of his generation as "Mr. Conservative Judaism." That was in part because of the many institutional roles he played within the movement, but it was even more a function of his articulate formulation, through both his writings and his lectures, of a centrist Conservative position.

On the institutional side, Gordis taught Bible at the Jewish Theological Seminary from 1931 into the 1980s, ultimately being awarded the named chair of Meyer and Fannie Rapaport Professor of Bible and Philosophies of Religion. Like Kaplan, then, he exerted a major influence on two generations of rabbinical students, and like Kaplan, his influence extended beyond his academic field of expertise to areas of Jewish thought. He also taught religion at Columbia University (1948–57), at Temple University (1967–74), and at the Hebrew University (1970–71), and he was the first Jew to teach Bible at the Protestant Union Theologi-

91

cal Seminary (1953–54). Remarkably, from 1931 to 1968 he also served as the rabbi of Temple Beth-El of Rockaway Park, New York, a large Conservative synagogue on Long Island, and thus, again like Kaplan, he combined the life of scholarship with the life of a congregational rabbi. In 1950 he founded one of the first Conservative day schools, renamed the Robert Gordis Day School in honor of his retirement in 1968. He served as president of the Rabbinical Assembly (1944–46), during which time the journal *Conservative Judaism* was founded and the first Conservative prayerbook, *Sabbath and Festival Prayer Book,* was published. He also served as president of the Synagogue Council of America (1948–49), and he was the obvious choice to chair the Commission on the Philosophy of the Conservative movement (1985–88), which produced *Emet Ve-emunah,* the first articulation of the philosophy of Conservative Judaism officially created and endorsed by all arms of the movement. For purposes of this volume on Jewish law, it is also important to note that he served on the Rabbinical Assembly's Committee on Jewish Law and Standards from 1946 until 1988, and in 1970 he chaired the Special Committee on the Revitalization of the Law Committee. While he wrote extensively on issues in the theory of Jewish law, he did not write rulings on specific issues. His activities stretched beyond the Jewish community, extending to church-state relations, interracial harmony and justice, and civic affairs.

In addition to his extraordinarily active career of service, Gordis wrote more than twenty books on biblical scholarship, Conservative Judaism, and the relationship of Judaism to contemporary problems. His book *Conservative Judaism: An American Philosophy* (1945) was the very first book ever to be published that articulated the philosophy of Conservative Judaism, and he returned to that subject in his later book, *Understanding Conservative Judaism* (1978), as well as in his last book, published posthumously, *The Dynamics of Judaism: A Study in Jewish Law* (1990). *Love and Sex* (1978), written for the Women's League for Conservative Judaism, won a National Jewish Book Award. His scholarship in Bible focused on the Book of Job and on the Five Scrolls read in the synagogue during the year (Song of Songs, Ruth, Lamentations, Kohelet [Ecclesiastes], and Esther). His books on theology and social ethics include *Faith for Moderns* (1960) and *The Root and the Branch: Judaism and the Free Society* (1962). As a rabbinical student, I had the privilege to study Job and the Five Scrolls with him, and I can attest that he brought his multiple interests into the study of Bible, enriching it for everyone. Many years later I served under his chairmanship on the Commission on the Philosophy of Conservative Judaism and its Editorial Committee, where I witnessed firsthand his masterful ability to hold together a clear middle ground among conflicting positions. Both in the speed with which he spoke and the energy he had for life, he well deserved the sobriquet his students lovingly gave him, "Rapid Robert"!

In the article below, Gordis responds directly to Reform, Orthodox, and Kaplanian approaches to Jewish law. With regard to Kaplan, he says, in very strong language, that "if we abandon the concept of Jewish law, we have unwittingly adopted the principles of Paulinian Christianity," for folkways are, in Gordis's view, not real norms, and thus Kaplan's theory amounts to antinomianism. Furthermore, "to define law in terms of sanctions seems to me to put the cart before the horse. Not sanctions create law, but law creates sanctions." He does not dwell on that for long, though, because Gordis believes that Jewish law does indeed have sanctions, theological ones: "For the believers in God, every wrong act has its tragic consequence reflected in the universe, and retribution is cosmic." Furthermore, obeying Jewish law brings its own rewards, and one feels the lack of those goods if one fails to obey what Jewish law requires. The Sabbath, for example, "brings deep and abiding rewards to the Jew" and "the failure to observe the Sabbath brings its punishment in the impoverishment of the spirit, the denudation of Jewish values, and the alienation from the Jewish community." We may understand the way in which divine benefits and sanctions operate differently from the way our ancestors did, but the rewards and punishments are nevertheless as real for us as they were for them.

This theological dimension also enables Jewish law to stretch beyond actions to motives and feelings, for while the state can punish me for assaulting my neighbor, it cannot demand that I cease hating him, as Judaism can and does. Similarly, Judaism demands not only that I refrain from beating my parents, but that I honor and respect them, which no state can mandate but which God can and does.

Who, though, determines Jewish law? In this essay, Gordis redefines Schechter's doctrine of "Catholic Israel" to refer only to those Jews who take Jewish law seriously. It is the practices of those Jews that, together with rabbinic rulings, shape Jewish law in our time. Any Jew can become part of Catholic Israel by making Jewish law part of his or her life, but only Jews who have done so may legitimately be counted among those whose practices must be considered in defining Jewish law. Thus the fact that the vast majority of American Jews eat unkosher food does not mean that the dietary laws are no longer binding, for Jews who take Jewish law seriously still overwhelmingly keep kosher. Gordis is aware that this establishes a moral and social anomaly, for how can a minority of Jews arrogate to itself the right to legislate for the majority? He maintains that such a situation can only be accepted on a temporary basis and that our contemporary challenge is to transform Catholic Israel from a minority to the majority of Jews.

Gordis also delineates in this article his methodology for evaluating Jewish laws. First, "the presumption should always be in favor of the traditional procedure." Thus "any Jewish practice *eo ipso* [in and of itself] has a claim upon us, unless it can be proved that it does not perform any of these functions, nor can it be reinterpreted to do so": (1) the cosmic or religious function, (2) the ethical or social function, (3) the esthetic or play function, and (4) the national or group-associational function. Note that he does not claim that these are simply four reasons that Jews may find Jewish rituals meaningful; he is making a much stronger claim: that even though we must begin with a bias toward the tradition, if a ritual does not fulfill any of these functions, even after efforts to reinterpret it, then it no longer functions as law. Gordis then articulates six methodological guidelines for how the new Committee on Jewish Law (later called "Committee on Jewish Law and Standards") should approach issues in Jewish law, which include not only careful study of traditional sources and the practices of Catholic Israel, but the use of legal techniques to define and justify a spectrum of acceptable observance from minimum to maximum, thus assuring pluralism. He also argues for the publication of guides for Jews so that they will know how to observe Jewish law as the Conservative movement understands it, as part of his attempt to transform the majority of Jews into what he defined as Catholic Israel.

Since Gordis had the opportunity to learn from Kaplan and to mark out a different path based on his objections to Kaplan, I thought that it would only be fair to include in this section Kaplan's response to Gordis, one of the chief exponents of what Kaplan calls the "Centrist" approach in Conservative Judaism. Kaplan here directly confronts Gordis's claim that Jewish rituals should continue to be treated as law, just as they had been in Jewish legal texts of the past.

While Kaplan himself maintained that "to achieve the purposes of ritual, even from the voluntarist viewpoint, calls for a formulation of norms or standards" that contribute to Jewish survival and enrich Jewish spiritual life, he argued that the legal approach to Jewish ritual that Gordis, among others, espouses cannot and should not be sustained. It cannot be sustained because there is no means to enforce rituals as law in societies with freedom of religion. It should not be because threats that ritual requirements will be enforced, which in a free society are perforce empty threats anyway, only lead people to resent the rituals. (He draws a parallel to American law: Americans who might have been persuaded by the temperance movement if it had appealed to their sense of morality and beneficence instead created "a wave of intemperance" and "a flouting of law in general" when they were forced to abstain from liquor by the Eighteenth Amendment to the Constitution.) Moreover, unlike the United States Constitution, the Torah does not have an amendment clause nor even provision for ongoing legislation, and if rituals are to be treated as law, there is no way to adjust them to new circumstances, even through liberal judicial interpretations of the law. Proof of that is that ever since Zachariah Frankel, Gordis's approach had been adopted, and it had yet (in 1956) to produce a single significant change in Jewish ritual law. Even the efforts of the Rabbinical Assembly to alleviate the condition of a woman "chained" to her first husband (an *agunah*) because he cannot or will not give her a Jewish writ of divorce are, according to Kaplan, lacking, for they depend on the couple agreeing to a clause in their wedding document contemplating their divorce. Instead, he says, contemporary rabbis should recognize the right of the woman to divorce her husband, a result impossible to achieve using only traditional legal methods of interpretation. Thus, according to Kaplan, with regard to rituals, we need to "salvage as much as possible of the good achieved by them in the past" by persuading Jews of their significance for our time. Although he does not say this in this essay, from his other writings and his own actions, it is clear that to do that Kaplan would have us first analyze traditional rituals for their spiritual content, discard those that no longer speak to us, change the form of those that need to be updated to be meaningful, invent new rituals to respond to new needs, and then educate Jews about the compelling meaning and messages of the Jewish rituals that we are promoting.

Gordis might admit that Jewish law has not yet been able to respond adequately to modern needs and sensitivities, but his response would be to renew our commitment to using traditional Jewish legal methods to accomplish that task. Kaplan's alternative, in Gordis's view, would undermine not only Jewish law but Judaism altogether, for a lawless Judaism is no longer Judaism in any recognizable form. It is important to see, though, that Gordis and Kaplan differ not only in their prescriptions for revitalizing Judaism in our day, but also in their very conceptions of law. For Kaplan, a demand is legal if and only if it can be and is enforced by a human government. For Gordis, a demand can be law if it is enforced by divine sanctions, and Jewish law is so enforced, even if it is not in the mechanical way that the Torah (especially Deuteronomy) envisions. Moreover, Gordis claims that a demand can be a law even if it is not enforceable, although he does not say much about how that can be so. We will need to pay attention to this issue—the definition of law it-self—as we proceed to the other thinkers in this volume.

How shall we evaluate Gordis's theory on its own terms? Gordis's approach to Jewish law is not "take it or leave it"; it seeks to integrate commitment to tradition and modernity, and that requires thought and judgment. To do that well, in turn, one must have both knowledge and experience: one must know Jewish legal texts and contemporary reali-ties, and one must have the wisdom to know when and how to fight for a change in Jewish tradition and when and how to fight instead for the traditional norm. Thus Gordis's approach is elitist, much as rabbinic Ju-daism has always been. Moreover, because Gordis's theory requires bal-ancing tradition and modernity, it will in practice often produce debate and differing conclusions. As a result, those who adopt his approach must at least tolerate and at best embrace pluralism and uncertainty; those who like clear, definitive instructions will not like this theory. Fur-thermore, because Gordis insists on employing legal reasoning to make any changes in the law, change will be slow and in some cases difficult to achieve, if it is possible at all. Because Gordis places authority in Jew-ish law in the hands of both rabbis and Catholic Israel, conflicts be-tween those two groups may result—and, for that matter, within each of those groups. Some would prefer a much clearer line of decision-making authority.

On the other hand, there are some clear advantages to Gordis's the-ory. It demands a sense of piety, lived out in practice, if one wants to have a say in defining Jewish law. That gives a distinctly religious sense to Gordis's view of Jewish law. Gordis's revision of Schechter's concept of Catholic Israel does seem right: in every community, it is those who take an active role that determine policy, and the same has been true his-torically and should be true now for Jewish practice. In this he is not cre-ating an exclusive club, for any Jew can join Catholic Israel by deciding to take Jewish law seriously, but he is identifying the group that does and should define the shape of Jewish law. Furthermore, Gordis's theory de-mands that legal decisions be made in a deliberate and thoughtful way; and as much as one may want clear instructions, one also wants recogni-tion of the fact that life itself is not simple, and that careful consideration of complex questions will have nuanced results. His theory is also au-thentically connected to the Jewish tradition, for he asserts a bias toward maintaining the tradition as it has come down to us and yet also main-tains an openness to change, exactly as the Rabbis of the Mishnah, Tal-mud, and Middle Ages operated. He thus preserves a sense of continuity with Jewish tradition and the authority that inheres in it. Finally, his view of the nature of law is broader and, frankly, more accurate than Kaplan's, for people do indeed obey laws for many reasons other than fearing punishment. Elliot Dorff will expand on that theme later, but in confronting Kaplan, Gordis began the discussion of how the authority of Jewish law is related to the nature of law in the first place.

⟪⟨⟆_____ ⟆⟩⟫

Authority in Jewish Law*

ROBERT GORDIS

IT SEEMS HIGHLY PROBABLE that the future historian will evaluate the great contribution of our teacher, Professor Mordecai M. Kaplan, toward the building of a vital Judaism in America not only in terms of his own original achievements, but also in the spirit of the rabbinic dictum: "Even greater than the agent is his achievement" (*Baba Batra* 9b). For over and above the seminal influence of his thought upon our movement from within, Reconstructionism has compelled us to face agonizing problems which we should have preferred to avoid. Only slowly and painfully has a literature on Conservative Judaism been growing up, and it is noteworthy how much of it has arisen as a reaction to the ideas which Doctor Kaplan has presented. Thus both those who accept his point of view in toto, as well as those who are unable to share it in large areas of thought are his disciples, drinking his waters, and being refreshed by his teaching.

This incalculable debt has been augmented by the series of articles, "Toward A Guide For Jewish Ritual Usage," recently published as the collective expression of the Reconstructionist Movement.[1] Our own reaction to the series may be summarized by the statement that the problems of Jewish ritual observance today are well set forth, but that the diagnosis is partial and the remedy markedly inadequate. But our concern here is not merely critical. These articles impel the leaders of Conservative Judaism, who are sincerely interested in the progress and intellectual validity of the movement, to grapple with this basic issue of Jewish law in the modern world. This paper is an effort to indicate the character of the problem and perhaps point the way to a solution.

Every student of Jewish life since the period of the Emancipation has noted the parlous state of Jewish observance. The organic pattern of Jewish traditional life has been shattered, and only vestiges are still maintained of such fundamental Jewish institutions as the Sabbath, the

---

*Proceedings of the Rabbinical Assembly 41–44, pp. 64–93 (1944).

holidays, the dietary laws, prayer and the study of the Torah. The fragments that are retained are often as ludicrous in their perverted sense of values as they are tragic in their implications for the future. The mourner who asks the Rabbi whether he may keep his shop open on the Sabbath of *shivah* week since mourning rites do not apply to the Sabbath is matched by the Jewess who wants to know whether she committed a grave sin by greeting a mourner during the same period, though her conscience does not trouble her about the *terefot* she serves in her home. It is no mere coincidence that these and similar questions are drawn from *Laws of Mourning,* one of the few sections of the *Shulhan Arukh* that may still be regarded as really alive, in practice as well as in theory!

John Erskine has said, "Nearly every one has religion, at least in the sense that he knows what church he is staying away from." It is only by that definition that most American Jews may be classified as Orthodox, Conservative or Reform, though there are the hosts of the "unaffiliated" for whom even this is too much religion.

Obviously the problem of Jewish observance is the crucial issue facing Judaism in our day. For even if we adopt a secular nationalist attitude toward the Jewish people like Ruppin, or a frankly assimilationist position like Jerome Frank, it is undeniable that the existence of the Jewish group as a recognizable entity, as well as the meaningful survival of Judaism as a spiritual force, is inconceivable without some regimen of ritual. Professor Louis Ginzberg pointed out long ago that *halachah* is far more fundamental in Judaism than *haggadah,* for ideas are volatile, but practices endure. If Jewish practice goes, virtually nothing remains.

Hence it is that the problem of Jewish ritual has been central in all attempts to adjust the Jewish heritage to the modern world. The very complexity of the problem forbids us to dismiss any of the attempted solutions without some consideration, if only to note and avoid their weaknesses.

THE REFORM ADJUSTMENT

Historically, the first attempt at a conscious adjustment of Jewish ritual to the modern world was made by Reform Judaism in Germany and in a more extreme form in the United States. To summarize the development of the entire movement in the broad Hegelian categories so beloved of German thinkers, traditional Judaism was the thesis, the Emancipation and the Enlightenment constituted the antithesis, and Reform Judaism emerged as the synthesis, the resolution of the conflict. Basically, the world-outlook of traditional Judaism was attacked as incompatible with the rationalism of the modern age. Even more energetically, it was opposed on the ground that it prejudiced the Jews' claim to emancipation, since it presupposed the existence of Israel as a national entity. The practices of traditional Judaism were challenged for both these reasons, as well as on the score of being cumbersome, outlandish and unesthetic by western standards.

Naturally, the degree to which Reform laity and leadership was prepared to scrap Jewish traditional observances varied with the individual, some going only as far as German Reform, which preserved a great deal of Jewish tradition, others as far as American Reform, which retained relatively little. Some leaders did not hesitate to decry circumcision and favored intermarriage. Theoretically, however, Reform in all its wings had a common platform: it surrendered the binding authority of Jewish law, and then left it free to each individual congregation to preserve such elements of the Jewish ritual as it found convenient or attractive, that is to say, religiously and morally edifying.

The principle underlying this process of selectivity was formulated in the Pittsburgh Platform of 1885. Sections 3 and 4 stated:

"We recognize in the Mosaic legislation a system of training the Jewish people for its mission during its national life in Palestine, and today we accept as binding only its moral laws, and maintain only such ceremonies as elevate and sanctify our lives, but reject all such as are not adapted to the views and habits of modern civilization.

"We hold that all such Mosaic and rabbinical laws as regulate diet, priestly purity, and dress, originated in ages and under the influence of ideas entirely foreign to our present mental and spiritual state. They fail to impress the modern Jew with a spirit of priestly holiness; their observance in our days is apt rather to obstruct than to further modern spiritual elevation."[2]

Actually, the Reform position was not altogether ingenuous. Thus at the Rochester meeting of the C.C.A.R. held in July 1895, a committee specially appointed to consider the question reported that "from the standpoint of Reform Judaism, the whole post-biblical and patristic literature, including the Talmud, casuists, responses, and commentaries, is, and can be considered as, nothing more or less than 'religious literature' . . . our relations in all religious matters are in no way authoritatively and finally determined by any portion of our post-biblical and patristic literature."[3] Out of deference to the Christian adulation of the Bible, the C.C.A.R. merely denied the authority of the rabbinical codes, saying nothing about the abrogation of Biblical law as well. As Gabriel Riesser had said of German Reform, "The Bible is treated gently (by Reform) because of its notable kinship with Christianity and on account of the august police." Reform was a type of Karaism in reverse—Karaism had begun by challenging the authority of the Talmud, and cleaving to the text of Scripture, but soon found it necessary, in order to make Biblical law function, to create its own Oral Law. Reform began in an anti-Talmudic spirit, and declared itself to be "Mosaic," but it quickly surrendered the binding authority of Biblical law as well. Even if the agitation against circumcision and the sentiment for intermarriage be dismissed as the vagaries of extremists, one has only to recall the virtual nullification of the Biblical laws on the Sabbath rest, fasting on Yom Kippur, divorce, the dietary laws and many others.

The tragic consequences of this consistent Reform policy became obvious in the succeeding fifty years, and in 1937 a new statement of Guiding Principles was finally adopted by the C.C.A.R. The revised statement shows the highest courage and intellectual honesty in modifying what has become "traditional" Reform Judaism. It adopted a considerably more favorable attitude toward the national elements in Judaism, such as Jewish ceremonies, the Hebrew language and the role of Palestine. This development is rich in promise for a deeper Jewish life in Reform circles and is to be greeted with favor.

Yet it is highly significant that the problem of authority in Jewish law is passed in complete silence in the later pronouncement.[4] It merely restates in more sympathetic fashion what had been set forth rather brusquely in 1885 when it declares:

"The Torah, both written and oral, enshrines Israel's evergrowing consciousness of God and of the moral law. . . . Being products of historical processes, certain of its laws have lost their binding force with the passing of the conditions that called them forth."[5] The Platform of 1885 and the statement of 1937 differ in the number of Jewish observances they would like to see preserved, but the basic philosophy is unchanged. Jewish tradition possesses no binding authority; there is no Jewish *law* for the modern Jew.

The drawbacks of the Reform attitude in its older and its newer formulations are self-evident. It makes anarchy ubiquitous and unity impossible of achievement. It destroys the sense of continuity that must link American Israel with the generations of the past and with their brothers throughout the world. Finally it empties Jewish life of so much of its content and warmth as to make it as lifeless and decorous as a corpse. Without binding authority, Judaism is powerless to evoke sacrifice, and without sacrifice, an ideal is doomed. The rewritten Platform of 1937 testifies to the inadequacy of the classic Reform version of Judaism, but in side-stepping the basic issue of the basis for Jewish ritual observance it has failed to solve the heart of the problem. One may doubt whether an attenuated Reform will prove more successful than the most self-confident Reformers of the pioneer ages.

THE ORTHODOX REACTION

A second adjustment of Jewish tradition to the modern world was attempted by Neo-Orthodoxy, whose great spokesman was S. R. Hirsch. This solution possesses the virtue of great simplicity. It meets the impact of the modern world by rejecting in *toto* the contemporary outlook on such religious and philosophic issues as inspiration, the higher criticism of the Bible, miracles, comparative religion, scientific law and the doctrine of evolution. Neo-Orthodoxy admits the difficulties and sacrifices entailed in the maintenance of Jewish law today but demands its scrupulous fulfillment, as being a divine imperative. For Jewish law to its minutest details is literally the command of God. It is true that

Jewish law bears the names of legislators, prophets and sages, but, they are passive instruments performing God's will, with personal backgrounds and historical circumstances playing no decisive part in the process. "Every regulation that an able student is destined to teach throughout time was already proclaimed to Moses at Sinai." (*Yer. Peah* 2,4) Thus Jewish law is the word of God, eternal, immutable, and forever binding upon Israel.

Neo-Orthodoxy, the classic form of which was expounded in Germany by the Frankfort school, made only two concessions to the modern age. It accepted the Reform theory that Jews now constitute merely *a* religious communion. The sole difference that sets its attitude apart from Reform is that it believes that in the distant future a supernatural Messiah will miraculously restore the nationhood of Israel. In the second instance, Neo-Orthodoxy brought within the precincts of Judaism the decorum and order characteristic of West-European life.

For certain minds seeking above all things the harbor of certainty, the power and appeal of Neo-Orthodoxy is undeniable. But its inability to meet the need of most modern Jews is equally clear. Its practical weakness is that it fails to reckon with the need for change, at least *de jure. De facto*, Orthodoxy has been forced to accept modifications which would have been undreamt of a few generations ago.

Perhaps even more important than the practical drawbacks of Neo-Orthodoxy is its weak ideological foundation. Modern historical science has demonstrated the evolutionary character of all human institutions, and Jewish scholarship has revealed the same process at work in Judaism. Orthodox scholars like David Hoffmann, in his critique of the Graf-Wellhausen theory, and Isaac Halevy, the author of *Dorot Harishonim,* in his onslaught on I. H. Weiss' *Dor Dor Vedorshav,* have rendered a superb service in exposing the weaknesses and errors of more radical scholars. Nonetheless they have been powerless to shake the conviction that Judaism has evolved through the ages, and, what is more, been responsive to environmental and even personal factors.

In fine, for a small compact group, Neo-Orthodoxy offers a way of life that is consistent and enduring, though at the cost of spiritual isolation from the modern world. But most modern Jews find it inadequate for their problems and needs.

THE MEDIATING PHILOSOPHY

The perils inherent in Reform's nullification of Jewish tradition and Neo-Orthodoxy's petrification of Jewish law led to the development of a mediating philosophy. This was particularly based on the achievement of Jewish scholarship, notably Zunz, Frankel and Graetz in Germany. The movement has never been fortunate in its name. Zechariah Frankel called it by the ponderous German title of *"positiv-historisches Judentum"*; in America, because of its accidental relationship to modern English orthodoxy, it bears the almost equally inadequate name of "Conservative Judaism." There is scant likelihood, however, of any change of nomenclature. Frankel's designation indicated its basic tenet: it accepted as basic the axiom that Judaism had developed historically, and then it adopted a positive, favorable attitude toward this historical product. What had been accepted as binding in Judaism could not be abrogated at will by any group.

As Professor Louis Ginzberg summarizes the viewpoint in his paper on Frankel, "for an adherent of this school, the sanctity of the Sabbath reposes not upon the fact that it was proclaimed on Sinai, but on the fact that the Sabbath idea found for thousands of years its expression in Jewish souls. . . . From this point of view, the evaluation of a law is independent of its origin, and thus the line of demarcation between biblical and rabbinical law almost disappears. . . ."[6] Vis-a-vis Orthodoxy, Frankel insisted that Judaism had evolved. In fact he played a great part in revealing the steps of the process. But vis-a-vis Reform, Frankel denied the right to set aside Jewish law and tradition for the sake of personal convenience or political emancipation.

Viewed against the background of the times, Frankel's theory is clearly an effort to create a counterpoise to Reform. Frankel had been revolted at the easy willingness of the delegates to the Brunswick Conference of 1844 to set aside the sancta of Judaism, but he decided to participate the following year in the Frankfort meeting. The break came on the apparently secondary issue of the language in which worship is to be conducted. When the conference voted that prayers could be offered in the vernacular and that Hebrew be retained in the service only in deference to the habits of the older generation, Frankel walked out of the sessions. Thus he bore witness to the national character of Judaism and the binding character of past Jewish practices as norms for the present. Unfortunately, Frankel never dealt fundamentally with the basis of authority, which is the crux of the problem.

It was left for Solomon Schechter to grapple with this issue. As Professor Kaplan has pointed out,[7] the two salient traits in Schechter's attitude were his stress on the primacy of Jewish scholarship and his emphasis on the importance of keeping Jewish life integral and unified. But Schechter did more—he was also aware that the conception of authority was the distinctive element in his outlook, setting it apart from both Orthodoxy and Reform. In his famous introduction to his "Studies in Judaism," he pointed out how modern Jewish historical scholarship had placed authority not in a literal Revelation but in "the conscience of Catholic Israel." "Judaism has distinct precepts and usages and customs, consecrated by the consent of Catholic Israel through thousands of years."[8]

Only through adequate learning would it be possible for Jews and particularly the rabbis to "know what is vital to Judaism and what may be changed with impunity." He disapproved of continual dropping of various ceremonies which he regarded as essential to religion as well as of unceasing innovations, which must, in the end, "touch the very vital organism of Judaism."

Schechter had notably deepened the concept of authority for Conservative Judaism, but even in his formulation, which was usually parenthetical and incidental to another theme, the will predominates over the intellect, that is to say, he was primarily concerned with a working formula rather than a logically perfect definition. He, too, had his gaze fixed on Reform, against whose inundating tide he sought to erect a dam. Yet it might not be overlooked that this general outlook was sufficiently grounded in reality to serve as the basis for the rapid progress of Conservative Judaism in America and even in prewar Germany, where Frankel's trend became dominant.

Nevertheless, for all its pragmatic value, the theory of Catholic Israel suffers from self-evident weaknesses. It has the virtue of recognizing the historical and evolving character of Judaism, but then it arbitrarily declares that what traditional Judaism has created until now must henceforth be maintained virtually unchanged. To cite Professor Ginzberg again, the norm according to Frankel was the Talmudic position that whatever observance is spread throughout the whole community must not be abrogated by any authority.[9] It thus creates a dichotomy in Jewish experience between the creative past and the degenerate present. Moreover, had the same doctrine been invoked in past centuries, the development of Judaism, and perhaps its very life, would have been halted. Finally, the practical application of the doctrine offers insuperable obstacles. If by Catholic Israel, whose practice determines what is binding in Judaism, we mean the majority of modern Jews, then we might as well eliminate the Sabbath, the festivals and the dietary laws, since they are violated by most Jews today. If, on the contrary, we subsume under the category of Catholic Israel the observant Jews only, the doctrine means a retention of the status quo, for by definition, an observant Jew is one who observes the Law unchanged.

For these reasons, in spite of the essential soundness of its emphasis upon the evolving nature of Judaism, the binding character of Jewish law and the centrality of Catholic Israel in that development, the theory as set forth by Frankel and Schechter proves unworkable in practice.

UNTENABLE GUIDELINES

The past few years have therefore witnessed the growth of a new approach to traditional Judaism, Reconstructionism. Within the last years, it has attempted to implement its attitude toward ritual by the publication of a "New Haggadah" and of the series of articles referred to above, entitled "Toward A Guide For Jewish Ritual Usage." The position there adopted may be summarized as follows: The traditional Jewish code of observance can no longer be maintained in its entirety. For practical and ideological reasons, many, if not most, modern Jews are not prepared to preserve it. The anarchy of Reform, the supernaturalism and reactionary character of Orthodoxy, and the indecision and lack of clarity characteristic of Conservatism render them all inadequate for modern needs

Hence a new rationale is needed. Every ceremony and rite must be judged in terms of its value as a method of group survival and a means to the personal self-fulfillment and salvation of the individual Jew.[10] We must reckon with the fact that a common pattern of observance is no longer possible. Jews in different lands, even those who vary in their social and educational levels, will diverge in their evaluation of specific rituals. All that may be expected today is a unity of ends; the means will vary sharply among groups and individuals.

Nor does "a stigma attach to those who permit themselves a wide latitude in their departure from traditional norms." For Jewish ritual is no longer to be regarded as law, but as folkways, if only because there can be no law without sanctions and we possess no agencies for enforcing Jewish observance or punishing any infraction of the codes. In fact, Professor Kaplan had urged the substitution of the term *minhagim* or "folkways" for "the commandments between man and God," in order to make it clear that "they lack the connotation of being . . . imperative."[11]

The proposed "Guide" then sets up criteria for judging the value of specific rituals in terms of the meaningfulness of their form, their content or both. It finally considers in some detail synagogue worship, the sabbath, and "dietary usages," retaining or modifying elements of the traditional codes in the light of the criteria previously developed.

This series has naturally aroused considerable discussion, both written and oral,[12] but here we wish merely to call attention to various details of both the theoretic formulation and the practical applications that are relevant to our purpose. It is not true, for example, that Conservative Judaism makes the survival of the Jewish people the justification of Jewish observance, or that traditional Jews observe the dietary laws "out of fear" and not "out of love." No doubt there are many who maintain Judaism generally out of the "fear of God," but many others are moved by the "love of God" as well.

Moreover, it is grossly insufficient to have unity of purpose with a variety of means, if only because, as John Dewey clearly pointed out, the means you have always with you, while the end belongs to an uncertain future. Given enough variety of means, no unity remains at all. Dr. Kaplan is undoubtedly correct in stressing the fact that traditional Judaism deprecated the effort to explain the meaning of the *mitzvot*.[13] But this attitude prevailed only during the earlier stages of the Jewish religion, before the impact of other cultures became more pronounced. When Judaism met Greek thought, whether directly as in Philo, or through the medium of Arabic civilization, as in medieval days, the search for the *ta'amay ha-mitzvot* (purpose of the commandments) became a central feature of Jewish religious thought and the subject of a considerable literature.

Thus the pioneer of Jewish philosophy, Saadiah, already classifies the commandments under two headings: *sichliyot* commandments, the reason for which is clearly evident, and *shimiyot*, those demanding obedience, though their meaning is not clear. By reinterpreting these categories in modern terms, we arrive at a sound classification of the *mitzvot*, (a) the rational commands, consisting largely of the ethical imperatives wherein Judaism is basically at one with all great religions and (b) the uniquely traditional forms, the product of historical factors in Judaism.[14] That the instruments of daily prayer are phylacteries and not a prayer-carpet cannot be justified on rational grounds, but is the consequence of a specific Jewish development. Nor need its justification be sought in the area of logic. Every personality, whether that of an individual or a group, includes rational elements, wherein it will resemble others. But the essence of personality resides in the non-rational elements, which alone are unique and distinctive. To attempt to build the human spirit purely from rational elements means to create an automaton, not a living organism.

BEYOND "FOLKWAYS"

The cardinal weakness, however, of the Reconstructionist approach lies, we feel, in its denial of the concept of Jewish law. Dr. Kaplan emphatically insists that ritual observances are not law but folk-ways, and he cites Vinogradoff to prove that law implies sanctions, the employment of force against the recalcitrant individual. Unless, therefore, we are prepared to reinstitute flagellation and the other Rabbinic punishments for the violation of the ritual commandments, Jewish ritual observances must be regarded by us merely as folk-ways. To deal with the practical implications of this attitude before considering its theoretic basis, it seems obvious to us that to declare Jewish observance merely a matter of folk-ways sounds the death-knell of Judaism as a normative religion. Nowhere is there a deeper "appreciation" of the beauty of Jewish "folk-ways" than among the labor Zionists, for example. The best book thus far written on the Jewish festivals emanates from a member of their circle. But a sympathetic attitude toward these customs, even an emotional relationship, is powerless to effect their observance. Undoubtedly, we prefer the observance of a Third Seder by the Labor Zionists to the Yom Kippur balls of the anarchists forty years ago, but what about the First and Second Seder?

If we abandon the concept of Jewish law, we have unwittingly adopted the principles of Paulinian Christianity. For it must be remembered that Paul was by no means uncompromisingly antinomian at the beginning of his career. On the contrary, his early attitude was one of toleration and even of commendation. In I Cor. 7:19 he declares, "Circumcision is nothing and non-circumcision is nothing, but the keeping of the commandment of the law." In Romans 2:25 he goes further and admits: "Circumcision verily profited, if thou keep the law." Yet beginning at that standpoint, it was a series of easy transitions that led him to the complete repudiation of Jewish ritual law and the retention only of the ethical commandments. Ultimately, Paul could insist that keeping the law was a mark of sin.

So much for the practical consequences of this negation of the concept of Jewish law. I confess, however, that I cannot follow the theory of the Reconstructionist approach either. To define law in terms of sanctions seems to me to put the cart before the horse. Not sanctions create law, but law creates sanctions. Vinogradoff, in the quotation cited by Dr. Kaplan does declare:

> "Every legal rule falls into two parts: first, a *command* stating the legal requirement, second, a sanction providing that, if the command is not obeyed, force will be employed against the recalcitrant person."

But he is speaking of legal rules regulating human relations, and here sanctions are a central feature, for this obvious reason: Legal codes that are concerned with the protection of the individual in society must interpose speedy and effective safeguards against aggression from other individuals. Protection and redress must be *immediate* in order to be effective, since the victim, being human, does not live forever! Hence laws *between man and God* which do not impose human sanctions are dead letters.

But for the religious spirit, the compulsion in law resides elsewhere than in the police power of the state. For the believers in God, every wrong act has its tragic consequence reflected in the universe, and retribution is cosmic:

> The shop *is* open; and the dealer gives credit; and the ledger lies open; and the hand writes; and whosoever wishes to borrow may come and borrow; and the collectors regularly make their daily round, and exact payment from man whether he is content or not. . . . (Ethics of the Fathers 3:20)

That is the essence of the religious outlook, which therefore regards the world as governed by the Divine law of justice, which is binding upon men even when no human penalties exist or can be enforced. Therein lies the significant contribution which religion makes to morality, its capacity to penetrate to areas beyond the reach of the law. The state punishes me if I hurt my neighbor, but hating him is no less a violation of law, though the courts are powerless to act. Beating one's old father is punishable by sanctions imposed by the police court; disrespect is not punishable by human agency, yet it is none the less binding. These and countless other ethical imperatives are law, not customs, practices or habits, yet no human, external penalty attaches to their violation.

These *a priori* considerations are reinformed by a consideration of Talmudic categories. No one will deny that to the Rabbis, the *mitzvot* were law, of binding power, yet every page of the Talmud refers to such concepts as "Free from penalty but forbidden," "unpunished in human law, but guilty by Divine law," "death at the hand of God." Recently, attention has been called to the phenomenon in Rabbinic law, where legal rules possessing human sanctions are transferred in the Talmud to the realm of ethics, with no external penalties.[15] In fine, human sanctions cannot serve as the marks of religious law.

But, it will be argued, Rabbinic Judaism regards every enactment of the ritual as well as of the ethical code as literally Divine, and violations of either are believed to entail Divine punishment. But for us today, Revelation rooted in the Divine as in all life, is a never-ending human process, with institutions and ordinances created by men in whom the Divine spirit works. Can we believe that the ritual code is enforceable with penalties? I submit that *in terms of our modern outlook,* it remains true for us today that the violation of Jewish ritual law is attended by Divine sanctions—*and that no other attitude is possible.* If we declare that the observance of the Sabbath brings deep and abiding rewards to the Jew, that it re-creates his spirit as it regenerates his physical and nervous system, that it brings him into communion with God, links him with the profoundest aspirations of Israel, and draws him into the orbit of Torah, then it follows inescapably that the failure to observe the Sabbath brings its punishment in the impoverishment of the spirit, the denudation of Jewish values and the alienation from the Jewish community, literally "that soul is cut off from its kinsmen."

We naturally picture the manner in which divine sanctions operate as different from the conception of our ancestors, because our conception of God has changed, but we cannot deny that Divine judgment operates in the world. For Conservative Judaism, murder and the infraction of the Sabbath are not on a par (incidentally they are not for Orthodox Judaism either),[16] but they are both violations of Jewish law, differing from each other as crimes, felonies and misdemeanors differ in American law and therefore entailing penalties of varying severity.

Moreover, and this is significant for the outlook of Conservative Judaism, which is based on the historical approach, the content of these categories will differ in time, *pan passu* with changes in conceptions and conditions. The commandment "Thou shalt not kill" was not at the time of its promulgation regarded as prohibiting clan vengeance, but as time went on this was subsumed under the category. First, the Torah limited the activity of the Avenger of the Blood in the case of an unpremeditated killing and established the cities of refuge. By the time of the Second Temple, clan vengeance under any circumstance would have been regarded as murder, pure and simple, had it ever been attempted. The same process of development at work may be observed in the current attitude toward lynching as a crime, concurred in by most, but not yet by all Americans. Some day, God grant it be soon, the mass murder of war will be recognized as part of the prohibition. Not only crimes, but misdemeanors, change with time, but these modifications do not invalidate their status as law.

Therein lies our differentiation from Orthodoxy. We likewise regard ritual observance as part of Jewish law, but our attitude toward law differs. We insist upon reckoning with the results of Jewish scholarship which illustrate with myriad of examples the flexible, evolutionary character of Jewish law. For us divine revelation is a never-ending process, but we recognize that Moses, Akiba, Maimonides and Karo had a greater need of revelation than the Brunswick Conference of 1844.

"CATHOLIC ISRAEL" AND AUTHORITY

Wherein does the authority of Jewish law reside, if revelation did not end at Sinai, or with the Mishnah or the Shulhan Arukh? The answer that Conservative Judaism requires is to be found in the doctrine of Catholic Israel enunciated in general terms by Frankel and Schechter. We need only to explore its implications in terms of our current trends and insights.

Frankel and his colleagues in Germany, and to a lesser degree Schechter in America, were concerned with erecting a dike against the flood-tide of Reform. Hence they evolved the conception of Catholic Israel, which called for the modern loyal Jew to identify himself with the accepted practice of the Jewish people. This concept was fundamentally a static principle, barring the way to change—a historical necessity in their day, when Reform threatened to sweep everything before it. Today, our concern is no longer with preventing extreme innovation but with establishing norms for orderly growth and progress. Yet because of its basic truth, the doctrine of Catholic Israel can prove equally fruitful in our present situation.

The conception of Catholic Israel is basically democratic. It declares that Jewish life is determined by no synod or conference or editorial board, but reflects the aspirations and attitudes of the Jewish people as a whole. Now, theoretically, democracy is, in Lincoln's classic definition, incidentally enunciated centuries earlier in the preface to Wyelif's Bible, "government of the people, by the people, for the people." Practically, however, no democratic government expresses the will of the entire people, but only of those sufficiently interested in it to exercise the franchise and obey the laws. The indifferent citizens who do not exercise the franchise, and the criminals convicted of an offense who forfeit their citizenship, constitute two classes that have no voice in the conduct of the government. At the opposite pole from the criminal are certain extreme idealistic groups, who voluntarily relinquish their rights in the state. H. D. Thoreau, the great New England naturalist, was a philosophical anarchist who wrote on the "Duty of Civil Disobedience." He remains a great American, but he was not consulted in the town meeting at Concord. Similarly, pacifists in the present national crisis are honored for their devotion to principle, and are not expelled from the American people, but they do not ask to decide the military and diplomatic policies of the government. In *posse*, democracy is the government of all the people; in *esse*, it is government by all elements of the people who recognize the authority of the law and actively express their interest, at least by going to the ballot-box. There are times when nearly all eligible voters exercise their franchise. Generally, the percentage is only a fraction, sometimes less than fifty per cent of the whole. Our government, however, remains a democracy, because potentially every American has a voice in the conduct of its affairs.

Apply this analysis to our problem and it becomes clear that Catholic Israel must be conceived differently from hitherto accepted views. On the one hand, it is not co-extensive with the Jewish people, nor on the other, is it restricted to those who observe the Law unchanged.

Catholic Israel is the body of men and women within the Jewish people, who accept the authority of Jewish law and are concerned with Jewish observance as a genuine issue. It therefore includes all who observe the law, whether formally Orthodox or Conservative or neither. The character of their observance may be rigorous and extend to minutiae, or it may include modifications in detail. Catholic Israel embraces all those, too, who observe Jewish law in general, though they may violate one or another segment, and who are sensitive to the problem of their non-observance because they wish to respect the authority of Jewish law.

Moreover, Catholic Israel is vertical as well as horizontal, that is to say, it includes the generations gone before, whose lives and activities have determined the character of the tradition transmitted to us. Their practice cannot permanently bar the way to growth, but it must necessarily exert influence upon our decisions regarding changes from accepted tradition. They cannot exercise a veto, but they must not be deprived of a vote.

That past generations should play an important role in determining the content of tradition for the present is not astonishing. The sales of "Gone With the Wind" were many thousands of times greater than that of "Hamlet," but the perennial appeal of the latter is more significant of its place in English culture than the "best-seller" qualities of the former. Catholic Israel is universal in time as well as in space.

In spite of widespread impressions to the contrary, Catholic Israel, those within the pale of normative Judaism, was never a monolithic mass, a homogeneous body. The divergences between Hillelites and Shammaites, the distinctions in custom between Palestinian and Babylonian custom, the differences among rationalist, mystic and traditionalist in the Middle Ages down to the *Hasid* and the *Mitnaged* in modern times, all these were often far-reaching, both in theory and in practice. Only the passing of time has blurred the lines and softened the acerbities of controversy.

The character and limits of these differences may be illustrated by two historical instances. Talmudic Judaism had its strict constructionists as well as its liberal interpreters, who greatly extended the scope of the Biblical text. The more liberal exegesis of Akiba generally prevailed over the stricter methods of Ishmael, yet the latter had a by no means inconsiderable influence upon Jewish law. When, however, centuries later, a group of strict constructionists, the Karaites, arose, who denied the entire validity of Talmudic law, they forfeited their right to determine the development of Rabbinic law.

Variations within Catholic Israel always existed. For obvious reasons, they are more marked today than in the past. Catholic Israel is no single, homogeneous group. It has its conservatives and its liberals, as has the American electorate. It is, however, restricted to those who accept the authority of Jewish law.

It need hardly be emphasized that this conception does not read any Jew out of the Jewish fold. It merely declares what should be self-evident, that only those should have a voice in determining the character of Jewish law who recognize its authority. Reform and secularist Jews will continue to select on a purely personal basis certain customs from the pattern of Jewish living that appeal to them. But since they deny the authority of Jewish law, they naturally cannot expect to be consulted in its development. It is true that in recent years, these groups have approved growing numbers of Jewish practices, a tendency eminently to be welcomed and encouraged. But the judgment of the Sages has particular relevancy to our problem.

CHANGE AND DEVELOPMENT

The conception of Catholic Israel, here proposed, sheds light on the process of change and development and the technique by which these changes are to be legitimized.

Changes in Jewish observance can become part and parcel of Jewish law only if they emanate from Catholic Israel, from those who accept the authority of Jewish law and not from those who, for whatever reasons, have broken with it. Thus the Prohibition Amendment was repealed not by the activities of the Capones and the Schultzes, but by the attitudes and behavior of law-abiding American citizens who opposed Prohibition. At the beginning, a small group of dissidents object to a given law, slowly they persuade others to adopt their opinion. When they increase in numbers, the enactment becomes a dead letter and ultimately disappears from the statute books.

This process of change and development in Jewish law is to be traced, not only during the great creative periods of the Bible and the Talmud, as modern Jewish scholarship has revealed, but even in the abnormal and chaotic history of the modern period. Before our eyes, radical changes are taking place, and this among those who live by Jewish law. The laws of *sha'atnez* and the prohibition of interest are virtually inoperative among traditional Jews, as is the formerly widespread custom of wearing a beard. Shaving, in spite of the five prohibitions involved, is almost universal, even without the shaving powder and the electric razor. The observance of the dietary laws today is generally accompanied by a willingness to eat dairy foods or fish in nonkosher eating houses. Recent inventions have created new problems of observance, and corresponding reactions, on the part of Sabbath observers. The telephone tends to be quite widely used (for social purposes), the radio and television perhaps a little less, and electric lights perhaps a little more. Yet increasingly, these acts are being performed by Sabbath observers. All these and similar modifications have occurred without guidance or even a conscious principle, but the principle does exist. It is Catholic Israel at work, who, if they are not prophets, are the descendants of prophets. (*Pes.* 66b.)

This recognition of Jewish law as the expression of Catholic Israel explains the fact that what was forbidden at one time and properly so may become permitted at another and with equal justice. For new conditions and attitudes impinge on the lives of men and accordingly modify the outlook and the practices of Catholic Israel. When East European Jews a century or more ago objected to the shorter, "German" coats of the *Maskilim,* it was not mere obscurantism, but a recognition that the surrender of the traditional Jewish garb was a symbol of a break with Jewish tradition. But as time went on, the new mode penetrated into traditional circles as well, and it now became innocuous.

Without presuming to decide here the Halachic issues involved, it is clear that some warrant for instrumental music in the synagogue may be found in Jewish tradition. Non-Reform circles were adamant in their objection to the innovation in nineteenth century Germany because they recognized that its introduction was directly a *hukat hagoy,* an aping of foreign customs; a conscious effort to pattern the synagogue after the Protestant Church. That factor is by no means negligible even today, but now when a traditional congregation introduces an organ it may be presumed to imitate some contemporary Jewish and not necessarily a Christian model. Of course, the decision with regard to such a step involves many considerations of a non-halakhic character as well.

If Jewish law is a constantly developing organism, wherein does its continuity lie? Precisely in its organic character. It has been pointed out that every living body is constantly engaged in breaking down and replacing its cells, so that within seven years, not a single cell remains unchanged in a human body. If this be true, how can we describe ourselves as identical with the personality we were eight years ago? The answer is obvious: Identity really means continuity, and continuity is preserved because the changes are gradual; we do not rise one morning to discover that every cell in us is new!

The process of growth is slow, it has its stresses and conflicts. By its very nature, every general law will work hardships in exceptional cases that require amelioration. But it remains law because we believe it to be binding and its observance or violation to entail consequences of good or evil.

FROM MINORITY TO MASSES

Having redefined Catholic Israel as those elements of the Jewish people that recognize the authority of Jewish law and are sensitive to the problem, we cannot overlook the ominous change that has taken place in modern times, in the ratio that Catholic Israel bears to the Jewish people as a whole. That Catholic Israel could be identified by Frankel and Schechter with virtually the entire Jewish people was due to the fact that until recently the two groups were practically coextensive. Today, Catholic Israel in our definition represents only a minority of American Jewry, and with the destruction of the European center, perhaps of world Jewry. A democracy in which only a fraction of the electorate is interested in the government is in grave danger, and the present status of Jewish religious life in America is equally intolerable.

In fact, a theoretical question may be raised as to the right of a minority to arrogate to itself the title of "Catholic Israel" and then undertake to "legislate" for the majority. If the final authority is vested in the Jewish people and Jews do not observe Jewish ritual, does not their practice or lack of practice become the modern standard of the Jew? Practically and theoretically, then, the concept of Catholic Israel as consisting of a minority is subject to challenge.

The answer lies in the conviction, and in the will behind that conviction, that the present status of Jewish observance is, or must be made, only temporary. To quote an analogy from American experience, we are now at the frontier stage of Jewish life in America. Every American is familiar with the frontier towns that sprang up all over America, particularly in the wake of the Gold Rush and similar mass movements. In these mushroom towns, the basic moral practice of American society was observed by a small and often impotent minority. Drunkenness, murder, gambling and sexual license were often widespread. Had the social behavior of these Western towns been perpetuated, it would have meant the collapse of the accepted moral code of America.

Instead, a contrary process took place. The minority gradually was able to institute law and order, and its standards ultimately became dominant. Where did a minority draw the authority to enforce its standards upon the majority? It derived it from the knowledge that its attitudes had the sanction of the entire American people, of whom it constituted an outpost. The weight of that authority ultimately prevailed, even though it was temporarily embodied in a minority. As Lincoln pointed out in his attack on the concept of "popular sovereignty" as expounded by Douglas, Americans would never have admitted the right of Mormons to practice polygamy in the territory they occupied as a majority. It is, of course, undeniable that the frontier spirit, as Professor Turner has stressed, exerted an abiding influence upon the American character and institutions, but the pressure of American life as a whole proved decisive for the frontier towns.

The analogy with the present status of Jewish life in America is striking. "Each man does what is righteous in his own eyes" is as valid a description of our age as of the days of the Judges. Pretending that the present chaos in Jewish life and observance is "the American way" and seeking to justify it or at least to acquiesce in it under some high-sounding formula are sheer self-deception, of which true spiritual leaders dare not be guilty. It may be granted that current American-Jewish practice will influence our future code of observance in many ways and must therefore be taken into account. But it is undeniable that there is need of reviving the mass of traditional Jewish rituals by interpreting them in the light of our modern attitudes and ceaselessly campaigning for their observance.

Therein lies a fundamental challenge of the current crisis to the Jewish spiritual leadership of today, one which has been unconscionably neglected. But the functions of the Rabbinate are not exhausted merely in agitating for Jewish observance. We must not only guide the practice of the people by expounding the values in Jewish ritual observance. We must, when changes are found necessary, create the instruments for bringing the change into the mainstream of Jewish tradition.

The technique for this latter function was evolved by the Rabbis of the Talmud. It resides in the process of interpretation rather than in nullification as a means of development. This contention, however, is frequently denied. It is argued that Akiba could draw fine-spun deductions from the Biblical text which actually were developments beyond it, because he believed it to be literally the Word of God and so both eternal in its application and significant in every syllable, and because the modern sense of historical change was lacking in his day. Since, however, for us, Revelation is no longer literal, but figurative, a process and not an act, and since we possess the modern sense of history, a similar procedure of interpretation is impossible.

This conclusion is, however, open to serious doubt. The Constitution of the United States is not regarded as the literal Word of God even by its most perfervid admirers, and no one believes that its authors foresaw the problems and conditions of our day. Yet the learned Justices of the Supreme Court find it perfectly sensible procedure to declare laws regarding radio chains, trade unions, the closed shop and public utilities "constitutional" or otherwise. By a process of interpretation of the letter of the Constitution, they seek to disclose its spirit and then make it relevant to contemporary needs.

Nor is this all. It is well-known that nine equally honest and reasonably competent judges will differ as to the constitutionality of a given law, basing their opinions on varying interpretations of the text of the basic document. The inference is clear that, barring an obvious infringement of the Constitution where no difference of opinion is possible, the Justices begin with an attitude on the social utility of a given law and then seek to validate their opinion by a study of the text.

Professor Morris R. Cohen points out that in human affairs, inventing and finding are not antithetical, so that "the process of law making is called finding the law." A judicial decision "decides not so much what the words of a statute ordinarily mean but *what the public, taking all the circumstances of the case into account, should act on.*" He argues forcibly against regarding this process as "spurious interpretation," pointing out that supplementary legislation by judges is not only inevitable but justifiable because *"to make a detailed description of specific human actions and their consequences forbidden or allowed would be an endless and impossible task."* (Italics his) He insists also, that while judges do and must make law, it would be absurd to maintain that "they are in no wise bound and can make any law they please."[17] The analogies with Jewish tradition and our present problem are obvious.

The process in Talmudic law was, as well as one can judge, entirely similar. When two sages differed on a given issue, the Biblical verses they cited were not the reason for their respective positions, only a legal justification. First came a felt need, often embodied in popular practice, then the process of interpretation of Scripture to give it continuity with tradition.

There is nothing in our modern concept of Revelation that makes this process either impossible or outmoded. The survival of the American way depends upon avoiding the Scylla of reaction and the Charybdis of revolution. So, too, the Jewish way of life depends upon our success in avoiding the unbending adherence to the *status quo ante* on the one hand, and wholesale nullification on the other. Our platform must be loyalty to Jewish law, as embodied in the practice and thought of Catholic Israel and subject to the changes adopted by Catholic Israel.

This democratic concept vests the full authority in the people, but that does not imply that the Rabbinate has no part to play in the process. On the contrary, the Rabbinate has a dual function to perform. When a change has already become part of the practice of Catholic Israel, the Rabbi of today, like his predecessors, has the duty of aiding its legitimatization by using the accepted principles of interpretation of the traditional Halachah. But long before this step is reached, the Rabbinate has the duty to guide the path of development of Jewish law by setting up criteria for Jewish observance, evaluating each specific element by those standards and then educating the people to adopt their attitudes.

CRITERIA FOR OBSERVANCE

The establishment of criteria for Jewish observance is no simple matter, as previous efforts in this direction have indicated. All the more reason, therefore, for another tentative approach:

A. Our attitude toward Jewish observance, as Professor Kaplan has indicated, is not neutral. We are definitely "prejudiced" in favor of Jewish observance. We do not approach Jewish life with a *tabula rasa,* any more than in any department of civilization. "The presumption should always be in favor of traditional procedure."[18]

B. In order that this principle serve as a practical guide, we may suggest, with apologies to Maimonides, a theory of negative attributes. Below we shall adduce four positive norms by which ritual is to be judged. Any Jewish practice *eo ipso* has a claim upon us, unless it can be proved that it does not perform any of these functions, nor can it be reinterpreted to do so.

   Thus four criteria may be briefly set forth as follows:

   I. *Cosmic or religious.* These are observances that bind us to the universe and lend a cosmic significance to the events of our ordinary life. Beautiful and meaningful ritual places such occasions as birth, puberty, marriage and death against the background of a vital universe and its Creator. They no longer remain accidents of animal existence. Such activities as eating or enjoying other pleasures are, by means of a blessing, invested with a sense of the Divine. The physical and nervous rebuilding of an organism through the Sabbath rest becomes part of the cosmic process.

Meaningful ritual invests human life with a sense of holiness. It declares with the unanswerable logic of beauty that man counts in the universe.

II. *Ethical or Social.* It is of the essence of ideals that they must be taught continually. Unlike the multiplication table, learning them by rote is insufficient, because life which, in the largest sense, depends upon them, is always conspiring through a thousand petty devices to defeat man's aspirations for peace, understanding and justice. As Einstein declared several years ago in an address on education, "With the affairs of human beings, knowledge of truth alone does not suffice. On the contrary, this knowledge must continually be renewed by ceaseless effort, if it is not to be lost. It resembles a statue of marble which stands in the desert and is continuously threatened with burial by the shifting sand. The hands of service must ever be at work, in order that the marble continue lastingly to shine in the sun."[19] To teach ideals perpetual-ly and yet avoid monotony is the special function of ritual. For, being symbolic in character, it lends itself to varying interpretations and avoids the perils of monotony. The *Sukkah*, the *Shofar*, the *Seder*, are rituals symbolizing ideals that can be reinterpreted anew and differently at each season.

III. *Esthetic or play function.* A principal reason for the fact that ritual observance, reverently and meaningfully executed, avoids the pitfalls of monotony is its esthetic character. Rituals constitute a source of poetry in life and offer an avenue of play for adults, who increasingly in our modern civilization find amusement in mechanical, vicarious and commercialized forms only. A religious service offers the adult the opportunity to sing; the Passover *Seder*, a chance to reenact a great drama; the *Habdalah* service, a bit of pageantry, which most grownups find nowhere else. It is symptomatic of the atrophy of the play function that adults who seek to re-introduce a ceremony into their practice after long disuse are self-conscious and uncomfortable about it. It is equally characteristic of the decay of vitality in the Reform synagogue that the congregation is passive and virtually inaudible, spectators rather than participants in a religious service. The esthetic, participating element in Jewish ritual is all the more essential for the psychic well-being of a people.

IV. Finally, Jewish ritual has national or *group-associational values*, linking the individual Jew to his people. While early extreme Reform sought to abolish *Milah* and decried it as a barbarous custom, the rite of circumcision possessed such strong survival-value that it has remained the universal mark of the covenant of Abraham. Even the dietary laws were never completely abolished by Reform. Until some years ago, the Register of the Hebrew Union College declared that the Dining Hall observed "some dietary laws." American Jewry reflects untold patterns of dietary observance, down to the Jew whose only rule is that he buys his *terefah* meat from a Jewish and not a Gentile butcher! Ludicrous as these variations are from the standpoint of traditional Halachah, they represent the periphery of a circle at the center of which is the full code of *Kashrut*. But all the degrees of observance recognize that the dietary laws draw the Jew close to his people and make him conscious of his Jewish allegiance.

In stressing the national element in Jewish observances, along with the other values inherent in them, we do not hesitate to affirm that whatever strengthens the bond of Jewish loyalty is a good, because we believe profoundly that Jewish survival is a blessing to the world. If that is not our profoundest conviction, we have no business trying to preserve either Judaism or the identity of the Jew.

C. It is obvious that the most valuable elements of Jewish traditional observance perform all these functions, the cosmic, the ethical, the esthetic and the national, and do them well. At times, an observance may perform only one or two of them, but do it to so transcendent a degree as to justify its retention.

By standards such as these the heritage of Jewish ritual must be evaluated. So vital is most of Jewish tradition that by and large, it can be maintained if properly interpreted. Some aspects require modification or reinterpretation or both, and others may need to be discarded. The function of the Rabbi is to foster the appreciation and observance of Jewish ritual and thus mold the attitude of Catholic Israel.

D. The final authority, however, rests with the Jewish people, though the formal retention, reinterpretation or surrender of Jewish observances should come from accredited rabbinical leadership. So long as some heart-beat of vitality may be detected in a custom, its value should be discussed with an eye to its resuscitation. But death is an unanswerable argument—if it has died utterly and completely, Catholic Israel has spoken, and there is no returning.

ACTION AND STANDARDS

It is obvious that the reinterpretation of the concept of Catholic Israel and the concept of the authority of Jewish law, as well as the suggested criteria for evaluating Jewish ritual observances here set forth, do not constitute a solution to the problem of modern Jewish religious life. They are rather the instruments for meeting the challenge which faces Jewish ritual today. There is crying need for a proclamation of the truth that the Jewish people without Judaism is an empty shell, and that Judaism without Jewish observance is a will o' the wisp. That truth must become transmuted into a campaign for Jewish religious life, active, personal, concrete.

Our movement is virtually the only agency on the American scene in position to undertake the effort for the revival and development of Jewish law, because we alone represent the modern interpretation of traditional Judaism. Thus Professor Salo Baron, who bears no official relationship to our movement, out of the fullness of his historical understanding says: "Neo-Orthodoxy, equally with Reform, is a deviation from historical Judaism. No less than Reform, it abandoned Judaism's self-rejuvenating historical dynamism. For this reason we may say that . . . the 'Positive-Historical Judaism' of Zacharias Frankel and Michael Sachs and the Conservative Judaism of America have been much truer to the spirit of traditional Judaism. By maintaining the general validity of traditional Jewish law and combining with it freedom of personal interpretation of the Jewish past and creed, Frankel and his successors hoped to preserve historical continuity."[20] He is clearly aware of the weaknesses of our movement, yet he declares: "It is Conservative Judaism which seems to show the greatest similarities with the method and substance of teaching of the popular leaders during the declining Second Commonwealth, inasmuch as clinging to the traditional mode of life, it nevertheless allows for the adaptation of basic theological concepts to the changing social and cultural needs. Perhaps also like early Pharisaism, it has thus far failed to develop a new comprehensive and uniform philosophy of Judaism."

But if we are to avoid the weaknesses of which Professor Baron speaks, Conservative Judaism, through the Rabbinical Assembly, must begin to grapple energetically with the issues of Jewish law. That we were right on the *agunah* question has been underlined with tragic clarity in the past few years. We are in desperate need of study and action, in the area of family law, in the field of Sabbath observance, the character of our Friday Evening Service and many other phases. Our laymen need a code of Jewish observance that will reckon with their practice but not surrender to it.

AUTHORITY IN JEWISH LAW

Our Committee on Jewish Law must become the center of our activity. It can do so only if boldly yet reverently it undertakes to formulate Halachah for Conservative Judaism. Its technique must include at least six elements: (a) a careful study of legal tradition with special concern for minority views, (b) a survey of present practices within the various sections of Catholic Israel, (c) an effort to establish optimum standards in terms of contemporary needs, (d) wherever possible, the delimitation of divergent patterns of observance varying from minimum to maximum, and corresponding to the phrases frequent in the traditional codes' "be lenient" or "be stringent." These patterns would clearly point out the varying importance of the details of observance, indicating the basically essential, the optional and the tangential elements in each area of practice, (e) the reinterpretation of traditional Halachah to validate those new practices found acceptable for today, (f) the publication of guides for American Jewry in various areas of Jewish observance, which would indicate the specific values inherent in each rite, as well as the method for observing it. A Guide to Jewish Practice for Conservative Judaism should combine the functions of a

Sefer Ta'amei Hamitzvot, a rationale for Jewish observance, and a *Shulhan Arukh,* a presentation of Jewish practice, couched in the modern idiom and sensitive to the human condition in our day.

The theoretic formulation of the Halachah for Conservative Judaism is the indispensable prelude to the practical tasks lying before the movement.

With the cooperation of the Jewish Theological Seminary and the participation of the United Synagogue, the Rabbinical Assembly must undertake an active campaign for Jewish living. In each community, some group, however small, would be enlisted in a Fellowship of *Haberim,* who, like the *Haberim* of the Mishnaic period, would undertake to maintain a higher standard of Jewish observance and study in their personal lives than the generality. There might indeed be several degrees of *Haberim,* depending on the extent and intensity of the Jewish program undertaken. Such fellowships offer a superb agency for channeling the reborn Jewish spirit for returning service men. Such a movement might well capture the imagination of American Jewry, civilian and veteran alike. The number who would be attracted by its intrinsic appeal and external glamor might be considerably larger than we dared to anticipate. The synagogue and the Jewish School, now largely impotent, would be reenforced by the most important members of the triad, the Jewish home, and Judaism would cease being a vicarious experience for most Jews, embodied in institutions and expressed almost entirely in financial contributions.

With such a platform and an appeal, Conservative Judaism would fulfill its destiny as the most vital force in American Israel. There will be many who will follow, many more who will listen, and many others, who, unpersuaded at the beginning, may be reeducated to the glory and satisfactions inherent in Jewish living.

If we prove worthy, in some slight measure, of our predecessors, it is given us to hope that we may again, as has happened in the past, transform the anarchy and ignorance characteristic of the pioneering stage into a rich, deeply-rooted pattern of Jewish life. Ezra and Nehemiah, who battled against intermarriage and the violation of the Sabbath in Palestine; Rab, who found an open valley in Babylonia which he fenced in (*Hull. 110*a); Moses ben Enoch, who helped lay the foundations of Jewish learning in Spain; all represent the rhythm of Jewish rebirth, which, *mutatis mutandis,* must be recaptured in America as well. Granted that the problems are infinitely more complicated than ever before, as Professor Kaplan has so thoroughly set forth, it too does not follow that our cause gains by inactivity or by surrender to the forces of dissolution.

In contradistinction to the Talmud and the authors of the Reconstructionist "Guide" alike, we feel that "if you have grasped for a little, you have not grasped."

Each rabbi, in isolation, has, for perfectly natural reasons, demanded too little rather than too much from his congregation in regard to ritual observance and Jewish study. What the individual cannot even hope for may often be achieved by organization—and that is the duty of our movement.

The history of human culture, no less than that of Jewish experience, has shown that ages of indifference and hostility to religion give way to periods of spiritual revival. The skeptical period of the eighteenth century, which itself conserved important religious ideals, gave way to the nineteenth century, which was, in many respects, a modern age of faith. There are more than a few signs, which the war experience has multiplied ten thousand fold, that modern men are seeking their way to God. I profoundly believe that it is easier, not harder, to win men for the traditional Jewish concept of the Living God as interpreted by our greatest teachers than for a reconstructed concept that denies His existential reality.

Judaism has no room for the anti-rational, for the *credo quid absurdum* attitude, but it does not exclude the emotional, the non-rational, the leap of faith across the abyss of the unknown. A recent radical writer declares: "Religion dissolved into ethicism is no longer religion. What is left to worship after dogmas and mystery have been taken away?"[21] For "dogmas" we may substitute "mitzvot," the obligations of Jewish law, interpreted in the light of our learning and our ideals. Without them, Judaism as a way of life is doomed. There is more than a little truth in the same writer's contention that "the rationalist reform of religion is itself a symptom of religious decay. On the whole, it has done more to accelerate the decay of religion than to prop it up."

Religion is in essence the all-embracing attitude of man toward the universe. It must therefore reckon with the unknown and mysterious in the cosmos as well as with the rational and the known. It dare not minimize the moral imperative to build a just society of just men. Yet to achieve this purpose, it must unfurl the banner of the Living God. To keep that faith ever vivid and real, ritual is essential, as we have seen. Our standpoint must be that ritual is part of Jewish law, possessing a strong sense of continuity with the past and an equally powerful capacity for growth and adaptation to the needs of the present. The crisis is already upon us, and so is the God-given opportunity. The day is short, the work is manifold. Let not the workers be indolent or disheartened, for the reward is very great. It may not be granted us to complete the work, but neither have we the right to desist from it.

NOTES

1. *The Reconstructionist*, Vol. VII, No. 13–16,18. The entire series has been republished under the same title in pamphlet form.
2. For a valuable survey of Reform, see David Philipson, *The Reform Movement in Judaism* 2nd ed. (New York, 1931). The full text of the Pittsburgh Platform is given in Philipson, *op. cit.*, p. 354 f.
3. Philipson, *op. cit.*, p. 358 f.
4. The details of the adoption of the Statement are extremely illuminating. At the 1936 meeting of the C.C.A.R. a proposed statement

of Principles was presented but was laid over to the next conference. This preliminary draft included the following statements:

For Reform Judaism, Torah represents the whole body of progressive religious values, from the covenant at Sinai to the present day. It is both Haggadah (lore) and Halachah (law). It sounds the eternal imperatives of faith and of duty. Though many of its ancient laws, ceremonial and civil, are no longer operative under the changed conditions of the present, "Law" continues to be an abiding element of the Torah of Judaism." . . . "To entrust ourselves voluntarily to the authority of the Torah, as interpreted by sound scholarship and by devoted spiritual leadership, in matters personal and social, is the supreme need of our spiritual life." (*Yearbook, C.C.A.R.,* Vol. XLVI, 1936, p. 90 f).

This entire material did not reappear in the final draft, nor was any reference made to it in any of the voluminous discussion reported in the Yearbooks of 1936 and 1937.

5. *Yearbook of the C.C.A.R.,* Vol. XLVII, 1937, p. 98.
6. L. Ginzberg *Students, Scholars and Saints* (Phila. 1928), pp. 206–7.
7. In the *Reconstructionist,* Vol. VI, No. 17, Dec. 27, 1940.
8. For these and similar quotations from his writings cited below, see the extremely useful paper by Myer S. Kripke, "Solomon Schechter's Philosophy of Judaism" in the *Reconstructionist,* Vol. III, No. 12 and 13, October 22 and November 5, 1937.
9. Ginzberg, *op. cit.,* p. 209.
10. *The Reconstructionist,* Vol. VII, No. 13, p. 9.
11. M. M. Kaplan, *Judaism As A Civilization,* p. 432.
12. As e.g. B. Z. Bokser, *A Criticism of the Suggested Guide to Jewish Ritual* (*Reconstructionist,* Vol. VII, No. 18, Jan. 9, 1942), and Jacob B. Agus, *"The Character of Jewish Piety"* (*idem.* Vol. VIII, No. 5, April 7, 1942.)
13. Cf. his "Reply" in the *Reconstructionist,* Vol. VII, No. 18, January 9, 1942.
14. Cf. S. W. Baron, *A Social and Religious History of the Jews* (New York 1937) Vol. I, p. 367.
15. See the suggestive paper by Dr. S. Federbusch, *"Mishpat Hahozer Le-Musar"* in *Hadoar,* Vol. XXI, No. 39, 40, now republished in his volume *"Hamusar Vehamishpat Beyisrael"* (New York, 1943), chap. 7.
16. Contrast the principle of *pikuach nefesh docheh shabbat* (*Shab.* 132a) and the doctrine *Ayn lecha davar sheomad bifnay pikuach nefesh . . .* (*Keth.* 19a).
17. M. R. Cohen, *Law and the Social Order* (New York, 1933) pp. 121, 131, 133, 146.
18. M. M. Kaplan, "Reply" cited above.
19. Albert Einstein, "Some Thoughts Concerning Education," in *School and Society,* Nov. 7, 1936, p. 589.

20. S. W. Baron, *op. cit.*, Vol. II, pp. 257, 394.
21. Bernard Noskin, "Socialism and Faith," in *The Jewish Frontier,* January 1942, p. 22.

REPLY*

Mordecai Kaplan

CORRECTING A MISCONCEPTION OF RECONSTRUCTIONISM

The article by Dr. Gordis dealing with "Authority, Permanence, and Change in Jewish Law" merits a reply from the point of view of those responsible for the publication of *Toward a Guide for Jewish Ritual Usage,* which he criticizes. Before commenting on the content of Dr. Gordis's article, however, I should like to correct a misconception about Reconstructionism which is implicit in some of his statements. He occasionally identifies the views expressed in the pamphlet, *Toward a Guide,* with essential Reconstructionist doctrine, and thus contrasts what he calls "the Reconstructionist approach" with that which he advocates. The mistake is a natural one and, for that very reason, it is important to correct it. It should be expressly stated that the platform of Reconstructionism is broad enough for both Dr. Gordis and the authors of the pamphlet with which he takes issue. All who conceive of Judaism as an evolving religious civilization—and this, of course, includes Dr. Gordis—are Reconstructionists, even though they may differ among themselves on some of the implications of this fundamental doctrine.

WHEREIN OUR APPROACH DIFFERS FROM DR. GORDIS'S

Dr. Gordis's criticism of our approach to Jewish ritual observance— meaning by "*our* approach" that of the authors of *Toward a Guide for Jewish Ritual Usage*—is significant, not only as a thoughtful expression of personal views, but as representative of a large body of opinion that disapproves of our attitude. He has made out a case against our

The Reconstructionist, Vol. 8, Nos. 14 and 15 (Nov. 13 and 27, 1942). Reprinted in Kaplan's *Questions Jews Ask: Reconstructionist Answers* (New York: Reconstructionist Press, 1956), pp. 264–276.

approach which is the more challenging because it is temperate and deliberate, and represents perhaps the best case that can be argued against us, from the viewpoint of the Conservative opposition.

The religious practice suggested by Dr. Gordis's viewpoint differs little from that which we would recommend. His opposition is directed not so much against the practices approved by us as against our theories, which he feels—and rightly so—involve a radical departure from traditional doctrine. We maintain them, nevertheless, because we are convinced that *only a radical change of attitude in respect to traditional observance can enable Jewish observance in our day to function as it should.* Jewish observance can only then be said to serve its purpose, when it contributes (1) to the preservation of the Jewish People and (2) to the satisfaction of the personal spiritual needs of Jews. Our position is that those *mitzvot* which, in tradition, are described as applying "between man and God" should be observed, insofar as they help to maintain the historic continuity of the Jewish People and to express, or symbolize, spiritual values or ideals which can enhance the inner life of Jews. *Their observance, however, should be reckoned with, not in the spirit of juridical law, which is coercive, but in the spirit of a voluntary consensus based on a general recognition of their value.* We shall, therefore, refer to our approach to Jewish ritual observance as *the voluntarist approach.*

In advocating that approach to Jewish ritual, we are not taking an antinomian attitude, as Dr. Gordis contends that we do. We insist that the concept of Jewish peoplehood, which is basic to the whole Reconstructionist position, involves the translation of ethical principles into concrete laws and institutions. We deplore and are endeavoring to correct the communal disorganization which has made the Jewish People impotent to enforce standards of ethical behavior in the relations of man to man. To compare our viewpoint on Jewish law with that of the Apostle Paul, whose fundamental effort was to dissociate the Christian Church from involvement in Jewish peoplehood, is misleading in the extreme. Nobody would call an American an antinomian merely because he does not believe in keeping the well known New England "blue laws" on the statute books.

To achieve the purposes of ritual, even from the voluntarist viewpoint, calls for a formulation of norms or standards. These norms must be determined by the two-fold purpose of contributing simultaneously to Jewish survival and the enrichment of the Jewish spiritual life. This must not be construed to mean that each specific rule must be effective directly toward the desired end, but that it must contribute to that end, in association with a whole pattern of conduct of which it is a part. Thus the rules prescribing the specific form of *tefillin* and *mezuzah* remain valid, if the use of *tefillin* and *mezuzah* is validated, as we maintain it is, by the criteria we have laid down. If, however, a particular rite, and not merely a specific regulation incidental to it, is of no service either to Jewish survival or to the spiritual enrichment of Jewish life, then it is valueless. If it operates to the detriment of Jewish survival, or runs counter to the spiritual welfare of Jewry, or of mankind, it has certainly no claim on the loyalty of modern Jews. These considerations, rather than *halakic* precedent and legalistic interpretation, should, in our opinion, determine the development of Jewish ritual for the Jew of today.

In contradistinction to this view, Dr. Gordis maintains a position which may be summarized as follows: Jews should persist in the traditional attitude which regards the *mitzvot she-ben adam lamakom* (precepts governing a man's relation to God) as falling within the category of juridical law. To do so, he maintains, need not involve acceptance of the Orthodox assumption that the law was supernaturally revealed. The authority of the *mitzvot* derives rather from the fact that they "are consecrated by the consent of Catholic Israel through thousands of years." This is the Conservative theory of the nature of Jewish legal authority as expounded by Zechariah Frankel, Solomon Schechter and others. When the changing conditions of life make the observance of a Jewish ritual precept infeasible, changes in the form of observance become necessary. Sometimes an observance has to be eliminated; at other times, a modification of it may suffice. But all such changes must be validated by an interpretation of Talmudic law. This interpretation should be liberal in spirit, taking cognizance of contemporary conditions and needs, but no change is legitimate without validation by interpretation and acceptance by Catholic Israel. Dr. Gordis's definition of Catholic Israel identifies it with "the body of men and women within the Jewish People who respect the authority of Jewish law, although they may violate one or another segment of it." This approach to change in Jewish ritual may, therefore, be appropriately designated the *legalistic approach.*

In defense of this legalistic approach, Dr. Gordis brings the following arguments: (1) It is in conformity with tradition, and hence makes for continuity in Jewish life. (2) It is feasible in accordance with this approach to effect changes in Jewish ritual by the method of interpretation. This feasibility is borne out by analogy with the method of interpretation employed in American constitutional law. (3) The legalistic approach makes it possible to retain the continuity of the *halakic* tradition, without accepting the Orthodox assumption, repugnant to our modern outlook, that Jewish ritual regulations were supernaturally revealed.

DOES THE LEGALISTIC APPROACH INSURE CONTINUITY?

The first of these arguments begs the entire question. In urging the legalistic approach on the ground that it will maintain the continuity of Jewish observance by very reason of its traditional character, Dr. Gordis assumes that that approach is adequate. But if that approach is adequate and if, being traditional, it is the approach which has been resorted to until now, how is it that there is a problem of Jewish ritual to discuss? Dr. Gordis does not deny the obvious reality of the break-down in Jewish observance in our day. Can he not see that that break-down could not have taken place if the traditional approach to observance had been adequate? To rely on the legalistic method of interpretation for effecting necessary change in ritual is to lean on a broken reed.

The legalistic approach was adequate in the past—that is until the era of the Emancipation—because the character of the Jewish community and the assumptions universally underlying Jewish belief exercised a coercive force on Jewish behavior. Membership in the Jewish community was then not optional and voluntary, because no other community would accept the Jew or afford him protection, aid and comfort in life, except at the price of conversion to Christianity or Islam, and complete severance from his kin and his People. The community, moreover, enforced its standards on Jews, with the full consent and approval of the state, by the use of excommunication and other effective coercive measures. In addition, all Jews were fully convinced that the ritual laws had been supernaturally revealed on Mount Sinai and that any Jew who transgressed them deserved to be punished. Thus, the uniformity of Jewish observance and the continuity of *halakic* tradition were dependent on faith in the coercive power of God, who acted partly through the social agencies of the Jewish community and partly through mysterious dispensations beyond human power.

Dr. Gordis only confuses the issue when he equates the modern conception of the operation of Divine law through the *natural consequences* of human behavior with the ancient conception. The rewards and punishments, in the ancient conception, were not natural consequences, but were *specially devised incentives* to secure adherence to a specific code. So long as this compulsive power of political, or quasi-political and theocratic, authority remained in effect, there was no problem of Jewish ritual observance. But that power is no longer in effect. The Jewish community lost its autonomy when Jews were incorporated into the body politic of the modern states. And changes in world outlook no longer permit Jews to believe that God exacts a penalty for every infringement of the Jewish code, or that all its rules are, in a *literal* sense, *mitzvot* or Divine commandments. In consequence, Jewish religious observances are being completely disregarded.

The disregard of those observances thus demonstrates the inadequacy of traditional methods of maintaining them when coercion can no longer be applied. That is why, assuming as we do the indispensability of religious observances to Jewish life, we are impelled to seek new ways of salvaging as much as possible of the good achieved by them in the past. *In the absence of all coercive power, it must be clear that a voluntarist approach is necessary, one that depends not on external authority to enforce its standards, but on the authority of spiritual conviction of the value of these standards.*

MORAL VS. JURIDICAL AND EXPERT AUTHORITY

When we no longer accept the Orthodox doctrine of the supernatural origin of the *halakah* and its supernatural enforcement, we have to base *halakah* upon human authority. There is, in the first instance, *juridical authority,* which is dependent on coercion. No system of laws regulating the relations *ben adam lahavero* (between a man and his fellow-men) can dispense with coercion. To attempt to do so would be to place the weak and innocent at the mercy of the strong and criminal. The second kind of authority is that of the expert. *Expert authority* does not gain, but loses, when backed by coercion. Bureaucratic methods that put the authority of the state behind the expert in the sciences or the arts ultimately cause their stagnation by removing them from the necessity of meeting the challenge of criticism and intellectual competition. Finally there is *moral authority,* which is based on the voluntary purpose of men to live up to the best of which they are capable, and to recognize as morally obligatory those forms of behavior which bring out the best in the individual and in society. Moral authority is destroyed by coercion, as every struggle for freedom of religion implies.

The voluntarist approach to Jewish religious observance proceeds from the conviction that, unlike the civil and criminal laws of the Oral and Written Torah, which must use compulsory sanctions for their enforcement in order to give effect to them, *the ritual regulations of the Torah are defeated in their very purpose by any effort to compel their observance.* At any rate, this becomes true as soon as we abandon the belief that God is directly concerned with enforcing compliance with them. The attempts of the Church in the Middle Ages to force the Jews to listen to Christian sermons were not effective in converting Jews to Christianity, and similar methods by the synagogue, such as were employed in the Middle Ages, to enforce Jewish conformity with ritual requirements will not win over our Jewish non-conformists.

Whatever norms we may wish to establish in regard to Jewish ritual observance belong to an entirely different category from those we may wish to establish in the relations between men and women, or between the individual and the society in which he lives. Since in common parlance, the term *law* is generally limited to rules that are enforced by the state, we prefer to designate the ritual *mitzvot* as *religious usages* rather than as laws. The term *law* as applied to them is a misnomer, and its use obscures their dependence in our day solely on moral authority.

If an example is needed to illustrate the danger of trying to reenforce moral authority by legal sanctions, in an area that does not directly involve social relations, the experience of the American People under prohibition should serve as an example. Advocates of temperance were to be found both in the ranks of prohibitionists and anti-prohibitionists. But the prohibitionists were not content to rely on moral authority to give effect to temperance. They approached the problem entirely from a legalistic angle and invoked the police power of the state to enforce prohibition. The result was such a wave of intemperance, and such flouting of law in general, that the 18th Amendment of the Constitution, embodying the principle of prohibition in the law of the land, had to be repealed in the interest of temperance and respect for law.

CAN LEGALISTIC INTERPRETATION EFFECT NECESSARY RITUAL CHANGES?

We do not mean to imply, in the foregoing discussion, that Dr. Gordis advocates the use of compulsion by the state or by the Jewish community, or that he relies on an anthropomorphic Divine Judge to enforce Jewish ritual regulations. What he would advocate, if the Jewish community were again to possess a certain coercive power over the individual, as is the case in the State of Israel, is not clear from his paper. But the main point of his contention is that, even without the exercise of that coercive power, which was once vested in the autonomous Jewish community, and without the Orthodox dogma of the revelations of the Torah and its legal implications, it still remains possible to develop Jewish religious observance and to effect necessary changes by treating ritual regulations as law. That is to say that, even without political or theocratic sanctions, Jewish ritual observance cannot only be preserved, but modified and developed by the same legalistic processes as were used when they had the backing of penal enforcement.

According to Dr. Gordis, the development of Jewish ritual law takes place through the actual practice of Catholic Israel and through rabbinic interpretation similar to that employed by the Supreme Court of the United States in interpreting the Constitution. "When a change has already become part of the practice of Catholic Israel," he writes, "the rabbi of today, like his predecessor, has the duty of aiding its legitimization by using the principles of interpretation of the traditional *halakah*. . . . When he finds the changes needful, even though the people have not yet recognized the necessity, he must urge their acceptance and then must find room for them in Jewish tradition." To prove that the legalistic method of interpretation does not depend for its validity on the Orthodox doctrine of *Torah min hashamayim* (the divine revelation of the Torah), he cites the application of the same method in the development of constitutional law by the interpretations of the federal courts.

If, however, we examine carefully the above statement, it is not difficult to see how misleading it is, and how it glosses over the impossibility of dealing effectively with ritual by methods of interpretation and development appropriate to those areas of the *halakah* that depend on external, coercive authority. When Dr. Gordis identifies "Catholic Israel" with "those who are loyal to Jewish observance," he insists on interpreting loyalty as consisting of the legalistic approach to Jewish ritual. For he can see no alternative to that attitude other than one of "hostility or indifference, which leads them to cast overboard the entire regimen of Jewish practice." He invokes the principle, "Greater is he who performs the commandment from a sense of obligation, than he who performs it without that sense," to justify the exclusion from "Catholic Israel" of those Jews who have shown an interest in reinstating Jewish observance, but validate their observance by other than legalistic principles. Dr. Gordis himself departs from the Orthodox definition of loyalty to the Torah. According to that definition the concept "Catholic Israel" is entirely meaningless and irrelevant in the matter of any kind of Jewish law. "Ye shall not add unto the word which I command you, neither shall ye diminish from it" (Deut. 4:2) is interpreted by Orthodox Jewry as demanding conformity to all such Biblical laws as the prohibition against shaving and against the wearing of *shaatnez* (clothing of mixed wool and linen), which Dr. Gordis, in the name of "Catholic Israel," has pronounced obsolete. It is therefore the height of arbitrariness to imply that people who validate their departure from traditional norms by legalistic interpretation belong to "Catholic Israel," while those who validate their departure by the voluntarist approach to Jewish observance are to be excluded from it.

We should like to know how Dr. Gordis would fulfill the duty of "aiding the legitimization" of the wearing of *shaatnez* and the shaving of the beard "by using the principles of interpretation of the traditional *halakah*." We are certain that any attempt on his part to do so would immediately be challenged by eminent halakists as illegal. According to "the traditional halakah," he would be castigated as *megalleh panim batorah shelo kahalakah* ("reading unwarranted meanings into the Torah").

THE ANALOGY WITH CONSTITUTIONAL LAW

Dr. Gordis's dilemma in dealing with these and similar modifications of Biblical and rabbinic law illustrates the fallacy of the analogy which he draws between the development of Jewish ritual law through interpretation and the procedure of the Supreme Court in dealing with the Constitution. It is not true that the Supreme Court legitimizes changes in the law based on the practice of the people. The Supreme Court, for example, could not have legitimized the abolition of prohibition, once prohibition was authorized by Constitutional amendment, or, for that matter, even if the abolition had been enacted by the legal statutory process of some State of the Union. The Supreme Court may not, of its own initiative, pronounce a law of Congress unconstitutional. Only when the legality of such a law has been called into question is it tested by submission to the judiciary. Since there can be no question about the legality of the enactment of the Biblical laws prohibiting *shaatnez* or shaving, no judicial interpretation by a rabbi could ever legitimize their abolition, if one were to follow the methods employed in the United States in developing Constitutional law.

But the weakest point in Dr. Gordis's far-fetched analogy is his complete oversight of the fact that the Constitution of the United States makes provision for its own amendment, while Jewish law makes no such provision. If, as Dr. Gordis contends, judicial interpretation allows sufficient latitude for any changes which, in the course of history, may become desirable, why was it necessary to introduce into the Constitution of the United States the provisions for that document's amendment? Surely it is easier to obtain a consensus among a majority of the Supreme Court than to pass an amendment to the Constitution. Nevertheless twenty-one amendments to the Constitution have been passed since its adoption by the Constitutional Convention in 1787, little more than a century and a half ago. Now the code of the

Torah was drafted thousands of years ago; yet Dr. Gordis wants us to believe that processes of development by judicial interpretation, plus such rabbinic *takkanot* as have been adopted from time to time within the framework of the Torah Constitution, are entirely adequate to meet the unprecedented and critical changes of modern times. Thus his argument from analogy with the development of constitutional law in the United States breaks down completely.

Dr. Gordis discusses at some length the criteria which, in his opinion, should guide rabbis in giving a liberal interpretation to Jewish law. They are, in effect, the same as those stressed in the *Guide for Jewish Ritual Usage*, namely, survival of the Jewish People and the enrichment of its spiritual life. We maintain, however, that observances which meet these criteria do not need to be validated by legalistic interpretation. On the other hand, those observances which fail to measure up to those criteria should be allowed to become obsolete.

WHAT HAS THE CONSERVATIVE APPROACH ACHIEVED?

Dr. Gordis apparently tries to forestall the criticism of the inadequacy of the legalistic process by conceding that it is necessarily a slow one. "It must be stressed, however," he says, "that the area of change will necessarily be small, relative to the extent of permanent values in Jewish ritual." That, however, is an understatement. The truth is that *the modern advocates of this method have produced no significant changes in the* halakah. Getting around the law by means of fictions is not *developing* the law. Although Dr. Gordis's formulation of the Conservative position is more fully stated and more explicit than earlier formulations of the Conservative viewpoint, nevertheless the general policy which he advocates has been under consideration ever since the days of Zechariah Frankel. Almost a century has thus elapsed since it was first proposed, and yet it has not legitimized a *single change* in ritual by the legalistic process. Not even the wearing of *shaatnez* or the shaving of the beard, of which Dr. Gordis approves, has been legitimized. And if these provisions particularly present difficulties because of their being stated in the Written Torah, it surely should have been possible, assuming the adequacy of the method of legalistic interpretation, to have legitimized a simplification of the rules of *kashrut* and desirable modifications in Sabbath observance. But nothing has been done about them.

Dr. Gordis cites, with a sense of satisfaction, the recent effort of the Rabbinical Assembly to modify, by the legalistic process, the law regarding the *agunah* (the wife whose husband has been missing without any witness of his having died, and who, according to Jewish law, cannot wed another for the rest of her life) for the emergency of the war. The proposed solution depends for its effectiveness on the acquiescence of couples, about to be married, to a procedure that contemplates contingencies involving divorce. The way to have dealt with the problem of the *agunah* should have been to enact the right of the woman, under specified conditions, to divorce her husband. This, however, would have involved not a mere process of interpretation but the assertion of the right and necessity to change existing law by legislative amendment, for the law as it stands permits only the husband to divorce his wife, but not the wife to divorce her husband.

However, the procedure in dealing with the *agunah* question is not really relevant to our problem and has been here referred to only because, notwithstanding its irrelevancy, it was brought into the discussion by Dr. Gordis. For marriage law is social legislation, which, in an autonomous community, would legitimately be accompanied by coercive sanctions and treated by the ordinary processes of law. Our contention as to the impropriety of such processes is limited to the area of the *mitzvot she ben adam lamakom,* or the ritual regulations. Whether, therefore, one agrees with our critique of the Rabbinical Assembly's handling of the *agunah* problem or not, one cannot escape the logic which renders inappropriate the use of the legalistic method for the development of religious observances. We, therefore, maintain that the voluntarist approach to religious ritual is not only more effective in bringing about necessary change and therefore more progressive; it is also more effective in safeguarding traditional *values,* and therefore more conservative than the legalistic and so-called Conservative approach.

B. JACOB AGUS (1911–86)

It was precisely at the same time—the late 1940s and early 1950s—that Jacob Agus wrote the philosophical essays that were to become the cornerstone of his later work in Jewish law. They were first published in the journal *Conservative Judaism* in close succession: "Torah M'Sinai" (February 1947), "Law in Conservative Judaism" (February 1948), and "Laws as Standards" (May 1950), the essay reproduced in this volume. Those articles, together with his Seminary lecture "Pluralism in Law" (Summer 1953), subsequently appeared as chapters 6, 7, 8, and 9 of his 1954 book, *Guideposts in Modern Judaism.*

In these writings Agus managed to develop what was arguably the most thoroughgoing philosophy of law for the Conservative movement. More than anyone else Agus spelled out not only what the Conservative approach to Jewish law was and should be, but why one should adopt it. This required him to articulate not only an approach to Jewish law, but also a theory of revelation and, ultimately, a theology. On each of these topics Agus's arguments combine the latest in then-current scientific theory with the knowledge gained through a historical approach to the Jewish tradition. As such, Agus quintessentially preserves all three of the characteristics that became the hallmarks of

Conservative Judaism: a theistic, personal God who commands; a historical approach to understand the Jewish tradition, including its legal texts and practices; and a willingness to integrate those first two principles in concrete legal decisions.

A quarter-century later, Agus returned to the subject of a Conservative philosophy of Jewish law. In his essay "Halakhah in the Conservative Movement" (1975),[2] he addressed the Rabbinical Assembly, the organization of Conservative rabbis, in very appreciative and hopeful terms. He understood the developments of the intervening years to be concrete indications of the accuracy and appropriateness of his own approach, and he suggested further plans to embody this philosophy even more in the future. As he put it then, "We must think of ourselves not merely as children of our forefathers, but also as ancestors of our children's children. We have to create fresh tradition."

Agus had not always thought that way. Raised in the Orthodox tradition, he was ordained by Yeshiva University in 1935. Even then, though, it was clear that he was testing the Orthodox convictions of his youth, for he completed a Ph.D. in modern Jewish thought at Harvard in 1939. His deep rethinking of his own Jewish convictions and his service as the rabbi of a Conservative congregation led him to affiliate with the Rabbinical Assembly in 1945, and he immediately became active in the task of formulating a distinctively Conservative ideology as a member of the Rabbinical Assembly's Committee on Jewish Law and Standards and its Prayer Book Committee. After serving as rabbi at congregations in several communities between 1935 and 1950, he founded Beth El Congregation in Baltimore and was its rabbi from 1950 to 1980, nurturing its growth from 90 to more than 1,100 families. He also taught at Temple University, Dropsie College, and the Reconstructionist Rabbinical College. He was a powerful force in ecumenical and racial relations, advocating trialogues among Jews, Christians, and Muslims and writing extensively on interfaith matters.

Because Agus had formal training in philosophy, his writings articulate a much more thorough and disciplined analysis and exposition of Conservative legal philosophy than that provided by most other thinkers of his time. Agus also combined his analytic ability with considerable creativity. Moreover, as we shall see, the Conservative movement effectively, if unconsciously, followed his lead in making some of its most critical legal decisions in the second half of the twentieth century. For these reasons—and also because Agus's theory is much less well known than those of other early and mid-century writers in Conservative legal theory—I will describe his views in much greater detail than those of most other thinkers in this book.

Agus asserted that the principle of Catholic Israel, which "militates against any break with other sections of the Jewish people" and which lay at the heart of Conservative legal theory as developed by Schechter and revised by Gordis, was no longer viable because the "masses of our people have already broken away from the ancient moorings of Jewish Law." In such a situation, he believed that the rabbinate and the laity together should constitute a bicameral legislative body that would effect the necessary changes to make Jewish law thrive in the modern world, using not only standard legal methods of interpretation and expanding or constricting the scope of precedents, but also *takkanot,* legislative enactments of changes.

TAKKANOT IN JEWISH LEGAL HISTORY

To understand Agus's view, then, I must say a few words about *takkanot* in the history of Jewish law. Jews living in modern Western societies are used to governments in which there are legislative, executive, and judicial branches. The exact relationships among those branches may vary from country to country, but each of them has a body elected to make new laws and revise or abrogate old ones. The authority of those bodies comes from the consent of the people to establish the government in the first place and the willingness of the vast majority of the population to abide by the laws that their representatives adopt.

Jewish law, though, begins with a radically different set of assumptions and operational principles. Not human beings, but rather God establishes Jewish law, and God proclaims twice in the Torah (Deuteronomy 4:2 and 13:1) that we are not to add to or subtract from that divine law. That means that the Jewish "Constitution," as it were, lacks not only an amendment clause, but even a legislative body to make or revise laws on an ongoing basis. Judges, however, are authorized to interpret and apply Jewish law in each generation (Deuteronomy 17:8–13). As a result, Jewish leaders, interested in making Jewish law relevant and vibrant in each generation, have expanded the judicial function—effectively enabling judges to make new laws under the guise of interpreting the Torah, including the Torah's demand that Jews should not veer to the left or right from what the judges in each generation tell them to do (Deuteronomy 17:11). Thus when American judges, for example, use their powers in an expansive mode to undermine laws that legislators have passed (e.g., United States Supreme Court decisions declaring unconstitutional and thus null and void state laws requiring racial segregation in schools, prayer in public schools, bans against abortion or homo-sexual sex, etc.), many Americans object to what they see as "judge-made law" on the grounds that legislators, rather than judges, are charged with making new laws. Indeed, the Supreme Court itself asserted just such a concern in refusing to declare unconstitutional state laws banning assisted suicide. In Jewish law, though, judge-made law is the standard operating procedure because there are no legislatures.

Even so, from time to time legislative enactments (takkanot) have become part of Jewish law. Some (takkanot hakahal) have been instituted by local communal leaders, and they gain their authority from the fact that the laws they adopt do not contradict the Torah but rather fill in gaps necessary for the community to run—just as zoning and taxation laws function in American society. Moreover, these takkanot are accepted by the community and are, in some cases, endorsed by the local rabbi.[3] Here the word takkanah is based on the meaning of the Hebrew root tkn as "establish," for nothing existed in these areas of law before the takkanot were adopted.

Some such takkanot—laws that establish new practices—come down to us not in the name of the lay leaders of the community but rather in the name of rabbis, and the Talmud even ascribes takkanot to the Patriarchs[4] as well as to Moses and Joshua[5] and other biblical figures. Other takkanot are ascribed to Ezra and the Men of the Great Assembly.

Other statutes (takkanot) instead change what was the established norm before, and they are thus more in the spirit of the meaning of the Hebrew root tkn as "fix." The Mishnah and Talmud record a number of such takkanot. One famous one was the measure (prozbul) instituted by Hillel to encourage potential creditors to lend money to needy borrowers even close to the sabbatical year, when the Torah would cancel such debts altogether. Rabban Gamliel the Elder and other rabbis instituted a number of other takkanot "for fixing the world" (mipnei tikkun ha'olam),[6] and Rabbi Yoḥanan ben Zakkai established nine takkanot after the destruction of the Second Temple to make the changes necessary to enable Judaism to function without a Temple.[7] In the Middle Ages, we hear of more such takkanot, perhaps the most famous of which were the two adopted in the name of Rabbenu Gershom prohibiting polygamy and requiring that a woman accept a writ of divorce for it to be valid. Other talmudic and medieval takkanot provide for the legally binding transfer of property in new ways, decree the punishment of flogging and even death for offenses not proscribed in the Torah, institute the punishment of incarceration, relax the procedural rules in criminal cases to allow circumstantial evidence, and dispense with the

Talmud's requirement of prior warning of a criminal when necessary to preserve public order. In modern times, the Chief Rabbinic Council of Israel in 1943 and 1944 adopted *takkanot* providing for the payment of court fees, the introduction of adoption as a legal institution, the legal duty of a father to support his children until they reach the age of fifteen (rather than six, as prescribed by the Talmud), and the decision to hold spouses and children equal in their rights of intestate succession, regardless of sex.[8] This last one changed the Torah's system of primogeniture and much of later Jewish law based on it.[9]

REASON AND REVELATION

With this as a background, we can now return to Agus. Agus argues that the law must depend upon a *combination* of reason and revelation. Revelation cannot be the exclusive source of Jewish law's authority because "there can be no inner correspondence between our present feeling and the events of several thousand years ago."[10] That is, even if we want to believe that verbal revelation took place amid thunder and lightning at Sinai, our own experience does not give us warrant for that belief, for we now do not experience such revelations. The Passover liturgy wants us to identify with the Exodus event when it proclaims that "In every generation a person must see him/herself as if s/he left Egypt," but even that liturgy recognizes that the best it can hope for is that contemporary people *see* (that is, imagine) themselves *as if* they had left Egypt. Thus immediate experience will not provide the necessary ground for Judaism for any Jews, living after the generation that stood at Mount Sinai, even if it did for those who were there. Thus when Agus asserts that revelation still has a role to play in modern-day faith, he does *not* mean divine, verbal communication at Sinai. What he does mean by "revelation" I shall discuss below.

Reason is also necessary for faith if one "is to escape the manifold pitfalls of unbridled superstition and unmitigated fanaticism." The religious bent in people is that which recognizes human limitations and dependence on factors beyond human comprehension and/or control. Keen awareness of those elements in our experience makes for passivity, acceptance, and thankfulness. Religious people are therefore all too prone to accept superstitions as absolutely true and to acquiesce to fanatic and sometimes downright immoral actions based on blind faith in what is presented as religious truths—often on the basis of some interpretation of the religion's official revelation. Reason, then, is necessary to counteract these inclinations.

Reason is also necessary to balance another common religious tendency, namely, the emphasis on inwardness. In some forms of mysticism, for example, one turns inward to find God, either with the help of revelation or as a substitute for revelation. Often this is accompanied by a disdain for reason and a denial of the reality of the physical world. For Agus, though, genuine piety requires a dialectic between subjectivity and objectivity. One must balance inner perceptions and emotions with reason and experience focused on the world outside us. "For the life of the spirit is not a static reflection and crystallization of the Truth, but a dynamic apprehension of it from every changing angle, in the ceaseless change of perspective from subjectivity to objectivity, and back again . . . To condemn objective piety [based on reason] on the grounds of inwardness is therefore to betray the marks of spiritual astigmatism."[11]

And finally, Agus notes, in our day revelation cannot fill in gaps left by reason. Saadiah Gaon (882–942), for example, had maintained that one reason why revelation is necessary is because reason gives us only general rules, and so we need revelation to give us the details as to how those rules are to be put into practice.[12] For Agus, though, revelation can no longer function in that way because "the dogma of 'Torah M'Sinai,' in its fundamentalist interpretation, is no longer a 'live' proposition to those who have made their own the spirit of Western culture and the modern methods of research in the history of religions."[13] In the past, Jews—perhaps even large numbers of them—may have believed that the text of the Torah that we have in hand is the literal word of God at Sinai and therefore supersedes all other forms of knowledge in its authority—and, indeed, sets the criteria for what will count as knowledge from any other source. In the modern world, however, that is no longer true. Western culture has all but totally triumphed among Jews, and therefore even religion must submit to the canons of reason for its analysis and validation. In such a context, Agus asserts, basing the authority of Jewish law on a literalist interpretation of the Torah *in the absence* of rational grounds for believing what it says is no longer even what William James would call a "live" option for contemporary Jews. Where reason seems to *contradict* propositions affirmed on the basis of the Torah, revelation would lose even more credibility in the eyes of moderns.

On the other hand, Jewish law's claims to authority, according to Agus, should not be based on reason alone. When one does this, as many nineteenth-century Jewish thinkers did, "the Law is stripped of every vestige of authority, the whole range of tradition is denied any inherent truth-value, and worship becomes a mere human exercise in mnemonics."[14] For if reason is the sole source of authority, everything else—law, beliefs, story, revelation, poetry, custom, history—becomes a handmaiden in its service, demonstrating or reinforcing rational principles in some way. This strips Jewish law of its inherent authority, making whatever sanction it has derive from, and dependent upon, human reason alone.

Reason, however, cannot sustain such a burden, and Agus provides four reasons to demonstrate why.[15] First, religious consciousness is a realm of unique values, *sui generis*, even as art and music, so that in it the concepts of ethics and aesthetics acquire a special tone and substance. Beauty is transmuted into a feeling of the Divine, duty is viewed as self-orientation to the Divine Will, and the measure of right and wrong is construed as the judgment of God.[16]

That is, even where reason can help us to understand phenomena like moral principles or aesthetic qualities, the very act of subjecting these phenomena to reason distorts them, for then reason sets the rules by which they are to be judged. They take on a completely different coloration and meaning, however, when experienced in the context of religion. If one's view of these phenomena is going to be adequate to their substance, then, one must use both reason and other avenues of knowledge appropriate to specific phenomena to know and understand them. In the case of Jewish law, the other appropriate approach is through revelation, as Jewish sources themselves assert.

Second, within religious consciousness all objects, animals, and persons are seen as creatures created by, and dependent on, a higher power. That is, religious people view our finite world as limited in its power and dependent on that which goes beyond it. This perception is not a reasoned inference, but rather "an immediate intuition of the transcendent." One recognizes such a perception of our finite world as appropriate without creating a rational argument to claim so; rather, the perception arises immediately from one's experience. It is like the experience of trying on a pair of eyeglasses: one immediately knows whether or not the view of the world they give you is right. If asked to do so, one may be able to supply some arguments to demonstrate that adjusting the focus in a specific way is best, but such arguments are not the basis of one's conviction that a particular setting of the eyeglasses provides a proper vision of the world; that comes from the experience itself. Reason is similarly not the sole ground of our religious knowledge.

Third, religion in general, and religious law in particular, develop organically. They are not the product of eternal, abstract truths applied in some ivory tower; they grow instead out of the continuing experiences of a community that affirms a religion's truths and lives by its laws. Because this is so, reason is really incapable of capturing much of the substance of Jewish law. Reason, after all, is universal in its nature, while Jewish law is particular to the Jewish people. Furthermore, a rational argument is, at least in theory, valid or invalid forever, while Jewish law is subject to changes over time. Jewish law derives some of its authority from the rational and moral purposes it serves, but the particular and developing qualities of Jewish law prove that that cannot be the whole story.

And finally, fourth, "revelation is an actual phenomenon, not merely a euphemism, and Judaism is a revealed religion." In other words, any interpretation of Judaism that denies its revelational base in favor of reason alone distorts Judaism.

Agus defines revelation as "the belief that truth and creative vision may come to man from God, thru [sic] channels other than the physical senses." He distinguishes three stages of revelation: (1) the intuition of the objective validity of ethical values; (2) an experience of the highest levels of religious feeling, designated "the feeling of the holy," "when the awareness of Divine mystery and majesty is the supreme note in man's consciousness," prompting one to dedicate oneself to God in the moral forms revealed in the first stage of revelation; and (3) "the covenant or destiny experience," when one acquires new insight and creative energy, such as the revelations that led to the emergence of Judaism in the midst of the pagan world. All people are recipients of the first two levels of revelation if they open themselves to receiving it, but the third stage is the possession of only a privileged few.

Just as the second stage of revelation includes and fortifies the first, so too the third stage proves "its authenticity by the intensification it affords to the first two phases of revelation. . . . Religion, in the specific or Jewish meaning of the term, is thus seen to be inherently related to the ethical ideal, as the roots of the tree are to its fruits." Agus, in fact, takes it as a specific mark of "the Conservative conception of the authority of Jewish law" that the higher phases are to be judged for their authenticity by their effect on the lower levels, for whereas the higher states of revelation gain in inspiration and in creative power over the lower ones, they decrease correspondingly in the quality of objectivity. . . . Thus, concerning every form of piety, it is legitimate to inquire whether it conduces to the good life of ethics, and in regard to every claim of Divine inspiration, it is necessary to employ the yardsticks of genuine piety, as we know it.[17]

Deuteronomy, the fifth book of the Torah, suggests two different criteria for determining whether a revelation is true. Chapter 13 says that if the prophet tells you to worship other gods, that proves that she or he is a false prophet. Chapter 18 makes prophetic authenticity depend upon whether the prophet's predictions come true. Agus's criterion of moral rectitude is neither of these, but it is closer to the first, for in both Deuteronomy 13 and in Agus's approach true prophets are to be recognized by the content of their words. Deuteronomy 13, though, makes the judgment depend upon the theological correctness of the prophet's words, while Agus focuses on their moral rectitude.

LAW NEITHER AS FOLKWAYS NOR AS A MEANS FOR JEWISH CONTINUITY NOR AS NATIONAL SPIRIT

As we have seen, Agus's commitment to reason forces him to deny an Orthodox, literalist understanding of the Torah that would locate the authority of Jewish law—ultimately, at least—in revelation alone. On the other hand, he also finds it necessary to show why reason cannot be the exclusive source of authority for Jewish law either. Probably the hardest battle he had to fight within the Conservative movement, however, was against three popular conceptions of Jewish law that base its authority on neither reason nor revelation, but rather on historical and/or sociological factors.

One such theory is that proposed by Mordecai M. Kaplan, to wit, that Jewish law consists of moral demands and folkways. Agus points out that conceiving of many of the commandments as folkways robs them of legitimacy as commandments and of authority to command unto death. Folkways lack historical authority to obligate, for Judaism from its very roots denied ancestral folkways in order to attain patterns of action that reflect divine truth. As he says in the selection below,

> Is the nostalgic reverence for parental practice to be glorified as an absolute imperative? Such a consummation would indeed offer a strange climax to the great adventure of Judaism, which began with a revolt against established customs and parental mores, as expressed in the command given to Abraham, "Go, thou, from thy land, the place where thou wast born and from the house of thy fathers."

Moreover, philosophically folkways lack the power to bind, which, for Agus, can only come from a deep conviction that Jewish law articulates divine truth:

> The motivation of Jewish piety was actually derived from a deep conviction in the truth of Israel's religious heritage, and the consequent

> common sense preference of eternal reward for temporary bliss. In this interpretation [of Jewish laws as folkways], however, the glory of Jewish martyrdom for the sake of Divine truth and the soberness of its mentality would be interpreted as the senseless stubbornness of a clannish people, fanatically isolating itself from the ways of the world, forebearing all mundane goods and spiritual values for the sake of mere tribal customs.

Furthermore, transforming Jewish law into folkways "lacks the moral quality, which alone evokes a sense of obligation and a feeling of consecration. Why should we strive with might and main to preserve folkways?"[18] Interpreting Jewish laws as folkways, Agus is convinced, could only appeal to a transitional generation that had lost the purpose but retained the sentiment of group survival for no good reason that it could give.[19]

A second conception of Jewish law, that of Aḥad Ha'am, views it as a bulwark to preserve Jewish national identity in the Diaspora. This approach, Agus acknowledges, is widespread among the American rabbinate and laity; it is invoked whenever there are appeals to preserving the "Jewish way of life"—or what has more recently been referred to as "Jewish continuity." Historically, however, Jews obeyed Jewish law out of religious conviction; the survival of Jewish nationality was an effect of such observance rather than its motivation. Indeed, it is not at all clear that the survival of every branch of a biological or historical group must be regarded as a supreme end in itself; the Nazi experience, at least, should call into question any philosophy that puts ultimate value in blood and folk. And finally, if preserving Jewish nationhood is the only reason to obey Jewish law, it should become obsolete now that the State of Israel has been established, at least for those who live there and even for those who choose to bask in its reflected national glory while living elsewhere.

A third understanding of Jewish law to which Agus objects goes to the very roots of the Conservative movement, appearing as it does in the writings of Zacharias Frankel and Solomon Schechter. It is the idea propounded by the "historical school" and rooted in nineteenth-century romanticism that Jewish law is the product of the national psyche (soul) that developed over time, and that it therefore must be maintained even if—perhaps especially if—it is irrational. Here again, though, "What is to prevent historic processes that functioned relatively well in the past to function poorly in the present, or even to cease functioning altogether?" Moreover, how can historical processes "be regarded as sources of absolute value, sufficient unto themselves?"[20]

LAW AS STANDARDS

These sociological/historical views, then, cannot provide a source of validity for Jewish law. They speak to the body of the law, not to its soul.
But if Conservative Jews are not, for reasons of historical accuracy,
going to see the Torah (much less later Jewish law) as the direct transcription of God's word, how can they understand Jewish law in a way
that preserves its authenticity and authority?

Agus articulates his task in this remarkably candid way:

> Let us begin our analysis then with a frank and clear rejection of the
> literalist Orthodox position. We do not believe that God dictated the
> Torah to Moses, as a scribe to a pupil, and that He had transmitted to
> Moses all the comments, interpretations, and inferences relating to it
> that were later recorded in the Oral Law. Having taken this step, we
> find ourselves still profoundly convinced of the importance of the Law
> and its supreme significance. But if these vague sentiments of reverence
> are to serve as the enduring foundations for Judaism of the future, they
> must be envisaged in all clarity as proven true in terms of the contem-
> porary situation and as rooted firmly in the eternal scheme of things.
> How then shall we think of Halachah?[21]

He outlines five elements of a viable answer to this challenge. It
must acknowledge that: (1) "The relationship of the Jew to God is the
incontrovertible starting point" of any theory of Jewish law that preserves the self-understanding and motivation Jews have historically had
in obeying it. (2) The commandments historically have been authoritative not only because they were seen as the word of God, but also because they purified human beings morally and served as worthy
instruments of piety. (3) The authority of the commandments traditionally has rested not only on the conviction that God commanded them,
but also on their acceptance by the Jewish People. (Thus, according to
rabbinic legend, "the Torah was offered to the other nations, but it is
not for them obligatory since they never accepted it.") (4) In addition to
the moral-legal basis of Jewish law, the Jewish people's historical memory also played a major role in affording authority to Jewish law. We all
were at Sinai, and we all, along with our ancestors and descendants,
agreed to become part of the covenant with God. (5) Finally, the precepts of the law constitute the minimal standards of the community; the
good person must rise above its demands and act beyond the letter of
the law.[22]

Taking these tenets together, Agus maintains, leads to a conception of Jewish law as "standards," or "divinely imposed disciplines of

the Jewish people." Agus stresses that the authority of Jewish law rests on both components of that formula, namely, God and the Jewish people.

In theological language, the authority of Jewish law derives from our love of God. Agus describes God as "the Pole of the Absolute, Ideal Personality"; using the language of physics, God is the ultimate point in the field of reality. In the love of God, then, "all moral and esthetic values are fused together into a new and creative unity." God thus functions dynamically as both the source and the goal of all human ideals, and the goal of all Jewish law "may be viewed as being motivated by the one sustained attempt to incorporate the love of God as a living reality in every phase of public and private experience." But it is not God alone who is the source of authority of the commandments, for love must be mutual. Therefore, Jewish law is both "Divinely inspired and self-imposed."[23]

Furthermore, it is multiple in character. Agus proposes that we think of Jewish law as a threefold ladder leading to God, corresponding to the three pillars of Jewish faith: Torah, worship, and good deeds. This model accurately describes both the accomplishments and the remaining challenges of those who climb high on one ladder while remaining on the lower rungs of the other ladders, and it also "permits us to regard all Jewish groups, seeking sincerely to elevate the level of spiritual life, as falling within the pattern of one common endeavor."[24] Thus, conceiving of Jewish law as comprised of these three standards enables us to understand and appreciate what we and others have done in striving for the divine goals of morality and piety, thereby engendering feelings of pluralism and cooperation within the Jewish community, while still depicting what we all have yet to do in striving toward the ideal.

TRADITION AND CHANGE

Legal expressions of piety—that is, reverence for God—are the body that enables the soul of piety—and, derivatively, of ethics—to become part of our lives. Without such concrete manifestations in ethics and law, our claims of commitment to piety would be empty.

> Religious seeing . . . is not only perception, but dedication and action as well. Thus, the original insight of Judaism was never simply Knowledge of the One God, but a consecration to the service of the One God. . . . Halachah is for us the way in which God's word is progressively being shaped into ways of life.[25]

Therefore, such legal forms must be preserved. Since they are easier to grasp than the abstract goals of morality and piety, though, laws tend to be conservative in nature, evidencing little room for changing the specific way in which they embody the moral and pietistic elements at their core. Therefore, while Agus is careful to say that legal forms must be maintained so that revelation in both its moral and religious aspects can enter our lives meaningfully, he also makes it clear that, in his opinion, laws are "identified as instruments" and must always be subject to evaluation according to the objective goals they are designed to advance. Put succinctly, morality and piety trump laws whenever the latter get in the way of the former or cease to further their goals.

> . . . the revealed character of Jewish legislation refers to the general subconscious spiritual drive which underlies the whole body of Halachah, not to the details of the Law. The vital fluid of the Torah-tree derives from the numinous soil of the Divine, but the actual contours of the branches and the leaves are the product of a variety of climatic and accidental causes.[26]

At the same time, "it is necessary to beware of the kind of changes that destroy the spell of the Law." Even if a given law begs to be changed because it violates our sense of morality or piety, Agus says, rabbis must take care not to change a specific law in a way that undermines respect for the law as a whole. "The new must be so delicately grafted upon the old that the health of the tree as a whole will not be affected."[27]

This, of course, complicates matters. However difficult it may be to recognize when a given law sufficiently offends our sense of morality or piety to require change, it is even harder to balance such considerations against the need to preserve the integrity of the corpus of the law. Judging the law by the objective standards of morality and piety entices one to change the law, or at least to be ready to do so. Concern for preserving the integrity of the law, on the other hand, prompts one to be wary about any change. In Agus's terms, morality and piety, which are "objective" in that they are values shared by everyone, come into conflict with the "subjective" ways individuals and groups have traditionally expressed these values in practice.

But that is precisely Agus's point: a Conservative position must find a way to balance both of these impulses, just as it balances reason and revelation. In contrast to the Reform position, which focuses on reason and change at the expense of revelation and continuity, and in contrast to the Orthodox position, which does the reverse, the Conservative position affirms both elements of these two pairs equally: reason *and* revelation, tradition *and* change. Similarly, in his 1975 restatement of his position, he stresses the importance of law *and* spirit (*halakhah* and *aggadah*).[28] This inclusiveness subjects the Conservative Jew to the tension inherent in balancing parts of the tradition that do not sit well together, and thus the simplicity, clarity, and confidence of those who embrace one or the other of the extremes of any spectrum are not available to the Conservative Jew. For Agus, though, the price is worth the gain, for the Conservative position is the only one that preserves both truth and Jewish authenticity:

> . . . the life of the spirit is a ceaseless movement between the two poles of objectivity and subjectivity. He who would keep his soul turned to the rhythm of truth must forever be on the move. He cannot stop at either pole and embrace the whole truth in his bosom; back and forth, he must move between the subjective and objective poles of the spirit, if he is not to petrify in static, sterile self-admiration. For reason and faith imply and fructify each other. . . .
>
> Coming now to the problems of Judaism proper, we maintain that our employment of a two-fold evaluation in the assaying of laws and ceremonies is true to the inward nature of piety. On the one hand, we accept the Halachah subjectively; on the other hand, we subject specific halachic precepts to criticism by means of the objective standards of piety and the good life that derive from the *yetzer tov* [good inclination] of modern thought and civilization. Both approaches are integral to the life of the spirit; we cannot afford to give up either one without forfeiting the soul of our faith.[29]

LEGISLATION AS A METHOD
OF CONSERVATIVE JEWISH LAW

Agus, though, does not have the usual notions in mind when he affirms the necessity to preserve Jewish law. On the one hand, he thinks that much more must be done than "business as usual" to engender observance of the law; he envisions, in fact, a vigorous campaign to make it a priority for the Jewish masses. On the other hand, though, he thinks that the process of applying Jewish law in our day also cannot be "business as usual"; it must instead be done using much more aggressive legal techniques. What marks both of these contrary moves—the one toward tradition, the other toward change—is balance and vigor, two characteristics that pervade Agus's thought.

First, on the side of tradition, Agus asserts that Conservative Judaism must not be characterized exclusively by the ways it has broken away from Orthodoxy. That would be to cast it in a solely negative light, defining it according to what it does *not* do or believe. Instead, the Conservative movement must devote itself with enthusiasm and energy to stimulating knowledge, observance, and piety among its adherents so that it is characterized by what Conservative Jews *do*. Toward that end, the movement "must undertake a campaign for the stimulation of a minimum of religious observances among our people, stressing in particular those precepts which contribute decisively and directly to the cultivation of the spirit of piety, such as the acceptance of regular weekly worship and study periods."[30]

Agus clearly would have liked more than "a minimum of religious observances," but he was enough of an educator to discern the difference between the ideal and the possible and the need to begin with something that could clearly be accomplished. Several of his colleagues apparently agreed with his assessment of the educational realities and with this aspect of his approach to Jewish law, for his idea of a campaign to engender observance was soon to be embedded in the responsum on the Sabbath, approved by the Law Committee, which he co-authored with two other rabbis. Whether or not one agrees with his strategy, it clearly indicates that Agus wanted to shift the momentum within the Conservative movement from what it denied to what it affirmed, and his campaign to engender observance among the many Jews affiliated with the Conservative movement was one aspect of Agus's understanding of a Jewishly serious movement.

While commitment to observance must be one mark of the Conservative movement, another must be its readiness to modify its content to achieve its moral and religious goals. Agus maintained that the Conservative movement's Law Committee, as constituted at the time, was "insufficient" to the task at hand. If the Conservative movement saw itself authorized only to interpret and apply traditional law, it would never get beyond the claims of the Orthodox to be the only authentic form of Judaism, for such interpretation and application of law is precisely what they do. Even if Conservative responsa generally prefer the lenient option within the traditional materials, the movement would not be distinctive in character and, worse, would always feel itself undermined by the learning and zeal of the Orthodox. Moreover, such an approach is based on an exaggeration of the degree of freedom embedded in traditional Jewish law, and if the Conservative movement does nothing else, it should not, as a movement dedicated to historical Judaism, misrepresent what the historical sources say.

The way out of this problem, according to Agus, was for the Conservative movement to have the courage and creativity to act on its own principles. What Jewish history does reveal is that various Jewish communities over time went beyond the interpretive method and enacted new laws (*takkanot*). As I explained above, sometimes these represented changes in what had been traditional practice, and sometimes they were simply positive law to address the community's needs not covered in the received law. In like manner, Agus asserted, "We need a law making body, not a law interpreting committee."[31]

Why have the Orthodox rejected such an approach? In large part, Agus averred, because they have an exaggerated sense of the deference that must be paid to earlier sources. They are, indeed, stymied by the authority they attribute to the rabbis and leaders of previous generations who, by that very fact, are for the Orthodox greater in wisdom and knowledge than any contemporary person or group could be. Such an approach, though, is not necessitated by the sources themselves, which demand that we have respect for previous generations but that judges in each generation may decide matters, as the Talmud says, "according to what their own eyes see." Therefore, the Orthodox methodology represents a *choice* as to how to read Jewish sources, and it is an arbitrary one at that, for it flies in the face of some of those very sources. Furthermore, the automatic Orthodox preference for the earliest decisions is "a mechanical principle of selection" of what should count in determining the law, rather than one based on the merits of any particular case. As such, it does not hold much promise for wisdom in applying Judaism to modern circumstances.

> If we follow the principle that the rabbis of our own days are incompetents and that the rabbis of the past were all-knowing, we undermine the very basis for development and growth in religion, even while we presume to speak in the name of religious progress. Obviously, the past cannot of its own momentum effectively progress in the contemporary world. Again, if we deny Divine sanction to the "Rishonim" [rabbis of the tenth to the sixteenth centuries] and grant it to the masters of the Talmud [completed c. 500 C.E.], or if we deny it to the Amoraim and Tannaim [the rabbis of the first through the fifth centuries C.E.], reserving it for the prophets [who lived between the ninth and the fifth centuries B.C.E.], we should be operating with a mechanical principle of selection, for which there is no basis in our philosophy of Judaism. . . . From our viewpoint, then, the present is more determinative than the past, and the immediate past more authoritative than the remote past.[32]

Agus proposed, then, that the Conservative movement make extensive use of the method of legislation (*takkanah*). He is careful to point out that that is a perfectly traditional way of doing Jewish law, evidenced in Jewish history from at least as early as the first century C.E. (indeed, arguably from the time of Ezra in the fifth century B.C.E.) and continuing throughout the Middle Ages and the modern period to contemporary times. Thus Agus thinks that there is ample precedent for using legislation as a legal method in our own time.

Moreover, that method is definitely needed now, for, as Agus asks rhetorically, "are not our time and circumstances so strikingly new as to justify the creation of new precedents?"[33] As we shall see, he has in mind not only the needs of contemporary Jewish society to make changes in the law, but also—and, perhaps, primarily—its need for legislation to reinforce practices that Jewish law already mandates.

In addition to these historical arguments, Agus supports the use of legislation on legal and philosophical grounds. Legally, as he points out, legislation was justified on the basis of Deuteronomy 17:11: "You shall act in accordance with the instructions they [the judges of your generation] give you and the ruling they hand down to you; you must not deviate from the verdict they announce to you either to the right or to the left." The "you must not deviate" *(lo tasur)* clause in the verse Agus calls "the magna carta of rabbinic legislation," and it is, indeed, as I described in chapter 2, the source of authority that the rabbis of the Talmud and thereafter used to stretch the law considerably in all directions.[34] If the Conservative movement is not going to restrict itself to the legal method of interpretation, and if, on the other hand, it is not going to abandon Jewish law altogether, then, according to Agus, it must embrace the method of legislation "or else disappear from the scene, as a movement."[35]

Philosophically, says Agus, "this principle [of *takkanah*] is fully in accord with our dynamic conception of revelation."[36] In addition to what he delineated about revelation in his essays in the late 1940s, described above, he elaborates further on his own concept of revelation in another essay included in his 1954 book, *Guideposts in Modern Judaism,* and in a subsequent book (published in 1983) as well.[37] In referring to "*our* dynamic conception of revelation" here, though, he undoubtedly has in mind any of the concepts of revelation within the Conservative movement that take into account the historical development of the Torah and understand revelation as continuing in our day through the work of contemporary rabbis and thinkers.[38] That tenet of continuous revelation, Agus maintains, also argues for contemporary rabbis to use the legal vehicle of legislation as they discern the will of God in new ways, of which only some can be reasonably derived from interpreting previous elements of the tradition. As he put it in 1975:

The religious experience of revelation has taken in Judaism the form of a succession of covenants with God, of which Joshua 24 is the archetypical account. . . .

Takkanah-legislation is in effect a periodic reenactment of the Covenant in regard to a specific problem. Continuous adaptation of the Law is therefore an expression of its vitality. The range of *takkanot* may be the world-fellowships of Israel, or the national communities, or the congregations, or *havurot* [groups of friends], or even families.

Every *takkanah* must be within the context of the overall Covenant made with all-Israel, as expounded in the "sacred tradition" of our people. But the various Jewish communities in different parts of the world are expected to enact *takkanot* for their own communities and on a temporary basis, *takkanot hakehillot*. Special *havurot* with their own *takkanot* were characteristic of the creative ages in Jewish history.[39]

PUTTING THE METHOD
OF LEGISLATION INTO PRACTICE

Legislation, then, is one mode of applying Jewish law that the Conservative movement must embrace. In the past, Jewish legislation has enjoyed two sanctions, "one deriving from the most sensitive conscience and the most creative scholarship of the age, the other deriving from the democratic principle of 'the consent of the governed.'" Accordingly, Agus proposes the establishment of two bodies: a "Jewish Academy," similar to the French Academy of Napoleon's time, consisting of selected rabbis, scholars, and laypeople; and periodic, joint special sessions of the United Synagogue and the Rabbinical Assembly empowered to accept or reject *takkanot* proposed by the Academy.

Agus deliberately called the first body "the Jewish Academy" and *not* "the Sanhedrin" so as to rule out from the beginning any pretensions to the authority that the ancient Sanhedrin had exercised (at least apparently) on its own: Agus's Academy would instead act like "the upper house" of a bicameral legislature whose actions would still need the confirmation of "the lower house" (i.e., the special joint assemblies he describes). Unlike the British Parliament, however, the Academy would take the primary role in studying issues and initiating suggestions for legislation. As such,

it should consist of the greatest men in our movement, those who have achieved distinction in the fields of scholarship, rabbinic leadership, Jewish education and social welfare. Like the [French] Academy, too, appointments should be made for life or for long terms—such appointments constituting the highest marks of recognition in our movement.[40]

The Academy would, in Agus's proposal, discuss not only matters of Jewish law, but also "principles and dogmas of faith, the latest developments in various fields of study bearing upon the philosophy of religion and ways and means of dealing with specific problems."[41] Thus, in his vision, it would function not only in the role of the current Committee on Jewish Law and Standards, but also in place of the Commission on the Philosophy of Conservative Judaism (which produced the first official statement of Conservative ideology in 1988), and perhaps also in place of some of the other current committees or commissions dealing with specific problems within the movement (like, for example, the Conservative Movement Council, which exists nationally, in the Pacific Southwest Region, and perhaps in some other regions, consisting of the presidents or their representatives of all the arms of the movement and which is used for joint planning purposes).

While Agus's proposal may be institutionally too cumbersome, demanding much too much of any one group of people, it has the theoretical advantage of making it clear at the outset that within Conservative Judaism, law, ideology, and social policy are not to be seen as disparate, independent entities, but rather as part of an integrated whole, each informing and affecting the others. This certainly has been a distinctive mark of much of what the Conservative movement has done in practice in the decades since Agus made his proposal.

Two points should be made about the membership of this body. First, in speaking of "the greatest *men* in our movement," Agus was probably simply using the language of 1948, when this was written, to refer to people of either gender. Female rabbis did not exist within the Conservative movement until 1985, and so he could not have imagined that possibility. He certainly knew of other women leaders within the movement, however, and he generally was supportive of expanding women's rights.

Second, it is interesting that Agus would include as members of the Academy not only scholars and rabbis, but also "laymen." In practice, the Committee on Jewish Law and Standards did not begin to include lay representatives until 1990, and then only as non-voting members and only as the result of political pressure exerted on the Rabbinical Assembly by the United Synagogue. A full forty years earlier Agus would have included lay leaders, presumably as voting members. While he does not justify that suggestion specifically, he presumably thought that the primary group that was to be responsible for shaping the beliefs, practices, and policies of the movement should include at least some representatives of the masses in whose name such pronouncements were being formulated. The Commission on the Philosophy of Conservative Judaism (1985–88) also had lay representatives—this time as full members—but there again they were added only after the rabbis and scholars had had time to begin the work on their own. As a member of both committees, I can attest that Agus was right long ago, for the lay members' contributions to the discussions of both groups have been both insightful and valuable.

Agus considered and answered several possible objections to the establishment of such an Academy. In response to the worry that using legislation as a legal tool would lead to antinomianism, especially in the context of the large gap between rabbinic and lay patterns of Jewish observance within the Conservative movement, Agus pointed out that the initial *takkanot* need not be negative, that, indeed, "There is no need for '*takkanot*' to sanction non-observance, but there is great need for '*takkanot*' to raise the level of observance." Accordingly, the Academy's "first task shall be to lead and guide our movement in a nationwide, '*tshuvah*' [return] effort, calculated to reestablish a minimum of observance among the members of our congregations . . . so that membership in a synagogue shall not be purely a financial transaction." The emphasis, in other words, should be on *takkanah* in the meaning of "establish" rather than in its meaning to "fix." It is only along with adoption by the rabbis and the laity of minimal standards of Jewish behavior that legislation would be considered to correct certain abuses in Jewish life, like the refusal of a man to grant a writ of divorce (a *get*) when there is no good reason for his unwillingness.[42]

Furthermore, as Agus points out, the principle of "Catholic Israel," first introduced to the Conservative movement by Solomon Schechter, would guard against any changes considered too radical by the Conservative community. Agus's proposal, in fact, gives that community a clear voice in determining Jewish law in a carefully delineated process, a voice laypeople lack when they can only react to the law established exclusively through rabbinic interpretation.

Another possible objection to such legislation is the dissension it might cause among the movements and within the Conservative movement itself. Agus dismisses the first as a serious concern on both practical and theoretical grounds. Practically, "uniformity of observance among Jewish people today is out of the question," and to wait for such agreement "would be tantamount in practice to the utter bankruptcy of our religious leadership." Theoretically, there is no reason to expect such uniformity, for the ways in which the Reform, the Orthodox, and the indifferent understand Jewish law bespeak convictions radically at odds with each other and with those of Conservative Judaism.[43]

The possibility of conflict within, and even defection from, the Conservative movement Agus takes much more seriously. The Academy he proposes, he says, should not dare try "to make up with one fell blow for a century of arrested progress." Caution and careful deliberation will be needed. On the other hand, though, he is convinced that the Conservative movement must adopt the way of legislation if it is to live out its ideological roots and if it is to do what must be done in our time to make Judaism a dynamic, living religion rather than a "desperate holding action" or merely a "way-station" to assimilation.

> The question raised by this objection, therefore, is a very fundamental one—to wit, is there room on the American scene for a Conservative movement, as distinguished from a Conservative way-station? To phrase the question is to answer it. There is not only room, but a crying need, for a Conservative movement. If there were no such steadily emerging movement, it would have had to be created. For our time calls for a bold constructive approach, which neither Reform nor Orthodoxy can give—the former thriving on the growing decay of tradition, the latter reduced to a desperate holding action.[44]

In sum, then, the Academy's purpose would be to function in *both* capacities that Agus demands of a living Jewish legal system: seriousness of purpose on the part of both the institutions and the individual members of the Conservative movement, as manifested by at least a minimum of observance of Jewish law, and, simultaneously, readiness to enact legislation to make the substance of Jewish law grow in appropriate ways to meet the needs of contemporary times.

AGUS'S OWN RESPONSA

Agus wrote several responsa for the Conservative movement's Committee on Jewish Law and Standards that illustrate his principles in concrete form. Undoubtedly the most famous of them is the responsum on the Sabbath, which he co-authored with Rabbis Morris Adler and Theodore Friedman. It secured the support of a majority of the Law Committee in 1950, and it has been the subject of much debate within the Conservative movement ever since.[45]

One immediately sees Agus's theory at work in the responsum's call for a program for the revitalization of the Sabbath. The protocol does not demand total observance, but rather has "as its immediate goal the acceptance on the part of the people of . . . basic indispensable elements of the Sabbath," which the responsum articulates in detail. The emphasis is on delineating and achieving Agus's "minimal standards." These include elements of traditional Jewish Sabbath observance, such as making preparations for the Sabbath, such as inviting guests, cooking food, showering, wearing clean clothes, and studying the weekly Torah reading, and the traditional Friday night home rituals. The responsum does not demand total compliance with all the requirements of Jewish law, however, and even those it includes are stated with room for individual adjustments. So, for example, attendance at public worship should happen "at least once on the Sabbath"; "One should refrain from all such activities that are not made absolutely necessary by the unavoidable pressure of life and that are not in keeping with the Sabbath spirit, such as shopping, household work, sewing, strenuous physical exercise, etc."; and "The type of recreation engaged in on the Sabbath should be such as is calculated to enhance one's spiritual personality in its intellectual, social, and esthetic aspects." The tone is clearly one of encouragement rather than one of obligation, and the content is explicitly directed at achieving the Sabbath's spiritual goals rather than asking for a blind obedience to the law as law.

The most controversial parts of the responsum, however, concerned riding to the synagogue and the use of electricity. The authors urged people not to use a motor vehicle on the Sabbath, both to enhance one's own repose and to encourage the family to spend time together, but they also said that "where a family resides beyond reasonable walking distance from the synagogue, the use of a motor vehicle for the purpose of synagogue attendance shall in no wise be construed as a violation of the Sabbath but, on the contrary, such attendance shall be deemed an expression of loyalty to our faith." The authors assert this because most Jews no longer know how to pray at home or to study Torah on their own, that "were it not for synagogue attendance on the Sabbath, there would be no prayer for most of our people" and no Torah study either. Furthermore, "in the spirit of a living and developing Halachah responsive to the changing needs of our people, we declare it to be permitted to use electric lights on the Sabbath for the purpose of enhancing the enjoyment of the Sabbath, or reducing personal discomfort or of helping in the performance of a mitzvah."[46]

The responsum itself announces three principles "implied in this program," principles in which Agus's philosophy is clearly evident:

(1) Despite the "cynical skepticism" that some may have about such a program of reconsecration, there have been many such efforts in the past, so that what we learn from history is that "[t]he Jewish religion does not favor the emotional excesses of the Christian 'revivalist' movements, but it fosters the principle of voluntary acceptance of a pattern of life." At the same time, the authors say, rabbis must be realistic in their demands of their community, for, as the classical Rabbis said, "To overreach is to court failure" *(tafasta merubah lo tafasta)*, "it is better to build a fence of ten handbreadths that is likely to stand than one of a hundred handbreadths that is liable to fall" *(tov asarah tefahim ve'omed mimeah tefahim venofel)*, and "it is better not to say a thing that will not be heeded" *(mutav shelo lomar davar she'eino nishma)*. All of these features of this approach are vintage Agus: creating a positive program for rededication; rooting one's approach in what Judaism has been historically; basing the authority of Jewish law, at least in part, on the voluntary acceptance of the people; and creating minimal standards that have a reasonable chance of being accepted rather than adopting an "all or nothing" attitude.

(2) The community power to enact ordinances is "virtually unlimited, provided its ordinances are made with consent of the resident scholars and provided further that they be inspired by the purpose of 'strengthening the faith,'" and such enactments should be made jointly "through their spiritual leaders and lay representatives." This is clearly Agus's program for using the legal vehicle of legislation *(takkanot)* to accomplish desired ends. Here the authors apply it to riding to the synagogue on the Sabbath and the use of electric lights, both of which they justify in this responsum in three ways: on narrow, legal grounds through scientific and halakhic analysis of what happens physically in the combustion chamber of an automobile and how that relates to the Torah's prohibition of lighting a fire on Shabbat (Exodus 35:3); on principled grounds of enhancing the joy of the Sabbath *(oneg shabbat)*; and, primarily, on the basis of the practical need of enabling Jews who would otherwise be unable to observe the Sabbath through synagogue services to do so.

(3) "The power of communities to make special enactments in behalf of the faith, through their spiritual leaders and lay representatives, is in turn a corollary of the principle of development in Jewish Law." This

development has historically included creating new practices and repu-
diating old ones. As the authors demonstrate through reference to a
number of talmudic and medieval sources, the authority for that development is based, at least in part, on the necessity for the community to
accept the law voluntarily for it to be valid; God's command is not
enough.[47] As we have seen, these principles are deeply rooted in Agus's
view of Jewish law.

Note that these decisions were not grounded only in considerations
of morality, aesthetics, piety, or practicality; they also follow from an
extensive analysis of the specific halakhic issues involved in driving and
using electricity. Thus, the theory used by the three authors was *not* to
replace legal reasoning, but rather to weave it into a broader consideration of how to accomplish the goals of the law in a contemporary setting. Since most Conservative congregants drove and used electricity in
any case, though, skeptics have commonly interpreted the responsum as
simply a way of giving retroactive sanction to the laity's practice, and
prospective sanction to those rabbis who wanted to do these things as
well—rather than how the authors presented it, namely, as part of a
concerted effort to revitalize Sabbath observance based on a serious
reading of Jewish sources.

Agus himself complained bitterly about the fate of the responsum
within the movement when the ruling was again discussed by the Committee on Jewish Law and Standards eleven years later (1961). Any
rabbi by himself, he points out, and even the rabbis together as a group,
could not possibly launch the revitalization effort on their own; from
the very beginning it needed to be a movement-wide effort:

> Our central agencies [by which he apparently means the lay organiza-
> tions of the Conservative movement] ignored this effort altogether,
> with the result that the Sabbath Revitalization effort remained merely
> an intra-Rabbinical Assembly project. . . . It would have been far bet-
> ter for the movement if the Sabbath Responsum had been directly en-
> dorsed by the Rabbinical Assembly [and not merely by the majority of
> the Committee on Jewish Law and Standards] and freely accepted by
> the United Synagogue and its affiliates. We should then have had truly
> autonomous legislation, bearing potent ethical-spiritual influence.

Agus noted that some rabbis objected to the self-declared status of
the responsum as a *takkanah,* preferring that the Conservative movement restrict itself to the more common legal method of interpretation.
He thanked the leadership of the Rabbinical Assembly for preventing a
vote from being taken on the floor of the Rabbinical Assembly convention intended to nullify its classification as a *takkanah,* and he argued

that, in our time, legislation is, in fact, the *preferred* way of achieving united action because it prevents the anarchy inherent in individual opinions:

> Actually, the sole difference between a *takkanah* and an interpretation is that the former is a *communal* enactment and the latter is a private opinion. It is clear that a conscious policy of limitless commentary, allowing free interpretation by individual rabbis, borders on anarchy. On the other hand, a communal enactment is likely to restrain arbitrary and extremist policies and to frame new enactments in the spirit of the tradition as a whole and of previous precedents.

There is still plenty of room for individual rabbis to make legal decisions based on their own authority as the local rabbi (*mara d'atra*, literally, "teacher of the place"), Agus maintained, but that role is properly restricted to matters of their own community. For example, an individual rabbi could decide *this* bottle of wine is kosher, but not whether, as a community, we are going to declare a principle that governs all consumption of wine in our day. That is, he draws the line "between *general* rules and *individual* applications," holding that in the former the way of legislation is the only one that prevents anarchy.

Along these lines, Agus said that the Committee on Jewish Law and Standards should get involved in setting *policy* for individual applications of the law, especially when the issues at hand occur on a regular and frequent basis. So, for example, it is proper that the Committee discuss whether this Sabbath responsum permits driving to a synagogue other than one's own to attend a bar or bat mitzvah (which Agus thinks is perfectly proper) or driving to visit the sick (which Agus thinks should only be done in an emergency). Given this, one wonders whether Agus has in effect undermined the status of the communal rabbi to make local decisions; he certainly has limited it considerably.

Agus argued against those who object to the responsum on the grounds that it widened the rift between the Conservative and Orthodox. If ecumenicism within Judaism is the issue, he points out, then relationships with the Reform movement should occupy the attention of Conservative leadership at least as much as ties with the Orthodox.

> Moreover, unity is neither desirable nor attainable by way of squeezing all of Jewish life back into "the four ells of Halachah," as it took form in the *Shulhan Arukh;* nor is it either desirable or attainable by way of fostering a rank anarchy of individual interpretations behind a facade of official loyalty to the Halachah; nor is it either desirable or attainable by way of negotiations between "spiritual statesmen on the summit" on

a *quid pro quo* basis. . . . To me, the only kind of religious unity which is salutary is the one that derives from the recognition of the distinction between the ethical-spiritual core of faith and the ritualistic-historical expressions of it. Hence, it is only in the growth of the liberal spirit that we can eventually attain the goal of creative unity.[48]

When Agus addressed the problem of the "chained woman" *(agunah)* in another responsum, his belief in the preferability of using legislation as a legal technique prompted him to object to the proposal put forward by Rabbi David Aronson. Rabbi Aronson suggested that the rabbinic court, based on the talmudic principle that the rabbis have the right to annul marriages, should issue a writ of divorce if the husband is missing or refuses to agree to a Jewish divorce (and the court finds his reasons for refusing are insufficient). Agus claims that this approach requires rabbis to issue a writ that says the opposite of what is in fact the case (namely, that the husband voluntarily divorces his wife). Moreover, it misunderstands the talmudic principle: it is really an assertion of the rabbinic prerogative to govern marriage law and to institute new procedures when necessary, and not a condition of marriage. "On this view, we have the right to analyze the problem of divorce and the *'agunah'* in basic terms." Agus does precisely that in suggesting a number of measures to deal with the various kinds of "chained women," including some suggestions openly based on the desire to equalize the status of men and women in marital law. In saying these things, Agus was objecting to a bold proposal on the part of Rabbi Aronson, another liberal Conservative rabbi, on the grounds that there are clear limits to our ability to interpret precedents responsibly to achieve the results we need and want, and that legislation is a much more honest and desirable method for doing so.[49]

Finally, it is interesting to note that Agus maintained his principles to the very end of his life. His 1982 responsum entitled "The Mitzvah of Keruv" deals with how the Conservative movement should balance its objections to intermarriage with its desire to attract the non-Jewish spouse to convert to Judaism. Here, he advocates communal action to assert the firmness required to resist intermarriage, for in a democratic country, people will not accept the authority of an individual rabbi but will understand and respect communal standards:

> . . . So long as the spirit of anarchy is kept within bounds, legal adjustments, even if far-reaching in character, may be enacted, without damaging the structure of authority within the movement.
>
> We live in a democratic age, where the supreme authority of a *mara d'atra* [local rabbi] is likely to be disregarded, if not resented,

while the collective authority of a national or world-wide body of representative rabbis, scholars and laymen is generally acceptable. A people, so religiously mature that it could glory in Rabbi Joshua's triumph over the mystical *bat kol* [voice from heaven] with the slogan, *lo bashamayim hi* ["The law is not in heaven"], can certainly be trusted in our day to understand that laws can be divine when they are man-made. But, they are not likely to tolerate the arbitrary tyranny of the resident rabbi or scholar, acting on his own judgment.[50]

AGUS'S 1975 RETROSPECT AND PROSPECT

In addressing the Rabbinical Assembly convention in 1975, Agus was enthusiastic about the developments of the intervening quarter-century and eager to undertake the next important steps toward putting his approach into practice. He pointed out, first, that "the Conservative tendency" from its earliest stages represented an integration of German and Russian Jewish expressions mixed with a heavy dose of American individualism and pragmatism. Further, he maintained that Solomon Schechter and Louis Ginzberg (1873–1953), the Seminary scholar who for fifty years had been the primary halakhic expert of Conservative Judaism, had both been moving in the direction he was proposing, thus giving his approach deep roots in the history of the movement.

There have historically been, in Agus's description, three ways in which Jewish law has changed, all three of which have occurred in the experience of the Conservative movement as well. First, "a more or less unconscious process of selective neglect and selective emphasis" has produced, in Agus's understanding, new forms of Jewish personal behavior. He gives a number of examples: adopting current American styles of dress and consciously choosing not to wear *arba kanfot* (an undershirt with the four fringes required by Numbers 15), *sheitels* (a wig for married women so that only their husbands see their hair), or a *kippah* (head covering for males) at all times; the non-use of *tevilah* (ritual immersion) by women after their menstrual period and prior to resuming sexual relations with their husbands and the neglect of the niceties of the laws governing menstruation *(niddah)*; the neglect of ancient rabbinic laws such as *tevilat kelim* (the requirement to immerse new utensils in a ritual pool), *afiyat akum* (the prohibition of eating food baked by non-Jews), *bishul akum* (the prohibition of eating food cooked by non-Jews), and *halav akum* (the prohibition of drinking the milk of non-Jews); the disregard of halakhic condemnation of those who are *mehal'lei shabbat* (violators of the Sabbath rules); and the eating of fish in restaurants.[51]

Second, through a conscious and deliberate interpretation of the law on the part of rabbis acting individually or jointly through a national institution or committee, the Conservative movement has, among other things: permitted the use of grape juice for kiddush during the Prohibition era (and presumably for those who medically cannot drink wine), endorsed the use of the "Lieberman *ketubah*," chosen not to enforce the laws of illegitimacy *(mamzerut)*, permitted use of electric lights on the Sabbath, decided to allow the Rabbinical Assembly's national Bet Din to solve the *agunah* problem through annulment, and "perhaps the most important decision of this category," appointed scholars who invoke the historical approach in the study of sacred Jewish texts—implicitly rejecting the authority of those scholars who did not use such methods, and thus creating the Conservative movement's own cadre of authorities to interpret and apply Jewish law.

Third, Agus sees several developments of the third quarter-century as embodiments of the legislative approach he himself advocates. Specifically, the *takkanot* that "resulted from the concurrent action of rabbis and laymen in formulating and carrying out congregational innovations" include mixed-gender pews, mixed-gender choirs, synagogue architecture directed forward with rabbis and cantors facing the congregation, abbreviated reading of the weekly Torah section, the elimination of some prayers and the recitation of others in English, the use of an organ in services, *aliyot* (Torah honors) for women, introduction of the bat mitzvah program and rite, riding to services on the Sabbath, and the late Friday night service. "A major *takkanah*," in Agus's view, was the adoption by virtually all Conservative synagogues at that time of the *Sabbath and Festival Prayer Book,* which includes (1) changes that transformed the traditional hope for restoration of animal sacrifices to a remembrance of the devotion of our ancestors who brought them, and (2) the change in wording that eliminated two early morning blessings in which Jewish men give thanks for not being created as a slave or as a woman, introducing instead blessings that express gratitude for being created free and in God's image. Although Agus admits that in some cases (e.g., mixed pews and the use of the organ in services) the rabbis were not consulted before the practice was initiated, "the acceptance of this action by local rabbis and their congregations renders it a *takkanah*." He therefore joyfully proclaims:

> I believe that we now have virtually completed the first chapter in the adjustment of Jewish law to American conditions . . . By and large, we are no longer plagued by the abyss between theory and practice which nullified our credibility in the past.[52]

In line with his assessment of what had occurred by 1975, Agus proposed that the process be taken further in a new, serious way. "We can now proceed to undertake the truly challenging task of developing new standards for personal and public life, through the application of the ethical principles of our tradition."

The one problem in accomplishing this was the absence of a clear cadre of laypeople with whom the rabbis can collaborate in applying the moral principles and insights of the tradition to new circumstances, for true standards must come out of the combined knowledge and deliberations of rabbis with laypeople who are both learned in a variety of disciplines and committed to Judaism. He therefore proposed the reestablishment of the *kallot* (conventions for study) of talmudic times, so that lay Jews who take Judaism seriously in their lives may consult with rabbis on applying the tradition to new moral circumstances, ultimately producing wise *takkanot* that would have the authority of both the rabbinate and Catholic Israel. In this way we would be doing nothing less than creating a new Talmud:

> The Talmud was not simply a folk-creation, nor yet a neat edition of academic learning. It stood between the two levels of culture, balancing the one against the other. It was made possible by the existence of a religious middle class: the *haverim* of tannaitic times and the *kallah*-sessions in Babylonia. This mediating group balanced the dialectic of the Torah-scholars by the pressures and ideals of the market-place. They made the difference between an organized community and a faceless mob. . . .
>
> Our greatest lack today is not so much the paucity of scholars as it is the loose and protean character of the laity in our movement. On the other hand, we have many religiously oriented attorneys, sociologists and political scientists whose expertise in their respective fields is quite as important as the rabbinic knowledge of our tradition. Any meaningful discussion of social issues must include their participation. I suggest that we begin to consolidate a firm core of men and women, consisting of those who undertake to attend institutes of learning on a regular basis—modern *kallahs*.[53]

Agus's idea is, at least to this author, downright exhilarating. It envisions giving Judaism new life and meaning in the lives of contemporary Jews by applying classical sources in an intelligent way to the problems—especially the social and moral problems—that confront us now. One can only do this, as he says, if one is fully cognizant of the previous development Jewish law has undergone and one is therefore convinced that a historically authentic approach can and should use all of the methods built into Jewish law for change and development. Moreover, just as one must be rooted in the past, one must recognize one's duty to the future, and that balance should guard against overzealous preservation of the past as it simultaneously keeps us from rash decisions that uproot us from that past. To strike the balance that will preserve Jewish continuity and yet speak meaningfully to contemporary circumstances, rabbis must take advantage of the general knowledge and the moral and Jewish sentiments of committed Jewish laypeople so that the resulting *takkanot* will be as wise an expression of the tradition and of the will of God as contemporary Jews can discern and formulate. The collaboration between rabbinic and lay leaders will also ensure that the *takkanot* will have authority as the product and practice of Catholic Israel.

The progress that Agus claimed the Conservative movement had made in adopting his approach by 1975 is, however, I think not as clear as he would like to believe. All of the modifications in Jewish practice that he mentions did indeed occur, but many of them only gradually made their way into most Conservative synagogues (e.g., roles for women in synagogue liturgy) and some have been reversed (e.g., enthusiasm for the late Friday night service and for the "cathedral style" architecture of Conservative synagogues of mid-century).

Moreover, Agus's classification of the changes into his three legal categories is highly debatable. So, for example, the responsum on the Sabbath that he co-authored is, despite its title as a "responsum," classified by Agus in this article as a *takkanah*, and I frankly doubt that many of the rabbis who voted for it saw it as that. They saw it instead, as the title suggests, simply as a responsum using the usual legal methods for writing responsa. One might agree or disagree with its reasoning, but it does not present itself, and was surely not understood, as new legislation, but rather as a rabbinic response to a question. A *takkanah* would not need the careful description (included in the responsum) of what goes on in the engine of an automobile to demonstrate that starting up a car is not a violation of a biblical prohibition of lighting a fire but, at most, of a rabbinic ordinance that contemporary rabbis may therefore weigh against other considerations. Agus's misclassification of legal developments is important to note because it demonstrates that the movement as a whole had not consciously accepted Agus's philosophy of law, even if it had acted in many instances in accordance with specific legal rulings growing out of that philosophy. The conscious reasons held by many of those who supported the new measures were consonant with many other philosophies of law as well, and I would guess that few people consciously embraced the approach and the program that Agus espoused.

That, of course, does not mean that his philosophy was faulty. It may just be that he was a man ahead of his time, that even if the Conservative movement did not adopt his philosophy of Jewish law then, it should now. It certainly has much to recommend it. At the same time, I frankly doubt that the Conservative movement in its present frame of mind is ready to make Agus's approach its own. Agus's philosophy of Jewish law fits squarely within Conservative Judaism as one possible option, but many within the contemporary movement are not ready for measures labeled innovations *(takkanot)*. On the contrary, the move to the right that has characterized all streams of Judaism since Agus spoke to the Rabbinical Assembly in 1975 has had its effects on Conservative Judaism as well, and so even those who support changes in the law prefer to package them as normative rabbinic rulings rather than as new legislation. Contemporary Conservative Jews feel the need for strong roots in the Jewish tradition more than they feel the need for what moved Agus so much —namely, to clean house legally and to face the future exuberantly.

AGUS'S LEGACY WITHIN THE CONSERVATIVE MOVEMENT

Jacob Agus, arguably more than any other Conservative rabbi of his generation, clearly and thoroughly articulated a philosophy of law appropriate for the Conservative movement, rooted in both reason and revelation, reflecting the developing history of Jewish law and its inherent values, and embracing both tradition and modernity in a conscious and serious way. One cannot help but admire the honesty and erudition of his approach as well as its concern for preserving tradition while making it compelling for contemporary Jews. He himself, however, wrote very few responsa for the Law Committee, and his proposal to use the legal technique of legislation *(takkanah)* has not been widely adopted by the Conservative movement. If anything, the movement has shied away from taking such steps, preferring instead to justify its actions within the more commonly used legal technique of interpretation.

In our own time, though, some of Agus's proposals have effectively been adopted, although without citing him as their ideological progenitor. The decision to ordain women, a major point of conflict within the movement, was not handled by the Committee on Jewish Law and Standards alone, but was rather entrusted to a movement-wide commission that took testimony from Conservative Jews in a number of cities. That commission ultimately reported to the Rabbinical Assembly convention, which directed its Membership Committee to accept applications regardless of gender once the Jewish Theological Seminary of America ordained its first woman rabbi, if the faculty of the Seminary were to vote to do so.[54] Even though this was not the procedure that Agus had proposed, this rather convoluted process reflected his belief that such significant actions be taken by the movement as a whole. His insistence that both laypeople and rabbis be involved was also evident in the process by which the Conservative movement framed its first and only ideological platform, *Emet Ve-emunah: Statement of Principles of Conservative Judaism,* for that was written by the Commission on the Philosophy of Conservative Judaism with representatives from all arms of the movement, including the Jewish Theological Seminary of America, the Rabbinical Assembly, the United Synagogue of America (later, of Conservative Judaism), Women's League for Conservative Judaism, and Federation of Jewish Men's Clubs. This was actually closer to Agus's model, for the Commission did not have to gain independent approval of any the movement's arms for its document. And finally, although I proposed in a responsum for the Committee on Jewish Law and Standards that there be a movement-wide commission to study areas of human sexuality, including, but not restricted to, the issues raised by homosexuality, with its recommendations reported to all of the arms of the movement, only the Rabbinical Assembly chose to take up the idea, creating a Commission on Human Sexuality with a mandate to study such issues and to report its findings to the Committee on Jewish Law and Standards.[55] None of these is quite what Agus wanted, but they all have elements of his proposals. He, however, laid the ideological groundwork for such an approach much more clearly than any of the people who initiated or carried out these most recent actions, and he did it thirty years or more before they happened! We may yet see the Conservative movement develop much more aggressively in ways he championed long ago.

In the following essay, Agus describes his objections to basing the authority of Jewish law in the folk (Kaplan), nation (Aḥad Ha'am), or people (the historical school), and he then articulates his own theory of seeing Jewish law as "the Divinely inspired and self-imposed disciplines of the Jewish people, undertaken for the purpose of elevating the level of individual and group life to the highest rungs of the ideals of Judaism." Judaism's moral ideals thus become the "goal and purpose" of Jewish law and thus the controlling factor in shaping the law, "while the ritual ceremonies are identified as instruments of relative value and significance." These "legislated spiritual disciplines" are inspired by God, but, in a kind of Copernican revolution, Agus asserts that "the efficacy of the *mitzvoth* consists not in their favorable effect upon the Divine Will, but in their influence upon the human soul, and their reward is supposed to be the automatic, natural rewards of a life dedicated to truth and goodness." He asserts: "To us, then, the laws of Judaism are disciplines and standards accepted for the sake of universal, spiritual ends," a clear foundation for all the interfaith work Agus did, for then other religions might have their own disciplines to move people to the same ends. Moreover, this provides a basis for pluralism among Jews too, "for our conception of a series of vertical standards permits us to regard all Jewish groups, seeking sincerely to elevate the level of spiritual life, as falling within the pattern of one common endeavor."

In evaluating Agus's approach, one wonders whether there are any bounds to Agus's acceptance of Jewish and interfaith pluralism—and, if so, how Agus would set them. Moreover, his theory entails a clear shift in the conception of Jewish law, for no longer is it "a binding Divine imperative" but rather "standards of piety." In Agus's own words, "Technically, this policy of setting minimal standards to meet contemporary realities may be expressed in halachic terms as a *ruling required by the time*. As our success grows, it may be possible to set a higher rung as the next immediate goal." Even then, though, the nature of Jewish law has changed, in Agus's Copernican revolution, from the dictates of God to "legislated spiritual disciplines" that Jews use to interact with God and to achieve universal ideals. And what happens if the minimal standards become the only thing Jews ever do, never advancing further? (To use Franz Rosenzweig's terms, what happens if "not yet" effectively and perhaps even consciously becomes "never"?) In fact, setting minimal standards poses the danger that people now observing Jewish law more intensely will stoop to the lower, communal standard, as the lowest common denominator in many areas of life often becomes the norm. On a communal level, this puts considerable power in the hands of rabbis, albeit with communal consultation and agreement, to change Jewish law through *takkanot*. In light of the Torah's prohibition of adding or subtracting to Jewish law and rabbis' consequent historical reticence to use that technique, however, and in view of its inherent ability to engender chaos into the legal system, should the legal vehicle of *takkanot* be used as extensively as Agus wants to do? What if the lay leaders cannot get their constituents to abide by even the minimal standards that the lay leaders themselves agree to?

Agus's theory also suffers from the same problem inherent in Gordis's approach, for they both clearly elevate the moral above the ritual. But how do we know which morals—and whose morals—trump which rituals? While Gordis would probably invoke the opinions and practices of Catholic Israel as the determinant of moral standards, Agus has described a specific decision-making body, the bicameral Academy, to identify the moral norms that the society should adopt and the times and places when they should override ritual requirements. But that is an eclectic procedure that gives the Academy the power to pick and choose as it wishes, thus giving it virtually total authority over Jewish law, and one wonders both whether that is wise and whether one will still be able to recognize God's hand in the law.

On the positive side, Agus's theory is realistic: he neither pretends that all Jews are committed to obeying Jewish law, nor does he turn a blind eye to the many Jewish commitments that Jews do have. On the contrary, his proposal seeks to build on Jews' current practices while pushing them to observe more through establishing achievable communal norms. His Academy would put rabbis and lay leaders in constant communication about matters of Jewish law, and that would undoubtedly elicit the lay leaders' cooperation in setting minimal standards and in encouraging greater observance. It would also involve the laity in the process of deciding difficult new issues in Jewish law, enabling rabbis to benefit from lay input in resolving legal issues. That is, the laity who, on Agus's theory, are made part of the educational and decision-making process are much more likely to participate in the shaping and ongoing practice of Jewish law than if they were only supposed to listen to their rabbis, an aristocracy of the learned elite. On both the theoretical and practical levels, Agus's theory preserves and justifies the divine authority of Jewish law well beyond ethnic folkways while yet providing for a clear mechanism for the legal education of the masses of Jews and for change.

Agus's theory embodies a bold theological and practical proposal. Judging by the Conservative movement's failure to embrace his theory enthusiastically, it may have been too bold. Only after the fact can we see that in several critical decisions since Agus wrote has the Conservative movement unconsciously followed his lead. But maybe that means that we need to confront the strengths and weaknesses of Agus's theory more seriously, for it apparently has in fact described the way in which the Conservative movement has functioned, even if Conservative rabbis and lay leaders are reticent to admit the ideological underpinnings that explain why they practice Jewish law as they do. Furthermore, Agus's theory may just be the recipe for future decisions in Jewish law and for future, ongoing practice of it, just as it has been in effect in the past.

Laws as Standards—
The Way of Takkanot*

JACOB B. AGUS

WHAT DOES JEWISH LAW, or more accurately, halachah, mean to us? We can scarcely deal with any issue in religious life today without first wrestling with this question with all the earnestness of which we are capable. To be sure, life is prior to thought, and often enough we may be called upon to act before our thought has been fully crystallized. But, in the realm of the spirit, nothing is ultimately significant and enduring that is not basically and essentially truthful, deriving from the fundamental convictions and dynamic motivations that constitute the permanent core of religion, and that remain eternally valid in the midst of a changing world. From a tactical viewpoint, peripheral considerations are frequently decisive, but we cannot build securely on a solid foundation if we do not envisage clearly the eternal validity and perennially fresh vital essence of Jewish law. What then is this vital essence? The Orthodox fundamentalist and the classical Reformist are at one in regarding this question as meaningless. The latter disdains a la St. Paul any "religion of laws," and the former is likely to stare aghast at the audacity of investigating what is obviously so simple. The halachah, in all its ramifications, is God-given. Both the Written and the Oral Laws were dictated to Moses at Sinai, and the laws that were subsequently instituted by the properly constituted authorities were also inspired by the *ruach hakodesh*. While areas of indetermination may remain here and there as a task for future generations, the *Shulchan Aruch* in its entirety, including the commentaries of *Shach* and *Taz*, was generally believed to "have been written with the aid of *ruach hakodesh*," so that the source of Jewish law was always the Divine Being. Even when a *minhag* attained the force of law, it was not because of a high estimate of the will of the *demos*, but simply because Israel as a whole was conceived to be holy and quasi-prophetic, sensing Divine truth in its innermost being.

To the literalist, then, Jewish Law, in all its life encompassing scope, was law, in the exact meaning of the term, since it was dictated by the King of the Universe and promulgated through His official channels. The Lord had concluded a covenant with His people, requiring them, as their part of the bargain, to observe His multiple commandments, in order that they might be prosperous in this life and blessed in the hereafter. In this mental world, God is envisioned as the austere King of Kings, promulgating laws for His subjects; as the King

Conservative Judaism, Vol. 6, No. 4 (Summer 1950), pp. 8–26.

Father in heaven teaching His children the proper rules of conduct; as the Judge at the end of days, sitting on His Throne of judgment, with the Torah in His lap; and as a diligent student of the same laws and principles which He has bequeathed to His people. Thus, the Law is either the expression of God's inscrutable Will, or the result of His kindness and solicitude for the best interests of His children, or the reflection of cosmic principles that inhere irrevocably in creation itself. In any event, the Law is superior to all human judgments and must be regarded as absolute in its validity and inexorable in its application.

The full stream of Judaism, through the ages, contained many trends, in addition to the massive current of naive piety. For the sake of clarity in analysis, however, the literalist mentality must be envisaged in all its naivete and inner consistency, in order that the full consequences of its rejection may be realized. Unfortunately, the debates concerning Halachah are all too frequently confounded by ambiguous phrases, which half conceal and half reveal mental attitudes that are themselves ambivalent, being compounded of both belief and unbelief.

Let us begin our analysis then with a frank and clear rejection of the literalist Orthodox position. We do not believe that God dictated the Torah to Moses, as a scribe to a pupil, and that He had transmitted to Moses all the comments, interpretations and inferences relating to it that were later recorded in the Oral Law. Having taken this step, we find ourselves still profoundly convinced of the importance of the Law and its supreme significance. But if these vague sentiments of reverence are to serve as the enduring foundations for Judaism of the future, they must be envisaged in all clarity as proven true in terms of the contemporary situation and as rooted firmly in the eternal scheme of things. How then shall we think of Halachah?

BEYOND FOLKWAYS

The Reconstructionists are best acquainted with the conception of "folkways" as the alternative to the Orthodox conception of the Divinely instituted *mitzvoth*. This conception implies that, in the past, the laws were simply the practices of Jewish people, some being derived from pre-Jewish sources and some growing out of their own experience and aspiration; that, in the present, their claim upon the individual is compounded of filial sentiment, national pride, the gregarious instinct and the need of the individual to seek and find his physical and spiritual salvation through the channels of community life; that, in the future, these ceremonies might well be replaced by different social organs that will respond more adequately to the then prevailing folk needs. The term "folkway" evokes the romantic admiration for plain people, who are free from the frequently disturbing and always challenging virus of rationality. It echoes the idealized image of the peasant that was so characteristic a feature of mid-nineteenth century nationalistic literature in Germany and Russia. It is idyllic, almost pastoral in its connotations, redolent of fields and forests, of pre-cityfied, even if not of pre-civilized existence. But, even while it thus echoes the cravings of romantic nationalism, it seems to speak in the scientific accents of the anthropologist, studying primitive societies, and the modern American sociologist, studying the ghettoes of European immigrants in our large metropolitan centers.

Nevertheless, in spite of its romantic undertones and its scientific resonance, the term, "folkways," can hardly be regarded as offering an adequate concept for Jewish law in our life. The amazing brilliance and insight with which it was developed assure for it a place in the history of Jewish thought, but, as a contemporary philosophy it is sadly inadequate. Primarily, it lacks the moral quality, which alone evokes a sense of obligation and a feeling of consecration. Why should we strive with might and main to preserve folkways? Their importance is supposed to reside in their inherent appeal and charm, not in any axiomatic claim to loyalty. Is the nostalgic reverence for parental practice to be glorified as an absolute imperative? Such a consummation would indeed offer a strange climax to the great adventure of Judaism, which began with a revolt against established customs and parental mores, as expressed in the command given to Abraham, "Go, thou, from thy land, the place where thou wast born and from the house of thy fathers." Nor does this state of mind in actual practice achieve more than the treasuring of "tallith" and "t'fillin" in public and private museums, the practice of visiting with the old folks on Yom Kippur and the crowding of synagogues for *yizkor*, leading perhaps also to the well-known facetious extreme of eating an extra Kosher dish in celebration of *yahrzeit*.

Certainly, if we pursue the implications of this concept backwards into the past and forward into life, we cannot but repudiate it with vehement finality. For, does it not present to us the image of our people, clinging to its ways and customs, in the face of direst consequences, for no reason save that those were indeed their ways and customs? The motivation of Jewish piety was actually derived from a deep conviction in the truth of Israel's religious heritage, and the consequent common sense preference of eternal reward for temporary bliss.

In this interpretation, however, the glory of Jewish martyrdom for the sake of Divine truth and the soberness of its mentality would be interpreted as the senseless stubbornness of a clannish people, fanatically isolating itself from the ways of the world, forebearing all mundane goods and spiritual values for the sake of mere tribal customs. Is the ardor of tribalism so beautiful a phenomenon, when we observe it among the backward peoples of this globe, that we should be tempted to reinterpret the Jewish past or reconstruct the Jewish present by means of it?—If today, we should see a people tenaciously clinging to its folkways to the point of sacrificing fortune, well-being and even life itself, in an environment where larger horizons, broader loyalties and a fuller life is possible, we should unhesitatingly condemn them as being both monstrously foolish and bitterly reactionary. If, then, the interpretation of Jewish laws as folkways is painfully inadequate to account for their historic function, it cannot serve as a proper vehicle for the momentum of loyalty to transmit its impetus for a creative life in the future. The ideal of clinging tenaciously to folkways, regardless of their intrinsic charm and worth, could only appeal to a transitional generation that lost the purpose but retained the sentiment of group survival, remaining, for no good reason that it could give, morbidly sensitive to the specter of the melting pot. In a balanced view, the so called "militant" survivalist, who deems group survival per se to be a supreme end of existence, is guilty of idolatry, religiously speaking, of vicious abstraction, logically speaking, and of sheer foolishness, practically speaking. Our ancestors were not guilty in any one of these respects; why should we expect our children, who are likely to outstrip us in worldly wisdom, to fall victims to these delusions?

THE LIMITATIONS OF NATIONALISM

Conceived in a totally different realm of discourse, the Achad Ha'amist conception of Jewish law as the "exilic garments" of Israel's soul is equally erroneous and misleading. In this view, the vast legal structure of the Jewish faith is interpreted as the product of the subterranean functioning of the national will to live. In the case of an individual, the powerful instincts of self-preservation generate ideas, attitudes and actions that are intended to guard his life, even if, on the rational level, they are "dressed up" in all kinds of rationalizations. The "real reason" for the multifarious actions of people is generally the impulse of self-preservation, though often enough people prefer to explain their actions in terms of "good reasons." In the same manner, the "real reason" for the progressive building up of the high fences of halachah was to assure the survival of the Jewish people, with the entire complex series of religious motivation serving only as the respectable facade for the dynamism of the national instinct. After the Babylonian exile, when the existence of Israel was placed in jeopardy, the national "will to live" began to weave the web of prohibition and interdictions, which had the effect of erecting an impassable barrier between Jew and Gentile and halting the trend of national dissolution. Later, as exile became ever more inexorably the normal state of Jewish existence, this tendency gathered momentum until, even as the turtle, the Jew came to carry his own home with him, wherever he went, permitting but a few chinks in his shell, for outside influences to penetrate.

On this interpretation, Jewish ritual law is indispensable from the standpoint of Jewish survival in the Diaspora. While Achad Ha'am was too inwardly truthful to maintain that religion should serve the ends of nationalism for the people of his generation, many of his followers agreed with Smolenskin and Lilienblum that the *mitzvoth* should continue to be regarded as the national commandments for Israel in exile.

In the United States, this cluster of motivations was a powerful factor among the Conservative-minded laity and rabbinate. One ventures to assert that in the sermons of all wings of American Judaism, the national motif is by far predominant whenever the so called "Jewish way of life" is preached. Implied in this interpretation is the estimation of group survival, not only as a biological instinct but also as a high spiritual obligation, so that the products of the national soul might be regarded as somehow "religious" as well. Echoes of the Halevian conception of Israel as a holy, prophetic people, that will in time be asked by all other nations "what the morrow will bring," were mingled with the sentiments of the Hebraic renaissance and the widespread hysteria of European nationalism, in order to furnish the composite apologia for Jewish ritual, that was actually in vogue in our own time.

Does this conception offer a valid interpretation of the past, adequate motivation in the present or eternal values for the future?—Obviously, it fails in all three domains. In respect of our historic past, a generation of nationalistic historians, led by Simon Dubnow, has not succeeded in hiding the incontrovertible fact that the fundamental motivations of Jewish life, all through the centuries, were derived from their religious convictions and that the survival of the Jewish nationality was an effect rather than a cause. In every generation, Jewish people were willing enough to compromise in regard to all nationalistic values, forsaking their land, language, mores, allegiance to an extra-national authority and accepting foreign national obligations, cultures and even irredentist sentiments with alacrity. But, they were adamant as the Rock of Gibraltar when the slightest tittle of the Law was involved, remembering the injunction that when a government is suspected of designs against the Jewish faith, resistance to the death must be offered even in so slight a matter as the proper manner of lacing one's shoes.

Nor can it be maintained that the survival of every branch of a biological or historical group must be regarded as a supreme end in itself. It is of the very essence of the ethical approach, to view all things objectively, to limit the value of every part by the consideration of the welfare of the whole, to think in terms of the unique value of every individual, not the group, and to view with extreme suspicion the tendency to glorify whatever is associated with the first person possessive pronoun. Certainly, if we judge the tree of romantic, biological nationalism by its fruits, we cannot but regard it as a most vicious and most insidiously corrupting aberration of the human mind. With Nazism as the logical culmination of the illogic of total tribalism, it would be the height of folly to regard the miracle of Israel's survival in the past and the rationale of its life in the present as being due to an inversion of the same dark philosophy of blood and folk.

As to the future, can any one seriously claim today that the nationalistic motive can be usefully employed as the foundation for Jewish law? Since the survival of Israel is presumably assured through the resurgence of the state of Israel, the nationalists in our midst can now afford to forego the aid of religious ceremonies. Those who take their national sentiments seriously will either go to Israel, or else be content to warm themselves by the reflected fire of Israel's reborn, secular life and culture. Those in whom the fervor of nationalism is of a lesser intensity will be prone to regard the establishment of the state of Israel and its gradual fortification as being a sufficient fulfillment of the impulse for group survival. Is not this the attitude of the vast majority of

America's immigrant nationalities that are even now commingling to produce the emergent American nation?—To be sure, the sudden resurgence of Israel's strength has moved many people to "accept" their Jewishness, but correspondingly this self-acceptance being a return to a normalcy of feeling is lacking in spiritual content and is quite incapable of opposing the assimilatory trend. On the contrary, it is likely to smooth the path of assimilation, by removing the Jewish feelings of inferiority and allaying the consciousness of Jewish "difference."

POSITIVE-HISTORICAL JUDAISM

Still a different version of the nationalist conception of Jewish law is offered by the so called "historical school," which was begun by Zechariah Frankel and expanded into impressive proportions by Solomon Schechter. To the historians of this school, history is a form of inverted prophecy and is therefore its own vindication. Jewish law, as it developed through the ages, is an organic product of slow gestation reflecting the inner genius and the profundities of the Jewish national character. Accordingly, no merely rational considerations can be allowed to outweigh the massive, historical processes, which echo the depths of the national soul by their very irrationalities. The spiritual history of a people, especially the structure of its laws, represents the gradual unfolding of its inner psyche. Hence, these laws must not be fundamentally disturbed; they should be allowed to change only in line with their own "positive-historical" grooves—for the law is the incarnation of the people's soul.

It is characteristic of romantic positions, founded as they are on the uncertain haze of emotion and the peculiarly conditioned slant of their adherents, that they reveal their weakness the moment they are fully expressed in unsentimental and objective terms. Thus, as here formulated, the historical approach is manifestly the outgrowth of an exaggerated emphasis on a half-truth. It is certain that the legal structure of a people deprived of a governmental authority is the means whereby its unity is maintained. It is also true that, in its creative period, the noblest ideals of a people are translated into the concrete terms of its legislation. But, considered a priori and in the abstract, what is to prevent historic processes that functioned relatively well in the past to function poorly in the present, or even to cease functioning altogether?—Historic processes in law, language, literature, politics and every other phase of culture are, after all, products of multiple factors and relative circumstances. How can they be regarded as sources of absolute value, sufficient unto themselves?

Actually, the plausibility of the "positive-historical" position is derived not from the intrinsic logic of its argument, but from the combined momentum of an ancient Jewish trend and a resurgent European reactionary movement. In appearance, at least, Jewish law seemed to be an independent domain, self-justifying and self-evaluating, regardless of fluctuations in the intellectual climate. Considerations of philosophy and theology appear to have been irrelevant to the unfolding inner logic of halachah. This fact is due, of course, firstly to the civil and public character of the major part of Jewish law. In such legislation, cognizance is universally taken of deeds, not opinions. Thus, in Greece and in Rome, as well as in Judea, charges of "atheism" were concerned with deeds, not with thoughts. Secondly, it is of the nature of the legal process for cases to be decided by reference to precedent and accepted maxims, rather than by a reconsideration of first principles. Thirdly, halachah was hammered out in its present shape largely by people who were entirely consistent in their religious views, but who were not rationalistic philosophers. Needless to say that it is a far cry from this statement of a historic fact to the value-proposition that philosophy, which is systematized common sense, *should* have nothing to do with halachah. It is a form of self-stultification that Maimonides would not even allow God to impose upon man. How can practice be permanently separate from its justification in theory? The centuries-long tendency to separate halachah from *aggadah* may have served a useful purpose in the Gaonic times, when it was set in motion, but it is not inherently justifiable. Men like Bialik and Rabbi Kuk, beginning from diametrically opposed starting points, agreed that only through the realignment of *aggadah* with halachah is progress in Judaism made possible.

In addition to reflecting the traditional independence of the domain of halachah, the "Positive-Historical" school expressed in the field of Judaism the nineteenth-century philosophy of German reaction. It was the legal historian Savigny, who first put forward the view that German law must not be radically modified, inasmuch as it reflects the unfolding soul of the German nation, thereby offering a rationale for the maintenance of the semi-feudal *ancien regime* against the challenge of the liberal forces unleashed by the French Revolution. Savigny transferred the Tertullianian reverence for the absurdities of dogma to the sphere of politics and law, maintaining that the seeming irrationalities of German law were the more sacred to the nation because of their evident unreason. His interpretation fitted in beautifully with the then current biological conception of the life of nations, as propounded especially by Herder and the Schlegel brothers. It was further deepened by the influential and profound works of Fichte, who expounded the thesis that the Germanic soul has a special affinity with *Vemunfi,* a form of reason that cannot be understood at all by the proponents of superficial rationalism, such as the French and Jewish liberals. Finally, Hegel climaxed the entire movement by his pedantic portrayal of the history of culture as being the invariant forms of the universal mind. The practical import of Hegel's conception was the representation of the Prussian state and its legal structure as the ultimate revelation of the Divine Being. For history is Divine Judgment, as it were, and its processes, as outlined in the past, mark out the grooves of change for the future.

It is in this intellectual atmosphere that it seemed so reasonable to base the validity of halachah solely on its "positive-historical" character. Stripped of these connotations, it becomes clear that the historical processes of halachah should be subject to reevaluation in terms of contemporary ideals, canons of criticism and necessities of circumstance.

LAW AND INSPIRATION

The common core of the three interpretations analyzed herein is the conception of folk, nation or people as accounting not merely for the external shape and historical character of the halachah, but as constituting the source of the validity and significance of Jewish Law. Manifestly, this sociological aspect of the law, revealing the massive group momentum inherent in it, cannot be gainsaid. No man lives alone, and the bonds of group loyalty, into which we fall by birth, constitute for us the natural matrix of our ideals, determining their external shape and slant. Against those who desert their natural groups to seek salvation elsewhere, the sociological argument is effective. But, to those who stay within, this phase is the body of the law, as it were, not its soul, and to attempt to base the value of law solely upon the character of the group is both futile and irrational. Only the absolute values of the spiritual life and the happiness of the individual Jew can be regarded as the axiomatic, irreducible foci of Jewish Law. For these are ultimates, in terms of which all group values must be judged.

To discover what halachah should mean for us today, we have to bear in mind firstly that the relationship of the Jew to God is its incontrovertible starting point. Secondly, in Judaism the laws were not only conceived as the word of God, but that they were so conceived because of their inherent worth as instruments of piety. True, they were God-given, but God is not a tyrant, imposing a yoke of obligations out of selfish need or sheer caprice. What does the Lord require of thee?—To fear Him, to love Him, and to walk in His pathways. The *mitzvoth* were given in order that men might be purified through them. Thirdly, the *mitzvoth* were not simply ordained for Jews by the fiat of the Lord; they became obligatory only when the Jewish people accepted them formally in the classic phrase, *na'aseh v'nishma*. Thus, the Torah was offered to the other nations, but it is not for them obligatory since they never accepted it. Fourthly, in addition to the moral-legal basis of halachah, there was always the consciousness of historic necessity, the ever present momentum of the past of which every generation must account anew. The Israelites at Sinai were historically committed already, because of the covenant with their ancestors, and the acceptance of all future generations is only in part voluntary and in part compelled by the realities of history. As the legend put it, the souls of all Israelites down to the end of time were gathered together for the theophany at Sinai. Fifthly, the precepts of halachah constituted the minimal standards of the community, by no means exhausting the full task and vocation of man. The good man must rise above the general level, *lifnim m'shuras hadin,* and Jerusalem was destroyed because its inhabitants insisted on the strict letter of the law.

Combining all these elements into one formula we arrive at the conception of halachah as the Divinely inspired and self-imposed disciplines of the Jewish people, undertaken for the purpose of elevating the level of individual and group life to the highest rungs of the ideals of Judaism. In this conception, the ideals of Judaism, insofar as they determine the standard images of the perfect individual and the perfect society, are recognized to be the goal and purpose of the entire halachic structure, while the ritual ceremonies are identified as instruments, of relative value and significance. The source of the validity of halachah is thus twofold—deriving in part from the consent of the people and in part from the inherent truth of the ideal embodied in it. If one grants supreme validity to any one ideal of Judaism, to the extent of desiring to share in the Jewish faith and destiny, then he cannot but accord a measure of authority to the legislation of the group as a whole. On the other hand, this allegiance to authority cannot be of an absolute character, since other values and ideals of his may conceivably be in conflict with the precepts of his people's legislation. The relative authority of any law is thus determined jointly by the degree to which it represents the common consent of our people and the measure in which it serves the highest ideals of Judaism.

The expression "divinely inspired and self-imposed" is intended to reflect the fact that the law is derived from both the insight of inspired titans of the spirit and the voluntary acceptance of the people generally. Of especial importance is the insistence on the Divine stamp of the central method of Judaism—the determination to translate abstract ideals into concrete ways of life for the people as a whole. Thus, the vague sentiment of loving God was concretized into the precept to pray three times daily; the recognition of our dependence upon Him, into the requirement to precede every new sensation of enjoyment by a blessing; the idle contemplation of His Nature into firstly the command to study the Torah day and night and secondly the ethically spelled out aspiration to emulate His ways as the infinitely perfect Personality. This method must be regarded as the cornerstone of Judaism, the one ideal which makes all other ideals practically meaningful and which transforms Judaism from a philosophy of monotheism into a monotheistic religion. It is compounded of a profound sense of personal consecration and a healthy regard for the conscience and welfare of the community as a whole.

This conception of the halachah is true to its historical character and development. While it describes the law as being the product of Israel, the two directions of religious love are interpreted as phases of one process. In our view, God is conceived as the Pole of Absolute, Ideal Personality in the back and forth flux of the multiple processes of reality, and the love of Him as the highest peak of the Divine process in the heart of man. For, in the love of God, all moral and esthetic values are fused together into a new and creative unity. If all ideals be conceived as dynamic motivations, deriving from God and leading to Him, then the love of God must be regarded as the parent-ideal, the living focus of the spiritual realm. And the entire halachah, in its manifold stages of growth and regardless of the diverse origins of some of its practices, may be viewed as being motivated by the one sustained attempt to incorporate the love of God as a living reality in every phase of public and private experience. Thus, a Maimonides may speculate on the ideal possibility of worshipping God in wordless silence and rite-less contemplation and recognize at the same time that for most people, such an ideal is all too frequently a snare and a delusion.

MOTIVATIONS FOR OBSERVANCE

No conception of Jewish Law is worthy of consideration if it does not truly capture some of the motivation which actually functioned in the historic past of our people. For we do not have either the desire or the will to create a new religion. Accordingly, we must inquire whether the interpretation of Law as legislated spiritual disciplines is indeed justified by the testimony of history.

In form, this conception is identical with the major part of halachah, the part that is described as *d'rabonon,* containing the officially authorized interpretations, *takkanoth* and *g'zeroth.* This class of ordinances is thought of as providing an outer area of disciplines intended to safeguard the inner area of Torah-itic *mitzvoth.* The exact boundaries of this area are subject to dispute, Maimonides having provided the widest conception current in rabbinic literature of the extent of the area of laws that derive their authority from the insight of the rabbis and their collective legislation. Obviously, from the standpoint of historical criticism, there is scarcely a shred of halachah that is not dependent in the last analysis on an authoritative rabbinic interpretation that was duly recorded at one time or another. As Maimonides put it in a different connection, "the gates of interpretation are not closed to us." The words of the Torah are sufficiently tractable to be incorporated into almost any system of legislation. But, the words of the living Torah have been frozen into rigid laws by layer after layer of rabbinic legislation. Thus, in the critical view, the distinction between Torah-itic and rabbinic laws vanishes, so that the final source is rabbinic *(d'rabonon).*

The realization of this truth need by no means be confined to those who repudiate the literal version of "Torah from Heaven." All who think in historical terms must find it difficult to resist such a conclusion. Hence, the extreme emphasis in halachic literature on the authority of scribes. Consider the implications of utterances such as the following:

> "Whoever disputes a word of theirs is as one who opposes God and His Torah, for all their words are of God, and even a Midrash of Moses himself, master of the prophets, could not possibly be set against their words, for their wisdom and *pilpul* is the word which God commanded unto Moses."
>
> (*Shaarei Tzedek*—Gaonic Responsa)

> "For they are assisted by the Shekinah, and it is not possible that their agreed opinions shall be contrary to the intent of the Torah. . . "
>
> (Kusari III, 41)

Now, the authority of the rabbis was not due to the mere fact of their election, but to their reputed saintliness, capped as it was believed to be by the gift of "Divine Spirit." The authority of the *Shulhan Arukh* was in no small measure due to the mystical visions of its author. Thus, the legislation of the rabbis, designated collectively as *d'rabonon,* coincides in form at least with the conception of Jewish law as outlined herein. It was believed to be "divinely inspired"; the disciplines were "self-imposed," for until and unless the people generally accepted a rabbinic ordinance it was considered as being automatically null and void. The purpose of rabbinic legislation was to maintain the "ideals of Judaism," as they understood them, identifying them on occasion with the ritual of the faith. Our conception of the ideals comprising the essence of Judaism belongs to the tradition of the prophetic-philosophic school of thought, to an analysis of which we shall now turn.

In order to understand the relationship of the substance of our conception, as distinguished from its form, to the basic currents of historical Jewish piety, we must launch upon an inquiry into the motivations that were supposed to underlie the rites and precepts of Judaism. What were the so called *ta-amai ha-mitzvoth,* the motives and purposes which, the Jew felt, supplied sufficient reason for his practice?— There were three categories of explanation, which functioned, sometimes separately, sometimes jointly, as the frames of reference for the reasons of the commandments. There was firstly, the mentality of folk piety, to which God was a quasi-human being, both King and Father. As King, His *mitzvoth* were commands that could not be questioned; as Father, it could be taken for granted that His Commands were somehow intended for the good of mankind, bringing with them life and blessing. A covenant was concluded between Israel and the Lord, requiring the people of Israel, as their part of the agreement, to serve Him in ways agreeable to Him. True, a faithful servant, will not pester His Master with demands for immediate reward, but the Lord could be trusted "to pay the reward of your work." Whether or not the intent of any particular *mitzvah* be apparent, the ultimate reason is to serve the Lord and to submit to His inscrutable Will.

In the philosophical current of Judaism, all arbitrariness and caprice is removed from the conception of God and the purpose of the *mitzvoth* is conceived to be unequivocally the spiritual perfection of the individual and the ethical perfection of society. The efficacy of the *mitzvoth* consists not in their favorable effect upon the Divine Will, but in their influence upon the human soul, and their reward is supposed to be the automatic, natural rewards of a life dedicated to truth and goodness. The core of Judaism, in this view, is the cluster of universal intellectual and ethical values, and all rites and ceremonies are merely the instruments of its implementation. Thus, Maimonides, after ridiculing those who revel in the occasional irrationalities of the Commandments, offers the classic formulation of the philosophic approach: "But, the matter is without question as we have mentioned—to wit, that every one of the 613 Commandments is motivated either by the purpose of imparting true ideas, or counteracting wrongful opinions, or the establishment of a just order, or the correction of injustice, or the training in good virtues, or the correction of evil practices. Accordingly, the purposes of all the *mitzvoth* fall into the three categories of true ideas, good virtues and the just order of society . . . Thus, these three categories are entirely sufficient to account for every one of the *mitzvoth.*" (Moreh, III, 31)

In the philosophy of Maimonides, the highest gift available to man is the attainment of a bond of union with Active Reason and the consequent assurance of immortality. This gift belongs primarily to the faithful devotees of the moral and intellectual life, and only secondarily to the observers of the *mitzvoth*, for the *mitzvoth* are instruments of the life of the spirit, and instruments sometimes fail to achieve their purpose.

The very clarity with which Maimonides presented the viewpoint of philosophical Judaism provoked a violent reaction among the naive believers and their defenders, as is amply demonstrated in the commentaries upon the "Guide" and the polemics that followed upon its publication. But, the sophisticated defenders of fundamentalist Orthodoxy cannot ever be satisfied with the mere reiteration of the naive viewpoint. For philosophy compels even its opponents to accept some if not all of its spirit. Thus, the anti-philosophical defense of the *ta-amai ha-mitzvoth* produced in the course of time a quasi-philosophical super-Orthodoxy, which is enshrined in the literature of *Kabbalah*. The logic of *Kabbalah* consists in a polar blend of the personalistic thinking of naive piety and the mechanistic thinking of rationalistic philosophy.

As a result, the Kabbalistic *ta-amai ha-mitzvoth* assume an automatic effect of the commandments upon the soul, but not in universal terms. Also, the commandments are related to cosmic forces, but not with the view of relating them to universal values. Every *mitzvah* is thought of as a chain descending from the spiritual world, bringing down holiness and achieving "unity" and bliss in the world, redeeming it from the power of evil—yes, redeeming even the Divine in the world, so that Israel Baal Shem Tov could even dare to interpret the phrase, "the Lord is your shadow," as meaning that the Deity is affected automatically and made to respond mechanically to our actions and intentions even as a shadow reflects the motion of a body. On the other hand, every sin is compared to a chain linking this world to the manifold worlds of uncleanliness, so that the sinner becomes chained and bound by his sin, even as the Hebrew word *assur*, meaning prohibited, also signified being "bound"—bound, that is, to the Satanic forces of evil.

The three systems of "reasons for the commandments" were not always kept rigidly apart, for it is a rare thinker who dares to be thoroughly honest and mercilessly self-critical. Jewish pietistic literature is particularly noted for its multifarious eclecticism. Also, the mystical current of piety, motivated by the urge of seeking the "nearness of the Lord," is oftentimes added to all of the three fundamental world-views in Judaism, making the process of analysis that much more difficult.

Indeed, one of the deeply rooted errors in Jewish historiography is the bland identification of mysticism with Kabbalah and the consequent failure to recognize the distinction between the several types of mysticism corresponding to the three fundamental patterns of Jewish piety. Nevertheless, upon analysis, the three systems of *ta-amai ha-mitzvoth* become easily distinguishable.

PHILOSOPHICAL PIETY

With this analysis in mind, it appears clearly that we today cannot accept either the naive type of philosophy of halachah or the Kabbalistic type. Only the current of philosophical piety, which relates the *mitzvoth* to the universal ends of the spiritual life, offers an approach adequate to our minds. This current, which was by no means confined to the technical literature of Jewish philosophy, always reflected Judaism at its best and at its noblest. The remark attributed to Aristotle that "all Jews are philosophers" does contain a grain of truth, since the impact of Judaism upon the cultural atmosphere of every age was almost always due to the tenacious conviction inherent in it of the supremacy and the ultimate triumph of the values of the spirit—a conviction which is of the essence of the philosophical mood.

To us, then, the laws of Judaism are disciplines and standards accepted for the sake of universal, spiritual ends. To be sure, even the most rarefied expression of philosophical piety was found in the past dogmatic elements. Thus, Maimonides exempted Moses from the general category of inspired thinkers, allowing for him a far greater measure of authority than his philosophy permitted. He also maintained that certain dogmatic beliefs, that were not true, were nevertheless to be accepted in order to avoid shocking the masses and disrupting the unity of the community. While we may readily concur in Maimonides' estimate of the value of dogma and uniform practice for the community of his day, we cannot but assert the obvious truth that in our day insistence on dogma and uniform practice could not possibly serve the cause of unity. In our age, such insistence could serve in fact only as a disruptive force, since only a fraction of our people subscribe to the totality of Jewish law.

If we remove from the philosophical pattern of Jewish piety the dogmatic elements which were never essential to it, we have a conception of Jewish law which is completely capable of meeting the challenge of our times. The builders of classical Reform sought consciously to build upon the foundations of what they termed "prophetic Judaism," thereby echoing a concept that was derived from the Christian reading of Jewish history. While this concept inspired the magnificent careers of some outstanding personalities, it could not serve as the basis for an enduring faith. The emphasis implicit in it could in fact only contribute to the trend of self-effacement, disintegration and dissolution, thereby making the claim of Christianity to be the rightful heir of prophetic Judaism appear to be incontrovertible. By contrast, philosophical Judaism is not individualistic, sentimental, vague and other worldly; it is sober, well-balanced, thoroughly grounded in the realm of eternal truth and eminently capable of translating the vital essence of Judaism into the realities of our time.

Viewing halachah as a set of standards and disciplines, we conceive of it as a vertical series, a ladder of Jacob, consisting of many rungs that lead from the earthly to the heavenly. There is ample precedent in traditional thought for this conception of multiple rungs in piety. Indeed, a better view still is to think of a threefold ladder, corresponding to the three pillars of the faith: Torah, worship and good deeds. Thus, it is possible to climb high on one ladder, while remaining on the lower rungs of the other ladders. This conception stands in clear contrast to the rigid uniformity of law, in the orthodox sense, that may be compared to a horizontal bridge, in which any breach is fatal. Thus, in halachah conceived as law, one is classed as a heretic if he defies any one precept consistently and consciously, even if he scrupulously observes every other commandment. In this view, compromise and adjustment could only be sponsored by the guile of the opportunist or the despair of the pietist.

On the other hand, our conception of a series of vertical standards permits us to regard all Jewish groups, seeking sincerely to elevate the level of spiritual life, as falling within the pattern of one common endeavor. No longer need the transgressor of one commandment look upon himself as living outside halachah, so that he no longer has any reason to cling to the rest of the commandments. It becomes possible to recognize the unity of the goal and the relative unity of the pathway, even while taking into account realistically the actual diversity in the standards accepted by different groups and individuals within the several groups. At the same time, this recognition is not a sterile formula intended to smooth the path of practical statesmanship; on the contrary, it is the one conception that makes possible a sustained endeavor in behalf of the continuous and steady raising of standards in Jewish life.

Realizing the vast gulf between halachah and the practices of the people, we may still reject the extremes of desperate Orthodoxy and wholesale repudiation and instead proceed to outline a series of standards that, given maximum effort, could become the accepted practice of our people. Then, we could look forward to a gradual and progressive lifting of standards and their extension to ever wider sections of our people. This could be done without presuming to change the Law save by the implication that the items not included in the program are regarded as non-essential.

The law, taken in its own terms, cannot be changed—leastwise by us. It is possible to speculate on eventual developments in Israel as resulting in sundry modifications, but, we, the writer and the readers of this essay, can no more change the law than we can change anything that belongs to the past. For, in its literal fulness, halachah is not to us a binding Divine imperative. The law could only be changed by people who truly live in it and by it—and it is a moot question, whether or not the inherent logic of being Torah-true permits change. In any event, while we certainly cannot think in terms of altering the law, we can and should reevaluate the law as consisting of standards of piety, of relative contemporary value and urgency. Selecting those of primary importance, we should consider them as the first step on the ladder of Judaism and bend all our efforts for their acceptance by as broad a section of our people as possible. Technically, this policy of setting minimal standards to meet contemporary realities may be expressed in halachic terms as *a ruling required by the time*. As our success grows, it may be possible to set a higher rung as the next immediate goal. In this way, we shall be making fruitful in our day the profound insights which underlie the structure of halachah.

Essentially, the question before us is whether to maintain the steadily disintegrating outer shell of halachah, or to permit its vital seed to produce nourishing fruits in our day. If we think of halachah as legislated standards and then consider the widening gulf between halachah and life, we cannot but be moved to undertake to bridge the gulf by setting standards for our people, which they might accept and which truly contain *ma-or sheba-ya-hadut,* the light which leads steadily upward.

C. ABRAHAM JOSHUA HESCHEL
(1907–72)

The other trained philosopher in the group of Conservative theorists in the mid-twentieth century was Abraham Joshua Heschel. Raised in a strongly rooted ḥasidic home and steeped in that tradition, he nevertheless completed a Ph.D. in philosophy at the University of Berlin, and his life and thought thereafer combined both worlds.

For several reasons, however, Heschel is rarely thought of as a philosopher. First, the philosophy he himself espoused was phenomenology, an approach that had some following on the European Continent in his time but very little popularity in North American philosophical circles. On the contrary, the dominant Anglo-American philosophical strain then was linguistic analysis, with a focus on the meaning of words to elucidate the meaning of the concepts underlying them, and there was a sense among such philosophers of intellectual, almost scientific, rigor. From that perspective Heschel's phenomenology seemed to be not philosophy at all, but poetry, and, truthfully, that is how it was perceived by the few philosophers of the time that read Heschel's writing. This was reconfirmed in their minds by Heschel's repeated references to the ineffable and mysterious, precisely at the time that philosophers were seeking to articulate as much as possible in words and thereby gain truth and clarity.

That view of his work is abetted by the very style Heschel used, which is much more suggestive and allusive than descriptive and precise. As Rabbi Chaim Weiner once told me, "The best way to read a lot of Heschel is not to," but instead to read one paragraph per day and let it carry you to whatever thoughts it prompts. That, indeed, is the way that many of Heschel's staunchest supporters find meaning in his work, very much like the way one reads a poem. The criterion of success is then not precision or systematics, but rather the extent to which the poem—or, in Heschel's case, the phrase, sentence, or paragraph—captures an important part of human experience, without regard to how the poem relates to anything else. The sheer popularity of his books suggests that many people have found that to be a meaningful way of reading Heschel.

Finally, during his lifetime Heschel was much more renowned as a rabbinic social activist than as a thinker. Heschel was possibly the most influential Jew in prompting the Second Vatican Council to adopt *Nostra Aetate,* a document that completely rewrote Catholicism's approach to Jews and Judaism. On the basis of that document, the Church, especially under Pope John Paul II, has gone very far in recognizing and honoring Judaism, the Jewish people, and the State of Israel, in admitting guilt for what the Church did and failed to do during the Holocaust, and in agreeing not to missionize among Jews.[56] Heschel's leadership in laying the groundwork for all of that through *Nostra Aetate* was nothing short of remarkable. He was also active in the civil rights movement, most dramatically when he marched alongside Martin Luther King in Selma in 1965 to protest segregation there. Along with Father Barrigan, he took an early and courageous lead in opposing the United States' involvement in the Vietnam War. His significant contributions to interfaith work, to civil rights, and to opposition to the Vietnam War have made him justly famous to many who have never read a word of his writings. Conversely, though, for many of his admirers his activities in these areas have almost obscured his writings, and that too has served to undermine his reputation as a serious theorist.

This conception of Heschel that strips away his philosophical import is, I think, both unwarranted and unfortunate. I acknowledge that Heschel's aphoristic language often makes it hard to analyze his work philosophically, for one is sometimes not sure how literally he means some of the things that he says. To make philosophic sense of him is particularly hard when what he says in evocative language in one place seems to contradict what he says in other places. One clear example of that is my own struggle to discern whether Heschel means to say that God revealed His will in distinct Hebrew words (which Heschel says in strong language in some places), or whether Heschel instead held that the Torah is a human *midrash* on the encounter with God (as he equally strongly says in other places).[57] In fact, in the first edition of my book (1977), *Conservative Judaism: Our Ancestors to Our Descendants*, I classified him as "Conservative I," together with other Conservative thinkers who believe in verbal revelation. But by the time I wrote the second edition (1996), Neil Gillman had convinced me that Heschel belonged better in "Conservative III," where the Torah is a human articulation of our experiences with God. Despite such difficulties—which, to be fair, can be found in examining some other philosophers as well—in my own teaching and writing I have done my best to articulate and evaluate Heschel's claims in standard philosophical form, and I am convinced that that can and should be done, that Heschel's approach to Judaism in general and to Jewish law in particular can and should be taken as a serious, philosophical set of claims.

So, then, what is Heschel's theory of Jewish law? On the very first page of his theology of Judaism, *God in Search of Man*, he maintains that there are three ways to reach God: through nature, revelation, and deeds. The book is then divided into three sections, in which he explores each of those three avenues to God. Of them, he maintains that the last, finding God in action, is the most important. In that book and in the essay that follows, he asserts that the Jewish way to God "is not a way of ascending the ladder of speculation . . . Our understanding comes by the way of *mitzvah*. By living as Jews we attain our faith as Jews. We do not have faith in deeds; we attain faith through deeds." That is, unlike Western thought, Judaism would not have us seek the true and the good through thinking about these abstract concepts or even through checking our hypotheses against experience in the scientific mode; instead, we must follow the commandments, and through them we will come to know God, the true, and the good. Accordingly, in a famous phrase in his book and in this essay, Heschel maintains that "[a] Jew is asked to take a *leap of action* rather than a *leap of thought*." That is, Jews are not asked to presume definitions and axioms, in the mode of deductive systems like geometry; they are instead asked to accept the commandments as the foundation of their view of life and infer from performance of the commandments the nature of God and thus of the true and the good. In this Heschel is echoing the oft-repeated talmudic doctrine, *mitokh shelo lishma ba lishma*, that one who obeys a commandment not for its own sake will ultimately come to fulfill it for its own sake.[58]

Heschel calls this "the ecstasy of deeds." The word "ecstasy" may call to mind someone in a trance, perhaps an exuberant one, but that is not what Heschel had in mind. He instead was referring to the etymo-logical origins of the word: *ec,* a form of *ex,* means "out of," and *sta* comes from the Latin meaning "to stand." Thus Jews are asked to "stand outside themselves," as it were, to try to look at the world not from their own, egocentric vantage point, but from God's point of view. God's commandments can enable us to do that.

> A Jew is asked to surpass his needs, to do more than he understands in order to understand more than he does. In carrying out the word of the Torah he is ushered into the presence of spiritual meaning. Through the ecstasy of deeds he learns to be certain of the presence of God.

Thus in his book Heschel tweaks the Orthodox who engage in "re-ligious behaviorism"—that is, those who think that the only important thing is to fulfill the commandments in all their detail and ignore all the while the spiritual goals of doing so. If one obeys the commandments mechanically, without the conscious intention of interacting with God, then one has lost the whole point of doing the commandments in the first place.

At the same time, in the essay reprinted below, addressed originally to Reform rabbis, he strongly asserts the necessity for maintaining the letter of the law, the routine, as well as its spirit. That is because "rou-tine breeds attention, calling forth a response where the soul would otherwise remain dormant." That is, without a regimen of required practice, we would quite possibly go through life without ever noticing the spiritual component of our existence or acting on it. Rituals and prayers required at specific times force us to stop and take notice of the moment and mark it. "Spirit is not something we can acquire once and for all but something we must constantly live and pray for." Indeed, when we want to pray, "who is able to extemporize a prayer without falling into the trap of cliches?" We need the set liturgy to give us words with which to express ourselves when we want to; the liturgy makes our dumb mouths sing.

In all parts of life, Judaism is not a state of the soul, a feeling, or in-wardness alone; it is "*an answer* to Him who is asking us to live in a cer-tain way. *It is in its very origin a consciousness of duty* . . ." We can only fulfill our duties to God and to our fellow human beings if we have the law to define how to do so. Just as we cannot know what we truly be-lieve unless we attempt to articulate our convictions, we similarly cannot be pious without expressing that piety in concrete forms governed by Jewish law. Thus we need "a unity of *faith* and *creed,* of *piety* and *ha-*

lachah, of *devotion* and *deed.*" Furthermore, those deeds may not be reserved for the occasional, peak moments alone; they must inform and penetrate the entirety of our lives, including both the most intimate aspects of it and also the public parts. Thus, contrary to the classical Reform movement's emphasis on ethics, Heschel pointedly tells his audience of Reform rabbis that "Jewish tradition maintains that there is no exterritoriality in the realm of the spirit. Economics, politics, dietetics [that is, the dietary laws], are just as much as ethics within its sphere." He is convinced that the good cannot exist without the holy, and so the Sabbath and other rituals through which Judaism separates the holy from the secular are critical aspects of cultivating a Jewish spirit.

On the other hand, we must never think of Jewish laws governing diet, the life cycle, and the seasons as merely "rituals, customs, and ceremonies," for that reduces them to mere manners. Instead, for us to be authentic to the Jewish tradition, we must perform those acts with inner devotion, *kavanah,* treating them as the Jewish tradition did, as *mitzvot,* as acts commanded by God and as our responses to God.

> Ceremonies, whether in the form of things or in the form of actions, are required by custom and convention; *mitzvoth* are required by Torah. Ceremonies are relevant to man; *mitzvoth* are relevant to God. Ceremonies are folkways; *mitzvoth* are ways to God. Ceremonies are expressions of the human mind . . . *Mitzvoth,* on the other hand, are expressions or interpretations of the will of God.

Finally, *mitzvot* are not just a human attempt to reach God; they are equally God's attempt to reach human beings. The very title of Heschel's book, *God in Search of Man,* expresses this important theme in Heschel's thought: God reaches out to us just as much, if not more, than we reach out to God. The *mitzvot* are one central way in which God does that, and obeying them is thus a critical way of ensuring that we do not make ourselves the measure of all things, but rather open our hearts, minds, and bodies to God.

Heschel's theory, like everyone else's, has its strengths and weaknesses. On the negative side, while he makes a strong case for intertwining law and theology—indeed, law with the whole of life—he never describes how this should be done. Because he himself never wrote a rabbinic ruling, we cannot discern his legal methodology from his own work, and he does not describe his proposed process in general terms either. Who should define how *halakhah* and *aggadah* are to be integrated in deciding any legal issue? How should that person or persons do that? Heschel is silent about the actual process of making legal decisions.

For Heschel, observing Jewish law came naturally, as a product of his own rich Jewish upbringing. That is not true for most Jews today, and so they may be understandably quite leery about taking a leap of action into a life of Jewish observance. Heschel's book *Man's Quest for God*, for example, describes his theology of prayer. This is all well and good for someone who knows Hebrew and is familiar with the traditional prayers, but how can he plausibly expect someone who does not read Hebrew to sit through three hours of a Shabbat morning service without understanding a thing and then return the next week, as part of a leap of action? Even those who read Hebrew may well find that the pace is too fast and the liturgy too expansive to commit to a life of traditional prayer. In a wonderfully descriptive phrase, Heschel describes the biblical prophets as "one octave too high" in that they demand moral perfection with little patience for human failings;[59] in demanding a leap of action into the universe of *mitzvot* Heschel himself may be an octave too high. The more popular phrase among mid-twentieth century Conservative thinkers may be more realistic and apt: one should think of a ladder of *mitzvot* that one climbs as best one can.

Furthermore, if someone tries a life of *mitzvot* and fails to connect with God in the process, why, according to Heschel, should that Jew continue to obey the commandments? Surely those in our tradition who advocated justifying obedience to the commandments for a variety of reasons *(ta'amei hamitzvot)* were wiser, for then if a given rationale fails to motivate someone to fulfill the commandments, perhaps one or more of the other justifications will work.

Along the same lines, Heschel's demand that Jews observe the commandments with the intention of reaching out to God and letting God reach us is certainly ideal, but that is a standard that few can reach very often—certainly not every day of their lives. What would that mean, then, for the life of a community? Could communal prayer—or observance of Shabbat, for that matter—ever satisfy the requirements of the law, given that a substantial proportion of the group at any given time undoubtedly falls short of reaching those spiritual goals? The Rabbis of the Talmud were wiser: they demanded *kavanah* for only a few lines of the liturgy,[60] for they knew that to interpret Jewish law to require more would mean that few people would ever fulfill the law.

In fact, Heschel's leap of action poses the reverse problem—namely, that people would leap from observing nothing into a version of fundamentalism. That, as we know, is all too common among *ba'alei teshuvah*, who sometimes not only take on everything at once, but also look down their noses at those who do not do exactly as they do. Heschel clearly does not want this, but in advocating a leap of action this result is all too likely. One clearly needs to balance one's new halakhic commitments with a sense of reason, process, and proportion—hardly the approach denoted by the language of a "leap" of action. A leap is especially dangerous in Heschel's thought, given that in this essay and elsewhere he completely separates Jewish law from ethics in order to make Jewish law a binding commandment of God rather than a moral demand flowing from human reasoning. One hears echoes of the problems evoked in the Torah's story of the binding of Isaac: Abraham was faithful, but was he morally right in obeying God's command rather than questioning it on moral grounds, as he had done earlier in arguing against the destruction of Sodom?

Conversely, Heschel maintains that we find God through our leap of action into a life of *mitzvot*. What would he say, though, to those who claim that they find God in ways that do not involve Jewish law— through playing the piano, for example, or surfing, or through close, personal relationships (*a la* Buber)—or even in ways that involve one or more violations of Jewish law, such as participating in the building of a house for a homeless family on Shabbat? In other words, how necessary is it to use Jewish law to find God? Is it only one way among many, or is it the best way, or maybe even the only way? If the latter, why is that so?

Furthermore, Heschel's theory depends heavily on his assumptions, just as every theory depends on the assumptions of its formulator(s). In Heschel's case, because he conceives of Jewish law as our reaching out to God and God's reaching out to us, one must believe in God in the first place. While he tries to demonstrate why we should believe in God in his 1951 book, *Man Is Not Alone,* by his 1955 book, *God in Search of Man,* he apparently changed his theory and classified the belief in God as "an ontological presupposition"—that is, an axiom that one must presuppose about the nature of being. Heschel's theory, then, requires not only a leap of action, as he says it does, but a leap of faith as well. The former may indeed prepare one to take the latter—action can lead to convictions—but ultimately Heschel himself takes a leap of faith as well. For those who are not willing to make both leaps, Heschel's theory, of course, is unavailing.

Even those who do believe in God may have difficulty swallowing the *mitzvot* as a whole, or any one of them in particular, as the will of God. If indeed, as Heschel says, the Torah is a human *midrash*, then how do we know that what it records is indeed the will of God? And how much the more so far all of the rabbinic developments of the law after the Torah was completed? And even if we think that the Torah articulated the will of God in its time, how do we know what the will of

God is for us in our time? Heschel himself made special arrangements for the bat mitzvah ceremony for his daughter, and so he clearly was not committed to, say, the *halakhah* as found in Shulḥan Arukh alone, but then how *do* we know that God now wants women to participate in public worship in ways that they did not before?

This problem produces yet another allied one: If the Torah is a human *midrash,* what is its basis of authority in the first place? In the essay that follows, he admonishes the Reform rabbis in his audience to recognize that the law must be based in the vertical history of the generations, and so clearly there is a historical and communal component in the law's authority, but he seems to want to say that, unlike Kaplan, the ultimate authority of the law is that it is our commanded response to God. But how do we know that we are doing God's will, if the text that announces that is itself a human document?

Some of this incompleteness and ambiguity, of course, is a function of the style in which Heschel wrote. One must say honestly that what his style gains in emotional power comes at considerable philosophical cost. Had Heschel written in a more descriptive, philosophical style, he might have recognized these questions and sought to answer them.

With all that said, Heschel presents us with some keen insights into the nature of Jewish law. It is, after all, one important way, and perhaps even the primary way, in which the classical Jewish tradition seeks to bring us into contact with God and God into contact with us. To fulfill the requirements of Jewish law does, as he says, at least ideally require us to pay attention to *both* its body and its spirit: religious behaviorism will not do if one is going to be both authentic to the tradition and also responsive to the God who commands. Conversely, religious spiritualism devoid of halakhic observance will also not do, for, ultimately, we are embodied persons who need to awaken our spirit through fixed regimens of practice. Moreover, his distinction between "rituals, customs, and ceremonies" and the *mitzvot* that we might classify as rituals is telling. It is indeed a theological error to describe the dietary laws, Shabbat, and the like as rituals rather than *mitzvot,* for the Jewish tradition certainly sees them not as inventions and conventions of human beings but rather as the commands of God. As much as I have difficulty with Heschel's separation of Jewish law from ethics, he certainly is right in asserting that the meaning of Jewish law is not only moral, but theological as well. And finally, Heschel is certainly right in suggesting that at its best, Jewish law can function to enable Jews to stand outside of themselves and their immediate concerns, so that they can see and value the world as God does and even find their way to God as God finds His way to us.

Toward an Understanding of Halachah*

ABRAHAM J. HESCHEL

BEYOND SYMBOLS

I came with great hunger to the University of Berlin to study philosophy. I looked for a system of thought, for the depth of the spirit, for the meaning of existence. Erudite and profound scholars gave courses in logic, epistemology, esthetics, ethics and metaphysics. They opened the gates of the history of philosophy. I was exposed to the austere discipline of unremitting inquiry and self-criticism. I communed with the thinkers of the past who knew how to meet intellectual adversity with fortitude, and learned to dedicate myself to the examination of basic premises at the risk of failure.

What were the trends of thought to which I was exposed at the university?

Kant, who held dominion over many minds, had demonstrated that it is utterly impossible to attain knowledge of the world . . . because knowledge is always in the form of categories and these, in the last analysis, are only representational constructions for the purpose of apperceiving what is given. Objects possessing attributes, causes that work, are all mythical. We can only say that objective phenomena are regarded as if they behaved in such and such a way, and there is absolutely no justification for assuming any dogmatic attitude and changing the "as if" into a "that." Salomon Maimon was probably the first to sum up Kantian philosophy by saying that only symbolic *knowledge* is possible.

In the light of such a theory, what is the status of religious knowledge? We must, of course, *give up* hope of ever attaining a valid concept of the supernatural in an objective sense, yet since for practical reasons it is useful to cherish the idea of God, let us retain that idea and claim that while our knowledge of God is not objectively true, it is still *symbolically* true.

Thus, symbolism became the supreme category in understanding religious truth. It has become a truism that religion is largely an affair of symbols. Translated into simpler terms this view regards religion as a *fiction*, useful to society or to man's personal well-being. Religion is not a relationship of man to God but a relationship of man to the sym-

*The Yearbook of the Central Conference of American Rabbis, Vol. 63 (1953), pp. 386–409.

bol of his highest ideals. There is no God, but we must go on worshipping his symbol.

The idea of symbolism is, of course, not a modern invention. New is the role it has now assumed. In earlier times, symbolism was regarded as a form of *religious thinking;* in modern times religion is regarded as a form of *symbolic thinking.*

It was at an early phase of my studies at the university that I came to realize: *If God is a symbol, He is a fiction.* But if God is *real,* then He is able to express His will unambiguously. Symbols are makeshifts, necessary to those who cannot express themselves unambiguously.

There is darkness in the world and horror in the soul. What is it that the world needs most? Harsh and bitter are the problems which religion comes to solve: ignorance, evil, malice, power, agony, despair. These problems cannot be solved through generalities, through philosophical symbols. Our problem is: Do we believe what we confess? Do we mean what we say?

We do not suffer symbolically. We suffer literally, truly, deeply. Symbolic remedies are quackery. The will of God is either real or a delusion.

This was the most important challenge to me: "We have eyes to see but see not; we have ears to hear but hear not." Any other issue was relevant only in so far as it helped me to answer that challenge.

I became increasingly aware of the gulf that separated my views from those held at the university. I had come with a sense of anxiety: how can I rationally find a way where ultimate meaning lies, a way of living where one would never miss a reference to supreme significance? Why am I here at all, and what is my purpose? I did not even know how to phrase my concern. But to my teachers that was a question unworthy of philosophical analysis.

I realized: my teachers were prisoners of a Greek-German way of thinking. They were fettered in categories which presupposed certain metaphysical assumptions which could never be proved. The questions I was moved by could not even be adequately phrased in categories of their thinking.

My assumption was: man's dignity consists in his having been created in the likeness of God. My question was: how must man, a being who is in essence the image of God, think, feel and act? To them, religion was a feeling. To me, religion included the insights of the Torah, which is a vision of man from the point of view of God. They spoke of God from the point of view of man. To them God was an idea, a postulate of reason. They granted Him the status of being a logical possibility. But to assume that He had existence would have been a crime against epistemology.

The problem to my professors was how to be good. In my ears the question rang: how to be holy. At the time I realized: There is much that philosophy could learn from Jewish life. To the philosophers the idea of the good was the most exalted idea, the ultimate idea. To Judaism the idea of the good is penultimate. It cannot exist without the holy. The good is the base, the holy is the summit. Man cannot be good unless he strives to be holy.

To have an idea of the good is not the same as living by the insight. "Blessed is the man who does not forget Thee."

I did not come to the university because I did not know the idea of the good, but to learn why the idea of the good is valid, why and whether values had meaning. Yet I discovered that values sweet to taste proved sour in analysis; the prototypes were firm, the models flabby. Must speculation and existence remain like two infinite parallel lines that never meet? Or perhaps this impossibility of juncture is the result of the fact that our speculation suffers from what is called in astronomy a parallax, from the apparent displacement of the object, caused by the actual change of point of observation?

THE URGE TO PRAY

In those months in Berlin I went through moments of profound bitterness. I felt very much alone with my own problems and anxieties. I walked alone in the evenings through the magnificent streets of Berlin. I admired the solidity of its architecture, the overwhelming drive and power of a dynamic civilization. There were concerts, theatres, and lectures by famous scholars about the latest theories and inventions, and I was pondering whether to go to the new Max Reinhardt play or to a lecture about the theory of relativity. Suddenly I noticed the sun had gone down, evening had arrived.

"When should the Shema be read in the evenings . . ."

(Berachot 2a)

I had forgotten God—I had forgotten Sinai—I had forgotten that sunset is my business—that my task is "to perfect the world under the kingdom of the Almighty."

So I began to utter the words "who by His word brings forth the evening twilight."

And Goethe's famous poem rang in my ear:

Ueber allen Gipfeln ist Ruh
O'er all the hilltops is quiet now.

No, that was pagan thinking. To the pagan eye the mystery of life is *Ruh*, death, oblivion. To us Jews, there is meaning beyond the mystery. We would say

Uber allen Gipfeln ist Gottes Wort.
O'er all the hilltops is the word of God.

The meaning of life is to do His will . . .

By His word cometh evening twilight

And His love is manifested in His teaching us Torah, precepts, laws.

Ueber allen Gipfeln is God's love for man—
"With everlasting love hast Thou loved thy people Israel
Torah, commandments, ordinances and judgments hast Thou
taught us."

How much guidance, how many ultimate insights are found in the
Siddur.

How grateful I am to God that there is a duty to worship, a law to
remind my distraught mind that it is time to think of God, time to disregard my ego for at least a moment! It is such happiness to belong to
an order of the divine will.

I am not always in a mood to pray. I do not always have the vision and the strength to say a word in the presence of God. But when I
am weak, it is the law that gives me strength; when my vision is dim, it
is duty that gives me insight.

Indeed, there is something which is far greater than my desire to
pray. Namely, God's desire that I pray. There is something which is far
greater than my will to believe. Namely, God's will that I believe. How
insignificant is my praying in the midst of a cosmic process! Unless it is
the will of God that I pray, how ludicrous it is to pray.

On that evening, in the streets of Berlin, I was not in a mood to
pray. My heart was heavy, my soul was sad. It was difficult for the
lofty words of prayer to break through the dark clouds of my inner
life.

But how would I dare not to *davn?* How would I dare to miss an
evening prayer? *Me-ematay korin et Shma.* "Out of *emah,* out of fear
of God, do we read the *Shma.*"

The following morning I awoke in my student garret. Now, the
magnificent achievements in the field of physiology and psychology
have, of course, not diminished, but rather increased my sense of wonder for the human body and soul. And so I prayed

"Thou has fashioned man in wisdom."
"Lord, the soul which thou hast given me is pure."

Yet how am I going to keep my soul clean?

The most important problem which a human being must face
daily is: How to maintain one's integrity in a world where power, success and money are valued above all else? How to remain clean amidst
the mud of falsehood and malice that soil our society?

The soul is clean, but within it resides a power for evil, "a strange
god,"[1] that seeks constantly to get the upper hand over man and to kill
him; and if God did not help him, he could not resist it, as it is said,
"the wicked watches the righteous, and seeks to slay him."[2]

Every morning I take a piece of cloth—neither elegant nor solemn,
of no particular esthetic beauty, a *talit,* wrap myself in it and say:

"How precious is Thy kindness, O God! The children of man take
refuge in the shadow of Thy wings. They have their fill of the choice
food of Thy house, and Thou givest them drink of Thy stream of delights. For with Thee is the fountain of life; by Thy light do we see

light. Continue Thy kindness to those who know Thee, and Thy righteousness to the upright in heart."

But, then, I ask myself: Have I got a right to take my refuge in
Him? to drink of the stream of His delights? to expect Him to continue His kindness? But God wants me to be close to Him, even to
bind every morning His word as a sign on my hand, and between my
eyes, winding the strap three times round the middle finger. I would remind myself of the word that God spoke to *me* through His prophet
Hosea:

> "I will betroth you to myself forever; I will betroth you to
> myself in righteousness and in justice, in kindness and in
> mercy. I will betroth you to myself in faithfulness; and you
> shall know the Lord." It is an act of betrothal, a promise to
> marry . . . It is an act of God, falling in love with His people.
> But the engagement depends on righteousness, justice, kind-
> ness, mercy.

THE DANGERS

Why did I decide to take *halachah* seriously in spite of the numerous
perplexities in which I became enmeshed?

Why did I pray, although I was not in a mood to pray? And why
was I able to pray in spite of being unprepared to pray? What was my
situation after the reminder to pray *Maariv* struck my mind? The duty
to worship stood as a thought of ineffable meaning; doubt, the voice
of disbelief, was ready to challenge it. But where should the engagement take place? In an act of reflection the duty to worship is a mere
thought, timid, frail, a mere shadow of reality, while the voice of disbelief is a power, well-armed with the weight of inertia and the preference for abstention. In such an engagement prayer would be fought in
absentia, and the issue would be decided without actually joining the
battle. It was fair, therefore, to give the weaker rival a chance: to pray
first, to fight later.

I realized that just as you cannot study philosophy through praying, you cannot study prayer through philosophizing. And what applies to prayer is true in regard to the essentials of Jewish observance.

What I wanted to avoid was not only the failure to pray to God
during a whole evening of my life but *the loss of the whole,* the loss of
belonging to the spiritual order of Jewish living. It is true that some
people are so busy with collecting shreds and patches of the law, that
they hardly think of weaving the pattern of the whole. But there is also
the danger of being so enchanted by the whole as to lose sight of the detail. It became increasingly clear to me that the order of Jewish living is
meant to be, not a set of rituals, but an order of all of man's existence,
shaping all his traits, interests and dispositions; "not so much the performance of single acts, the taking of a step now and then, as the pursuit of a way, being on the way; not so much the acts of fulfilling as the
state of being committed to the task, the belonging to an order in which

single deeds, aggregates of religious feeling, sporadic sentiments, moral episodes become a part of a complete pattern." (270)[3]

The ineffable Name, we have forgotten how to pronounce it. We have almost forgotten how to spell it. We may totally forget how to recognize it.

There are a number of ideas concerning Jewish law which have proved most inimical to its survival, and I would like to refer to two. First is the assumption that either you observe all or nothing; all of its rules are of equal importance; and if one brick is removed, the whole edifice must collapse. Such intransigence, laudable as it may be as an expression of devoutness, is neither historically nor theologically justified. There were ages in Jewish history when some aspects of Jewish ritual observance were not adhered to by people who had otherwise lived according to the law. And where is the man who could claim that he has been able to fulfill literally the *mitzvah* of "Love your neighbor as yourself"?

Where is the worry about the spiritual inadequacy of that which admittedly should not be abandoned? Where is our anxiety about the barrenness of our praying, the conventionality of our ceremonialism?

The problem, then, that cries for a solution is not: everything or nothing, total or partial obedience to the law; the problem is authentic or forged, genuine or artificial observance. The problem is not *how much* but *how to* observe. The problem is whether we *obey* or whether we merely *play* with the word of God.

Second is the assumption that every iota of the law was revealed to Moses at Sinai. This is an unwarranted extension of the rabbinic concept of revelation. "Could Moses have learned the whole Torah? Of the Torah it says, *The measure thereof is longer than the earth, and broader than the sea* (Job 11:9); could then Moses have learned it in forty days? No, it was only the principles thereof which God taught Moses."[4]

The role of the sages in interpreting the word of the Bible and their power to issue new ordinances is a basic element of Jewish belief and something for which our sages found sanction in Deuteronomy 17:11. The awareness of the expanding nature of Jewish law was expressed by such a great saint and authority as Rabbi Isaiah Horovitz in his *Shenai Luhot Ha-b'rit* [on that verse]:

"And now I will explain the phenomenon that in every generation the number of restrictions [in the *halachah*] is increased. In the time of Moses, only what he had explicitly received at Sinai (the written law) was binding, plus several ordinances which he added for whatever reasons he saw fit. [However] the prophets, the Tannaim, and the rabbis of every generation [have continued to multiply these restrictions]. The reason is, that as the venom of the serpent spreads, greater protection is needed. The Holy One provided for us three hundred and sixty-five prohibitions in order to prevent the venom from becoming too active. Therefore, whenever the venom of a generation grows virulent, more restrictions must be imposed. Had this [the spread of venom] been the situation at the time of the giving of the Torah, [those interdictions] would have been specifically included in it. However instead, the later ordinances derive their authority from God's command—'make a protection for the law'—which means 'make necessary ordinances according to the state of each generation' and these have the same authority as the Torah itself."

There are times in Jewish history when the main issue is not what parts of the *halachah* cannot be fulfilled but what parts of the *halachah* can be and ought to be fulfilled, fulfilled as *halachah,* as an expression and interpretation of the will of God.

There are many problems which we encounter in our reflections on the issue of Jewish observance. I wish to discuss briefly several of these problems, namely: the relation of observance to our understanding of the will of God; the meaning of observance to man; the regularity of worship; inwardness and the essence of religion; the relevance of the external deeds.

THE MEANING OF OBSERVANCE

From a rationalist's point of view it does not seem plausible to assume that the infinite, ultimate supreme Being is concerned with my putting on *tefillin* every day. It is, indeed, strange to believe that God should care whether a particular individual will eat leavened or un-leavened bread during a particular season of the year. However, it is that paradox, namely that the infinite God is intimately concerned with finite man and his finite deeds; that nothing is trite or irrelevant in the eyes of God, which is the very essence of the prophetic faith.

There are people who are hesitant to take seriously the possibility of our knowing what the will of God demands of us. Yet we all wholeheartedly accept Micah's words: "He has showed you, O man, what is good, and what does the Lord require of you, but to do justice, and to love kindness and to walk humbly with your God." If we believe that there is something which God requires of man, then what is our belief if not *faith in the will of God, certainty of knowing what His will demands of us?* If we are ready to believe that God requires of me "to do justice," is it more difficult for us to believe that God requires of us to be holy? If we are ready to believe that it is God who requires us "to love kindness," is it more difficult to believe that God requires us to hallow the Sabbath and not to violate its sanctity?

If it is the word of Micah uttering the will of God that we believe in, and not a peg on which to hang views we derived from rationalist philosophies, then "to love justice" is just as much *halachah* as the prohibition of making a fire on the Seventh Day. If, however, all we can hear in these words are echoes of Western philosophy rather than the voice of Micah, does that not mean that the prophet has nothing to say to any of us?

A serious difficulty is the problem of *the meaning of Jewish observance.* The modern Jew cannot accept the way of static obedience as a short-cut to the mystery of the divine will. His religious situation is not conducive to an attitude of intellectual or spiritual surrender. He is not ready to sacrifice his liberty on the altar of loyalty to the spirit of his ancestors. He will only respond to a demonstration that there is meaning to be found in what we expect him to do. His primary difficulty is not in his inability to comprehend the *Divine origin* of the law; his essential difficulty is in his inability to sense *the presence of Divine meaning* in the fulfillment of the law.

Let us never forget that some of the basic theological presuppositions of Judaism cannot be justified in terms of human reason. Its conception of the nature of man as having been created in the likeness of God, its conception of God and history, of prayer and even of morality, defy some of the realizations at which we have honestly arrived at the end of our analysis and scrutiny. The demands of piety are a mystery before which man is reduced to reverence and silence. In a technological society, when religion becomes a function, piety, too, is an instrument to satisfy his needs. We must, therefore, be particularly careful not to fall into the habit of looking at religion as if it were a machine which can be worked, an organization which can be run according to one's calculations.

The problem of how to live as a Jew cannot be solved in terms of common sense and common experience. The order of Jewish living is a spiritual one; it has a spiritual logic of its own which cannot be apprehended unless its basic terms are lived and appreciated.

It is in regard to this problem that we must keep in mind three things, a) Divine meaning is *spiritual* meaning; b) the apprehension of Divine meaning is contingent upon *spiritual preparedness*; c) it is experienced in *acts,* rather than in speculation.

a) The problem of ethics is: what is the ideal or principle of conduct that is *rationally* justifiable? While to religion the problem of living is: what is the ideal or principle of living that is *spiritually* justifiable? The legitimate question concerning the forms of Jewish observance is, therefore, the question: Are they spiritually meaningful?

We should, consequently, not evaluate the *mitzvoth* by the amount of rational meaning we may discover at their basis. Religion is not within but beyond the limits of mere reason. Its task is not to compete with reason, to be a source of speculative ideas, but to aid us where reason gives us only partial aid. Its meaning must be understood in terms *compatible with the sense of the ineffable.* Frequently where concepts fail, where rational understanding ends, the meaning of observance begins. Its purpose is not essentially to serve hygiene, happiness or the vitality of man; its purpose is to add holiness to hygiene, grandeur to happiness, spirit to vitality.

Spiritual meaning is not always limpid; transparency is the quality of glass, while diamonds are distinguished by refractive power and the play of prismatic colors.

Indeed, any reason we may advance for our loyalty to the Jewish order of living merely points to one of its many facets. To say that the *mitzvoth* have meaning is less accurate than saying that they lead us to wells of emergent meaning, to experiences which are full of hidden brilliance of the holy, suddenly blazing in our thoughts.

Those who, out of their commendable desire to save the Jewish way of life, bring its meaning under the hammer, tend to sell it at the end to the lowest bidder. The highest values are not in demand and are not saleable on the market-place. In spiritual life some experiences are like a camera *obscura,* through which light has to enter in order to form an image upon the mind, the image of ineffable intelligibility. Insistence upon explaining and relating the holy to the relative and functional is like lighting a candle in the camera.

Works of piety are like works of art. They are functional, they serve a purpose, but their essence is intrinsic; their value is in what they are in themselves.

b) Sensitivity to spiritual meaning is not easily won; it is the fruit of hard, constant devotion, of insistence upon remaining true to a vision. It is "an endless pilgrimage . . . a drive towards serving Him who rings our hearts like a bell, as if He were waiting to enter our lives . . . Its essence is not revealed in the way we utter it, but in the soul's being in accord with what is relevant to God; in the extension of our love to what God may approve, our being carried away by the tide of His thoughts, rising beyond the desolate ken of man's despair." (174)

"God's grace resounds in our lives like a staccato. Only by retaining the seemingly disconnected notes comes the ability to grasp the theme." (88)

c) What is the Jewish way to God? It is not a way of ascending the ladder of speculation. Our understanding of God is not the triumphant outcome of an assault upon the riddles of the universe nor a donation we receive in return for intellectual surrender. Our understanding comes by the way of *mitzvah.* By living as Jews we attain our faith *as* Jews. We do not have faith in deeds; we attain faith through deeds.

When Moses recounted to the people the laws of the covenant with God, the people responded: "We will do and we will hear." This statement was interpreted to mean: In *doing we perceive.*

A Jew is asked to take a *leap of action* rather than *a leap of thought:* to surpass his needs, to do more than he understands in order to understand more than he does. In carrying out the word of the Torah he is ushered into the presence of spiritual meaning. Through the ecstasy of deeds he learns to be certain of the presence of God.

Jewish law is a sacred prosody. The Divine sings in our deeds, the Divine is disclosed in our deeds. Our effort is but a counterpoint in the music of His will. In exposing our lives to God we discover the Divine within ourselves and its accord with the Divine beyond ourselves.

If at the moment of doing a *mitzvah* once perceived to be thus sublime, thus Divine, you are in it with all your heart and with all your soul, there is no great distance between you and God. For acts of holiness uttered by the soul disclose the holiness of God hidden in every moment of time. And His holiness and He are one.

WHY ROUTINE?

Why should worship be bound to regular occasions? Why impose a calendar on the soul? Is not regularity of observance a menace to the freedom of the heart?

Strict observance of a way of life at fixed times and in identical forms tends to become a matter of routine, of outward compliance. How to prevent observance from becoming stereotyped, mechanical, was, indeed, a perennial worry in the history of Judaism. The cry of the prophet: "Their heart is far from me" was a signal of alarm.

Should I reject the regularity of prayer and rely on the inspiration of the heart and only worship when I am touched by the spirit? Should I resolve: unless the spirit comes, I shall abstain from praying? The deeper truth is that routine breeds attention, calling forth a response where the soul would otherwise remain dormant. One is committed to being affected by the holy, if he abides at the threshold of its realm. Should it be left to every individual to find his own forms of worship whenever the spirit would move him? Yet who is able to extemporize a prayer without falling into the trap of cliches? Moreover, spiritual substance grows in clinging to a source of spirit richer than one's own. Inspirations are brief, sporadic and rare. In the long interims the mind is often dull, bare and vapid. There is hardly a soul that can radiate more light than it receives. To perform a *mitzvah* is to meet the spirit. But the spirit is not something we can acquire once and for all but something we must constantly live with and pray for. For this reason the Jewish way of life is to reiterate the ritual, to meet the spirit again and again, the spirit in oneself and the spirit that hovers over all beings.

At the root of our difficulties in appreciating the role of *halachah* in religious living is I believe, our conception of the very essence of religion. "We are often inclined to define the essence of religion as a state of the soul, as inwardness, as an absolute feeling, and expect a person who is religious to be endowed with a kind of sentiment too deep to rise to the surface of common deeds, as if religion were a plant that can only thrive at the bottom of the ocean. Now to Judaism religion is not a feeling for something that is, but *an answer* to Him who is asking us to live in a certain way. *It is in its very origin a consciousness of duty, of being committed to higher ends;* a realization that life is not only man's but also God's sphere of interest." (175)

"God asks for the heart." Yet does he ask for the heart only? Is the right intention enough? Some doctrines insist that love is the sole condition for salvation (the Sufis, *Bhakti-marga*), stressing the importance of inwardness, of love or faith, to the exclusion of good works.

Paul waged a passionate battle against the power of law and proclaimed instead the religion of grace. Law, he claimed, cannot conquer sin, nor can righteousness be attained through works of law. A man is justified "by faith without the deeds of the law."[5]

That salvation is attained by faith alone was Luther's central thesis. The antinomian tendency resulted in the overemphasis on love and faith to the exclusion of good works.

The Formula of Concord of 1580 condemns the statement that good works are necessary to salvation and rejects the doctrine that they are harmful to salvation. According to *Ritschl,* the doctrine of the merit of good deeds is an intruder in the domain of Christian theology;

the only way of salvation is justification by faith. Barth, following Kierkegaard, voices Lutheran thoughts, when he claims that man's deeds are too sinful to be good. There are fundamentally no human deeds, which, because of their significance in this world, find favor in God's eyes. God can be approached through God alone.

Paraphrasing the Paulinian doctrine that man is saved by faith alone, Kant and his disciples taught that the essence of religion or morality would consist in an absolute quality of the soul or the will, regardless of the actions that may come out of it or the ends that may be attained. Accordingly, the value of a religious act would be determined wholly by the intensity of one's faith or by the rectitude of one's inner disposition. The intention, not the deed, the *how*, not the *what* of one's conduct, would be essential, and no motive other than the sense of duty would be of any moral value. Thus acts of kindness, when not dictated by the sense of duty, would not be better than cruelty; while compassion or regard for human happiness as such is looked upon as an ulterior motive. "I would not break my word even to save mankind," exclaimed Fichte. As if his own salvation and righteousness were more important to him than the fate of all men. Does not such an attitude illustrate the truth of the proverb: "The road to hell is paved with good intentions"? Should we not say that a concern with one's own salvation and righteousness that outweighs the regard for the welfare of one other human being cannot be qualified as a good intention?

The crisis of ethics has its root in formalism, in the view that the essence of the good is in the good intention. Seeing how difficult it is to attain it, modern man despaired. In the name of good intentions, evil was fostered.

To us this doctrine is the essential heresy. Judaism stands and falls with the idea of the absolute relevance of human deeds. Even to God we ascribe the deed. *Imitatio dei* is in deeds. The deed is the source of holiness.

"Faith does not come to an end with attaining certainty of God's existence. Faith is the beginning of intense craving to enter an active relationship with Him who is beyond the mystery, to bring together all the might that is within us with all that is spiritual beyond us. At the root of our yearning for integrity is a stir of the inexpressible within us to commune with the ineffable beyond us. But what is the language of that communication, without which our impulse remains inarticulate?

"We are taught that what God asks of man is more than an inner attitude, that He gives man not only *life* but also *a law*, that His will is to be served not only adored, *obeyed* not only *worshipped*. Faith comes over us like a force urging to action. We respond by pledging ourselves to constancy of devotion, committing us to the presence of God. This remains a life allegiance involving restraint, submission, self-control and courage.

"Judaism insists upon establishing a unity of *faith* and *creed*, of *piety* and *halachah*, of *devotion* and *deed*. Faith is but a seed, while the deed is its growth or decay. Faith disembodied, faith that tries to grow in splendid isolation, is but a ghost, for which there is no place in our psychophysical world.

"What *creed* is in relation to *faith,* the *halachah* is in relation to *piety.* As faith cannot exist without a creed, piety cannot subsist without a pattern of deeds; as intelligence cannot be separated from training, religion cannot be divorced from conduct. Judaism is lived in deeds, not only in thoughts.

"A pattern for living—the object of our most urgent quest—which would correspond to man's ultimate dignity, must take into consideration not only his ability to exploit the forces of nature and to appreciate the loveliness of its forms, but also his unique sense of the ineffable. It must be a design, not only for the satisfaction of needs, but also for the attainment of an end," the end of being *a holy people* (175–176).

BEYOND THE HEART

The integrity of life is not exclusively a thing of the heart, and Jewish piety is therefore more than consciousness of the moral law. The innermost chamber must be guarded at the uttermost outposts. Religion is not the same as spiritualism; what man does in his concrete physical existence is directly relevant to the divine. Spirituality is the goal, not the way of man. In this world music is played on physical instruments, and to the Jew the *mitzvoth* are the instruments by which the holy is performed. If man were only mind, worship in thought would be the form in which to commune with God. But man is body and soul, and his goal is to live so that both "his heart and his flesh should sing to the living God."

Moreover, worship is not one thing, and living, another. Does Judaism consist of sporadic landmarks in the realm of living, of temples in splendid isolation, of festive celebrations on extraordinary days? The synagogue is not a retreat, and that which is decisive is not the performance of rituals at distinguished occasions, but how they affect the climate of the entire life.

The highest peak of spiritual living is not necessarily reached in rare moments of ecstasy; the highest peak lies wherever we are and may be ascended in a common deed. There can be as sublime a holiness in fulfilling friendship, in observing dietary laws, day by day, as in uttering a prayer on the Day of Atonement.

Jewish tradition maintains that there is no exterritoriality in the realm of the spirit. Economics, politics, dietetics are just as much as ethics within its sphere. It is in man's intimate rather than public life, in the way he fulfills his physiological functions that character is formed. It is immensely significant that, according to the Book of Genesis, the first prohibition given to man concerned the enjoyment of the forbidden fruit.

"The fate of a people . . . is decided according to whether they begin culture at the right place—not at the soul. The right place is the body, demeanor, diet, physiology; the rest follows . . . contempt of the body is the greatest mishap." Judaism begins at the bottom, taking very seriously the forms of one's behavior in relation to the external, even conventional functions, and amenities of life, teaching us how to eat, how to rest, how to act. The discipline of feelings and thoughts comes second. The body must be persuaded first. "Thou shalt not covet" is the last of the Ten Commandments, even though it may be the first in the case history of the aforementioned transgressions. While not prescribing a diet—vegetarian or otherwise—demanding abstinence from narcotics or stimulants, Judaism is very much concerned with what and how a person ought to eat. A sacred discipline for the body is as important as bodily strength.

In order to attain an adequate appreciation of the preciousness that the Jewish way of living is capable of bestowing upon us, we should initiate a thorough cleaning of the minds. Every one of us should be asked to make one major sacrifice: to sacrifice his prejudice against our heritage. We should strive to cultivate an atmosphere in which the values of Jewish faith and piety could be cherished, an atmosphere in which the Jewish form of living is the heartily approved or at least respected pattern, in which sensitivity to *kashruth* is not regarded as treason against the American constitution and reverence for the Sabbath is not considered conspiracy against progress.

Without solidarity with our forebears, the solidarity with our brothers will remain feeble. The vertical unity of Israel is essential to the horizontal unity of *kelal yisrael*. Identification with what is undying in Israel, the appreciation of what was supremely significant throughout the ages, the endeavor to integrate the abiding teachings and aspirations of the past into our own thinking will enable us to be creative, to expand, not to imitate or to repeat. Survival of Israel means that we carry on our independent dialogue with the past. Our way of life must remain such as would be, to some degree, intelligible to Isaiah and Rabbi Yochanan ben Zakkai, to Maimonides and the Baal Shem.

Let us be under no illusion. The task is hard. However, if it is true that the good cannot exist without the holy, what are we doing for the purpose of securing holiness in the world? Can we afford to be indifferent, to forget the responsibility which the position of leadership bestows upon us?

A wide stream of human callousness separates us from the realm of holiness. Neither an individual man nor a single generation can by its own power erect a bridge that would reach that realm. For ages our fathers have labored in building a sacred bridge. *We who have not crossed the stream, must beware lest we burn the bridge.*

MORE THAN MANNERS

Prompted by an intuition that we cannot live by a disembodied faith, many people today speak of the advisability of introducing "rituals, customs, and ceremonies."[6]

Is it symbolism that God desires? Is it ceremonialism that the prophets called for? Are *"customs and ceremonies"* the central issue of Jewish observance? "Customs *and ceremonies"* are an external affair, an esthetic delight; something cherished in academic fraternities or at graduation exercises at American universities.

But since when has esthetics become supreme authority in matters of religion? Customs, ceremonies are fine, enchanting, playful. But is Judaism a religion of play? What is the authentic origin of these terms —customs *and ceremonies?* I must confess that I have difficulty translating "ceremonies" into Hebrew. Customs—*minhagim*—have given us a lot of trouble in the past. *Minhagim* have often stultified Jewish life. According to Rabbenu Tam, the word *minhag*, custom, consists of the same four letters as the word *gehinom*.[7]

Let us beware lest we reduce Bible to literature, Jewish observance to good manners, the Talmud to Emily Post.

There are spiritual reasons which compel me to feel alarmed when hearing the terms customs *and ceremonies.* What is the worth of celebrating the Seder on Passover eve, if it is nothing but a ceremony? An annual reenactment of quaint antiquities? Ceremonies end in routine, and routine is the great enemy of the spirit.

A religious act is something in which the soul must be able to participate; out of which inner devotion, *kavanah*, must evolve. But what *kavanah* should I entertain if entering the *sukkah* is a mere ceremony?

Let us be frank. Too often a ceremony is the homage which disbelief pays to faith. Do we want such homage?

Judaism does not stand on ceremonies. . . . Jewish piety is an answer to God, expressed in the language of *mitzvoth* rather than in the language of *ceremonies.* The *mitzvah* rather than the ceremony is our fundamental category. What is the difference between the two categories?

Ceremonies, whether in the form of things or in the form of actions, are required by custom and convention; *mitzvoth* are required by Torah. Ceremonies are relevant to man; *mitzvoth* are relevant to God. Ceremonies are folkways; *mitzvoth* are ways to God. Ceremonies are expressions of the human mind; what they express and their power to express depend on a mental act of man; their significance is gone when man ceases to be responsive to them. Ceremonies are like the moon; they have no light of their own. *Mitzvoth*, on the other hand, are expressions or interpretations of the will of God. While they are meaningful to man, the source of their meaning is not in the understanding of man but in the love of God. Ceremonies are created for the purpose of *signifying; mitzvoth* were given for the purpose of *sanctifying.* This is their function: to refine, to ennoble, to sanctify man. They confer holiness upon us, whether or not we know exactly what they signify.

A *mitzvah* is more than man's *reference to God;* it is also *God's reference to man.* In carrying out a *mitzvah* we acknowledge the fact of God being concerned with our fulfillment of His will.

Is this religion of human will prophetic Judaism? Is this the spirit of "we will do and we will obey"?

Remember the words of Deuteronomy: "Beware, lest there be among you a man or woman, or family, or tribe, whose heart turns away this day from the Lord, our God . . . one who, when he hears the words of this sworn covenant, blesses himself in his heart, saying: I shall be safe (I shall have peace of mind), though I walk according to the dictates of my heart." (29:18 f.)

"Do not follow your own hearts" (Numbers 15:39). How can one pray "Help us, O God, to banish from our hearts . . . self-sufficient leaning upon our own reason" (The Union Prayer Book, p. 101), and proclaim at the same time that Judaism is basically a religion of man's will and choice?

Is it not our duty to insist that man *is not* the measure of all things? To deny that man is all and there is none else beside him? Don't we believe that God, too, has a voice in human life? Is it not the essence of prophetic Judaism to say: It is God who spoke to me, therefore I want to fulfill His will?

NOTES

1. *Shabbath* 105b. *Begufo* does not mean the body but the self or the essence of man; it is used by R. Abin as a paraphrase of *bach*, "in thee," Psalms 81:10. Compare the expression *Gufei Tora, Mishnah Hagigah* 1,8, which means "the essentials of Torah"; see also *Aboth* 3,18, *Gufei Halachot*.
2. *Sukkah* 52b.
3. [*Ed.:* Numbers in parentheses in this essay refer to pages of the author's *Man Is Not Alone*.]
4. *Exodus Rabba* 41,6.
5. Romans 3:28. "By the deeds of the law there shall no flesh be justified in his sight; for by the law is knowledge of sin."
6. Morton M. Berman, *The Survey of Current Reform Practice by Laymen,* delivered at the 42nd general assembly of the Union of American Hebrew Congregations, April 22, 1953.
7. See *Shiltey Giborim* on the Mordecai, *Gittin* 85a; also *Teshuvot Maharan Mints,* no. 67.

CHAPTER FIVE

Conservative Theories
of Jewish Law since 1970—Part I

WE WILL NOW TURN to nine theories of Jewish law that have been written since 1970 by rabbis affiliated with the Conservative movement. The order in which these appear is roughly chronological, in that chapter 5 includes selections written until approximately 1990 while chapter 6 contains expositions published after then. Many of these thinkers, though, have published on issues in Jewish jurisprudence (=Jewish philosophy of law) both before and after 1990, and so the ordering here is only approximate, tied primarily to the date of the specific excerpts chosen.

A. EDWARD FELD

Rabbi Edward Feld was ordained by the Jewish Theological Seminary of America in 1968. He served for many years as the Hillel Director at Princeton University, then as Rabbi at the Society for the Advancement of Judaism (founded by Mordecai Kaplan), and he is now Rabbi-in-Residence of the Seminary.

In his 1975 article that begins this chapter, Feld, like Kaplan before him, proposes that members of the Conservative movement should stop talking in legal terms. Feld agrees with Kaplan that in our modern, voluntaristic society, people need not identify with a religion at all; they are certainly not constrained by the government's police powers to obey specific religious rules, and the Jewish community no longer has such powers. As a result, "history has not dealt kindly with halakhah." Instead of a comprehensive legal system that governs all aspects of life, the

Enlightenment has enabled and convinced Jews to use civil law for everything except ritual matters and family law. Even the latter is increasingly observed in the breach, as Jews increasingly find unsavory the traditional language of a man "acquiring" a wife, together with its legal consequences, and as many Jews dissolve their marriages in the civil courts exclusively. And in a voluntaristic society, "you must ask whether a legal structure for religious ritual is relevant to the changed condition of modern Jewish life." True, the fact that Jews practice their religion in a variety of ways reduces our sense of unity, but, according to Feld, "our current pluralistic Judaism should not be viewed with regret for the loss of Jewish unity but should be welcomed as liberating."

Feld, however, adds another important factor to Kaplan's arguments as to why speaking of Jewish law no longer make sense—namely, that we have adopted a historical method of analyzing the Torah and later Jewish texts that makes it clear that the Torah is not literally God's word spoken at Mount Sinai. "Take away the notion of [verbal] revelation, and halakhah floats like a castle built on air." Indeed, it is simply inappropriate to use Jewish legal methodology (which presumes precisely such verbal revelation) because our historical consciousness has made our whole relationship to Jewish law relative to our judgment and circumstances rather than seeing it as the absolute command of God: "Biblical criticism, talmudic criticism—indeed, our entire newly discovered historical consciousness—have made our relationship to Jewish law relative. To simply graft the old halakhic process onto this new mode of thinking is to belie both the transformations that have occurred in our own understanding and the true underpinnings of the legal process. We may be traditionalist in *praxis* (practice), but our ideology is non-halakhic in that it is not charged with the absoluteness of biblical command." As a result, both because of the radical changes that the Enlightenment has brought to how we handle our civil legal affairs and our new historical consciousness, Jewish law is, for Feld, no longer law.

Feld differs from Kaplan in another important respect as well. Instead of Kaplan's use of communal consciousness and folkways to justify Jewish rituals, Feld proposes that we use Judaism's *aggadah*— its moral values, traditions, theology, stories, *and its traditions of practice*—to give us guidance and to shape our lives. Feld aims to be "both traditional and non-halakhic." To do that, Jewish law may well be part of the mix of elements from the Jewish tradition that influences us in our Jewish practice, but it should not be the only one, nor even necessarily the dominant one, and it certainly should not be treated as binding law. In fact, the details of the law should not matter as much as its goals, which, in essence, are to connect with God and the Jewish people.

He provides two specific examples of this. First, while Jewish law would allow violating Shabbat when life or health is threatened, in our own time, with our modern understanding of Jewish texts and the laws in them as not directly God-given, Feld would say that "if someone is sick on Shabbat we may call a doctor even though it is clearly not a matter of life and death." Second, during the winter families should be encouraged to light the Sabbath candles when they and their guests all assemble, even if that is hours after sunset (and thus technically violating Shabbat).

In these examples, notice that while Feld does not think that Jewish law is binding, he still looks to it for forms of expression and guidance. He takes the Rabbis' concern to save life and expands it to include less threatening forms of illness; he is not inventing a whole new value in saying that, but he is diminishing the relative importance of Shabbat in contrast to preserving health, which is also a deeply rooted Jewish value. Similarly, he still wants Jewish families to light candles with the appropriate blessings on Friday nights, as the Rabbis dictate, to mark the onset of the Sabbath. Unlike the Rabbis and subsequent Jewish law, however, he is preferring that positive rabbinic commandment to the negative commandment in the Torah forbidding the lighting of fire on the Sabbath (Exodus 31:3). As he says, however, we now know that despite Reform experiments to the contrary, the Sabbath will continue to be observed on Friday night and Saturday.

Feld recognizes that his approach may seem anarchic to some, but he claims that that is not the case. "On the contrary, rejecting halakhah can be a religiously liberating process through which new criteria of meaning are established and one's ritual life made holy." While I certainly applaud new efforts to make Jews' lives holy, those efforts will undoubtedly be manifold, varying even from person to person, and so I frankly do not see his words as an answer to the charge of anarchy. Feld is clearly right, though, when he says that those who take his approach seriously will not thereby have an easier time of deciding how to be Jewish. On the contrary, "this approach is more difficult than the halakhic system. One [that is, each Jew, not just each rabbi] has to examine, one has to make decisions; nothing is given." He says, though, that with all its difficulty, "ultimately this methodology is close to the needs of our age. We are a generation that questions all received tradition; everything has to be relearned; we glory in our autonomy."

While that may have been true of the Vietnam generation for whom Feld was writing in 1975, a generation later Jews seem to be seeking roots in tradition as much as, and perhaps more than, they are questioning authority. Nevertheless, in his 1994 book, *The Spirit of Renewal: Finding Faith after the Holocaust,* Feld continues to maintain his position about Jewish law:

> We will not look to the tradition for law, for an absolute guidance, for our circumstances and theology are conditioned by new events and understandings, but we can be sustained by the vocabulary that the tradition offers us for self-knowledge. We will not receive single-minded direction from our study of the tradition, but in engaging in open-ended argument regarding what we must do, we will be bounded by the values of survival and otherness, of the knowledge of evil and the will to do good, of the needs of the self and the need to reach out to the other. . . . This new calling has within it, for all its innovation, a deep connectedness with that earlier one.[1]

Furthermore, in a 2003 article, Feld called on Conservative Jews to recognize that we are really two camps: one, largely centered in the national organizations of the movement, that claims to be halakhic in both methodology and content and seeks to focus on deepening the Jewish knowledge and practice of the most committed members of the movement; and one, more representative of the members of Conservative synagogues, the ones the rabbis in the field are trying to serve, that is openly non-halakhic in their personal practices but want traditional practices in their public institutions—even though that means that they rarely attend them. He describes this second group as diffuse, without a clear program or methodology, but represented in the multiple worship services and levels of classes that synagogue rabbis are increasingly creating. I suspect that of the subgroups he describes within the rabbis of this second camp, he himself identifies with one or the other of these two:

> Others in this camp question whether halakhah is the right instrument to apply to the multiplicity of levels of observance which comprise the Conservative constituency—what is a proper halakhic response for one person at their level of observance may be inappropriate to another at theirs. Perhaps the very notion of a journey, of levels, has to be incorporated into contemporary halakhic response. Others feel that the insistence on the single defining quality of the Conservative movement as halakhic is increasingly used as a weapon to say "no" to anything new, to close down imagination and to stifle new thinking. These days, the Rabbinical Assembly's Committee on [Jewish] Law and Standards is used to making policy decisions for the movement, and public debate on issues is tabled.[2]

The thrust of that article, though, is that both sides had better start talking with each other seriously or the Conservative movement, dominated in its national organizations by the first camp, will shrink to the point of not being able financially to sustain those institutions, as more and more of that camp's constituency will be captured by a resurgent Modern Orthodoxy. "The heyday of the Conservative movement was the time where it was able to hold on to both poles," Feld points out, and "it would do our leadership well to try to promote dialogue between the two views. Blessing both sides of the debate may be the only way to achieve a dynamic, vital future."[3]

In many ways, Feld's own approach to Jewish law is based in Heschel's, but Feld takes Heschel's interest in *aggadah* much further than Heschel ever imagined—specifically, to provide an *alternative* to Jewish law, rather than simply to contextualize and augment it. Feld is suggesting a specifically non-halakhic but traditional form of Judaism that uses Jewish law (but does not see it as binding) and that reinterprets it using a nontraditional method (namely, every Jew individually and with non-halakhic forms of reasoning) in the name of achieving its goals in our time.

One problem with Feld's theory, of course, is that it veers quite far from traditional Jewish law in methodology, and potentially in content as well. Methodologically, Feld is entitling each Jew to interpret and apply Jewish law in the way that fulfills its goals in that Jew's life. That is not the same as saying to each person to do as he or she sees fit, the brand of autonomy popular in the Reform movement in the nineteenth and the first half of the twentieth centuries and still the operative principle for many Reform Jews today; Feld instead is imposing the criterion that whatever the Jew does must be done in the name of achieving the law's goals. Still, that takes authority away from rabbis, those designated as the legal authorities during at least the last nineteen hundred years, and places it in the hands of individuals, just as the Reform ideology does. In doing that, Feld, just like modern Reform thinkers such as Rabbi Eugene Borowitz, has to trust that each individual Jew has sufficient Jewish knowledge and sensitivity to recognize what the goal of the law is in each case—a questionable assumption given the level of Jewish knowledge of most Jews of our time.

In content, Feld's approach suffers from the same problem as the Reform focus on individual autonomy does—namely, how can he ensure that there will be any recognizable *communal* practice if everyone makes his or her own decisions? Feld recognizes that his approach may be "anarchic," but he does not explain how, with so many different paths taken by individuals, he would ensure that there would still be a coherent, Conservative community on either the local or international levels. In Feld's example of the Sabbath candles, classical Jewish law would specifically make the opposite choice, saying that the family should not light the candles after sunset because the Torah's prohibitions take precedence over the positive duty established by the Rabbis.[4] How else would Jewish law be changed if we were to follow Feld's lead? Indeed, if every Jew were entitled to make such decisions, how, if at all, would we be able to recognize Jewish practice as Jewish any more?

On the other hand, Feld's example clearly rings true to what many Jews do, including those who strive to make Judaism a serious part of their lives, for during the winter they simply cannot leave their jobs on Fridays early enough to begin Shabbat at its proper time. At the same time, they want to have a way of marking Shabbat off from the rest of the week, and they want to use the traditional method for doing so, even if it is done at a time that expressly violates Jewish law. Feld is also right in maintaining, as he does in his 2003 article, that the reality of the Conservative constituency is that it includes people taking multiple journeys, with few clear lines of definition of what is acceptable and what is not in a person's personal practice as he or she practices Judaism at various stages of life.

Thus as easy as it is to raise serious questions about Feld's theory, one must recognize that it articulates the reality for many Conservative Jews. This may be an indication that we are living in a post-halakhic age, as Feld claims, but not necessarily one that is unaffected by *halakhah* altogether. Instead, it may just be that many Jews now are, in terms that Rabbi David Lieber suggested to me three decades ago, *hovevei halakhah* (lovers of Jewish law) rather than *shomerei halakhah* (observers of Jewish law). For such people, while the methodology of making decisions in Jewish law has clearly changed radically, the content may not change nearly as much as is theoretically possible, precisely because they love Jewish practices as a way of concretizing Jewish beliefs, stories, and values and as a framework in which to bring family and community together. As a result, their *praxis* may reflect the tradition even if it violates the strict letter of the law. That will clearly not satisfy those who like order and definition, but it may not be nearly as chaotic as it might first seem, for many of those who join Conservative synagogues rather than Reform ones do so because they like traditional Judaism, even if they themselves do not practice it in accordance with the traditional requirements. This approach to Jewish law may, in fact, be exactly what Feld defines it as—an aggadic Judaism that is defi-

nitely different in method and even in some specific decisions from halakhic Judaism but is, in the larger scheme of things, not so different in
content and remarkably similar in goals to the Jewish law we have always known.

Towards an Aggadic Judaism*

EDWARD FELD

READING THIS JOURNAL, one frequently gets the impression that
Conservative Judaism is attempting to define itself as a halakhic movement. Discussions with Conservative rabbis have reinforced this impression: I have found even the most leftist rabbis including themselves
within the halakhic fold (although I note that they do so only through a
serious misconception of what the halakhic process is). It is therefore
necessary once again to explain the position of the person who does not
see himself as a halakhic Jew in the modern period (even though his religious practice may be traditional), and to show why Jewish law cannot serve any longer as the framework for Jewish religious life. There is
little that I have to say here that is new; rather, I write this because there
is no public voice among us enunciating the non-halakhic position.

I

Our changed concept of revelation, induced by our acceptance of modern biblical scholarship, alters the sacred character of the Bible and necessitates a new way of viewing the Halakhah. The authority of
halakhah stems from its intimate connection with the Bible, which is
why the Talmud went to such great lengths to link its sayings to biblical
texts. The foundation of the halakhic structure is biblical; the characteristic development of any specific law is established by the biblical verse
on which it is based. Ultimately, in the self-understanding of the tradition, Jewish law is meaningful because God commanded it. Thus, the
Halakhah is a system of mitzvot: revealed commandments. Take away
the notion of revelation, and halakhah floats like a castle built on air.

Yet we have been nurtured on an understanding of revelation that
stems from a critical analysis of the biblical text, different from and
more complex than the traditional understanding of revelation. For instance, we do not believe that the contradictions in the text of the

*Conservative Judaism 29:3 (Spring 1975), pp. 79–84.

Torah were put there to teach us a new halakhah; instead, we know that they are there because the Torah was written over a rather lengthy period of time. Thus, the very basis of talmudic exegesis is undercut. We may then relate to halakhah as tradition, but not as revelation, not as mitzvah. We ask a question of the biblical text that Rabbi Akiva would never have asked: what is divine and what is human in the commandments?

We know now that the record we have of the dialogue between God and man is not a mere transcription but a subtle mixture of the Word which is beyond words and its interpretation by men who wrote out of the spirit of the times and their own psychological perspective. Some rabbis were bold enough to take this view with regard to prophecy, but they could never hold it with regard to the law itself. That revelation had to be direct and unmediated (see Maimonides' Principles of Faith, numbers seven and eight); to question it would be to challenge the very authority of the Halakhah. But it is no longer possible for us to point to a specific passage of the Bible and say with certainty, "This is God's word to us." This new understanding of revelation undermines any simple-minded notion of mitzvah, and leaves halakhah dependent on an unsettled theological foundation.

CONSERVATIVE JUDAISM OFTEN LACKS the ideological rigor to confront these issues. Sentiment then overcomes reason, with the result that we can teach a critical understanding of the Bible and still not incorporate the conclusions of that scholarship into our religious lives. But ideology deeply affects our lives; by not confronting our intellectual situation, we allow the revival or continuation of modes of thought which essentially contradict what we most deeply believe. For the assumptions made by the Halakhah are not ours: we may observe Shabbat fully, yet we know that the seven day week is not inherently the primal order of time; we may observe kashrut because we believe that it holds Jews together and raises Jewish consciousness, that it is in part an ethical act, or even that it imparts a sense of the holy and is pleasing to God. But we do not really believe that God *commanded* us to keep kosher so that a Jew who does not keep kosher is violating God's will and cutting himself off from intimate connection with Him.

Biblical criticism, talmudic criticism—indeed, our entire newly discovered historical consciousness—have made our relationship to Jewish law relative. To simply graft the old halakhic process onto this new mode of thinking is to belie both the transformations that have occurred in our own understanding and the true underpinnings of the legal process. We may be traditionalist in *praxis,* but our ideology is non-halakhic in that it is not charged with the absoluteness of biblical command. And it is more than likely that this different ideological point of view changes our relation to the act. For instance, if someone is sick on Shabbat, we may call a doctor even though it is clearly not a matter of life and death. This is a new, more relative relationship to Shabbat than the halakhic one. Because Torah has lost the character of absolute command, it has also lost its absolute authority, and our understanding of it is much more complex than has been the case in the past.

II

History has not dealt kindly with halakhah. Fortuitously, the conditions of modern Jewish life liberate us from the necessity to maintain religious law.

Over time, the areas of life encompassed by Jewish law have continued to narrow: with the destruction of the Temple, the laws of sacrifice and ritual purity became inoperative (no one in Israel today seeks to reinstate this part of Jewish law—the Orthodox party seeks only to circumvent it); and with the Enlightenment and the breakdown of the Jewish community the civil code became inoperative. When we speak of the Halakhah, then, we speak of a law which has been reduced from its almost totally life-encompassing base to one that speaks only to very restricted areas: laws of marriage and divorce and religious ritual.

The laws of marriage and divorce are becoming increasingly problematic for the Jewish community. Certainly outside the state of Israel these areas of life are essentially ruled by the civil sector. The *ketubah,* for example, is meaningless in a society in which alimony and marital property relationships are fixed by the secular authorities. Religious divorce has only a residual and atavistic value when secular divorce is what is truly decisive for the dissolution of a marriage. With regard to Israel, the one country where halakhic marriage and divorce still possess the force of law, it is interesting that most of us are upset by the judicial practice there and advocate the introduction of civil marriage and divorce in that country too.

Most important, the essential concept underlying religious marriage is that of *kinyan,* property acquisition. Surely this way of looking at marriage is not very helpful to us, and will justifiably come under increasing attack in an age which is sensitive to feminist issues and challenges. In practice, we do not take the halakhot of Jewish marriage and divorce seriously. We might retain them for sentimental reasons or for aesthetic ones, but they do not have an absolute character for us. Rather, Jewish marriage and divorce are largely ceremonial, for the consequences of our taking these aspects of the Halakhah seriously would be disturbing if not unacceptable.

WHEN WE SAY WE ARE HALAKHIC JEWS, it is in the area of ritual that we most often maintain the primacy of Jewish law. Yet we must ask whether a legal structure for religious ritual is relevant to the changed condition of modern Jewish life. The most characteristic element of post-Enlightenment Jewish life is its voluntaristic nature. We have developed an attitude of religious pluralism; there are many different legitimate Jewish paths. The Halakhah, of necessity, had to define one unified religious path—Shammai was to have his day only in messianic times—but post-Enlightenment Judaism can afford to rejoice in the freedom of diversity. Our current pluralistic Judaism should not be viewed with regret for the loss of Jewish unity but should be welcomed as liberating. The modern Jew can choose the kind of religious life he wants; if he practices a religious act, he does so out of choice, not out of pressure from a tightly knit community.

I would think very few of us want to return to the enforced discipline of Jewish medieval religious life, but it is constraint that sustains the rule of law. If constraint is no longer needed, then is it a legal formulation of our religious life that is most relevant? Perhaps a more midrashic framework for Jewish ritual is most appropriate today.

For example, the traditional definition of work on the Sabbath was established in the classic thirty-nine categories of labor. It was necessary to define work in a formalistic framework so that its authority could be invoked to punish violators. In order to be enforced, a system of law has to be explicit, clear and objective, not subjective. Yet this can lead to religious absurdities: for example, one may carry a five hundred pound stone up and down in one's house and still not violate the law of work. Such absurdities necessarily arise from setting down any system of rules. In a voluntaristic Jewish community, however, might it not be more meaningful to talk about subjective categories of work?

The full force of this argument was brought home to me the first Shabbat of my married life. On Shabbat morning my wife went around the house watering the plants. I told her to stop, since it was a violation of the law. She replied that the plants should not have to suffer because it was Shabbat, and that she was not a farmer so the agricultural laws of Shabbat were just not relevant to what she was doing. It dawned on me that for urban Jews it might be a mitzvah to water plants on Shabbat. Surely, if we did this, a Jewish farmer would not assume that his working the farm was also in keeping with Shabbat.

III

What does it mean to be both traditional and non-halakhic? Let me attempt to answer by another example. My wife, Merle, and I celebrate Shabbat in a way which is fairly intense, and which others perceive as being fairly traditional. We usually invite guests for Friday night and try to have them come around sunset. Sometimes they are late or we are late and we start shortly after sunset. We sit down to the meal. Merle lights candles. We sing some *zemirot* and I make kiddush. Except for singing, we try to continue in reflective silence and darkness for a part of the mealtime.

Most people who have been present at our Shabbat table have felt something religiously meaningful communicated to them. Many have tried to incorporate elements of our Shabbat into their own lives. From a halakhic point of view however, we are violators of the Shabbat. After all, we often light candles after sunset. Yet it is important for us to light candles after the guests have arrived so that they can fully participate in welcoming the Shabbat, for it is in the context of this community that we feel Shabbat. Moreover, Merle and I feel it is important that we both have an active role in the ritual of beginning the meal. By the different acts of lighting candles and making kiddush we establish both our equal and our individualized participation. While from a halakhic stance what we do is a desecration of Shabbat, it is our non-halakhic point of view that gives our home its religious tone and mood on Shabbat.

TOO OFTEN THERE IS A SENTIMENTAL ATTACHMENT to the "total" halakhah based on a feeling that if we give it up, then we will plunge into an anarchic religious life in which all of tradition will be lost. On the contrary, rejecting halakhah can be a religiously liberating process through which new criteria of meaning are established and one's ritual life made holy.

One who is non-halakhic looks at traditional ritual, seeks to find the spiritual meaning in its essence and then tries to fashion the details of the religious action out of this aggadah. To be sure, this approach is personally more difficult than the halakhic system. One has to examine; one has to make decisions; nothing is given. But ultimately, this methodology is close to the needs of our age. We are a generation that questions all received tradition; everything has to be relearned; we glory in our own autonomy.

Classical Reform Judaism also challenged the supremacy of the Halakhah. Its mistake was that it soon transformed the changes it had made into a new halakhah. Once I was planning a service with a woman from a Reform background. When I argued for the inclusion of a traditional Amidah, she turned to a Reform Rabbi who was there and asked, "Are Reform allowed to say this?" That kind of Reform Judaism is really nothing but a new Orthodoxy. We need instead a dynamic system which should never become ossified into law. Halakhah of any kind, whether Reform or Orthodox, is no longer necessary in our community.

WE HAVE BEEN LIVING IN A PLURALISTIC COMMUNITY for more than a hundred years, yet the ultimate unity at the core of Jewish life has not been lost. We are all tempered by the same history; even our secular literature is nurtured by traditional religious texts. The overwhelming majority of Jews celebrate a seder of some kind. We now know that a Jewish Sabbath will be observed on Saturday, not Sunday, and that if we are to have a Jewish state it will be in Israel, not Uganda. What we have in common, then, is not established by the Halakhah but by our joint history, literature and set of symbols.

Over the generations Judaism became increasingly rigid as law was built to protect the Law, and the internal meaning of religious acts was frequently lost. The great danger of Orthodoxy is that it can make Torah, not God, the supreme god, and thus create a new heresy. If Jews are to find holiness once again, they must strip away the encrustations of the law and find the Divine within it. Religious ritual must be infused with religious meaning or there will be no Jewish renaissance.

Law as a religious form is necessary in a community which needs to have standards in order to compel obedience to them. It may also be necessary in a community which needs common rules for people to be able to live together at close quarters. It is not necessary in the changed condition of modern Jewish life—that is, in a voluntaristic pluralistic community.

Halakhah, like any legal system, must *objectify* universal standards. We are lucky to have arrived at a point where we can allow *subjective* religious standards—a new aggadic Judaism.

B. JOEL ROTH

Rabbi Joel Roth was ordained by the Jewish Theological Seminary of America in 1968 and completed his Ph.D. in Talmud there in 1973. An excellent and revered teacher, manifestly and deeply caring toward his students, he has influenced more than a generation of Seminary students through his serving as Dean of the Rabbinical School (1981–84 and 1992–93) and through his teaching on the Seminary faculty, where he is now Louis Finkelstein Professor of Talmud and Jewish Law. He also taught for two and a half years at the Conservative Yeshiva in Jerusalem, where he served as Rosh Yeshiva. He has been a member of the Committee on Jewish Law and Standards since 1978, a body that he chaired from 1984 to 1992. While he has written scholarly works in Talmud, his writings on Jewish law will concern us most here, including the responsa he has written for the Committee on Jewish Law and Standards and, especially, his book on the nature of Jewish law, *The Halakhic Process: A Systemic Analysis* (1986), from which the selections included below are excerpted.

As the subtitle of his book indicates, Roth seeks to understand Jewish law as a deductive system, much like geometry, with foundational definitions and axioms, and everything else—or almost everything else—following deductively from those. The beauty of such a system, of course, is that it is self-contained, and so if one accepts its premises and if a conclusion is validly deduced from those, then that conclusion follows with 100% certainty. That is the lure of any deductive system: it promises order and certainty.

The problem with any deductive system—in law and even in mathematics—is that life usually does not fit into neat categories with deductive conclusions. Thus as much as we are convinced that 2+2=4, as one learns more advanced mathematics, it becomes clear that that is true only if one begins with a base of 10 but not otherwise. Similarly, most of us are convinced of the truth of two postulates of Euclidean geometry—namely, that the shortest distance between two points is a straight line and that there can be only one line drawn parallel to any given line through a particular point external to it. In fact, your geometry teacher during the very first week of class may have sent you out, as mine did, to measure the distance between any two points with a string and a ruler to see for yourself that the former postulate is true, and the same rough-and-ready technique might well have convinced you of the second postulate as well. In the nineteenth century, however, Nikolai Ivanovich Lobachevsky (1826) and Janos Bolyai (1832) independently proved that the second postulate is false, and they generated a wholly different geometry ("hyperbolic geometry") based on the assumption that *more than* one parallel to a given line could be drawn through a fixed point and that the shortest distance between two points was a *concave* line. Later, Georg Friedrich Berhnard Riemann (1854) created yet another non-Euclidean geometry by assuming that the shortest distance between two points is a *convex* line. That shattered the confidence that most people had in the absolute truth of Euclidean geometry, but this mathematical speculation remained only an intellectual game until some fifty years later, when Albert Einstein demonstrated in his general theory of relativity that at the speed of light, lo and behold, the shortest distance between two points is in fact a convex line. These discoveries, of course, do not undermine the accuracy or usefulness of ordinary arithmetic or Euclidean geometry for most of the things we do in life, but they do demonstrate that even in mathematics a deductive system does not adequately encompass and explain all of reality.

If that is true of a deductive system in mathematics, which is intended to measure the more-or-less objective features of the universe, how much the more so is it true for law, which is created to govern the complex and ever-changing nature of a society. Nevertheless, the Continental European systems of law—as, for example, the French Napoleonic Code (1804), the Prussian Code (1813), and the Italian Civil Code (1865, revised 1942), versions of which still govern France, Germany, and Italy, today—are largely deductive in their nature and functioning. That is, to know what the law is you consult the code; judges may make decisions based on the code, but it is the code—and therefore legislators—who hold ultimately legal authority, not judges. In contrast, Anglo-American law is mostly case-based ("casuistic"). English law does not even have a constitution. The American legal system does

include both federal and state constitutions as well as collections of legislated laws, but in both systems the meaning and application of those
laws is ultimately determined by the courts. In doing so, the courts can
sharply narrow or expand the scope of the law, and they can even declare a law unconstitutional (according to either the federal or state constitution) and thereby make it null and void.

In this context, Roth chooses the former, Continental model for his
theory of Jewish law. He thus adopts what legal theorists describe as
"legal positivism"—that is, the doctrine that the law is totally encompassed by what the authoritative legal texts say it is. The legislators may
have had all kinds of reasons to enact a particular law—moral, social,
economic, political, or simply the pressure of time—but none of that
matters in interpreting and applying the law; what counts is what the
law actually says. As we shall see, Roth's positivism is not as pure as
that of some legal theorists because he introduces the notion of "extralegal" factors in determining the law, but like all positivists Roth's theory of law gives much less weight to those factors than to the stated law
itself. That is evidenced by the very term he uses: by describing such factors as "extralegal," he clearly conveys that for him they are, literally,
outside the law.

Roth borrows the German term *"grundnorm"* from the legal theorist Hans Kelsen[5] to name what Roth takes to be the deductive ground
for the Jewish legal system. In some ways, that is both fitting and ironic,
for the Germans, perhaps more than any other philosophers and legalists, have sought to put everything into a deductive system, whether or
not it fits. (Think of Kant and, especially, Hegel.) That is only partially
symbolic, though, because there have been some positivists even among
English philosophers, such as another theorist Roth cites, Sir John
Salmond, as well as Jeremy Bentham, John Austin, and A. Dicey.

In the opening pages of his book, included in the excerpt below,
Roth describes what he takes to be the *grundnorm* of Jewish law in
three separate ways: (1) "The document called the Torah embodies the
word and will of God, which it behooves man to obey, and is, therefore,
authoritative"; (2) "The document called the Torah embodies the word
and the will of God, which it behooves man to obey, as mediated
through the agency of J, E, P, and D, and is, therefore, authoritative";
and (3) "The document called the Torah embodies the constitution promulgated by J, E, P, and D, which it behooves man to obey, and is,
therefore, authoritative." In the latter two formulations, Roth is taking
into account modern biblical scholarship, according to which the text of

the Torah that we have in hand was edited from (at least) four different sources, which scholars have designated J ("the Jahwist source," in which God is described by His proper name, the tetragrammaton), E ("the Elohist source," in which God is described by the generic word for God, *elohim*), P (the Priestly source), and D (the Deuteronomist). In his first articulation of the *grundnorm,* Roth states the ground of authority as being God's will as articulated in the Torah, accepting it as a faith statement that the Torah does in fact do that and leaving aside all questions of how it was composed; the second articulation explicitly acknowledges J, E, P, and D as the mediators of God's will but continues to ground the authority of the Torah in that divine will; and the third says that even if one has doubts about God's role in the creation of the Torah but accepts it as authoritative on other (presumably human) grounds, the Jewish legal system can still be completely authoritative and function as a system on the basis of that acceptance.

Some may fault Roth for admitting the second and, especially, the third possibility for his *grundnorm,* for those options seem to distance the authority of the Torah from God. I, however, see his alternatives as a distinct strength of his theory, which then does not depend on any specific beliefs regarding God or the composition of the Torah. However one understands God—even if one is a complete atheist—and however one understands the Torah—from its being the direct and accurate transcription of the word of God to its being a totally human document—Jewish law is authoritative, according to Roth's theory, if one accepts the Torah as authoritative, for whatever reason one has for doing so.

The *grundnorm,* though, is not all that one must accept in order to make all of Jewish law authoritative: one must also accept the *methods* that rabbis have historically used to interpret and apply the Torah. After all, a classical Reform Jew could accept the Torah as authoritative *for its own time* but then maintain that revelation has progressed over the centuries and should now be interpreted by each individual Jew according to his or her own conscience. Or one might say, as the Karaites did, that the Torah is indeed the word of God but that it must be interpreted without the oral tradition. One might even, as Christians and Muslims do, say that the Torah is authoritative but so are later texts like the New Testament or the Koran. So Roth's theory involves a crucial extra step that he clearly assumes in his detailed description of rabbinic methodology but does not identify as a *grundnorm* of its own.

It is not only Roth's provision for biblical scholarship in defining his *grundnorm* that makes him clearly a Conservative Jew; it is also in his recognition of factors other than the texts of the Torah and the Oral Torah that shape Jewish law. While a few modern Orthodox thinkers (David Hartman most specifically) would acknowledge that as well, most modern Orthodox leaders (e.g., Norman Lamm, J. David Bleich, Moshe Tendler, Yeshayahu Leibowitz) would be wary of admitting such factors external to the texts of the tradition in interpreting it. As chapter 7 below discusses in some detail, Leibowitz in particular (who, like Roth, sees Jewish law as a closed system) would see consideration of human factors outside the system as sullying the divine authority of the Torah. Orthodox rabbis might, of course, consult experts in modern science, economics, politics, and other areas in order to understand the issues that these disciplines raise, but ultimately Orthodox decisions are based solely on applying the received texts to the current situation. Roth goes beyond that in acknowledging that at times the classical tradition itself introduced such elements into the decision-making process, sometimes even to the point of overturning received texts. (For example, some medieval rabbis maintained that the Talmud's medical cures are not to be followed in other times and places.) Roth provides a number of examples of such changes "because the times have changed" *(nishtannu ha'ittim)* as well as other rationales for changing the received law. In doing that, and in recommending that modern rabbis do so as well, he sees himself, as he says, as one who must "persevere as a member of a minority" who take both Jewish law and these extralegal elements seriously.

Roth's theory is thus consciously open to considering these other influences on the shaping of the law, both in studying the history of the law and in making decisions today. Roth describes four categories of such elements: (1) medical/scientific; (2) sociological/*realia;* (3) economic; and (4) ethical/psychological. For reasons of space, I have left out his book's extensive discussion of how these elements have played a role in the history of Jewish law, but the reader is encouraged to consult his book for that discussion. Moreover, Roth maintains that even if such factors lead a contemporary rabbi to interpret the Torah itself at variance with the way it has been interpreted in the past, that would not undermine the *grundnorm* demanding allegiance to the Torah. Rabbis should clearly do such things only sparingly and carefully, lest the continuity of the law be undermined; but when a contemporary rabbi does that, the authority that adhered to the original rabbinic interpretation of the Torah now transfers to its contemporary understanding.

Even though Roth describes the considerable scope that such factors have had in the past, he notes several limitations on their functioning. First, "our emphasis on the widespread use of extralegal factors in the halakhic system is in no way meant to imply that they play a part in every legal decision; there are many decisions reached on the basis of legal sources alone."

Second, such factors—and the experts who know about them—do not, in and of themselves, determine the law; only the rabbi does that. Rabbis may, and probably should, consider such expertise in their decisions, but Roth uses a vivid talmudic passage (Sanhedrin 75a) to point out that even if a person's life is, according to the doctors, at stake, only the rabbis can determine if the remedy that the doctors are recommending accords with Jewish law. Thus the proper role for these extralegal factors is to help rabbis think about their decision so that they might, for example, put more weight on a given stream of halakhic thinking rather than another when both appear within Jewish legal sources. So, for example,[6] even though a strong case can be made, based on the Talmud's understanding of fetal development, to allow not only the "morning-after pill" but even abortifacients like RU486 that work as late as six or seven weeks after fertilization, the rabbi may want to forbid such pills because of the major demographic problem that the Jewish community is currently having. Whether the rabbi chooses to be lenient or stringent, however, is solely the rabbi's decision and not that of doctors, demographers, or even the woman herself.

Third, "it would seem to be true that the more systematically severe the legal procedure, the more reticent *posekim* are (and should be) to make use of extralegal material." That is, the more a given extralegal factor would cause a disruption to the established legal system, the more serious the justification must be for using it to change the law and the more wary the rabbi should be in using it for that purpose.

The most important limitation on using these factors, though, is the very term Roth uses to describe them: "extralegal," outside the law. That immediately identifies the law with the received, written tradition. Other theorists of Jewish law would disagree with that perspective completely, pointing to the oral nature of most of the tradition from its very origins and the immense role that custom, morality, economics, politics, and even style have played in the history of Jewish law, especially as Jews spread all over the world. As a result, despite Roth's conscientious effort to demonstrate the role of such "extralegal" elements in the law, his theory seems to limit the scope and the methods of these elements far too much to be historically accurate, and many would find his definition of Jewish law too narrow a basis for making Jewish legal decisions in our own time.

That is especially so because of another characteristic of Roth's system. Roth is very liberal in defining what the *grundnorm* is, so that even those who believe the Torah is a totally human document may count as accepting it, as long as they also accept its legal authority. Those who do not accept the Torah's legal authority, however, are then completely out of the system; as with all deductive systems, you are either in or out, depending upon whether you accept the definitions and premises. But in our own day, the vast majority of the world's Jews would be defined out of Roth's system from the very beginning. That is a major problem, not only because it makes Roth's theory irrelevant to the vast majority of the world's Jews, but also because it leaves out many Jews who do in fact practice Jewish law, but not because they see the Torah (and later documents of the Jewish legal tradition) as legally binding. From the point of view of the tradition, that is surely not optimal; in fact, there is a long debate within the tradition as to whether one must have the proper intention to fulfill one's legal duties or whether doing the action required is enough, and those who require the proper intention would surely include that the Jew is trying to fulfill the will of God.[7] But for that group, even Roth's most liberal formulation of his *grundnorm* would not suffice, for it leaves God out of the picture entirely in establishing the legal authority of the Torah. My point here, though, is the reverse of that—namely, that there are many Jews who keep kosher, some form of Shabbat, engage in Jewish study and social action, etc., but do so for many reasons other than accepting the legal authority of the Torah. Some of these reasons are: they want any Jew to be able to eat in their home; they like how Shabbat affects themselves and their family; they enjoy the sheer intellectual give-and-take of Jewish sources or they study them to deepen their sense of linkage to the tradition; they are morally committed to Jewish norms of social action; etc. Roth's theory would include some Jews that classical sources would not—namely, those who do not see the Torah as divine but who accept the Torah as legally binding—and, more pervasively, it would exclude Jews who do in fact abide by Jewish law to a great extent but for reasons other than acceptance of the Torah as binding. That is a theoretical problem because Roth's theory thus seems to be factually inadequate insofar as it leaves out many Jews who in fact observe Jewish law and would be seen by others as observant; and it is also a pragmatic problem because Roth's theory makes it very difficult to have a genuinely pluralistic discussion because only those who accept Roth's premise have a voice in shaping Jewish law, leaving out those who obey the law for other reasons.

Another objection to Roth's theory concerns his methodology. While Continental systems of law do indeed operate in much the way that Roth describes, Jewish law has historically been much closer to Anglo-American law in its methods. The Torah itself does not have codes in the European sense of a systematic presentation of the law, topic by topic; its legal sections (especially Exodus 19–24, Leviticus 18–25, and Deuteronomy 12–25) are much more collections of judicial precedents. That becomes especially clear when one realizes that the Torah does not provide laws for many common occurrences, like how to conclude a business deal or how to get married. Moreover, the form of the Torah's laws is not always that of a complete statute. They do not always state the penalty to be imposed on the transgressor; sometimes only an absolute command or prohibition is enjoined as an expression of the absolute will of God. Contrariwise, sometimes the Torah adds the reason for the law, from the religious or ethical point of view, unlike the codes mentioned above, which give no reasons. It would be superfluous to state further that in the Torah, as is well known, religious and ritual regulations are found alongside legal ordinances without differentiation.

The Torah's ethical intent creates further disparity. The entire concern of the aforementioned European codes is to determine what is due to a person according to the letter of the law according to abstract justice, whereas the Torah seeks on many an occasion to go beyond strictly legal requirements and to grant a person what is due to him or her from the ethical viewpoint and from the aspect of the love we should all bear one another, since we all have One Heavenly Father. Cassuto therefore describes the Torah's collection of laws as "only notes on the existing laws" that were part of the oral tradition and accepted as customs of ancient Israelite society.[8] Furthermore, Menachem Elon, former Chief Justice of the Supreme Court of Israel who created the curriculum of Jewish law in Israeli law schools, has pointed out that systematic codes never fared very well in Jewish legal history, for as much as their authors specifically intended to make Jewish law clear and indisputable, the major codes of Jewish law have all been published with numerous commentaries, limitations, and objections surrounding them, thus indicating that Jewish law is not nearly as systematic as Maimonides, Karo, or Roth have tried to make it out to be. As Elon says with reference to Maimonides' Mishneh Torah:

> It would be difficult to find in all of halakhic literature another instance of a work that produced results so contrary to the avowed purpose of its author. Far from restoring to the *halakhah* its uniformity and anonymity, "without polemics or dissection . . . but in clear and accurate statements" (Mishneh Torah, Introduction), Maimonides' pursuit of that very aim be-

came the reason for the compilation of hundreds of books on his work, all of them dissecting, complicating, and increasing halakhic problems, resulting in a lack of uniformity far greater than before.[9]

Indeed, virtually every page of the Talmud is one argument after another, hardly the tone or product of a group that thinks in terms of established, defined, deductive, and authoritative legal systems. Rather, the history of Jewish law from its very beginnings in the Torah has been much more casuistic in nature, with all the unsystematic chaos that that entails. Even when the Mishnah gives a few examples of a legal principle and then says, "this is the general rule" *(zeh haklal)*, the Talmud often rejects even that amount of systematization by claiming that the Mishnah is actually referring to another case that you would not have known from the previous ones.[10] In rejecting a systematic approach, Jewish law loses the clarity and neatness that a system would have, but, like most Anglo-American philosophy and law, it gains a much clearer connection to reality and to the way that law actually functions in societies.

Another serious drawback of Roth's theory affects all forms of legal positivism: If the law is identified with texts, and if all considerations outside those texts are "extralegal" and therefore secondary in authority and import, change will happen very slowly, if at all. It is indeed unlikely that those who adopt this theory would be proactive in adapting Jewish law to the needs of modern times. In fact, in one area where Roth himself tried to be proactive, the halakhic ordination of women, he argues that a woman's acceptance of commandments from which she is normally exempt can legally enable a man to fulfill his own obligations to pray by responding "Amen" to her blessings during a service she leads. But the only way he can envision to enable women to serve as witnesses on documents for marriage or divorce is through a conscious change of the system as it has come down to us.[11] In that same rabbinic ruling, he worries that those who would make such a change lack the legal authority to do so,[12] a view he repeated when voting against the various responsa recently passed by the CJLS permitting women to serve as witnesses. That stance, of course, makes such changes impossible.

Finally, with Roth's understanding of the nature of the law, there can be no serious moral or social critique of the law. Instead, either the law is accepted forever as the criterion of what it means to be moral, or it loses any claim to morality. Those are clearly results that Roth tries to avoid by introducing his "extralegal" category, but in the end, his classification of morality as "extralegal" makes it far too weak a component of Jewish law if it is indeed to be what a moral God demands of us. This was evident, for example, in his 1992 responsum on homosexuality, in which he examined the text of Levitcus 18:22 thoroughly and used it to outweigh all other considerations.

On the other hand, the strengths of Roth's theory are many. If one does believe that the Torah is God-given—a belief that Roth's system does not require—then Roth's theory of Jewish law makes a clear distinction between God-given laws and human reasoning which, at most, can offer extralegal rationales to interpret God's will in a given way. Such a distinction would seem to protect the divine character and authority of the law from too much human interference. Roth's view also invests deep trust in the texts of the Jewish tradition and thereby honors them as holy. The systematic mode of thinking that he espouses promises to deliver a clear law with continuity and authority, and some part of all of us longs for certainty and order. Roth's approach also requires that we be humble in respecting the tradition and in not meddling with it too much. All of these are serious and significant strengths of viewing Jewish law as Roth does. As with every approach to Jewish law, the strengths of his theory must be measured against its weaknesses, for no human theory (my own definitely included!) will ultimately be adequate to describe and explain the phenomenon of Jewish law.

⚬⚬⚬

*The Halakhic Process: A Systemic Analysis**

BY JOEL ROTH

INTRODUCTION

The term *halakhah* is used in two different ways. It is generally used to signify the normative prescription or proscription that is the end result of the legal reasoning of a recognized *posek*, or legalist. When used thus, the term ignores the process that led the *posek* to his conclusion, and its meaning is limited to the resultant norm. When norms are severed from the decision-making process, they appear simple, clear, and definitive. "The *halakhah* forbids eating poultry with milk" sounds the same as "The *halakhah* forbids bowing to an idol." The statements themselves do not reflect that the former may be disputed by other

*New York: Jewish Theological Seminary, 1986, pp. 1–12, 231–234, 302–315, 375–377.

posekim (legalists), while the latter is universally affirmed by all *posekim;* or that the former was not always considered universally normative, while the latter was; or that the former is grounded in a rabbinic decision, while the latter is grounded in the dictates of the Torah itself. Both norms appear simple, clear, and definitive.

The term *halakhah,* however, is also used to signify the process by which legal conclusions are reached. In this sense the term refers to all of the factors that must or that might be considered by a *posek* before rendering his *pesak* (decision). When all of these factors are expounded together with the resultant norm, it rarely appears simple, clear, or definitive. It is, rather, complex, ambiguous, and replete with grounds for disagreement among *posekim.*

As indicated by its title, the primary focus of this volume is on the halakhic process, and not upon the actual norms. I have concentrated upon an analysis of the phenomenon of halakhic decision-making—the phenomenon of *pesak*—and not upon the phenomenon of obedience to the law.

As a legal process, *halakhah* is governed by systemic principles, that is, principles that *govern the way in which the process works,* as opposed to those that govern the determination of the law in any given case within the system. The latter are legal principles. Certain legal principles are also systemic principles, but many systemic principles are not legal in nature at all. The principle that the Supreme Court of the United States is the final arbiter of constitutionality is a systemic principle, but not a legal one. There is no specific case in which the knowledge of this principle will determine the final decision.

Systemic principles fall into two categories: explicit and implicit. Explicit principles are those that have been stated in the legal literature, while implicit principles are those that can be deduced from the legal literature, even though they have not been explicitly stated.

Among the explicit systemic principles of the halakhic system would be included:

1. In a dispute between earlier and later sages, the law follows the position of the later sages: *Hilkheta ke-vatraei.*
2. In a doubtful case the source of which is biblical, the stricter opinion prevails, whereas in a doubtful case the source of which is rabbinic, the more lenient position prevails: *Safek de-oraita le-ḥumera ve-safek de-rabbanan le-hakel.*
3. Rabbi X is sufficiently worthy to be relied upon in time of great need: *Kedai hu R. Peloni lismokh alav bi-she'at ha-deḥak.*
4. It is better that people should disobey the law inadvertently than that they should do so willfully: *Mutav she-yehu shogegin ve-al yehu mezidin.*

All four of the above are explicit principles because they have been stated in the legal literature. They are all also systemic because they embody principles that govern the process by which the system works. In addition, the former two are legal principles as well, insofar as each is sufficient in and of itself to determine the law in a given case.[1]

The principle that the halakhic system requires, not merely allows, the distinction between biblical and rabbinic injunctions, and the principle that the system affirms the possibility of co-opting sociological material in halakhic contexts, are examples of implicit systemic principles, since neither has been stated in the primary legal literature.

Clearly, implicit systemic principles are more problematic than explicit principles, since their "implicitness" makes it possible to deny that they actually exist. As a case in point, it is clear that many deny the existence of one or the other of the principles posited above, even if to others their existence is "irrefutably" implied by the legal literature.

The halakhic process, from the talmudic era through modern times, has been oriented more to the pragmatic than to the theoretical. The Talmud and the responsa are more directly comparable to case law than to treatises on legal theory. Even explicit principles—and surely implicit principles—generally lack thorough theoretical treatment in the primary sources. Analysis of most explicit systemic principles (and surely the discovery of implicit principles) must be based upon hypotheses gleaned from the primary sources inductively.

Analysis should reveal, first, whether and to what degree old systemic principles have remained stable, the degree to which they have been modified or abrogated, and whether new systemic principles have evolved. Second, it should test whether, under what circumstances, and to what degree data generally considered nonhalakhic (e.g., scientific, sociological, psychological) have been utilized in the decision-making process and are governed by systemic principles which validate their use within the system. And finally, it should demonstrate whether, how, and under what conditions new findings in rabbinic and biblical scholarship have been and can continue to be authentically incorporated into the existent halakhic process through the employment of systemic principles that legitimately govern their use.

The volume begins by distinguishing and examining the sources of all legal systems, including the halakhic. This leads, in Chapter 2, to an analysis of the concepts of *de-oraita* and *de-rabbanan,* the existence of which concepts is postulated as a fundamental systemic principle of the halakhic system. This analysis examines the difficulties inherent in the attempt to assign specific norms to either the category of *de-oraita* or the category of *de-rabbanan,* and deals also with the systemic principles that govern the relationship between the two categories. Chapter 3 introduces and defines the various kinds of legal questions that *posekim* deal with and explains the legal significance of the various types in relationship to one another. An appendix is added to Chapter 3 that analyzes several halakhic sources in the terms introduced in the chapter itself. By the beginning of Chapter 4 it will have become clear that the halakhic system allows an extremely broad discretionary latitude to its *posekim.* Therefore, the chapter itself is devoted primarily to an examination of the systemic principles that govern the use of precedent in halakhic decision-making.

In Chapter 5 we discuss the systemic principles that govern the source and scope of rabbinic authority, and by the end of the chapter we shall have discovered that the entire halakhic system is dependent upon its recognized authorities. Chapter 6, consequently, is devoted to discussion of the systemic principles that govern the qualifications of these authorities, both the academic and the characterological requirements for authority. Chapter 7 is devoted to an analysis of the systemic principles that govern the crucial question of rabbinic authority regarding matters that are *de-oraita*.

In Chapter 8 we shall deal with the systemic principles that govern the use of custom within *halakhah,* and in Chapter 9 I shall demonstrate that data generally considered nonhalakhic, have, in fact, always been legitimate factors in halakhic decision-making. I shall call these factors "extralegal sources," and, in addition, I shall analyze the systemic principles that have governed their legitimate use and prevented their illegitimate use. Since, however, discussion of many of the concepts involved in these extralegal sources is couched, in the modern world, in the specific terminologies of the physical and social sciences, while halakhic literature is generally prescientific, Chapter 10 is an editorial digression in which it is asserted that there is no special type of language that qualifies a decision as religious or nonreligious: The use of scientific language in halakhic decisions can be as religious, perhaps even more so, than disguising such factors in prescientific, but religious-sounding, circumlocution. And, finally, Chapter 11 is devoted to an analysis of the systemic principles that govern the legitimate use of the findings of modern rabbinic and biblical scholarship in halakhic decision-making.

NOTES TO INTRODUCTION

1. Principles such as the annulment of forbidden substances mixed with permissible substances in proportion of 1:60 *(bittul be-shishim)* or the right of an agent to serve also as a witness *(shali'ah na'aseh ed)*, for example, are legal principles alone, having to do only with the determination of the law in any given case, but not with the way in which the halakhic system functions *qua* process.

◖◖   ◖◖   ◖◖

CHAPTER ONE

Sources of the Legal System

THE NORMS OF ALL LEGAL SYSTEMS derive from two kinds of sources: historical and legal. Comprehending the difference between them is crucial to understanding the legal process *qua* process.

Legal sources are "those sources which are recognised as such by the law itself."[1] Historical sources are "those sources lacking formal recognition by the law itself."[2] Legal sources are norms the authority of which is accepted by and integral to the legal system; they serve as the sole *legal* justification of any new legislation and as the ultimate *legal* ground of judicial decisions. The myriad tomes of law, the *corpora* of judicial decisions, the various state and local constitutions or charters are all legal sources of the American legal system.[3] As these sources function within the system of American law, the philosophical, political, sociological, or economic factors that may have been instrumental in their becoming legal norms are considered to be irrelevant; these factors constitute historical sources, and are not accounted *legally* significant by the system. One reads occasionally of some judge who was forced to render a certain decision on the basis of valid statute, the origin of which had been clearly predicated on a reality different from that of the present. However, since the norm had never been amended or abrogated by the system, it remained authoritative and legal, and the judge was compelled to render his decision in accordance with it. His knowledge of the historical antecedents that gave rise to the norm in the first place was irrelevant. He could not decide *legally* in a manner contrary to its dictates.

The Jewish legal system is no different from any other in this regard. Its recognized legal norms operate independently of the historical sources that may have given rise to them. So long as a norm has not been amended or abrogated by the halakhic system, its origin as a reaction to Roman practice, as an emulation of Roman practice, or as a concession to the economic realities of Christian Europe, to suggest only several possibilities, is irrelevant to its validity as a norm of the halakhic system.

For this reason, historical sources are of a unique nature. At that point in time when they influence the introduction of new ideas into the legal system they are extremely important; yet their importance rests solely on the fact that their persuasive powers are sufficient to convince the authoritative *legal* body (or bodies) to incorporate them into the system as legal sources. Barring such incorporation, their influence on the legal system is merely potential, not actual, and regardless of their original importance, they fade into legal irrelevance once norms based on them are incorporated into the system as legal sources. So singularly unimportant to the functioning of the system are they, then, that inability to reconstruct the historical sources of any legal norm has no bearing whatsoever on the binding and authoritative nature of the norm.

Sir John Salmond summarized the difference between legal and historical sources as follows:

> The legal sources of law are authoritative, the historical are unauthoritative. The former are allowed by the law courts as of right; the latter have no such claim; they influence more or less extensively the course of legal development, but they

speak with no authority. . . . The legal sources are the only gates through which new principles can find entrance into the law. Historical sources operate only mediately and indirectly. They are merely the various precedent links in that chain of which the ultimate link must be some legal source to which the rule of law is directly attached.[4]

From the fact that historical sources are legally insignificant, it follows that the demonstration by scholars that the true historical sources of a given norm are different from what had generally been assumed is an interesting revelation, but legally insignificant. We shall return in due course to the implications of this statement for the halakhic system in particular. Salmond also wrote:

All rules of law have historical sources. As a matter of fact and history they have their origin somewhere, though we may not know what it is. But not all of them have legal sources. Were this so, it would be necessary for the law to proceed *ad infinitum* in tracing the descent of its principles. There must be found in every legal system certain ultimate principles, from which all others are derived, but which are themselves self-existent. Before there can be any talk of legal sources, there must be already in existence some law which establishes them and gives them authority. . . . These ultimate principles are the grundnorms or basic rules of recognition of the legal system.[5]

This statement of Salmond's reflects the Kelsenian theory according to which the nature of a legal system is such that all of its norms are derived from one basic norm, which is itself *presupposed* by the system. Kelsen writes:

If we ask why the constitution is valid, perhaps we come upon an older constitution. Ultimately we reach some constitution that is the first historically and that was laid down by an individual usurper or by some kind of assembly. The validity of this first constitution is the last presupposition, the final postulate, upon which the validity of all the norms of our legal order depends. It is postulated that one ought to behave as the individual, or the individuals, who laid down the constitution have ordained. This is the basic norm of the legal order under consideration. . . . That the first constitution is a binding legal norm is presupposed, and the formulation of the presupposition is the basic norm of this legal order.[6]

The concept of the basic norm is complex, yet indispensable. Its complexity derives mainly from the fact that this *grundnorm* is at once "metalegal" and "legal," that is, while its validity is presupposed by the system, it functions *legally* as a norm of the system.[7] Any attempt to prove the validity of the basic norm must belong to a realm other than the legal. To the extent that its validity can be proved at all, the proof must be theological, philosophical, or metaphysical. Yet it is this norm that serves as the ultimate basis of the legal system and has definite legal functions. Put succinctly, the orderly functioning of any legal order requires of its adherents a "leap of faith" concerning the validity of the basic norm of the system. Although leaps of faith do not fall within the realm of law, such a leap of faith is the ultimate validation of the legal system.[8]

Furthermore, it is important to grasp that presupposing the existence of a *grundnorm* is an amoral and nonvaluative act. The fact that a tyrant may have promulgated a constitution, obedience to which is the basic norm of a particular legal system, does not affect its status as a *grundnorm*. A postulated *grundnorm* is the *sine qua non* of a legal system, not a statement of the desirability, morality, or positive nature of the system. In many instances, such considerations will vary with the perspective of the viewer. The *grundnorm* of the American legal system was created as the result of an act of rebellion against a legal sovereign. To some, it was a necessary and ethical rebellion; to others, it was an immoral act of rebellion against the British crown. But even to this latter group, the *grundnorm* is the basic norm of the American system. Presupposing the basic norm of the American system is necessary in order to comprehend the functioning of the system, but carries no valuational implications whatsoever concerning the rectitude of the framers of the Constitution in postulating it. Thus, every legal system—democracy, monarchy, dictatorship, benevolent despotism—presupposes a basic norm; that fact, however, is independent of any consideration of the desirability of the system itself.

How, then, shall the *grundnorm* of the halakhic system be formulated so as to express the presupposed axiom that validates the system *legally?* The following seems reasonable and correct: The document called the Torah embodies the word and will of God, which it behooves man to obey, and is, therefore, authoritative.[9] Remembering that the basic norm is both "metalegal" and "legal," certain points follow. The first is that the individual legal statements of the Torah are legal sources of the system, i.e., they are norms the authority of which is accepted by and integral to the system. The second is that the concept conveyed by the rabbinic term *de-oraita* (norms having the authority of the *grundnorm* itself) is postulated by the system itself as a *sine qua non* of its functioning,[10] and implies, as well, a distinction (as yet undefined) between itself and the concept *de-rabbanan* (norms that are not *de-oraita*).

The third point is that any quest to establish the "truth" of the historical claims of the Torah is irrelevant to the halakhic process, since that quest seeks only clarification of the historical sources of the legal system, not its legal sources. Since in the halakhic system, as in all others, presupposing the existence of a *grundnorm* requires a "leap of faith," the truth or falsity of the historical claims of the *grundnorm* is legally irrelevant. Once norms are incorporated into the system as legal sources, the persuasive influence of the historical sources, originally so important, fades into legal insignificance.

Thus, it follows on one important level that the halakhic system *qua* system is independent of any considerations of the accuracy of the historical claims of its basic norm. Whether or not it is "true" that the Torah embodies the word and will of God is of great historical and theological significance, but of no legal significance. Even if one has traced the origins of the Torah to documents called J, E, P, and D, he may have uncovered the historical sources of the legal norms, but he has in no way abrogated the *grundnorm* of the halakhic system, which is *presupposed* by the system. As any number of observant scholars can attest, the system continues to function on the basis of its presupposed *grundnorm* regardless of the contention that the historical claims of the *grundnorm* may be inaccurate.

If one is so inclined, one may reformulate the *grundnorm* in the light of modern scholarship as follows: The document called the Torah embodies the word and the will of God, which it behooves man to obey, as mediated through the agency of J, E, P, and D, and is, therefore, authoritative. An alternative possible formulation might be: The document called the Torah embodies the constitution promulgated by J, E, P, and D, which it behooves man to obey, and is, therefore, authoritative. The first formulation has the advantage of incorporating God into the *grundnorm*. It is theologically self-evident that it behooves man to obey His will; thus, the "leap of faith" is simply in affirming that His word and will are mediated through J, E, P, and D. The second formulation obviates this "leap of faith" but replaces it with the presupposition that it behooves man to obey the will of J, E, P, and D. In either case, the halakhic system is ultimately predicated on a presupposition that it behooves man to obey the document called the Torah, regardless of the historical realities of its promulgation. Any discussion of the validity of the *grundnorm* must be nonlegal, i.e., philosophical, theological, or metaphysical. Legally, the *grundnorm* is posited and presupposed by the system to be true, and is therefore beyond discussion in a legal context.

The primary systemic assumption of the halakhic system, therefore, is the existence of an undeniable legal category that is called *de-oraita*. Any legal sources so categorized are, by definition, authoritative, since they are included in that document which, by presupposition, it behooves man to obey.

While the distinction drawn heretofore between legal and historical sources seems very precise, it has been justly criticized as too neat.[11] Surely it is the case that the line between the persuasive powers of historical sources, on the one hand, and their lack of legal recognition, on the other hand, is narrow indeed. Is there not a time at which the opinion of a great philosopher is incorporated into law not solely because he is persuasive, but because he is also authoritative? Does not the Congress of the United States often consider the historical sources of laws in determining whether or not the laws should be abrogated at present? Indeed, the same state of affairs obtains within the sphere of *halakhah*, too. Is the widespread acceptance of the *takkanot* (edicts) of Rabbenu Gershom or Rabbenu Tam, and their incorporation into the legal sources of so many communities, solely a factor of their persuasiveness, or also a factor of their authority?

Salmond himself was not oblivious to the problem. He wrote: "But the line between legal and historical sources is not crystal clear. . . . The distinction between legal and historical sources, while useful as a starting point, must not be pressed with too Procrustean zeal."[12] The implication seems to be that there might be, and often is, a nexus between legal and historical sources; while the distinction is real and extremely relevant, the two types of sources do not always function independently of each other. Thus, because modern scholarly investigation of Jewish sources concerns itself primarily with historical sources, we must, at some point, raise the issue of a nexus between the halakhic process and the findings of modern scholarship, a nexus governed by systemic principles.[13]

Since systemic principles, including those that are not legal principles and those that are only implicit, function as legal norms, that is to say, since the nature of systemic principles is such that any legislation or any judicial decision consonant and consistent with their requirements and stipulations is recognized as valid by the system, it follows that if one were able to articulate what the systemic principles were, it would be possible to determine with relative precision the validity and admissibility of any new legislation or judicial decision. (In practice, however, this is more likely to be true when one is dealing with explicit systemic principles than with implicit principles.[14] This is not because the premise is false, but because of the problematic nature of implicit systemic principles.)[15]

Furthermore, it follows that if we are able to determine those systemic principles that govern the nexus between modern scholarship and the halakhic process, it will be possible to determine with relative precision whether or not any new legislation or judicial decision is consonant and consistent with the requirements and stipulations of those systemic principles and, consequently, acceptable as valid by the system.

In anticipation of future detailed analysis, it should be pointed out even at this point how varied the grounds of dispute over such a determination might be. Disputants might disagree about whether the new legislation is consonant and consistent with the requirements of the systemic principle, while agreeing that if it were, it would be recognized as valid. They might disagree about the precise definition of the systemic principle, but agree that some such principle is, in fact, implicit in the system. They might disagree about the existence of such a systemic principle, yet agree that there are systemic principles that are operative and that address themselves to the nexus between modern scholarship and the halakhic process. Ultimately, the disputants may trace their disagreement to the question of the existence within the halakhic system of any systemic principle governing such a nexus.

NOTES TO CHAPTER ONE

1. P. J. Fitzgerald, ed., *Salmond on Jurisprudence,* 12th ed. (London: Sweet and Maxwell, 1966), p. 109. See also Menachem Elon, *Jewish Law: History, Sources, Principles* (Hebrew) (Jerusalem: Magnes Press, 1977), 1:211–13.
2. Fitzgerald, *Salmond,* p. 109.
3. Some of these are literary sources as well. For a definition of this term, see Fitzgerald, *Salmond,* p. 112, footnote (c), and Elon, *Jewish Law,* 1:211.
4. Fitzgerald, *Salmond,* pp. 109–10.
5. Ibid., pp. 111–12, quoted by Elon, *Jewish Law,* 1:213.
6. H. Kelsen, *General Theory of Law and State,* trans. Anders Wedberg (Cambridge, Mass.: Harvard University Press, 1945), p. 115, quoted by Lord Lloyd of Hampstead, in *Introduction to Jurisprudence,* 3d ed. (New York: Praeger, 1972), p. 302. Cf. H. Kelsen, *Pure Theory of Law,* trans. May Knight (Berkeley and Los Angeles: University of California Press, 1967), pp. 194 f.
7. Lloyd, *Introduction to Jurisprudence,* p. 279.
8. The question of the relationship between "validity" and "efficacy" is not relevant here. The present discussion is restricted to theoretical validation alone. A *grundnorm* and all of its derivative legal norms can be valid even if nobody abides by them. That this is the case can be demonstrated, at least on one level, by the fact that analysis of defunct legal systems is possible, culminating in the definitions of their *grundnorms,* which are their ultimate validations.

    Similarly, the present context of discussion permits ignoring the matter of sanctions and enforcement of the legal system. While it may be that one refrains from speeding in order to avoid the payment of a fine, the imposition of the fine is not what validates the law against speeding (although it surely enhances its efficacy). Rather, the imposition of the fine is itself the manner in which the courts demonstrate the validity of the law prohibiting speeding. Theoretically, the fine is legitimate only because the law for which it is a sanction is a valid legal norm—not vice versa.
9. Cf. Elon's formulation in *Jewish Law,* 1:215–16, and also his quotations from rabbinic sources, ibid., 1:216–17.
10. Since, the *grundnorm* of the halakhic system mentions God, and implies the concept *de-oraita,* it ought to be stressed that every legal system has its *de-oraita* equivalent, whether or not the *grundnorm* mentions God. Since the *grundnorm* is presupposed by the system irrespective of historical sources, the United States Constitution is no more *de-rabbanan* within the American system, because God is not part of the *grundnorm,* than the Torah is *de-rabbanan* in the halakhic system. In any system in which the *grundnorm* is embodied in a written document, that document is *de-oraita* in that system. Postulating God in the *grundnorm* be-

comes a much more relevant factor only when the amendment of the *grundnorm* is at issue.

11. See, for example, C. K. Allen, *Law in the Making*, 7th ed. (Oxford: Oxford University Press, 1964), pp. 268 ff. Elon takes note of the objections in *Jewish Law*, 1:213, n. 3, but opts for Salmond's distinction without further clarification.

12. Fitzgerald, *Salmond*, pp. 110–11.

13. Should it be the case that no nexus is possible, it would not follow that the system is not viable. The statement that the halakhic system operates independently of modern scholarship in no way implies its inability to confront new problems in general. It implies only that in confronting those situations, it does not permit the use of critical scholarship as considerations.

14. The phrases "more likely to be true" and "relative precision" are employed in order to imply recognition of the problems involved even with explicit systemic principles when they are not also legal principles. Examples (3) and (4) found on p. 2 [Editor's note: p. 222 in this volume] are paradigms. In (3), for example, the validity of the legislation or of the judicial decision can be determined only with relative precision because there may be a dispute concerning the applicability of the systemic principle to any given Rabbi X, or concerning the definition of the time in question as one "of great need." In this regard, then, explicit systemic principles that are not also legal principles share some common ground with implicit systemic principles.

15. See above, p. 2 [Editor's note: p. 222 in this volume].

〜 〜 〜

CHAPTER NINE

Extralegal Sources within Halakhah

UP UNTIL THIS POINT we have been concerned with examining the various legal procedures that lead to the determination of the law in the halakhic system: the resolution of questions of fact or law in the second sense, the exercise of judicial discretion, and the continued adherence to, or the rejection or modification of, precedented behavior or custom. We have noted frequently, however, that the system does not present us with objective criteria on the basis of which to apply to these procedures systemic principles like *Et la'asot ladonai heferu toratekha, Mutav te'aker ot aḥat min ha-Torah*, or *Le-migdar milleta*. Furthermore, while we have demonstrated the legitimacy of the exercise of judicial discretion, we have not considered the kinds of factors which might incline an arbiter to adopt one position over another or to reject a precedent or abrogate a norm or a custom. Regarding these factors, too, we shall see that the system does not provide objective criteria for determining their use.

In other words, we have thus far been dealing with the systemic machinery of the decision-making process and must now proceed to examine the factors that may legitimately be taken into account by *posekim* as they utilize the machinery. These factors constitute the extralegal sources of the halakhic system, which, although not themselves legal norms, nevertheless bear greatly on the determination of the law.[1] Among these factors are some that are stated explicitly in the literature as well as others that are implicit.[2]

Before we proceed, however, a crucial caveat is necessary. The fact that these factors are admissible as data in the decision-making process might lead to the idea that they are also, by themselves, capable of determining the law rather than merely affecting it. However, in truth, extralegal sources constitute only one among many kinds of information available for and subject to the arbiter's evaluation: It is *he* alone who determines the law. For example, icthyologists may offer data concerning the nature of the fins and scales of swordfish, but the *posek* alone can determine whether or not they fulfill the requirements of *senappir* (fins) and *kaskeset* (scales) required by Leviticus 11:9. Sociologists, demographers, and ecologists may offer data concerning the ability of the earth to sustain increasing numbers of humans in the next thousand years, but only *posekim* can determine whether those data warrant overturning the precedent that advocates large families for Jews. Chemists may provide analyses of the changes in chemical composition resulting from various steps in the processing of foods, but only *posekim* can determine whether these chemical changes affect the status of the finished foodstuff in relation to the laws of *kashrut*.

Moreover, since extralegal sources, although admissible, are not determinative, it follows that two arbiters can disagree concerning the actual significance of specific extralegal data. But it must be stressed, what they would *not* be in disagreement about is the potential significance (i.e., the admissibility) of extralegal sources in general.

The Talmud itself provides a clear case that reflects the fact that the law is determined by the sages, not predetermined by the data provided by extralegal sources.[3] The passage reads:

> Rav Yehudah said in the name of Rav, "It happened once that a certain man lusted for a certain woman to the point that he became ill *(he'elah libbo tina)*. They came and asked of the doctors, who responded that there was no cure for him other than intercourse with the woman. Said the sages, 'Let him die rather than have intercourse with her.'
>
> "'[Let her] stand before him nude.' [Said the sages,] 'Let him die, but let her not stand before him nude.'
>
> "'[Let her] speak with him from behind a partition.' [Said

the sages,] 'Let him die, but let her not speak with him from behind a partition.'"

Concerning this episode there was a difference of opinion between Rabbi Ya'akov bar Idi and Rabbi Samuel bar Naḥmani, one asserting that she was a married woman, and the other that she was unattached (penuyah).

The stringency of the sages can be easily understood according to the view that she was married, but what justifies the stringency according to the view that she was unattached? Rav Papa said that [the stringency was motivated by concern] for the ignominy of the family (pegam mishpaḥah).[4] Rav Aḥa the son of Rav Ika said that [the stringency was motivated by concern] lest Jewish girls become licentious with forbidden relations.[5]

One would have expected the sages to pay heed to the treatments prescribed by the doctors in order to save the life of the man. Yet in this case those prescriptions, the extralegal sources, were insufficient to warrant the abrogation of a norm, no matter how dire the consequences to the man. Having considered them, the sages concluded, legally, that they were outweighed by other factors that favored adherence to the accepted norm. The doctors provided the extralegal sources, but the sages determined the law.[6]

Extralegal sources can be divided into four basic categories, and this chapter will be devoted to the analysis of the systemic functioning of these categories of data in the resolution of questions of fact in the second sense, in the exercise of judicial discretion, in the adherence to or rejection of precedent, and in the abrogation or modification of norms.[7] While there are instances of overlap between the categories, the division into categories serves, nonetheless, as an indication of the types of concerns the sources reflect. We shall call these categories: (1) medical/scientific; (2) sociological/realia; (3) economic; (4) ethical/psychological. . . .

Before closing this discussion, however, several points need to be made.

First, our emphasis on the widespread use of extralegal factors in the halakhic system is in no way meant to imply that they play a part in every legal decision; there are many decisions reached on the basis of legal sources alone. Even more, it is frequently the case that legal sources that were themselves formulated on the basis of extralegal considerations are cited again and again without any reconsideration of those extralegal sources; the possibility of a nexus between the extralegal and the legal sources in these cases remain precisely that, a possibility, no more. If there is no impetus motivating the posek to elevate the historical sources to legal significance, they remain legally insignificant.

Secondly, since the question of whether or not the impetus motivating a posek to take any one of these actions is compelling can itself be a matter of legitimate maḥaloket, we have recognized the role that subjectivity plays in the halakhic system. But subjectivity, we have seen, need be neither capricious nor whimsical. While ultimately Ein lo *la-dayyan ella mah she-einav ro'ot,* no posek who is committed to the preservation of the legal system and to guaranteeing its continued viability, and who reflects both the academic qualification of *gamir vesavir* and the personal characteristic of *yirat ha-shem*[253] would allow himself the luxury of capricious or whimsical actions.

Thirdly, rabbinic exegesis of scriptural passages is very similar to the promulgation of norms, the clear difference between them being that rabbinic exegesis purports to be the *direct* interpretation of the *grundnorm* rather than the establishment of new norms consonant with its spirit. But given the similarity between these activities, we can surely expect the categories of extralegal factors we have found to be operative in the promulgation of new norms also to be reflected in the rabbinic interpretation of Scripture. And, indeed, this is the case. Can it be denied, for example, that the rabbinic explanations of the biblical verses detailing the case of the rebellious son[254]—which in the final analysis, seem to transform this matter into something purely theoretical[255]—were, in all probability, motivated by concerns we have called ethical/psychological? Is it not also probable that the forced interpretations of the biblical verses that form the basis for the institution of "warning,"[256] without which a person cannot be executed, were also motivated by ethical concerns?

And surely the laws of borrowing and lending at interest, as postulated by the sages,[257] reflect the probability that these interpretations were motivated by concerns of economic reality. Indeed, it seems more than probable that the words Rabbi Shimon puts into the mouths of usurers,[258] "Moses was a wise man[259] and his Torah is true[260] . . . and if he had known how much money one could make from interest, he would not have issued the prohibition," reflected more than the thoughts of sinners alone.

Borrowings from other legal systems, whether consciously or unconsciously, also reflect the influence of extralegal considerations. Such borrowings often incorporate the sociological reality into the Jewish legal system, sometimes intact and sometimes modified.[261]

Finally, it should be stressed that recourse to extralegal considerations is not restricted to any one kind of legal procedure. Their applicability, for example, is not restricted to a situation requiring the exercise of judicial discretion when there is no precedented position, or to one that requires overturning a precedented position in favor of a previously nonprecedented position, or one that requires the abrogation or modification of norms, or the reconsideration of the ostensible factual basis of a legal presumption. Nevertheless, it would seem to be true that the more systemically severe the legal procedure, the more reticent *posekim* are (and should be) to make use of extralegal material. That is, it is easier for them to invoke extralegal considerations in order to justify choosing one position over another if neither of the positions constitutes a precedent. They are more cautious about invoking them when the rejected position is a precedented one, and even more cautious in invoking them in order to abrogate or modify a matter of law in the first sense.

Indeed, the conclusion is inescapable that recognized systemic authorities can invoke these same categories of extralegal sources even in the exercise of their ultimate rights vis-a-vis matters *de-oraita*. In fact, a rereading of the sources quoted in Chapter 7 will demonstrate the accuracy of this contention (and also the fact that those sources reflect the same two nexus patterns between historical and legal sources that we have described in this chapter). Naturally, the greatest degree of caution would be exercised in the application of extralegal considerations to matters *de-oraita*, since they are part of the *grund-norm*, and abrogation or modification of them bears on the problem of *ultra vires*.[262]

In the final analysis, however, we must continue to keep in mind that terms like *easier to invoke, more cautious, even more cautious*, and *the greatest degree of caution* are not objectifiable. What may seem to one to reflect the utmost caution may seem to another to reflect insufficient caution, yet the dictum *Ellu ve-ellu divrei elohim ḥayyim* would apply to both. Ultimately, the only guarantee of the integrity of the halakhic system is the integrity of its recognized authorities.

NOTES TO CHAPTER NINE

1. We shall see that some of these factors reoccur with such regularity that they *appear* to assume the status of legal norms. For example, the economic consideration of *Hefsed*. See, however, n. 7 below.
2. It should be noted again that implicit principles are considerably more problematic than explicit ones, insofar as it is possible for some to deny that they are operative within the system at all, while others assert that their existence is "irrefutably" proven from the sources. See above, pp. 2f. [Editor's note: p. 222 in this volume.]
3. Sanhedrin 75a.
4. I.e., who would be embarrassed by the episode (cf. Rashi, ad loc.), since the episode would become a negative mark against them.
5. I.e., that inconsequential acts can lead to more drastic, and forbidden, results.
6. It should be noted tangentially that the factors that outweighed the advice of the doctors were also extralegal. According to the position that the woman was married, even a tinge of adulterous behavior outweighed the acceptability of non-normative, and easily misunderstood, behavior. According to the view that the woman was unattached, the possible social-psychological ramifications of compliance with the doctors' advice were judged more detrimental than the consequences of noncompliance. In theory, though, there could have been sages who disagreed with the ruling on the grounds that the tinge of adultery would *not* likely be misunderstood, or that the possible social-psychological ramifications of compliance *were* worth the risk in order to save a life—the latter being itself worth taking risks for.
7. However, see below, pp. 279ff. [Editor's note: not included in this

volume.] The following point, too, bears emphasis: that extralegal sources are admissble as considerations in the decision-making process is a *systemic principle,* i.e., a principle that *governs the process* by which the system works. No extralegal factor, however, can be a *legal principle,* since none is sufficient in and of itself to determine the law in any given case. Caution is urged against confusing *explicit systemic principles* regarding the use of extralegal sources, i.e., principles which can be called by a specific name, such as *Hefsed* or *Nishtannu ha-ittim,* with *legal norms.* The principle of *Hefsed,* for example, can never determine the law. When a sage decides a given case on the basis of the principle of *Hefsed,* he is claiming that in that case the systemic principle that allows the consideration of monetary loss as an extralegal datum is sufficient to warrant the apparent abrogation of a legal norm. The potential confusion arises primarily because the wording of the decision may contain a well-known phrase like *Mi-shum hefsed,* which can lead to mistaking the principle for a legal norm, the applicability of which to the specific case can be objectively determinable. *Implicit systemic principles* regarding extralegal sources are much less likely to be confused with *legal norms* precisely because they are implicit and are not expressed in specified words or phrases that identify them as systemic principles.

253. See above, chap. 6. [Editor's note: not included in this volume.]

254. Deuteronomy 21:18–21. Mishnah and Talmud Sanhedrin, chap. 8.

255. See the *baraita* on Sanhedrin 71a: "The case of a rebellious son never happened and never will. Why, therefore, is it written in the Torah? So that is should be expounded upon, and a reward be received for doing so."

256. Sanhedrin 40b–41a.

257. Bava Mezi'a, chap. 5.

258. Ibid. 75b. Cf. Yerushalmi Bava Mezi'a 5:13, 10d.

259. A euphemism for "a fool."

260. A euphemism for "nonsense."

261. On the pervasive Greek influence on Jewish law, see the writings of Prof. Saul Lieberman, including *Hellenism in Jewish Palestine* (New York: Jewish Theological Seminary, 1962) and *Greek in Jewish Palestine,* 2d ed. (New York: Philipp Feldman, 1965). On Roman influences, see Boaz Cohen, *Jewish and Roman Law* (New York: Jewish Theological Seminary, 1966). These volumes are merely examples of a vast literature. Much fertile ground remains for research into the borrowing process in every stage of halakhic development—both the borrowing of actual norms and the borrowing act of methods of study, analysis, and exegesis.

262. See above, pp. 201–204. [Editor's note: not included in this volume.]

ᘓ   ᘓ   ᘓ

CHAPTER TEN

The Language of Pesak: *An Excursus*

THIS CHAPTER CONSTITUTES a digression from the rest of the volume. It is motivated, as will become clear, by the subject matter of the previous chapter, and serves as an appropriate prelude to the subject matter of the next chapter.

Pesak, short for *pesak halakhah,* is the term used to denote both an actual halakhic decision and the argument that leads a *posek* to that decision. The legal sections of the Pentateuch, vast sections of the literary sources of the talmudic period,[1] the commentaries on the talmudic literature, from the *ge'onim* through the modern period, all of the responsa literature, and, most certainly, all of the codes fall within the broad category of *pesak* literature.[2] Indeed, most genres of classical Jewish literature contain elements of *pesak,* even when *pesak* is not their primary purpose. No two of the genres listed above are composed in the same literary style, and no two are identical linguistically. This, of course, is not to deny that later genres appropriated, to a certain degree, some of the vocabulary and style of the earlier ones, but to emphasize that each genre also added its own distinctively individual elements to the vocabulary and style of halakhic literature. Moreover, at each of its stages halakhic literature appropriated—again to a certain degree only—elements of the vocabulary, style, and method of analysis of the contemporary non-Jewish legal literature.[3] The introduction of foreign words, phrases, and idioms capable of expressing new ideas with greater precision than would have been possible in the primary languages of *pesak,* Hebrew and Aramaic, was never considered inimical to *halakhah.* Indeed, although Hebrew (itself containing significant amounts of Aramaic) has remained the most common medium of formal halakhic composition, it is not unusual to find halakhic discussions and decisions in languages other than Hebrew.

Halakhah is religious law and has always been so recognized by both its adherents and its authorities. Thus, since all of the genres listed above *are* part of halakhic literature, it follows that there is no particular literary style, no unique vocabulary, nor any specific method of analysis that qualifies as the *sine qua non* of halakhic literature. The responsa are religious even though their style is different from that of the Tosafot; the Tosafot are religious even though their method of analysis is not identical with that of the Talmud; and the Talmud is religious even though its vocabulary is very different from that of the Bible.

In the final analysis, the only prerequisite for qualification of a halakhic statement as legitimate *pesak* is that the vocabulary, style, and method of analysis used be capable of expressing legitimate *pesak.*

There is no intrinsic or objective reason, therefore, that the terminology of the social sciences, for example, should not be introduced into the *pesak* literature being written today. To introduce such language would be to do no differently than the talmudic masters who introduced Greek and Latin terminology and methods into their halakhic deliberations. For even if it is true that later generations did not always recognize that particular terms or analytical methods in talmudic *halakhah* were originally Greek, the same can certainly not be said of those who actually lived in the Hellenistic world and who themselves introduced these terms and methods. The point is that it was clearly inconceivable to any *tanna* or *amora* that any terminology or any method of analysis was, by definition, unsuited to the elucidation of the law. So long as religion and religious law are perceived as encompassing all aspects of life without exception, any tool that enhances the ability of *posekim* to grapple more adequately with any aspect of life cannot be ignored. Indeed, any *posek* who willfully ignores such a useful tool is being remiss in the fulfillment of his religious duty. There can be no discipline, science, or analytical method (or any vocabulary and style that express them) that is, by definition, irrelevant to an all-pervasive religious system.

The discussion of the role of extralegal sources within the *halakhah* in Chapter 9 should have made it abundantly clear that consideration of data derived from the social sciences, for example, is systemically valid in halakhic decision-making. Such data have always been taken into account, even when the social sciences lacked all but the barest rudiments of precise terminology and definable method. Now, therefore, that a vocabulary and a methodology have been fully developed by the social sciences, it is altogether proper that they be consciously used in the elucidation of the law.[4]

Nevertheless, two very different groups viewing *halakhah* from radically different perspectives, have come to the conclusion that the introduction of the vocabulary, style, and methodology of the social sciences into halakhic discourse would be somehow nonreligious in nature and, therefore, unacceptable. The first group views itself as highly committed to *halakhah,* while the second perceives itself as totally uncommitted to the system.

Those who view themselves as highly committed to *halakhah* think of it, with some justification, as a religious legal system that is unique in the modern world. In an age, they argue, when people were more religious and viewed all their decisions and actions in the light of religious values and religious law, the halakhic system was not unique; only the fact that it was Jewish distinguished it from other religious legal systems of the time. Today, however, when people do not view themselves as religious and committed to religious legal systems, *halakhah* stands virtually alone. So much is, indeed, accurate; it is the next step taken by this group that produces the difficulty. For they claim, albeit tacitly, that since the halakhic system is now *sui generis*, its uniqueness as a religious legal system would be seriously undermined if it were to accept the same terminology and methodology that has been accepted by and incorporated into modern secular legal systems. In essence, it is their view that any mode of legal expression and analysis that is utilized in nonreligious legal systems is, by definition, unacceptable in a religious system. It is, of course, with this tacit premise that we disagree, for its posits that the religious nature of a legal system is contingent upon the terminology it invokes and the methods it employs; the implication being that terminology and methodology, in and of themselves, are either religious or nonreligious.

Those uncommitted to *halakhah*, on the other hand, tend to claim that religious law is totally different in nature from nonreligious law, that the two realms are totally discrete and concerned with totally different subject matter. Religious law, they say, should be restricted to matters of ritual, dealing only with prayer, holidays, *kashrut*, and with those aspects of personal status that relate to religion; but damages, torts, property, contracts, etc., should be the concern of secular law alone. Indeed, they conclude, the types of considerations that are the hallmark of secular legal systems are, by definition, inappropriate to religious systems. Moreover, the employment of secular legal terminology and methodology in a religious system would result in its secularization. So the uncommitted, too, reach the conclusion that secular language and methodology weaken the religious nature of a religious legal system. Our disagreement with this group, of course, stems from our rejection of its major premise, that is, that religious law and nonreligious law are completely distinct realms of discourse.

A direct result of the argument of the committed is a theory we would call the "naiveté theory." This theory proposes that the best *posek* is the one who has no knowledge whatsoever of contemporary sociology, economics, psychology, history, or anthropology.[5] As a result of his noninvolvement in such matters, he is supposedly protected from the possibility of being influenced by them. It is assumed that as a result of his noninvolvement, his halakhic decisions will not consciously reflect any of the knowledge uncovered by these disciplines, and that he will, consequently, be free of the pressure to decide in a particular way that such knowledge might bring to bear. Since such knowledge falls within the domain of nonreligious legal systems, and since the unique legal system called *halakhah*, which is entirely religious, ought to be as free as possible from them, its authoritative *posekim* are, therefore, best confined to the "four cubits of *halakhah*." Only the decisions of such men can be truly religious, the theory proposes. Only the selfless commitment to the preservation of *halakhah* in its "purest" form will ensure its survival as a religious legal system.

There is, however, yet a third group of contemporary Jews (a small one, to be sure) who are committed both to the halakhic system and to the affirmation not only of the acceptability of extralegal data within that system, but also of the acceptability of the terminology and methodology that those data imply. Such a Jew often finds himself on the horns of a dilemma because of the two prevailing views on *pesak* that we have described. If, for example, he encounters a *pesak* on some matter other than ritual, and the matter is one with regard to which extralegal data should certainly have been taken into consideration, yet the *pesak* is written in a way that clearly indicates that the *posek* has either ignored such data completely or has taken it into account without consciousness of its extralegal nature, this member of the third group is disquieted because the *posek* seems to have been uninfluenced by possibly relevant extralegal concerns. If, on the other hand, he encounters a *pesak* that consciously utilizes the terminology and methodology that the extralegal data imply, this third-group Jew, continually bombarded by the image of the *posek* prevalent among the class we have called committed, is also disquieted. This time, however, he is disquieted because this type of *pesak*, which he can accept, is rejected by the large class of the committed on the grounds that the *posek* seems aware of and influenced by extralegal concerns. The image of the *posek* held by this third-group Jew, of an individual committed both to the halakhic process and to the admissibility within it not only of extralegal data, but of the terminology and methodology that those data imply, finds scant reinforcement in reality. The ultimate problem, of course, lies in the assumption, of both the committed class and the uncommitted class, that there is such a thing as religious language, which, by definition, excludes certain modes of discourse.

For a Jew who holds the third view to disregard the opinions of those who find the entire halakhic system irrelevant will not be difficult, since he does not even share a universe of discourse with them. To disregard those who claim to be committed to the same legal system as he is, is not as easy, for, although the system to which both affirm loyalty allows wide latitude for legitimate difference of opinion, the differences between them on this point cannot be called a legitimate *maḥaloket*: The disagreement is about the very nature and systemic functioning of the halakhic system. While disputants from within the same system may conclude A and not-A regarding a given issue (e.g., one concluding that swordfish is *kasher* and the other concluding that it is not *kasher*), they are not concluding both A and not-A about the system itself. Regarding disagreements of the first kind, we have long ago affirmed that both may be "right," for *Ellu ve-ellu divrei elohim ḥayyim*. But a dispute of the second kind reflects a fundamental difference of opinion regarding the systemic functioning of the halakhic process itself; it is not a case of *Ellu ve-ellu divrei elohim ḥayyim*. In this situation, one position must be the correct one and the other the incorrect; either the system functions in manner X or it does not.

Thus, the Jew holding the third view must react to the class of the committed in the same way as he reacts to those who find the system irrelevant. He must disregard their opinions.[6] Unfortunately, since the majority of those who affirm commitment to *halakhah* are not members of the third group, this Jew, in the final analysis, has no viable choice but to persevere as a member of a minority. To retract would be to acquiesce to what he knows to be false.

In essence, the position of the contemporary Jew who is a member of the third group is based upon four premises.

1. That the authorities *he* recognizes as legitimate are seriously en-
    gaged in *pesak halakhah;* that is, that the decisions of these au-
    thorities are legitimate halakhic decisions, made for the benefit of
    Jews who are committed to the halakhic system. In his view, these
    authorities are as prepared to be strict as they are to be lenient,
    and they are confident that their constituency will abide by their
    decisions, whether based solely upon legal sources or based also
    upon extralegal sources, whether the decisions reaffirm traditional
    precedent or invoke the ultimate right of recognized authorities to
    uproot a matter *be-kum va-aseh* (i.e., actively) from the *grund-
    norm* itself. No matter how small their constituency may be, their
    decisions are addressed only to it. If, because they are serious in
    their approach to *halakhah,* the number of their constituents
    should increase, so much the better. But even if their constituency
    does not increase, this will not cause them to compromise either
    their seriousness or their commitment.

2. That the halakhic system is an all-encompassing system and that
    there is no subject that is, by definition, outside the theoretical
    purview of *halakhah*. That social, ethical, and moral issues are as
    proper subjects for halakhic analysis as ritual matters; indeed, that
    it is possible to take *halakhah* into account even in some political
    matters. This is not to say, of course, that there will not be issues
    about which *halakhah* may, in fact, have nothing to say. One of
    the considerations to which a *posek* must attend before deciding
    on the relevance or lack of relevance of extralegal sources of a so-
    ciological nature, for example, is whether the sociological reality
    that may become legally significant reflects a desirable reality—a
    question about which, in the end, *halakhah* may have nothing to
    say.[7] Or, for example, before reaching a decision about whether or
    not to overturn the precedent favoring large families, a *posek* will
    have to consider the question of whether the earth can sustain
    more than a certain number of inhabitants, and whether the
    world's population is likely to reach that level. Although the an-
    swers to these questions may achieve legal significance, it is possi-
    ble that the *halakhah* itself will have nothing to say about these
    subjects. They are, by definition, extralegal sources.[8]

3. That there is nothing inherently religious or nonreligious about
    any language or literary style or method of analysis. Any language
    is acceptable if it reflects religious thought; it is the intent of the
    person who uses the language that determines whether or not the
    language reflects religious thought. Since modern language is ca-
    pable of expressing religious thought, no *posek* need shy away
    from employing it in *pesak*.

4. That just as the use of modern language is no deterrent to the
    expression of religious thought, so the use of modern analytic meth-
    ods and modes of expression is in no way inimical to religious
    thought; that, on the contrary, the use of modern analytic methods

allows for greater precision in defining and understanding the factors that impinge upon the religious decision-making process. For example, there is no question that the phrase *Ha-galut mitgabber aleinu* means "the socioeconomic-political reality in which the Jewish community finds itself";[9] nor is there any question that this English rendering of the Hebrew is far more precise and far more comprehensible to the modern mind than the original Hebrew. It makes clear what the Hebrew leaves ambiguous, namely, which factors of contemporary Jewish existence might be relevant to a halakhic position advocating the overturning of established precedent.

Indeed, the third-group Jew holds that it is positively desirable to analyze older material in terms of modern concepts, in order to understand it more accurately. The legal opinions of the schools of Hillel and Shammai, he maintains, are no less religious because they may be seen, in part, to reflect the different socioeconomic strata of the constituents of these schools. Whatever insights modern social science can contribute to a more precise and complete understanding of the development of Jewish law should be welcomed. Nor, even if the future brings new insights that contradict our present understanding, will this impugn the religious integrity of our earlier interpretation. It is self-evident that no generation can understand the past in greater depth than the state of its knowledge makes possible. Yet it is absurd for any generation to refrain from attempting to add its own contribution to the understanding of the past because it cannot be certain that its understanding will stand uncontested forever; the understanding of one generation is the starting point for the next. No responsible generation dare to think that it has nothing to offer in terms of increased understanding and depth. To do so is not only irresponsible, it is detrimental to the continued viability of the halakhic system itself.

And, finally, that since the insights of the present generation of social scientists are best understood when they are transmitted in their vocabulary and reflect their methodology, their vocabulary and their methodology must be co-opted for halakhic use.

Indeed, there is at least one sense in which the use of what is generally considered nonreligious language in modern *pesak* is a greater guarantee of the religious orientation of that *pesak* than the continued use of that which is generally considered to be religious language. The factors that influence decision-makers in the decision-making process influence them whether or not they are aware of it. Can it be denied that the rich man's perception of the world influenced the School of Shammai even though the members of that school were not consciously aware of it? Surely not. Similarly, a *posek* of the modern age also carries with him attitudes and biases of which he is not consciously aware. The "naive" *posek* is no less influenced by social currents and world upheavals simply because he pretends to be unaware that he is so influenced. Modern communications technology renders it impossible for him to be uninfluenced, no matter how strong his denial. It is surely no greater evidence of the religious dedication of a *posek* to allow himself to be influenced unconsciously by his cultural environment than to consciously acknowledge its influence and to subject as much of it as he is aware of to the same careful scrutiny and analysis as the legal sources he utilizes.

Indeed, it is possible to imagine that the schools of Shammai and Hillel would have exercised even greater care in reaching their decisions if they had been able to ask themselves whether a decision they were about to render genuinely reflected the "will of God," or whether it merely reflected the "will of God" as seen through the tinted glasses of greater or lesser wealth. They, of course, cannot be faulted for having failed to understand how the unconscious attitudes resulting from wealth or poverty can distort one's outlook, but a modern *posek* who deliberately refuses to make use of such knowledge and such insights that are available to him can, indeed, be faulted. He can no more dismiss as irrelevant the analysis of data available to him as a result of the advancement of human knowledge than he can dismiss as irrelevant the analysis of data available to him from the legal sources of the *halakhah* itself. Both can be rejected after they have been analyzed, but neither can be prejudged as irrelevant and requiring no analysis whatsoever.

Obviously, much terminology considered to be "religious" will continue to be used even in modern *pesak*. The ability to define with greater precision what elements a *posek* considers crucial in the determination of "justice," "righteousness," "uprightness," "morality" and "propriety" in no way undermines the religious values these concepts embody. These words I have just listed, and many others that are similar, will not disappear from the literature of *pesak*. The concepts they express will remain the religious bases of the decision-making process; all that will change is the misimpression that these concepts have a precise and objective meaning and application which transcend all elements of place and time, social and economic reality, and psychological and scientific knowledge.

Finally, the type of *literary style* demanded by modern *pesak* is one that reveals not only what the *posek* decides, but also the issues he has considered in reaching that decision. This, in turn, requires clarification not only of the options adopted, but also of the options rejected, and of the reasons for both. The more thorough, extensive, and detailed the exposition, the easier it will be to determine possible grounds for adopting a position other than the one advocated by the *posek*. Indeed, if such a style of *pesak* became widespread, the halakhic defensibility of most *pesak* would be enhanced. In the final analysis, such a style would result in the proliferation of legitimate *maḥaloket*, but all *Le-shem shamayim*, and all reflecting the idea that *Ellu ve-ellu divrei elohim ḥayyim*.

As modern *posekim* pursue their work, they should not be discouraged by the knowledge that later generations will find in their writings evidence that they, too, were influenced by factors of which they were unaware. No generation can be expected to be aware of matters which the knowledge of that generation does not allow. Each generation should be satisfied to bring to its halakhic literature all the knowledge available to it, and should be confident in the knowledge that, just as each past generation has, each future generation will do the same.

NOTES TO CHAPTER TEN

1. Halakhic Midrash, Mishnah, Tosefta, and both the Babylonian and Palestinian Talmuds. It seems most plausible that even Albeck, who denies that Rabbi Judah the Prince was himself at all interested in *pesak* in the Mishnah (see Hanoch Albeck, *Introduction to the Mishnah* [Hebrew] [Jerusalem: Bialik Institute, 1959], chap. 6), would agree that the Mishnah is *pesak*. For even if Judah the Prince was not himself rendering decisions, the sources he quotes were rendering decisions.
2. There are even significant elements of *pesak* in genres of literature not often thought of as containing *pesak*, such as religious poetry *(piyyut)*. See, for example, Tosafot Makkot 3b, s.v. *ikka*.
3. For the biblical period, see James Pritchard, *Ancient Near Eastern Texts* (Princeton, N.J.: Princeton University Press, 1955). For the early talmudic period, see above, chap. 9, n. 261. For the style and method of the Tosafot, see José Faur, "The Legal Thinking of Tosafot: An Historical Approach," *Dine Israel* 6 (1975).
4. We stress the social sciences because there has never been real objection to the use of the vocabulary and method of the physical sciences. However, see n. 5 below.
5. This list does not include the physical sciences. As we have seen in the medical/scientific section of chap. 9 (above, pp. 234–248 [Editor's note: not included in this volume]), the physical sciences function primarily in the resolution of questions of fact, not of questions of law. In such a situation, there would be no objection to ascertaining the makeup of a new substance in order to determine whether it is *kasher* or not.

   Yet even within the medical/scientific realm one can see ramifications of the "naiveté theory." For once a scientific source has been used to resolve a question of fact, one often detects a hesitancy to allow that resolution to be examined on the basis of *new* scientific evidence. As a theoretical example, suppose that "death" were defined as the "the cessation of a heartbeat and of breathing." Further, suppose this legal definition to have been arrived at on the basis of medical/scientific sources. If future scientific studies were to demonstrate that the moment of death is determined otherwise, one would suppose that to be sufficient grounds for reopening the question of fact (subject to the restriction, however, of not allowing the testifying scientific expert to determine the law). Yet the hesitancy we noted is reflected in statements like "The legal definition of death is different from the scientific definition," which could be true if it meant that the *posekim* had determined that other considerations favored the older position, even against the weight of new scientific evidence. If, however, such a statement intimates hesitancy on the part of the *posekim* to reopen the question simply because it has once been decided, it reflects acceptance on the "naiveté theory." The situation would be one in which a legal definition assumes the status of a legal fiction (i.e., a knowing and conscious perversion of the actual facts of the matter). While there is surely a place for legal fictions within the system (see above, p. 55 [Editor's note: not included in this volume]), they are always consciously fictional. Only a hesitancy to invoke the rights guaranteed to *posekim,* however, could convince someone to elevate what is ostensibly a reflection of actual fact to the level of legal fiction.

6. I.e., regarding the way the system functions *qua* system. Nevertheless, he is duty bound to study their decisions in order to determine whether or not some, in fact, reflect decisions he can find compelling. There can, after all, be cases in which such a Jew would find the argument of his theoretical disputant germane and cogent even from his own perspective of the way the system functions, and even if his disputant bases his argument upon a systemic premise which the "modernist" denies. Not every issue is one which *must* involve a dispute about the systemic functioning of the halakhic process.

7. The complexity of the problem is indicated by the possiblility that existing norms may influence a *posek*'s view on the desirability of instituting a new sociological reality. Thus, while judgments about the desirability of a regularized and dependable postal service will undoubtedly be made completely independent of halakhic influences, the same might not be said about an issue such as male and female coeducation. The latter issue is chosen purposely, because it is not a burning issue at present, already having been resolved by various groups one way or the other. It is surely probable that some *posekim* who decided that coeducation would be an undesirable sociological innovation were influenced, consciously or otherwise, by the fact that traditional halakhic norms do not reflect coeducation as a *desideratum.* Other *posekim,* on the other hand, may have decided that coeducation was desirable, no matter what existing halakhic norms indicated. That is, they assumed, consciously or otherwise, that although the traditional norms reflect a particular sociological reality, that did not preclude the possibility that some other sociological reality might be equally desirable.

It seems reasonable to posit that the influence of halakhic norms in such judgments will be stronger the less firmly entrenched the reality is in the world. As a particular reality becomes more and more entrenched, the likelihood of dispassionate consideration (i.e., consideration independent of existing halakhic norms) becomes greater and greater. Thus, for example, public nudity is likely to be forbidden by almost all *posekim* at present because they feel, consciously or otherwise, that the halakhic norms that apparently forbid it reflect not only *a* sociological reality, but *the* desirable sociological reality. If acceptance of public nudity persists for an extended period, the *posekim* of a later age may be more able to view the issue in terms of sociological desirability, independent of existing halakhic norms. Lest this seem farfetched, suffice it to say that it would be easy to demonstrate that the type of feminine clothing considered acceptable in almost all traditional circles today was decried as immodest and unacceptable by *posekim* who lived in an earlier age.

8. Here, too, we must reemphasize both the complexity of the problem and the fact that extralegal sources, while admissible, are not necessarily determinative. In addition to the extralegal questions mentioned here (which are not addressed unambiguously by the experts, and which therefore require the *posek* to choose the position he finds most convincing), the question of family size involves other extralegal questions as well, and a *posek* must weigh all of the answers before reaching a decision. For instance, there are sociological-ethical questions: Should Jews have large families, even if the earth could not support life if all groups did the same, because they are obligated to recoup the losses of the Holocaust? Should American Jews have large families in order to perpetuate their influence on American politics, not only for their own benefit, but also for the benefit of the State of Israel? And there are economic questions: Might large Jewish families be contraindicated by the parents' potential ability to support and educate their children appropriately, even if the earth can clearly support them physically, and even if there is enough food? How complex the halakhic issues are, and how fertile the grounds for legitimate *mahaloket*. While the answers to the above quandaries may well be issues about which *halakhah* itself has nothing to say, any *posek* will find the answers to them exceedingly significant, when he finally renders his decision.

9. See Tosafot Kiddushin 41a, s.v. *asur,* and above, pp. 257 f. [Editor's note: not included in this volume.]

   ◟◉ ◟◉ ◟◉

CHAPTER ELEVEN

On New Legal Sources

. . . THERE IS ONE MORE AREA in which the potential relevance of the *peshat,* when it is not identical with the accepted classical interpretation, is problematic, and that is when the passage in question is to be found, not in the Talmud or in later rabbinic sources, but in the Torah, the *grundnorm* itself.

As with rabbinic sources, if one can say about a verse in the Bible that one understands what it meant to the speaker/Speaker when he/He said it, one can say that he understands the *peshat* of the verse. Bible scholars, utilizing many of the same tools and instruments of research as rabbinic scholars, are often able to shed light on the *peshat* of a verse in the Torah, an illumination that frequently results in an interpretation of the *peshat* of the verse that was unknown to any of the classical Bible commentators. Often the newly interpreted *peshat* of the verse is also at variance with the rabbinic interpretation of the verse that purports to be its *peshat*.[189]

The question is: Does the newly interpreted *peshat* of the biblical verse have potential legal significance, just as the newly discovered or rediscovered *peshat* of a rabbinic source does; or does the fact that it is an interpretation of the *grundnorm* that is at variance with the classical legal interpretation of the *grundnorm* preclude its having even potential legal significance?

If one is willing to concede the possibility that the *peshat* of a rabbinic statement could have been known, lost, and rediscovered over a span of no more than twenty-five hundred years, it seems no more logically difficult to posit the same possible history for the *peshat* of a biblical statement, considering that the span of its life can far exceed twenty-five hundred years! It is no more illogical to assert that had the talmudic sages had access to the literatures of the ancient Near East, and had they known the cognate ancient Semitic languages, they would have brought that knowledge to bear on their interpretations of the Torah than it is to assert that had an *amora* had a sufficient knowledge of Greek, he would have brought it to bear on his interpretation of a tannaitic statement. And just as the assertion of a modern scholar of rabbinics that he understands the *peshat* of a rabbinic passage as it has not been understood since it was spoken in no way denigrates the interpretation of his predecessors, so, too, a similar assertion about a verse from the Torah by a modern Bible scholar in no way denigrates the interpretations of his predecessors.

Nor do any of the above assertions regarding biblical verses impugn or violate the status of the Torah as the posited *grundnorm* of the halakhic system. Even if a *posek* were to advocate the abrogation of a norm based on a rabbinic interpretation of a scriptural verse, and even if he were to affirm the Naḥmanidean position regarding the *de-oraita* status of such norms,[190] his *pesak* would not violate the sacrosanct nature of the *grundnorm* itself. Rather, it would be an instance of *Hem ameru ve-hem ameru*. The establishment of the meaning of the *grundnorm* has always been entrusted to the sages. Thus, if the sages at one time said that the Torah meant X, and the sages of another time said that it meant Y, the legal status of X would be *de-oraita* until abrogated by later sages in favor of Y, which would then assume *de-oraita* status. X may become null and void, but the status of the Torah as the *grundnorm* remains untouched.

As the precedented and codified interpretations of rabbinic sources remain normative except in the face of compelling reasons, so, too, the precedented and codified interpretations of the Torah itself would remain normative except in the face of compelling reasons to overturn the precedent. Indeed, much of this book has been devoted to analysis of the factors, conditions, and circumstances that warrant abrogating or modifying precedent. An entire chapter has been devoted to a discussion of rabbinic rights vis-a-vis matters *de-oraita*. If rabbinic rights extend to the point of active, outright, and long-term abrogation of norms of the Torah, rights exercised only under the careful aegis of God-fearing *posekim*, surely those same *posekim*, duly conscious of the complexities of the halakhic process and aware of the kind of circumstances that might warrant the adoption of a previously nonprecedented norm above a precedented norm, have the systemic right to utilize their status as the authoritative interpreters of *halakhah* even when the norm in question is found in the Torah itself.

NOTES TO CHAPTER ELEVEN

189. A very important distinction must be drawn here between two types of rabbinic interpretation of biblical verses. The talmudic sages had a very keen sense of the Hebrew language and knew very well that many of their exegeses were not the *peshat* of the verses they were purporting to explain. See, as a classical example, Rabbi Ishama'el's exclamation to Rabbi Akiva: "Because you interpret a *vav* as you do, a priest's daughter should be burned?" (Sanhedrin 51b). Even the rabbinic school of thought that denied that "the Torah is written in the language of man *(dibberah Torah ki-leshon benei adam)*" recognized that it was only the Divine nature of the text that allowed the sages to "read-in" to biblical verses meanings clearly not intended by the *peshat* of the verse. Examples of such non-*peshat* meanings abound: taking a phrase like *ish ish*, which on the level of *peshat* means "everyone," and interpreting it to have legal implications beyond its *peshat*; or interpreting the meaningless definitive article *et* to have legal implications.

We contend that such exegesis does not even *purport* to be the *peshat* of the verse, and that this was recognized by the sages who offered this kind of exegesis. Thus, regarding any such exegesis, the *peshat* is a historical source in its most restricted sense, i.e., lacking all recognition by the law itself, and completely irrelevant legally.

There are, however, biblical verses which the sages interpreted according to what they actually thought was the *peshat*. Many of these interpretations are denied as *peshat* by biblical scholars. The sages who interpreted *onah* (Exodus 21:10) to mean "regular conjugal relations" undoubtedly understood that to be the *peshat* intended by the Speaker. It is to differences between this kind of rabbinic explanation and modern interpretations that the present discussion addresses itself.

Admittedly, there are many gray areas with regard to which the *posek* must be very wary. Did the sages understand their interpretation of *le-olam* (Exodus 21:6) as being the Jubilee year to be *peshat* or not? Is their interpretation of *le-ot al yadekha* (Deuteronomy 6:8) as being a hand phylactery *peshat* to the sages or not? It is most likely that a *posek* would refrain from exercising any of the rights we have been discussing if it is unclear whether the rabbinic interpretation of a biblical verse is meant to truly represent the *peshat* or not.

190. Discussed at length in chap. 2. [Editor's note: not included in this volume.]

⟨⟨⟨⎯⎯⎯⎯⎯⟩⟩⟩

C. NEIL GILLMAN

Rabbi Neil Gillman was ordained by the Jewish Theological Seminary in 1960 and has been a member of its faculty ever since. He earned his Ph.D. in philosophy from Columbia University in 1975. Dean of the Rabbinical School of the Jewish Theological Seminary of America from 1970 to 1981, he is now Aaron Rabinowitz and Simon H. Rifkind Professor of Jewish Philosophy there. An innovative dean who created the first major curriculum reform of the rabbinical school in decades, a reform that is still the basis for the curriculum there to this day, he is also a beloved teacher, known for gently but firmly pushing his rabbinic and lay students to articulate and then critique their own theologies so that they get used to doing both of those tasks throughout their lives as part of a thoughtful, living faith. He is the author of four books and numerous articles, and the book from which the selections below are excerpted, *Sacred Fragments: Recovering Theology for the Modern Jew* (1990), won the National Jewish Book Award in Jewish Thought for 1991. He lectures extensively in synagogues, which is especially appropriate to his theory, one that focuses on Judaism as lived in the community.

For Gillman, community is key, but not primarily in the way that it was for Kaplan, as giving us a sense of belonging. That undoubtedly is important for Gillman too, as it is for all of us, but Gillman is more interested in the role that our community plays in giving us a lens through which to see life. That lens is partially articulated in a community's law and in the statements it makes about itself, but it is more graphically and completely described in its stories. Gillman is especially interested not in the stories of the events in a people's history, although how the community reacted to those events can indeed serve as a way to identify and describe its approach to life. One thinks, for example, of the conflicting Jewish perspectives on how to respond to power: the Hanukkah story urges us to fight for military victory against religious tyranny, which is in sharp contrast to the talmudic story in which Rabbi Yoḥanan ben Zakkai gave in to Roman military might for the sake of an agreement to let the Sanhedrin survive outside Jerusalem.[13] The former story counsels self-defense through military might while the latter counsels self-defense through diplomacy with the powers that be. As Gillman says, however, history can "help us understand how Judaism came to be what it is, but it cannot persuade us that it ought to remain that way today or that its institutions should have any claim on us. The historical approach has to be supplemented by a theological perspective that deals with Judaism's pervasive views of God and humanity, and their interrelationship."

Gillman is therefore most interested in a community's myths. He is *not* using that term in its colloquial meaning of a falsehood, as in the sentence "It is a myth that Elliot Dorff is a good baseball player." Many have misunderstood Gillman's thought precisely on that elementary point, even though he does his best to make this distinction clear. He is instead using the term "myth" in its anthropological meaning—namely, a community's historical "attempt to discern specific patterns in their experience, and to shape these patterns into a meaningful whole that gave order to their world." That is, myths are stories that describe a community's understanding of life, including how it perceives the present and past and the goals that we ought to strive for. If the myth is a live one for the community, then it articulates its fundamental convictions.

Martin Buber distinguished between p-faith (from the Greek word *pistis,* meaning knowledge, as in the English word "epistemology") and e-faith (from the Hebrew word *emunah,* meaning trust in something or someone). For the Greeks and Western intellectuals ever since, Buber said, and for Christians, faith has meant faith *that* something is true; for the ancient Hebrews and Jews ever since, faith instead means faith *in* someone or something that is trusted.[14] Whether or not he was historically right does not concern me here, but Buber's distinction can illuminate both Roth and Gillman: The theological and aggadic equivalent of Roth's *grundnorm* is in Gillman's theory the myth or myths in which the community places its trust. In both cases, the foundation of the theory rests on something that a community finds ultimately worthwhile, something evoking allegiance, something so trustworthy that one leads one's life by it. That kind of faith, in contrast to p-faith, does not come from propositions that are demonstrated to be true; it comes instead from generations of a community's experience passed on to each of its members and adopted by them, in turn, as they find the norm or myth a reliable and wise guide for their lives. They place their faith *in* that norm or myth.

A community might articulate its fundamental understanding of life in philosophical and legal terms as well, but stories communicate these truths much more effectively and are much easier to pass down from generation to generation. They also are much more emotionally compelling. That is because stories speak in concrete, graphic language, appealing not only to the mind, but to the imagination and actual life experience of the hearer. (Remember that most culture was heard, not read, until very recent times, and perhaps that is still true today.) Moreover, stories—especially multiple stories—can capture the complexity of life, as in the two Jewish stories cited above concerning the best way to live in a world in which we are buffeted by hostile regimes. Indeed, stories can point to the parts of life that we do not understand without taking a definitive stance about them; they thereby enable us to take note of the mysterious and ineffable parts of life, thus enhancing our vision of life as we live it, while avoiding the pitfall of making unsubstantiated and, indeed, unknowable claims. Stories can speak about the nature and purposes of life itself, good and evil, human suffering, joy, fears, hopes, community, loneliness, and even the meaning of death. Furthermore, while laws and philosophical statements can surely be reinterpreted and applied to new circumstances, stories almost beg for interpretation, asking the listener to interpolate his or her own experience into the story and, conversely, to read the story in terms of one's own experience. And since one's own life experiences change over time, the meaning of a favorite and retold story can change over time as well. Thus myths are emotionally compelling in ways that laws and philosophical arguments can never be.

As a result, as Gillman says, "In turn, the myth lent integrity and identity to its community, generated loyalty to its unique destiny, motivated behavior, and established deep and lasting affective impulses." That is, just as a community lends credence to myths by retelling and reinterpreting them constantly (think of the cyclical Torah readings and the Passover seder as examples), so too the stories lend a sense of identity to the community as the group whose lives are shaped by the same stories. Moreover, the Jewish tradition was especially fond of encouraging different interpretations of its stories, as witnessed by the free-wheeling style of classical Midrash, where interpretations do not have to be reconciled, as they do in law, but where each person can offer a new interpretation as simply *davar aḥer*, "another word" or another way of thinking about the story. This openness to new and differing interpretations helps to involve each and every Jew in deciphering the messages of the story, thus involving people in an ongoing converstaion on a very personal level. This emotional involvement in the tradition, in turn, helps to motivate Jews to obey the law that is rooted in the classical stories, most especially the core Jewish story: Exodus, Sinai, and the trek to the Promised Land. For it is in that story that the Israelites are freed from human masters to meet God at Sinai and there to enter into a covenantal relationship with God, including both love and duties on both sides, just as human covenants entail (e.g., the covenant of marriage). And in that story too we inherit another distinctive Jewish trait: hope for a Promised Land, which includes not only the Land of Israel and our commitment to Zionism but also our hope for a spiritual Zion, a perfected world in which peace, prosperity, and knowledge of God reign (see, for example, Isaiah 2:1–4 and Micah 4:1–7).

Myths can live and die, and myths can be broken. "A live myth is a myth that continues to work; a dead myth is one that has ceased to function. A broken myth is one that is acknowledged as myth." A live myth works in the life of a person or community as an accurate portrayal of that person's or community's convictions and a motivating factor to engage in the actions that, in the life of the community, stem from those convictions; a dead myth ceases to function in those capacities. A broken myth—that, is one that no longer communicates truths to us because we have experienced things that call the myth into question and maybe even contradict it—needs to be reinterpreted or replaced with another myth. Gillman cites the French philosopher, Paul Ricoeur, who speaks about three stages of belief: the first naivete, when the person believes the myth literally; the second stage of doubt, when either the whole myth or significant sections of it are seen as false or at best doubtful; and then the third stage, a state of "second" or "willed" naivete, when "we willfully accept the mythic structure precisely as myth and allow it to work for us as the poetic, dramatic, and imaginative creation that it is." In any case, "The issue is never myth or no myth but which myth, for myths are the only means available to us for comprehending complex and elusive dimensions of our experience. . . . What we cannot endure, simply because we are human beings, is the utter confusion or chaos that results from the absence of a structure of meaning by which to read our experience."

This means that myths do not simply exist; they can be probed, critiqued, changed, and even discarded. On what grounds are they judged? Gillman primarily focuses on the pragmatic criteria of whether or not they work for those who try to live their lives by given myths, that is, whether a given myth convinces and motivates a person or community. But then is every myth just as good as any other, as long as people believe in them? That is, can myths be objectively true or false, good or bad? One certainly would want to say, for example, that while the Nazi myth of Aryan superiority surely worked for the Nazis themselves before and during World War II and unfortunately still works for neo-Nazis today, it nevertheless is a pernicious myth that must be rejected on both cognitive and moral grounds. That is, we want to say that the Nazi myth told a lie about the nature of human beings and that that lie was morally atrocious. In *Sacred Fragments,* Gillman does not account for such a critique: he focuses only on whether a myth is alive, dead, or broken, not whether it is true or false, good or bad.

In any case, the life of *mitzvot* is rooted, for Gillman, in the central covenantal myth of the Torah. We obey the *mitzvot* because in some form we find meaning and direction for our lives in that myth. Because Gillman does not believe in an Orthodox view of revelation, however— that is, he does not believe that God spoke discrete Hebrew words at Sinai, a flawless copy of which we have in hand in any of the publications of the Torah—he does not accept an Orthodox view of the commandments either. In a direct objection to Joel Roth, he says:

> Just as the sense of covenantedness is very much alive, so is the commitment to the fact of *mitzvot,* or more precisely, to the fact of *mitzvah.* For if God did not dictate the content of the Torah, then He did not dictate the specific *mitzvot.* The immediate corollary of this conclusion is that it is not possible for us to speak of *the* body of *mitzvot* or of *the halakhah* as if it formed one clearly circumscribed, monolithic, internally consistent system. There never was such a system and there surely can not be one in our day.
>
> We should, instead, view the community of caring, committed Jews as a series of overlapping mini-communities, each of which centers itself about a body of *mitzvot* that it accepts as binding. Institutionally, these mini-communities organize themselves into three major coalition movements, Orthodox, Conservative, and Reform, with right-wing Orthodox (or the Hasidic communities) and left-wing Reform forming the boundary positions. . . .

He also includes Reconstructionist Jews and argues that even "Jews who do not formally affiliate with a synagogue or observe the rituals of Judaism, but work actively within the framework of what we call Jewish 'civil religion,' also belong in the picture, for they too feel a sense of coercion about their Jewish activity. It is not always clear, then, who is the 'observant' Jew and who is not; the dividing line is not sharp and clean."

Along the same lines, he pointedly speaks of the "limits of legalism," indicating his sharp distinction from Roth and truly any theory that puts primary emphasis on Jewish law. "The insistence on pre-scribed behaviors as the test of authentic Jewish expression is vulner-able to two charges. The first is that it inevitably breeds a routinized, mechanical form of religious life that tends to stifle inwardness and genuine emotion. The second is that the sheer omnipresence of the law can only loom as a burden to anyone who takes it seriously." Instead Gillman wants to see Jewish law as a vehicle for Jews in their various communities to express in actions their version of the Jewish mythic structure, which is and should be primary, both logically and experientially.

At the same time, because Judaism historically has so strongly connected its underlying understanding of life to specific, obligatory actions, "There is simply no religious authenticity in Judaism outside of a halakhic system—not necessarily *the* halakhic system that the tradi-tionalists exalt, but *a* halakhic system that concretizes our sense of covenantedness as a community to God." The critical thing, then, is not the identity of the body of commandments that one accepts as binding, but rather "the fact of *mitzvah*," that is, the fact that Jews draw some behavioral implications from the core stories. He is quick to point out that his view does *not* amount to a Reform position, in which individu-als choose for themselves what they think God wants of them; rather, the community is the critical defining agency of what is required. It is just that there are multiple subcommunities among Jews, and each of those will define the substance of the commandments differently: "This view denies neither the existence of parameters for what constitutes au-thentic Jewish behavior nor the fact of authority. It does insist, however, that both the parameters and the authority emerge out of the commu-nity." This, as he then points out, involves both pluralism and historical development, elements often missing in Orthodox theories of Jewish law.

Probably because Gillman assumes much wider acceptance of Ju-daism's moral demands than of its ritual commandments, Gillman de-votes no more space to Jewish morals but another complete chapter to rituals. In that chapter, he discusses a variety of theories of ritual that he rejects, including especially the theory of ritual as the direct command of God. He instead argues for seeing rituals as emerging, in some way, out of the religious life of the community, as he sees the origin of all commandments. He argues against those who would see Jewish rituals as anachronistic, and he also argues against Kaplan's view that rituals are merely folkways. "The symbolist position," which Gillman adopts, "goes beyond the folkways by locating the authority for the ritual pattern not solely in the community, but more significantly, in the community's sense of a cosmic order. Ritual draws its power from our intuitive human need for structure, which is the obverse side of our equally intuitive fear of chaos." That is, while both Kaplan and Gillman emphasize the communal authority of Jewish rituals, for Kaplan Jews should keep kosher, obey the rules of the Sabbath, and so forth, to increase their sense of belonging to the Jewish community, while for Gillman Jews should perform the rituals for theological reasons—namely, to remind them of their community's understanding of reality and to give them a sense of order and structure.

Gillman interprets rituals, then, as "a symbolic expression, in behavioral language, of the community's religious myth." As such, rituals do indeed identify the community and enable individual Jews and Jewish communities to mark specific space, time, and social structures as *kadosh,* as separate from others and, as Kaplan would say, more important. But for Gillman, they do even more. They are also a way of remembering and living out the community's fundamental convictions, those articulated in their myths. As such, rituals structure the reality of those who perform them, especially if they consciously have the myth in mind as they do them. "Rituals are public dramatizations that bring the myth into experience."

Gillman's theory, like all others in this book, has some distinct strengths and weaknesses. On the negative side, Gillman puts great emphasis on the various communities that create and live by their particular halakhic systems. But how can you have a community in the first place if there are radically different understandings of the core Jewish myths and the actions we should take to articulate them? Does his theory not amount to Reform Judaism, where each Jew decides for himself or herself how much of the Jewish interpretation of life to believe and how much of traditional Jewish law to obey? In fact, what defines an interpretation as still counted within the community in contrast to one that is unacceptable and therefore outside it? After all, in order for a flag to function as a flag, it must be shared by, and recognizable to, the whole community; the same could be said of the dietary laws, say, or the laws of Jewish marriage. When do individuals' interpretation of Jewish law veer so much from the mainstream that what they are doing can no longer be considered a fulfillment of Jewish law—or, for that matter, Jewish in any recognizable understanding of that term? And who gets to define the mainstream in the first place?

Gillman might say that this problem is worse in theory than it is in fact, for, after all, all the diversity among Jewish beliefs and practices has not prevented Jews from creating and sustaining the major movements in American Judaism. Moreover, for all of the diversity of modern Jews, Jews have been able to define Jews for Jesus and other messianic movements as outside the pale of the Jewish community. But the most recent national Jewish population study, according to which approximately half of all American Jews do not belong to a synagogue at all and many are intermarrying,[15] raises real questions about whether Gillman can safely depend on the existence of subcommunities within the larger Jewish community to define what is binding in Jewish law. Indeed, today we are having trouble defining even who is a Jew. In Israel, the situation is even more diffuse. Not only are there many splinter groups among the 20 percent of Israel's population who identify as Orthodox, but despite valiant efforts by the Conservative and Reform movements there, for the vast majority of the remaining 80 percent there are no clear institutions with which they affiliate to identify what is binding for them in Jewish law. For many Jews in both places, nothing seems to be legally authoritative. And if that is the case, is Gillman right in maintaining that "[t]here is simply no religious authenticity in Judaism outside of a halakhic system"? Historically that has certainly been true, but one wonders whether it is still true today and, if so, who defines that system.

More abstractly, if a Jewish myth is going to function as a communal myth, then there need to be some limitations as to the meaning of the myth and the members of the community who live by it in an acceptable way, but Gillman does not provide for such limitations. Indeed, in some passages he leaves it to individuals to decide what works for them and what does not, and that surely undermines the communal character and power of the myth.

From the other end of the spectrum, Gillman's view is much too undefined. This is definitely not a theory for those who want a clearly articulated and manifestly authoritative Jewish legal system. Gillman would undoubtedly agree with that critique, claiming that such a Jewish legal system was an illusion in times past and is even more so today. Still, there are many Jews who long for more unity and certainty than Gillman's theory provides. After all, according to Gillman's theory, a subcommunity of Jews can change the substance of Jewish law at any time, regardless of the long history of a given practice and regardless of what the rest of today's Jews are doing. That certainly does not make for continuity, unity, or even authority. Indeed, despite Gillman's clear distinction between "myth" as falsehood and "myth" as a perception of the real, those who take this stand have the uncomfortable feeling that if they go along Gillman's path, they will be making the definition and authority of Jewish law depend on quicksand, on stories that might just be fiction after all. Gillman, of course, would probably respond that such people have not gone beyond the first of Ricoeur's three stages and they must do so if they are going to have a mature faith. Still, the fact remains that for such people this theory is much too tentative and insecure, depending as it does on various communities' perception of reality, rather than on a clear command from God.

On the other hand, there are also major strengths to Gillman's way of understanding Jewish law. First of all, as he says, those who adopt it have much less chance of making Jewish observance mechanical or emotionally flat. On the contrary, as long as they keep in mind the underlying and primary perception of reality that leads to their practice, they will experience Jewish law not as a burden to be gotten around as much as possible, but as meaningful actions that remind them of their community's view of what is and what ought to be.

Second, Gillman's theory allows for pluralism and development in Jewish law, as he contends, for the law is constantly in touch with a community's perception of reality and the ideal. Both of those, in turn, can be influenced by contemporary science, morality, economics, and social concerns, and how much to allow those to influence the received tradition will often be debated, with some Jews changing their practice in light of such factors more often and some less often.

Third, Gillman's theory has the distinct advantage of rooting Jewish law in stories that are easily transmittable, open to ongoing interpretation, and emotionally compelling. Aside from the fact that this is exactly how the Jewish tradition was in fact transmitted historically, this has the educational and motivational advantages of making Jewish law something that Jews would find meaningful to carry out. That is because rather than rooting Jewish law in cold legalistic codes or abstract philosophical statements about God, stories root Jewish law in human experience. At the same time, unlike Kaplan, Gillman does not make God disappear from the picture, even with regard to ritual law, since any subcommunity's practice of the law reflects its understanding of not only human realities, but of the transcendent element of experience as well. Indeed, the very genre of myths would point Jews to asking and responding to the complex and critical aspects of experience that myths try to articulate, and in so doing Jews would be consciously basing their actions on how they understand themselves, other humans, the environment, and God.

Sacred Fragments:
Recovering Theology for the Modern Jew*

NEIL GILLMAN

THE CONTEMPORARY TRADITIONALIST UNDERSTANDS the covenant as a literal description of the God–Israel relationship, initiated by God with the biblical community and binding its descendants for all time. Those of us who do not accept a literalist view of revelation view it as the central symbol in the complex Jewish myth. The parallels with the Hittite treaties illustrate how a community uses institutions from its cultural milieu to understand its historical experience. To call the covenant a symbol in no way lessens its power. As long as we are human beings, we will invariably read our experience in terms of symbols or constructs. To the extent that we feel ourselves bound to the Jewish people in time and in space, to the extent that we feel its destiny to be ours, to the extent that we feel obligated to do whatever it is we do as Jews because of that bond, we are responding to the sense of covenantedness that has been transmitted to us from the past.

If we are to pinpoint the historical basis for whatever authority the classical Jewish reading of the world and human life has on us, it lies precisely in that vision of a people bound in covenant to God. Deuteronomy 29:9–14 reminds us that God's covenant was made not only with those who stood at Sinai but also "with those who are not with us here this day"—that is, with us, the descendants of that original community, to this very day.

COVENANT IN THEOLOGY

But *we* were not really at Sinai, and herein lies the problem of relying exclusively on history. History does illuminate the present. It helps us understand how Judaism came to be what it is, but it can not persuade us that it ought to remain that way today or that its institutions should have any claim on us. The historical approach has to be supplemented by a theological perspective that deals with Judaism's pervasive views of God and humanity, and their interrelationship.

Every tradition begins with a set of axioms or intuitive value claims that are implicit in its classical literature and shape its distinctive content. Typically these claims are never questioned, though their influence is pervasive. Take, for example, the claim that Judaism has no room for

*Philadelphia: Jewish Publication Society, 1990, pp. 44–47, 54–60, 224, 228–236.

the distinction between the realms of the "religious" and the "secular." There is no dimension of life that is even potentially free from God's concern or from religious obligation. Hence the all-encompassing nature of the *mitzvot*. A claim of this kind is simply axiomatic to Judaism; it neither requires, nor can it be given, any justification beyond itself.

Now to pursue the implications of that axiom. If we were to attempt to delineate God's ultimate purpose in revealing the Torah, it would have to be His concern with creating a certain kind of social order on earth. This is Judaism's acclaimed "this worldliness" as opposed to the alleged "other worldliness" of other religions. Granted, the distinction is not absolutely clear-cut—no religion focuses solely on one or the other—but we are dealing with emphases or priorities, and Judaism's emphasis is that religion must transform the world of everyday human activity. We will have a great deal to say about Judaism's view of the afterlife and the "world to come" later on, but these doctrines never induced a sense of apathy about our responsibilities here and now, and in this world.

If the task is to transform the social order in the here and now, then the focus of activity has to be the infinitely complex range of relationships between human beings in concrete life situations. It is true that spirituality, purity of heart, and devotion are important, and many of the *mitzvot* involve ritual behavior with no obvious or primary interpersonal referent. But again, we are dealing with emphases and priorities. A mere glance at the first chapter of the book of Isaiah establishes that God's priority is the interpersonal *mitzvah*, the fate of the widow, the orphan, and the oppressed—not sacrifices and prayer. To use the distinction that became so central to Christianity, Judaism insists that we are "justified" (i.e., rendered authentic or legitimate in the eyes of God) by our "works," that is by our behavior and not, as Pauline Christianity would have it, by our "faith;" and among these works, morality is primary.

Judaism is pervaded by a basic confidence in our human ability to do the right thing. It is dangerous to speak in such broad strokes about a long and complex tradition, but again, it contains relatively little of the pessimism or fatalism about the human being that one senses in other traditions. The Bible (for example, Genesis 6:5 and 8:21) preserves a remarkably clear-eyed appreciation of our ability to do both good *and* evil, and it is never naïvely optimistic that we will inevitably choose the good. But in no way is the evil outcome predetermined by the fact of our humanness, by our intrinsic character. We do not believe, for example, that Adam's sin left its indelible imprint on all future generations, as the Christian doctrine of original sin teaches. Our freedom is real and unquestioned, as is our ability to repent and, even more striking, God's readiness to accept genuine repentance (as, in Jonah, He accepts Nineveh's repentance) so that we may start afresh.

What should be mistrusted, however, is our reliance on our own intuitive human judgment as to what is good and what is evil in any one concrete situation. This, finally, is what, under the traditionalist interpretation of Jewish religion, justifies God's revelation of *mitzvot*. Every moment of our lives can bring us into a complex interpersonal relationship where values are in conflict, and where it is not at all clear

how we should act. Human intuition, the Bible assumes, is far from infallible. We are easily blinded by self-interest. The Jew confronts each
of these situations with the question: What does God demand of me
now? The answer is the *mitzvah*.

To be a member of the covenanted community, then, is to bind
ourselves to be partners with God in creating a certain kind of world
for ourselves and our progeny. The *mitzvot* are the means for bringing
this about. Their formulation in the terminology of law is our tradition's attempt to lend them a dimension of authority, a binding or
structuring quality that flows directly out of the assumptions of biblical theology and anthropology. . . .

MITZVOT AND THE JEWISH MYTH

The third version of the middle option on revelation, the version that
sees Torah as the classic embodiment of the Jewish religious myth,
claims that covenant and *mitzvah* are the two complementary corner-
stones of the structure of meaning through which our ancestors organized their experience of the world and of history. This myth was their
attempt to discern specific patterns in their experience, and to shape
these patterns into a meaningful whole that gave order to their world.
In turn, the myth lent integrity and identity to its community, generated loyalty to its unique destiny, motivated behavior, and established
deep and lasting affective impulses.

Myths, or portions of complex myths, can "live" or "die," and
they can be "broken"—these are commonly accepted terms in the language of the philosophy of religion. A live myth is a myth that continues to work; a dead myth is one that has ceased to function. A broken
myth is one that is acknowledged as myth. When a myth is broken, one
is tempted to respond in either of two ways: to proclaim it as dead, or
to deny its brokenness and retreat to literalism. But neither response is
necessary; a myth can be broken and still live.

A myth can be broken and still live because there is simply no alternative to myth making. The issue is never myth or no myth but which
myth, for myths are the only means available to us for comprehending
complex and elusive dimensions of our experience. Astronomers and
psychoanalysts know this very well. If we abandon one myth, it can
only be in favor of another. What we can not endure, simply because we
are human beings, is the utter confusion or chaos that results from the
absence of a structure of meaning by which to read our experience.

Even more important, once we have accepted the inevitability of
myth making, we begin to welcome the uncanny power that myths exercise over us. This post-literal or post-critical phase of the inquiry has
been dubbed, by the French philosopher Paul Ricoeur, a state of "second" or "willed naïvete." We willfully accept the mythic structure precisely as myth and allow it to work for us as the poetic, dramatic, and
imaginative creation that it is.

The mythic definition of Jewish identity as formed out of a
covenant with God and concretized in a series of behavioral obliga-

tions remains alive, however broken it may be for many of us. Its vitality emerges in the palpable sense of a shared history and destiny that binds Jews everywhere, even those who are not formally "religious" or observant. See how quickly Jews mobilize their energies to support the State of Israel or persecuted Jews wherever they may be. The very sense that their fate is our fate can only be accounted for by the sense of covenantedness.

That sense of covenantedness invariably gets expressed in some type of behavior or activity—not necessarily the ritual activity of the observant Orthodox Jew. It may be expressed in some form of social action on behalf of Jewish causes, whether local or international, such as the State of Israel or Soviet Jewry. But it continues to manifest the sense of Jewish covenantedness, and it is frequently performed with the same strong sense of obligation that accompanies traditional Jewish observance.

Finally, note the very distinctive mood that accompanies the performance of the ritual of circumcision whereby the male child enters into the covenantal community. There is joy, but it is mingled with a sense of awe, a palpable tension that is felt by all, participants and on-lookers alike. This is the most ancient ritual we have, dating back to Abraham and our very beginnings as a people. It is also a blood ritual, and the sign of the covenant imparted on the male child is indelible. Most of all it expresses the sheer fact of continuity, of another link in the chain of the generations.

At this moment, all of the features of Jewish identity come together: a shared destiny, an indelible bond, a commitment that defies historical forces, and a clear statement that that commitment has to be expressed behaviorally in the performance of a ritual that will forever transform the very body of the male Jew. There is no greater testimony to the power and efficacy of this ritual than the demand by many of our contemporaries for a parallel ritual celebrating the birth of a female child. In fact, many such rituals have emerged out of the community itself, frequently without official rabbinic sanction, simply as an expression of our impulse to celebrate another link in the chain of Jewish continuity.

Just as the sense of covenantedness is very much alive, so is the commitment to the fact of *mitzvot,* or more precisely, to the fact of *mitzvah.* For if God did not dictate the content of Torah, then He did not dictate the specific *mitzvot.* The immediate corollary of this conclusion is that it is not possible for us to speak of *the* body of *mitzvot* or of *the halakhah* as if it formed one clearly circumscribed, monolithic, internally consistent system. There never was such a system, and there surely can not be one in our day.

We should, instead, view the community of caring, committed Jews as a series of overlapping mini-communities, each of which centers itself about a body of *mitzvot* that it accepts as binding. Institutionally, these mini-communities organize themselves into three major coalition movements, Orthodox, Conservative, and Reform, with right-wing Orthodoxy (or the Hasidic communities) and left-wing Reform forming the boundary positions. Reconstructionism, representing one modern attempt to reconceptualize the relationship between the Jewish religion and the sense of Jewish peoplehood, sharpens the Conservative and Reform thrust. It might even be arguable, as noted above, that Jews who do not formally affiliate with a synagogue or observe the rituals of Judaism, but work actively within the framework of what we call Jewish "civil religion," also belong in the picture, for they too feel a sense of coercion about their Jewish activity. It is not always clear, then, who is the "observant" Jew and who is not; the dividing line is not sharp and clean.

This view denies neither the existence of parameters for what constitutes authentic Jewish behavior nor the fact of authority. It does insist, however, that both the parameters and the authority emerge out of the community. But once we deny verbal or propositional revelation, there is simply no escaping that conclusion. It is the community that decides for itself what will be considered *mitzvah* and it does so on its own authority. The assumption, of course, is that this process is taken seriously, not casually. It is clearly not taken this way by the entire community; substantial numbers of Jews have no interest in any of it. But many Jews do. In the final analysis, all we can do is speak to and for them.

The position also makes two assumptions about the nature of Judaism that are very much part of the modern consciousness: pluralism and historical development. Much has been made of the diversity and divisiveness that characterize Jewish life today. But never in the long course of Jewish history did all Jews agree on what they should do as Jews. That diversity—even in the content of the body of *mitzvot*—was always understood as both inevitable and a mark of vitality. It is all the more so today. One of the reasons for pluralism is that various segments of the community differ on which of the *mitzvot* are still binding, which are no longer binding, which new ones should be adopted, on whose authority, and when.

One example will lend concreteness to this discussion. The most divisive issue in the Jewish community over the past decade has clearly been the role of women in Jewish religious life. The range of options is very wide, from right-wing Orthodoxy, which continues to consign women behind a synagogue partition, to contemporary Reform, which offers full and equal participation in all ritual and liturgical roles. In the middle lie different versions of the Conservative position: Some allow a woman to be called to the Torah on notable occasions, others on any occasion; some allow her to go up to the Torah but do not count her in the *minyan* of ten Jews necessary for a formal service of worship, others do; and, more recently some accept the fact that she can lead the congregation in worship and serve as rabbi or *hazzan* if she wears a *tallit* and *tefillin* and obligates herself to perform all of the *mitzvot* that are binding on a Jewish male. In yet other Conservative circles, women are denied all of the above but are permitted to sit with the male members of the family in the synagogue sanctuary.

Each of these options constitutes a different response to the conflicting claims of tradition and modernity, or of theonomy and autonomy. Each represents a different consensus arrived at by a mini-community on what constitutes the legitimate parameters within the body of *mitzvot*. Each can be buttressed with precedents from the Jewish past, some emphasizing the traditional role of the Jewish woman, and others the prophetic call for justice and equality. Each assigns a different weight to factors that are not explicitly legal. There is inevitably a subjective dimension to the way all of these issues come together in the final decision. But all of the positions take very seriously the fact of obligation, all struggle with the issue of authority, and all claim to be authentic. The ensemble is clear testimony to the vitality and seriousness of the community as a whole.

THE LIMITS OF LEGALISM

From the outside looking in, the insistence on prescribed behaviors as the test of authentic Jewish expression is vulnerable to two charges. The first is that it inevitably breeds a routinized, mechanical form of religious life that tends to stifle inwardness and genuine emotion. The second is that the sheer omnipresence of the law can only loom as a burden to anyone who takes it seriously. Taken together, they draw attention to what has frequently been called, pejoratively, the "legalism" of Judaism, presumably as opposed to the spontaneity of other religious traditions that place greater, or even exclusive, emphasis on inwardness.

Both charges are serious; both point to real dangers that have to be recognized and opposed. It is true, for example, that prayer can easily become a matter of racing through paragraph after paragraph of prescribed words while our minds and hearts are elsewhere. And there are moments in the day-to-day life experience of the Jew where the sense of obligation seems unbearably weighty. We yearn to break free and express ourselves in a spontaneous way, to pray, for example, only when we are moved to do so and to say only the words that come to mind at that moment.

There are, of course, numerous biblical and rabbinic texts that teach explicitly that the *mitzvot* are the means, not the end of Jewish religion; that they are God's gift to us, designed to bring us closer to Him, not a barrier to His fellowship; that a *mitzvah* performed without emotion is religiously sterile. But it is also clear that religious devotion is singularly difficult to achieve, especially under the stresses and tensions of our day-to-day responsibilities. A case can be made that precisely in our day it is even more important than ever that a structure be available—moments designated for prayer, the Sabbath for rest, the Festivals for celebration—that impels us out of the everyday and creates windows of opportunity for religious feelings to emerge. Most of us need structures of this kind; few of us can generate spontaneity in a vacuum. There is always the danger that the structure will take on a life of its own. But usually we are aware of those moments, guard against them, and try to rekindle our inner life. Some of us are more successful than others, but at least we try.

Obligations can become burdensome but they can also generate genuine pleasure and a sense of privilege. At such moments, the rabbinic tradition of *simkhah shel mitzvah*, the joy that emerges in fulfilling a *mitzvah*, becomes palpable. But such moments can only be felt from the inside; their test is experiential, not intellectual or theological. In the final analysis, after all of the theology has been spelled out, the Sabbath has to be lived to be understood and appreciated.

There is simply no religious authenticity in Judaism outside of a halakhic system—not necessarily *the* halakhic system that the traditionalists exalt, but a halakhic system that concretizes our sense of covenantedness as a community to God. For all of its inherent dangers, this commitment is axiomatic to Jewish religion. It stems from our earliest attempts at religious and communal self-definition. The challenge is to view *halakhah* as the means, not the end of Jewish piety, to welcome the opportunities it provides for worship and celebration, and then to strive for that elusive blend of structure and spontaneity that has been the hallmark of Jewish religious living from time immemorial. . . .

RITUAL AS SYMBOLIC BEHAVIOR

Once we reject a literalist understanding of revelation, we can no longer view God as the active, initiating source of ritual practice. The alternative is to view ritual as emerging, in some way, out of the religious life of the community—a position that the three remaining approaches all share.

The first of these perspectives views ritual as a symbolic expression, in behavioral language, of the community's religious myth. Ritual is "symbolic" behavior in the sense, first, that it has no substantive effect on the world out there, except on the feelings of the one who performs the ritual; and second, because it shares the characteristic of all symbols, namely, that of standing for, pointing to, or participating in a reality that lies beyond itself. It is thus an expression, in behavioral language, of the community's religious myth. This myth, in the sense of the term discussed in chapter 4, renders this ultimate reality in more discursive or narrative terms; the ritual, in behavioral terms. Together, they form one complex whole, duplicating and reinforcing each other. The Bible, for example, refers to two powerful Jewish rituals, circumcision and the observance of the Sabbath, in each case, as an *"ot,"* or symbol; the first, for the covenant between God and Israel, and the other, for God's original ordering of the world at creation. This understanding of ritual reflects the theological perspective of this volume as a whole and we will return to it in greater detail below. . . .

RITUALS AND COMMUNITIES

There is no escaping ritual. Rituals are intrinsic to communities, be they as small as a family, a corporation, or a baseball team, or as large as the United States Army or the Jewish people. The nexus between ritual and community rests on our viewing ritual as a language; just as a community creates its language, the language itself creates the community. People who speak a common language share a sense of belonging. But in the company of people who speak a foreign language, we feel excluded. In fact, *every* community includes and excludes—and one of the ways it does so is through its distinctive language.

We are familiar with verbal languages that are unsurpassed for specificity and accuracy of content. They communicate the most complicated pieces of information clearly and distinctly. Ritual languages replace (or frequently supplement) words with specific gestures, ways of dressing and eating, or of shaping the most ordinary tasks of everyday life, such as preparing for sleep at night or getting up in the morning, of courtship patterns, life transitions, and the like. We call these behavioral patterns "rituals" because they carry absolutely predictable meanings—that's what makes them a language. These highly specific meanings enable them to be understood, or "read," by other people who "speak" the same ritual language, and thus to do the work of creating a community.

Take the community of contemporary adolescents, a striking example of how a community is held together by a set of highly coercive ritual patterns. In order to belong to this community, adolescents pay impeccable attention to how they dress, how they wear their hair, how they hold their bodies, what they eat, what songs they sing, how they court each other, how they deal with parents and teachers. To flout any of these rituals is to invite ostracism. It may have been fine a generation ago for an adolescent girl to go to school wearing penny loafers, a plaid skirt with a large safety pin on the side, a white blouse, and a cashmere sweater, but in the America of the late 1980s, this outfit would invite exclusion from the group. Such is the coercive power of these rituals—none of which, it need be added, were revealed at Sinai.

Rituals, like verbal languages, confer identity. That's how they create communities, for who we are depends in large measure on where we belong. They garb the social experiences of everyday life in the distinctive values of a particular group. In the process, a group acquires a distinctive identity, separate from others.

This "separated" quality is probably the basic meaning of the Hebrew word "*kadosh*." Much like the English word "distinguished," which can mean both "separate" and "special," *kadosh* begins by meaning "separate" and ends by meaning "special" or "sacred," "holy," "elevated." So the Sabbath day, according to Genesis 2:3, begins by being separated out from the other days of the week and then becomes a special day. The people Israel (according to Leviticus 19:2) are commanded to be "*kedoshim*" or distinct/special from other peoples, and the rest of that chapter describes the specific lifestyle that will accomplish this goal. Leviticus 11:44 also exhorts the people to become *kedoshim* as the climax of an extended list of forbidden foods. In both of these passages, the community is to be *kadosh* because God Himself is *kadosh*—the absolute paradigm of "separate"/"special"—in relation to the world and to other gods.

As much as these rituals serve to distinguish a community, they also transmit its identity from generation to generation. They are powerful pedagogic devices, largely because of their inherent theatricality. This theatrical quality is less evident in the rituals of daily life, but is very much evident in the grand set pieces of communal ritual such as the rites of passage—circumcision, marriage, and the rites surrounding death, burial, and mourning—or, in the celebration of the Festivals of the year, such as the Passover *seder*. The Passover Haggadah is both script and textbook; the *seder* table is both theater set and classroom; the rituals of drinking the wine, dipping the herbs, and eating, lifting, and lowering the *matzah* are both stage directions and experiential learning devices. The whole forms an elaborate pageant designed to teach the founding, or "master," story of this community to a new generation.

This metaphor of ritual as theater illuminates both its community-building role and its pedagogic function. Theater, too, creates community; in a play's most powerful moments, the proscenium collapses and the players and audience are drawn together in a shared experience. Again like great theater, ritual carries a powerful emotional charge. Verbal language may be highly specific, but body language is much more effective in expressing emotion. We hug our children, for example, but it would take pages of prose to convey the affection that emerges in the hug. Great educational moments always have an affective or experiential dimension; they speak to the heart and the senses as much as to the mind. Eating the bitter herbs and dipping our fingers into the wine at the Passover *seder* leaves an infinitely longer imprint on the child than the recitation of the Haggadah.

RITUALS AND MYTHS

Even the most convinced of secularists will find it difficult to deny the power of ritual to confer identity on a community and lend a sensory or poetic quality to its communal life. This, in effect, is the response of the folkways position to the challenge of anachronism. The question is: Can we go beyond this?

The symbolist position says that we can—by viewing ritual as an experiential expression of the community's myth. We have seen, in Chapter 4, that the signal function of a religious myth is to structure reality, to create a sense of cosmos or order in our lives. In the process, we acquire a place in the cosmic order and an accompanying sense of identity, security, and meaning.

The heart of the myth is its structuring role. Some structures are inherent in reality: day and night, for example, or animal and vegetable, male and female, heaven and earth, and life and death. These are part of the very nature of things. But other structures are cultural artifacts. Space and time, for example, in themselves are undifferentiated or homogenous; the division of space into inches, feet, yards, and miles; or the more complex differentiation of space through architectural design, the creation of special spaces such as temples and monuments, and the establishment of national boundaries and city limits is the work of human beings. So is the division of time into seconds, minutes, hours, days, weeks, months, and years; and certainly the determination of special times such as weekends, birthdays, anniversaries, or Sabbaths and Festivals.

The structuring work of the myth is reflected in both the intrinsic and the cultural distinctions. In the latter, it literally creates the structure: It determines, for example, when a day or a year begins and ends, when a week begins and why it has seven days; it establishes Festival days and special spaces, such as monuments and museums; and it creates sacred spaces, such as cathedrals and synagogues. Even where certain structures are inherently real, the myth determines which of these inherent structures it wants to highlight, which it chooses to ignore, and how it chooses to do the highlighting. Meat and milk, for example, may be inherently distinct, but there is no intrinsic reason why they can not be consumed together, whereas meat and vegetables, also inherently distinct, can. Or why males and females should be prohibited from sitting together in the synagogue but not around the dining room table.

Above all, a myth abhors undifferentiation or homogeneity, which it understands as incipient chaos, for human beings can not tolerate chaos. Cartons, for example, can be stored in a large, undifferentiated warehouse space; human beings demand rooms. If the space is to be lived in, it has to be divided into a kitchen, living room, bedroom, dining room, and the rest. The alternative engenders feelings of insecurity, rootlessness, and anxiety. The same applies to time. Try to imagine the sense of rootlessness that would result from going through life without the notion of a "day" or a "week," without a sense of when either begins and ends, without hours to mark off the working day or to tell us when the opera begins, or without special days devoted to leisure or celebration.

Myths function unconsciously. They are so ancient and authoritative that they become quasi-invisible. But those myths that shape human experience in a rich and distinctive way, that provide a living community with its *raison d'etre* and shape its sense of destiny, can not afford to remain invisible. They must be brought alive, into experience. To accomplish this, the community generates rituals. Rituals are public dramatizations that bring the myth into experience. They enable a community to bond together, live its myth in an overt way, and transmit it from generation to generation.

Rituals reflect the myth by almost invariably focusing on the interface between two structures, either two inherent structures or two structures that the myth wants to highlight. Wherever we find a ritual, we almost always find a structural distinction. The operative metaphor seems to be that of a "threshold," that is, the point where two structures meet. The ritual illuminates the threshold between these two structures, guides us from one structure into the other, and in so doing, brings the structural distinction into our awareness.

A number of examples. First, on the most literal level, the threshold of a Jewish home is marked by a *mezuzzah*, literally a "doorpost," but by extension, a tiny case containing the parchment with passages from the Torah that (according to Deuteronomy 6:9 and 11:20) we are commanded to place on the doorposts of our homes. The *mezuzzah* separates my home—with its associations of privacy, possession, security—from the outside world which is public, open, and hence potentially perilous (recall the blood on the doorposts of the Israelite homes in Egypt which protected our ancestors on the night of the Exodus, in Exodus 12:7). The *mezuzzah* effectively creates my private space which, by law, is inviolable.

On a much broader canvas, the Bible is replete with instances of the attempt to structure space. God commands Abraham (Genesis 13:17) to "walk about the land [of Canaan], through its length and breadth," as if to establish the coordinates of the space that he has been promised. Later, in the course of their trek through the wilderness—precisely!—the Israelites march in a highly structured order with the sanctuary at the center of the camp and the tribes arranged in precise order around the periphery (Numbers 2). This anticipates the later hierarchy of sacred spaces in biblical religion—the world as a whole, the land of Israel, Jerusalem, the Temple, the Holy of Holies, the Ark, and ultimately, the point between the two cherubim that were placed on the cover of the Ark, from where, according to Exodus 25:22 and Numbers 7:89, God will speak to the community.

Note, however, that in the desert experience, there is no inherently sacred space, no one spot that is fixed as a point of orientation for the spatial hierarchy. That point is wherever the Israelites set up their camp and locate the Sanctuary. Here, the community determines the spatial hierarchy. In the later tradition, the central point of orientation in the Jerusalem Temple is fixed by identifying it (according to 2 Chronicles 3:1) as Moriah, the place where God revealed Himself to Abraham as he was preparing to sacrifice his son (Genesis 22:14). This ambivalence prefigures the ambiguity with which later formulations of Jewish religion viewed the entire notion of sacred space for, in time, Jews were exiled from their land, the Temple was destroyed, and, in the course of an extended experience of exile (or displacement), Jewish religion reverted to the earlier notion that any spot on earth can become sacred simply by the decision to establish a synagogue for prayer.

But there is no ambiguity about Judaism's interest in structuring time. An elaborate set of rituals are designed to distinguish thresholds in time. We have liturgies to recite immediately upon waking up and immediately before going to sleep. We pray at sunrise and at sunset, and in each case, the liturgy notes the transition from light to darkness or from darkness to light, from day to night and from night to day. We mark the end and the beginning of a week with a Sabbath day, and we separate the Sabbath from the rest of the week by rituals of transition at its beginning and at its end. The rituals are called, respectively, *kiddush* and *havdalah*, which are synonyms and which literally mean "separating out." We have a ritual that marks the beginning of each month and a festival that marks the beginning of a new year. Two of our major festivals, Sukkoth and Passover, occur exactly six months apart and mark the natural transitions from summer to winter and again from winter to summer. Finally, we use rituals to mark the stages of human life: birth, puberty, marriage, and death.

Like space and time, social structures are also designated. Judaism has a ritual for creating a family (marriage), for dissolving a family (divorce), and for entering into a community (conversion). A Jewish male infant is brought into the covenanted community through the ritual of circumcision. The community as a whole celebrates its founding through a complex Passover festival during which it reenacts the events that brought it into being as a distinctive people. An elaborate set of rituals distinguishes the status of the male members of the community from the female, the adult members from the children, and in biblical times, the priests and Levites from the rest of the community.

Finally, a complex series of ritually determined distinctions shape the everyday life of a member of this community. They affect eating, dressing, sexual relations, interpersonal relations, and the rest. On the microcosmic level, the dietary laws, for example, force us to make explicit distinctions between meat products and milk products. Within the groupings of animals, fish, and birds, we distinguish between those members of each class that we may eat and those that we may not. On the macrocosmic level, the ensemble works to perpetuate a daylong and even lifelong sense of distinction between the life experience of this community and that of other communities, making this community *kadosh*—that is, "separate" and, eventually, special or "holy."

There is a clear overlap between the folkways position on ritual and the symbolist position; both see ritual as a way of conferring and transmitting identity within a communal structure. But the symbolist position goes beyond the folkways by locating the authority for the ritual pattern not solely in the community but, more significantly, in the community's sense of a cosmic order. Ritual draws its power from our intuitive human need for structure, which is the obverse side of our equally intuitive fear of chaos. That deeply human need is what makes ritual compelling. Jewish religion captures this compelling quality by viewing the Jewish ritual pattern as a system of law that it ascribes to a revealing God. But from this anthropological perspective, the reason this legal system is taken as binding in the first place rests in its responsiveness to the human need for order.

Finally, we call this position "symbolic" because it views these ritual patterns as having no substantive effect on the world. They don't change anything out there; they don't bring rainfall, assure safety and security, or cure illness. These ritual behavior patterns are themselves symbols in the sense described in chapter 4. They are not "signs"— mere human conventions that can be changed at whim like traffic lights. Rather, like a national flag, they point to, stand for, participate in, or draw their power from some dimension of reality that lies beyond them, precisely that dimension of reality that the community's myth tries to capture.

The Bible itself captures the symbolic quality of ritual by using the Hebrew term *"ot"* in reference to two major Jewish rituals, the Sabbath (Exodus 31:17) and circumcision (Genesis 17:11). The word itself is usually translated as "sign," but it is clear that in our technical, contemporary usage, "symbol" would be more accurate. Neither is a mere convention. Both have enormous affective power. Both draw their power from a central, founding event captured by this community's myth: in one case, God's original ordering of the universe in creation; in the other, the primitive binding together of God and Abraham, now Israel, in an eternal, covenantal relationship. In each case, the performance of the ritual is a reenactment—not merely a recalling—of that primal event. We recreate that original cosmic order by distinguishing the day on which God completed the work of creation and by stepping back from our own creative work, as He stepped back on the seventh day. In effect, every Sabbath is a temporary restoration of that primal sense of cosmos—which is why the talmudic tradition also understands the Sabbath as a foretaste of the age to come, when that original cosmos will be restored for eternity. We also reenact the primitive covenant with Abraham by introducing each newborn Jewish male into that same covenantal relationship.

On a broader scale, we as a community are commanded to be *kedoshim* (holy, separated out, distinguished) as God is *kadosh* (Leviticus 19:2). Our separateness points to God's. As we are distinct from other nations, so is He distinct from other gods. Each time we perform our rituals, we affirm His distinctiveness, for Israel is that community on earth that stands for, represents, or, in our terminology, "symbolizes" God's distinctive presence in the world.

The ultimate goal of the entire Jewish ritual system, then, is not simply to enable us to identify with this particular community, as the folkways position would have it but, rather, to capture in our personal lives an elaborate cosmic order which extends to God Himself as the ultimate cause and embodiment of that order. That's why our communal life is replete with divisions between the permitted and the forbidden—in what we eat, how we dress, how we conduct our sexual activities. The ritual system, then, points to, or brings into awareness the cosmic structures through which our community has organized its picture of the world.

───────

D. LOUIS JACOBS

Rabbi Louis Jacobs is currently rabbi of the New London Synagogue in London, England; Goldsmid Visiting Professor at University College, London; and Visiting Professor at Lancaster University as well. A product of Orthodox yeshivot at Manchester and Gateshead in England with undergraduate and doctoral degrees from London University, Rabbi Louis Jacobs's erudition and brilliance made him the obvious candidate to succeed Rabbi Isidor Epstein as Principal of Jews College upon the latter's retirement in 1962. In 1957, however, Jacobs had written *We Have Reason to Believe,* in which he affirmed belief in a historical approach to the texts of Judaism, including the Torah. That made him *persona non grata* within the Orthodox establishment, a painful story he retells in his 1989 autobiography, *Helping With Inquiries: An Autobiography.* Because of Jacobs's "heresy," Chief Rabbi Brodie not only refused him that advancement but also denied him reappointment as rabbi of his former congregation, the New West End Synagogue. After an angry public row, most of the members of that synagogue resigned and formed the New London Synagogue, with Dr. Jacobs as its rabbi. None of this deterred Rabbi Jacobs from maintaining his beliefs; quite to the contrary, he continued to write about them and to teach them in his synagogue, which, with the cooperation of its lay leaders, became the first Conservative/Masorti synagogue in England. Rabbi Jacobs is rightfully, then, known as the founder of the Masorti (Conservative) movement there and is still among its primary spokesmen.

A truly prolific author, Rabbi Jacobs has demonstrated the rare ability to write for widely varying audiences. He has written a number of books on Judaism intended for a popular audience. These are routinely "high popular culture": they do not assume a strong Jewish education, but they aim high in transmitting the tradition to lay people in a serious way. For example, between 1968 and 1976 he wrote a series of five books for Behrman House (the "Chain of Tradition Series"), designed for teenagers and adults with little Jewish knowledge. In that series he selected, translated, and explained, section by section, primary texts about Jewish law, mysticism, ethics, exegesis, and philosophy. He later wrote for Behrman House three introductory texts to Judaism for adults, *The Book of Jewish Belief* (1984); *The Book of Jewish Practice* (1987); and *Jewish Personal and Social Ethics* (1990).

A second genre of his writings focuses on Jewish theology, in which he not only explains the theologies of others but creates his own theology. This genre began with *We Have Reason to Believe* and includes *Faith* (1968); *A Jewish Theology* (1973); *God, Torah, and Israel: Traditionalism without Fundamentalism* (1990); and the restatement and reenforcement of his thesis in the first of those in his book, *Beyond Reasonable Doubt* (1999), the book from which our first selection from his writings is taken.

Yet a third genre of his writings, the largest corpus by far, is academic Jewish scholarship, which includes, among many others: *Studies in Talmudic Logic and Methodology* (1961); *Principles of Jewish Faith:*

An Analytic Study (1964); *Hasidic Prayer* (1973); *Theology in the Responsa* (1975); *A Tree of Life: Diversity, Flexibility, and Creativity in Jewish Law* (1984); and *Structure and Form in the Talmud* (1991).

The first selection below graphically illustrates Jacobs's ability to *synthesize* the traditional with the modern and the philosophical with the religious. He adamantly refuses to let traditional religious claims pass just because they are traditional; on the contrary, he exposes them to the most honest, thoroughgoing, far-reaching, and deep critique possible. At the same time, he is not prepared to ignore the distinctly *religious* meaning of classical Jewish texts and practices. Human beings may have crafted them all, but they did so, for Jacobs, in response to God. As he says elsewhere, "Revelation is a matter of faith rather than historical scholarship. Scholarly investigation into the authorship of the biblical books cannot by its very nature make any pronouncement on whether the author or authors of a biblical book were inspired."[16] Yet Jacobs himself clearly believes that the Torah is a divinely inspired book, and he comes to that conclusion on the basis of some reasons for his faith:

> It is exceedingly difficult, if not impossible, to account for the lofty teachings of the Hebrew prophets, the civilizing influence of the great Law of Moses, the history of a small people who found God and brought Him to mankind, the Sinaitic revelation itself and the spiritual power these books continue to exercise over men's souls, unless Israel really met with God and recorded in immortal language the meaning of that encounter. We can be skeptical of individual details in the Bible. We can dwell on the numerous parallels with Egyptian, Babylonian, and Assyrian *mores*. We can point out the striking resemblances between Hebrew poetry in the Bible and Canaanite hymns in praise of pagan gods. We are forced to recognize, to a degree quite beyond the imagination of our ancestors, the human element in the Biblical record. What cannot be seriously doubted is the 'something else' which has ensured that this and no other collection of books has become the sacred Scripture of a large proportion of mankind; that there are living Jews who regard themselves as the heirs to the Bible and no living Babylonians, Canaanites and Assyrians; that there is a Voice which speaks here in promise of great vision, of dreams of world peace, of holiness, justice, and mercy, of freedom and the unique worth of each individual as a child of God . . . For all our recognition of the dynamic rather than static quality of the tradition, the basic belief that it is all the work of God in co-operation with the humans who sought Him can reasonably be said to be based on experience, the experience of the prophets and law-makers in the first instance and the later experience of sages, thinkers, and undistinguished people who live by the great truths. The existence of the Jews does explain the existence of God. The Jews are the most powerful proof for God's existence. There is still great power in the appeal to tradition.[17]

Moreover, the ongoing meaning and import of those texts and practices depend on the extent that they continue to engage us with God:

> Revelation must be understood as a far more complicated and complex process of divine-human encounter and interaction and quite differently from the idea of direct divine communication of infallible laws and propositions, upon which the traditional theory of Halakhah depends. . . . Revelation is now seen as a series of meetings or encounters between God and man. The Bible is seen as the record of these encounters, as is the Torah throughout Israel's generations. It is not the actual words of the Bible that were revealed. These belong rather to the faltering human attempts at putting down what it signified for men to have felt themselves very near to God and how they reflected on the nearness to God of their ancestors.[18]

Thus the classical texts of the Jewish tradition are of human origin, but they were written in response to experiences of God. In asserting this, Jacobs espouses a view of Jewish scholarship and action that is at once brutally honest and yet fervently religious.

With regard specifically to Jewish law, he asserts, in general, that "The whole of the Halakhah is a mighty attempt at bringing holiness into the detailed affairs of life in this corporeal world."[19] In the first selection below, he acknowledges that the moral parts of Jewish law recommend themselves to all human beings on the basis of their reason and experience alone. Why, then, are they religious in any sense? Jacobs cites the medieval Jewish thinker, Saadiah Gaon (883–942), in stating that revelation is necessary because reason can only give us the basic principles of ethics, but we need revelation to inform us of the details of how those principles should be applied. Saadiah also maintained that revelation is necessary to ensure that we know what we must do even if our reasoning fails (some people, after all, are not very smart, and even the most intelligent of us make mistakes) or before it is developed (when we are children). Jacobs adds that even "granted the autonomy of ethics [from religion], religion is required to give an added dimension to life. The religious man sees his ethical concern as part of his total relationship with God. . . . By introducing the love of God into the picture, a different quality is imparted to man's ethical strivings. . . . Man is to live, it can be put, both horizontally and vertically," focusing both on earthly concerns and the relationship of those to God's ultimate purposes for our existence. Thus even though morals are open to all human beings to know and debate, Judaism adds a specific religious dimension to moral demands and thus enhances their scope and quality.

Jacobs asserts a similar claim for Judaism's ritual laws. He goes to some length in this selection to point out the massive human component in determining the exact shape of Judaism's ritual life, including the synagogue, the Sabbath and festivals, and prayer. Ultimately, as he says elsewhere, "the ultimate authority for determining which observances are binding upon the faithful Jew is the historical experience of the people Israel since, historically perceived, that is ultimately the sanction of Halakhah itself."[20] As he continues to note there, that might lead one to assert that Jewish law is exclusively the product of human beings and is to be understood, applied, and practiced as such, "that it is possible to have *mitzvot* ('commands') without a *metzavveh* ('one who issues the commands') or with the people Israel being the *metzavveh*." Jacobs, though, calls such an approach "a theological monstrosity," for it amounts to ancestor worship or worship of Jewish history, both forms of idolatry. (Kaplan, who saw Jewish texts and law as purely a human product, was at least honest enough to get rid of the category of Jewish law altogether, replacing it with moral norms built into nature and ritual folkways.) Jacobs instead asserts that for all the human involvement in producing and shaping Jewish law, it remains divine law because it is and always was intended as a response to God: "The *religious* appeal to history is that, whatever their origins, Jewish observances have come to be the most effective vehicles for the worship of God." That approach enables us to see that "it is not history that is being worshiped; it is the God who reveals His will through history."[21] In the first selection below, he explains in some detail how that religious element of Jewish ritual observance can be experienced by non-fundamentalist Jews who acknowledge fully and honestly the human shaping of those rituals. He maintains that any adequate philosophy of Jewish law must take account of that religious element—namely, the ways in which the rituals are our form of encountering and worshiping God.

To discern God's will through Jewish history and law requires that we first study those subjects honestly. Jacobs engages in just such a careful and extensive study of Jewish law in his book from which the quotations in the previous paragraph were taken, *A Tree of Life: Diversity, Flexibility, and Creativity in Jewish Law,* and he indicates some of the results of that effort in his discussion in the first selection below in describing how the laws of the synagogue and of the Sabbath and festivals came to be. Beyond such scholarship, though, one must see how those rituals, for all their human origins, function religiously as vehicles for encountering and worshiping God. Furthermore, to enable the ritual laws to fulfill that religious function, one must exercise *judgment*. Specifically, as he points out in the second passage from his writings included below (an excerpt from his earlier book, *A Jewish Theology*), one must distinguish between three types of traditional Jewish laws: those that are clearly beneficial, which we must retain and reinforce; those that are morally neutral but identify us as Jews, which we should retain as expressions of our traditional roots and communal identity; and those that are harmful, which we should find ways to change. The last of those include, in his examples, some of the disabilities of women in Jewish marital law, such as the case of an *agunah,* a woman tied to her first husband because he refuses to authorize a Jewish writ of divorce (a *get*) even though the couple has been divorced in civil law, in some cases for quite some time. At the time Jacobs wrote that piece (1973), that was precisely what the Conservative movement sought to resolve—and it did eventually succeed in finding halakhic ways to do so. One wonders what aspects of Jewish law Jacobs would classify today in this third category of "harmful" laws that need to be changed.

When studying Jacobs's writings, one of my students, Adam Naftalin-Kelman, asked a very perceptive question: What is Jacobs saying that is new in Conservative legal theory? After all, in some ways all of the Conservative thinkers that we have considered previously have also asserted in one way or another that we must be intellectually honest in understanding the texts and practices of our tradition and that we have to affirm tradition, on the one hand, and be ready to change it at times, on the other. As a result, I thought seriously about leaving Jacobs out of this collection. And yet I knew that I could not do that, not only because of Jacobs's importance in spreading Conservative Judaism to Europe, but also because he articulates his stance with a *combination and synthesis* of philosophical and scholarly depth that far exceeds that of any of the previous thinkers who make the same claims. Some of the earlier Conservative spokesmen have argued for this stance with great philosophical expertise, more have had depth in rabbinic texts, but nobody has argued as cogently for this Conservative stance on the basis of both traditional sources and philosophical acumen.

And yet, there are in Jacobs's theory, as in everyone else's, both strengths and weaknesses. In the latter category, Jacobs assumes, but never argues for, rabbinic determination of Jewish law; why should that not be in the hands of individual Jews or the Jewish community as a whole by something like a majority vote? In the first selection below, he acknowledges that some Jews will individually decide to use electricity on the Sabbath while others will not; how far does that flexibility go? And what are the parameters of rabbinic decisions? That is, to what extent is Jacobs willing to support rabbis' changing of traditional Jewish law in the name of correcting harmful results? He has recently taken a stance against rabbis performing commitment ceremonies for gays and lesbians, despite the harm that that refusal does to such people, and so there are clearly some limits implicit in his approach, but what are they? More broadly, Jacobs's theory, like that of many other Conservative thinkers, will clearly not satisfy those to the right or the left, for it is much too historical, open, and dynamic for those who require certainty in their belief and practice and much too communal and conservative for those who prize individual autonomy.

On the positive side, Jacobs's theory is extremely well rooted in traditional sources, as his extensive and thorough scholarship of Jewish law in all ages amply demonstrates. It is also philosophically honest and astute, for it clearly identifies that which scholarship can determine and that which depends ultimately on faith. Even for the latter category, Jacobs's writings clearly distinguish between a blind faith and a reasoned one. All in all, Jacobs's theory cogently articulates the grounds for one to be, as he says in another one of his writings, traditional without being fundamentalist—indeed, with being scrupulously honest while yet being firmly traditional.[22]

<hr />

SELECTION 1

*Beyond Reasonable Doubt**

LOUIS JACOBS

THE *MITSVOT:* God-Given or Man-Made?

An objection levelled again and again to views such as mine is: if what you say is true that the *mitsvot* are not direct commands given by God but the result of human reflection and adaptation over the ages, why should Jews obey them? Why should contemporary Jews be fettered by the tradition? It is rational to keep *divine* laws, for who is man to question the will of God? But why should human beings follow laws ordained by other human beings? Why should our lives be governed by the teachings of the masters of old, no matter how eminent, wise, and saintly they were? To reply to this challenge, it is necessary to con-

*London, England and Portland, OR: The Littman Library of Jewish Civilization, Valentine Mitchell and Co., Inc. 1999, Chapter 5 (pp. 106–131).

sider the meaning that can be given to the distinction between God-made and man-made laws.

The ethical precepts of Judaism present less of a problem than the purely ritual precepts in that the former are, in the main, those which human beings can understand and to which they respond of their own volition, those which they would carry out even if there were no divine commands. I discussed the relationship between religion and ethics from a Jewish point of view some years ago.[1] I repeat here only the salient points relevant to the theme of this chapter.

THE ETHICAL BASIS

A question much discussed by religious thinkers is whether the good in the ethical sense is good because God wills it to be so, or rather whether God wills it to be so because it is good. In other words, is there an autonomous ethic with only an indirect association with religion? To take the fifth commandment as an illustration, is it proper to honour parents because God has so commanded, or does God command it because it is right and proper? If the former is true, then conceivably if God had commanded us to despise our parents that would be right. But if the latter, then God, being God, could not possibly command us to despise our parents. Or, with regard to the eighth commandment, is it wrong to steal only because God has declared that it is wrong, or is it wrong to steal because it is intrinsically wrong and that is why God commands us not to steal? Although the biblical prophets were not systematic philosophers and would not have formulated the question in the form mentioned, yet from the prophetic books in the Bible it would seem that, for the prophets, justice and mercy are to be practised because human beings understand of their own accord that this is how they ought to behave, and the burden of the prophetic call in the name of God is for humans to be true to that which they already know is right. This is not, of course, to say that human beings always respond to what they know to be good. The prophetic demand is directed to people who know what is right but do not follow it in their lives. As Abraham Lincoln once said, 'It is not that which I do not understand in the Bible that bothers me. It is that which I understand only too well.'

In many of the pentateuchal laws the reason for their observance is stated, a reason which appeals to man's innate ethical sensibility:

> And a stranger thou shalt not oppress; for ye know the heart of a stranger, seeing ye were strangers in the land of Egypt.
>
> (Exod. 23:9)

> If thou at all take thy neighbour's garment to pledge, thou shalt restore it unto him by the time that the sun goes down; for that is his only covering, it is the garment for his skin: wherein shall he sleep? And it shall come to pass, when he crieth unto Me that I will hear; for I am gracious.
>
> (Exod. 22:25–6)

> Thou shalt not have in thy bag diverse weights, a great and a small. Thou shalt not have in thy house diverse measures, a great and a small. A perfect and just weight shalt thou have; a perfect and just measure shalt thou have; that thy days may be long upon the land which the Lord thy God giveth thee. For all that do such things, even all that do unrighteously, are an abomination unto the Lord thy God.
>
> (Deut. 25:13–16)

> Thou shalt not abhor an Edomite, for he is thy brother; thou shalt not abhor an Egyptian, because thou wast a stranger in his land.
>
> (Deut. 23:7)

A plain reading of the famous passage in the book of Micah (6:7–8) similarly suggests that man knows how he should behave and that that is what God wants him to do:

> Will the Lord be pleased with thousands of rams, with tens of thousands of rivers of oil? Shall I give my first-born for my transgressions, the fruit of my body for the sin of my soul? It hath been told thee, O man, what is good, and what the Lord doth require of thee; only to do justly and to love mercy, and to walk humbly with thy God.

So, too, does Isaiah appeal to his people:

> Wash you, make you clean, put away the evil of your doings from before Mine eyes, cease to do evil, learn to do well; seek justice, relieve the oppressed, judge the fatherless, plead for the widow.
>
> (Isa. 1:16–17)

The prophet Amos castigates Damascus, Gaza, Tyre, Edom, Ammon, and Moab for atrocities they have perpetrated, even though these peoples had received no divine law, the implication being that man is capable of discerning right from wrong by the natural light that is within him (Amos 1–2). Indeed, nowhere in the prophetic books are the 'nations' condemned for worshipping their gods—only for the ethical abominations such as child sacrifice associated with worship.

That to behave ethically does not require the authentication of a divine command is implied, too, in the rabbinic idea (Jerusalem Talmud, *Rosh hashanah* I:3) that God obeys His own laws. Quoting the Greek saying (the quotation is in Greek in Hebrew characters) that the law is not written for the king, the passage continues that a human king decrees laws for his subjects but he himself is not obliged to keep them, whereas God orders man to rise before the aged, and He did this Himself, as it were, out of respect for Abraham. The Babylonian Talmud *(Yoma 67b)* gives as examples of commandments 'which if they had not been written in Scripture should by right have been written' the laws concerning idolatry, immorality, bloodshed, robbery, and blasphemy. There is also the oft-quoted saying of the third-century Palestinian teacher, Rabbi Johanan *(Eruvin 100b):* 'If the Torah had not been given, we could have learnt modesty from the cat, honesty from the ant, charity from the dove, and good manners from the cock who first coaxes and then mates.'

Particularly relevant is the discussion in Sa'adya Gaon's *Sefer ha'emunot vehade'ot* ('Book of Beliefs and Opinions'), compiled in 933.[2] Sa'adya classifies the *mitsvot* of the Torah into the *rational* and the *revealed,* in which classification he was followed by subsequent Jewish thinkers. The rational precepts, which include the ethical, would be recognized as binding even without revelation. Revealed precepts (such as the dietary laws) are not irrational (there is a reason for them and they are not arbitrary), but here God's will is paramount. Obviously man would not know that he has to obey these precepts if it had not been revealed to him. He would not wear tefillin or refrain from eating pork if he were not *commanded* so to do, for how would he otherwise know that this is what God would have him do? But, Sa'adya asks, what need is there for revelation in connection with the rational precepts? If man can know them without revelation, if, as we say nowadays, they are autonomous and are kept because it is right to do so, not because they are enjoined in Scripture, why are they, in fact, revealed through prophecy? Sa'adya's basic answer is that revelation is required to avoid all uncertainty and for the precise details of how the rational precepts are to be carried out. Thus, for example, it is true that man would know by his own reason that it is wrong to steal, yet revelation is still required in order to inform man how property is to be acquired. Sa'adya seems to be saying that even without religion's precise teachings man's moral sense would still function, but it would be confused when it came to application. In Sa'adya's own words:

> A further example is that, although reason considers stealing objectionable, there is nothing in it to inform us how a person comes to acquire property so that it becomes his possession. It does not state, for instance, whether this comes about as a result of labour, or is effected by means of barter, or by way of inheritance, or is derived from that which is free to all, like what is hunted on land or sea. Nor is one informed by it as to whether a sale becomes valid upon the payment of the price, or by taking hold of the article, or by means of a statement alone. Besides these, there are many other uncertainties pertaining to this subject which would take too long and would be too difficult to enumerate. The prophets, therefore, came along with a clear-cut decision for each instance. Another example is the question of the expiation of crime. Reason considers it proper, to be sure, that whoever commits a crime should expiate it, but does not define what form this expiation ought to take: whether a reprimand alone is sufficient, or a malediction should go with it, or a flogging should be added. In the event that the punishment takes the form of

flogging, again, the question is how much, and the same applies to the malediction and the reprimand. Or it is possible that no satisfaction will be obtained except by the death of the criminal.

And again it might be asked whether the punishment should be the same for whoever commits a certain crime or whether it should vary from person to person. Then the prophets came and fixed for each crime its own penalty, and grouped some of them with others under certain conditions, and imposed monetary fines for some. For these considerations, then, that we have enumerated and other such reasons, it is necessary for us to have recourse to the mission of God's messengers. For if we were to defer in these matters to our own opinions, our views would differ and we would not agree on anything. Besides that, we are, of course, in need of their guidance on account of the precepts prescribed by revelation, as we have explained.

Sa'adya does of course believe in a direct divine revelation not only for the revealed precepts but also for the details of the rational precepts, and is no help for a non-fundamentalist approach. Yet Sa'adya's idea, followed by all who accept his distinction between the two types of precept, that there are precepts that do not in essence require a divine revelation because to observe them is innate to human nature, enables even those who prefer, for good reason, to think of revelation through the people rather than directly to them, to say that for the observance of the ethical precepts no direct revelation is necessary. As for Sa'adya's details of the precepts, these are indeed provided by the halakhah. What is required is to extend Sa'adya's 'the prophets' to the rabbis who teach the laws, to the Oral Torah. It may even be that Sa'adya himself included the rabbinic tradition in his use of the term 'prophets', since he was the great opponent of the Karaites, who rejected the whole talmudic tradition, and some of the instances to which he refers are, in fact, rabbinic, not biblical.

A further idea in connection with the relationship between religion and ethics is that, granted the autonomy of ethics, religion is required to give an added dimension to human life. The religious man sees his ethical concern as part of his total relationship with his God. This should not be taken to mean that there is a conflict between love of God and love of man, as George Orwell did, for instance, when he pronounced that you cannot love both God and man. On the contrary, the love of man is part of what is meant by the love of God. But, by introducing the love of God into the picture, a different quality is imparted to man's ethical strivings. Man has no need for the God hypothesis in order to appreciate the claims of the ethical side of human life. If a man has to invoke his religion in order to be good in the ethical sense, he is remote from the good as religion sees it. But the religious man believes that God *is* and that God's nature is such that every act of justice, love, and compassion makes for the fulfilment of

His purpose, every act of cruelty and oppression for its frustration. Man is to live, it can be put, both horizontally and vertically, open to earthly needs and responding to them as any other ethical man would do, but with his religious beliefs to add to the scene the glories of heaven. Such a way of looking at the matter does not depend on any fundamentalist understanding of *Torah min hashamayim*.

The Jewish mystics appear to see it in this way. Take, for instance, the great compendium of the Jewish religion *Shenei luhot haberit* ('The Two Tablets of the Covenant'),[3] known as the Shelah, by the German kabbalist, Isaiah Horowitz (?1565–1630). At the beginning of the book *(44b–45b)*, Horowitz discusses the obligation to love all God's creatures and its connection with the other great commandment to love God. Horowitz discusses the well-known story in the Talmud (*Shabbat 31a*) of the prospective convert to Judaism who requested Hillel to teach him the whole of the Torah while he stood on one leg. Hillel replied 'That which is hateful unto thee do not do unto thy neighbour. This is the whole of the Torah. All the rest is commentary, go and learn.' The medieval commentators were puzzled by this tale. What of the religious obligations of the Torah? Rashi suggests that Hillel was referring only to the ethical precepts, or that by 'thy neighbour' Hillel meant God. Horowitz draws on this to suggest that, in fact, both loves—of God and of one's neighbour—are really one, since God is One and all derives from Him. The love of one's neighbour is part of the love of God who created the neighbour. By loving one's neighbour one fulfils God's purpose. Horowitz adds a more mystical note. Since man is created in God's image, there is a divine spark in every human soul, so that the love of one's neighbour is quite literally the love of God.

Horowitz's summary of his view is interesting in itself, but also because it calls attention to character dispositions, which there is certainly no direct command in Scripture to cultivate:

> In truth, if you will examine the matter carefully, you will find that the majority of the precepts depend for their fulfilment on the command to love one's neighbour. First there are all the precepts regarding alms-giving, leaving the forgotten sheaf and the corners of the field to the poor, tithing, honesty in business, the prohibition of usury, and many others of a like nature. Then there are all the virtuous traits of character: compassion, kindliness, patience, love, judging others charitably, running to help them when they are in danger, not slandering them or bearing tales, not scorning or hating them or feeling envious of them, not flying into a rage, not being over-ambitious, these and thousands of other virtues depend on loving one's neighbour and only then can one become perfect by keeping both the positive and negative precepts. And even with regard to those precepts which have no connection with one's neighbour—the prohibition, for example, of forbidden food and of eating leaven on Passover—man will keep them *a*

fortiori. For if he loves his neighbour as himself, how much more will he love God Who loves him with an unqualified and true love, Who is Lord of the universe and to Whom all belongs, blessed be He. So you see that the command to love thy neighbour as thyself is the leg [referring to the would-be convert's demand that he be taught the whole Torah while standing on one leg] upon which the whole world stands. So you can see that 'thou shalt love thy neighbour as thyself' brings about 'thou shalt love the Lord thy God'.

THE RITUAL PRECEPTS

So far we have considered what Sa'adya calls the rational precepts. These do not necessarily need the spur of a direct divine communication for their authentication. But what of the precepts of which, Sa'adya says, we only know through revelation? Let us first examine the dietary laws as an example. The fundamentalist argument runs somewhat as follows. To observe the dietary laws, the laws of *kashrut,* involves a good deal of self denial. It is hard to be scrupulous in matters of diet, to refrain from eating certain foods, to have separate dishes for meat and milk, never to eat even kosher food in a non-kosher restaurant, but we willingly make the sacrifice because, we believe, this is what God will have us do. As the well-known rabbinic saying has it, 'A man should not say "It is impossible for me to eat swine flesh" but should rather say "It is truly possible, but what can I do since my Father in Heaven has so decreed?"' (Sifra on Lev. 20:26). But why submit to *kashrut* if the whole discipline may have originated in primitive taboos and was, in any event, not commanded by God but created by human beings, however spiritually gifted? The simple answer is that, indeed, there is little point in observing *kashrut* and the other ritual requirements of Judaism unless the motive for the observance is to obey a divine imperative. Where views such as mine deviate from fundamentalism is not on whether the precepts are commanded by God—many non-fundamentalists also believe that they are—but on how the command was conveyed. Historically considered, what the rabbinic saying is aiming at is that there is little religious value in otherwise apparently valueless observances unless these are undertaken out of a religious motivation.

Strictly relevant to this theme is the acute analysis of Maimonides in his *Shemonah perakim* ('Eight Chapters'—Introduction to *Pirkei avot,* ch. 6). Maimonides discusses Greek and Hebraic ethical ideals when these are in conflict. (Such a discussion could only have been held once Greek ways of thinking had begun, in the Middle Ages, to be considered in relation to Judaism. It was not, of course, and could not have been, possible in rabbinic times.) Who is the better man, asks Maimonides: the one who has no desire to do wrong or the one who wishes to do wrong but refrains by exercising constant self-control? The Greek thinkers appear to be saying that the better man is the one who has no desire to do wrong, no murder in his heart, no urge to take that which does not belong to him, no hateful or harmful thoughts. The talmudic rabbis, on the other hand, as in the quotation from the *Sifra*, seem to be saying the exact opposite. The rabbis seem to be saying that, ideally, a man should have the desire to do wrong, to eat forbidden food, for example, but should not do the wrong because his Father in Heaven has so decreed. Maimonides resolves the conflict by a neat (some might say, a too neat) distinction between religious and ethical laws. The rabbis are thinking of purely religious laws, and here the element of obedience to God's will will be paramount. The man who has no desire to eat forbidden food because, for example, he dislikes the taste or what he imagines to be the taste, does not abstain out of religious conviction and, since the act in itself is ethically neutral, his abstention has no religious value. His motive for abstaining is not for religious reasons. But the Greeks are thinking of ethical demands, and the rabbis would here agree that to refrain from murder by exercising self-control is to fall short of the purpose of the ethical laws, which, from the ideal point of view, seek to promote the good character which will ensure that its possessor has no wish in his heart to harm others.

FROM MAN-MADE INSTITUTIONS
TO DIVINE COMMANDS

In point of fact, most of the details of *kashrut* are not found in the Pentateuch at all. There is no reference to the laws of *shehitah*, which, say the rabbis, were given to Moses at Sinai. The prohibition on the cooking and eating of meat and milk together is derived by rabbinic hermeneutics from the verse which forbids seething a kid in its mother's milk, and the prohibition on cooking chicken in butter is said to be rabbinic. That one does not eat meat and milk at the same meal is also said to be rabbinic, a precaution against cooking them together. Again, according to the rabbis, the biblical prohibition on eating or drinking blood does not apply to blood that has been boiled or cooked, so that the whole procedure of salting meat before cooking is rabbinic. There is no escaping the view that a fundamentalist attitude involves the acceptance not of the literal words of the Pentateuch, but that the rabbinic interpretation is the authentic meaning of the pentateuchal laws, so that what non-fundamentalists are saying is that, seen historically, these rabbinic laws did not simply drop down from Heaven but are, like the pentateuchal laws themselves, the result of human co-operation with the divine in the creation of the Torah. Our approach is, indeed, new, and a departure from tradition, but does not involve any rejection of the *mitsvot* as the word of God.

In a lecture in Manchester a year or two ago I said, and it has been held against me by fundamentalists ever since, that I wear tefillin because my grandfather wore tefillin. This was taken to imply that the only reason I wear tefillin is because the tradition so demands, a position of ancestor worship I have never entertained for one moment. What I said was that the average Jew who wears tefillin does so as part of the pattern of his religious life, but that the sociological aspects of a ritual do not preclude the recognition of the ultimate religious sanction for its observance. True, I wear tefillin in the first instance because my grandfather wore them and my grandfather because his grandfather wore them. But, while the wearing of tefillin has now become sacred habit, it is a sacred habit by means of which Jews come nearer to God. Jews, before donning the tefillin, do, after all, recite the benediction 'Who has sanctified us with His commandments and has commanded us to wear tefillin.' They are saying in so many words that they wear tefillin because it is a religious obligation, an important part of traditional Jewish observance, even though they do not normally feel obliged even to consider how this particular practice came to be. The theological aspect is only relevant so far as the actual observance is concerned, not for any doctrine as to how the ritual came about. I do not deny that the attitude of the Breslau school, upon which my view is based, departs from the medieval philosophy of the *mitsvot* as direct commands of God. But it is a departure forced on us by the new knowledge of the history of Judaism. Fundamentalism may provide the certainty that many require in order to be observant, but history has shown that fundamentalism is untenable. A new philosophy of the *mitsvot* is required, but it is one still within the tradition itself (as discussed in Chapter 3 above) which can now be seen to be a developing tradition.

The best illustration of what is meant by revelation through the experiences of the people of Israel is provided by the institution of the synagogue. Even the fundamentalist, who holds that for religious institutions to be binding a direct divine command is necessary, has to admit that there is no such divine communication for Jews to frequent the synagogue. The whole institution of the synagogue has developed largely as a response to the destruction of the Temple, when communal prayer took the place of the sacrifices. Communal prayer itself is a later development. All the prayers in the Bible are individual prayers. The liturgy of the synagogue can be traced from its early beginnings. Many of the hymns were composed by medieval poets. The ever-popular *Lekhah dodi* hymn for welcoming the sabbath was composed by Solomon Alkabets as late as the sixteenth century.

With regard to the music of the synagogue, each community of Jews has its own melodies. Sephardi melodies are in the Arabic or Oriental modes, Ashkenazi ones in the German mode. In Western synagogues musical compositions go back to sixteenth-century Italy but, of course, there were musical accompaniments to the Temple service, and there has been a host of composers of synagogue music in the nineteenth and twentieth centuries. Even the mode of cantillation of the Torah differs from one community to another: the Sephardi differs from the Ashkenazi, and, in the Ashkenazi mode itself, there are differences between the German and the Lithuanian styles.

Architectural styles differ very widely from synagogue to synagogue. Rabbi Ezekiel Landau of Prague (d. 1793) was asked whether it is permitted to build an octagonal-shaped synagogue. He wrote in reply:

> With regard to the question whether it is permitted to build a synagogue with eight walls and eight corners or whether a synagogue must have only four walls and four corners and must be greater in length than in breadth. I am surprised at the questioner. What reason can he have had for supposing that it is forbidden? You were quite right to tell him that there is no reference to this in the *Shulḥan Arukh*. I go further and say that we do not find in any of the early Codes or in the Babylonian Talmud or in the Jerusalem Talmud that a synagogue is required to have any particular shape.[4]

There are many reasons why Jews go to the synagogue. Some go for social reasons or because they like the traditional melodies or the rabbi and the cantor (these institutions themselves having developed over time).

But the majority go to synagogue, in addition to other reasons, in order to worship their Creator. They do believe that it is the will of God that they should do so but, ultimately, that will is discovered through the very practice of worship in the synagogue. Jews go to the synagogue because that is what Jews do; and since that is what Jews do, how Jews worship God, it can be said that this is what God would have them do and is hence a divine commandment, albeit one not conveyed directly to passive recipients. To put it somewhat crudely, the synagogue is man-made, the institution itself, its forms, its liturgy, its melodies, its architecture, and everything else about it. But the men who made it were God-seekers who were followed by popular consensus, itself under the guidance of God. It is but a step—a very big step to be sure—to the application of this to the whole idea of revelation, a mystery even for the fundamentalist, as it is bound to be since no human mind can grasp the workings of the divine will.

Let us examine further the thought-provoking passage in the Talmud (*Shabbat 23a*) on the benediction to be recited when kindling the Hanukah lights. The passage reads: 'What is the benediction? Who sanctified us with His commandments and commanded us to kindle the light of Hanukah. And where did He command us? R. Avia said "Thou shalt not turn aside" [Deut. 17:11]. R. Nehemiah said: "Ask thy father and he will shew thee; thine elders and they will tell thee" [Deut. 32:7].' On this passage there is a huge debate between Maimonides and Nahmanides, concerning how it relates to laws introduced by the rabbis.[5] According to Maimonides, the passage means that the Torah itself orders us to obey rabbinic law. He ridicules, however, the notion that the passage means that one day this and that will occur in the days of the Maccabees, and that they will ordain that the Hanukah light has to be kindled, and that their ordinance must be obeyed. The passage should rather be understood to mean that there is a divine command that the ordinances of the sages of Israel should be obeyed whenever and for whatever reason they ordain them. Thus, in Maimonides' view, and this is repeatedly stressed by Orthodox thinkers today, all rabbinic law is ultimately biblical law. It follows that, in Maimonides' view, the only reason why a Jew is obliged to obey a religious law is because there is a command in the Torah for him so to do, and there is such a command to obey rabbinic law in the two verses quoted.

Nahmanides (Ramban), in his comments on this section of Maimonides' work, demurs. The two verses in Deuteronomy do not really deal at all with the question of laws ordained by the later rabbis. The first verse quoted, according to Nahmanides, deals with obedience by one of its members to the decision of the great court, the Sanhedrin. This does mean that there is biblical warrant for some teachings of the rabbis, but only when they are in the position of a Sanhedrin, that is, in their basic interpretation of the laws of the Torah, and in no way does this refer to institutions that are of post-biblical origin. The second verse is not in a legal context but is a simple plea to take note of the people's past. For Nahmanides, the two verses are what is known as an *asmakhta*, the term for an idea pegged onto a verse which is not its real meaning. For Nahmanides rabbinic law is precisely that, rabbinic and not biblical. Nahmanides does not tell us why, in that case, rabbinic law should be obeyed. Presumably he would have said that rabbinic law has to be obeyed, even in the absence of a direct divine command, because the Jewish religion requires later legislation by the sages in order for it to be preserved. Something of the sort is implied in the comment of the great twentieth-century *rosh yeshivah*, Rabbi Simeon Shkop (1860–1940):

> The Rambam holds that according to the Torah we are obliged to keep all that we have been commanded through *hazal*, and with regard to this it is said 'Thou shalt not turn aside.' But the Ramban, disagreeing with him, holds that this negative prohibition is only stated in the Torah with regard to that which *hazal* interpreted as the plain meaning of the Torah or that which they derived by means of the thirteen hermeneutical principles by which the Torah is expounded. But with regard to that which *hazal* innovated in order to provide a fence and a protection [i.e. rabbinic ordinances with the aim of protecting the Torah] there is nothing whatsoever in the Torah that we are obliged to obey their words. How I am astonished by such a statement! Can it be right that we are obliged to listen to the words of *hazal* without an admonition to do so in the Torah? Who is Lord over us except our Father in Heaven? If He did not decree that we must listen to the voice of *hazal*, who obliged us to do so? These things break the roofs [a talmudic expression to denote a very startling statement], and there is neither a carpenter nor a carpenter's apprentice ['carpenter' is a rabbinic synonym for a scholar] who can solve the problem. But I find a solution to this. According to the Ramban's theory we are obliged to obey *hazal* because our reason tells us so. Since they believed it to be good to ordain this and enact that, then that is what is true and good for us. Just as our reason concurs that we

should listen to the word of the Lord, so does it decree that we should keep all that *hazal* and our holy teachers decree.[6]

Be that as it may, historically considered we have in all this an anticipation of the idea that, whatever its origins, a ritual should be observed if its observance enhances the spiritual life of the Jew, though I am far from suggesting that either Nahmanides or Rabbi Simeon Shkop would even have thought of expressing such an idea. Yet, here too, when Jews kindle the Hanukah lights, they do so as part of their quest for the divine Will, and that is how the command is conveyed. There is also more than a hint here that the doctrine of the Oral Torah applies not only to actual laws given at Sinai but to the institutions of the rabbis, although, of course, the rabbis did believe in actual laws given to Moses at Sinai and they obviously would not have held that the Written Torah is itself a creation, so to speak, of the Oral Torah.

It has to be admitted, however, that the modern way of looking at the whole question of observance involves a strong degree of selectivity. On the fundamentalist view, to observe each *mitsvah*, together with every one of its details, is a divine imperative. The medieval thinkers did discuss the reasons for the *mitsvot*, but that the *mitsvot* must be kept in their entirety they did not and could not question. Before the Emancipation, Judaism presented itself as a package complete in itself. The medieval Jew followed the pattern of Jewish life which he was obliged to accept as totally binding in all its details, unless he wished to opt out of Judaism, which comparatively few ever thought of doing. The Emancipation and the Enlightenment brought in their wake an unravelling of the package, later aided and abetted by the introduction of the historical critical study of Judaism. The tendency among modernist Jews, even among those who kept the *mitsvot*, was to ask not so much why God ordained that we should keep the *mitsvot*, but rather why we should keep this or that *mitsvah* and, for the first time, the idea of relative value was introduced into the equation. To refer, again, to the question of *kashrut*, the modernist Jew who keeps the dietary laws will seek to discover what religious value there is in adherence to these laws. He will see such value in the preservation of the Jewish people or, in a more religious vein, in the promotion of holiness in daily living. This is, after all, the reason implied in the biblical injunction regarding these laws. But once the question of value is introduced, an element of selectivity is bound to be present.

It is all very well to argue, as I do in this book, that the *mitsvot* provide the Jew with a vocabulary of worship, but some of our values are those of Western society, and when the *mitsvot* are assessed against these values they do, not very often but certainly at times, come into conflict with the informed Jewish conscience. One thinks in this connection of attitudes towards women, or non-Jews, or the law of the *mamzer,* in which there is severe discrimination against innocent children.[7] Many non-fundamentalist but observant Jews have tried to face this acute problem. I have tried to deal with the vexed question, admittedly without too much success, in my book *A Tree of Life*. Here one can only say that it is possible, given the will, for the non-fundamentalist Jew to find the way to a solution by an adaptation of the halakhah, the legal system of Judaism, which, as historical investigation has shown, has been flexible and creative. After all, Jews no longer practise polygamy (even those Sephardi communities who did so until recently), no longer have slaves, and no longer avail themselves of the *herem*, nor do they treat heretics as if they are utterly beyond the pale, nor do Orthodox doctors refuse to treat non-Jewish patients on the sabbath.

It might be useful at this stage in the argument to examine Jewish life as it is actually lived. There are theoretical problems in connection with Jewish institutions, observances, feasts, and fasts, once the history of these has been discovered through scholarly research; but, as I have argued in this book, the history of how Jewish institutions came to be is irrelevant to Jewish religious life today. For practical purposes we need a vocabulary of worship. Let us see how this works.

Take the festival of Hanukah. We have noted the use of 'Who has commanded us' in connection with the benediction over the Hanukah lights, which can, without too much distortion, be understood as being commanded through the experiences of the Jewish people. Now, so far as this festival is concerned, the events it celebrates really happened. The Maccabees really did wage the wars and really did rededicate the Temple. But did the miracle of the oil really take place, or is it a legend? The arguments for the latter view are well known: the sole reference is in a comparatively late talmudic passage; there is no reference to it in the liturgy of the day; from the book of Maccabees it appears that the eight days of Hanukah are based on the eight days of the festival of Sukkot, which would have been celebrated had the Temple been in Jewish hands. And yet, legend or no legend, the celebration of Hanukah came to centre on the miracle of the oil. Homiletical discourses throughout the ages have interpreted the miracle of the oil as a symbol of the power of the spirit. On the sabbath of Hanukah the *haftarah* is from the book of Zechariah, containing the verse 'Then he answered and spoke unto me, saying: "This is the word of the Lord unto Zerubbabel, saying: Not by might, nor by power, but by My spirit, saith the Lord of hosts"' (Zech. 4:6). Moreover, there is much evidence that the kindling of the lights on Hanukah precedes by centuries the story of the miracle of the oil, and the connection of this with the pagan kindling of lights at the time of the winter solstice has often been noted. So what! Yes, Hanukah has had a history. Hanukah is man-made. Hanukah, and the stress on the miracle of the oil, is a creation of the Jewish people. But this creativity has inspired Jews to keep alive the flame of Judaism, and that is the best reason there can be for Jews to continue to celebrate this festival.

The festival of Purim presents problems of its own from the historical point of view. Did the events related in the book of Esther actually take place? Did King Ahasuerus really rule over the whole world, as some rabbinic *midrashim* seem to suggest, and did he wish to destroy all Jews at the request of Haman? Why is there no mention in any external sources of King Ahasuerus having a Jewish consort? Is the book of Esther a 'nationalistic' rather than a 'religious' book, as is suggested by the absence of the name of God? This kind of question has been aired in scores of books. And yet Jews, even if they allow themselves to doubt its historicity, still keep Purim. Why? Surely it is because the festival represents the persistence of Jews in surviving as Jews under the guidance of God. Haman has become a symbol of the vicious antisemite who cannot bear to live in a world in which there are Jews. As for the alleged vindictiveness of the story, for which reason some Reform Jews no longer celebrate Purim, it is a moral duty to rejoice at the defeat of tyranny. True, if the story in all its details really happened, there are questionable moral elements in it, but precisely here history helps us. In all probability it did not really happen, but antisemitism really happened and tyranny and oppression really happened and still happen, and it is the hope that these will one day be overthrown that is being celebrated on Purim. Yes, Purim is man-made and being man-made has questionable elements, but Jews have managed to override these elements in joyous celebration. The danger in the celebration of Purim is real. It could have led to an attitude of unbridled nationalism or exclusive particularism, to hatred of non-Jews or suspicion of their motives. That it did not do so is due partly to the 'fun' element in the festival: the Purimspiel, dressing up, imbibing strong drink, the parodies of classical Jewish literature, the Purim Rov and Purim 'Torah,' all of which allow aggressive instincts to be expressed without getting out of control. The horrible massacre in Hebron by Baruch Goldstein was, alas, provoked by the Purim story, but was an abominable act of murder decried and utterly repudiated in the name of Judaism by the whole of Jewry, except for the hateful fanatics who erected a stone in memory of the murderer.

It is when we come to the three biblical feasts—Passover, Shavuot, and Sukkot—that the historical question looms large. It is now axiomatic among biblical scholars that these were originally agricultural festivals in ancient Israel, transformed by being connected to historical events. With regard to Shavuot the transformation did not take place until fairly late rabbinic times, when it became the 'season of the giving of our Torah.' Also, the archaeological evidence points to the sojourn in Egypt of only some tribes, not all the Children of Israel. The question is, then, how much of the biblical story of the Exodus is in conformity with what actually happened in the past? Were there really around two million Israelites in the Exodus, and how could the seventy souls that came into Egypt have become such a large number of persons at the time of the Exodus? Again this kind of question is not relevant to practical Judaism. Historically minded Jews may express their puzzlement at these and similar aspects of the *seder* on Passover, but they do so as part of the *mitsvah* to retell the story, not as biblical critics or historians or archaeologists. Of course, if Israel was never in Egypt and no Exodus ever took place, it would be more than a little bizarre to celebrate a deliverance from an evil that never existed. To this our reply must be that, poetry or not, the story of the Exodus embraces the living tradition of a living people that the Exodus did happen, although the story received many embellishments through the ages. As Martin Buber put it, in the story of the Exodus we have 'sacred history,' *Heilsgeschichte*. It is saga rather than chronicle, poetic reflection on the facts of history rather than a sober account of them. And the message of freedom from bondage is a universal theme and is so considered by Jews who celebrate Passover, even while, as Jews, thinking primarily of their own freedom and giving thanks for it.

If Judaism is seen as having evolved through human co-operation with the divine, great caution should be exercised in drawing too neat a distinction between divine and man-made *mitsvot*. But if the question is raised whether Passover is man-made, the answer is that most of the features of the festival are acknowledged as human creations in the tradition itself. The prohibition on leaven and the obligation to eat matzah are both in the Bible, but it is in the rabbinic literature that we find the definition of leaven and when to eat matzah. That rice cannot become *hamets* is debated in the Talmud, the ruling being given that a dough made of rice does not constitute *hamets*. In the Middle Ages Jews in Germany, for various reasons, took it upon themselves not to eat rice or legumes on Passover, so that to this day pious Ashkenazi Jews do not eat rice or legumes on Passover, though for Sephardi Jews there is no prohibition. From the Bible it might appear that matzah has to be eaten during the whole of Passover, but as the rabbis understand it, the *mitsvah* to eat matzah is only binding on the first night of the festival. That one has to drink four cups of wine at the *seder* is a rabbinic rule, and the whole order of the *seder* night is based largely on Jewish custom in the sense that this is how Jews do it. And, here again, since it is man-made, the divine element only enters because Jews worship God on Passover in this, rather than any other, manner. A fundamentalist would object to the use of the word 'rituals' to describe the *mitsvot*. They are for him direct divine commands, and to call them 'rituals' is to cheapen them. But the non-fundamentalist, uneasy with the notion of a direct divine command because his knowledge of history does not allow him to see it that way, gladly employs the term 'rituals' to denote that they are the creation of human beings reaching out to God. And yet they are still *mitsvot*, divine commands in the sense that, if one can speak of what it is that God wishes Jews to do, this is what He wishes Jews to do.

In connection with Sukkot, all the details of how a sukkah is to be constructed—its minimum and maximum size, its shape, its covering, and the regulations regarding eating and sleeping there—are all as recorded in the Talmud and are not found in the Bible. That four species of plant have to be taken on Sukkot is mentioned in the Bible—though the idea that they have to be taken in the hand and waved to and fro is rabbinic. That the phrase 'fruit of a beautiful tree' means the *etrog* is stated only in the rabbinic literature, as are all the details regarding the size and shape of the four species. The festival of Simhat Torah is a new creation, dating from the geonic period (sixth–eleventh centuries), with its rituals developing in different ways among the Jewish communities of the world. That Sukkot has two days of festival at its beginning and end in the Diaspora is acknowledged to be rabbinic. In fact, the observant fundamentalist is misguided, from his own point of view, in stressing the idea that God gave every word and every letter to Moses. If this is the case, the question must present itself to him: how does it come about that, today, in our celebration of the festivals and in so many other matters, we practise our religion in a manner so different from the actual command of God? And it is not only the Orthodox who are fundamentalists. Some Reform Jews in the last century used to argue, as did the Karaites, that to keep two days of the festivals is sheer blasphemy in that it purports to improve on God's word. There is no recourse here and elsewhere but to accept that the festivals and all their details are man-made, in the sense that they are the result of human creativity, but, since they are directed to God, they are divinely commanded.

The man-made element in the festivals is seen most of all in Shavuot. As remarked above, the festival in the Bible is entirely agricultural and is an adjunct *(atseret)* to Passover, with no special rituals of its own except for the special sacrifices in Temple times. Even in the Mishnah, Shavuot is still known as 'Atseret.' But eventually Shavuot became the anniversary of the giving of the Torah, since, according to the book of Exodus, the theophany at Sinai took place on this date, in the third month of the year. Historically speaking, the whole idea of *the* Torah, comprising the whole of the Pentateuch as well as the Oral Torah, is not found at all in the Pentateuch itself, as I have noted previously. But once the Torah had come into its own, so to speak, in rabbinic times, Shavuot became the day *par excellence* on which is celebrated Israel's choicest gift—a gift, the non-fundamentalist would say, received not by passive recipients but through creative co-operation with the divine. From this point of view, Shavuot is truly the 'season of the giving of our Torah,' but the expression is not, for the non-fundamentalist, a statement about a particular date in history. It is rather a statement or declaration of what the Torah means for Jews in terms of the eternal verities. According to any reading of the situation, the later elaborations of Shavuot—the decorating of the synagogue with plants, the eating of dairy foods, the all-night vigil introduced by the kabbalists—are the result of Jewish creativity and are certainly man-made, yet no one thinks of rejecting them on these grounds.

Or take the festivals of Rosh Hashanah and Yom Kippur. There is no clear statement in the Pentateuch that the *shofar* has to be sounded on Rosh Hashanah. Since there is no pentateuchal basis for this, the Karaites did not blow the *shofar* on this festival. And, certainly, the details about the type of *shofar* that has to be blown, its size and the kind of notes to be sounded, as well as the accompanying benedictions and scriptural verses to be recited, are known to us from the rabbis, who provide us with the 'vocabulary of worship' to be used, and which Jews everywhere use, on this great day. For Jews, the sounding of the *shofar* means a call to repentance and to mending one's ways, as Maimonides said, although he refers to it only as a 'hint.'

Yom Kippur, in the Pentateuch, is chiefly a day of service in the Temple, and this is what it remained in Temple times. After the destruction of the Temple, the Temple service was referred to in the Avodah service of the Musaf prayer, but the emphasis became one of sincere repentance required of the individual Jew, the culmination of the Ten Days of Penitence, themselves the creation of the rabbis. To afflict oneself is enjoined in the Pentateuch, but it is the rabbis who explained this injunction to mean that we have to fast and who added the other 'afflictions'—to abstain from bathing, anointing with oil, wearing leather shoes, and marital relations. Jews who still observe these practices do so not necessarily because they are mentioned in the Bible, which, in fact, they are not, but because it has seemed very reasonable that this is the way a day of prayer and spirituality should be observed. The magnificent hymns of the day—well, some of them—are recited because, whoever were their composers, they still speak to our souls. Devout Jews know that these hymns and the melodies which accompany them are man-made, but refuse to see that as any reason for discarding them. On the contrary, if I may put it like this, a recognition of the human element makes it all the more religiously significant by calling constant attention to the fact that, in our religious life, we are reciting words composed by human beings like ourselves, even if we consider them to have been spiritually superior. In point of fact, a number of the *piyutim* are 'man-made' in another sense, in that they found entry into the prayerbook by a whim of the printers. It might also be noted that a feature of Yom Kippur mentioned in the *Shulḥan Arukh*, which used to be widely practised among the Ashkenazim, is hardly practised anywhere today, so far as I am aware, even among the *haredim*, with few exceptions. This is the practice of receiving a symbolic flogging on the eve of Yom Kippur. Why it has dropped out of practice can only be conjectured—maybe because it tended to invite ridicule—but drop out it did. This is a trivial matter in itself but is nonetheless relevant to our enquiry. To see the Jewish people as following practices that are man-made, by calling attention to the human element in the development of the Jewish religion, is also to see Jewish creativity in the omission of rituals which have had their day. Naturally, this latter principle has always been adopted with great caution, otherwise the Jewish people would have been in danger of allowing the whole house of Judaism to collapse by subjecting it entirely to its builders rather than its actual users. Behind it all lies the consensus of the Jewish people on what should be preserved of the tradition and what can safely be rejected. To call attention to the role of the Jewish community in the creation of Jewish institutions is not to adopt an attitude of ancestor worship or one which believes that the Jewish people can never be wrong. But how can we know when and where the Jewish people have created wisely or foolishly except by faith in the sound religious sense of the Jewish community as a whole, which, indeed, may at times have got it wrong but which has usually got it right? There is not much point in asking, for instance, whether the Karaites were right or wrong in their interpretation of the verse in the Pentateuch about not kindling lights on the sabbath, which, for them, means that Jews are obliged to sit in darkness all through the sacred day. Since our argument is that human consensus determines our ways of worship, then, indeed, the Karaites were right, in that their interpretation provided them with their vocabulary of worship, while the Rabbanites, whom we follow, were right in that their interpretation provided them with such a vocabulary. To ask 'but which of them does God Himself want?' is a little childish since Karaites and Rabbanites, Orthodox Jews and Reform Jews, all ask the same question, to which, short of a direct revelation, there is no answer. Yet, when all is said and done, history has decided, or, better, God has decided through history, that the Rabbanites have won out and that this, therefore, is the admittedly man-made Torah that God wishes us to keep if we wish to be faithful to Judaism as a religion.

We should, at this stage, look at the institution of the greatest significance to Jewish religious life, the sabbath. Whatever the origins of this tremendous day, without which, as the rabbis saw, there could be no Judaism worthy of the name, it appears in the Pentateuch, especially, as everyone knows, as the fourth commandment. Yet there are only one or two references in the Pentateuch to what constitutes *melakhah* ('work') on the sabbath. The Mishnah lists thirty-nine main classes of work:

> There are forty save one main classes of work: sowing, ploughing, binding sheaves, threshing, winnowing, cleansing crops, grinding, sifting, kneading, baking, shearing wool, washing or beating or dyeing it, spinning, weaving, making two loops, weaving two threads, separating two threads, tying [a knot], untying [a knot], sewing two stitches, tearing in order to sew two stitches, hunting a gazelle, slaughtering or flaying or salting it or curing its skin, scraping it or cutting it up, writing two letters, erasing in order to write two letters, building, pulling down, putting out a fire, lighting a fire, striking with a hammer, and taking [something] from one domain to another.
>
> (Shabbat 7:2)

It can be seen at a glance that these thirty-nine main categories of work are those which were involved in daily life in mishnaic times. They all have to do with the provision of food, clothing, and housing. Out of these there emerged, in the history of rabbinic Judaism, numerous applications of these main categories. The much later idea that it is creative work that is forbidden in order to hail God as Creator is fine, but, it must be said, there is no evidence for it in rabbinic literature.

In addition to the rabbinic development and interpretation of what constitutes work forbidden on the sabbath, there are prohibitions clearly of rabbinic origin such as *muktsah*, the handling of tools or money which may lead to the carrying out of forbidden work. To recite kiddush on the sabbath is derived from the injunction to 'remember the Sabbath,' but the derivation is of rabbinic origin, as is the injunction to eat three, instead of the usual two, meals on the sabbath.

Also of rabbinic origin is the lighting of sabbath candles—*ner shabbat*. In rabbinic times this meant that the home should be well lit on the sabbath but, in the Middle Ages, probably to counter the Karaite view that the home should be in darkness, special sabbath candles were introduced, over which the benediction is recited: 'Who has sanctified us with His commandments and has commanded us to kindle the sabbath lights.' This benediction is of importance to our investigation. Over a ritual unknown in both the Bible and the rabbinic literature, a benediction is recited in which God is thanked for *commanding* us. Can there be a better illustration that man-made laws are considered to be divine commands? The non-fundamentalist Jew who keeps the sabbath does not feel himself obliged to believe that all the thirty-nine types of work are to be refrained from on the sabbath because this was the direct divine command in the Torah. His sense of history will not allow him to accept this, which is why he is not a fundamentalist. But that in no way prevents him from seeing the sabbath, in all its details, in the language of tradition, as being a divine imperative.

At this stage in the argument, another cogent question can be put. Are you saying, then, that there is no difference between the fundamentalist and the non-fundamentalist? Is not your house of Judaism really only the same old house, except that you have entered it from the back door, while the fundamentalist, more honestly, has approached it from the front? What is the significance of your constant harping on direct versus indirect divine communication? Does it not all amount to the same thing? To vary slightly the metaphor of the door, are you not, without being aware of it, an Omar Khayyam?

> Myself when young did eagerly frequent
>
> Doctor and Saint, and heard great argument
>
> About it and about; but evermore
>
> Came out by the same Door wherein I went.

The differences between the two approaches may not, indeed, be too obvious at first glance, but unless I believed them to be real and important I would not have bothered to write *We Have Reason to Believe* and this book, and would have to conclude that Zechariah Frankel and the Breslau school were engaged in a colossal theological, though not historical, waste of time. In the realm of theory even if there were no consequences for practice, it is surely important to know the history of Judaism. According to the fundamentalist understanding, Judaism has had no history except one of single transmission from generation to generation of basically unchanging formulations. It is important to free the doctrine of *Torah min hashamayim* from the fetters of mechanistic fundamentalism. If it may be put in this way, it seems far more plausible and more true to the facts to say that God works through human beings in the disclosure of His word than that the Torah is an heirloom to be placed reverently on the shelf with only an occasional dusting. To see Judaism in historical terms also enables us to study the Torah in a new but refreshing way. It is no accident that fundamentalist Jews usually view historical studies with a strong degree of suspicion. They are right to do so from their point of view of static transmission. The idea of an unfinished Torah to be completed by humans does not affect in essence the doctrine that the Torah is divine. What is required is a new philosophy of halakhah, in which this creation of the Jewish people has not lost its dynamics. Yet, as I have said, there are problems in the new approach, especially in that it allows for selectivity.

If we examine the institution of the sabbath in this light, there is no logical objection to the acceptance by a non-fundamentalist of all the details of sabbath observance, since for him as well as for the fundamentalist the sabbath is mandatory. He will not smoke on the sabbath because he can appreciate that the discovery of how to make fire was one of the greatest steps towards civilization, and he will refrain from smoking on the sabbath as an acknowledgement of God as Creator. But he will find it hard to accept the notion, found in the sources, that to light a cigarette on the sabbath involves the death penalty, and that if he were to do this in the days of a restored Sanhedrin he would be sentenced to be stoned to death. He would be free from the crushing burden of direct divine communication that there is, in theory at least, the death penalty for this religious offence, flogging for another, and he would be glad that history has decided that such divine threats can no longer be operative.

Since, according to his view, the non-fundamentalist is free to choose which sabbath and other observances awaken a response in him, he may, in his personal life, though without any wish to offend others, choose, say, to switch on the electric light on the sabbath though he might not use electricity to cook or bake or shave. This is because the latter activities have long been part of sabbath observance, whereas a case has been made that switching on an electric light, since there is no combustion, does not fall under the heading of making fire. But that would be his personal choice, and he would do it in order to enhance his enjoyment of the sabbath. For the same reason he might decide that, whatever the halakhists say, to carry a handkerchief in the pocket on the sabbath does not involve the carrying from domain to domain referred to in the Mishnah, since people did not have pockets in their garments in mishnaic times. He will agree, if challenged, that he is not operating within the boundaries of the halakhah, but might feel free to depart from the halakhah in his personal life. Admittedly there is a grey area in all this, and there are undoubtedly severe tensions in the life of a non-fundamentalist who still believes it is right to be observant. I shall discuss this issue further in Chapters 6 and 11 of this book.

To give a different illustration of the non-fundamentalist attitude, we can take the Shema. The fundamentalist, in the unlikely event of being asked why he recites the Shema, would reply somewhat as follows: 'In Deuteronomy (6:4–7) Moses says: "Hear O Israel: The Lord our God, the Lord is One. And thou shalt love the Lord thy God with all thy heart, and with all thy soul, and with all thy might. And these words, which I command thee this day, shall be upon thy heart; and thou shalt teach them diligently unto thy children, and shalt talk of them when thou sittest in thy house, and when thou walkest by the way, and when thou liest down, and when thou risest up." Deuteronomy is the fifth book of the Torah delivered by God to Moses, and I therefore recite the Shema because God has told me to do so. I am aware that there is an opinion in the Talmud *(Berakhot 21a)* according to which "these words" mean words of the Torah and hence the duty to recite the Shema twice daily is rabbinic, but, then, I consider rabbinic law as laid down in the Talmud to have ultimate biblical and hence divine sanction. I know that I have to recite the Shema in the evening and the morning because the rabbis tell us that this is the meaning of "when thou liest down, and when thou risest up," which, say the rabbis, means at the time of lying down and at the time of rising up, that is, in the evening and the morning. Thus whenever I recite the Shema I am using God's actual words communicated (I know that God has no vocal organs and does not literally "speak") to Moses.'

The non-fundamentalist will put it all rather differently; he will say something like this: 'Deuteronomy was originally a separate book, probably the book discovered in the days of King Josiah and compiled shortly before then but, in any event, long after the days of Moses. It does contain the words of God for that time but is not itself the *word* of God. This it cannot be since it only became part of the Pentateuch when it was combined with the other pentateuchal books by an editor or series of editors, which means, since there are contradictions between Deuteronomy and other sections of the Pentateuch, that the Shema is not the words of Moses himself but what the Deuteronomist said that Moses said. I do not see the rabbis as infallible authorities but as great teachers, yet I must respect their ruling that one must recite the Shema daily, not so much because the rabbis say so but because all the evidence goes to show that the Shema was recited as part of the Temple service and has been recited by Jews throughout the ages. As a historically minded Jew, I am interested in how the Shema developed, but as a religious Jew the development is irrelevant to me. I recite the Shema because the words constitute a glorious affirmation of Jewish belief and, when reciting it, I share in the experiences of my fellow Jews, belonging to a community of faith reaching back to Deuteronomy and beyond. Since it is good to do this and since it provides me with a Jewish "vocabulary of worship," the only one that makes sense to me as a Jew, I believe that to recite the Shema is a divine command, albeit one communicated through the experiences of my people. By the same token I recite the words following the first verse of the Shema, which everyone admits were added in rabbinic times: "Blessed be the name of His glorious Kingdom for ever and ever."'

In effect, then, not only do both the fundamentalist and the non-fundamentalist Jew recite the Shema; they both do it in obedience to a divine command. The truth is that neither usually bothers to spell it all out. The religious Jew, fundamentalist or non-fundamentalist, is not necessarily concerned with theological or historical niceties. For all our discussion in this chapter on man-made versus divine precepts, it is the sociological factor that is decisive. A Jew acts out his Judaism within the context of the particular fraternity to which he belongs. A hasid will probably shout aloud the words of the Shema, and this will not only be tolerated but admired by his fellow-worshippers. A different, contemplative type of hasid may be lost in silent contemplation during a good part of his recitation of the Shema. A Lithuanian-type Jew will probably recite the Shema with clear enunciation of each word, as the rabbis advise. The custom of covering the eyes when reciting the Shema is observed by many Jews, but some Western Jews seem to believe this to be an ostentatious form of piety. What matters is that Jews recite the Shema in worship of the One God. By so doing they transform a man-made institution into a divine command.

NOTES

1. "The Relationship Between Religion and Ethics" in Gene Outka and John P. Reeder (eds.), *Religion and Morality: A Collection of Essays* (Garden City, NY, 1973), 155–72.
2. Part 3, chs. 1–3; trans. into English by S. Rosenblatt as *Beliefs and Opinions* (New Haven, Conn., 1948), 146–7.
3. [Amsterdam, 1648]; 2 vols. (Jerusalem, 1963).
4. *Noda biyehudah,* second series (Jerusalem, 1969), no. 18.
5. See Maimonides, *Sefer hamitsvot, Shoresh rishon* (Warsaw, 1883) and Nahmanides' comment *ad loc.*
6. *Sha'arei yosher* (Warsaw, 1928), section I, ch. 7, 18–19.
7. A *mamzer* is the child of a seriously forbidden union, and is only allowed to marry another *mamzer or* a proselyte.

SELECTION 2

*The Theological Approach**

LOUIS JACOBS

A SOUND THEOLOGICAL APPROACH will not fail to build on the findings of the Historical School. It will acknowledge that there is a *history* of Jewish observances and that these did not drop down ready made

A Jewish Theology (New York: Behrman House, 1973), pp. 224–232, 237–242 (selections from chapters 15 and 16).

from Heaven. It will recognise, for instance, that the dietary laws were not dictated in all their details by God to Moses but evolved gradually, frequently in response to outside stimuli. It will see the whole area of Jewish observances as growing naturally out of Israel's experience. But it will see the hand of God in all this, will see the "tree of life" that is the Torah as yielding no less nourishing fruit because it began its existence as an acorn. We believe in the God who speaks to us out of Israel's experience; Israel, the covenant people, dedicated to God's service and the fulfilment of His purpose. We believe in the God who, as Frankel said, reveals Himself not alone to the prophets but through Kelal Yisrael, the Community of Israel, as it works out and applies the teachings of the prophets. Yes, it is true, in a sense that the whole of the Torah is *minhag*, custom, growing through the experiences of human beings and interpreted by them in response to particular conditions in human history. But we go on from there to say that since this happened, since this is how God revealed Himself, then the *minhag* of Israel is Torah.

Either one sees power in the idea of submission to God's will or one does not see it. If one does, and very many sensitive religious people do, then there can be no greater value than the idea of a *mitzvah* as an opportunity of doing God's will. The Sabbath, for example, whatever its origins, is still the institution by means of which the Jew acknowledges God as his Creator and Creator of the whole world. Louis Ginzberg is right when he says that it is quite possible for a scholarly Jew to have exactly the same opinion as a German Protestant Professor as to how the Sabbath came into Jewish life, but come it did, and he can find it to be binding on him because it can bring him nearer to God as it brought his ancestors. Search the Bible from beginning to end and you will find there no command for Jews to build synagogues. And yet Jews do build synagogues and pray in them in their conviction that this is the will of God, since this is how Jews have expressed their religious strivings. We need a vocabulary of worship and this is provided by the *mitzvot*. That is their sanction.

These are the five attitudes. We have adopted the fifth because it seems the best way of understanding the meaning of Judaism for the modern Jew. We reject the first attitude because we cannot believe that Judaism wishes us to be obscurantist. We reject the second attitude because we see Judaism as something more even than ethics. We cannot accept the third attitude as it stands because we see Judaism as more than history. We do not adopt the fourth attitude because we see Judaism as more than sociology. But we believe in the fifth attitude, that Judaism is a religion, and a religious approach must see the *mitzvot* as ways to God. The sanction for the *mitzvot* is that they succeed in bringing men to God. Because they do this they are commanded by God.

While the approach to the *mitzvot* sketched here seems adequate in general terms, it cannot be denied that numerous problems arise when it comes to practical details. The problem of discovering a viable philosophy of the *Halakhah*—the legal side of Judaism—is acute. To consider in anything like a comprehensive fashion the whole range of *Halakhah* is really beyond the scope of a work on theology. It would require an investigation into Jewish law in all its ramifications. But some few suggested guidelines may perhaps be here attempted.

This approach we have adopted proceeds on the justifiable assumption that certain spiritual goods or values have become enshrined in Halakhic institutions, irrespective of their origins, and it is these which give the *Halakhah* its validity today. In this way the concept of *mitzvah* as divine command, giving *Halakhah* its spiritual power, can still be preserved even in a non-fundamentalist approach. But it surely follows that where the *Halakhah,* as it has developed, either does not promote such goods or is opposed to them, its claim on our allegiance is considerably weakened. It may then have to be relinquished entirely in loyalty to the good as taught by Judaism itself. The best way of seeing how this might work out in practice is to examine some of the instances where the *Halakhah* seem to promote no values or to be opposed to Jewish values. From this point of view Jewish observances can be divided into three categories: (a) the significant, (b) the meaningless, (c) the harmful.

THE SIGNIFICANT

Under this heading come observances such as the dietary laws and the Sabbath, *tallit, tefillin* and *mezuzah,* Yom Kippur and the other festivals. By "significant" in this context we do not understand a utilitarian approach to Jewish observance, that the dietary laws are hygienic and the like, but that the religious ideals of holiness and life's spiritual enrichment are enhanced by the observances. One can argue quite consistently that even if the dietary laws evolved out of primitive taboos and even if the Sabbath came originally from Babylon (and the world was not created in six days with God resting on the seventh), these institutions have become, through the historical experiences of the Jewish people, powerful vehicles for promoting holiness in daily living. The Jew who disciplines his appetites in obedience to a system developed in the service of holiness and who keeps the Sabbath as an affirmation that God is Creator, is loyal to a basic principle of Judaism, the sanctification of human life through action. Nor is it inconsistent for a Jew who argues in this way to be *totally* observant, to keep the Sabbath and the dietary laws as found in the *Shulhan Arukh* in all their details *(be-khol peratehem ve-dikduke-hem),* but the likelihood is that he will be less scrupulous than the fundamentalist since, on his view, the fear of transgressing a direct divine command does not affect his choice of what and what not to keep.

Such a Jew may, for instance, decide that switching on electric lights on the Sabbath is not an offence against the prohibition of making "fire." His argument is that even from the point of view of the traditional *Halakhah* there is room for permissiveness here (on the grounds that no *de-oraita* infringement is involved and that some authorities would favour a relaxation of the *de-rabbanan* prohibition for the sake of *oneg shabbat,* (see the sources quoted in *Proceedings of the Rabbinical Assembly of America,* Vol. XIV, 1951, pp. 135–137) and the fear of a *risk* of infringement *(safek),* which plays such a large role in the fundamentalist approach (perhaps rightly so, granted the fundamentalist premise), is considerably weakened, if not entirely neutralized, for the non-fundamentalist. Moreover, the motive for such a lenient interpretation is not pure expediency but to make the Sabbath less a day of gloom and discomfort and more a day of light and joy. This latter consideration will carry no weight at all with the fundamentalist, for whom the *Halakhah* expresses the direct voice of God. For the non-fundamentalist (horrid term, but what other is there?), however, operating within the categories of the religiously significant, a lenient interpretation of the *Halakhah* in order to enhance the Sabbath values is perfectly legitimate. Similarly the non-fundamentalist may decide to permit himself *kosher* food in a non-kosher restaurant since the traditional Halakhic objection to this is slight (the objection is to the *kelim* and the question of *noten taam lifegam* is involved, see *Shulhan Arukh, Yoreh Deah,* 103) and he will refuse to see the greater freedom of movement and social intercourse this provides him with as anything like a concession to base appetites in disloyalty to his religion.

THE MEANINGLESS

What of the prohibition of shaving with a razor and of *shaatnez* (a mixture of wool and flax)? On the fundamentalist view these are very far from meaningless. God commanded them and that is sufficient. But from the non-fundamentalist viewpoint it is more difficult to find meaning in these observances than in the Sabbath and the dietary laws, partly because these laws of shaving and *shaatnez* have never occupied so prominent a place in Jewish practice. To a far lesser extent can they be said to belong to the vocabulary of Jewish worship. It would, however, be precarious to argue that no meaning at all can be found in these laws. They can be interpreted, without distortion, as expressions of the priestly people idea, the people of God's covenant distinguishing themselves in matters of dress. If, as seems possible, these laws were ancient protests against idolatrous practices,[6] a comparison would be with a regiment wearing with pride a uniform worn by the soldiers of that regiment in a great heroic battle of old.

    Fundamentalism can be an attitude adopted towards the Talmud as well as to the Bible. The traditional *Halakhah* sometimes demands that laws of Rabbinic origin be obeyed even when the reason for which they were ordained no longer obtains (see I. H. Weiss: *Dor Dor Ve-Doreshav,* Vol. II, pp. 6f and Hayim Tchernowitz: *Toledot Ha-Halakhah,* pp. 194ff). The fundamentalist argument here is that laws laid down by the Talmudic Rabbis without dissenting voice have to be obeyed. The doctrine of the successive deterioration of the generations shows its influence here. "If the earlier scholars were like angels, then we are like men. But if they were like men, then we are like donkeys" (*Sabb. 112b*). The only good or value preserved by such an attitude is that of reverence for the past, but many of us today would question whether a slavish subservience to the past is, in fact, a value. The two most relevant instances are the prohibition of Gentile wine and of food cooked by Gentiles. Already in the middle ages some of the legal authorities argued for a relaxation of some of these laws on the grounds that the Gentiles among whom the Jews then lived were not pagans. If the test of religious significance is applied, it is difficult to defend the continued prohibition of Gentile wine and cooked food.

THE HARMFUL

There are (not surprisingly), in fact, very few of these, and they are largely in the area of women's rights. The most serious problem in the Halakhic sphere for the non-fundamentalist is where the present *Halakhah* is unjust. On any reading, justice is a basic imperative of Jewish life. How, then, can one countenance Jewish laws which themselves promote injustice? For the fundamentalist, again, there is no problem. On his view, all the laws were God-ordained and God is just. Somehow the apparent injustices in the law are compatible in ways we cannot see in this life with God's justice, in the same way as the instances of evil in the universe are compatible, in ways we cannot at present see, with God's goodness. The non-fundamentalist refuses this refuge. For him the laws were formulated by human beings in response to human conditions, under the guidance of God, to be sure, but subject to error like all other human institutions. The rationale for present-day loyalty to the law is that it preserves values, among them those of justice and equity. Where it patently does the opposite it can have no claim on the allegiance of the Jew.

The main instance of this kind of injustice is the case of the *agunah,* particularly when the couple have been divorced in civil law and the husband refuses to give his consent to the *get* (the bill of divorce) or will do so only if paid a large sum of money. It is true that a husband can find himself in the same position, but in that case legal remedy is at hand (the dispensation of 100 Rabbis and divorce without the wife's consent) so that, in this matter, the wife is in an inferior position.

What is to be done by the non-fundamentalist loyal in general to the *Halakhah* but painfully aware of this very hard case? The problem is, of course, a modern one because in Rabbinic times the Rabbis had the power of coercing the husband to give the *get* and, until recently, civil marriage and divorce were not available for Jews.

Tied up with it all is the problem of the *mamzer.* According to the Rabbinic interpretation of Deut. 23:3, the *mamzer* is a child born to an adulterous or incestuous union. This includes a child born to a woman and her present husband in civil law if she had not received a *get* from a previous husband. The *mamzer* may not marry (except if it be to one with the same status as himself), and his children and their children are in the same position. This law is in conflict with the basic principle of justice that children should not be punished for the sins of their parents, and, indeed, apart from this case, the *Halakhah* knows nothing of such punishment. Even if it be argued that the unfortunate status of the *mamzer* acts as a deterrent against adultery, it is surely stretching the matter beyond the limits of justice to apply the law to the case of failure to obtain a *get,* quite apart from the extremely dubious nature of a deterrent which operates by penalising innocent children.

It is true that all Halakhists are concerned with these problems, and various attempts at alleviation have been suggested so far without conspicuous success. The non-fundamentalist should add his voice to the demand for more determined efforts to deal with an unjust situation.

To sum up, Halakhic rules can be classified as significant, meaningless and harmful. The non-fundamentalist Halakhist will seek to deepen understanding of the significant, try to discover possible meaning in the apparently meaningless, and endeavour to mitigate the effects of the harmful without destroying the system as a whole. He will not necessarily be less scrupulous in his observance than the fundamentalist but if so will see gain in this rather than loss. He still has serious problems on his hands, but they are less acute than the problems of those who try to have Judaism without *Halakhah or* those who try to live as fundamentalists.

NOTES

6. See Maimonides, *Guide* III, 37 and *Yad, Avodat Kokhavim,* 12:7; Martin Noth, *Leviticus,* p. 143; Hastings' *Dictionary of the Bible, s.v. Hair,* p. 359.

ꞏ⧉ꞏ   ꞏ⧉ꞏ   ꞏ⧉ꞏ

CHAPTER SIXTEEN

Jewish Ethics

THE FINAL CHAPTER OF KAUFMANN KOHLER'S *Jewish Theology* is entitled: *The Ethics of Judaism and the Kingdom of God.* The inclusion of this topic in a work on Jewish theology is thus supported by the linking together of the ethical life with God's sovereignty. As Kohler says at the beginning of the chapter: "Jewish ethics, then, derives its sanction from God, the Author and Master of life, and sees its purpose in the hallowing of all life, individual and social." The relationship between religion and ethics has been discussed at length by religious thinkers. Many would disagree nowadays with the virtual identification of the *holy* with the *ethical.* But in any reading of Judaism the ethical dimension is of supreme importance. Judaism has always taught that God wishes man to pursue justice and mercy, to have a proper regard for his fellows, to make his contribution towards the emergence of a better social order. This is a constant theme in the Bible and in the Rabbinic literature, and over the centuries there has been produced a Jewish moralistic literature which draws on the Bible and Talmud to depict Jewish ethical life in its ideal form. The aim of this literature is to promote sound norms of good conduct and a noble character as the inspiration of the good life. Not that all the Jewish ethical teachers are in agreement on the basis of the ethical life or the details of what constitutes sound ethical conduct. These matters are extremely complex, and there is ample room for differences due to individual temperament and background. . . .

The above survey of Maimonides' ideal of the ethical life serves to demonstrate its power and nobility. It is a picture of life as lived by the Jewish sage; balanced, wise, kindly and life-promoting. Whether this is entirely relevant to the life of the Jew today is another matter. For all his greatness and towering genius, Maimonides was a child of his age. The noble life as conceived by the medieval moralists cannot be, as it stands, the ideal for life today, and a number of weighty objections can be argued against uncritical emulation.

For one thing, Maimonides' "middle way" owes a great deal to Greek influence. The Greek ideal of moderation in all things is based on the idea of harmony. Beauty is the result of a correct harmony in which everything is given its due weight but none to excess. S. D. Luzzatto in the last century went so far as to accuse Maimonides of what he called "Atticism," arguing that the Jewish ethical ideal demands an excess of generosity. It is the ideal of Abraham who sat at the door of his tent ready to welcome the hungry travellers and running out to meet them, not the prudential assessment of how far one should go in extending generosity to others. In fairness to Maimonides he has stated that the middle way is not for the saints. But Luzzatto would disagree that it is an ideal at all, to be followed by Maimonides' "sage" for example. The wisdom of Judaism demands an uncalculating type of generosity and a more spontaneous reaction to the call of the needy. In fact, it can be argued that Maimonides' whole attempt to record the ethical life in the form of rules and regulations and as part of a Code of Law is bound to fail precisely because, though idealistic sayings and maxims can act as an inspiration to character formation, by being frozen into unbending rules they destroy the freshness and spontaneity which are of the essence of the free-choosing good character.

Nor is Maimonides free from the idea of a dichotomy between body and soul. For all his rejection of the hermit ideal, the pleasures of the body are for him only a means of keeping body and soul together. The doctrine of doing things "for the sake of Heaven" comes very close, for him, to a rejection of any idea that the bodily appetites are themselves a divine gift. His attitude to sex is especially uncompromising. There is not the faintest trace of any notion of sex as a means of husband and wife expressing their love for one another. In a word, Maimonides' attitude is too detached, too coldly inhuman to serve us as the ideal. The Maimonidean ideal, too, has nothing to say about human culture, art, literature and music, for example. Maimonides' sage is either occupied in the accumulation of wisdom or engages in business or a profession to keep himself and his family. The question of the use of leisure does not arise for him because evidently he recognises no such concept.

Sagely conduct as described by Maimonides is sublime in its delin-
eation of the life of wisdom but is at the same time condescending and
patronising. There is no suggestion that the sage has anything at all to
learn from the simple virtues of the "people who walk in darkness."
The sage must keep himself aloof from the common folk, distinguished
from them in dress, speech and conduct. A case can perhaps still be
made out for the intellectual and spiritual aristocracy favoured by
Maimonides, but class distinctions even of this kind are viewed with
suspicion today and, on the whole, simply do not speak to our situation. If they move us at all, it is to protest.

In short, the Maimonidean ideal may win our admiration. It
hardly succeeds in attraction. Maimonides would no doubt say that
this is because we are "sick of soul." As he writes at the beginning of
this section: "Those who are sick in body taste the bitter as sweet and
the sweet as bitter. Some are so sick that they long for uneatable things
such as dust and charcoal and they loathe in proportion to their mal-
ady good food such as bread and meat. In the same way those who are
sick in soul love false opinions and long to hold them. They hate the
good way and are too lazy to walk in it and in proportion to their degree of sickness find it exceedingly hard to walk therein." But for
many today Maimonides' ideal is too narrow. It stresses too much the
conflict between the world and the soul and tends too much to imply
that God is at war with His creation.

If the Maimonidean sage were alive today, he might occasionally
watch television but only the educational programmes. He might even
go to the theatre and cinema but only if the performance promised to
raise significant moral issues, never if the prospect were that of enter-
tainment pure and simple. He would read scientific treatises and works
of edification and erudition but never thrillers or works of humour. It
is uncertain if he would ever go to concerts and to the opera. He
would have little appreciation of the delights of good food, wine or
conversation. It is doubtful if he would ever unbend to tell jokes. His
sympathy for the afflicted would be real and sincere, and he would
sacrifice much to help them in a disinterested way, but they would
probably miss the warmth which stems from the fellowship of men as
equals. He would be, in short, a prig.

This is precisely the problem in the ethical sphere for moderns.
The Jew of today acknowledges the great Jewish values taught in the
Jewish classics. He may be prepared to follow these even if they are
at variance with the civilisation in which he finds himself. He yields
to none in his admiration for the values taught in the Jewish tradition—that justice, compassion, righteousness, kindliness and the pursuit of holiness are divine imperatives. But, at the same time, he
knows of another set of values which have been particularly stressed
in the Western world: tolerance, artistic creativity, the use of scientific
method, social welfare, political endeavour, chivalry and the like,
and he does not find that these are always emphasised in the traditional thinkers. What is he to do in order to achieve a life of

wholeness and integrity? How is he to do justice both to the demands of the past and the claims of the present? Can there be a successful marriage between a theocratic view of life and the ideals of secular society?

There is certainly no easy solution to these problems. They belong to the tensions with which the modern Jew must live. Ultimately we all make up our minds on ethical questions by means of the general attitude we have towards life's meaning, and this in turn is an amalgam of complex ideas we have inherited as part of our cultural background. But the Jewish tradition is still a powerful guide containing an abundance of wisdom and stressing those values which have imparted quality to Jewish life at its best. A not too unsatisfactory way of trying to make this clearer is to examine how an ethical problem is actually dealt with in the Responsa literature. We take as one example among many a recent Responsum by Rabbi M. J. Breisch of Zurich.[7]

The following question was put to Rabbi Breisch by an Orthodox Jewish doctor. A young man of twenty, suffering, unknown to him or to his family, from cancer, became engaged to be married. Should the doctor inform the young woman of the truth? Rabbi Breisch came to the conclusion that the doctor is obliged to tell the young woman the truth. The verse: "Neither shalt thou stand idly by the blood of thy neighbour" (Lev. 19:16) teaches, according to the Rabbis,[8] that if one sees a neighbour floundering in the sea one must save him. Consequently, Maimonides[9] rules: "If a man sees his neighbour drowning in the sea or that robbers are making ready to attack him or that a wild beast is about to pounce on him and is able to save him, either by his own efforts or by hiring others to help, and does not do so he offends against the verse: 'Neither shalt thou stand idly by the blood of thy neighbour.'" Surely, argues Rabbi Breisch, this covers our case. Furthermore, there is the prohibition of placing a stumbling-block before a blind man, i.e. by allowing the girl to enter blindly into a marriage which is bound to cause her severe distress. These prohibitions override any considerations of professional etiquette.

Now the argument of Rabbi Breisch seems most reasonable, and we can accept it as supported entirely by our commonsense and general ethical outlook. But in that case what is added by finding the rule in the Jewish tradition? The answer is surely that it is encouraging to know that whatever we decide on such matters has a long history and that we are following in a rich tradition of questing for the will of God. Our "commonsense" view itself is partly fashioned, partly reinforced, by the truth as taught by the tradition.

What we are touching on here is, in fact, the perennial question of the relationship between religion and ethics. Modern man asks: "Why is it necessary for a revealed religion to tell me to do good; do I not understand this for myself? While admitting that it is often difficult to live under the requirements of moral duty, would I not still strive to do so even if I had no belief in revelation?"

This argument amounts to the assertion that man's innate moral sense is a sufficient guide for life's conduct. To make the same demand in the name of religion is superfluous.

There are many moves open to the believer in revealed religion. One is to claim the futility of referring to good deeds without consideration of God's revealed will since good deeds *are* good because God has so declared. Revelation is needed to define the good.

The objection to this approach is that it empties the term "good" of all its content. If a course of action is to be followed because God wills it, nothing is gained by calling such a cause "good."

The believer may reply that it is good to carry out God's will. But this can only mean that the "good" is not identical with God's will for otherwise it would be tautologous to say "it is good to do God's will." There is no escaping the conclusion that a thing is not good because it is in the Torah. It is in the Torah because it is good.

But in that case what is gained by having it in the Torah, the record of revelation? At this stage the believer may reply that although revelation does not function in order to define good conduct, it does serve as its guarantee.

Revelation, it can be argued, provides the momentum for the good life. Without revelation men would know what the good is, but would they pursue it? Would not their selfish grasping instincts prevail? The main objection to this is that it seems to imply what is demonstrably false, namely, that the atheist is always vicious. Nor is there much truth in the corollary that the believer is always virtuous.

A less vulnerable version of the argument is that the influence of revelation is to be seen not so much in the ethical life of the individual as in that of society. Religion, speaking in God's name, has created and sustained the background against which moral values can flourish.

The Hebrew Bible, with its strong insistence of justice and mercy, has fostered in Western civilisation a climate of opinion favourable to virtue and hostile to evil. There can, indeed, be a virtuous atheist, but he is living on the spiritual capital of believing ancestors.

There is much truth in this yet it does not provide a complete answer to our inquiry. Even in the West, to say nothing of other civilisations, some of the more important social reforms have been achieved through the efforts of avowed secularists, while the social conscience of believers has not always been beyond reproach.

Another reply is to argue that religion has little to do with being good in the ethical sense. Revelation is not for the purpose of teaching men how to behave well towards their fellow-men but how to worship God. Religion, on this view, is chiefly a matter of prayer and ritual, of meditation and contemplation, of a soul alone with God.

This kind of answer cannot possibly be acceptable to the believing Jew. Micah tells us that God does desire men to do justly and to love mercy, and this teaching is supported by all the prophetic voices in Israel. The Rabbis constantly remind the Jew that in addition to man's duties towards God there are God-ordained duties to men and that in many respects the latter are the more significant.

The most satisfying argument for the need for revelation in the ethical sphere is to appreciate that it opens up a new dimension for ethical man.

Revelation informs us that by living a life of honesty and integrity, by having a proper regard for his fellows and by practising righteousness and loving mercy, a man comes to have not only a better relationship with other human beings but a deeper relationship with God. To be good one does not need revelation, but it is important to know through revelation what God would have us be.

Judaism speaks of the nearness of God as the ultimate aim, and it teaches that man is never nearer to God than when he responds in love and sympathy to the needs of others. "Just as He is called 'gracious' be thou gracious. Just as He is called 'compassionate' be thou compassionate."

NOTES

7. *Helkat Yaakov*, Vol. III, No. 136, pp. 257–258.
8. Sanh. 73a.
9. *Yad, Rotzeah* I:14.

E. DAVID M. GORDIS

Rabbi David Gordis, with both ordination (1964) and a doctorate in Talmud (1980) from the Jewish Theological Seminary of America, has served as a Vice President at the University of Judaism and Executive Director of the American Jewish Committee, and since 1992 he has been President of Hebrew College in Boston. He has also served as the Executive Director of the Wilstein Institute of Jewish Policy Studies since its inception. An excellent teacher and an unusually creative and successful administrator, he applies his creativity and moral sensitivity not only to administrative matters, but to academic and Jewish legal matters as well.

This article, "Halacha as Process: The Jewish Path to the Good Life," was originally published in 1983 as one of the University of Judaism's *University Papers* series. In it, Gordis portrays Jewish law as one factor among others that comprise the Jewish heritage, a view shared by most theorists. Unlike theorists like Roth or even Dorff, however, Gordis maintains that Jewish law is not the primary way in which we should seek to apply the tradition to modern times. Ethics holds that place of honor for six reasons that he numbers and delineates, and for

Gordis ethics always must supercede law if there is a conflict between the two.

Moreover, in sharp contrast to Roth, Gordis claims that law is not systematic in the deductive sense of that word but rather operates in a broad context that includes the contemporary halakhic community, "other criteria" (including whatever is relevant to a given decision), and the individual. As he says, there is "a fundamental tendency of the Jewish tradition: when dealing with complexities and inconsistencies, the tradition prefers to sacrifice elegance and coherence if the price of that elegance is misleading and self-deluding over-simplification."

In the "interactive" process that Gordis describes for making decisions in Jewish law, he gives standing to the individual, a factor that is absent from earlier Conservative theories except, perhaps, Feld's and possibly Gillman's. Individual autonomy plays a major role in both classical and modern Reform theories, as we shall see in chapter 7, and more recent Reform theories like those of Eugene Borowitz would also have the individual take into account all of Gordis's other factors. In fact, at first blush, Gordis's theory looks very much like Borowitz's. Gordis, though, specifically makes the halakhic *community* a factor in making authentic Jewish decisions, a factor that plays a much less prominent role in Borowitz's theory, and Gordis would probably also maintain that there is a crucial difference in the *degree* to which he would give authority to the tradition as received. In the end, though, Gordis also specifically acknowledges the role of the individual in making Jewish legal decisions, an element in his theory that makes it unusual among the Conservative theorists we have considered so far.

That stance, of course, gives the individual both a privilege and a responsibility. Gordis himself recognizes that his interactional model for making Jewish decisions "places an enormous burden of responsibility on the Jewish community and on the individual Jew. It forces us to live with complexities, ambiguities, and uncertainties." This is certainly not a theory that will provide clean, indubitable answers.

Moreover, his approach "forces us to call upon the best that is within us in the constant interaction with Jewish tradition and its revitalization . . . We must call upon the resources with which we are endowed, our sensitivity, our knowledge, and our intelligence and attempt to maintain our tradition as an instrument for enhancing the quality of human existence." Thus his theory depends critically on the extent to which each individual can muster those qualities.

Even though Gordis invokes the halakhic community as an explicit factor in the process he describes, his theory gives legal standing to the individual as well, and that, in every case, raises the question of how the individual and community are supposed to interact in making Jewish decisions. Does this effectively place ultimate authority in the individual, who may take the halakhic community into account as much or as little as he or she pleases? Or does the community trump the individual when they come into conflict? Gordis does not decide that question, perhaps because what should happen may be different from case to case. But that raises real questions about the extent to which the result is a shared, communal "law" in any significant sense of that term.

Furthermore, while Gordis provides ample evidence that ethics has deeply affected the process of making Jewish legal decisions throughout the centuries, he veers from the tradition in maintaining that ethics, rather than law, is the central vehicle for making Jewish decisions about how we should act. In this, his stance is exactly that of his father, Robert Gordis. This position, though, incurs a number of problems. However much Jews of the past used their moral sensitivities to guide their decisions, in the end they needed to justify their decisions in legal terms. As I pointed out in the appendix to *Matters of Life and Death* (reprinted in chapter 6 in this volume) and more expansively else-where,[23] the genre of law, while in some ways problematic for morality, in other ways conveyed distinct advantages to Jewish decision-making. Among those are continuity, authority, and at least some degree of com-munal uniformity and identity. Abandoning Jewish law as the central mode for making Jewish decisions, even in favor of something as impor-tant as ethics, robs decisions of those important qualities.

Finally, it is not, in fact, clear that historically ethics has always trumped ritual law. The Talmud, for example, states that one must in-deed respect one's parents, as Leviticus 19:3 demands; but it also asserts that the juxtaposition in that verse of that command with the demand that we observe the Sabbath indicates that we must give respect to our parents only when they themselves obey God's law to observe the Sab-bath, for both the parents and the child are subject to God.[24] That, though, puts observance of the Sabbath above the moral norm to re-spect parents, in opposition to Gordis's theory. As I have discussed else-where,[25] the relationship between Jewish law and morality is more complex than the way Gordis portrays it.

Moreover, because Gordis places such a strong emphasis on ethics as a determining factor in making Jewish decisions, he needs to explain much more clearly how he knows what is morally demanded of us and the basis of the authority of those norms. Is he depending on some form of a natural law theory? On utilitarianism or some other form of consequentialism? On moral prinicipalism in the manner of Kant or W. D. Ross? On virtue theory?[26] As one would expect with any human theory, all of these conceptions of morality and its authority have both advantages and disadvantages, and if Gordis is going to depend on morality, he needs to enter the murky waters of deciding which moral theory he espouses, why he supports that theory, and how that theory can inform us of exactly what our moral duties are and why we should obey them.

Another Conservative rabbi and philosopher, Aaron Mackler, has created a theory similar to that of Gordis, in that he argues for a "holistic" approach to making Jewish legal decisions, including not only the legal texts that we have received, but also all other parts of the Jewish tradition and whatever else is relevant to the specific issue.[27] In this, Mackler, like Gordis, does not privilege Jewish legal texts over any of the other factors that should affect our decisions. Mackler, though, does not make ethics the supreme authority either; what is ultimately determinative in each case will, according to Mackler's theory, depend on the specific circumstances and the judgment of the one making the decision. For example, to decide whether to remove life-support systems from Mom, her adult children should consult her physicians, the family rabbi, other members of the family, and perhaps nurses, social workers, and Mom's close friends. Relevant factors to be considered include Jewish law, but also moral concerns, the patient's wishes, and the patient's best interests. The decision will therefore not come exclusively from a direct reading of Jewish law, and it may even violate what Jewish law seems to require. It will nevertheless be a Jewish decision to the extent that a Jew makes it with Jewish law and tradition as some of the factors included in the decision. Mackler's theory thus suffers from the same problems that Gordis's theory has in abandoning the central role of Jewish law in making Jewish decisions and in giving an expanded role to the particular person making the decision; but Mackler does not presume that ethics reigns supreme either, and so he does not encounter this last problem that I noted about Gordis's theory to the same degree, for he does not depend on ethics as much as Gordis does.

Nevertheless, Gordis's theory has some distinct advantages. It presents a rich context in which Jewish legal decisions should be made. In doing so, it makes clear that Jewish law does not exist in a vacuum but rather is the product of multiple interactions among all the factors that Gordis enumerates. Moreover, Gordis explicitly acknowledges the complexity of life and therefore the corresponding complexity of Jewish law as well. A good legal system should not, as he says, pretend that life is simpler than it is, for that would make the law irrelevant or seriously deficient in addressing the realities of life.

Finally, Gordis's motivation for creating his theory in the first place is both laudable and necessary—namely, to attract Jews to the Jewish tradition. He is absolutely right in asserting that if modern Jews are going to affirm their Jewish identity and roots, and if they are going to pay any attention to Jewish law, they have to come to know it as a deep reservoir of moral guidance. Certainly, Jewish laws that appear to modern Jews as patently immoral will undermine their allegiance to the Jewish tradition and must be changed for that pragmatic reason as well as the internal, theological, and methodological factors within the tradition itself that would demand such changes. But Gordis's point is more positive than negative: In accentuating the moral aspects of Jewish law, we provide Jews with a significant motivation to probe their tradition and to live their lives guided by it.

Halacha as Process:
The Jewish Path to the Good Life*

DAVID M. GORDIS

THE JEWISH PEOPLE HAVE LOST touch with its Halacha, and the gulf separating the Jewish people from its Halacha is the most severe internal problem facing Jewish life today. The Halacha, or Jewish legal tradition, is complex and varied. It includes the great law codes of Judaism, such as the Mishna, the Mishneh Torah of Maimonides and the Shulchan Aruch. It includes also Rabbinic commentaries on legal portions of the Bible, Talmudic discussions and a literature of inquiries and responses on legal matters spanning more than a millenium. The tragedy of Jewish alienation from the Halacha embraces within it such issues as the crisis of the family, the deterioration of interpersonal communication, the ascendancy of the ethic of self-centeredness and the "me generation," and the generally sensed decline in social and personal morality. The Halacha or Jewish way of life embodies the value system of the Jewish people. Is it any wonder, then, that those most detached from this repository of Jewish thinking, feeling and behavior so often fall victim to the assaults of assimilating forces and are lost to the Jewish people and to Jewish life?

Causes for the development of this gulf are complex. They include political, social, and psychological causes. Our principal concern here

---

University Papers (Los Angeles: University of Judaism, 1983), 16 pages.

is to explore the ideological foundations of this gulf and its implications, and to suggest a direction for bridging the gulf ideologically and didactically. The key to recreating the bridge between the Halacha and the Jewish people lies in an accurate understanding of the Halacha as process and of the interplay of ethical considerations with the Halachic tradition as received in each generation. This process was the source of the Halacha's vitality in the past, and it must be reconstructed if the Halacha is to live again in the minds and hearts of the Jewish people.

THE HALACHA AND MODERNITY

To state the matter briefly, the Halacha has by and large been associated with a world view which is perceived as antiquated and rooted in an ideology which is unacceptable to a "post religious" age. At a time when appeals to any tradition are generally suspect, the attempt to base a comprehensive system of belief and practice on a traditional theology and a pietistic historiography is bound to emerge unsuccessful. Traditional theological formulations and historiographical assumptions have been seriously questioned since the time of the Enlightenment. What was taken for granted not very long ago about the nature of God's revelation to people, about creation and about Scripture are certainly not accepted as axioms and are rejected by many reasonable and rational people. In the words of the well-known Gershwin song: "The things that you're liable to read in the Bible . . . it ain't necessarily so." And among the assumptions which are subjected to considerable doubt by the majority of the Jewish people are the authority of the Halacha and even its relevance.

The current apparent resurgence of religious fundamentalism among Jews and Christians as well appears to reverse this trend. In reality it does nothing of the kind. The return to "that old time religion" does not represent the triumph of the traditional ways of looking at the world over the forces of modernism and secularism. The flirtation with the nostalgia and esotericism of a pre-modern tradition represents a temporary withdrawal from the anxieties and pressures of a complex and conflicted world. It is a limited and ephemeral phenomenon. It solves no problems. It attempts to deal with difficult problems by pretending that they do not exist. The fundamental issues in the relationship of a tradition-bound people to its tradition in an anti-traditional age remain to be joined.

The distance between the Halacha and the people is not limited to any particular ideological groups in Jewish life. Those who reject the Halacha from a secularist point of departure elevate their rejection of the Jewish legal tradition to the level of ideological tenet. In so doing they voluntarily detach themselves from the Halacha. But those who accept the relevance or even the authority of the Halacha in their lives often reduce it by stressing its ritual and mechanical aspects, and ignoring the Halacha as applied to the relationships among people. In so doing they denude it of its profound significance and meaning as reflected in its ethical foundations in Prophetic and Rabbinic literature.

They overlook the fact that the Halacha is an instrument for effecting change and not an end in itself. They forget that the objective of the Halacha is to transform and ennoble the quality of our existence. This represents no less a gulf between the Jew and the true and authentic Halacha than the secularists' overt and conscious rejection of the tradition on ideological grounds. In certain ways it is even more pernicious, for it reflects a diminished and reduced conception of the nature of the tradition itself.

THE NATURE OF THE HALACHA

The magnitude of the crisis created by the alienation of the Jewish people from the Halacha is a corollary of the nature of the Halacha itself and of its majestic working papers and investigatory notes, the Talmud. Embracing as it does every area of human behavior, both public and private, social and individual, ritual and ethical; representing as it does the subtle contrapuntal interplay of broad underlying principle and specific imperatives of behavior; moving deductively from general to specific and inductively from life-generated specifics to general principles and values; illustrating brilliantly its somewhat elusive ambivalence toward its Biblical-constitutional base; venerating and canonizing but reworking, highlighting and setting aside as perceptions require through the Midrashic process; the Halacha in all these ways constitutes the fundamental repository of values for the individual Jew and for the Jewish people, and a methodology for applying these values to life. Within the Halacha are contained the principles and criteria which have guided the Jewish people in making choices, in establishing priorities, in devising approaches and techniques to analyze and deal with problems and to resolve issues which confront them. The life of our people through its history is reflected in the Halacha. The defining characteristics of our people, its spirit, its vision and its goals are contained within the Halachic tradition. This assertion stands independent of any specific ideological orientation towards the Halacha. It does not argue for or against the authority of the Halacha, for or against its divinity. It is a historical assertion, and as such it argues only for the relevance of the Halacha to an understanding of and association with the Jewish spirit in its living historical expression. The separation of the Jewish people from the Halacha must be viewed as no less than the alienation of the Jewish people from the texture and language, and ultimately from the substance of its value system.

HALACHA AND PROCESS

It is possible to speak of one meta-value in Jewish tradition, that is, one value which precedes other values because it concerns the nature of the generation and formation of values in Jewish tradition; I am referring to the strong orientation of the tradition to process in the formation of values and in their formulation. Jewish tradition does not characteristically convey values by stating them in declarative or apodictic style.

Values are conveyed through the struggles of great Jewish figures, as in the Biblical narratives, or through the struggle to deal justly with real-life situations and to apply principles to them, as in Talmudic dialectic or geonic responsa. This is not simply a characteristic of literary style; it is a fundamental characteristic of the mind-set of Jewish tradition. It seeks to engage the Jew in the decision-making process and to sensitize us to the complexities of decision making. For this reason, it is always necessary that we bear in mind when considering the Halacha not only the formulation of the law in the post-Talmudic codes, but also the substrata of discussion, the "give and take" in the Babylonian and Palestinian Talmuds and in the Talmudic commentaries.

The Jewish tendency to answer a question with a question is often commented upon by comedians. The humor has endured because of the underlying truth of the observation. We need only recall that even Maimonides, whose *Mishneh Torah* was intended in part to spare the student of the Halacha the need to have recourse to the intricacies of Talmudic dialectic, failed to substitute his elegant code of Jewish law for the Talmud as the dominant curriculum for the learned Jew.[1] He failed because he overlooked an important reality; when we detach the law from the Aggada, its ethical, ideological and ideational foundation, the result is a misconception and a distorted understanding of the nature of the law. So, too, to detach the Halacha from the dialectical substratum in the Talmud and the Codes brings about an inadequate appreciation of the nature of the Halachic enterprise and its emphasis on the process of welding principle to practice in the life of the people.

The emphasis on process is of crucial significance because it reveals a fundamental tendency of the Jewish tradition; when dealing with complexities and inconsistencies, the tradition prefers to sacrifice elegance and coherence if the price of that elegance is misleading and self-deluding over-simplification.

This is true in every area of Jewish thought: theological, ideological and legal. Sacrificing a degree of coherence and consistency, our tradition speaks on the one hand of a God who is both transcendent and forbidding, and on the other who is "near unto all who call upon Him in truth."[2] The liturgy states: "The superiority of man over beast is non-existent," and juxtaposes this conception with man "created in God's image." We are children of Abraham, and little lower than the angels. The legal tradition declares: "Both positions are the words of the living God"[3] in the face of irreconcilable inconsistencies.

In so doing, inconsistency for its own sake is not made into a virtue. Rather, when dealing with what appear to be compelling but conflicting truths about the nature of God, the nature of man or the nature of their interrelationships; and when approaching issues concerning which no clear consensus exists and where sensitive and informed people may differ, the imposition of a requirement of superficial coherence would impoverish the range of man's options. The tradition's role is to enrich and enhance our capacity to deal effectively and creatively with life and with experience. Such an imposed criterion of coherence is therefore unacceptable.

It is for this reason that process becomes central to Jewish concern. Exploration stimulates, illuminates, and enlarges one's vision. It represents an opening for growth and development. Conclusions stated in a form detached from the matrix of the investigation which preceded them can reduce man's appreciation of life's complexities and the capacity to deal with these complexities, using our creative faculties effectively.

Rabbinic Perceptions of the Halachic Process

The attitude of the tradition itself towards the Halachic process is an important illustration of the disinclination to oversimplify. Talmudic authorities no doubt felt themselves rooted in the Torah. They were Torah obsessed; Torah was the starting point for all they did, Torah being the divine word as revealed to Moses on Sinai. But though the fact of that revelation remained unquestioned, its content was the subject of a good deal of complex and apparently inconsistent speculation by the Talmudic authorities themselves.

The Palestinian Talmud reports a rabbinic comment which takes as its starting point an apparent redundancy in a Biblical verse:

> "Commenting on the verse: 'And God gave me the two stone tablets written by the finger of God and upon them (as) all the words which God spoke unto you on the mountain from within the fire on the day of assembly,' (Deuteronomy 9, 10): Rabbi Joshua b. Levi said: "Upon them, and upon them, all, (as) all, words, the words: (The verse intends to include) Torah (the simple meaning of the verse), (but also) Mishnah, Talmud (here meaning commentary on the Mishnah), and Aggadah. Even what the advanced[4] student is destined to teach in the presence of his master was already said to Moses on Sinai."[5]

In a similar vein:

> "Blessed be the name of the King, King of Kings who chose Israel from among seventy nations, as it is written: 'But the Lord's share was His own people, Jacob was His allotted portion.' And He gave us the written Torah containing intimations of matters hidden and concealed, and explained them in the Oral Law and revealed them to Israel."[6]

From these sources it would appear that the rabbis perceived of their own role as essentially stenographic in nature, communicating to the people what had been revealed to Moses on Sinai. These sources would imply a **reactive** role for the Talmudic authorities. One further source of this type may be adduced:

> "(On the verse): These are the statutes, the judgments, and the laws which the Lord established between Himself and the Children of Israel' (Leviticus 26,46): The statutes—these are the interpretations; the judgments—these are the laws; and

the teachings (Toroth)—this teaches that Israel was given two Torahs, one written and one oral."[7]

The foregoing sources would suggest that all of the tradition, the Pentateuch as well as the entire range of post-Biblical commentary and elaboration, was contained in the event of revelation to Moses on Mount Sinai.

A different selection of sources leads to a different rabbinic view of their own Halachic enterprise. These sources suggest a high degree of awareness on the part of rabbinic authorities of their creative role. They viewed themselves as creators and not simply communicators of the tradition:

> "(On the verse) 'And He gave to Moses,' (Exodus 31,18) (the anonymous Midrashic author asks rhetorically): Did Moses in fact learn the entire Torah? It is written: 'Its measure is larger than the earth and broader than the sea,' (Job 11,9), and did Moses learn it (all) in forty days?! Rather, The Holy One, Blessed be He, taught Moses general principles."[8]

"General principles" would imply something far different than a tradition which was revealed literally and in its entirety to Moses. This indication of a broader creative field for post-Biblical authorities is even clearer in other quite familiar sources:

> "The laws concerning the release of vows fly about in the air and have nothing on which to lean. The laws of the Sabbath, festive offerings, and violations of sacred property are like mountains suspended by a hair, for they have little Scripture and many laws."[9]

It might be argued that the intent of the passage is not to point to rabbinic creativity in these areas, but rather to indicate that the primary origin of these laws was not in the written Torah but in the *Torah Shebe'al Peh*, the Oral Law, which was equally divine in origin. If that were in fact the intent, however, the author would not have used such expressions as "flying about in the air," "having nothing on which to lean," or as "mountains suspended by a hair." The author intends rather to point out that the effort was made to link these areas of law with the limited relevant Scriptural material available, but that this effort was of limited success.

A final reference in this connection might be made to the charming and familiar account in the Babylonian Talmud of the visit of Moses to the academy of Rabbi Akiba.[10] After hearing from God that a man named Akiba b. Joseph was destined to derive "heaps of laws" from the decorative embellishments of the letters of the Torah which God himself was setting in place, Moses asks God if he might see Akiba at work. God obliges, and Moses finds himself seated at the back of a classroom in R. Akiba's academy. R. Akiba is lecturing and explaining the law to his students. Moses listens to the lesson and grows faint when he realizes that he does not recognize the material that R. Akiba is teaching. It is totally unfamiliar to him. Suddenly a student raises his hand and inquires of R. Akiba: "My teacher, what is the source of that law?" R. Akiba replies: "It is a law of Moses from Sinai." Upon hearing R. Akiba's answer Moses is reassured and recovers.

The tale is unequivocal in recalling that Rabbi Akiba's lesson, based ostensibly on the law of Moses from Sinai, was nevertheless incomprehensible to Moses himself. The charm of the story and, more important, its power and the very reason for its preservation is to convey the rabbinic consciousness of the fact that while they appealed to Sinai for the authority of their legislative activity, the rabbis understood the distance that separated them from Sinai. In telling this story, the rabbis asserted the creative and innovative nature of their own enterprise.

Several other sources relating to the rabbis' perception of their relationship to Torah as revealed on Sinai and of their own role as exegetes and legislators can be adduced. Those cited are adequate to demonstrate that though they certainly cannot be said to have viewed themselves as independent of the authority of the Sinaitic theophany or of the content of that revelation, neither can they be said to have viewed their relationship to Sinai and their function as purely reactive and stenographic. The best descriptive term for their own perception is that they interacted with the tradition as they received it.

I would like to stress here that once again this is an historical observation, not an ideological assertion. Whether or not the rabbis' self-perception is an appropriate model for contemporary Jewish life is the subject of disagreement among proponents of the several ideological groups which accept the binding character of the Halacha in some sense. I shall deal with that question below. That the rabbis viewed their relationship with the tradition as they received it in interactional terms is, it seems to me, a fact of Jewish history.

HALACHA AND ETHICS

We move now to the specific question of the relationship of the Halachah to ethics. The question requires immediate clarification, for "Halacha" and "ethics" belong to two different classes of words. "Halacha" represents a specific complex of laws and customs; "ethics" refers to a philosophical discipline concerned with the sources of criteria for evaluating moral conduct. In a strict sense the terms are not comparable. In considering the relationship between Halacha and ethics, what I mean to ask is: what role, if any, do values derived from some other source outside the Halacha have to play in establishing Halachic norms? Put another way, is the Halacha independent of, and should it be independent of, moral judgments that we might make on non-Halachic grounds? How should we deal with values which seem compelling when they conflict with Halachic norms?

Having argued for an interactive model as the best way to summarize and integrate the rabbinic authorities' stated perceptions of the nature of their relationship to the Halacha as received, we may now proceed to approach the question of the relationship of Halacha and ethics by asking: did the rabbis consciously or unconsciously apply an ethical criterion external to the Halacha as received to their legislative activity? I would argue strongly in the affirmative and would cite a few of the many examples which might be adduced.

The fourth chapter of the Mishna of Gittin cites several examples of enactments, *takkanot*, which were instituted on the basis of the principle *"mipne tikkun haolam,"* "for the improvement of the world." They include the prohibition of nullifying a *get* under such circumstances as would mislead a wife into believing that she had received a proper *get* when in fact what she had received was null and void.

In its discussion of the nature of the *tikkun haolam* referred to here, the Talmud furnishes two alternative explanations: one suggestion is that the intention is to protect the pious woman who will always refrain from remarriage on the chance that her *get* had in fact been nullified. The second suggestion is that the intent is to prevent the possibility of *mamzerim,* offspring of an adulterous marriage, which might result from a marriage entered into by a woman who assumed incorrectly that her *get* was valid. In the course of the discussion the Talmud cites Rabbi Simon b. Gamliel's recourse to the principle, "If so, what is the power of the court?" to support his interpretation of the enactment as meaning that subsequent to the enactment an act of nullification on the part of the husband simply had no force. The anonymous *amora* then asks:

> "Does a case, in fact, exist in which according to the law of the Torah the *get* is null and void and because of the principle of 'what is the power of the court?' we permit a married woman to remarry?!"

The much discussed response is:

> "Yes, all who marry do so on the authority of the rabbis, and the rabbis annulled this marriage."[11]

The commentators spent a good deal of time on this passage, and paid particular attention to the nature of the annulment. At issue is whether the marriage is being dissolved by the divorce originally written at the husband's request, or whether the annulment is in some sense independent of the *get.* This fascinating source deserves all the attention it has received, but we shall not dwell on it here. For our purposes it is sufficient to note that the *status quo ante* is changed by Rabban Gamliel the Elder because of the injustice and inequity which the law allowed. Furthermore, this change was instituted even at the price of a modification of the law of the Torah.

Other instances of *tikkun haolam* in the chapter include the introduction of the formula "and any other name by which he is known" into the language of the *get* to preclude abuses stemming from the intentional introduction of a flaw into the text of the *get*,[12] easing the requirements for the collection of the *ketubah,* or the husband's financial obligation undertaken at the time of marriage, by a widow,[13] and laws to alleviate the equivocal status in which Jewish slaves sometimes found themselves.[14]

I do not suggest that all enactments made because of the principle *mipne tikkun haolam* are based on ethical considerations. Some, such as Hillel's famous *prozbul,* which is a legal fiction created to circumvent the Torah's ruling that personal debts are cancelled automatically at the end of each sabbatical year, are designed to facilitate social intercourse. In several of the enactments, however, there is no doubt that the objective is to bring the law into line with what was considered ethically acceptable.

It should be added that the principle *of mipne tikkun haolam* is used not only to rationalize changes in the law but also to explain the basis for laws which do not explicitly modify the *status quo ante.* An example is the statement

> "The finder of lost property (who, upon returning the property might be expected to be required to take an oath that he was, in fact, returning all of the lost property which he had found) does not take an oath because of *tikkun haolam.*"[15]

The same holds true for the principle of *mipne darke shalom,* "in order to promote peace," which is stated to be the reason for the enactment of a number of laws.[16]

It is not possible to determine with certainty the motivation for the creation of the elaborate complex of restrictive legislation surrounding the imposition of the death penalty as summarized in the fourth through sixth chapters of the Mishna of Sanhedrin and in the Talmudic discussions of those chapters. Without doubt, externally imposed restrictions on the authority of Jewish courts entered into the picture. But after reading the instructions given to witnesses in capital cases in which they are confronted with the gravity of the testimony they are about to give, can one doubt that ethical considerations were paramount in the construction of this legislative complex?

"You must know, that capital cases are not like civil cases. In civil cases a person compensates his neighbor and is reconciled with him. In capital cases his blood and the blood of his descendants remain attached to him until the end of the world."[17]

It should be recalled that the context of this legislation is the Torah's prescribed death penalty for a range of offenses, both ritual and interpersonal in nature. There seems little reason to doubt that ethical criteria were significant in this area of legal development.

The Mishna of Baba Mezia presents a remarkable institution of Jewish law, an institution which as far as I know is an original creation of rabbinic law.[18] I refer to the institution of *ona'a,* literally "oppression," which refers in the general sense to such areas as *ona'at ishto,* "wounding the feelings of one's wife," and specifically to the provision for automatic cancellation of sale in the case of over-reaching by buyer or seller through exceeding a sixteen-and-two-thirds percent margin from the fair market value of a commodity. Fair market value was established by market officials. In relating the laws of *ona'a*, the Mishna reports a discussion which took place between Rabbi Tarfon, a second century *tanna* or rabbi of the period of the Mishna, and the merchants of the city of Lydda:

> "Rabbi Tarfon taught at Lydda: *Ona'a* (the amount the selling price may exceed established fair market value without invoking the buyer's right of cancellation of sale) is eight silver *ma'ahs* out of a silver *sela* (*sela* equals four silver *denarii* equals twenty four silver *ma'ahs*), one-third of the sale. (R. Tarfon was thus allowing twice the margin of profit which was the norm elsewhere.) The merchants of Lydda were happy. He said to them: The time period for cancelling the sale is (extended to) the entire day. They said to him: 'Let R. Tarfon leave us as we were,' and they resumed following the view of the sages (which limited the time of cancellation to that required to consult expert opinion).[19]

This conversation represents the attempt by R. Tarfon to adjust the law to meet the needs of the community of Lydda. His attempt appears to have been directed to the greater protection of the consumer. His negotiation with the merchants suggests an awareness of the adaptability of the law to the requirements of equity and fairness.

A remarkable passage occurring later in the same chapter of the Mishna deserves mention:

> "Just as there is *ona'a* in buying and selling so also there is *ona'a* in words."

This passage extends the notion of *ona'a* to the person who bargains with a storekeeper though he has no intention of buying, and to other instances of morally reprehensible behavior. This passage leaves no doubt as to the motivation of the entire institution of *ona'a*.[20]

A number of other instances could be adduced to demonstrate the active and conscious application of ethical criteria to the rabbinic legislative process.[21] The examples cited here should suffice to indicate that these criteria were contributory and at times critical to the process of the development of the Halacha.

ETHICAL CONSIDERATIONS AND THE CONTEMPORARY HALACHIC PROCESS

What remains to be established is the relevance of these historical observations for the nature of the contemporary Halachic process. I should like to propose that the contemporary Halachic community must apply ethical considerations to the Halachic process, and that in fact the Halacha cannot be unethical. We must never be in the position of defending a Halacha that does not reflect the highest ethical sensitivities of man on the grounds that the Halacha is unchangeable. To do so would in effect canonize human shortcomings.

To limit the scope and concern of the Halacha by eliminating from it ethical considerations and to allow a Halacha which we perceive to be unethical to remain unchanged is unacceptable on the following grounds:

1. The rabbinic perception of their role in the legislative process was historically accurate; interaction, in fact, did characterize the relationship of the people to their tradition. Interaction implies the application of external evaluative criteria to the tradition as received, and the subjection of that tradition to the independent judgment of a living community.

2. If one accepts the notion of the Halacha as the product of the interaction of God and man in time, rather than as the literal content of a single event of revelation, then one must accept the fact of man's role in the creation of the Halacha and of man's responsibility to participate in its creative development This necessitates the admission of a possibility of error in the tradition and the assertion of the capacity for growth, development, and progress towards higher levels of ethical sensitivity.

3. The basis of that independent judgment which is the corollary of the interactive model is man's capacity for moral discernment. The corporate moral judgment and growth of the Jewish community through time and the interaction of the moral consciousness of the individual Jew with the tradition as received give life to that tradition and validate its moral claims.

4. The claim for authority for the Halacha must presuppose a claim for its moral authority and stature. Once it is conceded that the Halacha is the product of divine-human interaction, no argument for the acceptance of anything reflecting less than the highest ethical standards can be countenanced. Human shortcomings cannot be canonized, nor can a claim of immutability be made for them.

5. The precedent of reliance on ethical criteria in the past creates the presumption that we ought to continue to accept these criteria in the present and for the future. This is an appropriate understanding of the "general principles" which were taught to Moses, transmitted by him to subsequent generations, and utilized creatively by successive generations of legislators.

6. Finally, the gulf described at the beginning of this paper, between the people and its Halacha, will not be bridged by a Halacha which does not represent the highest of which the human spirit is capable. A Halacha which does not represent moral excellence will never be a Halacha to which the Jewish people returns.

In sum, the interactive model of the Halacha which the rabbinic authorities perceived remains the appropriate model for the contemporary Halachic community because it is historically accurate and philosophically sound. Interaction implies that some set of criteria which is derived from outside the tradition as received must be applied to that tradition. That set of criteria must be rooted in man's capacity for moral development. The process of interaction should not be viewed as a conflict between the Halachic and the non-Halachic. It should rather be viewed as the *modus vivendi* of the Halacha, the way the Halacha lives. The Halachic process correctly understood presupposes the creative tension between the tradition as received and other criteria deriving from the creative capacities of the Halachic community and the individuals who comprise it.

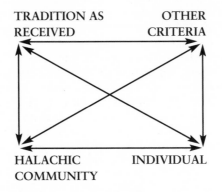

TRADITION AS   OTHER
RECEIVED   CRITERIA

HALACHIC   INDIVIDUAL
COMMUNITY

A graphic model for the functioning of the Halacha might be helpful; I have in mind a square, the sides of which are doubled-ended arrows and the corners of which are connected by diagonals. The upper left hand corner represents the tradition as received; the upper right corner represents other criteria. The lower left corner represents the community and the lower right corner represents the individual. All lines are vectors indicating influence and interaction in two directions.

The purpose of this model is to demonstrate the interaction of which I speak. The inputs into the decision-making process of the Halacha are both the tradition as received and other criteria: esthetic, sociological, psychological, and above all ethical. These two types of criteria, tradition as received and other criteria, influence the two loci of Halachic decision making, the community and the individual. The tradition as received is affected by other concerns, and other concerns affect the nature of the tradition as received.

On the community level both the tradition as received and other criteria are weighed in the decision-making process. In turn, the decisions entered into by the community influence the nature of the tradition itself as it is conveyed to the next generation.

The lower right hand corner represents the individual, for ultimately the decisions on the nature of the life to be constructed are made by the individual. The individual is influenced by the tradition as received which he or she has an obligation to study and pursue. The individual weighs both other considerations and the nature of the communal level decisions in reaching his or her own life pattern. That is the way the Halacha has operated in the past, and it is the way the Halacha must operate if it is once again to capture the heart and the allegiance of the Jewish people and to function in such a way as to transform the life of the Jew.

THE CHALLENGE OF THE INTERACTIONAL MODEL

The interactional model is not a simple conception of the Halacha. It places an enormous burden of responsibility on the Jewish community and on the individual Jew. It forces us to live with complexities, ambiguities, and uncertainties. It forces us to call upon the best that is within us in the constant interaction with Jewish tradition and its revitalization. It means that as we approach every new problem—e.g., the question of the role of women in Jewish ritual and public life, critical issues in areas of bio-ethics and science, dilemmas concerning the relationship of law and government, problems of social stratification and poverty—though we begin with the study of and with reverence for the tradition as received, this is but the starting point and not the end of our responsibility. We must call upon the resources with which we are endowed, our sensitivity, our knowledge, and our intelligence, and attempt to maintain our tradition as an instrument for enhancing the quality of human existence. We will make mistakes, and we may discover mistakes in what others have done. In those cases we must struggle to rectify and adjust and hope that we do better every step of the way. The alternative is unacceptable, for it reduces the Halacha to an unyielding and insensitive legalism which will neither move nor transform. That was never the nature of our tradition in any of its great creative periods, and it must not be the nature of our tradition in our day.

In a book published forty years ago Eliezer Berkovits, the distinguished Orthodox theologian, wrote:

"It (Judaism) cannot be 'preserved', it must move, it must progress; it must take up the thread where it has been left off; it must utilize all the potentialities of development which are included in the system of Halachah. We must apply Torah and not some formerly valid application of Torah to this new form of Jewish existence for which it was never intended. To make this possible we must transform the rigid authority of the Talmud back into the living authority of a national institution such as it was originally. This can only happen after we have, so to speak, given ourselves to the Talmud, so that it becomes again part of our cultural and religious experience. Only when Judaism has become the main spiritual force in us can it unfold itself through us. We have to reconquer the Talmud before Judaism can be freed from its present rigidity and further development can be made possible."[22]

More recently, the well-known Israeli philosopher Nathan Rotenstreich wrote aptly on the subject at hand:

> "The *Halakhah,* as a system of norms of human conduct in all areas, remains the key to the solution of the crisis of modern Judaism. But this system of norms must be reformulated, in the light of its basic principles, if the *Halakhah* is to be affirmed as a living body of laws and should not become merely a historical relic. For the modern Jew will not indefinitely adhere to Judaism because of its antiquity, but will do so because it contains valuable ideas to which he can subscribe. A commitment of this kind is not a unique act of judgment made at a particular time but a never-ending process. Each individual Jew is required to shape his life so that he is responsible for his deeds in all spheres of his experience—in his private and social life, in his relations with the world at large, and to God as the ultimate Judge of the Universe—and he will, therefore, subscribe only to norms which are consistent with his highest ideals, his intelligence and his knowledge. Even a secular Jew would not find it unreasonable to mold his life unceasingly in accordance with such norms. This idea of the *Halakhah* will find its own new expressions in the modern world. These new expressions may not be identical with some in the present-day *Halakhah*. But the tradition will be preserved and given new life even as it is changed."[23]

In order to regain its stature as the life-blood of the Jewish people, the Halacha must be revitalized, must be made to live again. Jews must be stimulated to invest time and energy in the study of the Halachic literature. Teachers of Halacha must intensify their efforts to excite their students with the role that every Jew is called upon to play in the process of a living Halacha. Jews must come to appreciate the Halacha as the best instrument we possess for enhancing the moral and spiritual quality of our lives. The Halacha must generate values but also reflect the best that is within us, particularly in the area of ethical sensitivity. Anything less will not work and does not deserve to work. If restricted and limited, the Halacha will remain by and large a relic on the antiquarian's shelf. If allowed to live, the Halacha can once again be the key to the transformation of the life of the Jewish people.

NOTES

1. On the fascinating question of Maimonides' motivation in writing the Mishneh Torah, see the extensive treatment in I. Twersky, *Introduction to the Code of Maimonides,* New Haven, 1980.
2. For example, contrast Isaiah Chapter 6 with Psalms 145,18.
3. Babylonian Talmud (B.T.) Eruvin 13b; Gittin 6b; Palestinian Talmud (P.T.) Berakhot 1,4; Kiddushin 1,1.
4. The translation of 'watik' is somewhat uncertain. The import of

the word is that the student referred to is the serious and advanced student, not the beginning student acquiring basic skills.

5. P.T. Peah 2,4.
6. *Midrash Tanhuma,* Noah, 3.
7. Sifra, Behukotai, 8.
8. Shemot Rabbah 41,6.
9. Shemot Rabbah 1,8.
10. B.T. Menahot 29b.
11. B.T. Gittin 33a.
12. B.T. associates this Mishna with the circumstances of a person (or city) known by more than one name. My understanding of the Mishna is that it is to be read in the context of the preceding law in the Mishna which dealt with intentionally sadistic behavior on the part of the husband. The specific abuse was the intentional introduction of a flaw into the *get* (suggested by the use of the intensive form of the verb *m'shanneh*) by modifying the name of the husband, wife, or city. The introduction of this formula validated the *get* despite this technical flaw and so represented a *tikkun ha-olam*. See also *Tosafot* ad loc.
13. Mishna Gittin 4,3.
14. *Ibid.,* 5.
15. *Ibid.,* 5,3.
16. *Ibid.,* 6,8–9. See also Mishna Shekalim 1,3.
17. Mishna Sanhedrin 4,5.
18. The contrast with the Roman law is striking. A. Berger states "In the classical law there was no requirement of a just price." (A. Berger, *Encyclopedic Dictionary of Roman Law,* Philadelphia, 1953, p. 649, s.v. "pretium iustum." See also *ibid.,* p. 636, s.v. "laesio enormis.") The notion of just price entered Roman law later.
19. Mishna Baba Mezia 4,3.
20. *Ibid.,* 10.
21. Reference should be made to one other remarkable passage concerning the marketplace. R. Simon b. Gamaliel modified the sacrificial requirements incumbent upon new mothers in order to control the market price of sacrificial birds. See Mishna Kerithoth, 1.7.
22. Eliezer Berkovits, *Towards Historic Judaism,* New York, 1943, p. 59.
23. Nathan Rotenstreich, *Tradition and Reality,* New York, 1972, p. 121.

CHAPTER SIX

Conservative Theories of Jewish Law since 1970—Part II

~~~~~~~~~~

F. ELLIOT N. DORFF

Elliot Dorff, author of this book, is Rector and Anne and Sol Dorff Distinguished Professor of Jewish Philosophy at the University of Judaism in Los Angeles. He is also a Visiting Professor at the School of Law of the University of California at Los Angeles (UCLA). Ordained by the Jewish Theological Seminary of America in 1970, he completed his Ph.D. in philosophy at Columbia University in 1971 with a dissertation in moral theory. Since then he has taught at the University of Judaism, serving also as Dean of its rabbinical program from 1971 to 1994 and Chief Academic Officer between 1980 and 1985. He has been a member of the Conservative movement's Committee on Jewish Law and Standards since 1984, for which he has written some fifteen responsa, and since 1996 he has served as Vice Chair of that body. He has served on several federal government commissions, including the Clinton Health Care Task Force (1993), the Surgeon General's Task Force to Form a Call to Action for Responsible Sexual Behavior (1999–2000), and the National Human Resources Protections Advisory Commission to review and revise the federal guidelines on research on human beings (1999–2002). He is currently a member of the Dialogue on Science, Ethics, and Religion Advisory Commission of the American Association for the Advancement of Science and the Carnegie Foundation's Project on Professional Education entitled "Life of the Mind for Practice Seminar," a Fellow of the Hastings Center, and a member of the Ethics Advisory Committee for the California Stem Cell Project. He has written over 150 articles and ten books on Jewish thought, law, and ethics, including two anthologies, *Contemporary Jewish Ethics and Morality: A Reader* (1995) and *Contemporary Jewish Theology: A Reader* (1999), both published by Oxford University Press and co-edited with Louis

Newman. He specializes in Jewish ethics, with books on Jewish medical ethics (*Matters of Life and Death* [1998]), Jewish social ethics (*To Do the Right and the Good* [2002]), and Jewish personal ethics (*Love Your Neighbor and Yourself* [2003]), all published by the Jewish Publication Society; *To Do the Right and the Good* was awarded the 2003 National Jewish Book Award in Contemporary Jewish Thought and Practice.

Throughout my career, I have had a hard time teaching my own writings, both because I am uncomfortable with the egotism inherent in presenting my own materials as *the* way to think about an issue, but also because after already formulating my ideas as clearly as I can (in print), it seems redundant at best to restate the same thoughts. Therefore, in contrast to my fuller exposition of other thinkers' ideas in my introductions to the selections from their writings, I will instead here simply summarize some of the foundations of my approach to Jewish law as articulated in articles that do not appear here. I will then call attention to the major themes of the selection included below and move directly to an analysis of the weaknesses and strengths of my theory.

One article that explicates the foundations of my thought about Jewish law is entitled "The Covenant: The Transcendent Thrust in Jewish Law," which first appeared in the *Jewish Law Annual*, vol. 7 (1988), pp. 58–96, and is reprinted in the Dorff and Newman anthology, *Contemporary Jewish Ethics and Morality: A Reader* (1995), pp. 59–78. There I present Jewish law, as the title of the article suggests, as best understood as the duties that arise from our ongoing covenant with God. In the first part of the article I describe the features of Jewish law that I think are best understood through the model of a covenant, and then, in the second half of the article, I try to anticipate and respond to some problems in using that model to understand and explain Jewish law. In using the covenant as a model, I am not only continuing a metaphor that the Torah uses many times, but I am also invoking associations with the biblical and rabbinic understanding of the relationship between God and Israel as that of a marriage, with God the groom and Israel the bride.[1]

Another article that articulates the foundations of my theory of law is entitled "Judaism as a Religious Legal System," and was printed in *The Hastings Law Journal* 29:6 (July 1978), pp. 1331–1360. (Since that may be hard for some to access, I should note that many of the points in that article are also discussed on pages 123–133, 187–257, and 421–434 for the book I wrote with Arthur Rosett, *A Living Tree: The Roots and Growth of Jewish Law* [Albany: State University of New York Press and New York: Jewish Theological Seminary of America, 1988] and, to a somewhat lesser extent, on pages 69–100 of my book, *Conservative Judaism: Our Ancestors to Our Descendants* [New York: United Synagogue of Conservative Judaism, 1996].) In Part I of the *Hastings* article, I discuss how Jewish law functions very much like secular legal systems, especially American law, in some respects—namely, the range of subjects it covers; its modes of enforcement by human authorities; its judicial methods for interpreting the law, changing it, and applying it to specific cases that allow it to retain relevance for new circumstances while still maintaining continuity and authority; and its interaction with custom. On the other hand, in Part II of that article, I indicate some of the ways in which Jewish law is a distinctly *religious* legal system by describing the religious influence on its legislative, executive, and judicial functions. Finally, in Part III, I describe some of the practical effects of the Jewish religion on Jewish law. My thesis, then, is that one must understand Jewish law *both* as a living legal system that uses techniques of interpretation, application, and enforcement familiar to American lawyers *and also* as a distinctly religious legal system affected by virtually every aspect of Judaism. In understanding and applying Jewish law, then, the trick is to discern when Jewish law does and should function like any other legal system, and when its religious setting should instead call forth a response that is more religious than legal in nature.

In light of some of the other theories of Jewish law we have discussed, it is important to clarify how I am using two words. First, throughout these articles, when I refer to Jewish law as "a legal system," I am *not* using the word "system" in the way that Joel Roth does—i.e., a deductive system of thought. Instead, I am using the word "system" in a much looser sense. That sense derives from my understanding of Jewish law as rooted in a living relationship with God. In that way it is much like a living organism, such as a human being. Some parts remain the same throughout much of its history but some parts change, sometimes rather radically and even unexpectedly, and every part influences every other part. Similarly, it is like human relationships, with parts that remain the same over time and other parts that change, sometimes rather radically, through the introduction of new aspects to the relationship, the dropping of old ones, and the modification in form of yet other elements. On the one hand, then, Jewish law is not simply a scattered list of laws or, even worse, the whims of a dictator that are subject to change at any moment with no stated reason required or forthcoming; it *is* an organic system of laws, after all, that has both continuity and authority. On the other hand, just as a living organism is not a deductive system, so too Jewish law, in my view, is not such a system; rather, it includes elements that interact with each other and with the surrounding environment in multiple ways that cannot be adequately explained by deductive reasoning alone and often cannot be predicted. As a result, those charged with interpreting and deciding the law must continuously engage in acts of *judgment* as to how to adapt it to the new circumstances. This may range from fighting against incursions from the outside; to assimilating some of them, perhaps with some modifications (the most common response of organisms and cultures to such influences from the outside); to adopting them in total. Furthermore, while in the Jewish legal system the official acts of judgment are in the hands of rabbis, Jewish law is now, and has always been, the product of the *interaction* between what the leaders of the people say and what those who are supposed to be governed by the law in fact do —between *din* and *minhag,* law and custom.

In all these ways, Jewish law is more like Anglo-American law than it is like European Continental law. Both Jewish and American law thus are legal "systems" in a much messier sense of "system" than Roth has in mind. Nonetheless, I think that viewing Jewish law as a living, religious, legal organism that is the product of our ongoing covenantal relationship with God is the most accurate way of describing both the history of Jewish law and how it functions at present. It also clearly brings God into the picture, for the legislative, executive, and judicial functions of Jewish law are all affected by its religious moorings and aspirations. (More elements of my *religious* understanding of Jewish law—specifically, how I think that Jewish law can be a path to knowing and interacting with God—may be found in chapter 3 of my book, *Knowing God: Jewish Journeys to the Unknowable.*)[2]

Second, as I explain in the article included below (the Appendix from my book, *Matters of Life and Death: A Jewish Approach to Modern Medical Ethics*), when I use the term "covenant," I am not using it in the way that Reform theologians like Rabbis David Ellenson and Eugene Borowitz are using the term—namely, to signify an individual Jew's relationship with God.[3] I am rather using the term in its more traditional meaning—specifically, as the Jewish *community*'s relationship with God, a relationship that involves legal obligations to God for all Jews. The *content* of those duties has changed over time and may change in our own era as well, but for me the *fact* that the covenant entails a whole host of such communal duties continues unabated.

Readers may be interested in two other places where I discuss aspects of my theory of Jewish law. Jews living in modern political contexts where freedom of religion—and, with it, freedom from religion—is guaranteed by law understand immediately that people have to be motivated to take on the many obligations of Jewish law that the government does not require them to accept. Modern Jews may be surprised to learn, though, that ancient Jews faced the same difficulty. After all, a bare forty days after God gave the Israelites the Decalogue amid thunder, lightning, and earthquakes, they were worshiping the Golden Calf. As a result, the Bible already recognizes that God's ability to punish us for disobedience will not suffice as the reason to obey the commandments; it therefore spells out many other motivations to do that, and the Rabbis later articulate even more. For an extensive treatment of the biblical and rabbinic motivations to obey the law, see my book, *Mitzvah Means Commandment* (New York: United Synagogue of America, 1989).

Second, in the Appendix of my book *Love Your Neighbor and Yourself: A Jewish Approach to Modern Personal Ethics*, I discuss the factors in religion that actually motivate immorality, and then I turn to the features of religion that may, and often do, lead us to be more moral than we would otherwise be. The factors that I discuss there that can have positive moral effect are: stories; history; family and community; leaders and other models; general values, maxims, and theories; theology; prayer; study; and law. However, any of these factors, including law, can be used mechanically, unintelligently, and even malevolently, and then it can actually guide us to adopt immoral attitudes and actions, those undoubtedly against the wishes of a beneficent God. In the selection included below, I address two related methodological questions— namely, what does Jewish law, when used properly, contribute to our moral sensitivity and action, and how should Jewish law be interpreted so that it can have that positive result?

My theory has inherent weaknesses, just as every other human theory does. It certainly will not appeal to those looking for a neat, clear answer to every question, for it presumes that Jewish law is evolving and that rabbis must use *judgment*—necessarily a subjective factor—in deciding how Jewish law in our day should respond to questions old and new. That will at least sometimes—and perhaps often—lead intelligent, highly educated, and morally sensitive people to different conclusions as they weigh all the factors that must go into a nuanced, Jewishly authentic, and wise Jewish decision for our time, leaving those who want definite and indisputable answers frustrated.

Even though it has a strong religious component, my theory of Jewish law does not pretend to give Jews a definitive articulation of the will of God, for it understands the Jewish tradition, and indeed the Torah itself, as the product of the ongoing interaction between God and human beings. As a result, it does not provide any guarantees that we ever have understood God correctly, or even that we do so now. I would argue, in fact, that no theory can guarantee that, for whatever methodology we adopt, we may all be wrong, for we are, after all, merely human. At the same time, I would also argue that we must trust our current communal understanding of God's will, derived from our most sophisticated efforts to understand and apply the Torah and the Jewish tradition; for our own best judgment of what God would have us do, reached through such a legal analysis, is all we have to go on. Still, that will not be comforting to those who yearn for certainty so that they can say without any doubt that they are doing and fighting for what God clearly wants.

On the other side, my covenantal theory will surely displease secularists, for it presumes that Jewish law has distinctive religious components, that Jewish law cannot, in fact, be understood properly without taking into account its religious character. Those factors include a divine role in the formulation of Jewish law and an even more profound divine role in motivating obedience to it.

Moreover, methodologically my theory will inevitably displease those to both the right and the left of me. On the one hand, while it sees Jewish theology, stories, history, maxims, prayer, and study as critical factors in Jewish experience that have continually interacted with Jewish law in the past and should do so also now and in the future (much more than Roth's extralegal factors would), it does, unlike Reform approaches, maintain that Jewish law is at the core of Jewish action and remains authoritative and binding. As a result, we have to play the legal game, as it were, in order to produce an authentically Jewish decision about any aspect of ritual or moral behavior. At the same time, unlike most Orthodox legal scholars, it does not isolate Jewish law from all other factors, trying to define its current dictates solely on the basis of past precedents. It instead requires rabbis first to study those precedents within their historical contexts and then to weigh them together with contemporary circumstances (economics, demographics, etc.) and a host of other Jewish forms of expression (stories, theology, history, morals, etc.) to make a considered, wise, and clearly Jewish judgment about what they think God wants of us now. Then it mixes things up further by taking into account past and current Jewish customs.

Worse still, while the interconnectedness of Jewish theology, morality, social and communal concerns, and Jewish law enriches the discussion of how the latter should be shaped and makes it conform closer to reality, the negative side of that interconnectedness is that any of those factors can then pose problems for Jewish law. In other words, the fact that I see Jewish law as embedded in Jewish theology, stories, history, prayer, study, and so forth means that as any one part of that complex organism that we call Judaism changes, it may have an effect on any other part of the organism, including Jewish law.

For example, if I believe, as I do, that Jewish law is at least in part the product of a beneficent God, how can I explain the Torah's provisions that any Jew who violates the Sabbath laws should be executed (Exodus 31:14–15); that enslavement of fellow Jews is allowed, although regulated (Exodus 21:2–11; Leviticus 25:39–43), while enslavement of non-Jews is not only allowed but even, at least according to some readings, a positive commandment (Leviticus 25:44–46); and that an illegitimate child and his or her descendants for ten generations may not marry a Jew (Deuteronomy 23:3) despite the fact that it was that child's parents who committed incest or adultery, thus making the child illegitimate, while the child was completely innocent? Surely one could historicize all of these laws, claiming that they were the view of God's will in biblical times but that both God's will and our perception of it have changed since then. But then how does one know that what we currently perceive as God's will is correct? Or is that too at best correct for our times? I actually do want to take such a historical approach, recognizing that we in our time must take the responsibility to make appropriate changes in the law to fit it to modern circumstances, just as our ancestors did in their time. That leaves us, as it left them, with the continuing problem of how we can ever know that we are correct in discerning the will of God.

This hard, epistemological question makes my theory depend on an abiding faith that Jewish law in its evolving forms is an accurate reflection of God's will at any given time, a faith that I know may be wrong in any or even all of our legal decisions. This epistemological predicament also makes my theory even more demanding, in requiring a keen sense of judgment and a deep tolerance for continual learning and reassessment of previous positions. To use my theory, one must both be seriously committed to pluralism and also psychologically able to ride the waves of change in human life in consort with the rest of the Jewish community, all the while keeping a clear focus on ultimate Jewish goals for life and on doing the best we can to discern and obey God's will.

This dilemma with respect to Jewish law is based on a deeper quandary in my theory with respect to God—namely, is my whole analogy to human covenants to describe the relationship between Jews and God apt? This model has a long history within the Jewish tradition in its favor, of course, but is it too anthropomorphic to describe our relationship with God? Does the covenant model, for example, bring God down too much to a human level in becoming a partner with us? Should we instead be talking about a much more transcendent and awesome God who would never deign to bargain with mere mortals? The Rabbis took the covenant model even further than the Bible did, for they maintained that they, human beings though they were, had the authority to determine the meaning of the covenant and that God had no right to intervene in that process.[4] Is all this sheer audacity and impertinence (*ḥutzpah*, we would call it in Hebrew), and should we stop pretending that we can interact with God in legal and covenantal terms similar to those we use in interacting with each other? After all, the biblical Job tried to take God to court and realized immediately that that would simply not work because God is the ultimate Judge and cannot be forced to submit to a legal case against Himself; should we not think likewise and abandon all this covenantal, legal framing of our relationship with God? In the first article cited above (p. 328), "The Covenant: The Transcendent Thrust in Jewish Law," I appeal to the tradition: despite its problems, our ancestors conceived of their relationship with God in this covenantal way, and so it ought to work for us, too. But is that enough of a defense? What if we Jews (and our ancestors) have been wrong all along?

Looking at the issue from the opposite end, does the Holocaust demonstrate that we were wrong in honoring God's law so much? In chapter 5 of my book *Knowing God*, I try to respond to that question, but ultimately even I would agree that to continue to trust in God and in God's law is an immense act of faith in our post-Holocaust era, even though such an act is one I personally espouse. In this faith, I am confirmed and comforted by the fact that the Jewish tradition itself was not at all blind to this problem, that from at least the biblical Book of Job to the present Jews have been struggling with the theological problem of evil—namely, how could a powerful, good God allow evils to occur, especially those natural evils (disease, earthquakes, etc.) that cannot be attributed to humans' abuse of their free will, as the Holocaust can be? I also agree fully with the tradition that God's oneness (monotheism) requires that God be associated with both the good and bad, for ultimately monotheism is a more adequate and compelling representation of the fullness of our experience than any theology that assigns evil to some other power or powers. After all, morally innocent people do suffer and morally culpable people do prosper, as the Rabbis acknowledged,[5] and if God is not involved in that reality, then God is not One and Omnipresent. Even if God is also involved in evil, I have faith (as did Jewish tradition) that God is generally good and demands good of us, and so I continue to believe in the ultimate goodness of God's law.[6]

In sum, then, my theory will not satisfy anyone who wants God alone, human beings alone (individuals or groups), or past precedent alone to decide what Jewish law should be in our time, and it likewise will not please those who want to deny binding authority to Jewish law altogether. In all these ways, my theory is, to put it bluntly, a messy view of Jewish law. Like some other theories we have considered (e.g., Gillman, David Gordis), my theory requires people to be pluralistic, willing to tolerate and even honor differences of opinion and practice, and yet also to know when and how to draw definitive lines about what simply cannot be justified as Jewish. Furthermore, it requires one to exercise such judgment on an ongoing basis, for the certainties of yesterday are not necessarily the certainties of tomorrow (or even of today)—and, in fact, may be overturned altogether. In other words, my theory requires not only a willingness constantly to reevaluate and possibly reshape any given Jewish law, but also to listen closely to others as they challenge one's own position on anything, including some things dear to one's heart. One needs a strong stomach to adopt my theory!

At the same time, my theory has some distinctive strengths. First, it is historically authentic, for Jewish legal decisions have been made in the way I describe through the centuries. The process of integrating all these factors was not always as conscious as I am trying to make it by articulating all the factors that influence Jewish law, and awareness of the historical context of precedents was surely not as keen in centuries past as it is now that we have modern techniques of historical analysis. Rabbis of all ages, however, certainly understood themselves to be the heirs not only of the Jewish legal tradition, but also of its theology, stories, maxims, and prayers, and they were keenly aware that their task was to find the best possible way of applying all of those factors to the conditions and needs of their time.

Because I make clear analogies to English and American law, we can learn from those legal systems without ignoring the differences between them and Jewish law. We can gain insights, for example, from comparing the legal *methods* used to interpret and apply cases in those systems, the *motivations* to obey the law, and even the *content* of the law, for my theory clearly portrays Jewish law as a legal system in many ways like Anglo-American law. At the same time, my theory clearly notes the differences between a secular legal system like American law and a religious system like Jewish law in calling attention to "the transcendent thrust of Jewish law," and those comparisons can also shed significant light on the assumptions and workings of Jewish law.

The covenant model that I use for Jewish law also makes it Jewishly authentic, for that is the oldest and most deeply rooted model in Jewish classical texts. My use of that model in its strong, legal sense of the term "covenant" hopefully sheds light on the authority and functioning of Jewish law at the same time as it gives the law strong Jewish roots. As Louis Newman has pointed out,[7] the covenant model as I use it also makes Jewish law an ongoing feature of the relationship between the Jewish people and God, rather than merely a static code. Along with this, my theory has the distinct advantages of making Jewish law open to change while still maintaining its continuity and authority within the context of an ongoing relationship with God.

Another important strength of my theory is true of most, if not all, Conservative theories of Jewish law, but it is worth restating—namely, that one can be completely intellectually honest. One does not have to pretend that Jewish law developed in a historical vacuum, influenced by God alone; one can—and, indeed, must—understand past precedents in their historical context as well as current conditions in order to apply received Jewish law intelligently and appropriately to our time.

For my theory, though, in formulating Jewish law for our time it is important to attend not only to past and present contexts, but also to all other relevant elements in Judaism—theology, stories, prayers, maxims, history, etc.—and relate them to the current situation. Only then can one appropriately capture the *organic* character of the relationship between ourselves and God, a relationship expressed in Jewish civilization in its entirety and in Jewish law in particular. If one takes note of all those factors, one at least has the proper method, I would contend, to arrive at a Jewishly rooted, wise, and morally sensitive articulation of Jewish law for today, one that will not only serve the needs of the Jewish people but will bring us closer to God.

Finally, my theory is also honest in its recognition of the difficult epistemological problems at the root of all human thought. For after all, in many areas other than religion and law we face the question of how we know what we think we know. For example, how do you know that this book in front of you exists? You might trust your senses, but, as Descartes pointed out, your senses sometimes deceive you, as when the oar in the water looks bent but in fact is not, as you determine when you lift it out of the water. And if knowing about physical things is hard, it is yet more difficult to know about abstract things like justice, hope, or beauty. Philosophers grapple with these questions, but in the end, however we respond to them, we do believe that we *can* know when there is a book in front of us and even when justice has been done, when there are grounds for hope, and when some things are especially beautiful. In a similar way, for all the underlying philosophical problems involved—problems that I readily acknowledge—I think that my view of God and God's law is well grounded in human experience and in Jewish tradition. Further, I would assert that it is about as adequate a view that humans can have. Like all human knowledge, my knowledge of God and God's law is not guaranteed to be accurate or ultimately provable, and surely other approaches may also be well grounded; in fact, I would count pluralism as a necessary facet of my theory and another of its advantages.[8] At the same time, in my book *Knowing God*, I argue that my own view—namely, that depicting God as a personality with a will who can and does engage in a covenantal relationship with us—although a stretch from human experience, is a reasoned one. So at least my approach is honest in its recognition of the philosophical problems involved and in the place of ultimate faith in knowing God and God's law.

While the selection from my writings below focuses on applying Jewish law to current medical quandaries, it can serve as an expression of some of the major features of my theory of law in general. The reader might keep in mind, though, the question of whether any of this would change if applied to other areas of life (such as poverty, war, or sexual ethics) and, if so, how.

⟨⟨Q_____Q⟩⟩

Matters of Life and Death: A Jewish Approach to Modern Medical Ethics*

ELLIOT N. DORFF

APPENDIX

The Philosophical Foundations of My Approach to Bioethics

RELIGION AND MORALITY

The Role of Religion in Making Moral Decisions

The more we deal with contemporary micro and macro issues in bioethics, the more we realize that deciding how to resolve them is not just a matter of determining what works or is affordable; it is also crit-

---

*Philadelphia: Jewish Publication Society, 1998, pp. 395–417 (including pp. 9–11, to which the Appendix refers).

ically a matter of our ultimate hopes and fears, of what we value in life, and of how we conceive of life in the first place. These concerns are the province of religion. The word *religion* etymologically means *linkages,* coming from the same Latin root meaning "to tie or bind," from which we also get the word *ligament.* And so it is that religions address the nature of our links to one another, to the environment, and to the transcendent. From such large pictures of how the world is, we base our hopes for how it should be, and thus values are rooted in the broader world views that religions provide. It is only when we have these ultimate perceptions and convictions in mind that we can sensibly make the specific decisions that contemporary medicine calls upon us to make.

Secular philosophies like those of Plato, Aristotle, Hobbes, and Marx also portray such pictures of reality, but they lack religion's popularity and emotional power. That is because religions not only present a given view of reality and a set of values deriving from it; they also link us to a community that shares these perceptions of reality, cherishes those values, and works for the realization of those hopes. Religions create communities committed to their ideologies by putting their specific understanding of reality into stories that can be easily shared, rituals that can help people live out their understanding of life and feel part of a group that shares it, and institutions that make it possible to teach and share the group's common convictions. These features make religion a powerful and popular way to speak about reality and to guide important decisions in life.

The Relationship between Religion and Morality: Four Theories

Religion, though, has not guaranteed moral behavior; in fact, sometimes religion itself is utterly hostile to it. Take, for example, the Crusades and the Inquisition, during which moral atrocities were committed in the very name of religion. Indeed, even some passages in the Bible are morally ambiguous at best and downright immoral at worst—texts like God's commands to bind and presumably murder Isaac, to kill all of the Canaanites as part of the conquest of the Holy Land, and to enslave non-Jews.[1] In the twentieth century, the worst atrocities were inflicted by the avowedly secular regimes of Stalinist Russia, Maoist China, and Nazi Germany. But moral abominations explicitly in the name of religion have continued, as fundamentalist Muslims terrorize or murder all who opposed them, including other Muslims, and as Baruch Goldstein and Yigal Amir killed in the name of their understandings of Judaism.

Why does religion sometimes lead to immoral action? For one thing, religious faith is built upon trust in God, but all too often that trust turns into credulity and superstition. More pervasively, the blind loyalty religion summons in its adherents, at least in some forms, works against their retaining a critical, moral sense that could criticize religion itself. Indeed, religious authorities have often discouraged or totally suppressed dissent, sometimes even to the point of executing dissenters and heretics.[2] In addition, religions have of necessity been organized into institutions, and so they suffer from all the moral weaknesses inherent in any institution. Conversely, many people we would clearly consider moral are avowedly secular, denying belief in any religion.

Since religion is neither sufficient nor necessary for moral behavior, then, and since sometimes religion actually produces immorality, some people conclude that religion and morality logically have nothing to do with each other. The two may affect each another, but like independent agents, their interaction may either benefit or harm.[3]

Others take the opposite view. Despite the evidence that religion can undermine morality, they hold, logic requires a religious basis for morality (a logical claim), or that social order and moral education both require a religious framework (an empirical claim). George Washington, Thomas Jefferson, and James Madison all endorsed some variation of this theory. Most Americans today likewise believe that even if nothing can absolutely guarantee morality, religion substantially increases its chances.[4]

Still others argue for a third way of viewing the relationship between religion and morality. Robert Gordis and David Hartman, among others, maintain that to be accurately described as religious, a person must behave morally. In other words, they view morality as a logical prerequisite for religion.[5]

The problem with this theory, however, is that it runs counter to how people understand themselves and others. That is, some people who consider themselves and are generally considered by others as religious nonetheless engage in gross moral turpitude, sometimes even being jailed for their behavior. Indeed, Jews' deep embarrassment at seeing newspaper photographs of Ḥasidim convicted of crimes would be unintelligible if such people automatically lost their religious status (and therefore ceased representing Judaism in the pubic mind) upon committing an immoral act. Thus, as much as Judaism demands and supports morality, morality is not by definition inextricably linked to Judaism.

In light of all the above, I hold yet a fourth thesis—namely, that *in Judaism, ethics and religion interact, and that they do so in both directions.* That is, some features of ethics can and should be used to direct and criticize religion, and conversely, some features of Judaism can both deepen and foster moral life. Thus while each can guide and enrich the other, it is also true that each can impede the other. Religion has been used to justify immoral behavior ranging from slaveholding to the assassination of Israeli Prime Minister Yitsḥak Rabin. Moreover, moral claims can produce conflicts with religion—as, for example, when a rally to help the poor takes place on Shabbat, or when moral considerations challenge norms embedded in religious texts (for example, the ban against homosexual sex). Yet because neither perspective controls the other or acts as a logical or empirical prerequisite for the other, religious people and institutions commit many amoral and even completely immoral acts, whereas secular people often behave quite morally. Often and ideally, though, morality and religion correct and support each other.

The Contributions of Ethics to Religion

How do morality and religion interact to their mutual benefit? Let us first look at how ethics can and should be used to guide and criticize religion—or rather, more specifically, the theology and practice of Judaism.

Theologically, the relationship between God and goodness as depicted in Jewish sources from the Bible to our own day has been ambiguous. Although God is generally held to be good, sometimes God commands or does things that are hard, if not impossible, to justify morally.[6] Moreover, in the experience of individuals and of the people Israel as a whole, both natural and human evils occur that make us question God's goodness or power—or even God's very existence.

Nevertheless, most of Jewish tradition teaches—and I concur with this view—that God must be construed as morally good, indeed, as the paradigm of what it means for us to be morally good.[7] Phenomena like childhood leukemia, where there is no human complicity on the part of the person afflicted and where the innocent suffer, though inscrutable, do not constitute sufficient proof that God does not exist or that God is amoral, immoral, or powerless; such phenomena are offset by the many instances of God's beneficence.[8] Thus, when faced with morally troubling phenomena devoid of human complicity, we must accept that we will never understand them and instead learn to cope with them. Such are the limits of human knowledge and understanding.[9]

On the other hand, when confronted with evils caused by human beings, our Jewish belief in a moral God who demands goodness requires that we do what we can to alleviate the effects of such evils and to prevent their recurrence in the future. This is the holy mission that Judaism establishes for us. Therefore, we dare not leave an immoral situation unchallenged, merely attributing it to the unchangeable will of an inscrutable or downright evil God.

Legally, this theology has even more far-reaching implications. For if God is "good to everything, and God's mercies are over all God's works," and furthermore, if God's laws are a manifestation of God's deep and abiding love, as the Psalmist and traditional prayer book proclaim,[10] then Jewish legal decisions must reflect these beliefs. Therefore, if a legal decision that seems justified by traditional sources, or even mandated by the majority of them, is not moral, it must be changed.

The classical rabbis made it very clear that the Jewish tradition they were shaping, which we identify today as normative Judaism, is *not* fundamentalist, even with regard to the Torah; it rests rather in the hands of the rabbis of each generation who interpret and apply it according to their own understanding of God's will.[11] It is, then, the way in which the rabbis of each generation understand morality that must govern how Jewish law is shaped to be morally good and, therefore, Godlike.

Because intelligent, morally sensitive, and committed Jews may disagree about the ethics and wisdom of any proposed decision, this methodological principle does not automatically require, or justify, any given decision in Jewish law. Yet the underlying morality of Jewish law, reflecting a moral God who commands it, should motivate its interpreters to aspire to make their legal decisions as morally exemplary as possible. Conversely, laws that are patently immoral must either be annulled altogether or at least so restricted in their scope as to make them effectively inoperable. Indeed, such reinterpretations of Jewish law on moral grounds have occurred in our own day, especially in respect to many laws defining the status of women. And by the same token, conflicting moral perspectives today fuel the arguments surrounding the status of homosexual relations.

Similarly, this fundamental commitment of Jewish law to morality, based on an underlying theology of a moral God who commands it, should also guide us as we face the many new issues in contemporary bioethics. In many such issues, the radical innovations of modern medical care make a mechanical or literal reading of traditional texts inappropriate. Instead, those who would apply Jewish law to these new circumstances must supplement their traditional learning with a keen moral sense of when and how to apply classical Jewish sources as a good God would direct us to do.

The Contributions of Judaism to Moral Theory and Practice

The second half of my argument—namely, that Judaism can contribute significantly to morality—applies to both moral theory (or "ethics") and moral practice ("morality").

On a theoretical level, Judaism affirms a particular picture of the world as it is and as it ought to be. It defines who we are as individuals, as a community, as parts of the environment, and as partners of God; and it provides ideals toward which we can and should strive. In so doing, Judaism places our moral decisions into the *context* of a larger vision of the world and our goals within it. Judaism thereby gives *meaning* to each of our moral efforts and provides *motivation* to meet our moral challenges. The beliefs of Judaism thus establish moral moorings for our specific judgments and acts.

Judaism also contributes to our moral behavior on a pragmatic level by strengthening the family and self-worth of both ourselves and others, as well as our moral restraints and aspirations. Through values, stories, rituals, and laws, Judaism reinforces the cohesiveness and moral effectiveness of our families and communities.

Another pervasive feature of Judaism that contributes mightily to our moral framework but is less often acknowledged in that capacity is *Jewish law*. Like Judaism as a whole, Jewish law does not guarantee moral sensitivity or behavior, but it makes their presence more likely in a number of ways. Since Judaism focuses so much on the legal expression of its views and values, much of our treatment of bioethics must be framed in legal terms. It is therefore worth spelling out here some of the ways in which Jewish law as a whole, and Jewish bioethical law in particular, helps to make people behave morally:

1. *Establishing a moral bottom line.* Law establishes a minimum standard of practice. Because many moral values depend on the mutual action of a number of people, the enforcement as law of a minimum moral standard enables a society to secure the cooperation necessary for such moral attainment. Furthermore, a beneficent act, whether done for the right reason or not, has its own objective value.

2. *Translating moral goals into concrete rules.* It is not just on a minimal level that law is important for morality; at every level of moral aspiration law translates moral insight and fervor into modes of daily action. Without that translation, our moral vision and courage lose their meaning and influence.

3. *Setting priorities among conflicting moral goals.* When moral values conflict, law provides a method for determining which value will take precedence over which, and under what circumstances. Non-legal systems commonly rely on the sensitivity and analytical ability of the individual or an authority figure to do that; law enlists the minds and hearts of legislators, judges, and the public at large. Although such a process does not guarantee wisdom, it does at least provide a greater measure of objectivity and hence a more thorough consideration of relevant elements.

4. *Appreciating the reality, nuances, and immediacy of moral issues.* In contrast to moral treatises, which are usually general and nondirective, judicial decisions respond to concrete cases in which judges make practical decisions. Thus in contrast to many "ivory tower" moral essays, legal precedents address reality in all its complexity and provide specific instructions for action. Much of the rabbis' sheer wisdom, in truth, can be attributed to the fact that they served as judges as well as scholars and teachers. Thus the legal context adds a sense of immediacy, nuance, and reality to moral deliberation.

5. *Preserving the integrity of moral intentions.* Law brings our motives into the arena of action, where we can see them clearly and work to change them if necessary. Law thus helps to preserve the integrity of moral intentions themselves, clarifying and verifying them in action.

6. *Balancing continuity with flexibility.* Because law operates on the basis of precedent, it preserves a strong sense of continuity in a moral tradition. On the other hand, through legal techniques—differentiating the present case from previous ones; limiting the scope of previous cases; finding other analogous cases in the tradition that lead to a different conclusion; redefining some of the critical terms involved; or, ultimately, issuing a *takkanah*, that is, a "fixing" or changing of the law—law preserves a reasonable amount of flexibility and adaptability.

Since this process is in the hands of rabbis, whose ordination signifies that they are both committed to the tradition and schooled in it, such changes will not happen cavalierly—especially if any one rabbi's decision enters into a larger discussion among many rabbis—but will instead enable appropriate change to take place over time.

7. *Preserving the coherence of a moral system.* If authorized judges in each generation—namely, rabbis—are entrusted with the task of legal interpretation for their communities, then even if there is disagreement among them, we can learn from their deliberations what counts as a Jewish approach—a norm formulated in the judicial line of precedents within Judaism—to a given issue. This is all the more true if the rabbis have a communal method of setting parameters for legitimate dissent among them; the Sanhedrin did that in times past, and the Conservative movement's Committee on Jewish Law and Standards functions in that way for the Conservative movement now.[12] To achieve a measure of coherence, even the Reform movement, which puts so much emphasis on individual autonomy, has shown renewed interest and creativity in developing its own legal response to moral issues by creating a Committee on Halakhic Inquiry and by publishing books of responsa.[13]

8. *Establishing and preserving the authority of moral norms.* Jews have historically adopted legal methods primarily because they believed that this was the only way to preserve the divine authority of the tradition. Rabbinic authority ultimately rests on Deuteronomy 17:8–13, which provides that in each generation questions about the law (and hence about what God wants) should be addressed to the judge of that generation. One may not, as the rabbis warn us, complain that this generation's judges pale by comparison with those of previous generations; instead, one must accept that "Jephthah in his generation is like Moses in his." Thus divine authority—and indeed continuing divine revelation—takes place in the form of judicial decisions throughout the generations.[14]

9. *Teaching morality.* The law serves as a tool for moral education as well. Although theories of moral education are many and diverse, the Jewish tradition has a clear methodology for teaching morality:

> Rav Judah said in Rav's name: A man should always occupy himself with Torah and good deeds, even if it is not for their own sake, for out of [doing good] with an ulterior motive he will come to [do good] for its own sake.[15]

Study of the tradition complements this largely behavioristic approach to moral education. On balance, though, the emphasis is on action:

> An excellent thing is the study of Torah combined with some worldly occupation, for the labor demanded by both of them

causes sinful inclinations to be forgotten. All study of the Torah without work must in the end be futile and become the cause of sin.[16]

The same educational theory is applied to moral degeneracy and repentance:

Once a man has committed a sin and repeated it, it appears to him as if it were permitted. Run to fulfill even a minor precept and flee from the slightest transgression; for precept draws precept in its train, and transgression draws transgression. If a transgression comes to a man a first and second time without his sinning, he is immune from the sin.[17]

Formulating moral norms in terms of law is thus very important educationally; for by so doing people are *required* to act in accord with moral rules as a step in teaching them how to do the right thing for the right reason.

In all of these ways, and undoubtedly in others, law contributes to our moral sensitivity and behavior as much as morality informs our law. The *interaction* between them improves both, especially when they are both put into the larger contexts of theology and religion.

Judaism has gone further than most other religious or secular systems of ethics in trying to deal with morality in legal terms. It is therefore not surprising that contemporary decisions in Jewish medical ethics flow out of the continuing *interactions* among Jewish religious thought, law, and morality. To isolate any one of these perspectives is to distort Jewish tradition. But to see and apply their interactions to contemporary concerns requires knowledge of and commitment to all three; a developed moral and legal sense; and the capacity for sound judgment, compassion, and wisdom.

LEGAL VERSUS NONLEGAL METHODS OF ACCESSING THE TRADITION

If religion can contribute to both moral theory and practice, as I have argued, how can someone looking for moral guidance access the tradition for its direction and moral insight? In other words, how can the tradition help us to confront the moral challenges of our age—especially those as markedly new as many of those in contemporary bioethics?

Judaism has historically depended upon a judicial mode for resolving moral quandaries, blending exegeses of the Torah and later rabbinic literature, precedents, and customs to arrive at a decision. Accordingly, almost all Jews who have written about biomedical issues in our day have used Jewish legal sources and methods primarily, if not exclusively. Yet within this commonality there are considerable differences. Conservative and Reform authors, for instance, differ from Orthodox writers in their ways of interpreting classical texts, the former two groups adding historical and cross-cultural considerations to the traditional commentaries used by the latter. Authors from these three denominations of

American Judaism, and their counterparts elsewhere, differ even more in the ways they apply those sources to contemporary circumstances and the degree to which they and their intended audiences feel obligated to follow the tradition, however it is interpreted. But most rabbinic writers in all three movements are united in their assumption that identifiably *Jewish* moral positions can only emerge through interpreting and applying the *legal* precedents and statutes of the Jewish tradition.

While this methodology is central to Judaism, it is by no means the only way to approach these matters. One could claim, for example, any of the following:

1. That the ultimate authority for differentiating right from wrong and good from bad is God (a "divine command theory"). Some who hold this theory maintain that God's will can be determined only by a literalist reading of a revealed text (for example, the Hebrew Bible, the Christian Bible).

2. That the authority to define God's will, including its moral aspects, should be invested not in a text but in a religious leader. Catholics, for example, understand the Pope as the ultimate authority in faith and morals, even when they disagree with him or disobey him.

3. That it is an individual's conscience that discerns God's will and thus determines what is moral and immoral. Both Catholics and Protestants assign such a role to the individual conscience, which is emphasized more or less according to the specific interpreter or adherent. The Reform movement in Judaism has similarly made individual autonomy the centerpiece of its ideology and methodology.[18]

4. That the person who makes moral decisions should not be a religious leader, whose authority is based on God, but rather a political one, whose authority is based on the power to enforce it ("Might makes right"). This is a secular version of the last two theories. In varying forms, this is the theory of Thrasymachus and Callicles in Plato's dialogues, and of Machiavelli and Nietzsche much later on,[19] and in practice it is the theory asserted by monarchs and dictators throughout history.

5. That moral decisions made for an entire democratic community should be determined by the will of the majority of citizens or their representatives or by some other expression of the communal will. This theory is either grounded on the pragmatic rationale that democratic decisions are the only way in which people with conflicting moral convictions can live together peacefully; or it is based on theories, such as those of Aristotle and Rousseau, holding that moral vision and consensus emerge from public debate. Since communities and nations do, and on this theory may, decide about the morality of a given act in different ways, such theories are inherently relativist—that is, they make moral judgments dependent upon, and only valid in, a given society. Even regions of a given country may, on this theory, take different moral positions. Consider, for example, the disparity between the laws governing sodomy in California, where sex between consenting adults is

legal regardless of the gender of the partners, and those in Georgia and Texas, where there is a law against even private, consensual homosexual sex between adults, a law that the United States Supreme Court affirmed in 1986 but overturned in 2003.

6. That good actions and policies are those that afford the greatest good for the greatest number, a view held by utilitarians and many American pragmatists. Theoretically at least, an objective calculus of benefits and burdens should be able to determine the correct moral decision in any given case.

7. That right and wrong can be determined on objective grounds, independent of the wishes or views of individual people or communities. Divine command and utilitarian theories are two forms of moral objectivism. Likewise, one could claim, along with Immanuel Kant, that moral principles are built into the structure of the human mind or, along with Saint Thomas Aquinas, that they are built into the very structure of nature. These principles define right and wrong and good and bad.[20] Although the methods by which one discerns these principles differ according to the particular theory, they usually involve an appeal to reason in some form.

8. That "good" simply means that the person using the term has a positive emotion toward the person or action being mentioned, and "bad" means the reverse. This view, advocated by the philosophers A. J. Ayer and Leslie Stevenson in the middle of the twentieth century,[21] stands at the other end of the objectivist-relativist-subjectivist spectrum. Such an emotivist theory of morality asks that we each simply consult our feelings toward the person or act being evaluated, without claiming that other people must or should share our own emotional reactions.

9. That there is no moral realm, that no decision is better or worse than any other, and that people should just do what pleases them.[22]

This is only a partial list of the methods people use to determine what is moral. Clearly, then, the Jewish preference for defining morality through a legal approach, while certainly long-standing and deeply entrenched within Judaism, is by no means the only way to do this.

Each of these methods has its benefits and drawbacks; none is perfect or totally without merit. I believe, though, that the Jewish tradition was wise in choosing to confront contemporary moral issues by using law because of the strengths of that method delineated above and the corresponding weaknesses of the alternatives.

Rules Versus Principles and Policies

To apply a legal method to contemporary medical issues, however, is not easy, for there are not many legal sources to ground such decisions. Although Jews have had a veritable love affair with medicine through the last millennium and even before, they have been no more able than non-Jews to extend or significantly improve a person's medical history.

It is therefore surprising that there are *any* precedents whatsoever on many of the subjects that currently concern us.

As soon as we look at the precedents that do exist, however, we see the difficulties in applying them to contemporary circumstances. For example, when we examine the precedents that have been widely cited to shed light on issues at the end of life, we find that some of them are not actually medical. They speak rather of Rabbi Ḥananyah ben Teradyon's responses to his students as they tried to relieve his suffering while he was being burned at the stake, and of Rabbi Judah ha-Nasi's handmaiden's interruption of his students' prayers on her behalf so that he could die. Other sources, though medical, bear little resemblance to modern medical contexts. They speak, for example, of the efficacy of putting salt on the tongue or hearing a knocking noise coming through an open window as ways to extend life. That is hardly the world of respirators and gastrointestinal tubes.

To address today's medical issues, then, Jewish law needs to be extended considerably. Contemporary rabbis must take on this challenge if Jewish law is going to be at all relevant to some of the most critical issues of our time. To do so, however, rabbis must face some deeply rooted philosophical questions about how to reconcile constancy with change—and, indeed, how to interpret and apply texts in the first place. What *should* be the methodology of Jewish law in addressing these radically new realities?

Contemporary legal philosopher Ronald Dworkin has elucidated an important distinction—between rules on the one hand and principles and policies on the other—that must inform such discussions.[23] Rules are norms to which there are no exeptions; they must either be followed at all times, or they must be changed. If rules conflict with each other, the conflict must be resolved by a higher-order rule specifically created to govern the authority and application of rules. A principle or policy, on the other hand, is a general guideline, set for either moral reasons (our "principles") or pragmatic ones (our "policies"), which can admit of exceptions when weighed against other moral or practical concerns.

Rules are most common in logic, mathematics, and games; but they exist in law as well. Such rules determine the hierarchy of laws—for example, a federal law takes precedence over a state law if the federal government has jurisdiction over the matter, and, in Jewish law, a mishnah has more authority than a *baraita*. Rules can also affect matters of content, but here it is often hard to determine whether a given norm is indeed a rule rather than a principle or policy. For example, does the First Amendment to the United States Constitution ban Congress from *any* impediment to freedom of speech—that is, is it a rule?—or does it establish a general norm restraining Congress from banning freedom of speech *unless* there is some important social reason to do so—that is, is it a principle or a policy? The language of the amendment itself can be interpreted either way, but later courts determined that the law was to be construed and used as a principle, not a rule. That is why yelling "Fire!" in a crowded theater is not constitutionally protected speech. Similarly, in Jewish law, the sixth of the Ten Commandments, "You shall not murder," sounds like an inviolable rule banning all forms of homicide, but the Torah itself permits killing others in war and self-defense.

This distinction has important implications for medical ethics. For example, one overarching axiom informing most Orthodox responsa on medical issues generally, and on euthanasia in particular, is that human life is sacred and therefore even small moments of it *(ḥayyei sha'ah)* must be preserved, whatever its quality. However, although Judaism certainly cherishes human life, it does *not* mandate the duty to preserve all human life under all circumstances at all costs. On the contrary, in some situations we are actually commanded to *take* a human life (for example, when execution is mandated by law, or when killing another is required to defend oneself), and in other cases we are obligated to give up our own life (specifically, when the alternative is that we ourselves must commit murder, idolatry, or incest).[24] In other words, Jewish law establishes a general *principle* to preserve life; but, like all other principles and policies, this one is open to being supplanted in given circumstances by specific considerations.[25]

Some rabbis have historically tried to establish general rules and to deduce rulings in specific cases from them, whereas others—the vast majority—have understood generalizations in the law as summaries of some decisions but not prescriptions for others. The former deductive approach was undoubtedly influenced by the medieval penchant for systematic structuring of both thought and law, and it produced the genre of codes; the latter casuistic method has its roots in the Bible and the Babylonian Talmud, and it has led to the genre of responsa.[26] Many rabbis in the last millennium have used both methods at various times; some (for example, Maimonides) have tried as much as possible to fit their decisions under the rubric of a well-defined rule, while most have preferred to reason analogically from a variety of precedents.

In any case, this distinction in method is crucial in contemporary biomedical cases for both methodological and historical reasons. Methodologically, a generalization that seems unexceptional in one era may be subject to serious criticism in another when circumstances have changed. If it is seen as a rule, to change it would require the wrenching task of either discarding the long-standing rule or weakening the absolute authority of all rules in the system by making an exception to this one. Normal legal reasoning, on the other hand, simply searches for other precedents within the law that seem more appropriate to the case at hand. One may not always find such precedents—in which case some serious revision of the law may be necessary—but this approach offers a considerably greater chance of extending the law aptly than merely invoking hard-and-fast rules. Moreover, arguing analogically from precedents is historically the *standard* method in Jewish law, and so following this method is actually adhering to the more traditional approach.[27]

Balancing General Guidelines and Individual Cases

The point needs to be taken yet further. Contemporary physicians and ethicists underscore the *complexity* of each case. Even when the medical diagnosis and prognosis of two people are identical, there may well be differences in temperament, values, family support, financial resources, and the like. Although these factors may not be relevant in analyzing the patient's *physical* status, they may well be very important in designing appropriate medical and nonmedical responses. Some scholars have therefore urged all concerned to pay attention not only to what Harvard psychologist Carol Gilligan has called the "masculine voice" in ethics—concerned primarily with rules and abstract principles—but also to what she calls the "feminine voice," which pays more attention to the specific human situation in which the decision is made, the relationships of the people involved, and the question of how a course of action will help or hurt the people *in this case*.[28] This approach has been compared to the more internally Jewish model of the Ḥasidim, who, at least by reputation, followed their emotions when dealing with specific cases that cried for compassion, in contrast to the Mitnaggedim, who were said to rely excessively on general norms framed by the intellect.

In large measure I agree with this call for increased attention to the details and nuances of specific cases. But this approach is neither distinctly feminine nor specifically ḥasidic.[29] Rather it bespeaks the Jewish tradition's long-standing insistence that individual cases must be decided on their own merits; that general rules may not substitute for careful consideration of the particular circumstances of the people involved; and that, more generally, law and morality are, and must remain, intertwined. Making decisions in specific cases does not eliminate the importance of articulating general standards—that is, commonly used principles and policies; one must just know when and how to use them. In the technical terms of contemporary ethicists, I am arguing neither for an exclusively situational ethic nor for a solely rule-based one (regardless of whether the rules are seen as deontological or consequentialist); I am arguing instead for a character-based ethic, in which both rules and contexts combine with moral moorings in philosophical/religious sources and moral education to produce moral sensitivity.[30] This approach represents a much richer—and, I think, much more realistic—view of how moral norms evolve and operate than is the exclusive attention to principles that has characterized much of moral theory until the twentieth century.

Weighing the Applicability of Precedents

This analysis, then, brings us back to our original question, namely, how can Judaism address contemporary medical realities radically different from those of the past? The methodological points I have made so far—that we must interpret Judaism's general rules as policies, not inviolable rules; that even general policies must be applied with sensitivity to the contexts of specific cases; and that we must nevertheless retain a legal method in making our decisions—all inform how we should apply Judaism to modern medicine. How, though, can we use ancient precedents that have at best a questionable relationship to contemporary medical contexts?

Despite radical differences between medicine in the past and in the present, Orthodox rabbis, by and large, have taken their customary, literalist approach. Some have indeed been ingenious in making it appear that the few ancient precedents available can reasonably determine the outcome of modern questions.[31] This process, however, ignores the historical context of past medical decisions and the crucial differences between medical conditions then and now. In Arthur Danto's felicitous phrase, such responses to the issues are paradigmatic examples of "misplaced slyness." Rabbinic sources, after all, did not contemplate the realities of modern medicine; nor, for that matter, did American legal sources as late as the 1940s. Therefore, depending closely on laws and precedents from times past to arrive at decisions about contemporary medical therapies all too often amounts to sheer sophistry. In such attempts the texts themselves are not providing clear guidance but are rather being twisted to mean whatever a particular rabbi or judge wants them to mean.

In a different form, though, this is simply legal method. To bring new situations under the umbrella of the law, judges in any legal system must often stretch precedents to make them relevant to new circumstances. Indeed, for a legal system to retain continuity and authority in current decisions, this *must* be done. Thus in our case, if a decision is going to be *Jewish* in some recognizable way, it *must* invoke the tradition in a serious, not perfunctory, way. One *can* do this without being devious or anachronistic *if one does not pretend that one's own interpretation is its originally intended meaning (its* peshat*) or its only possible reading.* The Conservative objection to many Orthodox readings of texts is thus based on both tone and method: not only do many Orthodox responsa make such pretensions, often with an air of dogmatic certainty, but they do so with blatant disregard for the effects of historical and literary context on the meaning of texts and indifference to the multitude of meanings that writings can often legitimately have.

In addition to such matters of intellectual honesty, literalist efforts to arrive at medical decisions today seem to be misguided on a purely practical basis. Even if we presume that our ancestors were consummately wise and perhaps even divinely inspired in making the decisions they did, there is no reason to suppose that their decisions would retain those qualities in our own setting. On the contrary, I am sure that they themselves would have insisted, as the Talmud does, that each rabbi now take a good look at "what his own eyes see" to be sure that his or her application of the tradition is deserving of the godly qualities of wisdom and kindness that we ascribe to Jewish law.

In our topic, this means that we, like medieval Jewish physicians and rabbis, should be prepared to deviate from the specific medical directions given in a particular precedent if contemporary medical conditions require a new application of Jewish concepts and values.[32] We want to root our decisions as strongly as possible in the tradition, but not at the cost of ignoring the significant differences between the medical setting of our own time and that of the past. We must therefore first judge whether or not medicine has changed significantly in the area we are considering, and, if it has, be prepared to stretch some halakhic and aggadic sources beyond their original meanings. We *should* do this in order to retain clear connections to the tradition not only in spirit and concept but even in expression. At the same time, we should openly state what we are doing—namely, that we are choosing both the texts to apply and specific interpretations of those texts in order to develop a Jewish medical ethic that carries traditional Jewish concerns effectively into the contemporary setting.

In insisting that we retain the legal form and substance of past Jewish law, I am disagreeing with Reform positions such as that articulated by Matthew Maibaum. He claims that the radical individualism and secularism of contemporary American Jews means that "to an increasing degree, trying to talk about Jewish medical ethics from a traditionalist point of view will impress no one." He objects to using not only the precedents of the past but even many of the concepts that underlie those precedents—concepts such as God's ownership of our bodies. Individual Jews, then, according to him, should not feel themselves bound by the tradition's laws or concepts but should rather use the tradition however they wish in arriving at their own decisions.[33]

It seems to me that his analysis makes one's claim to articulate a *Jewish* position much too tenuous. With such an approach, for example, how does one rule out anything as being contrary to Judaism? Why, indeed, would one be interested in developing a specifically Jewish approach to medical matters in the first place?

From one perspective, then, there is a methodological spectrum, in which positions are differentiated according to the *degree* to which individual Jewish sources are allowed to determine specific, contemporary medical practices. For most Orthodox rabbis, who read the classical texts of the Jewish tradition in a literalist way, such texts are totally determinative, and so the only substantive question is how a decision can be read out of, or into, those sources. For at least a segment of the Reform movement, the goal, as Maibaum says, is to show secular Jews that a given Jewish position "also happens to be immediately and centrally good for them." If this cannot be shown, then the whole tradition is "like a fine fossil or an elegant piece of cracked statuary; it is venerable, but is not relevant today."[34] I am taking a methodological position somewhere in between those two poles, affirming the necessity to root a contemporary Jewish medical ethic in the Jewish conceptual and legal structure of the past but recognizing that to do so honestly and wisely, we will have to make difficult judgments as to when and how to apply that material to substantially new settings.

The position I am affirming, however—largely identified with the Conservative movement in American Judaism—is not defined solely either by what it denies or by its comparison with others. On the contrary, central to its identity are its positive convictions about the proper way to understand and apply Jewish sources. In brief, Conservative Judaism affirms that to understand Jewish conceptual and legal sources properly—both early texts and their later interpolations through the generations—they must be studied in their historical contexts. The relevant similarities and differences between previous settings and our own can then be identified. With those in mind, to arrive at an authentically Jewish and wise decision, we should use legal reasoning, with appropriate attention to moral, economic, and sociological concerns and with continued awareness of the Jewish theological foundation concerning our nature as human beings created by and in the image of God. Sometimes traditional sources must be extended considerably to arrive at an apt decision, but the more a decision can be connected to classical Jewish legal and theological texts the better, for then continuity and the other advantages of a legal approach are more confidently assured. At the same time, we should always be careful to declare that ours is *a* possible reading of the tradition, among other possible readings, and we must argue for the one we choose by explaining the reasons that motivate us to adopt it.

The Impact of the Reader

There is one matter of method that is important in applying Jewish law intelligently to both old and new problems. Recent theorists of literature and law have increasingly pointed out the role of the reader in identifying the meaning of a text. Radical deconstructionists have even suggested that a text does not control meaning at all but rather that the meaning of a text is totally and exclusively what the reader wants it to mean. More moderate—and, I think, more accurate—understandings of this process draw attention to the crucial impact of the reader's background and goals in his or her understanding of a text but also acknowledge the role of the text in evoking and delimiting that meaning. Thus any given literary interpretation is generally and properly subject to critical evaluation based upon the degree to which it preserves the language, context, thrust, and apparent purpose of the text.

Legal texts are no different. Karl Llewellyn was probably the first to demonstrate the elasticity of legal texts and the corresponding effect of the reader in determining their meaning, and Ronald Dworkin and others have expanded on this point in recent times.[35] Ultimately, in legal texts as in others, what readers bring to the text is crucial in defining its meaning for them—at least as crucial as the text itself.

Lewis Newman has astutely and correctly applied these considerations to Jewish medical ethics. Acknowledging the critical role of the reader, he argues for semantic, methodological, and conceptual adjustments in contemporary Jewish bioethics.

Semantically, we should not, according to Newman, talk about what "Judaism" teaches on these matters, but rather what we, given our particular interpretive assumptions and our particular way of construing the coherence of the tradition as a whole, find within the traditional sources. That is, each rabbi can only offer *a* Jewish position, not *the* Jewish stance.

Methodologically, proponents of any given Jewish position must not simply state their reading of the tradition but must argue for it against other possible readings and, more broadly, describe how their ruling on a given issue fits into their own view of the tradition as a whole. They must, in the language of American jurisprudence, present "a *reasoned* opinion," not just an opinion.

Conceptually, Jewish bioethicists who adopt a legal mode must reflect greater knowledge and understanding of contemporary theories of legal reasoning and judicial interpretation. On the other hand, those who choose a nonlegal methodology should explain why; should demonstrate awareness of other modes in medical ethics; and, I would add, should articulate how their approach is identifiably Jewish.[36]

Only when these elements affecting any decision in Jewish medical ethics are made manifest can one fully understand the role that moral sensitivities can and should play in arriving at a ruling. Reform writers often speak as if contemporary moral sensitivities should replace traditional Jewish legal sources in shaping current policy. At best, they maintain, classical texts should be cited to reinforce what the writer thinks best on independent grounds. Orthodox rabbis, on the other hand, generally refuse to admit contemporary moral sensitivities as an independent source of authority; they deem authoritative only that which somehow can be deduced from the classical texts. Even those few Orthodox writers who openly speak about a moral component in halakhic decision making do so defensively, trying to justify why such components are legitimately considered.[37] Authors affiliated with the Conservative movement have been much more aggressive than their Orthodox colleagues in asserting a major role for ethical concerns, but unlike their Reform counterparts, Conservative rabbis use moral values as an integral part of the Jewish *legal* process by which contemporary decisions should be made.[38]

As a Conservative rabbi, I suppose it is no accident that I embrace this last approach,[39] but I also would argue that contemporary literary and legal theory can augment the usual arguments in favor of it. For it is not only that rabbis over the centuries have shaped the tradition with a conscious eye toward making it meet the highest moral standards; it is also that *any* reading of a text will involve the values and concerns of the reader. Thus moral considerations are quite properly part of the process of making decisions in contemporary Jewish law. We, as the interpreters of our tradition, have been taught by it to strive for the right and the good; and our understanding of what that means, although surely influenced by our tradition, is not exclusively shaped by it. We also bring our own contexts, with their inherent complexities, to our understanding of classical Jewish texts, and so our interpretation of those texts will inevitably—and properly—reflect those contexts and thus possibly differ from the readings of our ancestors. The point is that in reading our own concerns and our own moral sensitivities into the texts, we are no different from our ancestors; this is how texts must and should be read.

A Traditional, Dynamic Ethic for Our Time

I have described above a number of methodological principles:

- We should make our individual moral decisions within the context of our broader, religious convictions to give them intelligibility, coherence, and meaning.
- We should seek to maximize the contributions of religion and morality to each other and to minimize the dysfunctions in the relationship between them.
- We should retain a legal method with its inherent discipline, authority, continuity, coherence, and educational utility in making our moral decisions and in teaching moral sensitivity, recognizing all the while that the law must be continually tempered by its traditional and necessary interaction with morality.
- We should understand that Jewish law most often prescribes policies, not inviolable rules, and interpret and apply Jewish law accordingly.
- We should implement general policies with an appreciation for the nuances of a specific case.
- We should read texts in their historical contexts to understand them properly and to apply them intelligently to our times.
- We should be ever cognizant of the inevitable and proper impact of the reader and his or her context, goals, and values in interpreting and employing a text.
- We should understand that our awareness of the contemporary context does not vitiate the authority of the text but nevertheless opens the door, with appropriate argumentation, to contemporary moral perceptions and judgments.

In my view these principles must collectively shape the way in which we approach issues of bioethics in our time. Only then can our methodology be sufficiently dynamic to accommodate the revolutionary changes occurring in the world of medicine on an almost daily basis and yet remain unmistakably Jewish. Only then can we responsibly and wisely carry on the vital and religiously rooted tradition of medical care that we have inherited.

NOTES

1. The binding of Isaac: Genesis 22. The fate of the seven Canaanite nations: Deuteronomy 20:10–18; see also Exodus 34:11–16; Deuteronomy 7:1–6. The permission to enslave gentiles: Leviticus 25:35–46. For more discussion of biblical understandings of the relationship between God's word and the moral norm, see Elliot Dorff and Arthur Rosett, *A Living Tree: The Roots and Growth of Jewish Law* (Albany, NY: State University of New York Press

and New York: Jewish Theological Seminary of America, 1988), pp. 110–123. For rabbinic understandings of the relationship, see *ibid.*, pp. 249–257.

2. Morris Raphael Cohen has written polemically, but convincingly on this—although with more examples from ancient religions and from Christianity than from Judaism. See his book, *The Faith of a Liberal* (Salem, NH: Ayer, 1945, 1977), chapter 41, "The Dark Side of Religion," pp. 337–361.

3. Two people who hold that position, but for different reasons, are Kai Nielson, *Ethics Without God* (Buffalo, NY: Prometheus Books, 1973); reprinted in part in his article, "Morality and the Will of God," in *Critiques of God*, Peter Angeles, ed. (Buffalo, NY: Prometheus Books, 1976), pp. 241–357; and David Sidorsky, "The Autonomy of Moral Objectivity," in *Modern Jewish Ethics*, Marvin Fox, ed. (Columbus, OH: Ohio State University Press, 1975), pp. 153–173.

4. The evidence on that, however, is ambiguous. To take just one example, religious people (including some leaders of the Church) were counted among both those who actively cooperated with the Nazis as well as "the righteous Gentiles"—that is, those who, at the risk of their own lives and those of their families, hid Jews from the Nazis. To make matters yet more complicated, while most righteous Gentiles affirmed a belief in Christianity, they did not generally attribute their heroic acts to their religious beliefs but rather to their often unsophisticated, albeit deeply held moral conviction that it simply was not right to surrender Jews to the Nazis. See Pearl and Sam Oliner, *The Altruistic Personality* (New York: Free Press, 1988); Nechama Tec, *When Light Pierced the Darkness* (New York: Oxford University Press, 1986); and Mordecai Paldiel, *The Path of the Righteous* (New York: Jewish Foundation for Christian Rescuers and Hoboken, NJ: Ktav, 1993). I would like to thank my friend, colleague, and mentor, Rabbi Harold Schulweis, for these references.

A recent experiment by *Reader's Digest* provides another intriguing example of this ambiguity. The magazine's agents planted ten wallets filled with fifty dollars and identification information in a variety of places in twelve cities across the United States in order to determine whether the rate of return of the "lost" wallets would vary by the gender or age of the finders, the size of the city in which the wallets were found, or the depth of religious belief of the finders. A large number of those who returned the wallets said that they were motivated to do so by their belief in God: "Even those who don't regularly attend services credited religious lessons as a moral prod." The moral training received within the family, a personal sense of moral responsibility, and/or the desire to be treated similarly if they had lost their own wallet were, however, even more commonly mentioned as factors that prompted their honesty. See Ralph Kinney Bennett, "How Honest Are We?" *Reader's Digest* (December 1995), pp. 49–55; the quotation is on p. 55.

5. Robert Gordis, *The Dynamics of Judaism* (Bloomington, IN: Indiana University Press, 1990), pp. 50–68. Gordis maintains that, both according to the theory (aggadah) and practice (halakhah) of Judaism, ethics takes precedence over ritual, and moreover, the possibility "that God could command an immoral act is a notion completely unacceptable to Judaism" (p. 67). He thus titles the chapter where he makes and supports these claims "The Primacy of Ethics," by which he means both the legal and logical primacy of ethics over ritual and theology. Similarly, David Hartman maintains that "the divine power and mystery must never be used as a justification to undermine the category of the ethical" (David Hartman, *A Living Covenant: The Innovative Spirit in Traditional Judaism* [New York: Free Press, 1985], p. 97).

6. See Elliot Dorff and Arthur Rosett, *A Living Tree* (at note 1 above), pp. 110–123, for a discussion of such passages.

7. See, for example, Deuteronomy 32:4; Psalms 145:9, 17; B. *Sotah* 14a; *Sifre Deuteronomy*, Ekev.

8. I first argued this in response to Richard Rubenstein, who has articulately held in his various writings that the Holocaust, the nuclear threat, and overpopulation make it impossible any longer to believe in a beneficent God or, indeed, in a personal God altogether. See Richard Rubenstein, "Jewish Theology and the Current World Situation," *Conservative Judaism* 28:4 (Summer, 1974), pp. 3–25, and my response, *ibid.*, pp. 33–36.

9. To strip God of power or personality on this basis, as Harold Kushner (*When Bad Things Happen to Good People* [New York: Schocken, 1981]) and Harold Schulweis (*For Those Who Can't Believe: Overcoming the Obstacles to Faith* [New York: Harper-Collins, 1994]) have done in their theologies, is, I think, radically to diminish what we mean by God and to pretend that the complexities of our existence are simpler than they are. I would rather have honest perplexity in the face of some phenomena I cannot understand rather than believe in a neat, consistent system that ignores or sets aside by definition the parts of reality that do not fit it. That will mean, of course, that I must have some intellectual humility, but part of what it means not to be God, after all, is not to be omniscient. For more on this, see my book, *Knowing God: Jewish Journeys to the Unknowable* (Northvale, NJ: Jason Aronson, 1992), pp. 129–148.

10. The verse from Psalms: Psalms 145:9. The liturgist's understanding of God's law as the gift of God's love is expressed in the *ahavah rabbah* prayer in the morning service and in the *ahavat olam* prayer in the evening service, both immediately before the *Shema*: see Jules Harlow, *Siddur Sim Shalom* (New York: Rabbinical Assembly and United Synagogue of America, 1985), pp. 98–99 and 200–201.

11. For a thorough discussion of the rabbinic justification of the interpretive process, including the limits of its flexibility, see Dorff and Rosett, *A Living Tree* (at note 1 above), pp. 185–245. That rabbis must judge according to how their own eyes see things: B. *Bava*

Batra 131a, cited on p. 389 in Dorff and Rosett. For the impact of morality on the making and practice of Jewish law, see my article, "The Interaction of Jewish Law with Morality," *Judaism* (Fall, 1977), pp. 455–466.

12. There is no equivalent body among North American Orthodox Jews, who are badly splintered and who tend to follow a particular rabbi revered by their particular segment of the Orthodox community. Thus, until their deaths during the last decade, Rabbis Dov Baer Soloveitchik, Moshe Feinstein, and Menachem Mendel Schneerson served in the capacity of ultimate authority for the modern Orthodox, Agudat Yisrael, and Lubavitch portions of the Orthodox community, respectively. The Israeli Orthodox community has a Sephardic and an Ashkenazic chief rabbinate, but that office does not deter sharp criticism from other Orthodox rabbis, even of the same stripe—as, for example, the roundly maligned decision of the Ashkenazic Chief Rabbi to allow heart transplants. See *Assia* 14:1–2 (August, 1994) (Hebrew), where ten rabbis take issue with Rabbi Abraham Kahana-Shapira's decision to permit heart transplants. The three American rabbis mentioned above were rarely, if ever, subjected to such open rebellion.

The Central Conference of American Rabbis (Reform) has constituted a Committee on Halakhic Inquiry, and its chair, Rabbi Walter Jacob, has edited three books of Reform responsa, all published by the Central Conference of American Rabbis: *American Reform Responsa* (1983), *Contemporary American Reform Responsa* (1987), and *Questions and Reform Jewish Answers: New American Reform Responsa* (1992). Since Reform ideology champions the individual autonomy of each Jew to make religious decisions, however, these responsa function exclusively in an advisory capacity for Reform Jews. For two Reform theories on how that process should work, see the articles by Eugene B. Borowitz and David Ellenson in Dorff and Newman, *Contemporary Jewish Ethics and Morality* (New York: Oxford University Press, 1995), pp. 106–117 and 129–139. In the end, even a policy against intermarriage, overwhelmingly approved by the delegates to the 1985 convention of the Central Conference of American Rabbis, could not become binding on individual Reform rabbis, and in the intervening years it has actually become hard for Reform rabbis to refuse to perform intermarriages.

The Conservative movement tries to balance the authority of the individual rabbi for his or her community with communal norms. The Committee on Jewish Law and Standards validates acceptable options on issues that individual rabbis raise; if a responsum attains six votes or more (out of 25), it becomes a validated option within the movement. If two or more are validated, individual rabbis may use their own discretion as to which to follow. Even if only one option is validated, individual rabbis may choose to do otherwise. Three "standards" of the movement, however, have been adopted—forbidding intermarriage, requiring a Jewish writ of divorce *(get)* for remarriage, and defining Jewish identity through birth to a Jewish mother or halakhic conversion—and no Conservative rabbi or synagogue may violate those standards on pain of expulsion. For more on this, see Elliot N. Dorff, *Conservative Judaism: Our Ancestors to Our Descendants* (New York: United Synagogue of Conservative Judaism, 1996), pp. 151–192. This structure makes for plural practices within the movement within a given framework.

13. Three sets of books come especially to mind: the many books of responsa by Solomon Freehof, published by the Central Conference of American [Reform] Rabbis; the three books of new responsa that have already been published by that same body under the editorship of Walter Jacob (see n. 12 above); and the books published by the Freehof Institute of Progressive Halakhah, edited by Walter Jacob and Moshe Zemer.

14. For a thorough discussion of how this line of divine authority is understood in the biblical and rabbinic sources, see Dorff and Rosett, *A Living Tree* (at note 1 above), pp. 123–133, 187–198, and 213–245. The specific sources mentioned in this paragraph are the following: the Torah's attempts to differentiate true from false revelation: Deuteronomy 13:2–6; 18:9–22; examples of problems with false prophets: Jeremiah 23:16–40; that prophecy ceased after the Haggai, Zechariah, and Malachi died: B. *Sanhedrin* 11a; that interpretation (Midrash) took the place of prophecy: B. *Bava Batra* 12a; the comparative lenses through which Moses and other prophets see: *Leviticus Rabbah* 1:14; Jephthah in his generation is like Moses in his: T. *Rosh Hashanah* 1:18; B. *Rosh Hashanah* 25a–25b.

15. B. *Pesaḥim* 50b and elsewhere.

16. M. *Avot* 2:1.

17. B. *Yoma* 86b; M. *Avot* 4:2; B. *Yoma* 38b.

18. See, for example, Eugene Borowitz, *Renewing the Covenant* (Philadelphia: Jewish Publication Society, 1991), pp. 284–299; reprinted in Dorff and Newman, *Contemporary Jewish Ethics and Morality* (at n. 12 above), pp. 106–117. Rabbi David Ellenson, another important ideologue of the Reform movement, has pointed out that primarily because of the wide disparity between contemporary medical conditions and those of times past, some rabbis in all three movements have suggested using a "covenantal" model for making medical decisions centering on the individual's conscience. See David Ellenson "Religious Approaches to Mortal Choices: How to Draw Guidance from a Heritage," in *A Time to Be Born, A Time to Die: The Ethics of Choice* (New York: Aldine de Gruyter, 1990), esp. pp. 228–229; reprinted in Dorff and Newman, *Contemporary Jewish Ethics and Morality* (at note 12 above), pp. 129–139, esp. pp. 136–137. The articles he cites are these: Daniel H. Gordis [a Conservative rabbi], "Wanted—The Ethical in Jewish Bio-Ethics," *Judaism* 38:1 (Winter, 1989), pp.

28–40; Irving Greenberg [an Orthodox rabbi], "Toward a Covenantal Ethic of Medicine," in *Jewish Values in Bioethics,* Levi Meier, ed. (New York: Human Sciences Press, 1986), pp. 124–149; David Hartman [an Orthodox rabbi], "Moral Uncertainties in the Practice of Medicine," *Journal of Medicine and Philosophy* 4 (1979), pp. 100ff; and Eugene B. Borowitz [a Reform rabbi], *Choices in Modern Jewish Thought* (New York: Behrman House, 1983), esp. pp. 367–368, and "The Autonomous Self and the Commanding Community," *Theological Studies* 45:1 (March, 1984), pp. 34–56, esp. pp. 48–49. I would object to this approach on three grounds: (1) my appreciation of the *strengths* of a legal approach to the moral issues in life, as delineated above, and the corresponding weaknesses of the suggested alternative; (2) my conviction that personal responsibility *can* be retained in a properly understood halakhic system; and (3) my confidence that, when properly understood and applied, legal methods can enable Jewish law to treat realities as new as contemporary medical phenomena sensitively and wisely.

19. Thrasymachus: Plato, *Republic* 336B–354C. Callicles: Plato, *Gorgias* 482ff; 491ff. Niccolo Machiavelli, *The Prince* (New York: Modern Library, 1950). Friedrich Nietzsche, *Beyond Good and Evil,* Helen Zimmerman, trans. (New York: Macmillan, 1914), secs. 259–260; Nietzsche, *The Genealogy of Morals* (Garden City, NY: Doubleday, 1956), pp. 166–168.

20. Immanuel Kant, *Fundamental Principles of the Metaphysics of Morals,* First and Second Sections, T. K. Abbott, trans., from *Kant's Critique of Practical Reason and Other Works on the Theory of Ethics* (London: Longmans, Green, 1898), pp. 9–44. Thomas Aquinas, *Basic Writings of Thomas Aquinas,* A.C. Pegis, ed., 2 vols. (New York: Random House, 1945), vol. 2, pp. 3–5, 59–60, 85, 234–238, 335–342, 356–357, 748–750, 774–775; these are selections from Aquinas's *Summa Contra Gentiles,* book 3, chaps. 1, 2, 37, and 48, and from his *Summa Theologica,* questions 19, 20, and 91. All of these selections are reprinted in *Great Traditions in Ethics,* Theodore C. Denise, Sheldon P. Peterfreund, and Nicholas P. White, eds. (Belmont, CA: Wadsworth, 1996), 8th edition, pp. 105–124 and 179–198.

21. A. J. Ayer, *Language, Truth, and Logic* (New York: Dover, 1936, 1950), pp. 103–112. C. L. Stevenson, "The Nature of Ethical Disagreements," *Sigma* 1–2, nos. 8–9 (1947–48). Both of these selections are reprinted in Denise, Peterfreund, and White (see previous note), pp. 345–365.

22. For a good overview of how biomedical decisions have been made historically in other religions, both in theory and in practice, cf. Ronald L. Numbers and Darrel W. Amundsen, eds., *Caring and Curing: Health and Medicine in the Western Religious Traditions* (New York: Macmillan, 1986). For greater detail, see the series of books published by Crossroad (New York), in conjunction with

the Park Ridge Center in Illinois, entitled *Health and Medicine and the Faith Traditions,* with volumes on the bioethics principles and practices of the Anglican, Catholic, Islamic, Jewish, Lutheran, Methodist, and Reformed traditions. There is a plethora of books on secular approaches to medical ethics; two good ones, of many, are Tom L. Beauchamp and James F. Childress, *Principles of Biomedical Ethics* (New York: Oxford University Press, 2001), 5th edition; and William J. Winslade and Judith Wilson Ross, *Choosing Life or Death: A Guide for Patients, Families, and Professionals* (New York: Free Press, 1986). On the topic of our example, euthanasia, see, for example, Marvin Kohl, ed., *Beneficent Euthanasia* (Buffalo, NY: Prometheus Books, 1975); John Ladd, ed., *Ethical Issues Relating to Life and Death* (New York: Oxford University Press, 1979); and, more recently, *Must We Suffer Our Way to Death? Cultural and Theological Perspectives on Death by Choice,* Ronald P. Hamel and Edwin R. DuBose, eds. (Dallas, TX: Southern Methodist University Press, 1996).

23. Ronald Dworkin, *Taking Rights Seriously* (Cambridge, MA: Harvard University Press, 1977), pp. 22–31. That distinction is parallel to one commonly cited in Anglo-American law between absolute and rebuttable assumptions of the law.

24. The Torah mandates executing people for a long list of offenses; largely through specifying stringent evidentiary rules, the Rabbis narrowed the scope of this punishment considerably (cf. M. *Makkot* 1:10), but they retained it, at least in theory. The Talmud (if not the Bible) requires that, even at the cost of killing the attacker, we defend both ourselves (Exodus 22:1; B. *Berakhot* 58a; B. *Yoma* 85b; B. *Sanhedrin* 72a) and even others (the law of *rodef,* B. *Sanhedrin* 72b–73a; M.T. *Laws of Murder* 1:6–7; S.A. *Hoshen Mishpat* 425:1). The duty to give up one's own life when the alternative is to commit murder, idolatry, or incest is specified in B. *Sanhedrin* 74a. Note that the biblical phrase "and you shall live by them" (Leviticus 18:5) is a divine *promise* in the Torah, not a command, and in Jewish law it functions as the ground to justify overriding other commandments in order to save a life; it is *not* meant, either in the Bible or in later rabbinic literature, as a general command to save all human life in all cases.

25. See Daniel B. Sinclair, *Tradition and the Biological Revolution: The Application of Jewish Law to the Treatment of the Critically Ill* (Edinburgh: Edinburgh University Press, 1989), pp. 80–81, 88–89.

26. Umberto Cassuto has made this point with reference to biblical law codes, which, he says, "should not be regarded as a code of laws, or even as a number of codes, but only as separate instructions on given matters." See Umberto Cassuto, *A Commentary on the Book of Exodus* (Jerusalem: Magnes Press [Hebrew University], 1967), pp. 260–264. The Babylonian Talmud in B. *Eruvin* 27a and B. *Kiddushin* 34a expressly objects to treating the Mishnah's general rules as inviolable principles; moreover, in practice it

recurrently interprets general principles announced in the Mishnah (with phrases like *zeh ha-klal*) not as generalizations at all but rather as additions of further specific cases. See Jacob Eliyahu Efrati, *Tekufat ha-Savora'im ve-sifrutah be-Vavel uve-Eretz Yisrael* (New York: P. Feldheim, 1973), part 2, pp. 157–278, who points out that the Talmud interprets the phrase this way explicitly sixteen (or possibly eighteen) times among the eighty-five unrepeated instances in the Mishnah where this expression occurs. He claims that these discussions, limited to the Babylonian Talmud, are Saboraic in origin (i.e., from 500–689 C.E.). (I want to thank my colleague at the University of Judaism, Dr. Elieser Slomovic, for this reference.) With regard to the genre of Jewish codes, its methodological pros and cons, and its origins in medieval systematics, see Dorff and Rosett (at note 1 above), pp. 366–401.

27. The more radical option of instituting revisions in the law *(takkanot)* is also an available alternative within the methods of classical Jewish law, and, given the radically new realities of contemporary medical practice, one might reasonably argue that such revisions can be more easily justified in this area than in most others. I would agree, but I share the tradition's reticence to employ this method unless absolutely necessary (see Dorff and Rosett, *A Living Tree* [at note 1 above], pp. 402–420). We do not have much experience in dealing with many of the morally excruciating questions posed by modern medicine, and so at this point we have not yet had time to see if instituting revisions is required. I, for one, think that the classical methods of legal exegesis and analogizing, if used creatively and sensitively, are fully capable of producing appropriate guidelines to modern Jewish medical decisions, and I certainly think that we owe it to the tradition to try to use these more conservative methods for a period of time before resorting to *takkanot*.

28. Carol Gilligan, *In a Different Voice* (Cambridge, MA: Harvard University Press, 1982).

29. The first story I heard about Jewish law, in fact, came from my father. My grandparents and their children lived across the street from a large, Orthodox synagogue, of which they were members. Because of the proximity, my grandparents often hosted guests of the congregation for the Sabbath. One Friday afternoon my grandmother sent my father, then a lad of fifteen or so, to ask Rabbi Solomon Scheinfeld when the guests for that week were expected. Rabbi Scheinfeld served that congregation from 1902 to 1943, and, according to the *Encyclopedia Judaica*, he "was the recognized head of the city's Orthodox congregations during his tenure." The encyclopedia clearly refers to the camp of the *misnagdim*, for the Twersky family was firmly in charge of Milwaukee's Ḥasidim. When my father entered the rabbi's office, Rabbi Scheinfeld was literally in the process of deciding whether a chicken was kosher. As he turned the chicken over in his hands, he asked the woman who had brought it many questions about the

physical and economic health of her husband and family. After he pronounced the chicken kosher and the woman left the room, my father asked him why he had asked so many questions about her family. The rabbi turned to my father and said, "If you think that the kosher status of chickens depends only on their physical state, you understand nothing about Jewish law!" This, of course, attests only to the attitude of one rabbi in one instance, but if this is true for chickens, how much more so for human beings.

30. Stanley Hauerwas has probably been the preeminent exponent of this in the Christian world, as the very titles of his books indicate; see his *Vision and Virtue* (Notre Dame, IN: Fides Publishers, 1974); *Character and the Christian Life: A Study in Theological Ethics* (San Antonio, TX: Trinity University Press, 1975); *Truthfulness and Tragedy* (Notre Dame, IN: University of Notre Dame Press, 1977); and *A Community of Character: Towards a Constructive Christian Social Ethic* (Notre Dame, IN: University of Notre Dame Press, 1981). See also James William McClendon, Jr., *Ethics* (Nashville, TN: Abingdon, 1987); and Alasdair MacIntyre, *After Virtue* (Notre Dame, IN: University of Notre Dame Press, 1981) and *Whose Justice? Which Reality?* (Notre Dame, IN: University of Notre Dame Press, 1988).

31. Basil Herring's book, *Jewish Ethics and Halakhah for Our Time* (New York: Ktav and Yeshiva, 1984) is an especially thorough and fair presentation of the various Orthodox attempts to do this on many issues, including a number in bioethics.

32. Tosafot, *Mo'ed Katan* 11a; Jacob ben Moses Mollin, *Yalkutai Maharil* (Segal), cited in Fred Rosner, *Medicine in the Bible and Talmud* (New York: Ktav, 1977), p. 21; Solomon Luria, *Yam Shel Shelomo,* "Kol Basar," sec. 12; Joseph Caro, *Kesef Mishneh* commentary to M.T. *Hilkhot De'ot (Laws of Ethics)* 4:18; Abraham Gombiner, *Magen Avraham* commentary to S.A. *OraḥHayyim* 173.

33. Matthew (Menachem) Maibaum, "A 'Progressive' Jewish Medical Ethics: Notes for an Agenda," *Journal of Reform Judaism* 33:3 (Summer, 1986), pp. 27–33; the quotation is on p. 29.

34. *Ibid.* Despite my problems with Maibaum's position, he is definitely right in his call for Conservative, Reconstructionist, and Reform rabbis to articulate their respective views on medical matters in written form and to cull them into easily accessible collections so that lay Jews do not mistakenly think that the only Jewish views on these matters are those of the Orthodox, simply because they are the only ones in print. (And the Orthodox, who publish books with titles like "Jewish Bioethics," certainly do not let on that there are other possible Jewish approaches!) My book, *Matters of Life and Death: A Jewish Approach to Modern Medical Ethics* (Philadelphia: Jewish Publication Society, 1998), is, in fact, just such an effort.

35. Karl Llewellyn, "Remarks on the Theory of Appellate Decision and the Rules or Canons About How Statutes Are to Be Construed," *Vanderbilt Law Review* 3 (1950), beginning on p. 395,

and *The Common Law Tradition* (Boston: Little, Brown, and Co., 1960), Appendix C. Excerpts from these are reprinted in Dorff and Rosett (at note 1 above), pp. 204–213. Ronald Dworkin, *A Matter of Principle* (Cambridge, MA: Harvard University Press, 1985), pp. 159–177. For a good exposition of the deconstructionist position, cf. Stanley Fish, *Is There A Text in This Class?* (Cambridge, MA: Harvard University Press, 1980). For a critical review of the Fish/Dworkin controversy, see R. V. Young, "Constitutional Interpretation and Literary Theory," *The Intercollegiate Review* 23:1 (1987), pp. 49–60.

36. Louis E. Newman, "Woodchoppers and Respirators: The Problem of Interpretation in Contemporary Jewish Ethics," *Modern Judaism* 10:1 (February, 1990), pp. 17–42. Reprinted in Dorff and Newman (at note 12 above), pp. 140–160 and in Louis E. Newman, *Past Imperatives: Studies in the History and Theory of Jewish Ethics* (Albany, NY: State University of New York Press, 1998), pp. 161–184.

37. For example, Eliezer Berkovits, *Not In Heaven: The Nature and Function of Halakhah* (New York: Ktav, 1983), pp. 82–84; Shubert Spero, *Morality, Halakhah, and the Jewish Tradition* (New York: Ktav and Yeshiva University Press, 1983), esp. pp. 166–200; David Hartman, *A Living Covenant* (at note 5 above), esp. pp. 89–108.

38. For example, Robert Gordis, *The Dynamics of Judaism* (at note 5 above), esp. pp. 50–68; Simon Greenberg, *The Ethical in the Jewish and American Heritage* (New York: Jewish Theological Seminary of America, 1977), esp. pp. 157–218; and Seymour Siegel, "Ethics and Halakhah," *Conservative Judaism* 25:3 (Spring, 1971), pp. 33–40 and "Reaction to Modern Moral Crises," *Conservative Judaism* 34:1(September/October, 1980), pp. 17–27.

39. I think, though, that conflicts between rituals and ethics, however those terms are defined, are far fewer and therefore far less important than they are often touted to be. Moreover, I would claim that both rituals and ethics are authoritative within Judaism, neither necessarily always taking precedence over the other. Cf. my *Mitzvah Means Commandment* (New York: United Synagogue of America, 1989), pp. 7–9, 223–229.

G. ALANA SUSKIN

During the ten years that I have taught the course on which this book is based to rabbinical students at the Ziegler School of Rabbinic Studies at the University of Judaism and at the Rabbinical School of the Jewish Theological Seminary of America, I have repeatedly complained that nobody to date had written a feminist Conservative theory of Jewish law. Various women—and men—had written on how specific laws affecting women should or should not be changed, and others had written on the history of Jewish laws affecting women. Some of that writing represented truly groundbreaking research or creative contributions to Jewish ritual and liturgical life. Nobody, though, had attempted to create an overarching theory of law, addressing the kinds of questions I delineated in chapter 1 of this volume—questions like the nature of individuals and communities, the role of law in their lives, the grounds for the authority of the law (or lack thereof), the procedures by which law should be interpreted and applied, etc.

Finally, one of my students, Alana Suskin, took me up on my challenge. As an undergraduate she had completed a major in both philosophy and women's studies, and so she had a good background to probe these questions and formulate a response. After a year's independent study during which we both read feminist theories of Anglo-American law, Alana wrote the first version of the paper that follows. Ordained by the Ziegler School in 2003, Rabbi Suskin is now Assistant Rabbi at Adas Israel Congregation in Washington, D.C.

Suskin argues against legal positivism, claiming that there is ample justification within classical Jewish tradition to ground changes in Jewish law in the convictions and principles underlying the law rather than in the stated law itself. Thus even though classical Jewish law is not egalitarian, she argues that egalitarianism is implicit in its foundations and in the direction of its development. In doing so, she adopts a liberal, rather than a radical, form of feminism. That is, rather than arguing that there are significant differences between women and men that should be reflected in the law (as radical feminists would argue), Suskin, like liberal feminists, maintains that with the exception of their distinct roles in procreation the two genders are much more alike than unlike, and that the differences between them demonstrated in research by people like Carol Gilligan, Nel Noddings, and Deborah Tannen[9] are socially rather than biologically engendered. In some ways, though, this distinction is irrelevant to Suskin's theory, because for both camps of feminists "it is a moral necessity to make our roles more equal."

Since Jewish law, however, is not egalitarian, why should we not just abandon it? For those who maintain that Jewish law is divine, of course, the answer to that question is easy—we must obey Jewish law because God requires us to do so. Then, however, a second question becomes all the more pressing—namely, how can we interpret and apply the law to make it egalitarian when it has not been so for all of its history? Are we not then twisting what we take to be God's will? On the other hand, for those who deny divine authority to Jewish law but ascribe authority to it for other reasons, the question of why bother taking the trouble to keep it while yet changing it is more difficult to resolve. Suskin, however, affirms that for whatever reason one finds Jewish law binding, "identifying an egalitarian principle within Jewish law is a particularly pressing necessity if Jewish law and Judaism generally are to remain relevant—and if Jewish law is to continue to have any claim to divinity."

Drawing on the work of Judith Hauptman, Marc Stern, and Eliezer Berkovits, Suskin seeks to show that although it seems otherwise, egalitarianism is indeed built into classical Jewish law. Furthermore, she argues that Jewish theology requires egalitarianism through its principle of *kevod habriyot,* honor due to all human beings, and through its assertion that God wants us to increase holiness in the world.

Suskin then articulates several principles of her theory of law that must be put into play in order to make Jewish law egalitarian in our day. In these principles her liberal feminism comes to the fore. She is not arguing for a "separate but equal" approach to Jewish law, as radical feminists would; on the contrary, Suskin maintains that the burden of proof falls on anyone who would draw a distinction between what is required of men and what is required of women. She thus adopts a stringent position, a *humra,* making women obligated for all the commandments classically incumbent only upon men. Against those who maintain that that is effectively increasing the number of sinners (since all women who do not abide by these additional duties would now be seen as remiss in their obligations), she claims that her approach might actually diminish sinners, for it would show men that, contrary to what they might think, they need to take seriously the laws from which women have traditionally been exempt, for now no adult Jew is exempt from them. Suskin even plays with the possibility that with the exception of those elements of Jewish law directly relevant to sexual functions, the whole distinction between the genders should become legally null and void.

Finally, Suskin provides two examples of how her theory might work in practice. Her first example, abortion, illustrates how her approach might change both how Jewish law is decided and what it says on moral concerns. She points out that modern interpreters of classical Jewish sources on abortion have taken a position that is not only unnecessarily stringent—namely, that abortion is only permitted to save the life or health of the mother—but one that does not follow from the way that the Torah and Talmud understand fetal development. Sometimes people may choose to express their piety in ways beyond what the law requires, but in this case, men are deciding that women should do that. Worse, the men involved have left women out of the discussion altogether and have simultaneously ignored some circumstances in a woman's life that might well justify an abortion for reasons other than saving the mother's life or health. Suskin argues both for including women in future decisions about abortion and also for changing current articulations of Jewish law to be more in keeping with classical sources and to accommodate women's needs at the same time.

In her second example, drawn from Jewish ritual life, Suskin examines the exegetical reasons some give for restricting the *minyan* (the required quorum for communal prayer) to men. She then demonstrates that that reasoning is badly flawed and that a feminist approach would not only recognize that it is, but see it as a duty to interpret the law to include, rather than exclude, women.

As in the case of all theories, Suskin's approach has strengths and weaknesses. Those who are more convinced of the differences between men and women ("radical feminists," although the term "radical" evokes images of people yelling and screaming on picket lines and seems much too strong for many in this group) would undoubtedly object to Suskin's principle of equating men and women under the law in all but reproductive matters. As my friend and colleague at the University of Judaism, Rabbi Ben Zion Bergman, once put it, "Yes, men and women are equal, but *vive la différence!*" That approach, contrary to Suskin, would look for ways to recognize and celebrate the distinctive character of men and women in Jewish ritual and liturgical life and possibly even in Jewish family life.

My own favorite example of the latter strategy concerns lighting candles and leading the *kiddush* at home on Friday nights: according to traditional Jewish law, Jews of both sexes are obligated to do both for their household,[10] but by custom women usually light the candles and men recite the *kiddush*. In some homes one act or the other garners greater attention from family members and guests, and so the assignment is not inherently unequal. Moreover, even though by now Jewish art and stories have consecrated the moment of the woman lighting candles, there is nothing intrinsically male or female in either lighting candles or reciting *kiddush*, and single parents or same-sex parents could do both, and heterosexual couples might reverse these roles if, for example, the woman sings much better the man does. Still, this is one good example of how Jewish law might preserve both equality and difference.

In contrast to Suskin, I, for one, think that this model of gender-specific ritual behaviors should be extended to other areas of the law as well. For example, fathers and mothers are not, respectively, just sperm or egg donors, and their parenting roles, while overlapping in many respects, are not completely interchangeable. Explaining sex to a young adolescent, for example, is much more effectively done by an adult of the same gender, and with all the mixing of roles that has occurred in modern society, for children of both genders men still model what an adult male should be like (and what he should not or need not be like) and women model what an adult female should be like. So even though the parents' individual personalities, skills, and circumstances are often more important than gender in determining what each parent should contribute to the raising of their children, and even though the ancient Rabbis were speaking about a much more role-differentiated society than our own, their conviction that when both the father and mother are active parents, distinguishing in the law between mothers and fathers as two separate classes in considering such matters as custody laws and the responsibilities the parent of each gender has toward the children continues to make sense.[11] (This would obviously not apply to single or same-sex parents.)

Others, of course, will object to Suskin's whole egalitarian project. Some will claim that she is reading the classical sources in a very forced way, that they never implied—let alone demanded—that women be treated on an equal par with men. Others will dispute the wisdom of equating women with men, ironically taking a much stronger and more "radical" view of gender differentiation than I would. Some traditionally Jewish women would decry the fact that Suskin's theory forces them to become obligated for aspects of Jewish law from which they are traditionally exempt, and who is she to impose such duties on them when they do not want them? At most, this group would say, women should be given the option of taking on such duties, especially as we are still experimenting with the ways in which women might be more thoroughly integrated into communal Jewish life. Still others would say that her approach is theologically dangerous, for it imputes to God what we in our own generation want God to say in place of what God actually does say—or, at least, what God has been understood to say by Jews throughout the generations. Many Orthodox Jews would object to Suskin on one or more of these grounds, but some within the Conservative movement would as well.

On the other hand, Suskin's theory has some remarkable strengths. First, as I indicated earlier, this, to my knowledge, is the first time that anyone has written a full-blown feminist legal theory that is also distinctly Conservative. For that alone, Rabbi Suskin is to be congratulated.

Second, her theory is based on a close reading of Jewish classical legal and theological sources. One may disagree with her interpretation or application of those sources, of course, but nobody can legitimately dismiss her theory as Jewishly ungrounded.

Third, she demonstrates that her theory exists not only on the theoretical plane of abstraction but that, like all good theories, it has practical consequences. Again, one might disagree with her particular stance on abortion or on women counting as part of the *minyan,* but she demonstrates cogently (if not conclusively) that applying her principles might well lead to new conclusions in Jewish law.

Finally, she may well be right in her claim that failure to make women full and equal participants in Jewish life will, in our time, be bad for the Jews, the Jewish tradition, and even the authority of God. When men and women are increasingly treated equally in all other arenas of modern life, for Jewish institutions and laws to refuse to do so undoubtedly dissuades many modern Jews from getting involved in Jewish religious life. Furthermore, faced with such discrimination, they might well question the wisdom, authority, and moral goodness of both the Jewish tradition and God. So Suskin's theory challenges both those egalitarians who do not currently take Jewish law seriously and those Jews who do take it seriously but are not egalitarian. Just for the deep rethinking that her theory should engender in many of us we should indeed be grateful!

A Feminist Theory of Halakhah

ALANA SUSKIN

THE ROLE OF WOMEN IN JUDAISM has not remained unaddressed over the past fifteen years. Since the late 1980s, Jewish women, who long have been strong participants in the American feminist movement of the twentieth century,[1] have begun to look with interest into the role of women in Judaism. Since then, there have been sweeping changes in that role, many of which have been directly related to the changes in broader society, exposing many assumptions about women as a class as untrue, and forcing change not only in our secular lives, but requiring change in our religious lives as well. Nevertheless, one of the last areas to be explored has been Jewish women as halakhic agents. While there have been plenty of articles of the sort "let's all worship the goddess in us," very few feminists have taken on the topic of women within a traditional framework that recognizes traditional Judaism as valid and binding, but that also requires review of its attitude toward women. Dr. Judith Hauptman's *Rereading the Rabbis: A Woman's*

Voice (1998) was one of the first book-length attempts to address women and positive halakhic reinterpretation in any broad and serious way, but her work was a descriptive rather than a prescriptive work.

I intend to take a different direction in order to formulate a way to look toward the future in an organized, halakhic sense. I mean to assert in this paper that feminist principles of law must be adopted as fully operative principles of halakhic decision-making. Further, I mean to suggest that adopting such principles is essential for realizing the theological stances of traditional Judaism, and that such principles are *essential* to the survival of traditional Judaism. Finally, I will outline what such principles might look like (leaving space to revise at a later date, and not meaning to be exclusive of further expansion or elaboration) and will provide two specific examples of how it might be applied.

A SHORT SUMMARY
OF RELEVANT LEGAL HISTORY

While the ideal would be to begin by describing what a theory of law is at all, this proves to be an impossible task, as even the *Encyclopedia of Philosophy* throws up its (metaphoric) hands and says, "All the obscurities and prejudices which in other areas of philosophy surround the notions of definition and of meaning have contributed to the endlessly debated problems of the definition of law."[2] The best we can do is to begin with some very sketchy historical notions of law and add a few of the positions that help define the problem we address here.

As early as the Greek Sophists, there are attempts to develop distinctions between different kinds of law: the Sophists describe *physis* (natural law) and, in contrast, *nomos* (convention). By the time of the Romans, who exerted a strong influence on Jewish law, particularly in the arena of women, the Stoics have added a third category: they describe *jus naturale* or *jus gentium*, originally meaning a law applied to strangers but later extended to any legal practices common to all societies, in contrast to *jus civile*, originally the law of the city of Rome, but ultimately applied to any body of laws of a given community. Ulpian (170–228 C.E.) asserted that *jus naturale* applied to all animals, not just humans, as taught to them by nature.[3]

By the sixth century, when Justinian produced the *Corpus Juris Civilis*, the compilers of the *Institutes* section of this work seem to regard natural law as immutable divine law by which positive law may be evaluated.[4] By the early Middle Ages the Church Fathers added the notion of the *jus divinum*, as additional to and distinct from the other three types of law. In the seventeenth through nineteenth centuries, we begin to see the formation of legal ideas of individual rights that we still recognize in secular legal systems, such as those of Hobbes, Locke, and Kant, for example. For Hobbes, natural law is "the liberty each man has to use his own power as he will himself, for the preservation of his own nature, that is to say, of his own life."[5] Locke focuses on the social contract to address the question of obligation to obey law, despite the natural right to behave otherwise. Kant understands law as a formula expressing the necessity of action, but he also emphasizes the freedom to do as one wants as long as one does not interfere with the freedoms of others (a principle one might hear on any American street, if one were to frame such a question to random passers-by).

MORALITY AND LAW

Utilitarianism and positivism are two modern theories that have also had an important effect on how moderns think of the law and its purpose. Utilitarianism can be briefly explained as the principle of maximizing the good. Positivism in law is not so easily explained as it has apparently been used for a number of theories that are sometimes mutually exclusive, including:

1. A law is the expression of human will.
2. Legal decisions are determined by pre-existing legal rules, and courts either do, or should, reach their decisions only by reviewing the legal principles and the facts of the case and deducing the conclusion exclusively from the principles as applied to the case.
3. The idea that unless the law itself states the contrary, the fact that a legal rule is morally unjust does not make it invalid.
4. Where a legal system is in operation, there is a moral obligation to obey it regardless of the justness of its laws.[6]

The most common usage seems to be the second, although the third may also be relevant to our case. In fact, one argument often used against egalitarianism is that we cannot understand God's ways, and so laws that seem unjust may not be. As noted above, our main focus here is feminism, but certainly there is a challenge for any kind of egalitarianism from a divine document that includes slavery for Canaanites, and a lesser form of it for Jews; chatteldom for women; priests and Levites occupying a differing status from Israelites; the prohibition of their marrying widows, converts, and divorcees; disabled priests being forbidden from serving in the Temple, and so forth—implying a lesser status for those categories. We may not think that such distinctions are moral, but who are we to question God? Thus our human understanding of the justice of a claim or the lack thereof should be considered irrelevant to its authority. That is why the Torah insists that we may neither add to nor subtract from its laws (Deuteronomy 4:2 and 13:1).

These elements within the Jewish tradition that lean toward this definition of positivism are countermanded by a plethora of counterarguments that would oppose interpreting Jewish law using this type of positivism. Abraham, for example, argues with God and questions God's justice when he challenges God's decision to destroy Sodom and Gomorrah saying, "Shall the Judge of the world not do justly?" (Genesis 18:25). That indicates that there is a moral standard to which God can be expected to adhere rather than one that flows from God. Similarly, Zelophehad's daughters claim that God's laws of inheritance should treat them justly, indicating that as stated they were not just, a claim with which God ultimately agrees (Numbers 27:1–11). Rabbinic literature includes legal concepts such as *lifnim meshurat hadin* (we are responsible for moral duties beyond the letter of the law),[7] indicating that sometimes one must go farther than God's stated rule to do justice.

In addition, morality provides a challenge to Jewish law when one considers the identity of those who have been its interpreters. One of the feminist critiques of secular law is that until very recently it has been made exclusively by men. The traditional claim is that Jewish law was enacted by God. Nevertheless, even those who maintain that the *halakhah*, both oral and written, is completely divine must still recognize that from the time of the Mishnah until extremely recently God's will has been interpreted and applied *entirely* by men. This leaves us with a system of law in which the governed and the governing are not coincidental. The problem of such a system is that it makes it easy in the subtle (and not-so-subtle) shaping of law to support the needs of the governing group exclusively. Even though the Torah's legislation is presumably divinely just, in the process of interpreting and applying God's laws there are significant societal forces to exclude the needs or minimize the concerns of the governed where those needs or concerns do not overlap with the needs and concerns of the governors.

Eventually, one must address a fundamental question that guides the direction of how reinterpretation is to happen: Is the purpose of law to reflect society's norms, or is it to transform them? Are laws conservative or activist? This question becomes particularly important when dealing with religious law, *halakhah*, since ostensibly these laws serve the function of connecting us to God, who is just. Thus, do the laws stand to transform a society that is imperfect into one that has greater potential for godliness, or do we say that because the roots of the laws are in the divine law that God gave us, the laws must already be perfect and that no rabbi has ever made an error applying that law? But then we are returned to the question we asked earlier: From where do our notions of right and wrong come? If we say from the Torah exclusively, then how can we ever judge one of our precedents as immoral? If there are other sources for our sense of morality, when are we able to judge them as worthy of being included in our judicial system?

DOES JEWISH LAW
HAVE EGALITARIAN PRINCIPLES?

When dealing with the topic of *halakhah* and egalitarianism, we first have to ask what the categories are. In an article in *Tradition* (Summer 2002), Marc Stern outlines some of the reasoning that one needs to understand the relationship of egalitarianism to *halakhah*. While he does not specifically intend to deal with women and feminism, those topics are certainly covered by his logic. Specifically, he suggests four rationales for considering (general, not necessarily gender) egalitarianism "a binding norm"[8]:

1. *Legal:* The constitutional amendments after the Civil War and numerous civil rights statutes, presumably binding as *dina demalkhuta dina.*
2. *Pragmatic:* Equality advances Jewish interests on the whole. In a negative formulation, opposition to equality is likely to be fruitless and to generate hostility to Judaism and Jewish law that is not outweighed by any contrary interest.
3. *Moral:* Derived from either religious sources (e.g., the story of the creation of human beings) or from general moral principles not contradicted by religious sources.
4. *Empirical:* Jews are biologically, psychologically, intellectually, or morally no different from others and thus have no claim to special treatment.

These rationales, while clearly meant for a more general argument about egalitarianism between Jews and non-Jews, can also be applied to egalitarianism in dealing with women. Those who oppose egalitarianism for women tend to do so by denying the fourth argument: that women are not substantially different from men. Such a refusal of egalitarian principle can be addressed in three ways. First, there is overwhelming evidence that women and men are *not* substantially different from one another, with the exception of some specific reproductive mechanics.[9] Second, where there appear to be some superficial differences, it is difficult to argue that those asserted differences are not the *result* of differential treatment of men and women in society, particularly since as women and men take on more egalitarian roles in society, many of those differences have, in fact, fallen away. A number of them also appear to be related more to dominance-submission roles than to sexual geography. A very good example of this is the purported speech differences reported by Deborah Tannen. Further research shows that many of those speech patterns occur among any group that is subordinate, including employees to bosses, citizens in general to authority figures, and minorities to the dominant, majority group. Third, even disregarding that, as Jews are not different from non-Jews, if equality is a moral good within general society, then it must also be a moral good within Jewish society. Since Jews have in fact supported equality for women in, for example, the workplace, it follows that Jewish life, too, should at least be examined on the basis of its practices regarding men and women.

It should be clear from the above that I am asserting a liberal, rather than a radical, theory of feminism. What I mean by this is that there are two types of feminism that have vied for prominence over the last 200-plus years. Radical feminism, sometimes called essentialist feminism, is the idea that women and men have certain essential characteristics that make them up and distinguish them. This kind of feminism is the sort that argued for the women's vote on the grounds that women were less corruptible than men and would come in and clean up the government. Like that assertion, most of the assertions of this type of feminism do not stand up to extended scrutiny, although it is in fact the strain of feminism that has become prominent since the late 1980s in a slightly more sophisticated form. In this type of feminism the attempt is to celebrate difference. The problems arise when one actually attempts to (a) uncover what the differences actually are and (b) figure out a way to emphasize difference without reenacting the same dominance-submission patterns that caused the sexism in the first place. Like the doctrine of separate but equal in the schools, radical feminism has never been successful in accomplishing these tasks. It is also the kind of feminism that is usually (although not inevitably) found among the so-called "Orthodox [Jewish] feminists."

Liberal feminism is a somewhat less unified phenomenon. It is composed of a number of different kinds of feminisms, from those who argue that there are few, if any, differences between men and women, to those who argue that there are differences, but they are socially imposed and maintained, to those that argue that even if there are biological differences, it should be considered a moral obligation to lessen them as much as possible. As an example of the last of those forms of liberal feminism, if we discovered that men were biologically worse at mathematics (as many held during the Renaissance), we would be obligated to help them by providing special education in school until they were able to master such an important and useful skill for modern life. Because the debate between radical and liberal feminists has not been conclusively resolved (despite the evidence being strongly in favor of sex differences being largely sociological, and strongly superficial), the question at hand at the moment is really not which of these theories is true, but what to make of them. It is perfectly reasonable to remain agnostic about whether men and women are biologically different and still assert that it is a moral necessity to make our roles more equal.

Another question that egalitarianism raises is: Why obey Jewish law at all? If one is committed to egalitarianism and if traditional Jewish law is sexist, why not toss it out altogether, claiming that its sexism demonstrates that it is not divine? On the other hand, if one believes that it is divine, then why not attempt to live with it as it is?

Those who are not committed to Jewish law altogether, of course, would find its sexism just another reason to ignore it. Those who do not believe that *halakhah* is divine may, however, yet be committed to it for other reasons. If that is so, they will want to work within it to make it more egalitarian, just as those who believe in its divinity would want to do. For both of the latter groups, I maintain that the principles that I elaborate below are, in fact, entirely within the system. The goal of this exercise is to take an implicit principle and make it explicit.

Furthermore, I assert that identifying an egalitarian principle within Jewish law is a particularly pressing necessity if Jewish law and Judaism generally are to remain relevant and if Jewish law is to continue to have any claim to divinity. It is clear from our texts that God desires justice—indeed, the Torah, both oral and written, reiterates this often. The Sifrei[10] reports, "'And the daughters of Zelophehad drew near': When the daughters of Zelophehad learned that the land would be divided among the tribes to the males but not to the females, all of them gathered together to consult with each other. They said: God's mercy is not like the mercy of human beings. Human beings have mercy upon the male more than upon the female, but God is not thus; rather, God's mercy is upon both males and females, as the Torah says, '[God] gives mercy to all flesh.'"

There is an implication in this passage of two things. First, it is clear that the Rabbis themselves recognized that there was an unjust inequality, and that that inequality does not originate with God. Second, because this passage is derived from the story of Zelophehad's daughters (Numbers 27:1–11) there is an implication that God is waiting to be asked. In other words, in the story, God surely knew that Moses had parceled out the land only to the males of the tribes and yet did nothing—until these women came to Moses and demanded their rights. The result was less than egalitarian, but it was undoubtedly an improvement. This and other aggadic materials can lead us toward an understanding that, indeed, it has long been part of the tradition to recognize that women's unequal treatment before the law is an artifact, not of God's doing, but of human attitudes.

Dr. Hauptman maintains in her book that over time the Rabbis moved toward increasing "rights" for women. This implies that the Rabbis recognized the humanity of women. Unfortunately, the main way that the Rabbis were able to act was through increasing protections for women. While it was certainly a step forward to recognize women as agents, albeit limited ones, protecting women is a form of maintaining the status quo and leaves the underlying problem alone. Much like giving money to the poor without teaching them a trade or providing real living-wage jobs, it is not true justice to put a band-aid over the symptoms, letting the wound fester.

Some of the Rabbis' attempts to equalize the status of women, however, have been in direct response to women's desires for more equal roles. A wonderful example appears in B. Ḥagigah 16b. It says there, "R. Jose said: Abba Eleazar told me: Once we had a calf that was a peace-sacrifice, and we brought it to the Women's Court, and women laid their hands on it—not that the [ritual of] laying on of the hands has to be done by women, but in order to gratify the women." Marc Stern comments, "Hazal recognized long ago that women wanted a fuller and more equal access to ritual observances than would have been the case had they observed only mitsvot they were obligated to perform. They accordingly permitted women to perform semikha on korbanot 'in order to give pleasure to women,' even though this involved looking away slightly from a rabbinic prohibition. Yet they are explicit: it was the demand of the women for equal roles that moved Hazal."[11]

Nevertheless, while this follows the pattern of the daughters of Zelophehad in that the women asked and the Rabbis responded, it is still a position of women speaking from a subordinate position, saying: Please let us do something. This is not an amelioration of power imbalance, or an increase in equality. It maintains the hierarchy that raises up men into a position closer to God and allows them to generously throw a few crumbs to women.

It is clear that in order to deal with the problem of inequality there must be three things: (1) an emphasis on responsibilities over rights or protections, (2) a theological underpinning, and (3) a voice for women. I will address each in turn.

RESPONSIBILITIES OVER RIGHTS OR PROTECTIONS

In Judaism, humanity is expressed through one's public responsibilities and through the obligations one has to the community and to God. It is often said that feminism is "about choice." I strongly disagree with this. Even secular feminism will fail if it only makes more choices available without addressing the need for women to be responsible to take on certain tasks. For example, there is very good evidence that the economic status of women is closely linked to the extent of their power and equality in society. In societies where women contribute more materially to the family or community, they are more valued and more equally treated. When the society delegates roles to women such that they make less of a contribution, their treatment falls accordingly. This happens in individual families, where, for example, economic dependence is often a hallmark of domestic violence, as the male partner isolates his wife or girlfriend and prevents her from leaving or getting help; but it is most prominently on a societal level that duties determine status. Therefore, women have a responsibility to make an economic contribution to their family and community, and it needs to be roughly equal to that made by the men of that society. Simply saying that women should be free to have a choice about whether or not to work is not appropriate because it reinforces societal patterns of inequality. Since this paper is not a discussion of women's economic status in secular society, I will only mention, but not expand on, the current research on how such a pattern produces continuing glass ceilings and the recent push for women to stay home with their children.[12]

The same is true in traditional Jewish society: the public obligations of men are where power is derived. As long as women are not both fully obligated and fully part of the decision-making process for both men and women, we are not living up to the Torah. That is just starting to happen within the Conservative movement, but how far we have to go is indicated by the great discrepancy between the number of women and men on the Committee on Jewish Law and Standards.

THEOLOGICAL AND LEGAL SUPPORT FOR A FEMINIST JEWISH STANCE

Legal methods are procedurally necessary for *halakhah*. That is, for a judicially based, divine legal system like *halakhah* to work, legal authorities need to act as if cases were determined by pre-existing precedents and laws, and courts must reach their decisions primarily by reviewing the received law and the facts of the case. However, such an approach cannot provide a basis for searching for and invoking principles within the law that have heretofore remained hidden or undiscovered.[13]

I offer here a possible (although obviously not the only) theological underpinning for this project. It has the benefit of remaining entirely within the halakhic system; however, it will be unsatisfying to those who prefer the positivistic stance that excludes appeals to God as a part of the legal mechanism. What I want to suggest is that God gave us the Torah as part of an ongoing project to make us holy. Since God, being omniscient, knew that a nation just liberated from slavery would not be able to comprehend a non-hierarchical society, God deliberately gave us the Torah written ambiguously enough that we would need to interpret it. (This is similar to Maimonides' contention about the reason why God commanded animal sacrifices: it was a temporary measure to fit the customs of the era.[14]) Similarly, the Rabbis maintain that the Torah includes a few cases whose *only* purpose is to be expounded. So, for example, the Talmud states about the rebellious son, "But it never happened and never will happen. Why then was this law written?—That you may expound it and receive reward," *derosh vekabbel sekhar,* as it says also about the leprous house, on the same page.[15] Certainly, God wishes us also to expound and learn from those situations that actually do happen, and even those that may have happened at one time but no longer do.

God wishes of us to move as a nation toward partnership, toward a more holy understanding of ourselves and the world, and so God created the language of the Torah in such a way that we would have to re-examine the precedents we have set as we developed. The cases in these days are not the same as those of earlier days. We may be free to revisit them because they are different in kind, for we are in a different place developmentally—just as one does not judge an eight-year-old in the same way as one does a fifteen-year-old.

Eliezer Berkovits suggests that the Mishnah's rule that one court may not abrogate the words of another unless it is greater in wisdom and number[16] is a specific principle: "A fellow *Beth Din* [court] is a contemporaneous one; not in the chronological sense, but contemporaneous in the continued identity of the situation, of the nature of the problem, of the needs and ethical quality of the individual and society."[17] Even the rulings of 50 years ago are not the rulings of a fellow court—the world is simply too different—let alone the rulings of a court of 1000 years ago, or twice that. As the Talmud instructs, each generation must judge after their own eyes.[18]

The Torah, both oral and written, insists on rationality, not stagnancy. The concept of *sevara* insists that we act so. Berkovits asserts that, "In a number of Talmudic passages it is taken for granted that the *sevara* is no less authoritative than the biblical text itself.[19] For example, in B. Bava Kama 46b, it says quite plainly, "*Ha lama li kera?! Sevara hu!*—What do I need a prooftext for? It's logical!"[20] Other commentators also have a sense of moral development, most famously Maimonides in Part III, chapter 32 of his *Guide for the Perplexed,* in which he suggests that God established sacrifices for Israel because they needed them at the time but not as an eternal duty.

Berkovits notes, "Occasionally a new law that departs from a prevailing rule may be created by a *sevara* . . ."[21] Through arguments that span the course of several chapters he shows that, in his words:

1. Principles from a *sevara*, sound common sense, logical reasoning, have the validity of a biblical statement.
2. The Torah itself makes reference to a ruling by a *sevara*, assumes it to be known, and by comparison to it establishes its own ruling in a case which the *sevara on its own would not have been able to give the biblically required decision.*
3. A *sevara* may be so convincing that it may compel one's conscience to suppress the plain meaning of a biblical injunction and force upon a verse in the Bible a meaning that it can hardly bear textually. . .[22]

Finally, we also traditionally understand that the Torah has extreme regard for human emotion, economic liability, and honor. The principle of *kevod habriyot* (honor due one's fellow human beings) appears numerous times in the Talmud, asserting, with specific examples, that it even overrides a negative precept of Torah.[23] Given the above principles, it is clear that there lies within the Torah tradition support for reinterpretation to be made in accordance with egalitarianism.

Similarly, Marc Stern notes,

> The egalitarian trend that might have been dismissed in the middle of the last century as a fad cannot be so dismissed today . . . [How should interpreters deal with it?] One must take note of the fact that some *mitzvot de-rabbanan* [commandments initiated by the rabbis] have been allowed to fall out of use . . . Nor should we ignore the number of legal devices used to avoid the potentially harsh effect of Torah laws. . . . Our conception of the Jewish family was changed irrevocably by the *takkanot* [legal amendments] of Rabbeinu Gershom abolishing polygamy and (more crucially) unilateral male divorce . . . What devices did the Torah confer on *talmidei hakhamim* [scholars] to adjust to changing circumstance? There are many . . . Rabbenu Tam was notoriously unrepentant when challenged about these leniencies. It was, he said, a *mitsva* [commandment] to allow Jews to earn a living. It would be ironic if economic realities could affect halakhah, but not moral ones.[24]

The Torah is a prescriptive document; God gave it for the purpose of making us holy. It has become clear that the trend of both secular society and Jewish tradition is toward greater equality and more care about *kevod habriyot*. It is a matter of common sense to recognize, given both economic and social realities, that feminism is a necessity of Jewish development and holiness. Further, it may well be that developments in secular law historically come at least partially from the Jewish tradition's drive toward greater holiness. It would be ironic if we, who have attempted throughout history to live up to our Torah and in so doing have effected the development of greater egalitarianism in secular law, were to stop now.

A POSSIBLE PLAN TO GIVE WOMEN A VOICE IN JEWISH LAW

The following is my prescription for how we should be implementing halakhic reinterpretation along feminist lines:

1. *There are no such things as "women's issues. . ."* Women's voices have to be heard as lawmakers, but it is not enough for women to be heard as advocates in court, or as *mikvah* ladies. When power is limited, it is limited, and in the Jewish community power is wielded through the judiciary—i.e., the rabbinate. There is no halakhic reason why women cannot be *poskot* [those who make authoritative rulings in Jewish law] even in the most traditional of Jewish communities. Women need to be part of the conversation—all of it. There is no Jewish topic that does not affect both men and women. Furthermore, women's decisions need to affect men as well.

An interesting model for this is that of the *tallit* [prayer shawl]. I first ran across this idea in an online essay, which I have since been unable to relocate. The wearing of a *tallit* by women began to be popular around the time of the beginning to the DIY ("Do-it-yourself") *ḥavurah* movements in the 1970s. When this began, *tallitot* were mostly polyester, white and blue or white and black; in some very traditional congregations, they were wool, but again white and blue or white and black, or in a few cases, white and white. When women began wearing *tallitot*, part of the ambivalence about how women should wear them was expressed through women trying different kinds of *tallitot*. Since there are no legal requirements of a *tallit* other than it have four corners to which the requisite fringes are attached, women started tie-dyeing them, wearing them in different shapes, different colors, and even different fabrics, such as painted silk or soft rayon.

After some time, many men realized that they were wearing boring *tallitot*, that there was no halakhic reason for them to wear boring *tallitot*, and that they did not *have* to wear polyester, black and white *tallitot*. Shortly, men, too, began wearing *tallitot* that were more expressive of their own aesthetics and their own feelings about which traditional verse moved them enough to be put on the *atarah* [the "crown," or upper band of the shawl]. Today, there is hardly a synagogue around the country, including Orthodox ones, where a colored *tallit* cannot be found. There is an entire industry devoted to producing beautiful *tallitot*—and we now have a widespread new custom of *hiddur mitzvah* [fulfilling a commandment in an aesthetically beautiful way] via the adoption of a *mitzvah* by women. It seems to me that this is a wonderful metaphor for how halakhic reinterpretation ought to happen regarding women. It is not enough to "add women and stir" (see point number 3 below). When women participate, it means that the roles of both men and women must change; otherwise attempts to include women have not really changed anything.

2. *Or are there?* On the other hand, on *halakhot* that directly relate to women's bodies and reproductive status, it is even more essential that women are part of the conversation—but that is not enough. For some topics, it is necessary that the Jewish community raises these matters anew and revisits them halakhically now that women can speak for ourselves and participate in the conversation about what the *halakhah* really means.

Catherine MacKinnon[25] asserts that it is the performance of sexual acts that is the crux of gender inequality. In her view, dominance and submission as enacted through sexual performance and taught as normative in media and other social venues (billboards, movies, and pornography among other places[26]) are actually central to how men and women view each other and themselves: that men are the standard, and women are the deviation, and that the purpose of the deviators is to be sexual things for use.

While such a view is a rather cynical, and, in my opinion, melodramatic summation of the situation, it nevertheless is at least partially supported by the evidence. I do not think that there has been any sort of great conspiracy by "the man" (as it were) to keep women down, but certainly a brief view of traditional texts and their views of women makes clear that in structuring marriage as *kinyan* (purchase) the Rabbis maintained as law significant features of chatteldom. In fact, it is a reasonable question to ask whether any traditional marriage today is halakhically binding since it requires women to understand that they are giving themselves over as chattel to do so, and no—or at least very few, certainly fewer than the number of Jewish women who marry—modern women would in fact agree to this.

Are there halakhic alternatives? Perhaps, but we Conservative Jews have not explored them sufficiently as of yet, so far concerning ourselves more with two-ring ceremonies that (again) deal with some of the superficial inequities without dealing with the underlying power imbalance. Who knows, perhaps a good solution would actually fix the *agunah* problem once and for all, as well.

3. *Add women and stir is not enough.* There cannot just be more women's voices in the conversation; the voices of both women and men need to take egalitarian principles into account. I say egalitarian rather than feminist because while feminist principles need to be brought into our judiciary, there are—at least today—broader problems of class that are not being addressed in our community as well. Those problems concern, for example, who has access to texts through access to day schools, summer camps, etc.

This also affects women and, again, affects women disproportionately because we have to run to make up for the past in which girls and women were not given the opportunity to study and, according to some, not even allowed to do so. So what are these egalitarian/feminist principles?

a. When there are two possible options, the one that makes women equal should not only be favored, but the other option needs to be recognized as not acceptable. This is much like the status of slavery: Although slavery is halakhically permitted, few would rule in its favor today, given the ethical implications of slavery. Those that did make such a ruling would be shunned from most communities as engaging in morally abhorrent practices.

This is the very minimum in a traditional community, but it is not enough. To live it, it is necessary to live by the rule of *lo'eg larash heref osehu*—that one who mocks a pauper blasphemes his Maker. In B. Berakhot 18a this is cited against a person walking in a cemetery with *tefillin* on his head or while reading from a Torah scroll, or reciting the Shema within four *amot* [cubits] of a corpse. Surely if we must take such care with the dead, it should be equally incumbent to do no less for the living. Thus, for example, I know someone who has taken upon himself to never be counted in a *minyan* that does not count women; that I only know of one such Jewish man is sad. When honors and responsibilities are not available to women, men are obligated to also turn them down.[27] Granted this may cause a dilemma in communities where women are not counted in *minyanim*, or for *aliyot*, or the role of *shaliah*, but in all places that insist upon men having a role that women may not, men may not take them either. At the very least, men should understand that they are responsible not to take on such honors and responsibilities as respecting the principle of *kevod habriyot* and in order to avoid *lo'eg larash*.

b. Jewish laws that exclude women must be revisited. Except for laws that deal specifically with reproductive matters, there should be no difference in treatment of men and women. This is the first step in establishing that broader, mutual feedback in the example of the *tallit* that I mentioned earlier, in which change affects not only women, but also men.

c. On the other end, men must also be seen as needing to participate more in family life. Thus the idea that women were exempted from positive time-bound commandments because of family responsibilities should be used as the beginning of a discussion about reassessing family responsibilities. We no longer see women as chattel, subject to men's whims to the extent that women may not do positive *kavod* [honor] for their parents because their husband's desires take precedence. We would see that as abusive, which it is. Nor is it acceptable for women to be working the second shift (that is, doing all or most or even more than half the childcare and house cleaning in addition to working a full-time job). This is not, as many social conservatives would have it, a mandate for taking away women's jobs; rather, it is a requirement that men share more of the responsibility for their family. When we say that women must be considered obligated publicly, the way men have been in the past, we must also say that men are obligated privately, as women have been in the past. Rabbis, then, as the judiciary, must not view the laws as a means to support the status quo; to the contrary, we must be an activist court to ensure that justice is done and the vulnerable are removed from their vulnerable position, not simply protected within it.

d. We must understand the enforcing of the equality of women as a *ḥumra*, a stringency. We are not making a *kula*, a leniency, when we rule that women are obligated for all the *mitzvot* that our tradition imposes on men; we are making a stringency.

Toward this end, we must address the arguments against giving women these responsibilities along the lines of "we don't want to increase the number of sinners." There is a strong response: to the contrary (and along the lines of the *tallit* feedback loop) we are actually improving the chances of reducing the number of sinners. In secular life, we are accustomed to the ideology at least (even if it is not always quite borne out in practice) that women and men are equal in rights. Since in Judaism we speak not in the language of rights but of obligations, most American Jews view those obligations much in the way that in secular law we view rights. As a result, when Jewish men see that Jewish women seem to have a choice about whether or not to do certain things in Jewish practice, that they are not obligated, the men—perhaps unconsciously, and perhaps not—understand themselves also not to be obligated, that *halakhah* is a choice. What appears to be happening is that we are losing the sense that Jews are obligated. If we are more stringent about women being obligated, it is likely to have the effect of increasing men's participation in obligatory *mitzvot*.[28]

On the other side of the argument, it is condescending to give women a choice to obligate themselves or not. We Jews live in a system of obligation: choice about whether or not to obligate is the same as saying "you still really do not count."

Thus, contrary to the *teshuvah* (rabbinic ruling) by Rabbi Joel Roth,[29] we should assume that women are obligated *a priori*, that our community has developed to the point that the majority of women consider themselves the equal of men. Instead of requiring that women who wish to be considered equal in obligation take steps to make themselves such, as Roth stipulates, it should be the woman who does *not* wish to be considered equal who must speak up and say that she does not wish to be—and this should be a temporary measure: no more than 100 years. This would actually be more in keeping with how our communities already work; Rabbi Roth's *teshuvah*, as I understand he himself admits, simply does not happen.

e. Finally—and this is a very radical step that I am not certain of yet, but I suggest as a possibility—it may be that in applying Jewish law, we should view *ishah* (woman) and *ish* (man) as empty terms. There simply may not any longer be referent objects attached to these concepts. I do not mean, of course, that there are no *men* and *women*— the English words no longer carry the freight of the Hebrew terms that are associated with halakhic judgments that make women secondary. There may be *zakhar* and *nekeivah*, and there may be some few exceptions related to reproduction and nursing, but by and large it may be necessary to view *ish* and *ishah* as we do *ben sorer umoreh*, that is, defined out of existence, or even as *sotah* (the woman suspected of adultery and subjected to the water rite of Numbers 5)—something necessary in the time of the Temple, but outside the requirements of the Temple cult, simply no longer possible to use or exist. It may be time for us all to be *adam*, simply human.

A CASE STUDY: ABORTION

One example of how one could address law as a feminist is the case of abortion. The basic sources are as follows: In B. Yevamot 69b there is a story of the daughter of a priest who is widowed shortly after marriage to an Israelite; the ruling is that she may partake of *terumah* (the priestly portion) during the forty days following the consummation of her marriage despite the fact that she has become a widow. Since permission to eat *terumah* is only for the daughter of a priest who is unmarried, or a widowed daughter who has no children, and since we could not know whether she is pregnant at this point, by inference, during the first forty days we consider the fetus "as water." This is confirmed by the Mishnah in Niddah 3:7 (30a), which declares that a fetus aborted fewer than forty days following cohabitation does not create the *tum'ah* (impurity) of childbirth specified in Leviticus 12:2–5. Nor, according to *Mishnah L'melekh, Hilkhot Tum'at Met* 2:1 does it cause the *tum'ah* that is caused by a corpse if it is expelled within forty days after conception. However, according to Rabbi Joseph Trani, abortion at this stage, while not prohibited because of the fetus being a life, is considered a form of self-mutilation, because the fetus is considered a limb of the mother.

The Conservative movement's Committee on Jewish Law and Standards came to the following opinion, as appearing on the movement's website (edited):[30]

> The Status of a Fetus: In the modern debate on abortion, many religious traditions view a fetus as equivalent to an existing human life, even from conception. While Judaism sees the fetus as valuable and sacred as potential life, the sources indicate that it is not equivalent to a person.
>
> One source for understanding this attitude comes from the Torah in Exodus 21:22–23: "If two men are fighting and wound a pregnant woman so that the pregnancy is lost, but no 'great harm' occurs, he will be fined as much as her husband assesses, and the matter will be placed before a court." Such a case is not considered murder. However, "If 'great harm' does occur, it is a case of *nefesh tahat nefesh,* 'life for life.'" In other words, the Torah draws an important distinction: causing a miscarriage of the fetus is a civil wrong resulting in monetary compensation (implying the fetus is not a person), while killing the mother is considered to be homicide.
>
> Finally, there are opinions that differentiate the "potentiality" of life, depending on how far along the pregnancy is. Several sources regard a fetus as a partial person after the first

forty days (before which some talmudic sources regard it as "mere fluid" and are more permissive). However, after forty days, if a spontaneous or induced abortion occurs, a woman is required to undergo the purification process identical to that which follows giving birth, implying that some aspect of "personhood" has been attained.

However, cases where abortion might be considered do not always fall into such clearly defined categories. What about cases where a test indicates the child may have a genetic disorder, such as Tay Sachs? Does a family's ability to economically support an additional child have any relevancy? If a pregnancy or additional child may result in psychological harm to the mother, is this comparable to physical harm? Is abortion following rape or incest allowable?

Individuals, and the rabbis they consult in attempting to deal with such situations, weigh all of the above attitudes, expressed in many additional source texts. In particular, while the sources are clear regarding abortion due to a physical threat to the mother's health, sources are divided regarding situations which cause psychological harm. Some sources tend to be lenient in such cases, especially early on in pregnancy. On the other hand, there is a strong tendency to be as restrictive as possible, lest lenience be seen as minimizing the seriousness of the act of abortion. In 1983, the Committee on Jewish Law and Standards of the Rabbinical Assembly arrived at the following summary position on abortion.

Conservative Movement Statement on the Permissibility of Abortion

Committee of Jewish Law and Standards, Adopted on November 21, 1983: Jewish tradition is sensitive to the sanctity of life, and does not permit abortion on demand. However, it sanctions abortion under some circumstances because it does not regard the fetus as an autonomous person. This is based partly on the Bible (Exodus 21:22–23), which prescribes monetary damages when a person injures a pregnant woman, causing a miscarriage. The Mishnah (*Ohalot* 7:6) explicitly indicates that one is to abort a fetus if the continuation of pregnancy might imperil the life of the mother. Later authorities have differed as to how far we might go in defining the peril to the mother in order to justify abortion. The Rabbinical Assembly Committee on Jewish Law and Standards takes the view that an abortion is justifiable if a continuation of pregnancy might cause the mother severe physical or psychological harm, or when the fetus is judged by competent medical opinion as severely defective. The fetus is a life in the process of development, and the decision to abort should never be taken lightly. Before reaching her final decision, the mother should consult with the father, other members of her family, her physician, her spiritual leader, and any other person who can help her in assessing the many grave legal and moral issues involved.

Both Rabbi Trani's position and that of the CJLS are relatively stringent positions—namely, that while the fetus is not a human being, there are reasons to prevent the woman from aborting it. Both positions assume attitudes that the *halakhah* simply fails to support: the Talmud does not appear to actually believe (as the CJLS ruling says) that, "The fetus is a life in the process of development, and the decision to abort should never be taken lightly." While the Talmud, of course, cannot plausibly be interpreted to suggest that one should take the decision lightly, especially in light of the danger the procedure involved in those times, our tradition seems far more interested in the woman's physical health than in the fetus. This position corresponds to its view that the fetus is like a limb of its mother—that is, that she would be causing *herself* harm to remove it—not that she's killing an independent being or a "life in the process of development," whatever that is.

Thus both Rabbi Trani and the CJLS fail sufficiently to take into account the woman's agency in the process of making the decision and her possible reasons for not wanting to carry a pregnancy to term or to bear a child and/or raise it. Now that abortion is clinically quite safe—safer, in fact, than actually carrying a child to term—we can question whether viewing abortion as self-mutilation still holds true. Moreover, it would be useful to consider whether there might be non-medical (or non-psychiatric) reasons why it would permissible for a woman to abort—at least early on.

In fact, the positions offered by Rabbi Trani and the CJLS are both far more stringent than those of the Talmud. That and other considerations mean that, according to the principles I enunciated above, it is necessary to revisit the case, bringing women to participate in the *teshuvah* process, and taking into account the opinions and experience of women with abortion—and perhaps of pregnancy and child-bearing and -rearing, as well.

What we would want to do is go back and re-examine some of the other sources, such as Rabbenu Tam, who comments on B. Yevamot 12a that women who are permitted to use contraceptive devices to prevent pregnancy are permitted to "insert a tampon"—i.e., a device to cause a just-fertilized egg to be expelled, and not to implant in the womb. If early-stage abortion were prohibited, then Rabbenu Tam could not have advised this course of action.

Rabbenu Nissim, in his commentary on B. Ḥullin 58a, says that we need not consider the well being of a fetus that has not yet emerged into the world. Also, the Mishnah in Arakhin 1:4 (7a) states that a pregnant woman who is sentenced to execution must still be executed, as long as she is not in labor. The Talmud on this passage comments "Of course!" Rabbi Joseph Trani argues that this amazement would be out of place if destruction of a fetus in any way was like taking a human life: Indeed, the Talmud instructs that the woman should be struck on the abdomen to cause the death of the fetus prior to that of the condemned woman, in order to avoid the indignity that would be inflicted on her body if the fetus emerged after her death.

In general, we have adequate reason to assert that Jewish law in fact supports a very *lenient* view of abortion. If asked to rule on a case of a woman who was considering an abortion, say because she was economically unable to handle the raising of a child, I would be inclined to suggest that if one aborts the fetus before the fortieth day, it is permitted to do so, although *not encouraged* if there is no danger to the health or life of the woman. Since, however, Jewish law clearly does not view feticide as equivalent to homicide, particularly during the first stage of pregnancy, we would be wrong not to permit a woman who feels unable to bear a child to rid herself of the fetus. I would also suggest that if it is possible, the woman should try to have a chemical, rather than a surgical abortion, as it could be less considered to be "wounding oneself."

Theoretically speaking, abortion is not considered murder in Jewish law up to the point that the head emerges. However, after the time of the Talmud, the trend has been to forbid abortion, except in cases of a threat to life, and more leniently, health. This is rather strange, as the Talmud certainly sees other reasons where abortion might be permissible. Furthermore, the prohibition of abortion based upon its being self-injury fails to take into account the variety of reasons why a woman would need to abort a child, such as her vulnerability, both physically and economically, when she is with child, and economic hardship has indeed always been a reason for rabbis to look leniently upon halakhic rulings.

Reasons given for these stringencies against abortion include some condescending ones, such as that women will come to use abortion as birth control. That is an unlikely proposition in the event that there is any other kind of birth control available. (I grant that in poor communities that is frequently not the case, making it a priority to push governments to support family planning organizations.) It does sometimes happen as, for example, in cases of spousal abuse that it is easier for women to get an abortion than prevent a pregnancy, and in such cases we should certainly be considering other interventions before we worry about the abortion's permissibility. As anyone who has gone through an abortion could explain, however, it is an extremely unpleasant procedure, for which no one would volunteer if it were possible to avoid.

Other reasons for restrictions on abortion include the offensive, like telling women that children are a blessing, and that we should maximize the possibility of family life. Clearly, if a woman is seeking an abortion, that child is not a blessing for her. Moreover, that argument assumes the conclusion, since by Jewish law, the fetus is not a child, certainly not at the point at which abortion is legally available in this country for any reason other than a threat to the woman's life or health.

Since the case of abortion is not a ritual matter, we need not be too concerned with the third and fourth principles. The principles with which we are most concerned for such a case are those that insist on hearing women's voices as part of the halakhic process, as well as those requiring us to take into account what sorts of structures are in place to maintain or interfere with women's equality. I specifically chose abortion as a case because it is directly related to something that affects many women very deeply. When we fail to respond to a matter like this in a feminist way, we are maintaining social structures that disempower women. The topic of abortion is also interesting for the way it comes up: What it notably does not do is arise as a discussion of how to prevent pregnancy, how to create a system for women to care for children that they are unable to maintain through their own salaries, or something else relevant to the life and hopes of the woman; it comes up rather as a question about ritual purity and determining whose life to save. It is interesting that while economics has traditionally been a reason for leniency in other areas of the law, it is expressly excluded by the CJLS as a possible reason for abortion, despite the *halakhah*'s clear leniency about the matter.

A SECOND SAMPLE CASE: *MINYAN*

Another possible case to consider (just for variety, and for the sake of dealing, albeit briefly, with a ritual matter) is the question of what constitutes a *minyan*. Based upon the third principle, women could explore the Talmud's definition of the minimum number to constitute a community as ten men (exclusively) based upon the verse in Numbers 14:27 that calls the ten spies who report back bad things about the land of Israel "an evil congregation" (B. Sanhedrin 2a).

Perhaps one would draw the (rather obvious, actually) conclusion that to the contrary, namely, that it should mean not exclusively men, since there are clearly places in which the word *edah* includes women. For example, in the very next Sabbath's Torah reading, God in Numbers 16:20–21 tells Moses and Aaron to separate themselves from *ha'edah hara'ah hazot*—this evil congregation—so that God can destroy them, but allows Moses to warn the *edah,* the congregation, to get away from the homes of Korah, Datan, and Abiram. They do so, and Korah, Datan, and Aviram, *together with their entire families,* are swallowed up. This implies that *edah* refers to all of Israel—not just the men—in the cases of both the Israelites who are getting quickly out of the way as well as the women of the families of these three ringleaders. Certainly, we could take the number as a minimum number, but we should not take all the details of the case of the ten spies, for then every *minyan* would have to be of evil people as well!

INCREASING HOLINESS THROUGH A VITAL, FEMINIST, AND TRADITIONAL WAY TO UNDERSTAND AND APPLY JEWISH LAW

In summary, traditional Judaism certainly has a strong basis for reconsidering the role of women broadly within the tradition. What we have heretofore lacked is a set of principles to use in addressing *halakhah* with the goal of engaging the embedded idea of equality between women and men. If traditional Judaism is to remain a holy system, we need to implement such principles in order to move toward the ultimate goal that God has set for us: to connect to God and increase holiness in the world.

NOTES

1. Many people are unaware that feminism has a long history prior to that of the American movement. Not only has feminism existed as far back as the early nineteenth century in America, but it was also extant in France as far back as prior to the French revolution. See the works of Dr. Claire Moses on this latter topic, such as *Feminism, Socialism, and French Romanticism* (1993) and *French Feminism in the Nineteenth Century* (1984).
2. *Encyclopedia of Philosophy*, Paul Edwards, ed. (New York: Macmillan, 1967), vol. 5/6, p. 264.
3. *Ibid.*, pp. 254, 256. This idea of Ulpian's does in fact crop up in the Talmud from time to time as well. For example: "R. Yohanan observed: If the Torah had not been given, we could have learned modesty from the cat, honesty from the ant, chastity from the dove, and good manners from the cock, who first coaxes and then mates . . ." (B. Eruvin 100b).
4. *Ibid.*, p. 256.
5. *Leviathan*, section 14.
6. *Encyclopedia of Philosophy*, vol. 5/6, p. 419.
7. *Lifnim meshurat hadin*: B. Bava Kamma 99b–100a; B. Bava Metzia 24b, 30b; etc. Other rabbinic categories that express this expectation of going beyond the letter of the law come in negative forms, such as *kofin al midat Sedom* ("we coerce a person [to act otherwise] with regard to a trait of Sodom"—B. Eruvin 49a; B. Ketubot 103a; B. Bava Batra 12b, 59a, 168a), *kofin oto ad sheyomar rotzeh ani* ("we force him until he says, 'I want to!'"—B. Ketubot 49a–49b), *ein ru'ah hakhamim nohah hemenu* ("the spirit of the Sages is not happy with him"—M. Bava Batra 8:5; B. Kiddushin 17b; B. Bava Kamma 94b; B. Bava Metzia 30b, 48a) and also positive forms, like *lifnim meshurat hadin* and laws derived from Proverbs 3:17, "Its ways are pleasant, and all its paths are peace" (B. Yevamot 15a, 87b; B. Nedarim 62a; B. Gittin 59b). For a brief discussion of these concepts, see Elliot N. Dorff, "The Interaction of Jewish Law and Morality," *Judaism* 26:4 (Fall 1977), pp. 455–466, esp. pp. 456–459. For a broader treatment of this theme, see Menachem Elon, *Jewish Law: History, Sources, Principles*, Bernard Auerbach and Melvin J. Sykes, trans. (Philadelphia: Jewish Publication Society, 1994), vol. 1, pp. 155–189.
8. Marc Stern, "On Egalitarianism and Halakha," *Tradition* 36:2 (Summer 2002), p. 6.
9. For an exhaustive examination of studies purporting sex difference, and refuting such consistent attempts to show there is such difference, see Carol Tavris, *The Mismeasure of Woman: Why Women Are Not the Better Sex, the Inferior Sex, or the Opposite*

Sex (New York: Simon and Schuster, 1992). In general, since this is such a short paper, I will try to dispense with endnotes, summarizing, rather than citing from her work.

10. On Numbers 27:1, paragraph 133 of the Horowitz edition.

11. Stern (at note 8), p. 21.

12. Just in case it is not already completely obvious, it is a cycle: Women still do the majority of housework and childcare, meaning that even when they work outside the home, they still have two additional full-time jobs when they return. When all women work outside the house, making equal money in society, there will be more of a push to create a system where there is better daycare and where men do a more significant proportion of those jobs. There have been oceans of ink spilt on this topic. For an introduction to the problem of women's economic contributions and differential expectations, see the early groundbreaking work by Arlie Russell Hochshild and Anne Machung, *The Second Shift: Inside the Two Job Marriage* (New York: Viking Penguin, 1989).

13. Nevertheless, the advantage of such a principle is that once it is discovered, there is good reason to believe it has been there all along, and so not only does it fit into the positivistic schema, but it *should* be used to reinterpret cases that formerly did not apply such a principle!

14. Maimonides, *Guide for the Perplexed*, Part III, chapter 32.

15. B. Sanhedrin 71a.

16. M. Eduyot 1:5. For a discussion of this precedent, see Elliot N. Dorff, "Towards a Legal Theory of the Conservative Movement," *Conservative Judaism* 27:3 (Spring 1973), pp. 65–77, esp. pp. 69–72.

17. Eliezer Berkovits, *Not In Heaven: The Nature and Function of Halakha* (New York: Ktav, 1983), p. 56.

18. B. Sanhedrin 6b; B. Bava Batra 130b–131a.

19. Berkovits (at note 17 above), p. 3.

20. This kind of thing appears both in the commentators and the Talmud itself in a number of places. See also B. Ketubot 22a, and *Nimukei Yosef* on B. Bava Metzia 47b, for examples suggested by Berkovits.

21. Berkovits (at note 17 above), pp. 5–6.

22. *Ibid.*

23. B. Berakhot 19b; B. Shabbat 81b, 94b; B. Eruvin 41b; B. Megillah 3b; B. Bava Kamma 79b; B. Menaḥot 37b–38a.

24. Stern (at note 8 above), pp. 22–23.

25. Catherine A. MacKinnon, *Toward a Feminist Theory of the State* (Cambridge, MA: Harvard University Press, 1989), chapter 7.

26. Not to mention children's television—something I recently noticed while watching cartoons with a friend's child!

27. See the extremely wonderful article by Esther Ticktin, "A Modest Beginning" in Elizabeth Koltun, ed., *The Jewish Woman* (New York: Schocken Books, 1976), pp. 129–135. Everyone who believes that women can be separate but equal should be required to

read this article. On second thought, everyone should be required to read this article.

28. A *very* non-feminist argument in favor of complete equality of obligation might be that it is a *hora'at sha'ah* (a decree of the hour, a temporary measure) in order to get men to fulfill their obligations!

29. Joel Roth, "On the Ordination of Women as Rabbis," in *The Ordination of Women as Rabbis: Studies and Responsa,* Simon Greenberg, ed. (New York: Jewish Theological Seminary of America, 1988), pp. 127–185.

30. www.rabbinicalassembly.org/contemporaryhalakhah.

H. RAYMOND P. SCHEINDLIN

Raymond Scheindlin was ordained by the Jewish Theological Seminary in 1965 and earned his doctorate in Arabic literature from Columbia University in 1971. After serving on the faculties of McGill and Cornell Universities, he returned to the Seminary in 1974, where he served on the faculty and as Provost from 1984 to 1988. He is now Professor of Medieval Hebrew Literature there and Director of the Seminary's Shalom Spiegel Institute of Medieval Hebrew Poetry. He is the author of six books, including one on medieval Hebrew secular poetry (*Wine, Women, and Death,* 1986) and a companion volume on medieval Hebrew religious poetry (*The Gazelle,* 1991). He also translated Ismar Elbogen's monumental history of Jewish liturgy (1993) and wrote a translation and commentary on the Book of Job (1998).

In some important ways, this article is atypical of the others in this book. First, this is an article primarily about prayer rather than law. I have nevertheless included it because within his discussion of prayer Scheindlin suggests how he views Jewish laws governing prayer and Jewish law generally, and in doing so he articulates an approach to Jewish law that others have not suggested. In fact, this article began as an oral presentation in the Seminary's adult study program in 1991, a tape of which I heard; I immediately began using that tape in my course on theories of Jewish law within the Conservative movement, and I urged Scheindlin to publish his presentation. I am grateful to him for taking the trouble to revisit that presentation and articulate it in written form for the purposes of this volume and for the benefit of us all.

Second, as Scheindlin himself says in the very first paragraph, although he has written extensively about Jewish liturgy and taught it regularly, he is "unused to speaking about it personally." But that, of course, is what all of the authors in this volume are doing. Most do it in more academic and theoretical terms, presenting their views as interpretations of previous Jewish law, interpretations buttressed by extensive references and argumentation and consciously open to critique. Even so, each of the authors in this volume clearly intends to describe and defend his or her own view of Jewish law as he or she understands and lives it. Scheindlin just makes that personal connection more explicit than most. He says, in fact, again in the first paragraph, "I cannot draw on authority to support my ideas in this area; all I can do is lay them out as a personal presentation without documentation."

What, then, is Scheindlin's view? In the second and third paragraphs of this essay, he announces "two principles right at the beginning"— namely, that he believes neither in normative rules nor in a definitive theology. Judaism provides *opportunities,* in his view, that we may or may not take advantage of. If you choose to engage in nothing Jewish, that "would not make you a bad person or even a lost soul. I would not even feel sorry for you, or lament that you are missing something." Scheindlin is clearly very serious in asserting Judaism in general, and Jewish law in particular, as *an option* for Jews that may enrich their lives, but only one among many such options that include other forms of cultural expression.

As Scheindlin makes clear later on, he sees all cultural expressions as vehicles to enable people to express themselves, "to express something we wanted to express but had not thought of consciously or did not have the means to express." Even the most articulate of us cannot put all of our thoughts and experiences into language; language only works on "simple everyday things or things that are capable of being compressed into neat logical sequences, but when we try to express our more intimate feelings, language turns out to be a clumsy tool." Some of us are better at using language than others, and so we need to use the work of others to help us identify our own feelings and express them. But even people who are good with words cannot articulate everything in the realm of feelings: they need to use language indirectly and suggestively rather than descriptively to capture their feelings and experiences, and they need to draw us into their feelings and experiences to help us recognize and express our own. They thus use poetry and stories rather than propositions. Some abandon words altogether, using music, art, or dance to accomplish these ends.

Jewish law, then, becomes yet another way to articulate our inner being. It is not by any means the only way to do this, and for many it may not be the most effective way. If that is so, so be it; if one finds some other means to connect with one's inner being and express it, one should grab hold of it and use it, and so much the worse for Jewish law.

And yet Jewish law *can* serve this spiritual purpose. Scheindlin, I would imagine, would focus on rituals in particular as a way in which Jewish legal institutions can accomplish this function because they constitute a kind of poetry in action. The joy of the Shabbat table and the warm feelings of tradition, family, and community that it engenders are clearly what draws people to it and gives that ritual its meaning. It is not just the aesthetic quality of the ritual objects, the special way we are dressed and the table is set, the singing, and the food that express what Shabbat is about—although its meaning certainly includes all of those factors; the rituals, though, point beyond themselves to a reality that we can only partially capture in language, to the passage of time and to the larger meanings of family, community, the Jewish tradition, and Creation itself. Similarly, the *sukkah* expresses our joy at harvest time, the fulfillment that comes from the cooperation of human work and the forces of nature to produce these gifts of the land, and at the same time the *sukkah* symbolizes our sense of the fragility of life and the temporary and weak hold we have on such gifts. Mourning rites graphically help us express our feelings of bereavement, sadness, and worry about our own future without the presence of the one who has died, and simultaneously our fear of our own demise some day in the not-so-distant future.

Scheindlin specifically admits that he cannot call on any divine or human authority to confirm his approach; to the extent that Jewish law has any authority, it would derive from its effectiveness to express what we feel on such occasions and cannot adequately convey in language. Moreover, "feel," as Scheindlin is using the term, is not just an emotional or aesthetic category; it is also a cognitive category, for we feel— or experience—aspects not only of ourselves, but of the world outside us. We thus learn truths about life and the world in which we live through such rituals—or, if we choose, through music, art, poetry, or learning how to do anything well. (In this Scheindlin's use of "feel" expresses the same thesis, but from the opposite direction from the way the Bible uses the verb "see" [ra'ah], which means not just to look out at the world to learn something about it, but to experience it emotionally. Both Scheindlin and the Bible intend to indicate that we *both* learn truths and feel emotions in our interaction with the world.) That, of course, makes the authority of Jewish law highly individualistic, for it succeeds with some and not with others in performing these cognitive and emotional tasks.

Even though Scheindlin asserts that Jewish law can accomplish these ends and he thus chooses to incorporate aspects of Jewish law into his own life, he objects to seeing law as a system of binding norms. He thinks that people can be moral without it and immoral with it. Moreover, to see it as binding undermines its spiritual purposes. Very much similar to Martin Buber in this, Scheindlin maintains that to see Jewish law as an authoritative system would put our Judaism into a straitjacket, making it impossible to express our own individual selves. That is, he not only claims that individuals may choose to practice Jewish law to the extent that they please—including not at all—but he also avers that to see Jewish law as a binding legal system ruins its ability to function as an art form, its ability to enable us to express ourselves. As he says,

> Judaism is my art form. I have experimented with several varieties of Judaism in the course of a lifetime of being actively Jewish and many years as an academic specialist in Judaica. I have tried *halakhah* and strict observance, but came to realize that this is not my vehicle. It does not work for me, partly because I am not of a legalistic temperament but also because of what I see as an inherent flaw in the system. The halakhic system seems to me to be not so much a method for serving God as it is an attempt to legislate culture. I would rather see being Jewish as analogous to being Irish or Italian—as an identity that has many components, including traditions, folkways, and even (unspoken) rules, but that is not legislated as a legal system. I understand that *halakhah* has religious meaning for others, and perhaps the loss is mine, but I can only be who I am, just as I can only believe what I believe.

What are the weaknesses and strengths of this artistic approach to Jewish law? Because it is highly individualistic, it has the same problem that other such theories have—namely, how do you create a community on such grounds? Scheindlin might answer that it is the group that shares the artistic opportunities that Judaism provides, including its textual tradition, that constitutes the community of like-minded souls, much as those who share an interest in Mozart or Shakespeare constitute a community as well.

That explains how the isolation of this approach can be overcome, but it does not describe how the group can form communal norms. Scheindlin is not interested in such norms; for him, one can *choose* to live one's life according to Jewish law, but the law has only the authority that individuals give it. Anything more than that—in particular, any attempt to claim that Jewish law is binding—is, for Scheindlin, not only unfounded but counterproductive. After all, if the purpose of culture in general and the law in particular is to enable people to express themselves, then one has to allow people to do that in their own terms; it is impossible to "legislate culture," to force people to express themselves in specific forms. That, of course, undermines the very possibility of legal rules that require everyone in the group to act in a particular way.

One wonders, though, exactly how far Scheindlin would want to push this notion of individual expression. In order for people to express themselves, they have to use forms—verbal, artistic, musical— that can communicate their feelings. If one is satisfied to express oneself in ways that nobody else understands, then, indeed, no rules need govern one's expression. But if one also wants to *communicate* to someone else, as in the case he mentions of the couple sharing intimate feelings through the woman's piano playing, then some shared conventions are necessary. (Philosophers of language refer to this as the problem of the status of private languages: If they cannot serve in the communicative role that we normally expect from languages, they may not properly be termed "languages" at all.) But every convention consists of rules that must be followed if the parties sharing that convention are to communicate successfully. The rules of grammar of the various human languages are obvious examples, but so are the harmonies of music and the styles of art. In each case, a novice—or, on the other end of the spectrum, an extremely creative user of the convention—can twist the rules to some extent and can still be understood, but there are clear limits to that elasticity. At some point, it is no longer the same language, and only people who speak the new language can use it to communicate. Consider the difficulties contemporary English speakers have, for example, in understanding Chaucer's English, let alone those speaking in another Latin-based language like Spanish or French. For that matter, while Americans can usually understand the English of Britons or Australians, that is not always the case, both because of the accent and also because of the different use of words and expressions in these communities. So if Scheindlin is serious about Jewish culture as a mode of communicating our inner feelings, experiences, and perceptions, even he would have to admit some binding rules incumbent on all who want to use that culture as their art form. As

Mordecai Kaplan noted, a flag can only function as a flag if everyone both in the group and outside it recognize it as the group's flag, and that requires strict rules as to its colors and shapes. How, then, is this different from legislating culture in the area of moral and ritual practice?

At the same time, there are some distinctive strengths to Scheindlin's approach. Its individualism enables—even encourages—people to "live and let live." Rabbis and other Jews might encourage their fellow Jews to take advantage of the opportunities that Judaism has to offer to express their innermost feelings, but there is no obligation to do so. As a result, those Jews who do choose the Jewish option will pursue it with the relish and passion of their own convictions; they will never become what Heschel derogatorily called "religious behaviorists." (This is similar to Franz Rosenzweig's distinction between *Gesetz* and *Gebot,* between those who obey Jewish law as an outside burden imposed on them, in contrast to those who obey it as part of their individual relationship with God;[12] but for Scheindlin the passion comes from the ability of Jewish law to articulate our inner feelings, while for Rosenzweig it comes from its ability to reinforce our relationship with God.)

Moreover, while Scheindlin shares Mordecai Kaplan's cultural orientation to Judaism, he focuses much more than Kaplan does on the artistic and expressive functions of Jewish law. That transforms the character of Jewish law: It is not, as it is for Kaplan, just folkways, holding the community together through common symbols; it is rather the means by which those who choose to use these communal symbols express their own, individual experiences, feelings, and perceptions. As such, this theory will clearly have great attraction for many contemporary Jews who seek some form of inner spirituality, whether in Judaism or outside it. This includes not only the "baby boomers" that sociologist Wade Clark Roof calls "seekers"; it includes also Jews of many ages who are initially convinced to get involved in things Jewish by the sheer aesthetics of Friday night around the Shabbat table, the *sukkah,* and many other experiential aspects of Jewish ritual life. As such, for all its differences from the conceptual world of classical and rabbinic Judaism, and for all its problems of forming community together with communal norms, Scheindlin's theory has the distinct advantage of describing the spiritual and artistic elements that first draw many Jews to serious Jewish commitments and that later sustain those commitments, even when some of those Jews find that they are making Jewish law a part of their lives for other reasons as well.

The Inner Art of Prayer

RAYMOND P. SCHEINDLIN

ALTHOUGH I HAVE A GREAT DEAL of experience speaking about the Jewish liturgy—that is one of the subjects I teach at the Jewish Theological Seminary—I am unused to speaking about it personally. And although I have a lot of experience writing about Jewish literary texts, I have generally done so as an academic, my writing based on research and documented by footnotes. I devoted several years to translating the classic modern study of the Jewish liturgy, a book that contains no fewer than ninety-nine pages of footnotes, from which I learned a great deal about the sources and history of the Jewish liturgy. But I also learned that no earlier authority speaks for me on this subject, and that no one else's liturgical or religious system works for me. I cannot draw on authority to support my ideas in this area; all I can do is lay them out as a personal presentation without documentation.

It will be worthwhile to enunciate two principles right at the beginning. My Judaism does not embrace normative rules. It does not tell you what you should do or what you should believe. It offers you opportunities, which you may or may not decide to take advantage of. You may be able to take advantage of some Jewish ideas and practices but not of others. You may even find that none of it works for you. This would not make you a bad person or even a lost soul. I would not even feel sorry for you, or lament that you are missing something.

The other principle is that I do not have an active theology. I decided a long time ago not to worry about trying to bring my ideas about religion and God into line with reason, or even to try to give them a tight formulation. My attempts at theology have taken me no further than the conviction that there is more to life and the universe than we may have yet succeeded in pinning down; but whether that additional something is God and the divine, i.e., something transcendent and unknowable, or whether it is something that we will ultimately understand with the tools of logic and science, I cannot say. I do feel quite certain that if it is divine, it is far beyond concern with my activities, thoughts, and speech.

Yet prayer has been most consistently at the center of my religious life. It is the vehicle for the expression of my otherwise inexpressible inner self as well as of my Jewish identity.

PRAYER AS A FORM OF EXPRESSION

When I pray, I am not obeying a halakhic rule that one is obliged to pray. I may choose to pray in a halakhic manner, but not out of obligation. When I pray, I am not addressing a sentient being other than myself; I do not conceive of God as doing something analogous to what I do when I listen to another person speaking. Yet when I pray, I am not faking. My behavior and feelings when I pray are strong enough and have been consistent enough over enough decades to convince me that something real is happening to me, that what I am doing is not empty behaviorism. Though I do not mean the words of my prayer literally, there is meaning in it; but the criterion of literal truth is too clumsy to help identify the meaning or justify the act.

I have come to understand the impulse to pray by means of analogous experiences that are available in everyday life. When we read a poem, we adopt the poet's assumptions, whether in real life we agree with them or not. The truth that the poet is getting at requires that we go along with him for a little while. This truth lies below the level of the words, or, we might say, above the level of the words. In reading a poem, we temporarily adopt a doctrine that may be logically false or run contrary to our normal opinions and beliefs in order that we can come closer to a truth that we do share with the poet.

Christopher Smart was a well-known eighteenth-century London madman who would stop strangers on the street and insist that they pray with him; Samuel Johnson, who knew Smart, defended him, saying that it was more irrational not to pray at all, and "I'd as lief pray with Kit Smart as anyone else." But with all his eccentricities, Christopher Smart wrote poetry, including the following lines from his "Rejoice in the Lamb."

> For I will consider my cat Geoffrey.
>
> For he is the servant of the living God duly and daily serving him.
>
> For at the first glance of the glory of God in the East he worships in his way.
>
> For this is done by wreathing his body seven times round with elegant quickness.

We may assume that Christopher Smart had a cat named Geoffrey, but that is the end of the literal truth in this poem. Yet the poem works immediately and intuitively on every one of us. The poem embodies a truth, but the truth is under the surface of the words. Geoffrey is a projection of Christopher Smart's piety, his vision of all nature as alive and aware of and glad for the gift of life; it is a projection of Smart's sense of being a servant of God. Projecting his personal piety onto his household pet is a literal falsehood, but even a religious skeptic will find it moving, will identify with the speaker—madman though he was—and catch in his words a whiff of Smart's (and his own) love of God. The feeling may vanish later, but it leaves a trace on the reader's soul.

It is the same with Emily Dickinson's "I heard a fly buzz when I died," patently a false statement. Did Kublai Khan actually build a stately pleasure dome in Xanadu? Is there even a place called Xanadu?

I do not know, and it does not matter. We can experience what the poet wants us to experience by accepting his premises for a while and seeing where they lead. Once we have gone there, we can return to real life. But we can never return completely; we have been changed by the experience. I personally do not believe in the Trinity, but John Donne's sonnet "Batter my heart, three-person'd God" expresses a religious mood that does not depend entirely on Christian doctrine, but an attitude or spirit that is available to Jewish or even secular readers if they look for the universal behind the particular.

This is true of fiction as well. "Once upon a time" never introduces a true story; the minute we hear this phrase, we know to expect something that is literally false, but something that may be true in a larger sense. I would not like to enter a reality contest against Huckleberry Finn or Anna Karenina; they are more real than any of us.

Let us tackle this matter of the relationship of prayer to poetry from a different direction. Who is the addressee of a love poem? When the poet says, "Shall I compare thee to a summer's day?" does he have a real person in mind? Shakespeare scholars debate this question, but it does not matter at all to us when we read the sonnet or listen to it read. I read it alone, not to anyone else, and I hear someone speaking—not to me, but to whom? Even if I imagine that I am saying the words myself, I do not need to have a particular person in mind. Then why bother with the whole exercise of writing and reading love poetry? Because the exercise enables me to identify things that are inside me, feelings and attitudes that are released by the poem. The poem is a vehicle for my emotional and intellectual life. By imagining a beloved to whom I might say, "Shall I compare thee to a summer's day?" I can approach the truth of love and language. By imagining that I am speaking to God, I can get to the truth of my soul.

The need for this indirect approach arises from the failure of language. Language enables us to get a good grip on simple everyday things or things that are capable of being compressed into neat logical sequences; but when we try to express our more intimate feelings, language turns out to be a clumsy tool. Using it directly almost never results in a satisfyingly accurate and full expression of intertwined ideas or strong emotions. Poetry is a technique that man has devised for using language indirectly and thereby getting a better grip on the more complicated truths. Another technique is music, which does away with words altogether; it is more efficient than language for expressing emotions, though not nearly as efficient for everyday chores like finding out what time it is or for solving algebra problems. Poetry is a kind of compromise, bringing together a musical element (rhythm, rhyme, strophic structure, and other sound devices) with imagery and other kinds of indirect means of expression, and retaining the possibility of making direct statements when appropriate.

Prayer, poetry, and music are closely related forms of expression. We respond to all of these forms when, and to the extent that, they express things that are already inside ourselves. Besides, they sometimes bring to the surface things that are inside ourselves that we were not aware of until we came into contact with the prayer, the poem, or the music. The artist who made the work has an insight about life and people—perhaps he himself would have been incapable of expressing it in direct statements—that he, being an artist, could bring to the surface using indirect means. We respond because he saw and expressed something that is already inside us that we would otherwise not have noticed. The artwork does not teach us something new. It enables us to express something we wanted to express but had not thought of consciously or did not have the means to express. The relationship between the prayer, poem, or music resembles the way Socrates, in one of the dialogues of Plato [*Meno*], teaches the slave the Pythagorean theorem: not by explaining it to him but by asking him questions that enable him to bring the eternal idea that was inside him all along to the surface. (At least, that is the way that Plato interprets what happens between Socrates and the slave.)

I learned this early in life, because when I was a small boy, in the days before television (well, in the days before we slightly backward Scheindlins had television), my father used to read poetry to me. He read me poems that any educator would say were too hard for me, that were far beyond my experience of life, that could only frustrate, even intimidate a child. Such poems as William Cullen Bryan's "Thanatopsis" and Milton's "Il Penseroso," they would say, were not age-appropriate for a nine-year-old. Yet through these sessions, I learned that words could be vehicles of strong feelings and ideas, and I learned to identify my own feelings and ideas in other people's writing. Slightly older, I found that certain feelings or situations would remind me of lines of poetry I knew. There was comfort in knowing that I had not been there first, that a wise writer had gone ahead and had these experiences and found a way to formulate them, to bring them to the surface.

When I came to rabbinical school and began studying Judaica seriously, I came to realize that the Jewish tradition works the same way with Scripture and liturgy. When we find ourselves in Scripture, we call it midrash; when we find ourselves in liturgy, we call it *kavanah*.

In all these works of art, we see something of ourselves and we see something beyond ourselves. This thing that is beyond ourselves is not so far away that we cannot tell it is there, but it is too far beyond ourselves for us ordinary people to articulate. An artist is a person, as I understand it, who articulates it for us. We use his articulation of this remote but identifiable truth to satisfy our own inchoate sense that something else lies beyond us and to satisfy our own yearning to take part in that something. One of the great ironies of life is that we are so constructed as to be able to sense that there is something out there, yet lack the power to express or explain it. We yearn intensely for contact with that something beyond. To express that yearning, we need professional help, because it is beyond most of us.

In speaking about the beyond, I am not necessarily referring to anything supernatural. It exists in the nearly universal intuition that beyond the world of phenomena there is something numinous that draws us to itself—something that myriad pictures and concepts of God have been devised by the various cultures of the world to explain or at least to capture in words. If you are inclined that way, you can apply what I have just said to the God of Israel. But the idea that something exists that is beyond our reach is present in every human enterprise. It may be found, for example, in the effort to do something perfectly. To do anything really well—to run, to play music, to love, to write a perfect sentence, whatever you throw yourself into—you can imagine what it would be like emotionally to do it perfectly, to outdo yourself, yet only rarely in a lifetime do you succeed. The irony is that we can imagine achieving perfection; we are given the vision—but not the power.

Why are we able to conceive of that which we cannot attain? And if we cannot attain it, why do we yearn for it so? We have to suppress thinking about it most of the time or we would live in frustration, but few people are completely dead to the problem. To get through life, most of us have to adjust to that fact that we can only do what we can do, can only see as far as we can see. Some of us dedicate ourselves nevertheless to trying to achieve perfection; this can become a destructive obsession, or, for the very few, it can actually lead to the desired result. Most of us eventually shrug our shoulders and give up. At some early point in our lives we confront the challenge, experiment to decide which way is ours, and shelve it. We suppress the yearning for perfection, but it does not really go away.

PRAYER WITHIN THE JEWISH FRAMEWORK

Culture provides us with tools for satisfying the tension between what we can conceive and what we can achieve. By culture, I do not mean going to concerts or art galleries or buying designer items; I am using the term the way sociologists use it, to mean the totality of behaviors and attitudes characteristic of an individual community. As members of society, we inherit tools of life and expression that we share with other members of our society. We may inhabit several cultures at once, each of which provides us with its own typical media and tools to deal with our inner tensions and longings.

One of the cultures in which I function—one of the cultures that has created the set of problems that I live with and that has given me the tools to live reasonably comfortably with them—is Judaism. Within Judaism, prayer is one of the main vehicles for focusing the yearning for the ultimate, one of the chief outlets for expressing the frustration of this unfulfilled desire. Prayer, for me, is not the worship of God. It is a form of expression deriving from one of the cultures that have shaped me, Judaism, and it has counterparts in the other cultures that I inhabit.

Art does not exist outside a particular culture. There has to be material for the artist to work with, or art would be pure abstraction. These materials do not consist only of paraphernalia such as paints and marble and catgut, but they include the whole system of themes, symbols, and language that everyone, the artist included, inherits. Judaism is the material I work with. To me, Judaism is a vehicle of self-expression, and at its most highly developed, it is an art form parallel to music, poetry, or painting. Like them, it points toward truth, and gets further in the direction of truth than mere observation or reason can. Like them, it attempts to capture truth in such a way that the act of capturing truth itself becomes beauty.

All art forms are the application of a set of skills to the artist's conception of truth, which he finds within himself. The radiance of the outside world touches a photographic plate inside him that controls his vision, or perhaps rather a photoelectric cell that controls his actions. The result of this interaction between outer and inner world is the work of art, whether painting, poem, song, or prayer. The poet, the artist, knows the truth not so much by looking outward as by looking inward; he has the power to catch what is outside in his inner mirror and, working from what he sees, to take action that brings to others not the outer stimulus, which is available to all, but his inner vision, which to them is revelation. This capturing of the outer world in the inner self and conveying it outside again would appear to be one of the greatest satisfactions that life has to offer.

The power to do what I am describing is probably innate; most of us try our hands at it at one time or the other in the course of our lives, usually when we are young, and give up. But as with all other aptitudes, some people are more gifted than others. You may have in your extended family one of those child geniuses who, at age five, sit down at the piano and play right off some music heard on the radio or a CD, such as Beethoven's Ninth, though they never had a lesson and cannot even completely reach the keyboard. This is what we call "gifted." Others master the skill through a combination of love and diligence, and they may get to be so proficient that the rest of us cannot tell the difference between them and the truly gifted. I believe that all of us are born with more or less the same impulses, even the same potential, but that some of us—the geniuses—are born with the switch turned on, while the rest of us have to labor at figuring out where the switch is and how to operate it, and once past a certain age, it never works quite as well. None of these techniques comes automatically to most people. The more we work at building our technique, the better we can perform and the more expressive we can be. You know this if you have taken piano, drawing, dance, or tennis lessons. Then there are those who affect the manner of artists, though having neither genius nor having devoted themselves to mastering the technique.

All this applies to Jewish behavior and liturgy as much as to the art forms just mentioned. To begin at the bottom: if you buy a beautiful matzah cover, that is definitely a Jewish experience, though not in itself a very rich one. That it is beautiful does not make you an artist, and that it is Jewish does not mean that it expresses much for you. As with any art, performing Judaism well involves a vast amount of training; and as with any art, even appreciating it involves a good deal of work and commitment.

We cannot all make a painting or play a sonata; we cannot all even get what a Rembrandt or a Glenn Gould is doing. Both performance and judgment involve mastery. Similarly, you cannot experience fully what prayer has to offer without a tremendous amount of discipline and application. I have chosen to devote my discipline and application to something that, for biographical reasons, came naturally to me, and you should choose to put your discipline and application where it is most natural for you. Mine is the Hebrew language: the Bible, classical Jewish writings, and ritual skills are the sphere in which I function naturally. To them. I have devoted a lifetime of attention, and they have provided me with the tools with which to see the world and to express what I see.

Performing the Jewish liturgy does not just mean learning how to perform the synagogue service; it fits into a larger context, just as playing the piano does not involve just playing notes. There needs to be a larger musicality. In both liturgy and piano playing, technique and book learning are an essential foundation; but technique alone is merely pedantry. You can play your scales perfectly and still not make music. Conversely, even scales can be music when played by someone who has mastered technique and has something to say. For such a person, even scales can express an inner life. Jewish liturgy is not a spontaneous outpouring of the soul; it is a complex and difficult ritual that, like piano playing, has to be mastered in order to achieve expressivity.

I found myself once alone with a married couple, both musicians, in a small concert hall with a piano. The wife was a pianist, and she began noodling on the piano and then playing real pieces that she had performed earlier in her career. After a while, it became evident that by playing she was actually speaking to her husband. Although I was there by invitation, they drifted into their own private world and forgot about me. He stood by her, and when she would finish one piece, he would name another and she would play it, if she thought she still could, and it seemed that by doing this, they became engaged in a nostalgic review of their married life. I became more and more uncomfortable, but did not dare break the spell by leaving. At last, she launched into the familiar Beethoven piece called "Für Elise." Probably everyone who has ever taken piano lessons has had to work on this elementary piece, and I doubt any professional pianist has ever programmed it on a recital; yet here was a woman who had devoted a lifetime to mastering the most complicated works in the piano repertoire playing for her husband—and a forgotten visitor—this simple piece from childhood, focusing a lifetime habit of expressivity on a bagatelle. It was a truly moving performance. Where one has a lot to say and massive skill with which to say it, even a rudimentary children's piece can be performed movingly.

Different forms of expression work for different people. Sometimes even a masterpiece speaks not to us but only to others. But there is no reason for despair: something else will probably speak to us. How do we find what speaks to us? Or better, how do we find our own vehicle that will permit ourselves to speak? This depends on the range of our experience—have we exposed ourselves to sufficient vehicles of expression?—and on whether we have exerted ourselves to master the form.

Judaism is my art form. I have experimented with several varieties of Judaism in the course of a lifetime of being actively Jewish and many years as an academic specialist in Judaica. I have tried *halakhah* and strict observance, but came to realize that this is not my vehicle. It does not work for me, partly because I am not of a legalistic temperament but also because of what I see as an inherent flaw in the system. The halakhic system seems to me to be not so much a method for serving God as it is an attempt to legislate culture. I would rather see being Jewish as analogous to being Irish or Italian—as an identity that has many components, including traditions, folkways, and even (unspoken) rules, but that is not legislated as a legal system. I understand that *halakhah* has religious meaning for others, and perhaps the loss is mine, but I can only be who I am, just as I can only believe what I believe.

Nor can I think of Judaism as an ethical system. I know that there is an ethical system within Judaism, but I do not see that as Judaism's defining feature. My observation of life has led me to believe that some people are ethical and others are not, irrespective of their other beliefs and affiliations. Most people have a sense of right and wrong, though some people do not act on it; most people do not act on it at all times; and a very few, like Iago, are devoid of it. The ratio is probably the same among Jews and non-Jews, observant and nonobservant. Those who have an inclination toward the ethical will find their sources for it in Judaism and will be able to quote maxims from the Bible and the Rabbis, but the real source is their own inclination.

To me, much of the satisfaction afforded by being Jewish is being part of an ancient chain of tradition of words and texts. Working with the words, and thereby with the personalities, thoughts, and feelings of centuries gives me a concrete sense of cultural rootedness and lends specific shape to my historical identity. I can perceive this feeling in dealing with the liturgy and other Jewish texts, as I can in those rituals that I voluntarily observe.

In fact, those texts keep me in touch with other roots besides the Jewish ones. We Jews who experience Judaism through texts are more in touch with the roots of Western civilization than most other people. We are among the vestiges of the Greco-Roman world. Hellenism intersected with Judaism from the time of the conquests of Alexander the Great: in antiquity itself, the age of our founding texts; in the Middle Ages, the age of Jewish philosophy; and in the age of modern science, beginning in the sixteenth century. So much of our culture was formed either as a reaction to Hellenism, as a defense against Hellenism, or as an adaptation of some aspect of Hellenism; every moment along the continuum of post-Hellenistic Judaism can be seen as a key to a larger world that we have to know in order to know who we are. Knowing that world helps us to know Judaism, but knowing Judaism can also help us to understand that world.

As for prayer: as prayer opens windows into a world of feeling and intuition, it links us to our past. When I read the Torah, I am a link in a very long chain that shapes my identity; it is a ritual of personal and communal self-definition, as well as a reenactment of the moment that marks the beginning of the Jewish people as recounted in Nehemiah, chapter 8, describing how the Torah was first read in public. I enunciate the words, and add my own meaning to the centuries of interpretation that preceded me; thus they serve both as a key to my own inner life and as a form of historical identification. When I serve as cantor on the High Holidays, I am the high priest and the representative of the whole history of medieval Hebrew liturgical poetry. In both cases, the historical continuity is directly related to the scholarship to which I have devoted my career.

And then there are the recurring themes of prayer—praise, thanksgiving, petition, and repentance. These themes reflect genuine feelings that are inside of us and that come to the surface whenever we enter into a meditative mood and think about life. Our prayers express them very well; our prayers are actually the overflow of these aspects of our inner life. The prayers of praise and thanksgiving that recur in infinite varieties in our liturgy from the Psalms through the medieval poets are an overflow of my gratitude. The prayer of petition is the overflow of my deficiency. The prayer of repentance is the overflow of my error, of my sin. The way traditional Jewish culture formulates these expressions is to imagine them as addressed to God, and that works every bit as well as the address to the beloved in a love poem. I do not need to do what my remote ancestors did—take the personification literally. To me, the personification is a literary device that is very effective in helping me to release the attitudes that are in me. That is a good thing to do, because these attitudes are the product of a religious impulse that one can experience even without having a concept of God: the unverifiable but overwhelming certainty that there exists a mysterious something that is larger than the world and larger than our minds, some mysterious force that underlies yet transcends the universe and interpenetrates all things, something to which we aspire to unite ourselves so that we may realize our potential to be greater than we are. The Jewish tradition provides a vast system of metaphors for dealing with that nearly universal sensation.

Furthermore, it seems to me that transcendence and immanence lead to the same point, for looking into myself, I see the mysteries of the universe just as when I look out to the farthest reaches of nature. The mystery of the heavens and the mystery of the mind seem to be the same. Solomon Ibn Gabirol, a medieval poet, put it very well:

> Three things there are together in my eye
> that keep the thought of Thee forever nigh.
> I think about Thy great and holy name
> whenever I look up and see the sky.
> My thoughts are roused to know how I was made
> seeing the earth's expanse where I abide.
> The musings of my mind, when I look inside—
> At all times, O my soul, bless Adonai.

The poet's vision moves from the most distant, most untouchable realm, the sky, which recalls God's lonely essence; to the earth, which, closer in, makes him meditate on the creation of material reality; and finally it reaches his own power of thought, which brings him back to the name of God. Innermost and outermost worlds are one.

My God does not issue orders. He is the transcendent mystery inside myself and beyond the world, the intimate beauty and horror that I occasionally glimpse directly but that I am more often sensible of only indirectly through doors and mirrors. These doors and mirrors include nature, human love, accomplishment, art. They all point toward the unseen vital force that drives us all, fills us with feelings, aspirations, yearnings, joys, and sorrows beyond what we can see or quantify or name. This core of life is God. Consciousness of this core is spirituality. Ordering one's life to make one conscious of that in a regular way is religion. Judaism is one such religion—the one I happen to have been born into and that I have cultivated.

Employing a craft to enable one to participate in this core of life is art. Prayer is one such craft. The great striving of the human spirit is the striving to see that core and to speak of that core. And no one speaks of it better for me than Walt Whitman, in a poem with which I shall close:

A noiseless patient spider—
I marked it where on a little promontory
it stood isolated,
marked how to explore the vacant vast surrounding,
that launched out filament, filament, filament
out of the self, ever unreeling them, ever tirelessly speeding them.
And you, O my soul, where you stand
surrounded, detached, in measureless oceans of space
ceaselessly using, venturing, throwing, seeking
the spheres to connect them
till the bridge you will need be formed,
till the ductile anchor hold,
till the gossamer thread you fling catch somewhere,
O my soul.

I. GORDON TUCKER

Gordon Tucker is the rabbi of Temple Israel Center of White Plains, New York and Chairman of the Board of Directors of the Masorti Foundation. He is also a former dean of the Seminary's Rabbinical School (1984–92) and Assistant Professor of Philosophy there, where he continues to teach. He was ordained by the Seminary in 1975 and completed a Ph.D. in philosophy at Princeton University in 1979. Author of

Heavenly Torah, a translation of, and commentary on, Heschel's book on classical rabbinic theories of revelation, Tucker is well known both for his keen and creative mind, his deep fund of Jewish and general knowledge, and his warm spirit.

In this section's article, Tucker does not intend to lay out his own particular theory of Jewish law but rather to justify the structure by which the Conservative movement makes its Jewish legal decisions. He does that through a deep analysis of the legal and theological roots of the system. Most of the Conservative theorists explored above—those that see Jewish law as binding—decide matters of Jewish law as individual rabbis and, for some, as members of the Committee on Jewish Law and Standards, which formally approved Tucker's paper. That makes this justification of the method used to make such decisions a fitting way to complete these two chapters on Conservative theories of law since 1970.

A long-standing member of the Committee on Jewish Law and Standards (CJLS), Tucker undertakes in this article to justify the structural feature of that committee that allows for different, but equally valid rulings on any given issue. He does that to fend off both of two contradictory approaches that have been proposed within the movement: (1) that if a central committee exists within the movement to deal with matters of Jewish law, it should be strictly advisory so as to preserve the ultimate authority of the local rabbi; and, conversely, (2) that when the Committee has ruled on an issue, all rabbis of the movement should be bound to rule in accordance with an approach that the Committee has validated. Tucker instead charts a middle path, the one embodied in the structure of the Committee since the 1985 revision of the Rabbinical Assembly Constitution.[13]

Specifically, he argues that in some, few areas rabbis should indeed be bound by decisions of the Committee—namely, when the Committee (and, later, the annual convention of the Rabbinical Assembly) adopts a Standard of Rabbinic Practice. Rabbis or synagogues that violate a Standard are subject to expulsion from, respectively, the Rabbinical Assembly or the United Synagogue of Conservative Judaism. As of this writing, only three such Standards have been adopted: one prohibits Conservative rabbis from officiating at the marriage of a Jew to a non-Jew, one requires a Jewish writ of divorce (a *get*) before a Jew who has been married and divorced in civil law may remarry in Jewish law, and one defines Jewish identity as a function of matrilineal descent or halakhic conversion. Many, many more areas of Jewish practice are widely shared within the Conservative movement, but only those three have been embedded in Standards with the authority to constitute grounds for expulsion if violated.

In all other matters, Tucker argues, rabbis are and should be free to accept the decisions of the Committee or to act on their own authority in choosing to do something else. Rabbis who make a decision about Jewish law in response to questions of individuals or for the institution they serve in accordance with a validated decision of the Committee can rightfully claim not only their own individual authority as a rabbi (and perhaps the rabbi of that institution) but also the authority of the CJLS in supporting their judgment. Rabbis who act either in absence of a decision of the Committee or contrary to one cannot, of course, claim that the CJLS supports their ruling. In practice, most Conservative rabbis abide by decisions of the Committee when it has ruled on a given topic, and that empirical fact and the expectation that normally rabbis will follow CJLS rulings give the movement much of its coherence and identity. Those factors also make the decisions of the CJLS more than merely advisory. Nevertheless, Tucker strongly defends the right of individual rabbis to take a stand on their own. That prerogative has explicitly been granted to individual rabbis since the Rabbinical Assembly's rules governing the Committee changed in 1985, but Tucker demonstrates that that should be the case not only to allow for pluralism and the practical realities of the movement, but also to continue one side of a long debate within the rabbinic tradition with regard to the *theology* underlying this practice.

Specifically, Tucker traces two streams within classical rabbinic literature. According to both, the law is determined by the majority of judges. For one stream, though, the decisions of the majority did not allow for any dissenting practices and, in fact, led to sanctions for those who disobeyed ("majoritarianism with authoritarianism"); for the other, though, while the majority determined the decision for the community, individual rabbis retained the authority to rule and act otherwise. As Tucker points out, these two distinctive rabbinic positions reflect not only a matter of differences in legal procedure, but also differences in theology. For the former, "Religious truth was determinate, and it was determined by the court's majority. From that view followed the sanctions invoked by Rabban Gamliel and all of his intellectual successors." For the latter, though, "majority decisions are a best approximation to a truth which God has decided to leave indeterminate to humans, and are thus both the culminations of rounds of debate and dissension, and the preludes to further such rounds." According to this group, anyone who follows the majority can rest assured that he or she is obeying God as far as the majority of rabbis understands God's command on any particular issue, but the majority's decisions "do not . . . forbid or prevent individuals who can investigate on their own, and who can study, understand, and critique those very decisions, from coming to their own conclusions, following their reasons and their consciences." This view, in other words, is much more humble in its assertions about what we human beings can know about God's will: The majority may define what most learned Jews think is appropriate, but they may all be wrong, for we are all, after all, human beings with limited human knowledge. Permission for individual rabbis to rule otherwise, then, does not rest on the practical fact that the majority's decisions cannot always be enforced, or even on the virtue of tolerance for other opinions; in Jewish sources it rests rather on the recognition of our human inability to know with certainty what God wants of us. Here we have a persuasive justification for the majoritarianism without authoritarianism that we seek—and that characterizes the relationship between the CJLS and the individuals and institutions of the Conservative movement.

Some, however, would give a utilitarian argument for demanding obedience to the majority's position. They would say that even if we can theologically justify both a majority view and individual minority views, we should require adherence to the majority's rulings in order to maintain the unity of the Jewish people. Admitting other positions as authoritative for those who find them persuasive, this argument goes, would fragmentize the Jewish community.

In answering this utilitarian argument, Tucker invokes the argument provided by the legal philosopher Robert Cover (who, incidentally, was a committed and informed Conservative Jew) in favor of the American system of courts, where federal, state, and municipal courts have differing jurisdictions, and federal courts in different regions of the country may produce conflicting rulings. To paraphrase a rabbinic source, "How can one study Torah under such circumstances?!" That is, how can Americans have a coherent system of law with all this diversity of opinion? Cover understands the risks to the coherence, unity, and clarity of such a system, but he points out that a regimented, unified system would sacrifice other goods—specifically, appropriateness to local circumstances and creativity: "The multiplicity of centers [for generating norms] means an innovation is more likely to be tried and correspondingly less likely to be wholly embraced. The two effects dampen both momentum and inertia." As Tucker applies this idea to Jewish law, the delicate balance between the CJLS and the individual rabbi in the Conservative movement "allows for religious and halakhic creativity locally, where the need for it first arises, and where its authenticity can best be evaluated. This is a precious resource indeed, and it should not be lightly dismissed for the sake of an elusive 'uniformity' which will disappoint tomorrow those whom it satisfies today."

Tucker thus provides a thoughtful argument for what may seem to some as too loose and to others as too limiting a structure to make Jewish legal decisions and to implement them. We need *both* a coordinated body to make decisions for the movement *and* ways to preserve pluralism within a broad spectrum of Jewish practice, for both theological and practical reasons. Furthermore, one of two significant streams of classical rabbinic opinion recognized the same needs and the same theological limitations of our knowledge of God's will and sought to create a similar structure. The system in place in the Conservative movement, then, is not only theologically and practically wise, but historically authentic.

Still, this system comes with its problems. First, there is, after all, another stream within Jewish sources, the one that Tucker dubs "majoritarianism with authoritarianism," and so at best Tucker's defense of the Conservative movement's structure represents a choice of one classical rabbinic theology over another. Those who make the other choice not only have rabbinic sources to support them, but they also gain a stronger sense of clarity, unity, and authority: There is, on this view, only one correct way to interpret and follow God's will.

The problem with the authoritarian alternative, of course, is exactly what drives Tucker and the Conservative movement to prefer the other approach—namely, how can a human being know for sure what God wants of us now? Even if one accepts the Torah as the definitive announcement of God's will, we human beings must still *interpret* it to determine what we think it means, and so from the very beginning there is a critical, human—and therefore fallible—element in the way we decipher God's will. But the problem is worse. The Torah itself, after all, asserts that God sometimes changes His mind,[14] and so even if we are certain about what God wanted of us at the time of the giving of the Torah, how do we know that that is what God wants of us now? After all, we would *expect* a good and knowing God to tailor divine commands to the realities of our time, just as any good human legislator would do. Finally, as Tucker says, the strain of rabbinic thought on which the Conservative movement's methodology is based preserves a degree of flexibility, relevance, creativity, and pluralism far greater than what is available to those who believe in the authoritarian line of thinking. Thus, as I pointed out when discussing Joel Roth's theory in the previous chapter, Jewish law, like Anglo-American law and in contrast to European Continental law, has historically sacrificed clarity and deductive certainty for truth, an accurate depiction of human life, and relevance, and the Conservative movement's approach follows that historically Jewish choice. In doing so, it has already fostered pluralism while interpreting and applying Jewish law in new ways, in particular with regard to the place of women in Jewish law

and society. Its structure promises to provide both continuity and necessary innovation in the present and future as well, as the CJLS deals with
many new moral and social problems to make Jewish law a source of
meaning and guidance for Jews in all aspects of life.

*[Editor's note: For those who do not understand Hebrew, I have
translated the Hebrew terms that Rabbi Tucker uses in the middle
of sentences but not the sources he quotes because he summarizes
the import of each source before or after he cites it. In addition,
the reader will find translations of some of the sources he cites in
chapter 2 above; notes in the text will refer the reader to the
specific page where the translation can be found.]*

A Principled Defense of the Current Structure and Status of the CJLS*

GORDON TUCKER

INTRODUCTION

Every so often in the history of the Rabbinical Assembly, concerns are
raised about the structure of the Committee on Jewish Law and Standards (henceforth: CJLS), and whether it adequately serves both the ideology of the movement and the needs of the RA's members. Such
discussions surrounded its creation in 1927, its restructuring in 1948,
and various changes in its by-laws. Indeed, my own earliest, and still
most vivid memory of a spirited exchange on the floor of the RA Convention, was the heated debate at the 1976 Convention, during which
members presented a resolution which stated, among other things, that
the CJLS, as then structured, "weakens the authority of all rabbis,
whether the individual rabbi agrees or disagrees with the majority decision of the Committee. . . . In this way, the Mara D'atra becomes less
and less his own congregation's interpreter of the classical sources of the
Jewish tradition."[1] The resolution called for the CJLS to be dissolved,
and to be replaced by a "Panel on Jewish Law," which would have had
the authority to respond only to individual rabbis who had sent in

*In *Responsa 1991–2000 of the Committee on Jewish Law and Stan-
dards of the Conservative Movement*, Kassel Abelson and David J.
Fine, eds. (New York: Rabbinical Assembly, 2002), pp. 759–772.

queries, and which would not have produced published, authoritative responsa. Although the resolution was defeated, it did enjoy some significant and vocal support. It is perhaps worth remembering that the opposition to the central authority of the CJLS in that instance, and in other similar ones, came from members dissatisfied with what they considered liberalizing decisions of the Committee. To them, the authority of the מרא דאתרא [local rabbi] meant not legal atomism and chaos, but their right to issue פסקי הלכה [legal decisions] in accordance with their own consciences and religious convictions, taking the histories and needs of their communities into account.[2] There was then, and I believe still is, a strong majority in the RA that believes in the importance of a central Law Committee with significant scholarly and moral authority in the movement, and which simultaneously is committed to a certain inalienable authority that each local rabbi has in the area of halakhah. There is surely a tension here, and the rules of the CJLS have, in their fluctuation over the years, reflected that tension. But the argument of this paper will be not only that the CJLS structure accurately mirrors the political and professional dynamics of the Conservative rabbinate, but that it also conforms best to our religious convictions, and indeed to corresponding tensions evident in many, diverse classical sources on halakhic authority.

To be more specific, it is this conception of the role and the authority of the CJLS that I will be defending here:

> The CJLS is the central body in the Conservative movement for halakhic discussion and decision making. Its authority derives from the assent of the members of the Rabbinical Assembly that there should be a central body composed of members who have significant expertise in Jewish law, and who are willing and able to devote a significant amount of time to researching, discussing, and debating halakhic matters that affect Conservative Rabbis and the movement generally. The CJLS thus brings a much-needed consolidation and focusing of legal opinion to what otherwise would be an overly decentralized and chaotic field. For this reason, the CJLS can be said to be the halakhic voice of the movement as a whole, and it is thus undesirable and inconsistent with Rabbinical Assembly aims for there to be other law committees or panels that publicly issue responsa in the name of Conservative Judaism. (An exception to this observation is the authority explicitly granted to the Masorti movement's panel to issue responsa on דברים התלוים בארץ [matters unique to the Land of Israel].) Because it is a body that seeks to coalesce judgment around particular halakhic opinions, and not simply to give voice to individually held positions, it is right and proper that six members of the CJLS be required to define an authoritative opinion. Because it is a body that is ultimately here to provide service and guidance to Rabbinical Assembly members, it is also right and proper that authoritative opinions not be categorized by the number of votes that they received, and that they not be binding on Rabbinical Assembly members in a coercive

sense, but rather only in the sense that we are bound by our covenant to one another to give extraordinary weight to CJLS responsa in reaching our own legal decisions. Should a Rabbinical Assembly member choose, upon study and consideration, not to follow any CJLS position on a given matter, he or she would thus be unable to claim any authority or backing for that position from the CJLS, a "sanction" which in some circumstances could be substantial, in others not. Some constituencies of the movement, such as the United Synagogue, can choose and have chosen to bind themselves to follow only authoritative CJLS opinions. And finally, the CJLS may, as a legislative initiator, propose to the Convention a Standard of Rabbinic Practice, which would coercively apply to all Rabbinical Assembly members. The plenum of the Convention actually enacts the Standard. Thus, it could be said fairly that halakhic authority in our movement is shared. It ultimately resides with the Mara D'atra, though by covenant the CJLS in practice serves as the authoritative guide for legal decisions, and by Rabbinical Assembly rules, the CJLS and the plenum share the legislative power to enact the Standards that define, in part, our legal boundaries.

And now to the defense.

MAJORITARIANISM AND AUTHORITARIANISM

The CJLS operates on what I shall call a "modified majoritarian principle" for which there is, apparently, no real precedent in pre-modern Jewish life. It is a "modified" majoritarianism because, as is well known, we do not have "majority" and "minority" opinions as such, and even positions that do not enjoy a majority, or even a plurality, on the CJLS can be authoritative Committee pronouncements. Yet it is majoritarian in the sense that votes are taken, and CJLS rules define a threshold (six votes) below which opinions are דעות יחידים [opinions of individuals] and are denied Committee sanction. We will turn our attention to the CJLS's characteristic modifications of majoritarianism a bit later. For now, we must focus on majoritarianism in any form as a Jewish religious construct.

The adherence in Rabbinic Judaism to the majoritarian principle is among its most basic postulates. It is classically formulated in any number of texts, and for our present purposes two of these will illustrate the point sufficiently:

1. ולמה מזכירין דברי היחיד בין המרובין הואיל ואין הלכה אלא כדברי המרובין.[3]

2. רבנן פליגי עילווך ויחיד ורבים הלכה כרבים או דילמא רבנן כוותך סבירי להו.[4]

Both of these texts incidentally make it quite clear that the issue of majoritarianism is inseparable in Rabbinic Judaism from the equally important matter of the authority of the rabbinic court. For the text in עדויות [Eduyot] goes on to restrict severely the circumstances under which a court's rulings may be overturned, and the text in ברכות [Berakhot] implies that Rabban Gamaliel's sons would have disregarded their father's ruling (on the latest hour for reciting the evening שמע [Shema]) had a majority of his contemporaries ruled differently. We shall return to this connection presently. For now, it is clear that the Rabbinic view of the law allowed for it to be determined by a majority vote, and that was quite a stunning departure from the biblical view that God's law is mediated through prophets or oracular devices, which are assumed to be unambiguous and with respect to which majority views are irrelevant. The Rabbis knew they were doing something quite different from what prophets had done, and that in some sense their own enterprise was incompatible with prophecy and the direct divine authority it claimed. Consider this passage from the Sifra:

אלה המצות: אין נביא רשאי לחדש עוד דבר מעתה[5]

which retroactively nullified the innovative power of any prophet after Moses, in apparent flat contradiction of the plain intent of Deuteronomy 18.[6] Even more to the point, Maimonides, in the introduction to his commentary on the Mishnah, states what he believes to be the fundamental difference between rabbinic activity and the activity of all prophets other than Moses (who is referred to here as הנביא [the prophet]):

ומי שלא שמע בו פירוש מפי הנביא ע"ה... הוציא דינים בסברות במדות
השלש עשרה... שהתורה נדרשת בהם... וכשהיתה נופלת המחלוקת היו
הולכים אחרי הרוב כמו שנאמר אחרי רבים להטות. ודע שהנבואה אינה
מועילה בפירושי התורה ובהוצאת ענפי המצות בשלש עשרה מדות אבל
מה שיעשה יהושע ופנחס בענין העיון ובסברא הוא שיעשה רבינא ורב
אשי.[7]

In fact, not only is prophecy obsolete, one may not even legitimately think of reviving it:

וכן... שאמר בדין מדיני התורה שה' צוה לו שהדין כך הוא והלכה כדברי
פלוני. הרי זה נביא השקר ויחנק–אע"פ שעשה אות–שהרי בא להכחיש
התורה שאמרה לא בשמים היא.[8]

And yet, despite the ideology that saw prophecy as a dead institution of the past, some Rabbis, certainly, saw themselves as the *successors* of the prophets:

אמר רבי אבדימי דמן חיפה מיום שחרב בית המקדש ניטלה נבואה מן
הנביאים וניתנה לחכמים. אטו חכם לאו נביא הוא? הכי קאמר אע"פ שניטלה
מן הנביאים מן החכמים לא ניטלה. אמר אמימר וחכם עדיף מנביא.[9]

[Editor's note: This passage from Bava Batra 12a is translated on p. 27 above.]

These are strong and bold statements attributed in this text to two different אמוראים [amora'im, talmudic rabbis] of different places and different generations. And indeed, it has many echoes in talmudic and later rabbinic literature. This has important implications. Among other things, it means that the negation of prophecy did not necessarily mean that the rabbinic court would forego the authority that the prophets enjoyed. Rabban Gamaliel claimed precisely that kind of authority on a number of fa-

mous occasions, and although he attributed what some viewed as his
high-handedness to utilitarian social/political motives,[10] others after him
went beyond utilitarianism to make stronger claims about the majoritarianism of the rabbinic court. Nahmanides, for example, in his comment on
Deut. 17:11—לא תסור מן הדבר אשר יגידו לך ימין ושמאל ["Do not veer
from what they (the priest or judge) tell you to the right or left"]—began
with Rabban Gamaliel's utilitarian justification for the domination of the
majority, but then went on to a more metaphysical claim:

כי על דעת שלהם הוא נתן לנו התורה אפילו יהיה בעיניך כמחליף הימין
בשמאל וכל שכן שיש לך לחשוב שהם אומרים על ימין שהוא ימין כי רוח
השם על משרתי מקדשו ולא יעזוב את חסידיו לעולם נשמרו מן הטעות
ומן המכשול.[11]

Here we have the claim that there is a Divine Providence which warrants
that the majority of the court will invariably be right, and thus a justification for the court taking on the authority of the prophet, to the point
of the most severe sanctions against those who would defy its rulings.

The point of the texts brought in the previous paragraph is that it
would be a mistake to celebrate the Rabbis' majoritarianism as a clear
triumph of democracy or decentralization of religious authority; on the
contrary, their majoritarianism operated within a clearly defined elite
circle, and the court constituted by that circle was endowed with the
authority of the priest or the prophet, in that failure to submit to the
discipline of its rulings was punishable by death.[12] The Rabbis may
have opened up the univocal and uncompromising biblical 'כה אמר ה
["So said the Lord"] into a process of debate and vote, but they still operated under a very authoritarian rubric. Once the debate and the vote
were over, dissent was, at least theoretically, to be suppressed. Whatever
"democratization" was inherent in the move from prophet to published
text was all but nullified by the rigid authority claimed by the majority
on the basis of the Deuteronomic לא תסור ["Do not veer"].[13]

Such, at least, was the theory. A closer consideration of the issue,
and examination of some of the relevant texts, reveals, however, that
majoritarianism was not necessarily and inexorably bound up with the
authoritarianism symbolized by Rabban Gamaliel. For some in the
Rabbinic world, the break with prophecy was more complete and
more fundamental.

To understand this other mindset, I think it important to reflect on at least one aspect of the history of the verse in Exod. 23:2:
לא תהיה אחרי רבים לרעות ולא תענה על ריב לנטות אחרי רבים להטות ["You
shall neither side with the multitude (or mighty) to do wrong—you shall
not give perverse testimony in a dispute so as to pervert it in favor of the
multitude (or mighty)"]. Biblically, the meaning of the verse is, after all,
fairly clear: "don't follow a majority when it is wrong." And certainly,
the biblical view was that although a majority may have rejected, e.g.,
Jeremiah's instructions condemning the formation of alliances against
Babylonia, Judeans loyal to God were expected to follow the prophet's
"minority" view. A referendum, even if conducted solely among the
prophetic elite, would have been irrelevant to the biblical mind.

Rabbinically, however, something unusual and striking happens to this very clear verse. In Mishnah Sanhedrin 1:6, for example, it is taken for granted that אחרי רבים להטות ["to pervert it in favor of the multitude"] means "follow the majority," the exact opposite of its plain meaning. The understanding of the phrase לא בשמים היא ["It is not in heaven"], attributed to רב ירמיה [Rabbi Jeremiah] (oh, the irony of the name here!) in בבא מציעא נ"ט: [Bava Metzia 59b] goes so far as to say that the majoritarian view is a constitutional principle by which God is, therefore, also bound. Now, why in biblical Judaism was it so clear that a majority should not necessarily be followed, and why in Rabbinic Judaism was it so clear that a majority must be followed? The reason, I believe, is this: from the point of view of biblical Judaism, there is a truth, quite independent of the majority, that can be gotten through a prophet, or perhaps through the priestly אורים ותמים [breastplate]. From the point of view of Rabbinic Judaism, however, the statement כה אמר ה' ["So said the Lord"] is constitutionally forbidden, as much as would be a law that outlawed political dissent in Massachusetts. Rabbinic Judaism, in this understanding, is about the notion that we can't get religious truth directly. The majoritarianism of the Rabbis thus can be understood as flowing from an epistemological agnosticism, a conviction that what David Hartman has called the "immediacy" of the biblical period[14] is forever gone. And thus, the new reading and use of אחרי רבים להטות ["to pervert it in favor of the multitude"] and such well-worn phrases as אלו ואלו דברי אלקים חיים ["These and those are the words of the living God"] must be seen for what they are: dramatic changes in the very definition of religious truth.

From this point of view, majoritarianism is not a matter of גזרת הכתוב [what a biblical verse demands], a new form of quasi-prophetic authority, but is rather born of a coming to terms with what truth means in the post-biblical and pre-messianic condition of epistemological indeterminism. It is our best tool for getting at religious truth, and thus the debates that precede the vote, and even the dissents that follow it, are integral parts of that quest for truth. This is no mere speculation; it is, in fact, reflected in a variety of rabbinic texts that decidedly do not see majoritarianism as being inevitably wedded to authoritarianism. One such text will suffice for the moment. It appears in the Palestinian Talmud, Tractate Sanhedrin, as a comment on the Mishnah which states the general principle that in both monetary and capital cases, the majority is to be followed:

אמר רבי ינאי אילו ניתנה התורה חתוכה לא היתה לרגל עמידה מה
טעם וידבר ה' אל משה אמר לפניו רבונו של עולם הודיעיני היאך היא
ההלכה אמר לו אחרי רבים להטות רבו המזכין זכו רבו המחייבין חייבו
כדי שתהיה התורה נדרשת מ"ט פנים טמא ומ"ט פנים טהור.[15]

[Editor's note: This passage from Y. Sanhedrin 22a is translated on p. 31 above.]

Were it not for the last phrase, this text might also have been interpreted in such a way that the majoritarian principle was one dictated by גזרת הכתוב [what the biblical verse demands], and thus consistent with a Rabban Gamaliel-type exercise of coercive power. But

כדי שתהיה התורה נדרשת ["so that the Torah can be interpreted"] seems
to say more than that, and its significance was picked up by Moses
Margoliot in his commentary on the Yerushalmi:

הודיעני היאך ההלכה: שלא יהיה בה ספק. א"ל זה אי אפשר. אלא
אחרי רבים להטות וכו' מפני שהתורה צריכה שתהיה נדרשת במ"ט
פנים לכאן ולכאן ואם אני מגלה לך ההלכה שוב לא תהיה נדרשת
בהרבה פנים.[16]

The פני משה [P'nei Moshe] is making the following point: If there is
any גזרת הכתוב [what the biblical verse demands] operative here at all,
it inheres only in God's decision not to allow religious truth to be unambiguous and univocal. But given that decision (which is, like all of
God's decisions, ultimately inscrutable), the majority enjoys no pro-
vidential guarantee, nor any special metaphysical status. It is simply
that the way, the best way, to approximate religious truth ever more
closely is to foster the debates out of which a majority emerges. The
way in which פני משה [P'nei Moshe] here draws out the language of
the ירושלמי [Jerusalem Talmud] makes it further clear that diversity in
debate, and even a certain indeterminacy, is "good" for Torah—it is
the way in which Torah should be pursued. And the truly remarkable
thing about the ירושלמי [Jerusalem Talmud] here is that it retrojects this
all the way back to Mount Sinai. Unlike the ספרא [Sifra] and the רמב"ם
[passage by Maimonides] at which we looked earlier,[17] Moses himself
(whom רמב"ם [Maimonides] had called הנביא ["the prophet"]) is, according to this text, already in the post-prophetic age!

We have thus seen that there are two possible readings to the majoritarianism by which the decisions of the rabbinic courts have always
been characterized. One of these is that the "procedures" changed, as it
were, in post-biblical times. That is, the prophetic revelation was replaced with the sittings and votings of rabbinic courts, but the metaphysical and epistemological status of the pronouncements remained
essentially the same. Religious truth was determinate, and it was determined by the court's majority. From that view followed the sanctions invoked by Rabban Gamaliel and all of his intellectual successors.[18] But
there is another reading of the rabbinic majoritarianism, which we have
begun to see emerge. That is the interpretation under which majority decisions are a best approximation to a truth which God has decided to
leave indeterminate to humans, and are thus both the culminations of
rounds of debate and dissension, and the preludes to further such
rounds. We shall now spell this alternative view out just a bit more.

MAJORITARIANISM
WITHOUT AUTHORITARIANISM

The theory under which all associated with the Rabbinic community
owed unquestioning allegiance and obedience to the majority decisions of
the court certainly did not operate unexceptionally. It was not just pivotal
figures of the early period, such as Rabbis Eliezer and Yehoshua, who reg-
istered dissents and were said to have paid prices for those dissents. It

seems from other texts, about later Sages, that the habits of asserting independence from majority decisions persisted. Consider an account given in
the ירושלמי [Jerusalem Talmud]. The Mishnah states that:

אין נוטעין ואין מבריכין ואין מרכיבין[19] ערב שביעית פחות מל' יום לפני
ראש השנה ואם נטע או הבריך או הרכיב יעקור.

Now the ירושלמי [Jerusalem Talmud] tells the following story:

לא עקר פירותיו מה הן? רבי בא רבי לא הוון יתבין בצור אתא אתא עובדא
קומיהון. הורי רבי לא ישפכו פירותיו. א"ר בא אני לא נמניתי עמהן
בעלייה.[20]

The context makes it clear that a vote had been taken to add the additional and extraordinary sanction that if one (a) had violated what was
a protective injunction pertaining to ערב שביעית [the thirty days before
the beginning of the sabbatical year], and (b) had also neglected to
obey the sanction that required uprooting the sapling planted during
the extended protective period, that one also (c) had to dispose of the
fruit of such a tree when it was matured. But the text also makes it
clear that רבי בא [Rabbi Ba], not having been part of the voting body,
would not agree to such a proliferation of גזרות [restrictive decrees],
and felt free to rule on his own, as he saw fit.[21]

What makes the behavior attributed to רבי בא [Rabbi Ba] and others so striking to us is the fact that the juridical authority claimed by
the Rabbis under לא תסור ["Do not veer"] seems so strong.[22] Let us be
specific about what a majoritarianism without authoritarianism must
overcome, in terms of the textual tradition. One of the most famous of
all the authoritarian texts is the one from the ספרי [Sifrei], constituting
a comment on Deut. 17:11:

לא תסור מן הדבר אשר יגידו לך ימין ושמאל–אפילו מראים בעיניך
על שמאל שהיא ימין ועל ימין שהיא שמאל שמע להם.[23]

*[Editor's note: This text from Sifrei Deuteronomy is trans-
lated on p. 29 above.]*

The impact of this comment is potentially enormous, and it seems unequivocally to support the idea that the decisions of the rabbinic court
have been endowed with a special status that transcends human reason,
and therefore commands human assent.[24] What complicates the situation, and opens up alternative understandings, is an apparently diametrically opposed baraita which appears in the ירושלמי [Jerusalem
Talmud]. It reads as follows:

יכול אם יאמרו לך על ימין שהוא שמאל ועל שמאל שהוא ימין תשמע
להם? ת"ל ללכת ימין ושמאל–שיאמרו לך על ימין שהוא ימין ועל
שמאל שהוא שמאל.[25]

*[Editor's note: This text from Y. Horayot 1:1 is translated on
p. 29 above.]*

Many efforts have been made to harmonize and reconcile the baraitot
in the ספרי [Sifrei] and the ירושלמי [Jerusalem Talmud]. The one that

will be of most interest to us here, not only because of its persuasiveness, but also because it comes from a rabbi of the modern era, is that of David Zvi Hoffmann. Hoffmann notes that there are two verses in Deuteronomy that give a command with the words לא תסור ["Do not veer"]—in 17:11 (the one we have looked at already), and in 28:14 ולא תסור מכל הדברים אשר אנכי מצוה אתכם ימין ושמאל ["Do not veer to the right or to the left from any of the commandments that I enjoin upon you"]. In 28:14, the word אנכי ["I"] is spoken by God, and therefore Hoffmann claims that we have here two potentially conflicting commands. One commands unswerving obedience to the rabbinic court (at least as the Rabbis understood 17:11), and the other commands unswerving obedience to God. That Hoffmann recognizes these as a potential conflict already demonstrates that he rejects the metaphysical view of the authority of a rabbinic majority (for the metaphysical view identifies that majority with the unitary will of God). Moreover, Hoffmann says that according to 17:11 (and thus the ספרי [Sifrei]), one who wishes to follow the court without doing any study or investigation of one's own is fulfilling religious obligations fully. Indeed, Deuteronomy and the ספרי [Sifrei] state the imperative so strongly in order to give lenient decisions of the court greater authority: "The לא תסור ["Do not veer"] had to be pronounced absolutely for the High Court as, otherwise, it would not have any validity, as many an individual would have denied recognition to a decision that rendered things easier out of scruples of conscience."[26] However, one who chooses to investigate and study further, and who comes to the conclusion that the majority of the court is mistaken, must reckon with the לא תסור ["Do not veer"] of Deut. 28:14, which commands unswerving obedience to the commands of God. The court has no unbreakable monopoly on legal competence. Here are Hoffmann's strong and far-reaching words: "But on the other hand, so says the Baraita of the Yerushalmi, the second לא תסור ["Do not veer"] has been pronounced for the word of God with all the more emphasis and absolutely. *For the Torah has been given as an inheritance directly to the whole community of Jacob, and no edict of the authority is able to delete even one word from the Torah. . . .* In this case there is thus a conflict between the two לא תסור ["Do not veer"] and the individual has to decide for one of them."[27] For Hoffmann, the issue was clear. The majoritarianism of Rabbinic law is not גזרת הכתוב [what the biblical verse demands], which every individual, no matter who he or she is, is obligated to submit to. It is rather a divinely sanctioned accommodation to the indeterminacy of religious truth (also divinely ordained, according to the ירושלמי סנהדרין [the passage from Sanhedrin in the Jerusalem Talmud] and the פני משה [P'nei Moshe] cited above, n. 15 and n. 16). The court's majority provides for the promulgation of the best consensus (of the community which looks to the court) as to what God's commands are. Once promulgated, those decisions are all that members of the community need follow to remain in good standing and good conscience. They do not, however, forbid or prevent individuals who can investigate on their own, and who can study, understand,

and critique those very decisions, from coming to their own conclusions, following their reasons and their consciences.[28]

Here we have a persuasive justification for the majoritarianism without authoritarianism that we seek—and that characterizes the relationship between the CJLS and the individuals and institutions of our movement. It is significant that this defense can not only be extracted from the classical texts (both normative and narrative), but is also explicitly and forcefully given in the writings of a traditional halakhist of the modern era—one who understood well what the forces of emancipation had irrevocably done to make a rigid, centralized, halakhic authoritarianism unwise. Indeed, it was not just Hoffmann in Germany who articulated this. For roughly at the same time that Hoffmann made his argument cited above, a similar interpretation of the baraita in the ספרי [Sifrei] was given in Eastern Europe by Naphtali Zvi Yehudah Berlin, the נצי"ב [Netziv, an acronym for his name] of Volozhin. The נצי"ב [Netziv] understands a comment in the שאילתות דרב אחאי גאון [She'iltot of Rav Aḥai Gaon] to be a reaction to a peculiarity in the text of Deut. 17:10. In that verse we are told: ועשית על פי הדבר אשר יגידו לך מן המקום ההוא אשר יבחר ה' ["You shall do what they tell you at the place that the Lord has chosen"]; and in 17:11 we are told: על פי התורה אשר יורוך... תעשה לא תסור מן הדבר אשר יגידו לך ימין ושמאל ["You shall act according to the instruction (Torah) they teach you. Do not veer from what they tell you to the right or left."]. Here is the נצי"ב's [Netziv's] commentary:

ומקרא דעל פי התורה וגו' מיותר שהרי כבר אמר ועשית על פי הדבר וגו' ותו מאי הוא על פי הדבר ומאי הוא על פי התורה? משום הכי מפרש דאמר משה לפני המקום יתברך בזמן שלא יהיה המקום אשר יבחר ה' קיים מה יעשו? וא"ל על פי התורה וגו'. נמצא דבזמן שבהמ"ק קיים מה שיאמרו הסנהדרין אפילו שלא בהוכחה מכללי התורה ישמעו. אבל בזמן שאין בהמ"ק קיים דוקא על פי התורה.[29]

[Editor's translation: The verse, "According to the instruction" (Deut. 17:11) is superfluous, for he [Moses] already said "And you shall do what they tell you, etc." (Deut. 17:10). Moreover, what is the meaning of (the two different phrases), "what they tell you" and "according to the instruction"? Therefore one can explain that Moses said before God: In an era when the "place that the Lord has chosen" (i.e., the Temple in Jerusalem) no longer exists, what should one do? God said to him: "according to the instruction..." Thus when the Temple exists, whatever the Sanhedrin says, even without proof based on the principles of the Torah, they should obey; but when the Temple does not exist, only "according to the Torah" (that is, only if they link their instruction to the Torah should the people follow it).]

That is, a metaphysical aura may have surrounded the court at the time when the Temple stood, but that is all (safely?) in the past now. For the נצי"ב [Netziv], normal rabbinic practice demanded that reasons be given for rulings of the court (for he understands the otherwise superfluous word תורה [Torah] as "reasoned teaching" rather than as "pronouncement"). For those who had the competence to evaluate the court's proceedings, the court's authority extended no further than the persuasiveness of its arguments. The נצי"ב [Netziv] underscored this even more vividly in his commentary on the Torah:

אבל בזמן שאין בהמ"ק קיים אזי דוקא על פי התורה אשר יורוך... וכל
הדרשות אמת והתורה כפטיש יפוצץ סלע.[30]

[Editor's translation: But in a time when the Temple no longer stands, then one must obey specifically what they (the rabbis of the time) teach you . . . and all their interpretations are true, and the Torah is "like a hammer smashing a rock" (Jeremiah 23:29). Editor's note: See p. 30 above.]

We need no better summary of this position than that.

In order to conclude this section, a few words should be said about the utilitarian argument (attributed, as we've seen, to Rabban Gamaliel himself) that, irrespective of what one believes about the metaphysical significance of the rabbinic court, obedience to central authority serves to prevent undesirable fragmentation and sectarianism in the community. It has already been noted above that Hoffmann's and Berlin's endorsements of the right of the individual to diverge from the court's rulings on the basis of conscientious study and consideration are significant in the light of the fact that they are both nineteenth century, post-emancipation halakhists. Indeed, the contemporary Jewish world is marked not only by an irrevocable religious decentralization, but also by theological views which would seem to make the disutility of strongly sanctioned religious authority outweigh whatever gain might be expected from the point of view of promoting halakhic uniformity. Now a structure marked by a central interpretive body which is paralleled, and in some sense rivaled, by the halakhic authority of each individual מרא דאתרא [local rabbi] is not unlike other familiar structures with parallel or overlapping jurisdictions. The late Robert Cover gave a principled defense of the jurisdictional complexities, redundancies, and rivalries in the American federal system against those who have argued for the desirability of a more uniform, linear flow of legal authority. It is an instructive defense for our purposes. For like those who have criticized the Conservative movement's legal structure (with local decisors somewhat beholden to, but still independent of, the CJLS) as incoherent and haphazard, there have always been those who have looked at concurrent and overlapping jurisdictions in the United States as "an accident of history and a . . . malformed jurisdictional anomaly that we have endured, but not loved, for so long."[31]

But there is another way to view such complexities, argued Cover; not as a "dysfunctional relic," but rather as a product of a coherent evolution, which persists because of its strong functionality. He gave a number of interesting and compelling defenses of the maintenance of rival jurisdictions, but perhaps the most intriguing one—and one we would do well to heed—concerns the benefits of legal innovation that jurisdictional complexity and decentralization opens up:

> There may be with respect to many matters a potential for a unitary national norm. . . . However, more typically we rely upon a regime of polycentric norm articulation in which state organs and lower federal courts enjoy a great deal of legislative autonomy. This multiplicity of norm articulation sources provides opportunities for norm application over a limited domain without risking losses throughout the nation. This proliferation of norm-generating centers also makes it more likely that at least one such center will attempt any given, plausible innovation. . . . The multiplicity of centers means an innovation is more likely to be tried and correspondingly less likely to be wholly embraced. The two effects dampen both momentum and inertia.[32]

Stated in our terms, this argument means that, in addition to all the principled reasons we have given for maintaining the distinctive and delicate balance between the CJLS and the מרא דאתרא [local rabbi], our movement's structure allows for religious and halakhic creativity locally, where the need for it first arises, and where its authenticity can best be evaluated. This is a precious resource indeed, and it should not be lightly dismissed for the sake of an elusive "uniformity" which will disappoint tomorrow those whom it satisfies today.

The analogy to a federal system should not be thought strange here. Indeed, we have not only theoretical statements on local autonomy from such sources, ancient and modern, as have been cited above, but historical precedents as well. H. H. Ben-Sasson, for example, characterized the status of the well-known ועד ארבע ארצות [Council of Four Lands] as follows:

> The Council of the Lands of the Polish Crown originated from the rabbinical court at the fairs held in Lublin. It acquired the status of a central bet din [court] because of its activity during the meetings of merchants and heads of the communities and because famous rabbis participated in its deliberations. . . . Even at the zenith of the activities of the councils, the autonomy of the individual community, which had its own independent boroughs, was undiminished . . . the bet din was competent to adjudge disputes among the constituents of the council, or between the council and its constituents.[33]

The ועד [Council] functioned for over 200 years, and served a crucially important centralizing function. But it did not supplant local juridical competence, unless issues affecting the polity as a whole came before it.[34]

Hundreds of years earlier, Rabbenu Gershom (early eleventh century) had already put together a similar kind of "federal system," at least as it is described by Finkelstein:

> [T]he traditional unity of the Jewish people had at last been disrupted. . . . Whereas previously the Jews throughout the world had looked to some central authority to guide them in matters of religious observance, each community now had its

own traditions. . . . Rabbenu Gershom undertook no less a
task than that of bringing all these scattered communities into
a federation. . . . [T]he idea of a democratic federation had
never been fully developed in Israel. There had been obedience
to constituted authority, but this authority was always based
on that of past ages. Rabbenu Gershom proposed to establish
a voluntary constitution among the communities that would
claim its authority solely from those whom it governed.[35]

Menahem Elon, in fact, understands the era of Rabbenu Gershom and
its aftermath to have been a sort of watershed in Jewish jurisprudential
history. It was, he tells us, at that time that central courts, like those of
the Babylonian Geonim, ceased to function as master "receivers" to
which all questions of consequence were transmitted. Local halakhah
began to make its existence felt:

כאשר אנו מציינים, שעיקרה של חליפת השאלות ותשובות מתקופה זו
ואילך היתה בתוך כל מרכז ומרכז, אין כוונת הדברים לומר, שמכאן ואילך
נותקו קשרי השאלות ותשובות בין המרכזים השונים. מתחילתה של תקופה
זו, ובמשך כל הזמן שלאחר מכן, מצויות בידינו ידיעות רבות על שאלות
ותשובות, שנשלחו ממרכז אחד למשנהו... ההבדל העקרוני, שחל מבחינה
זו בין השו"ת בתקופת הגאונים לשו"ת שבתקופות שלאחר מכן, היא
איפוא בכך, שבתקופת הגאונים עיקרן ורובן של השאלות באו למרכז
שבבבל, ולאחר מכן היתה חליפת השאלות ותשובות העיקרית בתוך
אותו מרכז ורק חלק ממנה התנהל גם בין המרכזים השונים.[36]

The local halakhah that was developing became prominent enough to
have moved Rabbenu Tam, in the twelfth century, to make a sweeping
statement (which was, admittedly, close to a דעת יחיד [the opinion of
only one rabbi], but noteworthy nonetheless). He claimed that a majority can enforce its will on the minority only if the latter explicitly agreed
to that majority's authority in advance.[37] If such points of view existed
concerning the legislative power of central courts (i.e., concerning תקנות
[enactments]), about which there was always greater utilitarian concern
about community harmony, how much more so would local autonomy
be accepted with respect to interpretive, or judicial functions.

These several precedents are illustrative of how our judicial and
community history often knew delicate balances between central authority and local autonomy. They should quell fears with respect to
our own particular version of non-authoritarian majoritarianism as
embodied in the CJLS. There is, indeed, not only nothing to fear, but
perhaps blessing as well. As Cover put it:

It seems unfashionable to seek out a messy and indeterminate
end to conflicts which may be tied neatly together by a single
authoritative verdict. . . . I, ultimately, do not want to deny that
there is value in repose and order. But the inner logic of "our
federalism" seems to me to point more insistently to the social
value of institutions in conflict with one another. It is a daring
system that permits the tensions and conflicts of the social order
to be displayed in the very jurisdictional structure of its courts.[38]

The creation and maintenance of the central authority of the CJLS witnesses to the value all Rabbinical Assembly members place on "repose
and order." But we, too, are a kind of federalism, with local rabbis
playing the role, if we may say so, of lower, local tribunals. The tensions between the CJLS and the מרא דאתרא [local rabbi], which we
have lived with since 1927, witnesses to our readiness to be "daring,"
and to uphold a structure which reminds the Jewish world, and ourselves, of theological principles that we recognize in our classical
sources, and in which we deeply believe.

CONCLUSION

This paper has been a principled defense of, not a realistic resignation to,
the current structure and status of the CJLS. That is, the previous sections have reviewed the textual and theological bases for the authority
traditionally vested in the majoritarian procedures of rabbinic courts.
We have seen that two alternative views (at least) are possible with respect to this matter: the first has been seen to flow from metaphysical beliefs about the divinely bestowed authority of the court's majority
decisions, and the second has been seen to result from a theological conviction about epistemological indeterminacy in the post-prophetic age.
Each one of these views carries with it implications concerning the rights
of minorities and of individuals not on the court, implications which
sharply diverge one from the other. While each view can consistently be
maintained, it has been argued here that the second view is most in keeping with the history and theology of the Conservative movement, appropriate for the decentralized condition of the modern Jewish community,
and amply supported by halakhic sources, ancient and modern. Indeed,
the CJLS already operates under procedures quite different from traditional rabbinic majoritarianism. It has, since 1967, not even designated
its opinions as "majority" or "minority" opinions, and it has done so
out of a conviction that the majority of the court should not be granted
a monopoly on legal competence and authority. What we have argued
for, to wit a "majoritarianism without authoritarianism," thus applies
with even greater force to the CJLS, with its already modified majoritarianism. Reaffirming the responsibility of each מרא דאתרא [local rabbi] to
study and consider CJLS opinions, and reaffirming the right of that
מרא דאתרא [local rabbi] to choose even a halakhic path not chosen by
the Committee (except, of course, in cases where a Standard has been
promulgated by the CJLS and the Convention), should be seen not as a
challenge to the legal and moral suasion which the CJLS will always
wield. Nor should it be spoken of apologetically as a haphazard quirk of
the movement, made necessary by political contingencies. Rather, it
should be understood as an extension of the very logic that has created
the CJLS and its internal rules, and as our faithfulness to obligations to
God and to community that, as David Zvi Hoffmann observed, will
sometimes live in tension. It is hoped that this paper may facilitate not
only a new understanding of the current structure and status of the
CJLS, but a new pride in it as well.

NOTES

1. *Proceedings of the Rabbinical Assembly* 38 (1976): 318.

2. The 1976 episode, and a host of other important details of CJLS history through 1980, is described thoroughly in the unpublished paper, "The Clearing House: A History of the Committee on Jewish Law and Standards," by George Nudell.

3. משנה עדויות א': ה' [M. Eduyot 1:5].

4. בבלי ברכות ט. [B. Berakhot 9a].

5. ספרא בחקתי י"ג:ז' [Sifra Beḥukkotai 13:7].

6. Verses 14–22 of that chapter set forth the obligation to heed the teachings of a prophet who has been granted a revelation by God, and who correctly predicts a wondrous event. The need for a "sign" obviously presumes some new, innovative, perhaps even startling statement by the prophet. Indeed, the context of this section is equally clear that Israel is being singled out from the nations in the following sense: the other nations rely on "readings," of the stars, or other phenomena or forces of nature. Israel is not to "read" that which is there, but is to be granted continually renewed revelations from God, through a prophet.

7. רמב"ם, הקדמה לפירוש המשניות [Maimonides, *Commentary on the Mishnah*, Introduction].

8. רמב"ם, משנה תורה, "הלכות יסודי התורה" ט':ד' [Maimonides, *Mishneh Torah*, "Laws of the Fundamental Principles of the Torah" 9:4]. Again, the contradiction of Deut. 18:14–22 is noteworthy.

9. בבלי בבא בתרא י"ב. [B. Bava Batra 12a].

10. רשב"ע. גלוי וידוע לפניך ולא לכבוד בית אבא עשיתי אלא לכבודך שלא ירבו מחלוקות בישראל—בבא מציעא נ"ט: ["Master of the Universe, it is revealed and known to you that I did not act for the honor of my father's house but for Your honor, so that there would not be controversies in Israel"—Bava Metzia 59b].

11. רמב"ן, פירוש התורה, דברים י"ז:י"א [Naḥmanides *Commentary on the Torah*, on Deuteronomy 17:11].

    The ספר החינוך (ע"ח) [*Sefer Ha-Hinnukh*, par. 78] formulates this in its own way:

    ...רבויי הדעות יסכימו לעולם אל האמת יותר מן המעוט. ובין שיסכימו לאמת או לא יסכימו לפי דעת השומע. הדין נותן שלא נסור מדרך הרוב.

    ["With a multitude of opinions they will come to the truth more than if there are only a few. And whether, *according to the opinion of the listener,* they (the majority) decide correctly or not, the law is that we may not deviate from the majority opinion."]

12. This, of course, is the law of the זקן ממרא [the rebellious elder], which the Rabbis transferred to their courts from Deut. 17:12, where it applies to the authority of the כהן [priest]. The analogous authority of the biblical prophet is stated in Deut. 18:19, where the death penalty is not explicitly stated, but the ominously threatening sanction אנכי אדרש מעמו ["I (God) will exact punishment from him"] gives the imagination clear direction.

13. Deut. 17:11. We shall have occasion to return to this verse and its exegesis a bit later.

14. See David Hartman, *Conflicting Visions* (New York: Schocken, 1990), pp. 19–30 ("Joy and Responsibility").

15. ‏(כ"ב.) ד':ב' ירושלמי סנהדרין‎ [Y. Sanhedrin 4:2 (22a)].

16. ‏פני משה, ירושלמי סנהדרין ד':ב'‎ [*P'nei Moshe*, Y. Sanhedrin 4:2].

17. See n. 5 and n. 7 above.

18. I am referring here, at least, to the interpretation on such sanctions given by ‏רמב"ן‎ [Naḥmanides] (see note 11 above), whose understanding is by no means idiosyncratic and isolated, nor even original to him. As we've seen, however, the text in ‏בבא מציעא נ"ט:‎ [Bava Metzia 59b] attributes to Rabban Gamaliel a prudential/utilitarian, rather than a metaphysical/epistemological motive ‏(שלא ירבו מחלוקות בישראל)‎ ["so that there would not be controversies in Israel"]). I shall take up the utilitarian point of view explicitly only briefly in this paper, long enough to illustrate that once the metaphysical point of view is countered with a plausible alternative, the conditions of Jewish modernity to which we have become accustomed present, in addition, a ready counter to the utilitarian argument for attaching nearly inviolate authority to majority decisions.

19. The reference here is, of course, to grafting part of a tree onto another tree of the same species. Grafting across species is forbidden whether or not it is the sabbatical year.

20. ‏(ל"ג:.) ירושלמי שביעית ב':ו'‎ [Y. Shevi'it 2:6 (33d)].

21. Essentially the same story is told, with some different names (though ‏רבי בא‎ [Rabbi Ba] is still the main character) in ‏ירושלמי מעשר שני‎ ‏א':א' (נ"ב.)‎ [Y. Maaser Sheni 1:1 (52c)]. A different story which also illustrates an ambivalence about the authority attached by some to court majorities is found in ‏תוספתא אהילות י"ח:י"ח‎ [Tosefta Ohalot 18:18].

22. Since ‏רבי בא‎ [Rabbi Ba] explicitly said ‏אני לא נמניתי עמהן‎ [I am not numbered among them], this is not a claim that he was somehow flouting the law of the ‏זקן ממרא‎ [the rebellious elder], which was not taken to apply to non-members of the voting court. Rather, it is a claim that the general, but unmistakable spirit of so many texts that the rabbinic court was to be the legal authority seems to be violated by the kind of cavalier statement attributed to ‏רבי בא‎ [Rabbi Ba] and others. See what follows in the main text of the paper.

23. ‏ספרי דברים קנ"ד‎ [Sifrei Deuteronomy 154].

24. It won't do to argue, as some have tried, that the words ‏מראים בעיניך‎ ["It seems to you"] in themselves allow us to conclude that this rule applies only when one only "suspects" that the court has made a mistake, but not when one "knows" it, since there are parallels to the ‏ספרי‎ [Sifrei] passage in which the text reads simply ‏מראין‎ ["It seems"] (which should probably be understood as ‏מורין‎ ["We teach"]) and ‏אמרו לך‎ ["They said to you"]. See David Zvi Hoffmann, *The Highest Court*, trans. Paul Forchheimer (New York: Maurosho Publications, 1977), pp. 111–112.

25. ירושלמי הוריות א':א' (מ"ה:) (Y. Horayot 1:1 [45d]). An interesting question here is just what the proof text appealed to by the ירושלמי [Jerusalem Talmud) is, if any. The problem is that consultation with a concordance confirms that there is no such verse as ללכת ימין ושמאל ["to go right and left"]!

26. David Zvi Hoffmann, *The Highest Court* (see n. 24 above), p. 116. One cannot help being reminded here of the dissatisfactions voiced in the past against what were viewed as overly liberal majority decisions of the CJLS, and the desire of those who identified themselves as liberals to defend the central authority of the CJLS. See, again, the Nudell paper (cited above in n. 2) and the 1976 *Proceedings of the Rabbinical Assembly.*

27. David Zvi Hoffmann, *op. cit.*, pp. 116–117 (emphasis mine). Hoffmann is primarily speaking of occasions on which the individual scholar, acting as local jurist, would follow what his competent understanding told him was the will of God, rather than accept an overly lenient decision of the court. The substance of Hoffmann's argument, however, is equally valid for, and can be easily extended to, other cases in which the individual who is competent in halakhic texts would feel compelled to diverge, in teaching and practice, from the majority of the central court. Such occasions might include judgments that an overriding ethical imperative underlying the halakhic system itself had been neglected by the court's majority.

28. These last two sentences correspond rather closely to two of the characteristics of the status of the CJLS set forth at the beginning of this paper. Specifically, it is perfectly in order and normative for individuals (lay or rabbinic) in the movement, and indeed, for entire institutions such as the United Synagogue, to accept only authoritative decisions of the CJLS as their halakhic imperatives. At the same time, it is also normative and proper for rabbis, particularly those who are charged with making halakhic decisions for congregations, to study CJLS opinions and to come to their own decisions, even if they do not coincide with any CJLS opinions. That is the point of the ירושלמי [Jerusalem Talmud] in הוריות [Horayot] (see n. 25 above), and indeed, the בבלי [Babylonian Talmud] as well (see ב הוריות [Horayot 2b], the section ending with the words דטעו במצוה לשמוע דברי חכמים ["where they erred in the commandment to obey the words of the Sages"]).

29. העמק שאלה על שאילתא נ"ח (משפטים), אות ל"ז [*Ha-amek She'elah* on She'ilta 58 (Mishpatim), #37].

30. העמק דבר. על דברים י"ז:י"א [*Ha-amek Davar,* on Deuteronomy 17:11] (emphasis mine).

31. Robert Cover, "The Uses of Jurisdictional Redundancy: Interest, Ideology, and Innovation," in *William and Mary Law Review* 22 (1981): 640.

32. *Ibid*, pp. 673–674.

33. H. H. Ben-Sasson, "Councils of the Lands," *Encyclopaedia Judaica* (Jerusalem: Keter Publishing House, 1972), vol. 5, pp. 995–996.

34. No exact analogy between the ועד [Council] and the CJLS is being claimed here. The sole point is that the co-existence of a central body with agreed-upon judicial powers and local centers of authority has good precedents in Jewish life. Nevertheless, the CJLS's role in initiating Standards of Rabbinic Practice can perhaps be seen as analogous to the handling of such polity-wide issues by central organs of authority in the past. Indeed, Standards are small in number, and are generally confined to such issues as conversion, Jewish status, etc. in which the crossing of jurisdictional lines makes reliance on each מרא דאתרא [local rabbi] either impractical or nonsensical.

35. Louis Finkelstein, *Jewish Self-Government in the Middle Ages* (New York: Philipp Feldheim, 1964), pp. 21–23. Finkelstein's work included as well, on pp. 257–264, the enactments of the Frankfurt Synod of 1603. That Synod had to "beg of every Rabbi who is not a member of this council to agree to these decisions . . ." (Section 9). Again, we see the balance between the central body with legislative power ceded and recognized by the communities, and the local rabbis who, like רבי בא [Rabbi Ba] centuries earlier, seemed to be able to say אני לא נמניתי עמהן בעלייה ["I am not counted among them"].

36. מנחם אלון, המשפט העברי (ירושלים: הוצאת מגנס תשל"ח), כרך ב', עמ' 1232–1233 [Menahem Elon, *Jewish Law* (Jerusalem: Magnes, 1978), 2:1232–1233 (Hebrew)].

37. Elon (see previous note), vol. 1, p. 581. Also see Elon's discussion in vol. 1, pp. 549–550, concerning the tendency, after the time of Rabbenu Gershom, for there to be ordinances and rulings of a local nature that were not expected to be adopted by all Jews.

38. Cover, *op. cit.*, p. 682.

CHAPTER SEVEN

Some Comparative Theories
to the Right and Left

FOR MUCH TOO LONG, many Conservative Jews understood themselves only in terms of what they were *not:* they were not Orthodox and not Reform, and so by default they were Conservative. While it is definitely true that Conservative Judaism is, from one perspective, the middle movement, agreeing with Orthodox Judaism in some respects and with Reform in others, the problem with understanding it only in those terms is that it robs Conservative Judaism of its positive assertions, making it seem philosophically wishy-washy. As the old joke goes, the Orthodox are crazy, the Reform are lazy, and the Conservatives are hazy. Pragmatically that is a problem, for with most Jews holding college degrees, contemporary Jews want to have a good idea of what the movement stands *for* if they are going to identify with it and invest their resources of time, energy, and money in it. But the problem is not only pragmatic; it is also theoretical. To depict Conservative Judaism as simply some ambiguous, noncommittal, and nonconfrontational form of Judaism describes it falsely, for from its inception Conservative Judaism has made some serious assertions about the nature of Judaism in general and of Jewish law in particular.

One way to illustrate this truth is by describing many of the theories of Jewish law within the Conservative movement in all their variety, as the previous four chapters have done. Those theories articulate in various ways how the Conservative movement understands what Jewish law *is.* One way to understand anything, though, is to become clear about what it is *not.* In fact, the very word "define" in English (like *lehagdir* in Hebrew) means to draw borders around, thus mapping out what is within the phenomenon being defined and what is outside its bounds. So in this chapter I will compare the theories presented above with some theories in the other movements, with the hope that the previous chapters have amply dispelled the old impression that Conservative Judaism is only what it is not.

In what follows, I will be particularly interested in those approaches in the other movements that come closest to Conservative Judaism, for in considering them we will arrive at a much sharper picture of where the borders are on both the right and the left. The modern Jewish movements, though, are made up of individuals, each of whom has his or her own understanding of Judaism. Moreover, people affiliate with one movement or another for reasons that are compelling to them personally. In that process, some Jews find that one movement clearly fits their own approach to Judaism. Others find themselves philosophically either on the left end of one movement or the right end of the other; the one they ultimately choose often depends not primarily on their beliefs, but rather on the accidents of their personal biographies—with whom they grew up and associate now, where they went to school, whom they want to influence and, possibly most importantly, how they want to see themselves and their families and among whom they want to be accepted.

Like the people affiliated with the various movements, some theories fit clearly within one movement or another, while others lie near the borders and thus test the boundaries. It is precisely the latter that give us a clearer sense of what defines each movement's unique approach to Jewish law, for they define where and why a given theory is still Reform (or Orthodox) while another one very much like it in some respects is nevertheless Conservative. The lines between movements, after all, are not hard and fixed; what exists instead is a *spectrum* of theories of Jewish law, and it will be instructive to see where, and if, lines can be drawn that more or less define the differences between the movements in their approaches to Jewish law. However things fare at the borders, theories at the center of each movement look quite different from one another, and so I will also consider some more mainstream articulations of the other movements' approaches to Jewish law.

Since this is a book on theories of Jewish law primarily within the Conservative movement, I will not be presenting nearly the number of variations within the other movements as I did for the Conservative movement. My goal is simply to supply a representative sample at the border and in the middle of each of the other movements to clarify where the Conservative movement is distinctive. Readers interested in any of the other movements' approaches to Jewish law should, in all fairness, consult books devoted to that. Moreover, because this book focuses on Conservative theories of Jewish law, I will not include extensive readings from each of the theorists in the other movements that I examine in this chapter; instead I will summarize their theories with appropriate quotations from their writings so that readers of this volume can hear them in their own words, albeit in an abbreviated fashion.

One word about the term "movement" in these comparisons. Neither the Conservative nor the Reform movement is a monolith; there is a spectrum of belief and practice within each one. Moreover, there is no such thing as "the Conservative (or Reform) movement, Incorporated." Each consists of a number of organizations that share an approach to Judaism and cooperate on a number of projects. Still, institutionally it makes sense to speak of a Conservative (or Reform) movement because of the institutional framework, albeit loose, that links Conservative (and Reform) Jews to one another and gives them a sense of a coordinated mission and enterprise.

None of that is true for the Orthodox, who are badly splintered into a variety of groups, from Modern Orthodox, to Agudah, to a variety of Hasidic sects. These groups are not linked institutionally at all; on the contrary, they sometimes even question the Jewish legitimacy of the other groups. The closest that any of these groups comes to a "movement" is the Modern Orthodox, with its primary seminaries (Yeshiva University in New York and Hebrew Theological College in Skokie, Illinois), its rabbinical organization (Rabbinical Council of America), and its congregational body (Union of Orthodox Jewish Congregations) working together on some projects. Thus the term "movement" throughout this chapter refers less to an institutional structure than it does to the ideological convictions and Jewish practices of people who consider themselves part of a given movement.

One other introductory comment. This chapter is *not* intended as a comparison of the movements. For that, on the ideological level one would need to delve into many more thinkers among the Orthodox and Reform than I have done here, to ensure a representative sample. On the institutional level one would ask such questions as how each movement makes halakhic decisions, whom it deems to be Jewish and whom it construes to be a rabbi, the scope of authority of the individual rabbi, and how it treats Jewish marriages, divorces, and rabbinic ordinations performed by other movements. This chapter is instead about the *boundaries* between the movements, concerning the issue of legal theories, and so while it examines a centrist thinker among the Orthodox and the official platform statements of the Reform movement for the sake of comparison, it also deliberately compares a thinker on the left wing of Orthodoxy with Conservative thinkers, and it probes the places where the platform statements of the Conservative and Reform movements overlap. In my view, the movements, qua movements, have clear differences in both philosophy and practice, as I have described elsewhere;[1] moreover, I think that the availability of diverse movements is ultimately good for both Jews and Judaism, and so I would be among the last to pretend that those distinctions do not exist. This chapter, though, is about the borders, where things get much fuzzier than they do at each movement's core.

A. AN ORTHODOX THEORY AT THE CENTER OF ORTHODOXY: YESHAYAHU LEIBOWITZ

Yeshayahu Leibowitz (1903–94), Professor of Organic and Biochemistry in the Natural Science Faculty at the Hebrew University in Jerusalem and Professor of Neuropsychology in the Medical Faculty there, remained a Professor of Philosophy there after retiring from the science faculties in 1973. Most of his writings were in those scientific fields, but he also was a prolific writer on Judaism in general, Israel, and Jewish law. Other centrist Orthodox thinkers on Jewish legal theory include, for example, Joseph B. Soloveitchik (e.g., *Halakhic Man,* 1983), Norman Lamm (*Faith and Doubt,* 1971), and David S. Shapiro (*Studies in Jewish Thought,* 2 vols., 1975, 1981).

Leibowitz has an approach to Jewish law that is clearly Orthodox and representative of what many other Orthodox Jews believe, for he believes that Jews are under an unstinting duty to serve God according to Jewish law. Leibowitz takes that common Orthodox (and Conservative) tenet to its logical extreme: The service of God must be for its own sake; its purpose is *not* to achieve spiritual, moral, or physical perfection, nor is it to achieve social goals. Thus if you are obeying Jewish law to make you feel good, to identify with Jewish history or community, or even to make you more moral, you are not, according to Leibowitz, obeying the law for the right reason. In fact, you are engaging in idolatry, putting human beings before God; for acting in conformity with the *mitzvot* to fulfill human needs is no longer primarily about God, but rather about the human beings who have made their own needs the definition of what God wants: "the Halakhah . . . addresses a man's sense of duty rather than his emotions or inclinations."[2] He uses this, in fact, to contrast Judaism with Christianity, for Jesus dying on the cross indicates God's submission to human needs, in sharp contrast to Abraham's binding of Isaac, "the highest symbol of the Jewish faith," which represents human beings bending their will to God's.[3]

Leibowitz's totally heteronomous approach to the nature of Jewish law—that is, his view that it comes from a source outside the humans who are subject to it (namely, God)—also affects his view as to how Jews should fulfill it. Jews do that correctly only at those times when they least want to do so but nevertheless act in accordance with the law because God commanded them to do so. As Leibowitz says with regard to prayer,

> The spontaneous prayer ("when he is overwhelmed and pours out his complaint before God") a man prays of his own accord is, of course, halakhically permissible, but, like the performance of any act which has not been prescribed, its religious value is limited. As a religious act it is even faulty, since he who prays to satisfy his needs sets himself up as an end, as though God were a means for promotion for his welfare. As in the case of any Mitzvah, prayer—especially prayer—is religiously significant only if it is performed because it is a Mitzvah. Its religious value is minimal when it is performed out of free inclination.[4]

Along the same lines, in sharp contrast to someone like Heschel, who speaks not only of the necessity of human pathos and intentionality in worshiping God (in contrast to "religious behaviorism") and even of divine pathos in God's search for human beings, Leibowitz says:

> Most characteristic of the Halakhah is its lack of pathos. The Halakhah does not depend upon the incidence of religious experience and attaches little importance to the psychic urges to perform extraordinary deeds. It strives to base the religious act, even in its highest manifestations, on the permanent habit of performing one's duty. "Greater is he who performs because he has been commanded than one who performs without having been commanded."[5]

Leibowitz's stance thus echoes a famous rabbinic comment in the Sifra:

> Rabbi Elazar ben Azariah says: How do we know that a person should *not* say, "I do not want to wear *sha'atnez* [a forbidden mixture of linen and wool; see Leviticus 19:19 and Deuteronomy 22:11]," "I do not want to eat the meat of a pig," "I do not want to have sex with someone forbidden to me," but rather [he should say,] "I indeed do want to [do all these things], but what can I do given that my Father in Heaven decreed on me [not to do them]?" [We know that that is what one should say because] the Torah says, "And I have set you apart from other peoples to be Mine" [Leviticus 20:26], which requires that one must separate oneself from sin and accept upon oneself the yoke of the Sovereignty of Heaven.[6]

Leibowitz asserts that Jewish faith and *halakhah* cannot be separated. While he acknowledges and even celebrates the fact that historically differing beliefs have been accepted among Jews, that liberality comes to a crashing halt when it comes to *halakhah*. Not only has relinquishing the duty to do *mitzvot* put communities outside the pale of Judaism historically, but so has calling into question the theological grounding for the commandments: "Halakhah is founded on faith, yet at the same time constitutes this faith. . . . The Halakhah is not an external wrap clothing Jewish religion or faith. It is the sole form in which they can be embodied, the collective manifestation of Judaism."[7] This form excludes all others:

> Judaism as a specifically defined entity existing continuously over a period of three thousand years was not realized in philosophy, literature, art, or anything other than halakhic living. Hence whoever is able to achieve religiosity only through the channels of Judaism, or whoever is interested in the Jewish manifestation of religiosity, must, willy-nilly, come to grips with the religious praxis of Judaism, with the world of Halakhah.[8]

Moreover, "The belief that the substance of Jewish faith can be retained when the Halakhah is adapted to human needs, whether these be material, spiritual, or mental, is mistaken."[9] Thus, for Leibowitz, Jews must not only affirm the obligatory nature of *halakhah*, but they must see it as such simply because God commanded it.

Leibowitz, though, goes further still: It would be a serious error to seek meaning in each and every commandment that one fulfills not only for theoretical reasons, but for practical ones as well, for "Only a small minority of men determine their way of life by conscious deliberation made in full awareness, and even they direct their actions by principles and conscious deliberation only on rare occasions—their moments of 'poetry.'"[10] As a result, Jews must instead focus on fulfilling the commandments as a matter of routine. Failure to adopt such a routine "has only loosened the reins and set free forces of darkness and agents of horror which had been restrained only by customary routine."[11]

Leibowitz's theory of Jewish law is very Kantian, although in a religious rather than a moral sphere. Kant thought that one does something moral only when one acts *against* one's own best interests and out of a pure sense of moral duty. Like Kant, Leibowitz speaks of Jewish laws in terms of categorical (absolute, unexceptionable) imperatives that are binding under all conditions and that are only fulfilled when done not for one's own sake but out of a sense of duty to God. (Unlike Kant, of course, Leibowitz thinks that the imperatives come from God rather than from human reason.)

This raises an old question: Are there any beliefs that a Jew must af-

firm in order to be a Jew? If so, which ones, and in which form? Moreover, who has the authority to decide those questions?

While Leibowitz may be right historically in asserting that until the
modern period *halakhah* was always a component of Jewish identity,
for the last two hundred years some Jews—and, for at least the last hundred years, most Jews—no longer make it part of their lives and yet they
still do identify as Jews. Minimally, this raises an empirical problem for
Leibowitz's theory, for if most Jews no longer judge themselves in terms
of Jewish law, let alone practice it, what reality does Leibowitz's theory
describe? Moreover, if Leibowitz were right, there would not be very
many Jews doing "religious" acts, even among those who in practice
fulfill the commandments, for many do so at any given time for reasons
other than as their duty to God.

But problems exist on the theoretical level as well. In insisting that
Jews obey the law only out of duty toward God, Leibowitz, like some
other Orthodox theorists and unlike others, specifically ignores the long
history in Jewish tradition, *from the Torah on,* of finding rationales for
obeying the commandments, in addition to seeing observance as obedience to the will of God.[12] In fact, throughout history some very prominent Jews, Maimonides perhaps most famous among them, thought that
part of the binding character of Jewish law derived from its rationality
and its fulfillment of human needs, that God was not simply an arbitrary dictator who needed to be obeyed no matter what. There are
voices like that of Leibowitz, of course, in the Jewish tradition; but such
understandings of God usually apply to what *God* has done, not what
God has willed *us* to do in the *halakhah*. Perhaps the most clearly articulated of these is found in the talmudic story of Moses questioning God
about Rabbi Akiva's awful death and getting the response, "Silence!
That is what I have decided."[13]

The only way in which Leibowitz takes history into account at all—
and, along with it, the social, moral, and economic factors that enter
into Jewish law—is in maintaining that the binding halakhic norm is defined by God-fearing individuals for their own time. In other words,
such humanistic factors may not be part of the Jew's motives to obey
the law, but they may enter into the process by which the content of the
law is determined. As he says,

> "[T]he religion of Israel, the world of halakhah, and the Oral Law,
> was not produced from Scripture. . . . In cybernetic terms, one can de-
> fine the relation between Bible and Halakhah as one of feedback: The
> halakhah of the Oral teaching, which is a human product, derives its
> authority from the words of the living God in Scripture; at the same

time, it is the Halakhah which determines the content and the meaning of Scripture.[14]

This, though, is highly perplexing, if not downright inconsistent. How can *halakhah* gain its authority from "the words of the Living God *in Scripture*" (emphasis added) if *halakhah* is also determining the actual "content and meaning of Scripture"? If Scripture is not clear enough in telling us what God wants us to do so that human beings have to interpret and apply it, how can the *halakhah* retain the pure divine authority that Leibowitz ascribes to it? That is, as soon as human beings have to intervene to determine what God demands, is it not the case that we only know what *human beings think* God wants of us?

Moreover, Leibowitz declines to discuss how revelation happens, and this is a serious flaw in his theory. After all, if we are not clear about *how* revelation happens—or even *if* it happens—then how do we really know that God wants us to live a life of *mitzvot*? God does not directly respond every time a Jew performs one of the commandments or says a *berakhah* thanking God for giving them to us. It is therefore impossible to know if obeying the commandments is really desirable to God unless one has a very clear understanding of how God's will comes to us through revelation, an understanding that Leibowitz does not provide. But that undermines his theory, for if God does not desire *halakhah*, then doing the *mitzvot* for God serves no purpose—and may even anger God!

In asserting that Jews should make fulfilling the commandments a routine, for otherwise "the forces of darkness and agents of horror" will be set free to have their dastardly effects, Leibowitz seems to be providing readers with a societal reason to adhere to the *mitzvot*. It is fascinating to see how he does the very thing that his theory rejects—namely, suggesting that one obey the *halakhah* in order to fulfill human needs.

We must also ask whether routine is really beneficial. One could argue that routine leads to a fundamentalist style of life, lacking creativity and depth. In Heschel's terms, that kind of routine can all too easily make for "religious behaviorists" who lose all sense that their actions are supposed to connect them to God and serve as a response to their Creator.

Leibowitz's view has the distinct advantage of a strong sense of divine authority, but it simultaneously has the disadvantage of detachment from the long Jewish tradition of finding rationales other than "the command of God" to obey the commandments. That makes his theory historically inauthentic. Indeed, while it fits nicely with Rabbi Elazar ben Azariah's opinion in the Sifra, it violates an oft-repeated principle in the Talmud that those who cannot obey the law for its own sake should obey it *not* for its own sake, for in doing so they will come to obey it for its own sake.[15] In a similar way, most moral theorists and, indeed, most people, would say that those who act in compliance with a moral rule that happens to be in accordance with their own best interests, or simply because they want to act in that way, have indeed acted morally, Kant notwithstanding. That is, in obeying the dictates of both Jewish law and morality, the purity of intention demanded by Leibowitz (and Kant) is not required, seldom achieved, and arguably not the ideal in the first place. Such theories not only fail to capture the reality of life lived in accordance with Jewish law (and morality); they are downright austere and even mean, for they impose a standard that most people find impossible to attain most of the time.

Leibowitz acknowledges that the content of the law has evolved throughout the ages as it has been interpreted by rabbinic authorities.[16] Those who have the authority to function in this way must be truly learned and dedicated to serving God. The focus here for Leibowitz is that those seeking to interpret God's will must do so free of their own self-interest. He believes that those who change the law for moral, social, or economic reasons have humanity in mind and not God. Such changes are thus antithetical to the theological basis of Jewish law and thus to the essence of Jewish law itself. As he says, "[I]t is the intention of realizing the Torah in life that distinguishes the shaping of Halakhah by the preceptors of the Oral Law from its modification at the hands of the Reformers."[17] Leibowitz's words here are telling: he embraces "shaping" of the law but not "modification." How do they differ? "In rendering their decisions, the former [proper rabbinic authorities] are guided by considerations which appear to them grounded either in the Halakhah itself or in the conditions necessary for halakhic observance. The latter [Reformers] act out of motives which reflect not a sincere attempt to understand the Halakhah itself but rather a desire to adapt the Halakhah to a variety of human needs, cultural, moral, social, and even political."[18]

Along these lines, Leibowitz asserts that Judaism and ethics cannot be merged for two reasons. First, while ethics seeks to govern the relationships among human beings on the assumption that each person is worthy of respect, Judaism does not view human beings as inherently valuable. Humans attain worth only because they are made in the image of God. Leibowitz says, "[T]he duty of love toward one's neighbor is not a corollary of man's position as such but of his position before God."[19] He points out that even the commandment "Love your neighbor as yourself" ends with "I am God."[20] Thus all commandments governing our relationships with other human beings are not grounded in our duties to other human beings (the realm of ethics) but rather in our duties to God.

Beyond that, "[M]orality can be neither Jewish nor non-Jewish, neither religious nor irreligious. Morality is morality. The attempt to fuse morality and religion is not a happy one."[21] That is because morality deals with human issues, while the Torah deals with divine concerns. Leibowitz, in fact, says that the attempt to find moral values in Judaism is "Lutheran, not Jewish."[22]

But if that is the case, what are the "conditions necessary for halakhic observance"? It would seem that most people would define such conditions as precisely the social, moral, economic, and political considerations that Leibowitz shuns. Why *would* the law change if not for these reasons? In making such claims, Leibowitz ignores the real issues that go into defining the law in each generation, including precisely these factors. He thinks instead that "God-fearing men" make their decisions solely in response to God's demands. But even in trying to determine what God wants of us, any good rabbi will take into account multiple factors that affect the human beings involved.[23] Had Leibowitz paid more attention to that, he might have seen that those exact same concerns affect people's motivations to obey the law as well. That, of course, would sully the purity of the theological motive he demands, but it would have brought him closer to the truth of both why Jews act in conformity with Jewish law and what makes the law moral, wise, and, ultimately, godly.

Leibowitz himself has difficulty maintaining the line between what he construes as justified reasons to change the law and unjustified ones. On the one hand, he claims that women should not put on *tefillin;* because God did not command women to do so, their donning *tefillin* would be solely in response to their own needs and not God's. It would be exactly like "engaging in something like a sport or a hobby" and "would be religiously pointless."[24] On the other hand, Leibowitz finds the notion that women should be barred from study of the Torah intolerable. That is because although studying Torah *(talmud Torah)* is a commandment for men, it also "enables the Jewish person to share the Jewish cultural heritage and its spiritual content."[25] He says that "Keeping women away from Talmud Torah is not to exempt them from a duty (as is the case with some other Mitzvot) but is rather to deprive them of a basic Jewish right," that keeping them at home and away from study "does not grant women equal partnership in sustaining spiritual life. . . . The perpetuation of this attitude within Judaism and the

Jewish religion is intolerable in the Jewish world of today."[26] But why does study of Torah have spiritual benefits while wearing *tefillin* does not? And why, for Leibowitz, does something like a woman's spiritual benefit matter in determining God's *halakhah*? Is that not changing God's law for the sake of fulfilling a human need, which is precisely what Leibowitz claims to be theologically and legally illegitimate?

Whatever its strengths and weaknesses, Leibowitz's theory clearly demonstrates some of the differences between Orthodox and Conservative understandings of Jewish law. Instead of viewing it as if it occupies a Platonic, divine realm separate and apart from the realities of people's lives, as Leibowitz and many other mainstream Orthodox Jews do, Conservative thinkers universally acknowledge that Jewish law has always been rooted not only in God's commandments as stated in the Torah and the ongoing oral tradition, but also in the social, economic, moral, and even personal realities of the people charged with obeying it. Such factors have always affected both the motivations that have led people to obey it and the substance of the law itself. Moreover, the placement of Jewish law not only in the divine-human encounter but also in human, historical context means that Conservative thinkers readily acknowledge that Jewish law has changed over time— and should continue to adapt to changing circumstances now—in response to human needs as well as to divine ones. Ultimately, this is a difference not only in the methodology of how Jewish legal texts are to be interpreted and applied, but also in theology: for Conservative thinkers maintain that God lives in a dynamic, ongoing relationship with us and so God's will (or at least our understanding of God's will) may change with changing circumstances. In contrast, many Orthodox theologians, like Leibowitz, understand God's will to be definitively stated in the law with little, if any, room for change; thus while people can change with time, God is strangely limited to what He said at Mount Sinai.

B. AN ORTHODOX THEORY AT THE BORDER OF CONSERVATIVE JUDAISM: DAVID HARTMAN

Rabbis Eliezer Berkovits, Irving Greenberg, David Hartman, and Emanuel Rackman and Professor Tamar Ross are all Modern Orthodox thinkers whose theories of Jewish law bear remarkable resemblances to Conservative approaches. Although I could use any of them for this purpose, I will use Hartman to illustrate just how difficult it sometimes can be to distinguish an avowedly Orthodox theory from a Conservative one.

Although Hartman has spent most of his adult life in Israel and may therefore be construed to be ineligible to represent North American Orthodoxy, even at its fringes, he was born, raised, educated, and ordained in the United States, served a congregation in Montreal before emigrating to Israel, and continually interacts with North American rabbis and laypeople whom he invites to the Shalom Hartman Institute, which he established in Jerusalem for pluralistic Jewish study. Furthermore, his major treatment of Jewish law, for which he was awarded a National Jewish Book Award in the United States, was written in English and published in the U.S. Clearly, then, his theory of law was intended to influence North American Jews, especially his fellow Orthodox Jews, in their thinking about Jewish law. Finally, to this day, Hartman identifies as Orthodox. Other Orthodox Jews may doubt his Orthodoxy, but that is just the point in using his theory, for it indeed tests the borders between Orthodox and Conservative approaches to Jewish law.

The very title and subtitle of Hartman's book on Jewish law, *A Living Covenant: The Innovative Spirit in Traditional Judaism* (1985), announce that he, in sharp contrast to Leibowitz, construes Jewish law to be living (i.e., dynamic) and innovative while yet traditional. As he states in the first pages of the introduction to his book, he wants to dispel conceptions of Jewish law that would paint it as legalistic and inducing passivity (Marx's "the opiate of the masses") and instead locate the vivid spirit and activism inherent within Jewish law. He then announces his thesis:

> In contrast to the above characterization of the Torah and Judaic spirituality, this book attempts to characterize Judaism in terms of a covenantal anthropology that encourages human initiative and freedom and that is predicated on belief in human adequacy. I argue that a covenantal vision of life, with *mitzvah* (divine commandment) as the central organizing principle in the relationship between Jews and God, liberates both the intellect and the moral will. I seek to show that a tradition mediated by the Sinai covenant can encourage the development of a human being who is not afraid to assume responsibility for the ongoing drama of Jewish history. Passive resignation is seen not to be an essential trait of one whose relationship to God is mediated by the hearing of *mitzvot*.[27]

He then specifies that he will "not argue against the viability of secular humanism. Nor do I claim that a system of ethics must be founded on the authority of divine revelation." In fact, later in the book he appeals to morality as part of the broader, covenantal context of Jewish law that must continually interact with it to make it whole. Moreover, he specifies at the outset that the viability of Judaism is not established through a critique of other faiths; he is *not* interested in showing that "Judaism is unique or superior to other faith communities." At the same time, he will argue strongly "for the significance of Jewish particularity, not for its uniqueness."[28] If one did not know the author, this last sentence could easily be construed as being written by Mordecai Kaplan, for it expresses exactly the latter's theory about the nature of the Jewish people.

Hartman uses the covenantal metaphor, not only because that is the Torah's own metaphor, but also to call attention to the tension that must exist between "the dignity of the autonomous self and unswerving commitment to the community": "Since the covenant is made with the people as a whole and not with Jews as individuals, the ample scope it gives to individual spiritual self-realization cannot exist in isolation from a communal political consciousness."[29] Even though he acknowledges that the covenant theme in the Torah is rooted in ancient vassal treaties, he wants to downplay the Torah's metaphors of king and father in favor of the prophets' metaphor of husband and wife to depict the relationship between God and the People Israel[30] and the Rabbis' metaphor of God as our teacher. "Marriage is an invitation to enter a relationship that is close and intimate but that does not abolish the individuality of either partner. . . . The self remains autonomous, but it is an autonomy in which the relational framework is fundamental to one's self-understanding."[31] Similarly, "God, as teacher, encourages His pupils to think for themselves and assume intellectual responsibility for the way Torah is to be understood and practiced."[32] Both of the latter metaphors also have the advantages of minimizing the role of reward and punishment in the relationship, focusing instead on the love between the partners and on their ongoing relationship.

That continuing, covenantal relationship between God and the People Israel leads Hartman to a clearly dynamic theory of Jewish law:

> Torah, therefore, should not be understood as a complete, finished system. Belief in the giving of the Torah at Sinai does not necessarily imply that the full truth has already been given and that our task is only to unfold what was already present in the fullness of the founding moment of revelation. Sinai gave the community a direction, an arrow pointing toward a future filled with many surprises. *Halakhah,* which literally means "walking," is like a road that has not been fully paved and completed. . . .
>
> The covenant is not a purely legal obligation; it is a total relationship. The logic of a legal system cannot do full justice to the relational

framework of the covenant built upon the metaphors of God as lover and teacher. . . .[33]

Hartman here is clearly different from people like Yeshayahu Leibowitz in the Orthodox world and Joel Roth in the Conservative movement, both of whom depict Jewish law as a deductive system, but Hartman is remarkably close to Dorff's covenantal theory, which employs the same biblical and rabbinic metaphor and draws from it some of the same conclusions.

Rabbi Joseph Soloveitchik, Hartman's teacher and one of his chief influences, maintains that we should obey Jewish law as a "lonely man of faith" who comes into the world with autonomy and creativity but also with complete dependence on God (*Lonely Man of Faith,* 1965, 1992). Soloveitchik thus accepts God's law as law out of sheer terror, much as the Israelites did under the influence of the thunder, lightning, and earthquakes at Mount Sinai. Hartman, however, thinks that Soloveitchik underestimates the role of human beings in defining the law. Worse, "[s]uch an attitude can have dangerous implications. When the faith experience is insulated from outside criticism, there is a risk of moral sloppiness and religious arrogance. . . . When the faith commitment has been insulated from and unresponsive to rational criticism, there is nothing that cannot be justified in the name of tradition."[34] Hartman expressly includes Western culture and spirituality as areas that "should be examined critically by Jews but also recognized as a stimulus to internal Judaic reappraisal and renewal."[35] He also disagrees with Leibowitz's claim that the only proper reason to obey the law is out of obedience to God.

Instead, Maimonides is Hartman's primary model, for Maimonides affirms a real faith in God as he also provides for rabbinic creativity. Moreover, Maimonides is a model for Hartman in asserting that nothing in Jewish law should be inconsistent with reason or ethics:

> . . . For myself, it is the Maimonidean-Aristotelian spirit that guides my approach to the *mitzvot.* For Maimonides, *mitzvot* are essentially related to the well-being of the community and the building of a healthy moral character. . . .
>
> Israel's uniqueness is not ontological but normative: it reflects the sanctifying power of Mosaic legislation to rescue human beings from idolatry and allow them to show what it means to be created in the image of God. . . . Moral concern is not an appendage to the life of faith. It flows from the total covenantal relational identity of one committed to the life of *mitzvah.*[36]

Hartman states this not only as a governing principle of his theory, but as a rule to be applied in practice:

> . . . I allow that the Torah may challenge some accepted current pat-
> terns of behavior, but I cannot imagine that it requires us to sacrifice
> our ability to judge what is just and fair. The covenant invites a com-
> munity to act and to become responsible for the condition of its
> human world. This invitation to full responsibility in history would be
> ludicrous if the community's rational or moral powers were negated in
> the very act of covenantal commitment. . . . That means that the devel-
> opment of *halakhah* must be subjected to the scrutiny of moral cate-
> gories that are independent of the notion of halakhic authority.[37]

Such moral norms are not restricted to, nor dependent upon, Judaism:
"Parallels to the ethical *mitzvot* in Judaism can be found in many other
civilized religious or nonreligious communities. The question of what
makes for a viable social and moral order is not a problem confined to
the particular context of a Jewish state."[38] In fact, identifying moral
norms and living a moral life does not require religion or revelation at
all: "Human history has shown that individuals are capable of developing viable ethical systems not rooted in divine authority."[39]

What, then, is the relationship between Jewish law and morality?
For Hartman, Jewish law is simply one effective way among others to
live a moral life: "The *halakhah* . . . does not give authority to what
constitutes moral character, but rather is a way of life that effectively
fosters those principles of healthy moral character dispositions that are
known through reflection on the nature of the human individual."[40] The
fact that other nations and religious groups seek to be moral in no way
diminishes the importance of morality for Judaism; on the contrary,
"the divine power and mystery must never be used as a justification to
undermine the category of the ethical."[41]

As much as Hartman emphasizes the rational and moral aspects of
halakhah, he insists that it is improper to reduce Judaism, as some
Reform leaders have done, to ethical imperatives alone. The nonrational
commandments, the *ḥukkim*, give the Jewish people identity and give
them forms through which to worship God: "Many of these *ḥukkim*,
as *mitzvot* that structure Judaic particularity and provide a vivid framework for expressing the community's particular passion for its God, resemble intimate family customs. Through them the community builds
familial solidarity grounded in a common memory and destiny. . . .
They complement and absorb the ethical."[42] Jewish life and law would,
in fact, be greatly impoverished if they were reduced to the moral:

> A family seriously committed to the ethical life does not only engage in
> social and political action. The family enjoys music, art, strolling in the
> country, intimate family meals and discussions, and the joy of just

being together in familial solidarity. . . . Ethical seriousness is not the only value in the covenantal appreciation of the religious life; the community and social action do not exhaust the yearning of the religious soul for God. Prayer, religious awe, and the nonrational retain their place in the religious life even as one makes the ethical a controlling category for the development of *halakhah*.[42]

I have quoted extensively from Hartman's book because his theory is so radically different from what most people expect from Orthodox writers. He surely has not eliminated the divine basis of the authority of Jewish law, but he certainly has toned down its emotional impact and ultimate determining power, for now human reason and morality play critical roles in defining what the law requires. God is no longer just a commanding God who expects Jews to obey passively; God is rather the Jews' covenantal partner, who does indeed expect things of us—just as marital partners expect things of each other and teachers expect things of their students—but who also is significantly affected in those demands by how the human partners respond to those commands. God is even, on this view, prepared to change His will as a result of human moral and rational critique of the law. This is indeed a far cry from Leibowitz and sounds, in both its covenantal and moral emphases, remarkably close to Dorff. Dorff, though, draws some other implications from the covenantal theory for both relations among Jews and interfaith relations, and he explores the ways in which law and morality interact much more thoroughly than Hartman does; in fact, Hartman himself states that "My book does not attempt to work out the way in which ethics can control halakhic development, nor does it try to establish the limits of tolerance and pluralism,"[44] both of which Dorff explicitly tries to do in his writings.

With all this emphasis on the law's historical development, ethical grounding, and "innovative spirit," to quote the subtitle of Hartman's book, what makes Hartman's theory Orthodox? He himself surely sees it as such. When I was once on a panel with him, I suggested that his theory sounded more Conservative than Orthodox. He smiled and shrugged his shoulders, but then he tried to defend its Orthodoxy by pointing out that he was basing himself on the Talmud and Maimonides. Those are certainly classical Jewish sources; but they are sources shared by all Jews, and he is interpreting and using them to form an understanding of Jewish law and a methodology for applying it that is very much like mine, much more so than most other Orthodox writers.

Furthermore, in practice few Orthodox Jews think about Jewish law in the way he does, and even fewer Orthodox rabbinic rulings use the methodology he describes. On the other hand, many Conservative Jews think of Jewish law in exactly the way he does, and many of the rulings of the Committee on Jewish Law and Standards apply Jewish law in just the way he suggests. In truth, if I had not identified the author of the excerpts quoted above, most readers would justifiably identify the approach described in those excerpts as Conservative.

What makes Hartman's theory Orthodox, then, is primarily a matter of factors external to the theory itself. Hartman, after all, grew up within the Orthodox world, was ordained by Yeshiva University, and served as the rabbi of an Orthodox congregation before emigrating to Israel. Most Orthodox rabbis stay within Orthodox circles, many of them not even joining the local Board of Rabbis; Hartman, in sharp contrast, has actively fostered contacts with Jews and rabbis of all stripes. Still, he identifies himself as Orthodox and prays and lives within an Orthodox community. Furthermore, even though he shares many elements of most Conservative theories of Jewish law, including their concern for interpreting classical Jewish texts and Jewish law in historical context and applying the law with moral and other human concerns in mind, he nevertheless may not implement his theory in the ways that the Committee on Jewish Law and Standards has. On the contrary, another important factor identifying his theory as Orthodox is the group he wants to convince, and that is, first and foremost, his own Orthodox community.

In the end, then, one must understand that the border between Orthodox and Conservative theories of Jewish law, as manifested in a theory like Hartman's, cannot always be determined by the content of the theory alone. How people see themselves and the community they choose to join, after all, are not only a function of what they think; all kinds of biographical factors play a role in that—even for philosophers like Hartman.

Another thinker who occupies the border between Orthodox and Conservative Judaism but from the opposite direction is David Novak. Unlike Hartman, Novak began in the Conservative movement. He was ordained by the Jewish Theological Seminary of America, and he served Conservative congregations for some fifteen years. He was also a member of the Rabbinical Assembly's Committee on Jewish Law and Standards and the Commission on the Philosophy of the Conservative movement, the group that produced *Emet Ve-emunah,* the only official platform statement of the beliefs of the Conservative movement. He ultimately left the Conservative movement over the issue of ordaining women and was a founding member of the Union of Traditional Conservative Judaism, an organization that later dropped the word "Conservative" from its title. Now a professor at the University of Toronto, his extensive writings manifest a clear understanding of the historical development of the Jewish tradition, very much in the Conservative mode, but his practice is Orthodox. Still, he is proud that his daughter is part of a women's *minyan* in the Chicago area. Novak, then, is a good example of a person who tests the definition of the right end of the Conservative movement as Hartman tests the left end of Orthodoxy.

This fuzziness at the borders does not undermine the significant differences that usually characterize Conservative theories in contrast to mainstream Orthodox ones like those of Leibowitz and Soloveitchik —and the specific rulings that grow out of those disparate approaches. It only means that while one can generally differentiate the middle of one movement from the middle of another with clarity, there are some people whose theories and/or practice straddle the line and make it more fuzzy. This may be intellectually frustrating, but it should not be surprising: Life, after all, does not come in neat intellectual boxes, and so we should expect that real people take stances that do not fit into clear categories. For that matter, some people who usually fit quite nicely into one or another of the movements most of the time may on occasion surprise us by their position on a given issue. (Some would say that about my own position on homosexual marriages and ordination: While otherwise I am very squarely in the center of the Conservative movement in both theory and personal practice, on that issue I am way on the left end.) There is thus a *spectrum* of positions, and while the middle of each of the three categories that mark the Reform, Conservative, and Orthodox positions on the Jewish spectrum can be described quite clearly and can be easily distinguished from each other, the exact dividing points between each of the movements is harder to characterize.

C. THE BOUNDARY ON THE LEFT: THE MAINSTREAM OF THE REFORM MOVEMENT

Anyone who has had experience with the Reform movement during the twentieth century would certainly have noticed that it has taken some major steps to the right during that time. In mid-century, it was unusual for Reform congregations to allow men to wear head coverings during worship, let alone insist on it; now men in Reform services commonly wear not only a head covering but also a *tallit,* and some women do that too. In 1975 the Reform movement produced *Gates of Prayer,* which has considerably more Hebrew than the old *Union Prayer Book* (1895, last revised in 1940) had. The new Reform prayer book, *Mishkan Tefillah* (2005), includes even more of the traditional liturgy. There were no Reform day schools in 1950; today there are a number of them. Reform movement summer camps for children and families have blossomed. Some Reform congregations now have kosher kitchens, for many Reform rabbis and some Reform lay Jews now observe the Jewish dietary laws. The Reform movement has also not only changed its anti-Zionist stance of the years before the founding of the State of Israel, but it has founded congregations and communities there and has aggressively acted to change Israeli law to permit Reform Judaism to flourish there. The Reform rabbinate's Responsa Committee, established by Rabbi Solomon Freehof in the 1960s, has become ever more productive in responding to Jewish legal questions from a Reform perspective. Its publications and those of the Freehof Institute of Jewish Law have made major contributions to Jewish legal practice and thought.

1. Theory

These changes in practice have produced parallel changes in the official platform statements of the organization of Reform rabbis, the Central Conference of American Rabbis.[45] Its first statement on Jewish law, adopted as part of the Declaration of Principles at the 1885 Pittsburgh Conference ("the Pittsburgh Platform"), stated the following about Jewish law:

3. We recognize in the Mosaic legislation a system of training the Jewish people for its mission during its national life in Palestine, and today we accept as binding only its moral laws, and maintain only such ceremonies as elevate and sanctify our lives, but reject all such as are not adapted to the view and habits of modern civilization.

4. We hold that all such Mosaic and rabbinical laws as regulate diet, priestly purity, and dress originated in ages and under the influence of ideas entirely foreign to our present mental and spiritual state. They fail to impress the modern Jew with a spirit of priestly holiness; their observance in our days is apt rather to obstruct than to further modern spiritual elevation.

This was clearly a rejection of Jewish ritual laws, except those that "elevate and sanctify our lives." The latter expressly do not include the dietary laws or "dress"—clearly intending head covering for males at services, possibly the *tallit* as well, and probably also *tefillin.* The Sabbath and festivals would be observed, but not necessarily according to the traditional laws governing those holy days.

The second Reform platform statement, adopted more than fifty years later as "The Guiding Principles of Reform Judaism" in Columbus, Ohio in 1937, was much more sanguine about traditional Jewish practices. While it specifically maintains that "certain of its [the Torah's] laws have lost their binding force with the passing of conditions that called them forth," the accent has shifted dramatically from the negative to the positive. The document is divided into three parts—A. Judaism and Its Foundations; B. Ethics; and C. Religious Practice—and the parts relevant to Jewish law, quoted below, very much encourage Jews to make traditional Jewish practice part of their lives:

A-4. *Torah.* . . . The Torah, both written and oral, enshrines Israel's ever-growing consciousness of God and of the moral law. It preserves the historical precedents, sanctions, and norms of Jewish life, and seeks to mold it in the patterns of goodness and of holiness. Being products of historical processes, certain of its laws have lost their binding force with the passing of the conditions that called them forth. But as a depository of permanent spiritual ideals, the Torah remains the dynamic source of the life of Israel. Each age has the obligation to adapt the teachings of the Torah to its basic needs in consonance with the genius of Judaism. . . .

B-6. *Ethics and Religion.* In Judaism, religion and morality blend into an indissoluble unity. Seeking God means to strive after holiness, righteousness, and goodness. The love of God is incomplete without the love of one's fellowmen. Judaism emphasizes the kinship of the human race, the sanctity and worth of human life and personality, and the right of the individual to freedom and to the pursuit of his chosen vocation. Justice to all, irrespective of race, sect, or class, is the inalienable right and the inescapable obligation of all. The state and organized government exist in order to further these ends.

B-7. *Social Justice.* Justice seeks the attainment of a just society by the application of its teachings to the economic order, to industry and commerce, and to national and international affairs. It aims at the elimination of man-made misery and suffering, of poverty and degradation, of tyranny and slavery, of social inequality and prejudice, of ill-will and strife. It advocates the promotion of harmonious relations between warring classes on the basis of equity and justice, and the creation of conditions under which human personality may flourish. It pleads for the safeguarding of childhood against exploitation. It champions the cause of all who work and of their right to an adequate standard of living, as prior to the rights of property. Judaism emphasizes the duty of charity, and strives for a social order which will protect men against the material disabilities of old age, sickness, and unemployment. . . .

C-9. *The Religious Life.* Jewish life is marked by consecration to these ideals of Judaism. It calls for faithful participation in the life of the

Jewish community as it finds expression in the home, synagogue, and school and in all other agencies that enrich Jewish life and promote its welfare. The Home has been and must continue to be a stronghold of Jewish life, hallowed by the spirit of love and reverence, by moral discipline and religious observance and worship. The Synagogue is the oldest and most democratic institution in Jewish life. It is the prime communal agency by which Judaism is fostered and preserved. It links the Jews of each community and unites them with all of Israel. The perpetuation of Judaism as a living force depends upon religious knowledge and upon education of each new generation in our rich cultural and spiritual heritage.

Prayer is the voice of religion, the language of faith and aspiration. It directs man's heart and mind Godward, voices the needs and hopes of the community, and reaches out after goals which invest life with supreme value. To deepen the spiritual life of our people, we must cultivate the traditional habit of communion with God through prayer in both home and synagogue.

Judaism as a way of life requires, in addition to its moral and spiritual demands, the preservation of the Sabbath, festivals, and Holy Days, the retention and development of such customs, symbols, and ceremonies as possess inspirational value, the cultivation of distinctive forms of religious art and music, and the use of Hebrew, together with the vernacular, in our worship and instruction.

Without knowing that these paragraphs are part of official Reform tenets of faith, one might well think that they were written for Conservative Jews. The practices common in Reform congregations and among Reform Jews at the time were markedly different from those common in Conservative synagogues and households, and there is no specific mention in the document itself of such Jewish rituals as the dietary laws or *tefillin*. Furthermore, there is no claim here that Jewish law is binding, whether one sees the point in it or not; the only motivations listed appeal to *individual* Jews to adopt Jewish practices to enrich their lives and fulfill Jewish ideals. Still, the rabbis who wrote and approved this document were clearly trying to deepen the Jewish roots of their constituents.

By 1976, the date of the third Reform platform statement, the practices of Reform synagogues had become more traditional. By that time, the new Reform prayer book, *Gates of Prayer*, had already been issued a year earlier, and it contained much more Hebrew than the *Union Prayer Book* had. Still, it was not nearly as traditional as the Silverman prayer book commonly used in Conservative synagogues; *Gates of Prayer* offered the rabbi a variety of options for Friday night and Saturday morning services, all of which were considerably shorter than the traditional liturgy. Furthermore, Reform synagogues then, as now, commonly did not schedule Sabbath morning services altogether unless there was a bar or bat mitzvah. Some Reform rabbis and laypeople were keeping kosher, and some were wearing a head covering and a *tallit* in services. The Reform movement in the 1960s was heavily invested in the civil rights movement, to the point that some Reform rabbis were worried that Judaism for themselves and their congregants had been reduced to civil rights activism. By 1976, though, there was a turn to more traditional practices for both the individual and the community. The platform statement reflects that, in asserting that while the founders of Reform Judaism emphasized only the moral parts of Judaism, Reform rabbis now wanted to reinforce the many other parts of Judaism as well, including a number of Jewish rituals that are specifically mentioned, even "daily religious observance."

One underlying principle of Reform Judaism that had characterized it in practice from its very beginnings but had surprisingly never been expressed in its 1885 and 1937 statements was finally articulated in 1976—namely, the autonomy of each individual Jew to decide which Jewish practices to adopt. The 1976 statement tries to achieve a balance between accepting the tradition as part of one's life and making an autonomous choice, by asserting that to make an intelligent choice Jews must first study the tradition. Thus this statement's paragraph relevant to Jewish law, quoted below, represents a breakthrough in both articulating the governing assumption of individual autonomy for the very first time and simultaneously asserting that intelligent use of that autonomy makes demands of knowledge and judgment:

4. *Our Religious Obligations: Religious Practice.* Judaism emphasizes action rather than creed as the primary expression of a religious life, the means by which we strive to achieve universal justice and peace. Reform Judaism shares this emphasis on duty and obligation. Our founders stressed that the Jew's ethical responsibilities, personal and social, are enjoined by God. The past century has taught us that the claims made upon us may begin with our ethical obligations but they extend to many other aspects of Jewish living, including: creating a Jewish home centered on family devotion; lifelong study; private prayer and public worship; daily religious observance; keeping the Sabbath and the holy days; celebrating the major events of life; involvement with the synagogue and community; and other activities which promote the survival of the Jewish people and enhance its existence. Within each area of Jewish observance Reform Jews are called upon to confront the claims of Jewish tradition, however differently perceived, and to exercise their individual autonomy, choosing and creating on the basis of commitment and knowledge.

Finally, in 1999, again, ironically, in Pittsburgh, the Central Conference of American Rabbis adopted its most recent *Statement of Prin-*

ciples for Reform Judaism. While the Pittsburgh Platform of 114 years earlier had emphasized the ways in which Jews and Judaism should be part of a universal, human culture, the 1999 statement focuses on affirming Jewish tradition, albeit in dialogue with modern culture and within the boundaries of personal autonomy. This is clear from the very first paragraph of the Preamble, which explains the reason for writing the document as a response to today's conditions "when so many individuals are striving for religious meaning, moral purpose, *and a sense of community*" (my italics); the last of those would have been anathema to the Reform rabbis of 1885, who were trying to rise above individual communities and nations to form a universal, human culture.

The second paragraph of the Preamble presents even a more stark contrast to the tone and direction of the 1885 statement: Instead of stating all the parts of the Jewish tradition that Reform Jews should discard, the 1999 statement strongly affirms Jewish tradition:

> Throughout our history, we Jews have remained firmly rooted in Jewish tradition, even as we have learned much from our encounters with other cultures. The great contribution of Reform Judaism is that it has enabled the Jewish people to introduce innovation while preserving tradition, to embrace diversity while asserting commonality, to affirm beliefs without rejecting those who doubt, and to bring faith to sacred texts without sacrificing critical scholarship.

If the second sentence read instead "The great contribution of Conservative Judaism . . . ," the rest of the paragraph would clearly articulate how Conservative Judaism understands itself! This is clearly a much more traditional form of Reform Judaism, one much closer to Conservative Judaism and harder to distinguish from it. While that statement refers to a number of issues other than law, on the specific point of enabling "the Jewish people to introduce innovation while preserving tradition," compare it to the folling paragraph from the official statement of the beliefs of the Conservative movement, *Emet Ve-emunah: Statement of Principles of Conservative Judaism:*

> We in the Conservative community are committed to carrying on the rabbinic tradition of preserving and enhancing Halakhah by making appropriate changes in it through rabbinic decision. This flows from our conviction that Halakhah is indispensable for each age. As in the past, the nature and number of adjustments of the law will vary with the degree of change in the environment in which Jews live. The rapid technological and social changes of our time, as well as new ethical insights and goals, have required new interpretations and applications of

Halakhah to keep it vital for our lives; more adjustments will undoubtedly be necessary in the future.[46]

As will be described below, important differences between the two
movements in both theory and practice remain, but these paragraphs
bespeak a remarkable similarity in current self-perception.

The 1999 document is divided into three sections—God, Torah, and
Israel—just as the Conservative movement's Statement of Principles,
Emet Ve-emunah, is. In the section on Torah, the Reform document
says this about the commandments:

> We affirm the importance of studying Hebrew, the language of Torah
> and Jewish liturgy, that we may draw closer to our people's sacred
> texts.
>
> We are called by Torah to lifelong study in the home, in the synagogue,
> and in every place where Jews gather to learn and teach. Through
> Torah study we are called to *mitzvot*, the means by which we make
> our lives holy.
>
> We are committed to the ongoing study of the whole array of *mitzvot*
> and to the fulfillment of those that address us as individuals and as a
> community. Some of these *mitzvot*, sacred obligations, have long been
> observed by Reform Jews; others, both ancient and modern, demand
> renewed attention as the result of the unique context of our own time.
>
> We bring Torah into the world when we seek to sanctify the times and
> places of our lives through regular home and congregational obser-
> vance. Shabbat calls us to bring the highest moral values to our daily
> labor and to culminate the workweek with *kedushah*, holiness,
> *menuchah*, rest, and *oneg*, joy. The High Holy Days call us to account
> for our deeds. The Festivals enable us to celebrate with joy our peo-
> ple's religious journey in the context of the changing seasons. The days
> of remembrance remind us of the tragedies and the triumphs that have
> shaped our people's historical experience both in ancient and modern
> times. And we mark the milestones of our personal journeys with tra-
> ditional and creative rites that reveal the holiness in each stage of life.
>
> We bring Torah into the world when we strive to fulfill the highest eth-
> ical mandates in our relationships with others and with all of God's
> creation. Partners with God in *tikkun olam*, repairing the world, we
> are called to help bring nearer the messianic age. We seek dialogue and
> joint action with people of other faiths in the hope that together we
> can bring peace, freedom, and justice to our world.
>
> We are obligated to pursue *tzedek*, justice and righteousness, and to
> narrow the gap between the affluent and the poor, to act against dis-
> crimination and oppression, to pursue peace, to welcome the stranger,
> to protect the earth's biodiversity and natural resources, and to redeem
> those in physical, economic, and spiritual bondage. In so doing, we

reaffirm social action and social justice as a central prophetic focus of traditional Reform Jewish belief and practice.

We affirm the *mitzvah* of *tzedakah,* setting aside portions of our earnings and our time to provide for those in need. These acts bring us closer to fulfilling the prophetic call to translate the words of Torah into the works of our hands.

In all these ways and more, Torah gives meaning and purpose to our lives.

Note several features of the new Reform statement. While Zacharias Frankel had left the organization of Reform rabbis in the 1840s to form what became Conservative Judaism because the Reformers were moving away from a largely Hebrew liturgy to one in the German vernacular, the Reform rabbis of today state openly that Hebrew is important for both study and prayer. In the third section of the document, they go yet further: they "urge Jews who reside outside Israel to learn Hebrew as a living language."

This statement encourages Torah study of all kinds, and the rationale is not intellectual stimulation or cultural rootedness, but rather because "[t]hrough Torah study we are called to *mitzvot.*" Here the Reform rabbis are following an ancient talmudic dictum, where the Rabbis of the Talmud decided that study is greater than action because study leads to action.[47]

Moreover, the Reform rabbis here are clearly articulating a new focus on a life of following the commandments, and indeed a new language of *mitzvot.* Although they never translate that term as "commandments," probably because that would lead to all kinds of questions about the authority and enforcement of such commands, they do describe the *mitzvot* as "the means by which we make our lives holy" and even as "sacred obligations." The former definition suggests that doing them is a good idea, but voluntary: one may not, after all, want to make one's life holy or even understand what that means. The latter definition, "sacred obligations," indicates instead that there is an obligatory character to them, that they are not a matter of autonomous choice. Yet it leaves out explanations of some crucial aspects of such "sacred obligations"—namely, who imposes them (God, the Jewish people, Jewish tradition, or some combination of these); whether or not individual Jews may autonomously decide to opt out of such obligations or ignore them; how we know what exactly we are obligated to do; whether these obligations are subject to change and, if so, by whom, for what reasons, and through what process; and what the consequences are for failing to fulfill such obligations. The document, in other words, is fuzzy on the exact nature of the *mitzvot* and their relationship to modern Jews, and it fails to describe some of the most important features of a philosophy of law. Still, it is remarkable that the document speaks in such traditional terms, a clear indication of the new direction in which the rabbis of the Reform movement want to take it.

That is made even clearer by the document's assertion that while Reform Jews have observed some of the *mitzvot* in times past, "others, both ancient and modern, demand renewed attention as the result of the unique context of our own times." One can only guess what the authors of the document had in mind, but current Reform practice would indicate that the "ancient" practices they might have referred to would include such rituals as circumcision, the dietary laws, *kippah* (although that is not so ancient), *tallit,* and maybe even *tefillin,* regular prayer, and all of the specific holidays and life-cycle ceremonies that they mention in the succeeding paragraphs. The "modern" ones probably refer to new rituals for welcoming baby girls into the Jewish community and a host of other new rituals for women, as well as some new rituals that have been created in response to modern history, such as Holocaust Remembrance Day *(Yom Hashoah)* and Israel Independence Day *(Yom Ha'atzma'ut).* Note also that the document reaffirms the Reform movement's historical emphasis on Jewish moral norms, this time spelling them out in much greater detail than in any previous platform statement.

Finally, note that the 1999 document never makes explicit reference to individual autonomy. It continually refers to "we," as evidenced in the paragraphs quoted above, and it includes a strong statement of community identity: "We are Israel, a people aspiring to holiness, singled out through our ancient covenant and our unique history among the nations to be witnesses to God's presence. We are linked by that covenant and that history to all Jews in every age and place." The closest the document gets to affirming a role for individual decisions is in the Preamble, which "acknowledges the diversity of Reform Jewish beliefs and practices" and which "invites all Reform Jews to engage in a dialogue with the sources of our tradition, responding out of our knowledge, our experience, and our faith." But even here the language is in the first person plural, and it is unclear whether the framers intend that individuals decide what to take from the Jewish tradition—as a matter of philosophy, and not just as a matter of fact due to freedom of religion in Enlightenment countries—or whether they intend to move to a more communitarian form of decision making. Reform colleagues tell me that this is a source of tension within the current Reform rabbinate.

For all of its embrace of traditional practices, the new Reform statement differs markedly from Conservative Judaism in both theory and practice, in how the law is to be both understood and applied. Thus, immediately after the paragraph cited above, *Emet Ve-emunah* says the following:

> While change is both a traditional and a necessary part of Halakhah, we, like our ancestors, are not committed to change for its own sake. Hence, the thrust of the Jewish tradition and the Conservative community is to maintain the law and practices of the past as much as possible, and the burden of proof rests on the one who wants to alter them.[48]

Furthermore, in contrast to individual autonomy, *Emet Ve-emunah* specifically asserts that "Authority for religious practice in each congregation resides in its rabbi (its *mara d'atra*). It derives from the rabbi's training in the Jewish tradition, attested by his or her ordination as a rabbi, and by the fact that the congregation has chosen that rabbi to be its religious guide."[49]

Thus with all of the serious movement of the Reform rabbinate toward more traditional practice, the principle of autonomy still governs, in sharp contrast to Conservative movement theories that routinely speak in communal and legal terms. Within the autonomous context of Reform Judaism, its use of the term *mitzvot* remains unclear in its degree, scope, and grounds of authority. Indeed, the very existence of a Responsa Committee might be seen as an anomaly: How can there be a legal ruling if everyone is to choose what to do independently? The Committee is, at best, a vehicle to give Reform Jews *advice*, which is surely a worthwhile thing in itself but not the same as a legal *ruling*, as pertains to the authors' intent or the receivers' understanding and action.

2. Practice

The decidedly traditional turn in the 1999 document and in the life of the Reform movement in recent years has led some in the Reform and Conservative movements to question whether there are any longer any distinctions between them worth noting and maintaining. So, for example, Rabbi Paul Menitoff, current Executive Director of the Central Conference of American Rabbis, now claims that in the near future there will be no Conservative movement because the Reform movement has basically come to articulate what most Conservative Jews do in their personal and family practices in such areas as Sabbath observance and the dietary laws. Moreover, on controversial issues, such as interfaith marriages, same-sex marriages, the ordination of homosexuals as rabbis, and patrilineal descent, Menitoff maintains that most Conservative laypeople agree with the liberal stances that the Reform movement has taken.[50]

Some people who argue this way hark back to Milton Steinberg's distinction between Orthodox and liberal Jews in his 1947 book, *Basic Judaism*. They maintain that, as Steinberg predicted, we are now entering a "post-denominational age," in which all boundaries among liberal Jews have become meaningless and even inaccurate and misleading.

That was exactly the thesis of Reform Rabbi Clifford E. Librach in his September 1998 *Commentary* article, "Does Conservative Judaism Have a Future?" In it he claims that the Conservative movement has lost its rootedness in tradition and that, with the increasing traditionalism of the Reform movement, the Conservative movement no longer has a distinct identity or mission. As part of his argument, he cited my own liberal stand on homosexuality and my claim in an earlier article[51] that custom drives Jewish law on the status of women.

I responded to him in a letter published in the January 1999 issue of *Commentary*[52] that both my personal practice and also the overwhelming (sometimes unanimous) approval that my rabbinic rulings for the Committee on Jewish Law and Standards enjoy, indicate that I am somewhere in the middle of the movement. On the particular issues of homosexual unions and ordination, however, I am definitely on the left end of it, and so my own stance on homosexuality cannot be invoked to show where the movement as a whole is. Moreover, in contrast to those who have the same view as I do about homosexuality within the Reform movement, I feel the necessity of arguing for these changes in halakhic norms in halakhic terms, and that is a burden of proof that few, if any, of the Reform writers feel or respond to. On the latter issue, the status of women in Jewish law, an appeal to custom is not a new approach at all; as I demonstrated in my article, the classical Rabbis did the same thing on this very topic.

To move to Rabbi Librach's broader point, he admits that the ideologies of the two movements remain substantially different, but he claims that the realities of the two movements are no longer distinct. As a traditional Jew, I certainly welcome the efforts on the part of the current leadership of the Reform movement to increase the Jewish education and practice of Reform Jews. In the meantime, however, in my response to him I pointed to some very real differences in practice that continue to mark the Conservative movement from the Reform movement—namely:

1. Every Conservative congregation that has a kitchen has a kosher one. Few Reform congregations have kosher facilities, and in those that do, kosher meals are simply one option that they provide.
2. Approximately 95% of Conservative synagogue worship is in Hebrew. Current Reform liturgy employs more Hebrew than was used in past Reform prayerbooks, but even the most Hebraic services in *Gates of Prayer* use Hebrew for less than half the service.
3. Every Conservative synagogue holds services on Saturday mornings, while Saturday morning services take place in most Reform congregations only when there is a bar or bat mitzvah.
4. Every Conservative synagogue that can do so holds morning and evening services daily. I know of no Reform congregation that does so.
5. Conservative day (and supplementary) schools spend more time on Jewish studies and focus more on traditional texts than do their Reform counterparts. Similar curricular differences characterize adult education in the two movements, including conversion programs and even the schooling of future educators and rabbis.
6. When a Jewish couple divorces in civil law, Conservative rabbis require that they procure a Jewish writ of divorce *(get)* before remarriage is permitted. Reform rabbis do not require this document, with the result that, according to Jewish law, children from a woman's second, civil marriage are Jewishly illegitimate *(mamzerim)*.
7. Despite considerable sociological pressure, the Conservative movement continues to define Jews in the traditional way—namely, as the children of Jewish women or as those who have been converted to Judaism according to the demands of *halakhah*. The Reform movement also includes as Jews those whose fathers, but not whose mothers, are Jewish, and not all Reform rabbis insist on the traditional rituals of conversion.
8. Conservative standards forbid full synagogue membership to non-Jews, even if they are married to Jews, although many Conservative synagogues are seeking ways to welcome the non-Jewish spouses of members in ways that do not violate *halakhah*, especially if they have agreed to raise their children as Jews. Many members of Reform congregations are non-Jews, failing to fulfill any standard of Jewish identity.

I then concluded the letter as follows:

The list could go on. Suffice it to say that, contrary to Rabbi Librach, the Conservative movement remains the voice of traditional, modern Judaism in our time, just as much as it was in times past. As these differences amply demonstrate, the much-ballyhooed transdenominationalism that Rabbi Librach and others affirm is greatly exaggerated.[53]

Thus despite the fact that both the 1990 and 2000 National Jewish Population Studies have demonstrated that Conservative and Reform laypeople share much in their patterns of *personal* observance and in their attitudes toward the topics that Rabbi Menitoff listed, the *institu-*

tional practices that I listed above still divide the movements considerably. In light of these differences, the movements are significantly distinct in our own day. Furthermore, I would guess that it is unwise to predict what will happen in the institutional future of the movements. A look at such predictions about the movements fifty years ago and what has in fact happened should give any putative prophet pause.

D. TO THE LEFT OF THE REFORM RABBINATE:
SECULAR JEWS, ARTHUR WASKOW,
AND ARTHUR GREEN

While the Reform rabbis' platform statements have moved toward more tradition over the years, others in the Reform and the new Renewal movements have taken stances on Jewish law further to the left. There are some Jews, of course—indeed, statistically a very large percentage—who do not affiliate with any synagogue or even with a secular Jewish institution, and many, if not most, of those practice very little of Jewish law. They may put up a *mezuzah,* with or without a kosher parchment scroll; they may have some kind of seder meal on the first night of Passover, possibly with very little telling of the Exodus story and thus not much more than an extended family meal (one that is probably not kosher for Passover); and they may light the Hanukkah lights—but such Jews do very little else. They may be perfectly moral human beings, and they may even engage extensively in social activism, but they rarely do so as an expression of their Judaism, and certainly not out of a sense of being divinely commanded. Such Jews are precious to the Jewish people nonetheless, and other Jews must do all in their power to attract them to a deeper and broader expression of their Judaism. Much to its credit, the Reform movement has succeeded more than any of the other movements in encouraging such people to do that, and the Federation of Jewish Men's Clubs has recently taken on that task within the Conservative movement. In addition, in 1969, Rabbi Sherwin T. Wine founded the Society for Humanistic Judaism, which consists of synagogues dedicated to a secular philosophy of Judaism.[54] Thus much to the left of the Reform rabbis' statements are the views and practices of many, many Jews who are secular by default or in principle.

In between these two poles to the left of the Conservative movement—the Reform rabbis on the more traditional, right end, and secular Jews on the left end—there have been several writers who have taken more liberal positions than the Reform rabbis have espoused but who have very much affirmed the importance of Jewish practice, unlike secular Jews. Two important writers of this type are Rabbis Arthur Waskow and Arthur Green.

Arthur Waskow

Arthur Waskow, who earned a doctorate in United States history in 1963 from the University of Wisconsin, has served as one of the founders of the Jewish Renewal movement (1969–present) and Director of the Shalom Center, a division of ALEPH: Alliance for Jewish Renewal that focuses on Jewish thought and practice to protect and heal the earth. An amazingly creative and morally concerned Jew, he has prodded Jews from right to left on the religious spectrum to act in response to the moral challenges of our time. Author of *Godwrestling* (1978), *Godwrestling: Round 2* (1996), and *The Seasons of Our Joy* (1982; revised edition 1991), it is his book, *Down-to-Earth Judaism: Food, Money, Sex, and the Rest of Life* (1995) in which he comes closest to articulating a philosophy of Jewish law.

In the section of his book about food, he openly states his methodology as one that "reshapes Jewish values" to connect the idea of *kashrut* with other traditional Jewish concerns about ecology, understood in a broad sense.[55] Such values would include *tza'ar ba'alei ḥayim* (preventing cruelty to animals), *bal tash'ḥit* ("not ruining" the earth, protecting the environment), *shemirat haguf* (protecting our bodies), *tzedakah* (justice—in this case, sharing food with the poor), *berakhah* and *kedushah* (the blessing and holiness that we must affirm when we eat). But then he and his group of Renewal Jews in Philadelphia realized that to draw on these values in any serious way would require research into how the Jewish tradition has worked with these values to arrive at specific decisions. Both the decisions themselves and the reasoning that led to them would be important for a thoroughly grounded, but also modern, Jewish approach to food: He is committed "[n]ot necessarily to follow the same paths of thought or decision, but to wrestle with a Judaism that draws on the wisdom of all Jewish generations, not our own alone. Once we have done this, then indeed our generation must decide for itself."[56] Through this process, he created his concept of "eco-kashrut," a list of principles and practices that declares food fit, or kosher, only if it satisfies not only the ritual practices involved in the traditional laws of keeping kosher, but also the environmental and other moral concerns embedded in the values he listed.

Waskow, though, is keenly aware, on a methodological level, that some values may conflict with others:

For example, some might treat the principle of *oshek* (not oppressing workers) as paramount, and use only products that are grown or made without oppressing food workers (products, for example, grown in one's own backyard or neighborhood garden, or that come from a kibbutz where all the workers are also co-owners and co-managers). Others might make the principle of *bal tashchit* (protection of the environment) paramount, and put *oshek* in a secondary place, perhaps applying it only when specifically asked to do so by workers who are protesting their plight.[57]

He therefore affirms a methodology in which individuals prioritize their values and make decisions accordingly, with all members of the group understanding and respecting others' rankings through differences of emphasis and interpretation. In fact, "there might be so many ethical values to weigh that it would be rare to face a black-and-white choice in a particular product," and so "[c]hoices would depend more on balancing and synthesizing underlying values than on an absolute sense of Good and Bad, more on a sense of Both/And than of Either/Or."[58]

The individualism in this approach and also its Jewish and moral seriousness become explicit in Waskow's section on sex, where he invokes the American values of "consent of the governed" and "freedom of religion" to argue for a democratic way of making decisions for the group while respecting individual differences:

On the one hand, this means that Jewish practice is shaped not by a small elite of rabbis alone and not by the past alone, but by a much larger body of all who are in covenant with each other, with the past and future, and with the Divine. On the other hand, it means a deeper respect for individual conscience and individual practice within a voluntary Jewish community, rather than automatic and universal obedience to *halakha*.[59]

Such a theory, of course, raises all the familiar questions that we have seen with any theory that provides considerable room for individual choice. Does such a metholodology give us norms that *require* us to act in specific ways, or does it articulate only expressions of our will—maybe even the will of the majority? In other words, are the results genuinely moral and prescriptive or only descriptive of what people want? (As G. E. Moore pointed out in the early part of the twentieth century, "desired" does not necessarily mean "desirable.") Moreover, the community that Waskow was talking about was a small discussion and friendship group that did not really need to do things cooperatively. How would this methodology work for larger groups of Jews, or for the entire Jewish people? What would be necessary to make a decision: consensus, a simple majority, or some other percentage of the participants?

And how would he then account for another American value, namely, individual rights? Or, for that matter, would any decision be made by the group at all? Even though he would have us "wrestle" with Jewish sources, in the end the decision is our own, and so what makes it authentically Jewish? Would all Jews count equally, or would those who know more about the Jewish tradition or the given issue count for more? (Remember that in the United States, anyone of the proper age may run for Congress but judges must have law degrees. Which of those models would Waskow use, and why?) At least in theory, coherence, authority, and continuity seem to be in short supply for his theory, as does the distinctly Jewish character of his approach.

And yet, at the same time, its individualism and democracy allow for immense creativity, and Waskow demonstrates that in his own writings. He also demonstrates that creativity in his activities on behalf of moral causes and in his innovative rituals to mark the seasons of the year and of life. These are clear advantages of interpreting and applying the Jewish tradition as he does.

He clearly is taking a much more individualistic approach to Jewish law than the Jewish tradition and most Conservative writers do (with the possible exceptions of Feld and Scheindlin). In using Jewish law per se as one source for making decisions but not the only one, he does reflect some of the Conservative writers discussed above, but most of them would privilege the law as the primary mode for determining Jewish norms while in various ways using other parts of the tradition in interpreting it. Like the two most recent platform statements of the Reform rabbis, Waskow wants Jews to confront the tradition, which his approach takes very seriously; but one gets the strong sense from his writings that he is more interested in "reshaping" Jewish law than in perpetuating the received tradition—a sense that one does not get from the latest Reform platforms. Even though he and his colleagues call their movement "Renewal" for good reasons, it has many of the elements that led the founders of the Reform movement to their choice of name, for much more than conserving the tradition, Waskow thinks that it is necessary to reform Judaism in order to renew it.

Arthur Green

The same kind of approach is suggested by Arthur Green, Philip Lown Professor of Jewish Thought at Brandeis University, Dean of the Rabbinical School at Boston's Hebrew College, and formerly President of the Reconstructionist Rabbinical College. Ordained by the Jewish Theological Seminary of America in 1967, he completed his doctorate at

Brandeis in 1975 in Jewish Thought and has written widely on Hasidism and other forms of Jewish mysticism, including some books devoted to his own creative theology. His books in the history of Hasidism include *Tormented Master: The Life and Spiritual Quest of Rabbi Nahman of Bratslov* (1981) and *A Guide to the Zohar* (2003). His books articulating his own theology include *Seek My Face, Speak My Name* (1992) and *Ehyeh: A Kabbalah for Tomorrow* (2003).

In his published 1994 lecture at Hebrew Union College, "Judaism for the Post-Modern Era," Green describes the new generation of spiritual seekers in much the same way the sociologist Wade Clark Roof does[60]—spiritually serious, but individualistic and unwilling to accept tradition just because it is tradition. Instead, for this new generation at the beginning of the twenty-first century, religion must meet their needs or they will abandon it. Green suggests that in order to meet the needs of such people, current leaders of liberal forms of Judaism (for whom he speaks, in the first person) remember that they too were seekers in their youth:

> We liked Martin Buber's distinction between *religiosity* [that is, institutional religion] and *religion* [that is, individual spirituality], and shared his feeling that too much had been frozen in the old forms of Jewish observance. But as leaders of liberal Jewish institutions we too became defenders of another version of institutionalized religion, and perhaps lost some of our attunement to that religiosity.[61]

Instead, Green says, leaders of liberal forms of religion must engage in a *teshuvah* (return) of their own: "This may mean a washing out of our mouths of some of the 'answers' we have provided for the Jews we serve, when we should have just told them that we too were seekers. We too were attracted to the life of faith without being literal believers in the revealed authority of Judaism and its practices."[62]

To rejuvenate Judaism in such a spiritual way, Green suggests using the Jewish mystic tradition and shaping it into a new form. Judaism's central metaphor, according to Green, is standing at the foot of Sinai and passively receiving the Torah.

> The Judaism of the foot of the mountain has not much room for seekers. Torah has already been given; we live in the afterglow of revelation. For purposes of praxis, there is a Set Table [*Shulhan Arukh*] where we can look up how it is we are to live, what to do in any given situation. Our question—which does go on in classical Judaism, to be sure—takes the form of commentary, but commentary to a text that is already given, already fixed in its primary meaning. And the event of revelation,

the moment of encounter between the divine and the human, is to be seen through the distant veil of generations, *dor dor ve'sofrav, dor dor u'sefarav,* each writer and book adding another layer of distance.[63]

Instead, Green argues for a completely different metaphor, the mouth of a well or a never-ending stream, where the seeker continually encounters God anew. That will not entail abandoning the classical texts of Judaism, but it will mean that we must read them in the mystic way, seeking the meaning behind the texts.

> But Jacques Derrida and Walter Benjamin, among the fathers of the post-modern mind, are here to remind us that on one level we have no such fixed text at all. The revelation is silent, beyond speech, beyond the confines of both mind and language. It is we (in our terms, in the person of Moshe Rabbenu) who put it into words, who create the *torah shebikhtav* [Written Torah] that is really the first layer of commentary on the silent *Urtext* [original text] that we can only call *torat ha-shem* [the Torah of God]. We were transformed, dazzled, shaped into a revolutionary new nation by an encounter with that silent Presence, with that level of Being, with that rung of Mind. The Torah-text emerged, over a period of generations, from our attempt to live in the light of that transforming encounter. While I am not suggesting for a moment that we as Jews can or should leave that sacred written text behind, I am saying that we have to learn to recover what lies behind and within it. Standing at the mouth of the well, a source or *makor* that never runs dry, whence revelation pours forth like a never-ending stream, will do us better than being at the foot of a mountain, which, the rabbis tell us, loses all sense of holiness once the single event of revelation is over.[64]

Green here is explicitly using the Jewish mystic model of seeking the esoteric meanings of the Torah. He cites both the Kabbalah and the Ḥasidic masters as his predecessors in this endeavor. Most of the Jewish mystics of the past adhered to Jewish law, interpreting it mystically in their search for underlying theological and moral meanings not obvious in either the plain meaning of the Torah or its classical interpretations. Unlike them, and unlike even the assumptions of the more antinomian strains in Kabbalah and Ḥasidism whose authors nevertheless assumed that the Torah was fixed, Green is suggesting a more radical form of mysticism, in which the text of the Torah itself is seen as a human interpretation of the encounter with God—a view that Green learned not only from the postmoderns he cites but also from modern biblical scholarship and from his mentor, Heschel. Green, though, takes this insight much further than Heschel and many biblical critics do: *Because* the Torah is a human reaction to God, we must get beneath it to encourage contemporary Jewish seekers to find their own encounters with God. The Torah and its classical rabbinic commentaries may serve as a guide for that search, but they do not establish a Set Table in either theology or law, for revelation of God—of the One, as Green calls ultimate reality—is ever gushing forth. Therefore our response to the One may and perhaps should change daily.

This is clearly a more radical form of reconstruction of Judaism than we have seen so far, but it is not intended to establish a way out of Judaism. Quite to the contrary, Green is explicitly creating this theology and theory of law to articulate a reason and method by which modern Jewish seekers can find meaning in their Jewish heritage rather than leave it for Buddhism, Hinduism, or other religions or spiritual practices. Furthermore, Green is not just trying to appeal to the current market of spiritual seekers because that is today's fad. He is instead suggesting that these seekers' quest is everyone's journey and was, in fact, the project of the creators of Kabbalah and Hasidism, as well as for our biblical and rabbinic forbears. All those people satisfied themselves, however, with different responses to their quest.

Green is thus claiming that the theological searching of contemporary Jews need not force them out of the bounds of Judaism if they and current Jewish leaders only understand that Jews in all ages have been deeply involved in just such a quest. To do that, current Jewish leaders must admit that they too are still involved in that same project and that they lack neat and convincing answers to some of everyone's most pressing questions and needs. Rabbis and others who have engaged in that searching for years may serve as guides for spiritual newcomers, but they cannot serve as authorities in either theology or law, for each person must shape his or her own response to the One.

There is in this approach, of course, very little basis for community and very little acknowledgment of the ways in which the communal aspects of Judaism serve to draw Jews to affirm their Jewish identity. Furthermore, in Green's theory neither theological nor legal authority exists. There is no Set Table for Jewish practice, little less any authoritative interpreters of it. These are obviously major points of difference with most Conservative theories of Jewish law. Moreover, in Green's theory, Jewish identity altogether is in question. Jewish seekers would remain Jewish only to the extent that they find—or are taught to find—the Jewish tradition meaningful. That imposes an immense burden on rabbis and other Jews interested in perpetuating the Jewish tradition, for they no longer can satisfy themselves with teaching those who are already interested in Judaism or convinced that they have no alternative, but they rather must now act as Jewish salespeople, as it were, trying to show skeptical Jews that Judaism can help them in their spiritual quests and can do so more effectively than other traditions can.

And yet there are some distinct strengths in Green's approach. First, Wade Clark Roof and Green are undoubtedly right in their sociological depiction of many Jews of the current generation, and if Judaism is going to survive, Jewish leaders must take that seriously and must find ways to respond to the new generation's spiritual needs. Green's approach is surely one way to do that, for it consciously roots such individualistic searches for the spiritual in older Jewish sources written by people who sought to respond to the same needs. Furthermore, those Jews who indeed find such meaning in Jewish sources are likely to become very committed to Judaism, for they will have a strong sense of its relevance to their lives and their own ownership of their form of Judaism. While the theory gives no guarantee of this, perhaps such Jews will ultimately find themselves living out their Jewish commitments and expressing their own spirituality through reinterpreting and practicing many of the same commandments that have characterized Judaism for centuries.

E. A POSITION ON THE LEFT BORDER OF CONSERVATIVE JUDAISM: EUGENE BOROWITZ

Finally, Eugene Borowitz has affirmed a position very much like Clifford Librach's; but while Librach maintained that the *practices* of those within the Conservative and Reform movements are similar, Borowitz claims instead that his own *theory* of Jewish law, Reform rabbi and theologian though he be, is functionally equivalent to Conservative theories, including mine.

Eugene Borowitz is Sigmund L. Falk Distinguished Professor of Education and Jewish Religious Thought at the Hebrew Union College-Jewish Institute of Religion in New York City, where he has taught since 1962. He holds doctorates from Hebrew Union College and Teachers' College, Columbia University, and he won a National Jewish Book Award for his book, *The Masks Jews Wear* (1973). He is probably best known as the founder and long-time editor of *Sh'ma: A Journal of Jewish Responsibility*. A revered and beloved rabbi and professor within the Reform movement, he is known for challenging students to articulate clearly and thoughtfully their own positions on theological issues. A mark of the esteem with which he is held in the Reform movement is that he chaired the committee that wrote the 1976 platform statement for the Reform rabbinate, *Reform Judaism: A Centenary Perspective.* Author of twelve books, one articulates his theory of Jewish law, namely, *Renewing the Covenant: A Theology for the Postmodern Jew* (1991).

It was in response to that book that I was asked to write a review for the journal *Conservative Judaism.* I did so, describing the real innovation Borowitz had made in Reform thought—namely, to say that for a Jew to exercise autonomy responsibly in choosing a form of Judaism, he or she must be a "Jewish self" and not just a "self." That is, Jews need to learn and experience their tradition before they can appropriately and responsibly choose which parts of it to affirm and practice in their lives. At the same time, I said that this emphasis on individual autonomy marked his theory as distinctly Reform and not Conservative. Rabbi Borowitz, a good friend and sparring partner, then wrote an Open Letter to me in the pages of a subsequent issue of *Conservative Judaism,* claiming that I had misunderstood his intentions, that he was not writing as a Reform spokesman but as an individual who had a particular theory of law, and that his theory was very similar to my own. I, in turn, responded to him, and we both regard the exchange as a wonderful example of how friends and colleagues can respectfully—and, hopefully, insightfully—disagree.

Rabbi Borowitz liked our exchange so much that he had the exchange printed separately and distributed to every Reform rabbi in the Central Conference of Reform Rabbis. I liked it very much too, and so I am including it below as a clear example of how someone to the left of the Conservative movement institutionally may not be so far from it in theory and possibly even in practice. Rabbi Borowitz, in any case, would claim that!

⟪❧ ⎯⎯⎯⎯⎯ ☙⟫

*Autonomy vs. Community**

ELLIOT N. DORFF

THOSE WHO HAVE READ from the prolific writings of Rabbi Eugene Borowitz in the past will not be at all surprised that this work of his is clearly written, personally honest and unpretentious, penetrating in its criticism of alternative approaches, fully aware and appreciative of both the Jewish tradition and the contemporary context of Jewish life, morally and theologically urgent and, throughout, thought-provoking.

Conservative Judaism 48:2 (Winter 1996), pp. 64–68.

These are some of the characteristics that we have come to expect of Eugene Borowitz and—all too often—to take for granted. Through his own writings and through the dialogue he has encouraged through *Sh'ma,* the journal he founded and edited for three decades, he has set both the intellectual and the moral standards for what serious, open and respectful Jewish discussion should be.

This book is the quintessence of all the qualities Rabbi Borowitz has manifested in the past. Ideas that were only tentatively put forward in early books like *A New Jewish Theology in the Making* (1968) and *How Can a Jew Speak of Faith Today?* (1969) have now come to full exposition. Rabbi Borowitz has proven to be as relentless in the pursuit of clarity, truth and Jewish responsibility in his own theology as he has been in examining the work of others, and we are all the better for it.

It is, then, very much in the spirit of Eugene Borowitz that I want to take him on frontally in this review. I know that he will understand—and I certainly hope that everyone else will too—that I do so with genuine love for the man and with deep appreciation for his work. At the same time, we have an honest disagreement over how Jews should think about their Judaism and express their convictions in action, and the nature and reasons for that must be stated clearly, rigorously and yet respectfully. That is the model he has set for us.

This book does not present itself as a distinctly Reform theology, but it certainly is one. Indeed, it would be hard not to be, given that Rabbi Borowitz has been the prime Reform ideologue for a generation. Like Reform ideologies from the days of Abraham Geiger, Borowitz's approach places the ultimate source of authority on matters of both belief and practice in the individual person. To believe and act responsibly as a contemporary Jew, to be sure, the individual must learn as much as possible not only about modernity but also about traditional Judaism and the various ways people have proposed to integrate the two. That is the clause Rabbi Borowitz wrote into the 1976 Centennial Perspective of the Reform Movement—specifically, "Within each area of Jewish observance, Reform Jews are called upon to confront the claims of Jewish tradition, however differently perceived, and to exercise their individual autonomy, choosing and creating on the basis of commitment and knowledge"—and it is the thrust of what he writes in this book.

Here, though, Borowitz has definitively spelled out for his theology how locating the locus of authority in the individual amounts to anything more than each person doing whatever he or she wants to do about his or her own Jewish identity. Borowitz does this through his concept of "the autonomous Jewish self." All moderns living in Western countries have inherited the right to make their own decisions regarding religious belief and practice from the Enlightenment philosophies that shaped Western governments. That is the "autonomous" part of "the autonomous Jewish self." The individual Jew, however, is not simply an isolated person who happens to choose to affirm his or her Jewishness; rather, from the moment of birth or conversion, each Jew must see himself or herself as an autonomous *Jewish self.* That is, we modern Jews, *as an integral part of who we are as people,* are Jews just as much as we are individuals. This means that we do not begin our inquiry into our own identities with a clean slate, free to choose whatever we like; we begin, instead, *as Jews,* and therefore as part of the Covenant between God and Israel.

This conception of our individual identities automatically and immediately imposes upon us covenantal obligations to do God's will. We may, and will, perceive what God wants of us in our own individual way (the autonomy again); but however we understand God's covenantal command, we have a duty to perform it—the Jewish part of our autonomous Jewish self. Like other duties, religious obligations do not reduce to our desires. On the contrary, religious duties often require us to do what we otherwise would not want to do. As a result, in affirming covenantal responsibilities, Borowitz is saying that there are teeth to the covenant, that God not only likes us, does things for us and wants to be associated with us, but demands things of us.

Those familiar with the writings of Martin Buber and Franz Rosenzweig will see in Borowitz's approach something falling in between theirs. Indeed, Borowitz acknowledges his debt to them. Like both of them, Borowitz begins with the individual as the fundamental reality. That is the mark of all existentialist theories. Borowitz, however, grants the individual much more room to determine the content of Jewish duty than Rosenzweig ever did. For Borowitz, I am *not* obligated to do whatever I can do of traditional Jewish law, as I am for Rosenzweig, for as I individually understand God's will, God may not want me to follow all of Jewish law (or, for that matter, any of it) in modern times. On the other hand, for Borowitz I am not simply an individual who relates to God, as I am for Buber; I am, for Borowitz, a *Jewish* individual, and so the duties that derive from that relationship inevitably have a distinctively Jewish character. This, then, is the theory behind the operational statement that Borowitz wrote into the Reform movement's Centennial Perspective in 1976—that I must *"confront"* the claims of Jewish tradition *because I am a Jewish self;* that I will and, in modern times, may understand them in my own way ("however differently perceived"); and then I will and may make my choices as to how to believe and act as an *autonomous* Jewish self.

My problems with this theory are, in essence, the reasons why I am a Conservative Jew and not a Reform Jew. First, to be a serious Reform Jew along these lines is a *very* tall order. One must first learn both the Western and the Jewish traditions thoroughly so that one's choices can be informed and intelligent. One must also learn how to recognize the voice of God through all of this so that one knows how God wants one to integrate tradition and modernity. I do not doubt that Eugene Borowitz has the requisite knowledge and powers of judgment to make his theory work, but I doubt that many others do. The amount of Jewish and general education needed for such a theory to work—to say nothing of the demands of theological training and moral sensitivity—is simply too great for most Jews to master. I frankly doubt whether the educational systems currently in place in any of the movements could produce many people with all of these qualifications, let alone a whole cadre of Jewish people with them, and I question whether even the ideal Jewish educational system—however that is defined—realistically can hope to achieve the goals of Borowitz's method of applying Jewish law.

It is precisely here where the Conservative approach, for all of its difficulties, is actually easier. Like Borowitz, I too want Jews (most especially myself, but not only me) to adopt a form of Jewish belief and practice that integrates the best of tradition and modernity. In the Conservative way of doing things, though, I do not have to depend exclusively upon my own resources to decide how to do that. Instead, I participate in a *community* of people who are on the same quest, and we make those decisions *as a community* in the ways in which that traditionally has been done—through rabbinic decisions, individually and collectively, and through the interaction of law with custom. We may, of course, all be wrong, for we are, after all, human, but that would most assuredly be true also for our Orthodox coreligionists who unavoidably interpret and apply traditional Jewish texts according to their own human abilities and those of the rabbis they respect. We in the Conservative movement, in my view, are in a better position to discern God's will than the Orthodox are because we openly recognize the human component of revelation from the beginning and therefore are more keenly aware of the need to differentiate the human from the divine in those texts as we make decisions for our time. On the other hand, though, like the Orthodox and unlike Borowitz, the Conservative approach requires us constantly to check our own understanding of God's will with that of other Jews. This complicates and delays the process of making decisions, but it also relieves me of being solely responsible for the Jewish decisions I make—a Jewish and moral burden that few of us can bear intelligently and responsibly.

In addition to these practical problems with Borowitz's theory, I have some Jewish and some philosophical problems with it. From the point of view of the Jewish tradition, of course, individual Jews are not vested with the right to make decisions as to what they should believe and practice. That is a communal, and ultimately a divine, matter. Borowitz, of course, would claim that modernity has irreversibly denuded Judaism and the Jewish community of that kind of authority and that, furthermore, individual autonomy in matters of religion is a good thing. I have problems with both of those claims, but suffice it to say that a move to individual autonomy *at the very least* is a significant move *away* from traditional Judaism. That makes the "Jewish" in "the autonomous Jewish self" seriously attenuated in its meaning.

But let us look at the claims underlying virtually all of Reform thinking from Geiger to Borowitz. Is individual autonomy "all that it has been cracked up to be"? I, for one, am most grateful for the Enlightenment and for its American offshoots in granting me and all others under their sway political freedoms that include freedom of religion and of speech. I not only thrive under those freedoms in a practical sense; I think that they are an important new addition to what we mean by the concept of the sanctity of the individual created in God's image. Such sanctity *requires* mutual respect among people of all religions and denominations who honestly are seeking to discover God in their lives.[1]

In our own time, though, we have come to see that just as communal authoritarianism can destroy the individual respect required by that divine image, so too can autonomy left unchecked. Individuals *should* have choices in important areas of their lives; I would even go so far as to say that, in political matters at least, the burden of proof should be on the government to show why individuals should *not* have a choice in a particular area. What we want from religion, though, is not simply to congratulate us for what we would have thought or done on our own anyway; we want religion to *broaden our concerns, give us guidance, and challenge us to be better than we would have otherwise been.* If religion is going to do those things, autonomy must be balanced not only with divinity but with community.

Borowitz spends six chapters on the issue of community and speaks eloquently about the sociality of Jewish spirituality. After all is said and done, though, that sociality does not, for Borowitz, require obedience of Jewish law "however differently perceived" (to borrow a phrase) and so I frankly doubt that he has successfully protected those who follow his approach from the dangers of autonomy run amok. We need a better *balance* between autonomy and community, and the emphasis, if there is to be one, should, in the area of religion, be on community, for only then can religion fulfill its functions. But that judgment, again, makes me Conservative and Borowitz Reform.

Finally, the very Enlightenment theory on which Borowitz's emphasis on autonomy is based is currently—and, I think, correctly—coming under attack. Contrary to the classical Enlightenment thinkers like John Locke, we do not exist as individuals in some state of nature and then autonomously decide to enter into a social contract. Instead, as people like the French Jewish philosopher Emanuel Levinas and "communitarians" like Amitai Etzioni have pointed out, our very being is social. We come into the world with relationships already built into our existence. Those relations immediately impose duties upon us. The nature and extent of those duties, and the way Jewish law is related to this analysis of the origin of duty, are matters for lengthy discussion well beyond the scope of this review essay; but that line of reasoning is, I think, much closer to the truth and to the grounds for a meaningful theory of Jewish obligation than is one based on autonomy—even one modified by the adjective "Jewish."[2]

All of this is not in any way to deny the importance of this book. Here we have the premier Reform theologian articulating clearly and passionately why Jews who believe in autonomy as a cornerstone of their religious faith should nevertheless see themselves also as subject to Jewish duties. This certainly has been the emphasis of many Reform theologies of the past. Here it is not only stated, but closely reasoned and tied to a wider theology of the relationship of Jews to each other, to Torah and to God. Borowitz here delivers on the promise of his earlier conception of Covenant within a Reform context, spelling out its meaning, grounds and implications as he has never done before. Watching him do that in the careful way he always does was a sheer delight. Ultimately, as I indicated above, I have practical, Jewish and philosophical problems with the approach that Rabbi Borowitz adopts, but I have been genuinely enriched by this book. By letting us in on his own informed and immensely thoughtful and skillful theological wrestling, Eugene Borowitz has shown all of us just how deeply we all can and should probe the foundations of our own faith.

NOTES

A review of Eugene B. Borowitz, *Renewing the Covenant: A Theology for the Postmodern Jew* (Philadelphia: The Jewish Publication Society, 1991), xiv + 319 pages.

1. I have developed the theological basis for such pluralism with non-Jews in my article, "The Covenant as the Key: A Jewish Theology of Jewish-Christian Relations," in *Toward a Theological Encounter: Jewish Understandings of Christianity,* Leon Klenicki, ed. (New York: Paulist Press, 1991), pp. 43–66. I have addressed the same concerns regarding differences of belief and practice *within* the Jewish community in my essay, "Pluralism," in *Frontiers of Jewish Thought,* Steven T. Katz, ed. (Washington, D.C.: B'nai Brith Books, 1992), pp. 213–234. Both have been reprinted in my book *To Do the Right and the Good: A Jewish Approach to Modern Social Ethics* (Philadelphia: Jewish Publication Society, 2002), chs. 2 and 3.

2. See my book, *Mitzvah Means Commandment* (New York: United Synagogue Youth 1989), especially pp. 81–96, for a brief comparison of these two theories as applied to Jewish law.

The Reform Judaism of Renewing the Covenant
An Open Letter to Elliot Dorff*

EUGENE B. BOROWITZ

I'M DEEPLY GRATEFUL FOR YOUR searching review of *Renewing the Covenant.* To be given serious attention is itself a considerable gift but you are also gracious enough to say many nice things about my work

---

Conservative Judaism 50:1 (Fall 1997), pp. 61–65.

over the years and that truly touched me. Many thanks indeed for your great-heartedness. Yet as you surely know, the greatest compliment of all is to have a thoughtful reader probe your ideas with great care and respond to them from the depths of his or her understanding. I was particularly happy that you devoted a significant part of your review to my effort to transform the old Enlightenment-Kantian view of the individuality of the self into something far more congenial to Judaism. As I see it, there is far more overlap in our views than your analysis indicates though I agree that we differ in significant part.

You perceive a great divide between us because you insist that my book must be read "as a distinctly Reform theology . . . Indeed, it would be hard not to be, given that Rabbi Borowitz has been the prime Reform ideologue for a generation." As a result, though I climax my "theology of post-liberal Jewish duty" with my notion of "the Jewish self"—self-consciously not "the autonomous Jewish self" of my 1984 article—you believe I must not be saying anything much different from what Reform thinkers of prior generations said. All my talk aside, you insist that self overwhelms Jewishness with all the usual deleterious consequences for our Judaism.

Two things about this assertion particularly surprise me. The first stems from your careful emphasis on my six chapters rejecting the isolated selfhood of the Enlightenment and Kant, a notion that dominated the older Reform Judaism (and most of American Jewish non-Orthodox apologetics). Post-modern Jews, I argue, need to recontextualize selfhood for Jews as Covenantal, that is, to see the Jewish self as an individuality fundamentally grounded in God and the Jewish people's relationship to God. Moreover, even though you know that "This book does not present itself as a distinctly Reform theology," you insist that "it certainly is one." Since you claim that "Reform" necessarily calls for the supremacy of utterly individual autonomy, you can insist that I must also be making the isolated self the arbiter of Jewish duty. You say I write clearly and probingly, so either I cannot mean what I say or else I misunderstand its implications.

I do not know how I can persuade you that "I am not now and never have been a card-carrying Reform ideologue." As to my role in preparing our Centenary Perspective document, I became Chair of the Committee that wrote it only because a previous Commission—of which I was not invited to be a regular member—failed to do so despite several years of meetings. A series of political necessities then brought the CCAR to turn to me. So though you twice credit me with inserting some specific language in it, my colleagues, vigorous exercisers of their autonomy and doughty defenders of their political diversity, never extended such deference to me. They wrote the text in session line by line. Overnight I put my notes (now in the American Jewish Archives) of what they had agreed to say into connected prose. They then went over the whole thing again—as later did the whole membership in a floor debate of the draft. In short, I am not the Reform Robert Gordis, z"l.

Instead, I have always tried to think academically about Jewish belief and its consequences. None of my models—Cohen, Baeck, Kaplan, Buber, Rosenzweig and Heschel—ever did their thinking as part of a movement or in the context of its ideology. They simply tried to think through the truth of Judaism in their day as best they could understand it, and I have spent my life attempting to emulate them. Only one of my books for adults and only a few of my articles deal with Reform Judaism. For over three decades I have addressed myself to and written about that overwhelming mass of modernized Jews who, regardless of labels, exercise the right to make up their own minds about what they will believe and do as Jews. Having been misunderstood when I tried calling these people "liberal" Jews, I attempted to nail down my meaning in *Renewing the Covenant* by mostly speaking about "non-Orthodox" Jews. When I mean Reform Jews there or anywhere, I say so.

If you would like some specific if rough examples of my view of Reform Jewish decision-making today, look at my *Reform Jewish Ethics and the Halakhah* (Behrman, 1994). That book, with all its faults, e.g., its fourteen issues were tackled by teams of students who did term papers as my kind of Reform *poskim,* will show you the distance between my functioning theory of duty and the one you have imputed to my theology. Even though the students are far more Kantian than I am, you will not find "autonomy run amok" in any of their papers.

You see three issues dividing us: practicality, Jewishness and philosophy. The first, practicality, has two parts: the heavy burden of being a responsible (Jewish) self and the role of community in our decision-making. I agree few of us can know all we need to know to make a significant decision. When I need help in such cases, I do what most people do: consult experts and read the most responsible literature I can find. I see no reason why responsible Jewish selves will not do the same on matters where Judaism is relevant. Thoughtful Jewish writing on contemporary problems today continues to expand, one reason I take it that you and I often seek to make our own views known and do all we can to see to it that rabbis and Jewish educators are increasingly knowledgeable.

You say that the Jewish self will not care as you do about what the Jewish community says on an issue. Maybe "your" Reform Jews are supposed to believe that, but not if they took my views seriously. In addition to what you correctly said about my situating the Jewish self inextricably in the Jewish people, consider what I wrote about proper Jewish decision-making as the climax to my argument in *Renewing the Covenant* (pp. 288–295). There I explain in some detail that as a result of its Covenanted situation, the Jewish self should make decisions based on: (1) what it believes God wants of it as a member of the Covenanted people; (2) which means it will be concerned with what the Jewish community today is saying on this topic (more of this below); (3) but the experience of Covenant being fundamentally historical, what rabbinic tradition said on the topic must be given reverent attention; (4) as must the messianic, future-oriented thrust of the

Covenant. But all those vectors finally come to rest (5) in an individual self whose individuality is not extinguished for all that it is utterly bound up with God and the Jewish people's relationship with God, historically articulated, presently lived and projected to the End of Days.

My six chapters and my second vector should make plain that I insist on community concern among Jews and know nothing of the unattached self in Judaism. If that means that I am not a Reform Jew by your standards, then so be it. It is equally clear that I am not your kind of Conservative Jew, for I do not closely identify "community" with rabbinic law-making as you do.

The issue of law, however, requires me to inquire about your "practicality" in making it so central a tenet of Conservative Judaism. For years Conservative rabbis have lamented the inability of the movement to create a laity that would let their lives be disciplined by Jewish law, and recently a good number of rabbis and laypeople who took law seriously abandoned Conservatism for a movement of their own. Realistically, then, how practical is it to ask Conservative Jews to live by Jewish law? Of course, if by "law" you mean little more than "standards," the term with which law is linked in the title of the Rabbinical Assembly Committee dealing with issues of duty, then little divides us. No self-respecting Jewish self could object to hearing about communal standards; that would only help clarify one important factor in determining Jewish duty.

We disagree, however, about the possibility and desirability of law fulfilling its common function, being authoritative in our lives. You charge that my sense of "sociality does not . . . require obedience of Jewish law." You are right. But has the Conservative movement, which has made law central to its ideology, yet found a way to "require obedience of Jewish law"?

Your second objection to my position is that Jewish tradition knows nothing of individual Jews being given "the right to make decisions about what they should believe and practice." I agree that in sanctioning even a Covenantally limited autonomy, I, and certainly the Reform Jews who are more radical than I am, have moved away from classic Jewish faith. But by Maimonides' standards of *epikorsut,* the Conservative view (like that in Reform) that there is a significant human factor in revelation instantly puts you too in our situation. The issue here is not, as you suggest, a simple realism about what modernity has done to us all but rather how we evaluate what we have learned about the conjunction of human dignity and self-legislation. You are too sensible not to value much that this notion has brought us, and you affirm its lasting significance when it does not degenerate into radical individualism, a plague I equally deplore. But I argue that modernity, by teaching us this new sense of self, has made a major, lasting, spiritual contribution to Judaism—or, to be more direct, that this notion is contemporary revelation, a new insight into God's will and thus a present indication of our ongoing Covenantal responsibility. That is, I believe, the theological substrate to the endemic practice of most of contemporary Jewry: listening to their leaders but then exercising what they take to be their sacred right, making up their own minds about what they will and won't do. Community creates duty, as you say, but that is a far cry from anything like authoritative law.

This brings me to your final charge against me, that I have ignored the philosophical attack on the radical individualism of the Enlightenment. That makes sense only if one demands that the rejection of the Enlightenment and Kantian self which I have specifically called "postmodern" and "post-liberal" doesn't mean what it says and I have no choice but to be a defender of the kind of individualism you take to be the unchanging essence of Reform Judaism.

I shall allow the defense to rest there. But I must, however, point out that the authority of the self operates in contemporary Jewish law more significantly than you have acknowledged. On the simplest level, why is it that I know that I will find your forthcoming book on Jewish medical ethics highly persuasive, where a similar book by David Novak will be somewhat less so and the writing of J. David Bleich on the same topic will likely touch me only informationally? Surely what divides this trio is not what the legal texts objectively say, for you will all study the same ones. It is also not substantially a matter of consulting the community (though I imagine that your disparate reference groups will have some influence on you). Rather I suggest that we are dealing here with the way in which the self makes itself felt even in legal decision-making. One factor in decision-making, not the only or the most significant matter in the process, is simply who you are as a person and how you act on that individuality. Were you a different person, you would not be the *posek* [decisor] we know you to be, the author of your *shitah* [approach].

Or let me give a case more internal to the Conservative movement. Consider the situation of Conservative rabbis faced with a split decision of the Committee on Jewish Law and Standards. How do they finally reach a decision about a difficult issue? The critical texts can apparently be read in at least two ways, and they cannot ask the community to settle the matter for it is just its leaders who are themselves of two minds. I suggest that in significant measure they will follow my five-part schema: they will seek to determine what God now wants by filtering their living religiosity through Jewish history, the community's present experience and its ongoing messianic aspiration and, finally, subject the whole to the reality of who they individually are and what they personally believe. You and they may take step three—studying Jewish law and lore—with a somewhat greater sense of obligation than I might, but we shall all be following the theology of Jewish duty explicated in *Renewing the Covenant*.

This line of argument can proceed one final step. You assert, in distinguishing yourself from the Orthodox, that there is a significant human element in legal decision-making, and your open acknowledgment of it enables you "better [to] discern God's will" than they can. By what authority is that position put forward as a fundamental principle of your Judaism? It cannot be on the basis of Jewish law and tradition, for they do not grant human beings that much power. It cannot be claimed that it is self-evident, for not only do our Orthodox deny it but so do all fundamentalists and secularists. I suggest that the Conservative sages who founded your movement did so on their own authority as scholars, people of piety and participants in many aspects of modern culture. In brief, they acted on the authority of their autonomy, literally, their right to be self-legislating. And those who have since joined the Conservative movement have done the same thing in a somewhat lesser fashion. You have more investment in autonomy, Covenantally recontextualized to be sure, than you are willing to admit—or so I see it.

I hope you will take the length at which I have written as a token of my great personal esteem for you and your writings over the years. I have learned much from you in the past and look forward to doing so in the future. I do hope you will have the opportunity to respond to what I have written here, and I will look forward to hearing from you about it.

Matters of Degree and Kind
An Open Response to Eugene Borowitz's
Open Letter to Me*

ELLIOT N. DORFF

I LOVE BEING CHALLENGED BY YOU! Your letter, as you undoubtedly hoped, forced me to reread your book, especially the chapters to which you refer. I also pondered your letter for quite some time.

I admit that I first read your book through the prism of your earlier writings and your long association with Reform Judaism. While I recognized that there is much that is new in *Renewing the Covenant*— most especially your redefined and recontextualized idea of the Jewish self—I did not appreciate the extent to which you wanted to distinguish this work from both your own previous writings and from Reform thought in general. For that I apologize. (Incidentally, Rabbi Robert Gordis, z"l, was no more independent in crafting *Emet Ve-Emunah:*

Conservative Judaism 50:1 (Fall 1997), pp. 66–71.

The Philosophy of Conservative Judaism than you report that you were in editing the Reform Movement's *Centenary Perspective*. Rabbi Gordis did not write the first draft of any of the sections of *Emet Ve-Emunah*, and the commission charged with writing it debated every sentence—indeed, virtually every word. His good sense, energy, and wide respect within the movement, though, permeated our discussions and kept them on track—a role that, I would bet, you played too.)

On rereading *Renewing the Covenant*, then, I would agree that we are closer than I had previously thought. From one perspective, what separates us is indeed, as you suggest, a matter of degree: I take studying Jewish law and lore with "a greater sense of obligation" than you do. That, though, is not only a difference in background or temperament; it is also a difference in conviction, one, I think, that ultimately amounts to a difference in kind.

As I see it now, the distinction between us centers around our conceptions of law. You draw a sharp distinction between "standards" and "duty," on the one hand, and "authoritative law," on the other. Do you mean to suggest by that that norms become law only when they are enforced? That is certainly a possible understanding of law, but it is an awfully narrow one, one which, I think, does not do justice to how either secular or religious law operates. Think, for example, of Prohibition. There you had nothing less than a Constitutional amendment, with the full force of the federal government behind it, and yet it failed as a law and ultimately had to be repealed. Why? Because, I would suggest, the authority of any particular law or any legal system is based on a whole range of factors—communal acceptance of the law or legal system as generally wise, moral, practical, or all three; a sense of covenantal promise to abide by the law, whether one agrees with it or not (Do you really like every American law?); love of country; fear of chaos; a desire to be part of a coherent, well-integrated community; and perhaps even an aspiration to create an ideal society. Even though the vast majority of Americans obeyed the Prohibition Amendment and the laws enacted to carry it out, the police forces of the United States and of the several states combined were not sufficient to enforce those laws on the small percentage of Americans that disobeyed them—precisely, I would suggest, because the other elements noted above that make a law authoritative were missing.

If Prohibition graphically demonstrates in a secular legal system the limitations of restricting law to that which is enforced, the Golden Calf incident does the same in Jewish law. Just a short forty days after the awesome thunder, lightning, and earthquakes of Sinai, the Israelites were already worshipping the Golden Calf! The Bible was thus not only philosophically sophisticated but pragmatic and wise in suggesting nine separate motivations to abide by Jewish law, and the Rabbis added several more; I discuss these at some length in my book, *Mitzvah Means Commandment*.[1] Religious legal systems, like Jewish law, add motivations to obey to those inherent in secular law—motivations like the aspiration for holiness, the drive to complete a divine mission, and love of God.[2]

This affects our discussion in two ways. First, while I too would distinguish between authoritative law and moral standards, I would not draw the line nearly as sharply as you do. In my view, law can be amoral or even immoral, as a dictator's dictates may be. Nazi Germany's laws obviously come to mind. But when a secular legal system, like that of the United States, strives from the very beginning to embody moral values—in America's case, to secure individuals' "unalienable rights" (the Declaration of Independence) and to "establish Justice, insure domestic Tranquility, provide for the common defence, promote the general Welfare, and to secure the Blessings of Liberty to ourselves and our Posterity" (the Preamble to the Constitution)—then the law becomes permeated with moral concerns. I am not claiming that American society was ever morally ideal or is now; I am only claiming that the law is used in America not only as a tool for social peace and defense, but also for moral goals like justice, liberty, and the general welfare.

That is even more true for a religious legal system like Jewish law, which is, according to the Torah, given by a God of justice and mercy and which demands that we strive to be holy like God and to "do the right and the good in God's eyes" (Deuteronomy 6:18). Once again, because human beings are fallible and because the conditions of life and moral sensitivities change, Jewish law as it has come down to us does not always articulate the highest moral standard, and it certainly does not guarantee that those who follow it will necessarily be moral. Nevertheless, much of Jewish law does indeed set a high standard of morality for us, for Judaism, perhaps more than any other legal system on earth, strives to embody moral norms in legal form. Judaism cannot totally succeed in that effort, for life is too complex for any legal system to cover every possible eventuality. Moreover, life changes too much over time to be guided sensitively by the specific rules of the past. Hence there will always be a realm of moral duty and an even larger realm of moral goals beyond the limits of the law, and the law itself must be continuously subjected to moral critique. Nevertheless, a great deal of the authority of Jewish law derives from its moral base— whether or not Jewish law is enforced.

Moreover, while some of the other rationales enunciated in classical Jewish sources for obeying Jewish law have changed in our day in form or even in substance, and while now, as in the past, some motivations may persuade a given Jew more profoundly than others, many of the biblical and rabbinic reasons to live in accordance with Jewish law can and do apply to Jews today no less than in the past. One may still feel bound to obey Jewish law out of a sense of owing God, or due to one's Covenantal promise, or because one sees the life guided by the law as wise, or because one is motivated by respect for, or love of, God. For all these reasons, then, I maintain that Jewish law is fully authoritative for us today, even without human enforcement.

Second, my own understanding of the authority of Jewish law—and of its history—leads me to a different picture than you have of the role of the individual in the system. Yes, certainly, the Enlightenment gave us a new appreciation of the independence of the individual as a source of autonomous will and even moral values, and yes, certainly, I share both your gratefulness for those lessons and your commitment to individual liberty. The Enlightenment amounted to nothing short of a revolution in human thought, one that brought us many boons. Your book, more than any other I know, consciously tries to integrate that modern sense of individualism into a new approach to Jewish life and law.

In some ways, I want to strengthen your position by pointing out that even in the predominantly communitarian world of classical Jewish law individuals always had a role in formulating it. On the other hand, though, I would claim that classical Jewish law framed the role of individuals in shaping the law in ways that are not only different from the one you propose, but, I think, ultimately healthier for both individual Jews and for the Jewish community.

By sheer coincidence, I read your letter to me just after grading a series of midterm examinations for a class I am teaching in Mishnah, and the Mishnah I asked my students to translate and explain was Rosh Hashanah 2:9. There the rabbinic titans, Rabban Gamliel and Rabbi Joshua, clash, and Rabbi Akiba and Rabbi Dosa ben Harkinas do their best to console and advise Rabbi Joshua. That Mishnah is, of course, a resounding statement of communal authority over the individual, for ultimately Rabbi Joshua must submit to the superior authority of Rabban Gamliel. What is remarkable about that story, though, is that Rabbi Joshua does not immediately capitulate to Rabban Gamliel's decree; Rabbi Joshua must be convinced of either the correctness of Rabban Gamliel's decision or, failing that, of at least the legitimacy of Rabban Gamliel's authority to impose his decision. Moreover, as Louis Finkelstein, Jacob Neusner, Joel Gereboff, and others have demonstrated, the rulings of the classical rabbis were critically dependent upon their individual personalities, circumstances, and philosophies of life. Thus if you expect to warm to my treatment of Jewish medical ethics in my forthcoming book more than you have liked David Novak's or J. David Bleich's readings of Judaism on that subject—and I deeply appreciate your support!—it is only because of the same personal factors that have affected Jewish law from time immemorial.

I would go even further. You say that the significant human element that I ascribe to Jewish law "cannot be on the basis of Jewish law and tradition, for they do not grant human beings that much power." Yes they do! After it is all said and done, our Judaism is the religion of the Pharisees, not of the more fundamentalist Sadducees of their time or the Karaites of later generations. The Pharisees, our "Rabbis," insisted that rabbis in every generation had to determine the substance of the law, that it was wrong to refuse to do that on the grounds that previous generations had judges like Moses and our generation's judges pale by comparison (*T. Rosh Hashanah 1:17; B. Rosh Hashanah 25a–25b*). The Rabbis furthermore maintained that after the destruction of the First Temple, revelation would come in the form of the Rabbis' interpretation of the Torah, even to the point of asserting that a new, fully recognized revelation from God Himself could not overpower the authority of each generation's rabbis to determine the content of revelation in their time *(B. Bava Metzia 59b)*. Some Orthodox rabbis deny this inevitable and divinely authorized human element in discerning God's will, but they are misrepresenting rabbinic Judaism, as articulated in the texts I just cited and in many others, and they are deceiving themselves; after all, if God's will is so transparent as to be clear without any human interpretation, how can Orthodox rabbis disagree among themselves? Moreover, those rabbis who refuse to recognize the effects of their own methodology on their decisions are, I repeat, less well able to discern God's will than those who acknowledge the human element in the ongoing process of legal midrash. A striking formulation of this point was written by Rabbi Emanuel Rackman, an Orthodox rabbi himself, in his article *"Challenge to Orthodoxy,"* reprinted in his book, *One Man's Judaism,* pp. 262–283.

(Incidentally, on this point we disagree as well in our interpretation of Maimonides. Maimonides takes the rabbinic idea that "the Torah was given in the language of human beings" further than the Rabbis ever did by painstakingly spelling out in Part I of his *Guide for the Perplexed* the literal meanings of many of the metaphors in the Torah. Moreover, in his *Mishneh Torah* (Laws of Rebels, Chapter 2), he explicitly supports the authority of rabbis in each generation to make decisions, even, at times, against the Torah. These parts of his writings indicate that he surely assumes that "there is a significant human factor in revelation" in both its process of transmission and in its legal products—although obviously not to the extent of assigning the writing of the entire text of the Torah to human beings, as modern scholarship does.)

My understanding of the place of individuals in shaping classical Jewish law thus makes your question all the stronger: if individual rabbis in all their individuality have influenced the outcome of Jewish law, why do I put so much emphasis on the community of rabbis as the ones who determine its substance? Why not think of the Jewish community much more broadly, as you do, to include each individual Jew as the one who makes that decision?

I embrace the rabbinic method for defining Jewish law because, in part, Jews have done so for generations, and I want the historical rootedness I gain in retaining this method. I also want the coherence and community that come with the rabbinic method; I fear that individualism, even in your modified form, will lead to anarchy and isolation. I also believe, as I said in my earlier statement, that individual Jews—indeed, individual rabbis, myself certainly included—do not have the expertise or wisdom to make these decisions on their own. You yourself describe the process by which individuals make decisions as consulting others when they do not know what to do; I simply want to institutionalize that process—and retain a stronger sense of community and legal coherence at the same time—by putting Jewish decisions in the hands of those who know Jewish law in addition to the realities of modern life. They, of course, may have to consult experts in other fields in formulating their decisions, just as judges in any legal system do. But the decision will then be rooted in Jewish sources and thus become recognizably Jewish to all who examine it, even to those who disagree with it. For all these reasons, we must take seriously the lessons not only of ancient times, but also of recent years, when we have increasingly come to recognize the proper limits of individualism, even of the Jewishly informed and committed self of whom you speak.

This, then, brings me to the last issue, the relationship of the rabbis to the laity. On the one hand, you valorize the position of the individual—the Jewish self—in making Jewish law. In your letter, though, your example of how your brand of Jewish individualism would work in practice is the series of essays written by your rabbinical students; that hardly argues for how lay Jews will live by your theory. In the next paragraph, when arguing that lay people can indeed do that, you again urge us to "do all we can to see to it that rabbis and Jewish educators are increasingly knowledgeable." It is, of course, true that if Jewish professionals do not know Judaism, they cannot help lay Jews to know it; but your theory requires that each individual Jew knows enough to make responsible Jewish decisions. It is the possibility of that that I question in asking about the practicality of your proposal. Indeed, historians like Jacob Neusner assert that even at the time of the Pharisees most lay Jews did not know enough to practice Jewish law accurately, let alone enough to make decisions in Jewish law.

What I would assert, though, is that the laity as a group do indeed have halakhic power through their communal practices, their *minhagim* (customs). Jewish law throughout the ages has been the product of an interaction between the spiritual leaders of the community (whether prophets or rabbis) and its members. In Jewish law, as in American law, sometimes law creates new customs; sometimes law repudiates common customs and seeks to uproot them; sometimes customs undermine laws; and sometimes customs serve as the source of new laws. In all of these interactions between law and custom, the community as a whole has an immense effect on the shape of the law. That role for the laity, though, is decidedly communal, and even though the entire community may adopt a practice objectionable to the rabbis, I would much rather trust the community as a whole than individual lay members in it—just as I would rather trust the community of rabbis rather than individual rabbis, including myself.

In sum, then, it may indeed be, as you say, that much of our disagreement stems from the greater sense of obligation that I assign to studying Jewish law and lore and to acting in accordance with it. I think, though, that some of the matters that divide us stem from differences in convictions about the nature of law and the respective roles of rabbis and lay people in determining its rules. With all that, we share a deep commitment to the Jewish tradition, and I love to be prodded to rethink the nature and grounding of my own commitments by your probing questions and creative ideas. May we continue to engage together in this ongoing wrestling with God and with Judaism for many years to come.

NOTES

1. *Mitzvah Means Commandment* (New York: United Synagogue of Conservative Judaism, 1989). These arguments are presented in shorter form in the book I wrote with Arthur Rosett, *A Living Tree: The Roots and Growth of Jewish Law* (Albany, NY: State University of New York Press, 1988), pp. 82–122 and 246–257.
2. For a discussion of the ways in which Jewish law is similar to a legal system in some ways and very different in others—including the motivations of those who abide by it—see my article, "Judaism as a Religious Legal System," *Hastings Law Journal* 29:6 (July 1978), pp. 1331–1360.

CHAPTER EIGHT

Sample Illustrations
of Conservative Legal Theories at Work

IN CHAPTER ONE, I illustrated why theories of law matter by contrasting Jewish and American law on a variety of issues and by describing why one should care about theories of law in the first place. As I explained there, one of the reasons that theories of law matter and that one should care about them is that they can sometimes lead to specific conclusions about what the law should be and how it should be enforced that are different from the results that would be reached if one used another theory. This pragmatic reason to pay attention to theories is surely not the only one, as I explained there, but it is an important reason. Theories often have a direct effect on the substance of the law and on the motivations to obey it; sometimes that influence is immediately clear, and at other times one must analyze the law a bit more closely to see the effects of the theory underlying it.

To illustrate this with regard to Conservative theories of Jewish law, this chapter will examine some responsa validated by the Conservative movement's Committee on Jewish Law and Standards, as well as some other materials produced by the movement to teach Jews about some aspects of Jewish law. Because the Committee on Jewish Law and Standards has produced a large, varied, and rich store of responsa, and because other arms of the movement in North and South America and in Israel have further added to the treasury of Conservative legal materials, this chapter makes no claim for anything approaching completeness. (A partial list of such materials appears in the bibliography on page 524.) Any Conservative responsum or educational material about Jewish law can and should be examined for the legal theory that it assumes, but this chapter will necessarily focus on only a few of these items. Even with regard to the selections included here, my interest will be only those parts of the texts that exhibit how legal theories have shaped them and provided motivation for Jews to heed them. Hopefully that will be enough to make the point that Conservative theories of Jewish law indeed have had a pronounced effect on Conservative practice, and also to illustrate how readers can analyze other Conservative writings for the legal theories that undergird them. Similar remarks apply to legal writings produced by members of Judaism's other movements.

A. A RESPONSUM ON THE SABBATH

Perhaps the most well-known—and the most maligned—responsum that the CJLS ever approved was the 1950 responsum on the Sabbath. Often referred to, especially by its critics, as "the driving *teshuvah*" because it permitted driving to the synagogue for services on Shabbat when a Jew faced the choice of either driving there or not going at all, that understanding of it misrepresents both its content and intentions. Its actual title, "A Responsum on the Sabbath," much better describes its content, for it articulates a comprehensive plan to increase Shabbat observance.

While some legal questions, such as directions for building a *sukkah,* can be answered by a straightforward reference to earlier responsa or codes, the authors of this responsum, Rabbis Morris Adler, Jacob Agus, and Theodore Friedman, maintain that modern conditions require a much more serious analysis and response if Jews in significant numbers are to be convinced to observe the Sabbath. They point to three factors that make a simple reference to earlier Jewish law on the Sabbath inadequate: the acceptance of Jews into the larger society with the accompanying economic pressure to follow the larger society's calendar, including work on the Sabbath (often the busiest day of the week for businesses); the invention of electricity; and the invention of the automobile. Both of the latter two factors could never have been anticipated by earlier Jewish scholars, and so modern rabbis using any legal theory must decide how to understand them within the framework of Jewish law. Moreover, the automobile has made it possible for people to live in much less dense housing patterns than was previously necessary, with the result that many Jews depend on the car to get from place to place and so they no longer live within walking distance of the synagogue. Rabbis can, of course, ignore this new societal reality and thereby maintain the purity and full authority of the received law; but they can only do so by simultaneously classifying most Jews as sinners and making Jewish law insensitive to modern realities and thus irrelevant to modern Jews. The authors, in sharp response to such an approach, maintain that Jewish law requires more of rabbis than that, and that it is a disservice to both Jews and Judaism to interpret the law in such a way that most Jews cannot and will not follow it. They thus state their theory of law at the very outset:

> Our duty as rabbis is not exhausted when we cite the law as it has been understood and practiced, and ignore the conditions of life in the midst of which, or the thoughts of men by whom, that law is to be followed. One of the great responsibilities of this age in our history is to release the life-giving and life-enriching powers that inhere in our tradition, by relating that tradition to modern life. Changing conditions threaten an inert system of law. The Halachah lived and functioned in our history because it has traditionally been characterized by resiliency and responsiveness to life. The very designation of Jewish law as Halachah [from the Hebrew root meaning to go] suggests its capacity for movement and reveals the intent of its architects and builders to change it with a genius for vital adaptability to the moving and changing scene.[1]

Putting this another way, they want to make sure that the details of the law do not get in the way of the larger purposes of the law. In this case, that goal is to "revitalize" observance of the Sabbath among the majority of modern Jews who have let it drop out of their lives. Toward that end, the three authors propose both legal changes and an educational program.

Three things characterize their efforts. First, theirs is a program for their time and place:

> The program that we propose, then, is not to be regarded as the full and complete regimen of Sabbath observance, valid for all Jews for all times and for all places. On the contrary, it is aimed to meet the particular situation that confronts us, a situation without parallel in the long annals of Judaism. Our program seeks to reintroduce into the lives of our people as much Sabbath observance and spirit as we may reasonably hope our people will, with proper education, accept.[2]

Their proposal, in other words, is to create a "ladder of observance," a metaphor popular among Conservative rabbis and theorists, so that people who cannot or will not observe the Sabbath in strict adherence to all of its laws will not abandon it altogether, but will rather do what they can to observe part of it. Thus those Jews who cannot fully observe the Sabbath should nevertheless light the Sabbath candles to usher in the Sabbath, make all preparations for the Sabbath before then, attend public worship for at least one of the services of each Sabbath (Friday night, Saturday morning, or Saturday afternoon), and "refrain from all such activities that are not made absolutely necessary by the unavoidable pressures of life and that are not in keeping with the Sabbath spirit, such as shopping, household work, sewing, strenuous physical exercise, etc."[3] Note that this list specifically does not include desisting from one's gainful employment on the Sabbath, even though that is a major part of traditional Sabbath observance, for the intended audience is those who cannot do so for economic reasons. At the same time, before providing this list of immediate goals, the responsum specifically states that they are partial and temporary: "Emphasis on this immediate program should in no wise militate against the ultimate objective—the cessation of all gainful employment on the Sabbath. It is in the conviction that only the immediate can lead to the ultimate that the following program is proposed."[4]

Second, the authors maintain (with the justifications that we shall examine) that to accomplish the goal of revitalizing the Sabbath in the lives of most modern Jews, some leniencies in the law are necessary—specifically with regard to electricity and driving to the synagogue to accommodate "the geographical growth of the average American city." In a few cases, however, such as Manhattan and Jerusalem, Jews continue to live in dense housing patterns and do not need to use a car to attend synagogue services on the Sabbath. The authors therefore specify that their program must be adapted to local needs, that it is dependent on "the discretion of the local rabbi."[5] This, of course, is the recognition of the long-standing authority of the *mara d'atra,* the rabbi of the specific community and the important role of that rabbi to apply Jewish law appropriately to the needs and conditions of his or her particular community.

Third, and finally, this whole effort is to be seen in not only a legal context, but an educational one as well. As they say toward the end of their responsum,

> We cannot too strongly emphasize that our views in regard to the use of electric lights and the automobile on the Sabbath are not separable from the total program for the revitalization of the Sabbath as herein suggested. To take these elements out of the context of the entire national and local effort required for the strengthening of the basic institution of the Sabbath would be to subvert the spirit and the purpose which animate our decision.[6]

In addition to those three factors, this responsum illustrates several other important methodological features that one commonly finds in Conservative responsa. Specifically, like many other Conservative responsa, this one points to historical development in Jewish law to root the ruling in that history. So, in responding to the decline in Sabbath observance among the majority of Jews, they say: "Actually, there were many occasions in Jewish history when the seemingly hopeless process of decay was arrested and even reversed by a determined and courageous act of reconsecration."[7] They point, for example, to multiple times in the Bible when the Israelites concluded a new covenant with God after a period of straying from obedience to the law and even outright worshiping of foreign gods. As another example, they mention a responsum of Rav Yehudai Gaon, in which a community inquires whether laymen should put on *tefillin* during morning prayers or whether that would be an act of arrogance on their part and the practice should be restricted to the great men of the community. Thus barely two centuries after the completion of the Talmud the practice of every man putting on *tefillin* each weekday morning had declined, despite clear biblical and talmudic mandates to do so, and this decline was corrected not only by Rav Yehudai's responsum (ruling) that laymen should don *tefillin* each weekday morning, but also by "determined efforts of education, culminating in the re-acceptance of standards of piety."[8]

In such efforts, though, one must pay attention to the Talmud's warnings that *tafasta merubbah lo tafasta*, "to overreach is to court failure," and *tov asarah tefaḥim ve'omed mimeah tefaḥim venofel*, "it is better to build a fence of ten handbreadths that is likely to stand than one of a hundred handbreadths that will probably fall."[9] Thus contemporary rabbis must not immediately expect full observance of Jewish law, for that is self-defeating; they must instead interpret Jewish law in a way that makes demands that most Jews can and will fulfill. Sometimes that will be one step on the way to fuller observance; the authors clearly see their list of minimal communal standards for Sabbath observance in just such a way. Sometimes, though, rabbis had to recognize that a previous law is unworkable in modern times:

> Numerous illustrations may be cited of laws and practices which have become so obsolescent that few, if any, Jewish leaders would campaign for their reintroduction. Thus the prohibition against milk and bread made by Gentiles, the requirement to dip newly purchased dishes in the *mikvah*, or to abstain from newly harvested grains, *chodosh*, are examples of laws that have quietly lapsed. We may recall also the lapse of the laws governing the lending of money, of *sh'mittat k'safim*, the inauguration of *heter iska* and its subsequent obsolescence.[10]

The authors use these examples not to claim that any of the laws relevant to their topic (the Sabbath) should be seen as having lapsed, but rather to illustrate the importance of human input in the development in Jewish law. As a matter of legal principle and procedure, though, rabbis must always recognize that when a given law is no longer widely practiced, they must make a strategic decision as to whether to fight hard to reinstate it, even if gradually, or to let it fall into oblivion, in the manner of some laws in every legal system.

Another methodological feature of this responsum that is common to most other Conservative responsa is that it seriously tries to derive its conclusions from the received tradition. The authors justify their leniencies on both electricity and driving to the synagogue on the Sabbath by applying halakhic precedents to the scientific processes by which electricity is produced and automobiles operate. One may disagree with the authors' judgment, of course, but that would be the same kind of dispute among interpreters that occurs often in the history and current practice of Jewish law. The authors, after all, specifically did *not* come to these conclusions through amending the law or ignoring it; they instead investigated the new technology that makes electricity and automobiles possible and then applied talmudic and later Jewish legal precedents to those new realities. This is definitely typical of Conservative responsa; it is, in fact, the standard operating procedure.

Two other methodological features of this responsum, though, are the direct result of the participation of Rabbi Jacob Agus among its authors. First, the responsum specifically calls for a joint campaign of the Rabbinical Assembly and the United Synagogue which "should have as its immediate goal the acceptance on the part of the people of the following basic indispensable elements of Sabbath observance."[11] This is clearly based on Agus's view that Jewish law must be the product of a bicameral legislature, consisting of the rabbinate and the laity, if it is going to be obeyed in our modern, voluntaristic society. Rabbis' knowledge of both the law and modern circumstances can enable them to apply Jewish law to current circumstances, but only the willingness of the laity to accept the law will make it a reality of contemporary Jewish practice. It was precisely the failure of the Rabbinical Assembly as a whole (rather than just the CJLS) to endorse and energize the proposed program, and the similar failure of the United Synagogue to adopt it, to gain the acceptance of the laity, and to pursue it vigorously that Agus blamed for its failure eleven years later (1961):

> Our central agencies [by which he apparently means the lay organizations of the Conservative movement] ignored this effort altogether, with the result that the Sabbath Revitalization effort remained merely an intra-Rabbinical Assembly project. . . . It would have been far bet-

ter for the movement if the Sabbath Responsum had been directly endorsed by the Rabbinical Assembly [and not merely by the majority of
the CJLS] and freely accepted by the United Synagogue and its affili-
ates. We should then have had truly autonomous legislation, bearing
potent ethical-spiritual influence.[12]

Second, while the authors straightforwardly apply Jewish precedents
to the questions of electricity and driving to the synagogue, they invoke
their power to enact ordinances in creating the minimal standards of
Sabbath observance that they seek to have the laity accept. With regard
to that list, the responsum specifically states that "the power of a community to enact ordinances in the field of religious life is virtually unlimited, provided that its ordinances are made with the consent of the
resident scholars and provided further that they be inspired by the purpose of 'strengthening the faith' and intended only for their own time
and place."[13] In support of that claim, the responsum notes the remarks
of Maimonides, Rabbi Jacob Emden, and Rabbi Moses Isserles to that
effect; to quote the last of those, "when new circumstances develop that
were unknown to the ancient authorities, it is permitted to institute new
enactments."[14] This clearly reflects Agus's theory that changes in Jewish
law legally can, and sometimes should, be made through communal
takkanot that can both introduce new leniencies or stringencies in the
law and also establish minimal communal standards—precisely the kind
of minimal standards that the responsum articulates.

B. THE ORDINATION OF WOMEN

1. *The Study Commission*

The decision to ordain women, clearly one of the most controversial
changes in the history of the Conservative movement, ironically was not
made through the usual procedures of the Committee on Jewish Law
and Standards. A minority of that committee, presumably (but not explicitly) on the basis of rabbinic rulings written by Rabbis Aaron Blumenthal and Phillip Sigal on the eligibility of women to serve as leaders
of worship, had voted in 1974 to permit women to be ordained. Neither
the Jewish Theological Seminary in New York nor the Seminario in
Buenos Aires, the only Conservative rabbinical schools in existence at
the time, however, then made admission to rabbinical school open to female candidates.

Instead, the decision came about in a most unusual way. Specifically, when the Rabbinical Assembly, assembled in convention in May

1977, was about to vote on whether to admit women ordained by other institutions to membership, Seminary Chancellor Gerson D. Cohen asked the Assembly, in view of its long and close relationship to the Seminary, to table the resolution until the Seminary had a chance to consider ordaining women itself, so that the first woman to be admitted to the Rabbinical Assembly would be a Seminary graduate. The Assembly acquiesced, and it passed a resolution asking the Chancellor to establish a study commission "whose membership shall reflect the pluralism and diversity of the Conservative Movement"[15] that would issue a report by the 1979 convention.

The commission Chancellor Cohen appointed consisted of fourteen members. It included Chancellor Cohen and his assistant, Rabbi Gordon Tucker; two Seminary professors (Haim Dimitrovsky and Seymour Siegel); three congregational rabbis (Fishel Pearlmutter, Elijah Schochet, and Wilfred Schuchat); and seven lay members of Conservative synagogues, including three women. The Commission's work lasted for fourteen months, and it met with rabbis and lay leaders in eight different cities in North America between July and December, 1978, to get a better idea of where the movement overall stood on the issue. According to Rabbi Tucker's final report, "Although no tally was made, or indeed ever contemplated, it was manifest that the overwhelming majority of those who chose to testify at these meetings strongly favored the ordination of women."[16] Ultimately, the Commission itself voted 11 to 3 to endorse that recommendation. (The three who voted against that recommendation were Professor Dimitrovsky and Rabbis Schochet and Shuchat.)

The majority justified its recommendation on the basis of legal, moral, and "other" considerations. The report states at the outset and repeatedly thereafter that the Commission was committed "to the notion that legitimacy within Conservative Judaism must be measured first and foremost by an *halakhic* standard."[17] Thus while ethical and other considerations played a role in their decision, halakhic concerns were paramount.

Legally, then, the Report points out that most of the modern rabbi's duties—teaching, preaching, counseling, community organization, interfaith activities, fundraising, Zionist activities, and officiating at baby namings, bar or bat mitzvah ceremonies, and funerals—do not present any halakhic impediments for women. In the few areas where there are halakhic questions about whether a woman may serve in a rabbinic capacity, such as witnessing and signing a wedding contract *(ketubah)*, a writ of divorce *(get),* or the documents of conversion, or leading the congregation in prayer as the *sheliaḥ tzibbur* (the one chanting the services as agent of the community), women rabbis could simply avoid such activities by asking men to do them. Moreover, already then there were some halakhic opinions of the CJLS that would permit women to act in some of these capacities. The Commission concluded that

> The *halakhic* objections to the ordination of women as rabbis center around disapproval of the performance by a woman of certain functions. Those functions, however, are not essentially rabbinic, nor are they universally disapproved, by the accepted rules governing the discussion of *halakhah* in the Conservative Movement. *There is no direct halakhic objection to the acts of training and ordaining a woman to be a rabbi, teacher, and preacher in Israel.*[18]

When turning to moral concerns, the Commission specifically stated that "there was no agreement among Commission members concerning precisely what the relationship is or ought to be between *halakhah* and ethics."[19] The Commission did agree, though, that in many areas of Jewish law "the developmental history of the *halakhah* exhibits a strong tendency to approach ever more closely an ideal ethical state" and that, "echoing the opinion of Rav that the *mitzvot* were given us to 'refine us,' the Commission accepted the view that the commandments have among their chief purposes the ethical perfection of the individual and society."[20] The ethical mandate in this case, as the Commission saw it, was to permit women to become rabbis, both because "The basic ethical principle underlying the democratic society in which we live—a principle that has deep roots in our biblical-rabbinic tradition—is that each person should have at least a legally equal opportunity to pursue a chosen career"[21] and also because permitting girls to study with boys throughout their lives the very same subjects, as the Conservative movement does, and then suddenly barring women from continuing their Jewish education at the final, highest stage is unjustifiable, especially since there is no clear halakhic reason for doing so.[22]

The ethical concerns that the Commission considered against ordaining women included two matters. First, is it fair to admit women to rabbinical school when it may be the case that they will have difficulty finding jobs after ordination? The Commission decided that it was not clear that women rabbis would have such difficulty and, in any case, women candidates could be given fair warning that, given the experience of women rabbis in the Reform and Reconstructionist movements, they could face some discrimination. Second, is it fair to impose this decision on those who do not want to see women ordained? To that the

Commission noted that failing to ordain women was also making a decision and that the minority that opposed it did not have the right to block the majority who favored it, especially because there was no clear legal objection.

Finally, the Commission noted some other considerations. These included the fact that 74% of the Rabbinical School student body voted in an opinion poll to admit women, that the vast majority of the people interviewed also supported that move, and that it became clear that a considerable number of women—many more than first anticipated—wanted to become Conservative rabbis. Furthermore, the failure to ordain women would deprive the Conservative movement of 50% of its otherwise available pool of talented and committed potential rabbis.

The Commission ultimately recommended that the Seminary admit women to the Seminary's Rabbinical School as quickly as possible—namely, in September of 1979. The Chancellor, however, decided to submit the whole issue to the Seminary faculty, seeing it not as a strictly religious issue, on which he could set policy by himself or with an advisory committee of rabbis, but as an academic issue regarding qualifications for admission. The Seminary faculty split badly on the issue, and it was tabled.

Before we proceed to the aftermath of these events and its implications for how Jewish law is determined within the Conservative movement, let us note several features of the unusual procedure just described. The agreement between the Rabbinical Assembly and Chancellor Cohen did not refer the matter to the CJLS, the body usually charged with interpreting Jewish law for the movement, presumably because it had already issued majority and minority opinions on the issue. Furthermore, Chancellor Cohen, acting as *mara d'atra* of the Seminary, presumably had the authority to decide the matter on his own. He recognized, however, that this was an explosive issue, one that might well have major repercussions for the Seminary and the movement as a whole, no matter how it was decided. He also clearly wanted to retain the centrality of the Seminary within the movement in educating its rabbis. The Commission that he appointed and headed, then, is probably best understood legally as an advisory commission to the *mara d'atra*. Local rabbis have always had the option of garnering advice from other rabbis or laypeople. Furthermore, rabbis who have any hope of being listened to and obeyed, let alone of keeping their job, have always directly or indirectly considered how their community will respond to alternative possibilities of interpreting the law. Thus while the Commission was a very formal structure to gain such information and advice, the functions it served in shaping Jewish law are anything but unprecedented.

Note also that the Commission understood Jewish law to be the primary determining factor in the matter. Thus even though the Commission was not established as a body to determine Jewish law for the movement, it understood that whatever it decided had to be rooted in Jewish law because that was the movement's central commitment. Furthermore, the Commission's report clearly distinguishes between biblical and rabbinic laws in the degree of flexibility they have; that again is a classic Jewish legal distinction, however difficult it might be at times to decide whether a particular law is biblical or rabbinic in its authority. Thus even though the Commission's decision was revolutionary in the eyes of some, it did root itself in classic halakhic sources and methods.

Finally, note that while the Commission declined to describe the precise way in which Jewish law and ethics are related, it did assert that Jewish law must be read to purify Jews, along the lines of the talmudic sage, Rav. Thus while moral norms do not substitute for the law or trump the halakhic process, they do definitely play a critical role in shaping the law, defining as they do the norms by which it is to be assessed as well as its ultimate goals.

2. The Seminary Faculty

Several years later, when the Rabbinical Assembly was again set to vote on admitting women rabbis ordained by other movements to membership, Chancellor Cohen decided to revisit the issue with the Seminary faculty. Before the summer of 1983, he invited faculty members to write formal rabbinic rulings or other forms of written response to the question of whether the Seminary should ordain women. Those writings would be distributed in September for the whole faculty to read, and a new discussion and vote would take place in October of that year.

Most of the written materials presented then were ultimately published in the book *The Ordination of Women as Rabbis: Studies and Responsa* (1988), edited by Seminary Vice-Chancellor Simon Greenberg. It includes materials written by nine Seminary faculty members who argue for or against ordination on a variety of grounds. Rabbi Joel Roth presented a halakhic justification, and it was his opinion that formed the basis of the ultimate faculty vote to admit women.

Rabbi Roth's first question is whether women can voluntarily take on obligations that classical Jewish law does not impose on them and whether, if they do, such obligations have the same status as duties imposed by Jewish law on men. Through a careful analysis of sources, he determines that women can choose to obligate themselves for *mitzvot* from which traditional *halakhah* exempts them—or at least, that there is sufficient halakhic justification for ruling that they do. They must understand, though, that once they assume all the obligations from which they are traditionally exempt, they sin if they fail to fulfill those additional duties, just as a man does; if they do not take on that burden of possible sin, then they are not really assuming the obligations but only doing some optional things. In this part of the responsum, Roth is reporting the various stances of the issue in earlier texts, making inferences from them for this issue, and choosing among them, in a straightforward, halakhic style that could equally well be used by an Orthodox rabbi.

In section 2 of his responsum he discusses three possible ways for making women eligible to serve as witnesses on, for example, wedding and divorce documents, but he does not think that any of them is sufficient. Furthermore, he worries that if women do serve in that capacity, the documents will be invalid and will threaten the unity of the Jewish people. Still, he clearly is using a Conservative methodology here, for he openly recognizes that the ban on women testifying is rooted in the Rabbis' view of the women of their time as nonconversant with the world of the courtroom at best and unreliable and prone to exaggeration at worst. He presents several arguments to show that "it is the rabbinic image of the nature of women which is the sole justification for the prohibition. I consider the opinion that the modern image of women does not justify the prohibition, and that this change from the rabbinic image of women is desirable, to be self-evident."[23] The Rabbis, though, proclaimed that the Torah itself prohibits women from testifying, although the Rabbis themselves carved out some exceptions to that rule; Roth, then, has to address how we can overturn a rabbinic interpretation of the Torah. He discusses three ways to do that, each with its advantages and disadvantages, and ultimately he recommends that the Seminary faculty abrogate that prohibition, proclaiming that that is "the ultimate *halakhically warranted* act. It is not a *not-halakhic act.*"[24] This clearly is not the kind of methodology likely to be found among Orthodox rabbis these days, and it is surely not the kind of historical reasoning likely to be found in that world. It is rather distinctly Conservative in both its analysis of the law and its suggested method for fitting the law to modern realities.

As for the title "rabbi" itself, in section 3 of his responsum Roth finds no legal objection to granting it to a woman or to allowing her to serve as a judge, as long as the parties accept her as such. This, again, is based on straightforward halakhic reasoning, choosing among precedents from which the writer can deduce the desired result.

Finally, in section 4 of his responsum, Roth opposes adopting a *takkanah* making all women equal to men in their Jewish obligations because that "would result in the creation of a large class of sinners where none now exists."[25] At the same time, he does not want to bar women who choose to take on the duties from which they are halakhically exempt from doing so. As a result, he adopts a middle stance: those women who do assume all the *halakhic* obligations from which they have traditionally been exempt will then be eligible to lead the community in prayer and count as part of the quorum for prayer; those who do not, will not.

In sum, then, he makes two recommendations: that the faculty exercise "the ultimate systematic right of the learned who are committed to the *halakhah* to openly and knowingly abrogate the prohibition against women serving as witnesses";[26] and that even without that, women should be admitted to rabbinical school and be allowed to serve as leaders of prayer and count as part of a *minyan, on condition that* they accept upon themselves all of the duties incumbent on men, including, for example, daily prayer with *tallit* and *tefillin.* "Should a woman renounce her obligatory status, she would be required to cease functioning as a rabbi."[27]

The faculty did not deal with women serving as witnesses, as Roth had wanted; that was left for the CJLS to do, as I shall discuss below, in two different responsa adopted in 2002 and 2004, respectively. The faculty did vote, however, to adopt Roth's justification for admitting women to rabbinical school, and so since October 1983, when the vote was taken, to the present, women are permitted entry on condition that they openly assume the duties of obeying all the commandments, including those from which the tradition exempted them.

Note how unusual this whole process was. It was not the CJLS that decided the matter, even though some of its decisions were invoked in the commission's report; it was rather the faculty of the Seminary. The faculty was never before or ever after asked to vote on a religious question. Indeed, there were many at the time who questioned the right of those members of the faculty who were themselves not halakhically observant to vote on this issue. On the other hand, there were also many who questioned the right of those professors who affiliated with the Orthodox movement to make a decision for the Conservative movement. As a result, after these events, Chancellor Cohen established an advisory committee consisting of those Conservative rabbis on the faculties of the Seminary and the University of Judaism to help him make future religious decisions for the Seminary. As one of the members of that committee, I had the distinct sense that he regretted not having referred the matter of ordination to such a committee in the first place, so as to avoid both challenges to the faculty's authority to decide such a matter.

Moreover, Rabbi Roth's responsum as well as that of Rabbi Mayer Rabinowitz (another member of both the Seminary faculty and the CJLS) were never officially approved by the CJLS, and neither was the earlier responsum by Rabbi Phillip Sigal on which the CJLS had apparently based its decisions in 1974, cited by the Commission Report. The Sigal responsum was officially tabled on November 7, 1984 by a vote of 13–2, with the provision that it nevertheless be included in the *CJLS Proceedings*.[28] The responsa by Rabbis Roth and Rabinowitz, both printed in the volume edited by Simon Greenberg, *The Ordination of Women as Rabbis*, were voted into the permanent record of the CJLS on that same day without discussion, but they are not officially sanctioned positions of the CJLS.[29]

All of this is highly irregular, but it points to the fact that some legal decisions within the movement are made by bodies other than the CJLS. In this case, it was the Seminary faculty. Another instance of this procedure may be seen in the Solomon Schechter Day School Association's standards for member schools, which includes a rule for admission of non-Jewish students on a temporary basis that was never considered by the CJLS. In addition, of course, the *Va'ad Halakhah* (Law Committee) of the Rabbinical Assembly's Israel region has issued five volumes of responsa on its own, and it continues to produce more. All of this should serve to put the CJLS in perspective: It certainly is the central body for addressing questions in Jewish law for North American Conservative Jewry, at least most of the time (the issue of the ordination of women being a clear exception); but the authority of the CJLS for Israel's Masorti Jews and for Conservative Jews in Europe and South America is much less clear.

C. FOUR RESPONSA ON WOMEN AS WITNESSES

In 1974, Rabbi Aaron Blumenthal submitted an oral responsum, not uncommon at the time, on "The Status of Women in Jewish Law," in which he blamed the influence of Roman jurisprudence for the rabbinic concept that women suffered from "lightness of mind." He dismissed that view as probably wrong then and certainly no longer applicable in our day, and ruled, in the language of the responsum that he later committed to writing, "that a woman may serve as a witness in all matters equally with a man."[30] Seven members of the CJLS voted against it, but six voted for it. According to the rules of the CJLS at the time (and, for that matter, now as well), that number of members voting for the responsum constituted enough of a plurality to make it a valid option within the movement, making women eligible to sign documents of marriage, divorce, and conversion as witnesses.

The rules of the CJLS changed in 1985 to require that votes be taken only on written opinions, and the fact that the CJLS had in 1974 voted without the chance to read and think about what they were affirming made many within the movement uneasy about basing their actions on that earlier vote. When the question arose in 1999 as to whether the issue should be revisited, this time with written responsa before the Committee, a straw vote indicated a very slight majority in favor of doing that. Those voting against reconsidering the issue argued that the current CJLS would only repeat the same close split that the CJLS of 1974 had produced, and the process of disagreeing on this matter would only serve to further divide the movement. Those voting for revisiting the issue argued that the 1974 vote was effectively inoperative because even though Rabbi Blumenthal's paper was subsequently published, the CJLS had not voted based on a careful reading of a written paper. This, in and of itself, is a mark of modernity: In ancient times, all arguments were oral, but the majority of the CJLS of 1999 did not trust that form of argumentation or record.

Ultimately three members of the CJLS produced responsa that were voted on by the CJLS. Rabbi Myron Geller, in his paper, "Woman Is Eligible to Testify," argues that the same Rabbis who interpreted the Torah to exclude women from serving as witnesses created exceptions to that rule, thus indicating that even they did not support a blanket prohibition for women to act as witnesses. Specifically, based on a *takkanah* ultimately attributed to Rabban Gamliel the Elder, the School of Hillel accepted the School of Shammai's view that a woman may remarry even on the basis of her own sole testimony that her husband has died.[31] Once that *takkanah* was established, the Rabbis proceeded to expand the areas where women's testimony was acceptable and to develop a general principle to justify that.[32] Specifically, where two witnesses were required, only men could testify; but since a husband could rely on his wife's assurance that seven clean days had passed since her menstrual flow had ended and that they may therefore resume sexual relations, with regard to all ritual prohibitions, where a single witness was sufficient, women qualified to serve in that capacity.[33]

Furthermore, Rabbi Geller notes that while the Shulḥan Arukh excludes as witnesses those Jews who disobey Jewish law, Rabbi Uziel, writing for the Israeli Supreme Rabbinical Court in 1946, accepted all such testimony because the original ban was not based on the Torah itself but rather on the expectation that transgressors of the law could not be trusted to give reliable testimony; now that, "for our many sins," many Jews transgress the law, the court must assess whether the particular witnesses are likely to tell the truth, whatever their degree of piety.[34] Rabbi Geller concludes,

> Since women and transgressors are normally listed together amongst *p'sulei edut* [those unfit to give testimony] and since both are excluded *d'oraita* [as a matter of Torah law], it is fair to say that both biblical rules are based on the same reason, that is, concern about false testimony. The exclusion of women is not at all scriptural fiat, *g'zeirat ha-melekh,* and the only question is their credibility. When there is no reason to suspect that a woman's testimony is distorted by her exclusion from society or her subjugation to some male, there is no reason to exclude it. If we are able to make a case, which I believe is unquestioned, for *shinnui ha-'itim* ["a change in times," i.e., new circumstances requiring new laws], there is simply no basis for continuing any exclusion of women from testifying either to establish the facts or to constitute a religious ritual such as *kiddushin* [betrothal] . . . We authorize female rabbis and qualified laywomen to serve as witnesses for *kiddushin* [betrothal], *gittin* [writs of divorce], *giyyur* [conversion], or in any capacity governed by *halakhah.*[35]

The several discussions that the CJLS had about this paper focused not so much on the halakhic justification for expanding the ancient *takkanah,* for everyone on the Committee recognized the significant change in circumstances that has taken place in the position of women in contemporary society and the resultant need to recognize that women now know general society as well as men do and can think independently of men. The primary concern was rather about the effect of Rabbi Geller's ruling on couples (and especially women) divorced with a writ of divorce signed by a woman as a witness. If that document's legitimacy is called into question, the woman would still be technically married to her first husband. Therefore, if she remarries and has children by her second husband, that relationship would be categorized by Jewish law as adulterous, and her children would be halakhically illegitimate *(mamzerim),* who, according to the Torah, may not marry a Jew for ten generations.[36] Even though the CJLS had approved (by a vote of 15 in favor, 3 opposed, and 3 abstentions) an extensive paper by Rabbi Elie Spitz on March 8, 2000, that effectively nullified the category of illegitimacy by using the mishnaic Rabbis' maneuver of refusing to hear testimony that someone was illegitimate, many on the CJLS were nevertheless concerned that Jews divorced through Conservative procedures not be classified in that irreparable category by Orthodox authorities if the people involved or their children decide to become Orthodox. Marriage and conversion can always be redone if a person or couple decide to become Orthodox, and any children born to a couple whose first wedding was halakhically challenged would nevertheless be perfectly legitimate; but the children of a second marriage after a divorce declared invalid because of a female witness would be harmed for life—indeed, for generations.

In response to this concern, Rabbi Susan Grossman wrote a responsum, *Edut Nashim K'edut Anashim* (The Testimony of Women is Like the Testimony of Men), that was also approved by the CJLS. Rabbi Grossman in principle accepts Rabbi Geller's conclusion that women are *legally* eligible to serve as witnesses in all ways that men are, but she delegates the question of using women as witnesses in divorce procedures to the Joint Bet Din of the Seminary and the Rabbinical Assembly, as a matter of its internal *policy* in carrying out its primary function of supervising divorce procedures within the movement.

Rabbi Aaron Mackler, concerned with the same issue, instead invokes the medical model of informed consent, where patients have to be competent to understand what the possible outcomes are for their agreement to a medical procedure to be morally and legally valid. Even then, there are times when a physician must not acquiesce to a patient's informed wishes:

> Rabbi Geller appeals to the model of informed consent for *gittin,* as well as for other documents. In health care, even advocates of informed consent acknowledge competing ethical concerns that could prevent a health care professional from going along with a patient's desired course of action. Ruth Faden and Tom Beauchamp write that "the physician is of course enjoined from doing harm if interventions inflict unnecessary pain and suffering on patients." Ethical principles, including those of providing benefit and avoiding harm, "can have sufficient weight under some conditions to override respect for autonomy." As Rabbi Miriam Spitzer observes in responding to Rabbi Geller's position, "Nor is the response of 'informed consent' convincing. Those who will be most hurt by these issues [namely, the children and later descendants of a woman's second marriage after being divorced with a *get* signed by a woman] are not in a position to give consent, informed or otherwise."[37]

The model of informed consent, with the limitations professionals morally must impose when a client or patient can be seriously harmed if their desired course of action is carried out, leads Rabbi Mackler to the following conclusion:

> Women may serve as witnesses. In principle, this acceptance of women's witnessing applies in all realms and to all documents. In practice, however, special concerns arise from the rejection of women's witnessing by some Conservative and virtually all Orthodox rabbis. For marriage (*ketubbot* and *kiddushin*) and conversion *(giyyur)*, women should only serve as witnesses with the informed consent of the individual(s) directly affected, and following a prudential judgment by the rabbi that the involvement of women witnesses would not impose undue risks in the particular case. Because of practical concerns for the well-being of individuals and of *klal Yisrael* [the Jewish community], women should not at the present time serve as witnesses for *gittin* [writs of divorce].[38]

Several things should be noted about this entire discussion. First, all four responsa—by Rabbis Blumenthal, Geller, Grossman, and Mackler—acknowledge that the ability of women to serve as witnesses, although approved in certain kinds of cases, was historically limited. That is, all four are honest about the history of this matter in Jewish law. At the same time, they all recognize that the circumstances that led to women being disqualified—their isolation from community life and their economic dependence on men—have now changed, and so the reasons to distrust their ability to give honest and reliable testimony no longer exist. The responsa invoke a reason to change the law that medieval sources used in a number of areas—namely, *shinnui ha'ittim,* a change of times that requires a corresponding change in law. Thus the changes that they propose could equally have been made during the Middle Ages, had the status of women changed then to be what it is now. Still, one gets the distinct flavor of a Conservative responsum in these writings from their ready use of historical perspective.

Second, all four responsa deal with the claim that the ban on women's testimony is rooted in the Torah. They all explicitly or implicitly accept that if the ban derived from "the decree of the King" without any rationale attached to it, then no change in times or circumstances could warrant a change in the law. That is, they all accept the authority of the Torah to make decrees on our practice that we do not understand or agree with. In this case, however, the Torah itself is not clear about whether women may testify; it is the Rabbis who interpret the Torah that way. The four respondents argue, then, that the reason the Rabbis interpreted the Torah as they did is because in their time women's social and economic circumstances cast doubt on whether they could know communal life well enough to testify accurately about it and whether their economic dependence on men would make them afraid to testify truthfully to something their husbands did not want them to say. The Rabbis themselves demonstrate that this is the case by their own acceptance, as early as the first century C.E., of women testifying in matters that they would be likely to know and report accurately. The respondents then argue *not* for a complete change in the law—a new *takkanah*—but for a much lesser change, albeit a significant one, namely, expansion of the scope of the Mishnah's *takkanah* to make women eligible to testify on many more subjects where testimony is needed.

Third, even though all four are convinced that the halakhic basis for making women eligible to testify is strong, they come to differing conclusions as to what should happen in practice. Rabbis Blumenthal and Geller argue that we should do in practice what our legal analysis has concluded—namely, consider women eligible in all areas where men are. Rabbis Grossman and Mackler, however, argue that forming our practice by our principles might be noble but also harmful to our constituents in the case of women signing Jewish writs of divorce. Rabbi Mackler goes further, suggesting that even in other documents, congregants have to be duly informed of the risks involved in having a woman sign as a witness and the rabbi must ascertain that for this particular person or couple the risks would not be great. Thus even when Conservative rabbis agree on the legal analysis of a given issue, they may disagree as to how best to apply it to the practical realities of life. In approving all but Rabbi Mackler's responsum, the CJLS indicated that these are valid differences in judgment and that local rabbis had to evaluate the arguments and their own particular situation in deciding which one to use. Thus here again the role of the local rabbi *(mara d'atra)* is critical.[39]

D. A RESPONSE TO MISCARRIAGE

The very first responsum written by a female rabbi to be approved by the CJLS was that of Rabbi Debra Reed Blank on March 6, 1991. It actually was written in response to another responsum on the subject written by the Conservative movement's very first woman rabbi, Rabbi Amy Eilberg. As I said at the CJLS meeting at the time, "This marks a milestone for the Conservative movement and for Jewish law in general in two ways. First, this is the first responsum written by a woman rabbi, possibly the first in history, and certainly the first to be approved by the CJLS. Second, it is wonderful to know that female rabbis can disagree with each other just as much as male rabbis do!"

Rabbi Amy Eilberg argued in her 1990 responsum—the first to be submitted by a female rabbi for consideration by the CJLS—that when a couple suffers a miscarriage, they should be viewed as mourners, and therefore they and their community must go through full Jewish mourning rites. She pointed out that in our time, couples who become pregnant assume that with modern medicine each pregnancy will result in a birth. That obviously is not true, but we should respond to the couple's emotional state. Emotionally, the couple feels as if the fetus is already a child for whom they were planning and about whom they were dreaming. That is especially true in our time, when Jews commonly marry later than in times past and therefore may often have trouble becoming pregnant in the first place. As a result, they have much invested in the success of each pregnancy. If they then experience a miscarriage, their emotional state is indeed similar to that of mourners, and they need the full support of their community that Jewish mourning rites afford.

In discussing Rabbi Eilberg's responsum, the CJLS certainly understood and appreciated the need for a Jewish response to miscarriage in our time, even though the classical tradition passed over miscarriage with no ritual or other obligations on anyone. Part of the reason why a response to miscarriage is needed in our time is that women's issues are no longer confined to women but are rather openly discussed by both men and women. Thus women are not, and should not be, expected to simply suffer in silence when a miscarriage occurs—and, for that matter, neither should their husbands. Furthermore, as Rabbi Eilberg rightly pointed out, in light of modern medicine miscarriage in our day is both less expected and less accepted as simply a fact of life, and it has more significance for the long-term prospects of the ability to procreate for a couple that begins trying to have children in their thirties rather than in their teens.

At the same time, the CJLS was deeply worried that treating miscarriage as an occasion for full mourning rites would effectively classify the fetus as a full human being, and that would undermine the stance of the Jewish tradition and the CJLS on abortion. After all, if the fetus were a human being, then abortion should always be prohibited, as the Roman Catholics maintain, for then abortion would be, at best, killing one human being in order to save the life of another. The Jewish tradition from chapter 21 of Exodus on, however, classifies the fetus as having a lesser legal status than the woman bearing it, and the Mishnah draws the implication from that distinction that before the head emerges we must dismember the fetus to save its mother if her life is threatened in childbirth.[40] Especially in the context of consistent attempts by Catholics and others to make abortion illegal in the United States, many members of the CJLS asserted that we dare not provide any opening to anyone misconstruing our position to allow abortions when there is an elevated risk to the woman's life or health (physical or mental) over that of normal pregnancy and, when there is a clear threat to her life or health, to actually require an abortion.

Rabbi Debra Reed Blank, in her alternative responsum, "Response to Miscarriage," specifically responds to these concerns: "Our tradition has always been careful to make a distinction between a fetus and a person, holding that 'personhood' comes only with birth."[41] She therefore argues that both the man and the woman in a couple that has suffered a miscarriage should be treated not as mourners but as ḥolim, as ill—psychologically and, in the case of the woman, possibly physically as well. The appropriate Jewish response is thus fulfilling the commandment of bikkur ḥolim, visiting the sick. Rabbi Blank takes care to note that Jewish law classifies mental as well as physical distress as illness, for in the standard prayer for healing we pray for both "healing of soul and healing of body." She therefore rules that friends and family need to pay attention to the psychological and emotional suffering of both the man and woman as well as to the woman's physical pain, if any. As in all cases of fulfilling the commandment of visiting the sick, friends and family must assess the particular needs of the people involved and seek to meet them, while simultaneously taking steps to ensure that their ministrations are welcome and helpful rather than intrusive and irritating. The rabbi and friends can assess if the couple wants others to know and, if so, who, and they can offer to include them in the prayer for healing in the synagogue or in their private prayers. For some couples or individuals, immersing in the mikvah helps to mark the transition from their previous state to the present one and helps them to heal after their pregnancy loss. If the couple feels uncomfortable with making the miscarriage public and does not want visitors, one can still check whether they need help with something in particular—shopping, childcare, etc. Rabbi Blank's self-perception of what she is doing in this responsum is this:

> Throughout I shall be dealing with patterns that have always, in fact, been permissible. In that sense, my paper is not a halakhic innovation. However it is necessary to say these things in writing because there has

been a widespread misconception that Jewish law proscribed these behaviors in the case of miscarriage.[42]

That, however, understates the case, for, as she notes, the common practice until now has been for there to be no communal reaction to miscarriage at all. While she is, as she says, simply invoking the established
modes of fulfilling the commandment of visiting the sick, she is applying
them to a new group of people—namely, couples who have suffered a
miscarriage. In that sense, her responsum is indeed innovative, a mark
of the increasing attention in our time to the use of Jewish rituals to
meet the emotional needs of both women and men, needs that were formerly either ignored or consciously suppressed. Recognizing this, Rabbi
Eilberg, who strongly disagrees with Rabbi Blank's approach to the
matter, says that "Any new halakhic response to pregnancy loss is a step
forward in demonstrating to the members of our movement that halakhah does respond to the most profound events in their lives."[43]
Rabbi Blank's responsum was approved by the CJLS on March 6, 1991,
by a vote of seventeen in favor, one opposed, and three abstaining.

One feature of the CJLS rules is also illustrated by this case: CJLS
members may write concurring or dissenting opinions to approved responsa, and such opinions, although not official CJLS positions, are included in the record of the CJLS. In this case, Rabbi Eilberg not only
voted against Rabbi Blank's responsum, but wrote a formal dissent. In
it, she maintains that Rabbi Blank's approach misstates the facts:

> A mother and a father who have lost a fetus by miscarriage are not
> sick. They are grieving. This is not a disease, not illness; their experi-
> ence has nothing to do with pathology—either physical or mental.
> What they have suffered is a loss, and what they need most of all is ac-
> knowledgment of the reality and profundity of that loss, and support
> in their grieving process.[44]

In fact, even if we pay attention only to the mother's physical state, she
is "almost always less sick than a woman with the flu."[45]

Rabbi Eilberg admits that the support that visitors provide for the
sick may be helpful to the grieving couple, but seeing such efforts as a
response to illness rather than to mourning misstates another important
feature of this situation—namely, that many illnesses pass in a short
amount of time and leave no mark, while "grieving a pregnancy loss
quite normally may take a full year"[46] and, especially if the couple does
not later succeed in having a desired child, the painful memory of this
lost opportunity may last a lifetime. It is especially important to mark

the need to publicly grieve a pregnancy loss because "many of their loved ones deny this loss with misguided if not insensitive approaches like, 'You can always have another one' or 'At least you never had the chance to know him or her and love him or her.'"[47]

Furthermore, Rabbi Eilberg notes that "there is now a voluminous literature on the psycho-social dynamics of pregnancy loss" and that doctors, nurses, chaplains, and social workers routinely encourage parents to name the miscarried fetus, to plan a memorial service, and to keep a memory book to help them identify the object of their loss so that they can mourn it and thereby separate from it. Whether this is advisable for miscarriages in the first or second months of pregnancy is debatable, for statistically approximately 50% of conceptions miscarry in those two months, often before the woman is even aware that she is pregnant. For miscarriages later on in pregnancy, however—particularly beginning with the fourth month, when most couples presume that the risk for miscarriage has largely passed, when the parents can now see their child on a sonogram, and especially when the mother and even the father may begin to feel the baby move—health care professionals do indeed advise the methods Rabbi Eilberg describes for couples to cope with their loss, for by then the couple assumed that they were having a baby and maybe even chose a name and bought furniture and clothes for their expected infant.

Rabbi Eilberg is fully aware of the concern expressed by many members of the CJLS to make it crystal clear that for the Jewish tradition the status of the fetus is less than that of a full human being, and she even agrees with that; but while "halakhically, philosophically, or legally" the fetus is not a person, *emotionally* for the couple it is. Therefore,

> To refuse Jewish parents the essential comfort of hearing their rabbi and community acknowledge the reality and pain of their loss—because of the philosophical consideration that our use of the word "baby" may affect the Supreme Court debate—is, I believe, to communicate to the parents something very sad. Your doctor understands what happened to you, your nurse understood, the social worker at the hospital understood. Your rabbi is not willing to call this loss by its right name. In short, your Jewish community is not here for you.[48]

She instead recommends using the traditional Jewish mourning rites but in a modified way—*keriah* (tearing one's clothes), a modified burial service, a meal with a small circle of family and friends, one day of *shivah*, and reciting *kaddish* for thirty days.

Rabbi Eilberg makes a good case for distinguishing between illness and grief, and she rightly points out that what couples feel after a miscarriage is the latter. Why, then, did the CJLS overwhelmingly support Rabbi Blank's paper in preference to Rabbi Eilberg's? It was clearly the Committee members' worry that responding to miscarriage with mourning rituals would muddy the distinction in status between a fetus and a baby, thus endangering and perhaps even undermining the basis for Jewish law's approach to abortion. The Committee preferred deliberately to misinterpret a grieving couple's emotional state rather than risk overturning the propriety of abortion when the mother's physical or mental health required one.

The important thing to note here is that this is a difference in weighing the *significance* of the factors that would argue for one approach or the other. This illustrates clearly that the strength of a responsum is not solely a function of how thoroughly the author has researched past Jewish legal literature; it also critically depends on the author's *judgment* of what factors should count the most in reaching a decision. All parties can agree in identifying the relevant facts of the situation, but they may disagree in their judgment as to how best to respond to them legally. In this case, such a difference in weighing the competing factors led Rabbis Blank and Eilberg to use different legal categories to formulate a response to miscarriage. While courts clearly may be engaged in decisions that have serious consequences for the parties involved when the judge is asked simply to apply clear law to the case at hand, this kind of case, where the issue is a matter of deciding which legal category to use in the first place, is an example of what U.S. Supreme Court Justice Benjamin Cordozo called "the serious business cases" of the court, for such a decision affects not only this case, but also all future cases of the same sort. Jewish law has similar cases, and the dispute between Rabbis Blank and Eilberg is a good example of this.

E. TWO RESPONSA ON THE END OF LIFE

Another pair of responsa that respond to a given issue that constitutes a "serious business case" in Cordozo's sense are the two responsa approved on December 12, 1990, on end-of-life issues by Rabbis Elliot N. Dorff and Avram Reisner.[49] Without examining the lengthy reasoning and the multiple issues at the end of life that both of them treat, suffice it to say that Rabbi Reisner uses the category of *goses* (a person just about to die) as his controlling category, although he expands it to include patients not only in the last three days of life, as many interpret it, but as much as a year away from death—despite the fact that an early source characterizes such a person as "a flickering candle" and even moving the person is forbidden, lest one be the direct cause of his or her death. Rabbi Dorff, on the other hand, using that image, restricts the category of *goses* to the time when it is indeed a threat to the person's life to move him or her, often hours (rather than days or weeks) away from death. Rabbi Dorff instead employs the talmudic category of *tereifah* to designate a person from the time when it becomes clear that he or she has a terminal, irreversible illness—this despite the fact that classical Jewish law only removed the culpability of someone who killed such a person *after the fact* (the murderer is *patur*) and did not use it to exempt doctors and others from taking steps to cure such a person *before the fact* (it is not *mutar* to fail to intervene).

Thus both Rabbis Reisner and Dorff stretch traditional legal categories in an effort to gain guidance from the Jewish tradition as to how to treat very ill people in our time. They feel the need to do this because the Jewish tradition, like all others, could not have even contemplated the range of medical abilities currently available to keep dying people alive; it certainly did not rule in such cases. The Kantian problem thus becomes acute: Kant pointed out that when we cannot do something, we need not ask whether we should, but as soon as we *can* do something, we must ask the moral and legal question as to whether we should, for the fact that we *can* do something does not necessarily mean that we *should*. We could, of course, maintain in a positivistic mode that Judaism has nothing to say about these new circumstances because our ancestors did not rule on them—and some very serious Jews and legal thinkers would say exactly that—but that comes at the great price of making the Jewish tradition totally irrelevant to many modern issues. Rabbis Reisner and Dorff reject that approach and instead prefer to stretch traditional legal categories, if necessary, in order to apply the tradition to new circumstances and thus make it relevant and instructive.

This difference of opinion about which fundamental legal category to apply leads Reisner and Dorff to some differing conclusions as well—or, perhaps, their differences of opinion on the concrete issues led to their differing choice of which legal category to employ. Exactly what motivates a rabbi or judge to decide in a given way is often unclear, resembling the proverbial "chicken and egg" controversy. Sometimes it is indeed clear that a given intellectual analysis has led a rabbi or judge to a given conclusion, and sometimes, conversely, it is clear that the rabbi or judge began with a given desired result and then found a way to justify that result within the law. Often it is not clear which of those processes is happening, especially when both factors (and others as well) work in tandem to produce a decision.

In any case, Reisner and Dorff use their differing fundamental legal categories to justify the same conclusions for about 80 percent of the issues they treat but different conclusions on the other 20 percent. Because both responsa are lengthy, closely reasoned, and detailed (together they occupy 86 printed pages in the Spring 1991 issue of the journal *Conservative Judaism*), Rabbi Reisner wrote a summary statement indicating where the two responsa agree and differ. The major differences include these three:[50]

1. Both rabbis would allow withholding or withdrawing machines from a terminally ill patient, and both endorse hospice care where the goal has changed from cure to comfort because cure has been deemed by competent physicians to be impossible or at least highly unlikely and possibly also painful; but Rabbi Dorff would also permit withholding or withdrawing medications from such a patient, including artificial nutrition and hydration. Rabbi Reisner would permit withdrawing and withholding medications from such a patient only if the patient completed a valid treatment directive to that effect, but in his opinion even such a directive cannot justify withholding or withdrawing artificial nutrition or hydration, for he sees those as food rather than as medication.

2. Rabbi Dorff sees a person in a persistent vegetative state as an impaired life (a *tereifah*), just as one with a terminal illness, and therefore he would allow withholding or withdrawing machines and medications from such a person, including artificial nutrition and hydration. Rabbi Reisner requires full maintenance of a person in such a state.

3. Both rabbis endorse pain relief, but Rabbi Reisner would allow the use of only that amount of morphine or other drugs that the physician can administer with assurance that the drug will not hasten the patient's death. Rabbi Dorff would allow even greater amounts of such drugs as long as the physician's intention in administering them is to save the patient from pain, even though the doctor knows that the increased dose may also hasten the patient's death; Dorff would prohibit the exact same dosage of drugs if the physician's intention were instead to bring about the patient's death faster. Put theoretically, Dorff accepts the "double effect argument," where the doctor does something with a permissible intention even though he or she knows that it may lead to a prohibited result (in this case, hastening the patient's death), while Reisner does not accept the "double effect" argument. In classical Jewish sources, one is not responsible for what one does not intend to do *unless* one knows ahead of time that a given, unintended result is inevitable (*p'sik reishei v'lo yamut?*, literally, "Can you cut off a chicken's head such that it will not die?"). Dorff takes refuge in the fact that pain thresholds among patients, the rate at which they metabolize medications, and differing body mass among patients all make the specific amount of medication that will cause death in any given patient uncertain and there-

fore not an instance of *p'sik reishei*.

Aside from the inherent importance and timeliness of their topic, these responsa are significant for several reasons. They were not the very first issues in bioethics that the CJLS addressed; as early as 1953, the CJLS approved a responsum by Rabbi Theodore Friedman permitting blind Jews to accept cornea transplants from cadavers, and in 1958 the CJLS approved a responsum by Rabbi Isaac Klein permitting Jews to donate their bodies to science or medical schools for first-year anatomy classes.[51] Several responsa on abortion were approved on August 23, 1983, including one that had been written by Rabbi Isaac Klein in 1959. The explosion of developments in medicine in the 1970s and 1980s, however, led Rabbi Joel Roth, then Chair of the CJLS, to establish a Subcommittee on Bioethics in 1990 to deal with all of the new issues in that area that rabbis and lay Jews were asking about, and these two responsa on end-of-life issues were the first to come through that process. That subcommittee has been very prolific, and in 2000 the Finkelstein Institute of the Jewish Theological Seminary published a collection of the CJLS rulings on bioethics to that date as a book edited by Rabbi Aaron Mackler, entitled *Life and Death Responsibilities in Jewish Biomedical Ethics*. Thus the responsa on the end of life by Dorff and Reisner are important not only because of the significance of the subjects they treat, but also because methodologically they illustrate a dispute over which legal categories to apply when responding to a new issue (a "serious business case") and because they are the product of a new procedure of the CJLS.

When Rabbi Kassel Abelson became Chair of the CJLS in 1992, he followed Rabbi Roth's lead in establishing subcommittees in several other areas. The CJLS now has subcommittees on all of the following: Bioethics; Family, Gender, and Human Sexuality; *Kashrut* (the dietary laws); Halakhah and Special Needs; Conservative Movement Publications; and Business Ethics. The subcommittees of the CJLS do not function in the way that subcommittees do in Congress, for a responsum does not have to be voted out of a subcommittee in order to be considered by the full CJLS. The purpose of the subcommittee is instead to give authors a first response to their draft so that they can revise (and hopefully improve) it before presenting it to the entire committee. Where there is no relevant subcommittee, the CJLS considers the author's draft directly, but most responsa are now considered by subcommittees first.

Finally, these responsa illustrate two other features of Jewish law generally and Jewish law within the Conservative movement in particular. First, both Dorff and Reisner extensively consulted physicians and researchers in end-of-life care, sometimes through their writings and sometimes orally. In fact, the subcommittee interviewed several experts in the field as a way to help Dorff and Reisner—and ultimately the whole CJLS—learn what they needed to know to apply Jewish law intelligently to these new areas of medicine. In Jewish law, as in other legal systems, expert testimony cannot substitute for the law; that only the rabbi or judge can determine. But rabbis and judges and the legal rulings they produce can benefit immensely from experts in the areas they are considering.

Second, when these two responsa came to a vote, several members of the CJLS voted for both of them. In some cases, such members believed that both were legitimate expressions of Jewish law as applied to these new areas. A few other members articulated their intention that the two balance each other in the areas in which they differed. There is nothing in the rules of the CJLS to prevent members from voting for two conflicting responsa for these or other reasons; when two or more responsa are approved on a given issue, that indicates the pluralism within the movement. On the other hand, most often only one responsum on a given issue is approved, and that then indicates the unity of the movement in those areas of the law.

F. EDUCATIONAL MATERIALS ON JEWISH LAW: RABBINIC LETTERS ON INTIMATE RELATIONS AND ON POVERTY

Finally, we will look at a different genre of Jewish legal material produced by the Conservative movement. As their name indicates, responsa (literally, "questions and answers," *she'elot u'teshuvot*) are intended to answer questions in the law. Sometimes, though, the law is clear, but many Jews do not know it or understand the various reasons to follow it. Those educational and motivational goals led the Leaders Training Fellowship (a youth group consisting of those teenagers taking at least six hours of Jewish studies each week during the academic year) to produce a series of pamphlets in the 1950s written by Rabbi Chaim Potok, mostly on issues in Jewish ethics. Those same goals have led United Synagogue Youth to produce a whole series of excellent source books on various aspects of Judaism, including a number on aspects of the theory and practice of Jewish law. Women's League for Conservative Judaism has published a book on Jewish prayer. The Federation of Jewish Men's

Clubs, in conjunction with the University of Judaism, has produced the Art of Jewish Living series written by University of Judaism Vice President Ron Wolfson, with books explaining both traditional practices and creative ways to implement them on Friday evenings at home, at the Passover seder, at Hanukkah, and when comforting mourners; they are now published and distributed by Jewish Lights. And in addition to many scholarly and liturgical works, the Rabbinical Assembly is about to publish a collection of essays on Jewish rituals and another on Jewish ethics intended to explain how Conservative Jews understand many areas of Jewish practice.

In 1996 and 2000, however, the Rabbinical Assembly published two rabbinic letters, one on intimate relations and the other on poverty—namely, *"This Is My Beloved, This Is My Friend" (Song of Songs 5:16): A Rabbinic Letter on Intimate Relations*; and *"You Shall Strengthen Them" (Leviticus 25:35): A Rabbinic Letter on the Poor.* The first was the product of the Rabbinical Assembly's Commission on Sexuality, and even though it was an educational document rather than a set of legal decisions, it, like most Rabbinical Assembly publications that have to do with Jewish law, was approved for publication by the CJLS. The Letter on Poverty was the product of the joint Rabbinical Assembly/United Synagogue Commission on Social Action. Both were written by Rabbi Elliot Dorff in conjunction with these groups, in order to educate the movement about two important areas of Jewish law.

Why the form of a Letter? I explain that in the Prologue to the *Letter on Intimate Relations:*

> This rabbinic letter is an effort on the part of the Conservative rabbinate to talk openly about matters of human sexuality and intimacy with the members of our movement. Although sex is certainly not the whole of life, it is an important part of it, and so it should be part of the discussion that we Jews have about the norms by which we live. The Jewish tradition has much to say about this area of life, as it does about most, and much of what it says is as compelling to us now as it was to our ancestors. Judaism has a distinctly positive view toward sexuality as the gift of God, and it articulates values and rules for this area of life that make it the pleasurable, yet holy, activity it was meant to be.
>
> In times past, great rabbinic authorities wrote letters to the Jews of their generation to convey Judaism's message concerning human sexuality and intimate relations. Probably the most famous is *Iggeret Ha-Kodesh*, attributed to Rabbi Moses ben Nahman (Nahmanides, 1194–1270), but we also have manuals on these matters written by, or attributed to, Rabbi Moses ben Maimon (Maimonides, 1135–1204), Rabbi Abraham ben David of Posquieres (1125–1198), and others.[52]

They used the format of a letter *(iggeret)* or a manual rather than a rabbinic responsum *(teshuvah)* because in these essays they were not called upon to rule on a specific question in Jewish law but rather to educate their readers to the accepted rules of the Jewish law and the concepts and values that underlie them. Their audience, then, was not primarily other rabbis, but the entire Jewish community. Moreover, they used the form of a letter or a manual, rather than a responsum, because they wanted to be personal in tone as well as in content regarding this most personal of areas.

This letter, then, follows a traditional form for discussing these matters. In our own time, when Jews live under conditions remarkably different from those of the past, we need all the more to explore how we can and should synthesize our Jewish commitments with modern realities and sensitivities. Even within the ranks of those who otherwise obey Jewish law strictly, the laws and values of Judaism on matters of sexuality and intimacy are, unfortunately, observed too often in the breach, and that is true as well for those who in other areas are not very religiously committed.[53]

This letter is therefore intended to address all Conservative Jews, whatever their level of knowledge and commitment. It is written in response to our duty as rabbis to both Judaism and the Jewish community to teach the tradition so that Judaism can affect not only our public and professional lives, but our personal lives as well. As such, it is part of the Rabbinical Assembly's agenda to address contemporary concerns of Jewish continuity, for only when Jews know what Judaism says about important issues will they appreciate the reasons why they should practice it and teach it to the generations to come.

How do these Letters and the other educational efforts of the Conservative movement in legal education relate to Jewish legal theory? In one obvious respect, these publications attempt to explain both *how* and *why* to follow Jewish law in a given area. Thus before discussing the details of what Jewish law would have us do and refrain from doing in our intimate relations, the Letter on Intimate Relations devotes the first of its four sections to a description of the concepts and values that Judaism would have us use in shaping all of our human relationships, including our most intimate ones. The Letter on the Poor describes in its first section why I, as a person and as a Jew, should be interested in helping the poor and willing to do so, and, as that Letter articulates, the motivations go well beyond general, humanitarian feelings. (The version of that Letter that I published in my book, *To Do the Right and the Good: A Jewish Approach to Modern Social Ethics,* also includes a list of a number of reasons why I might well *not* want to help the poor!) These educational efforts assume modern conditions in which Jews living in countries where there is freedom of and from religion must be shown *why* they should take on these obligations and shape their lives in accordance with Jewish law. Then, when they have that intention, in many cases they have to be shown *how* to do so as well, either because they do not know much about Jewish law or because new conditions raise problems or questions as to how traditional Jewish law should be applied in our time.

The other important theoretical component of these efforts goes to the core of Judaism and Jewish law. In the Torah itself, God commands Moses a number of times to "Speak to the Israelite people and say to them . . ."[54] Moses is not to teach the law only to the elders; this was *not* to be an esoteric tradition, held in secrecy and confidence by a privileged few. This was instead to be a tradition shared by the masses. To make sure that that is the case, the Torah insists that once every seven years, Jewish "men, women, and children"—and even "the strangers in your communities"—gather to hear the entire Torah read and explained.[55] Parents have the specific duty to teach their children Torah, a duty shared, according to the Rabbis, by grandparents as well, but already by the first century the Rabbis had established schools to ensure that all boys learned the tradition, whether or not their parents were educated or wealthy.[56] Girls and boys both learned the tradition informally from what they saw going on in their homes and communities. These Letters and other educational publications of the movement, then, constitute a modern form of carrying out the strong duty in our tradition to teach Jews Jewish law, show them how it is to be applied to contemporary circumstances, and motivate them to obey it.

EPILOGUE

The Unity within the Diverse Conservative Theories of Jewish Law

THIS BOOK HAS PRESENTED a variety of theories of Jewish law within the Conservative movement. The diversity within the movement in its approaches to Jewish law should therefore not be in doubt. At the same time, it is important not to exaggerate that diversity, for much unites the movement as well in its approach to Jewish law. Here, at the end of a book that presents the diversity within the movement, then, it is important to remind readers of the *unity* within Conservative Judaism in its approach to Jewish law so that people "do not lose the forest for the trees." Some of these unifying factors include the following: a strong interest in Jewish law as a central feature of what it means to be Jewish; a sense that Jewish law makes an important claim on us (most would say it is "binding" or "authoritative"); a recognition that Jewish law has changed in substance throughout history and therefore must be studied and applied with that historical development in mind; a clear rooting of Jewish law in Judaism's larger context, including its views of God and humanity (its theology and anthropology), its stories, prayers, economic and social conditions, and its sense of morality; and a deep commitment to make Jewish law articulate how a good and just God would have us act in our time and place.

As the chapter comparing Conservative theories to other theories demonstrates, other Jews share some but not all of these commitments. Moreover, even the elements they share with the Conservative movement they often interpret and apply differently.

What is clear, then, is that quite apart from our differences with the other movements, the Conservative movement asserts some important convictions about the nature of Jewish law as articulated in the unity and variety that characterizes the theories presented in this volume. Its ultimate commitment is to learn Jewish law, to make it a vital part of our own lives, to enrich it by judiciously applying it to modern times, and to pass it on to the next generation in a way that is historically authentic, personally and socially meaningful, morally sensitive and challenging, and worthy of God who would have us follow it.

> Take utmost care and watch yourselves scrupulously, so that you do not forget the things that you saw with your own eyes and so that they do not fade from your mind as long as you live. And make them known to your children and your children's children: The day you stood before the Lord your God at Horeb, when the Lord said to me [Moses], "Gather the people to Me that I may let them hear My words, in order that they may learn to revere Me as long as they live on earth, and may so teach their children." You came forward and stood at the foot of the mountain . . . The Lord . . . declared to you the covenant that He commanded you to observe . . .

> (DEUTERONOMY 4:9–13)

BIBLIOGRAPHY

SUGGESTIONS
FOR FURTHER READING

Many of the authors whose work has been included in this book have written widely about topics not directly relevant to their theories of Jewish law. In this Bibliography, however, I have restricted the entries to their writings about legal theory or closely related issues (e.g., their view of revelation, their treatment of ethics), together with the work of other people writing about their theories (the "secondary literature").

Obviously, the secondary literature is very sparse or non-existent with regard to more recent theories because not enough time has elapsed for thinkers to digest and live with their theories to identify their strengths and weaknesses. Indeed, my commentary on their theories in this book often represents the first published description, appreciation, and critique of them. At the extreme, for two authors whose work is included in this book, this is the first time that they have written about their theory of Jewish law. Thus most of the entries in chapters 5 and 6 are other works that the authors have written, rather than the work of other people analyzing and evaluating their theories.

To make this bibliography as useful as possible, I have organized it by chapter so that readers can quickly find other materials on the topic or thinker that interests them. This means, however, that in a few cases I have listed a book more than once—specifically, when it is relevant to the topics of more than one chapter of this book. Finally, I have not repeated in this list the writings that have been republished in this book, even though, in my judgment, they are the most important and/or understandable writings of the author expressing his or her theory of Jewish law; readers can find the sources of those readings in the Permissions section at the end of this volume and at the footnotes at the beginning of each reading.

515

CHAPTER ONE:
BRINGING THE TOPIC DOWN TO EARTH

A. On Conservative Judaism

Dorff, Elliot N. 1977; 1996. *Conservative Judaism: Our Ancestors to Our Descendants.* New York: United Synagogue of America; second, revised edition: New York: United Synagogue of Conservative Judaism.

Elazar, Daniel J. and Rela Mintz Geffen. 2000. *The Conservative Movement in Judaism: Dilemmas and Opportunities.* Albany: State University of New York Press.

Gillman, Neil. 1993. *Conservative Judaism: The New Century.* West Orange, NJ: Behrman House.

Golinkin, David. 1990. *Halakhah for Our Time: A Conservative Approach to Jewish Law.* New York: United Synagogue of America.

Gordis, Robert. 1978. *Understanding Conservative Judaism.* New York: Rabbinical Assembly.

Nadell, Pamela S. 1988. *Conservative Judaism in America: A Biographical Dictionary and Sourcebook.* New York: Greenwood Press.

Waxman, Mordecai, ed. 1958. *Tradition and Change: The Development of Conservative Judaism.* New York: Rabbinical Assembly.

B. On the Nature of Philosophy

Cahn, Steven M. 2000. *Exploring Philosophy: An Introductory Anthology.* Oxford: Oxford University Press.

Perry, John and Michael Bratman. 1998. *Introduction to Philosophy: Classical and Contemporary Readings.* New York: Oxford University Press, 3rd edition.

Warburton, Nigel. 2004. *Philosophy: The Basics.* New York: Routledge.

Westphal, Jonathan. 1998. *Philosophical Propositions: An Introduction to Philosophy.* New York: Routledge.

C. On Theories of Law

Cohen, Marshall, ed. 1983. *Ronald Dworkin and Contemporary Jurisprudence.* Totawa, NJ: Rowman and Allanheld.

Feinberg, Joel. 2003. *Problems at the Roots of Law: Essays in Legal and Political Theory.* Oxford and New York: Oxford University Press.

_____ and Hyman Gross, eds. 1991. *Philosophy of Law.* Belmont, CA: Wadsworth Publishing Company, 4th edition.

Raz, Joseph. 1980. *The Concept of a Legal System.* Oxford: Clarendon Press.

CHAPTER TWO:
THE BIBLICAL AND RABBINIC ROOTS
OF CONSERVATIVE LEGAL THEORIES

Dorff, Elliot N. 1996. *Conservative Judaism: Our Ancestors to Our Descendants.* New York: United Synagogue of Conservative Judaism, pp. 49–95.

_____ and Arthur Rosett. 1988. *A Living Tree: The Roots and Growth of Jewish*

Law. Albany: State University of New York Press and New York: Jewish Theological Seminary of America.

Elon, Menachem. 1994. *Jewish Law: History, Sources, Principles.* Bernard Auerbach and Melvin J. Sykes, trans. Philadelphia: Jewish Publication Society, 4 vols.

Hecht, N.S., B.S. Jackson, S.M. Passamaneck, D. Piatelli, and A.M. Rabello, eds. 1996. *An Introduction to the History and Sources of Jewish Law.* Oxford: Clarendon Press.

CHAPTER THREE:
EARLY CONSERVATIVE THEORIES OF JEWISH LAW

Zacharias Frankel

Davis, Moshe. 1965. *The Emergence of Conservative Judaism.* Philadelphia: Jewish Publication Society.

Parzen, Herbert. 1964. *Architects of Conservative Judaism.* New York: Jonathan David.

Schorsch, Ismar. 1991. "Zechariah Frankel and the European Origins of Conservative Judaism." *Judaism* (Summer 1991): 344–354.

Solomon Schechter

Bentwich, Norman De Mattos. 1938. *Solomon Schechter: A Biography.* Philadelphia: Jewish Publication Society.

Davis, Moshe. 1965. *The Emergence of Conservative Judaism.* Philadelphia: Jewish Publication Society.

Fierstein, Robert E. 2002. *Solomon Schechter in America: A Centennial Tribute.* New York: Rabbinical Assembly.

Ginzberg, Louis. 1928, 1958. *Students, Scholars, and Saints.* Philadelphia: Jewish Publication Society. Reprinted in Seymour Siegel, ed., *Conservative Judaism and Jewish Law.* New York: Rabbinical Assembly, 1977, ch. 1.

Karp, Abraham. 1998. *Jewish Continuity in America: Creative Survival in a Free Society.* Tuscaloosa: University of Alabama Press.

Oko, Adolph S. 1938. *Solomon Schechter: A Bibliography.* Cambridge, England: The University Press.

Parzen, Herbert. 1964. *Architects of Conservative Judaism.* New York: Jonathan David.

Schechter, Solomon. 1896. *Studies in Judaism.* New York: Macmillan; republished as *Studies in Judaism: First Series.* 1911, 1945. Philadelphia: Jewish Publication Society. Republished in *Studies in Judaism.* Piscataway, NJ: Gorgias Press, 3 vols.

———. 1908. *Studies in Judaism: Second Series.* Philadelphia: Jewish Publication Society. Republished in *Studies in Judaism.* Piscataway, NJ: Gorgias Press, 3 vols.

———. 1909. *Some Aspects of Rabbinic Theology.* New York: Macmillan; republished as *Aspects of Rabbinic Theology:* 1961. New York: Schocken.

———. 1915. *Seminary Addresses and Other Papers.* Cincinnati: Ark Publishing.

———. 1924, 1945. *Studies in Judaism: Third Series.* Philadelphia: Jewish Publication Society. Republished in *Studies in Judaism.* 2003. Piscataway, NJ: Gorgias Press, 3 vols.

Starr, David Benjamin. 2003. *Catholic Israel: Solomon Schechter, A Study of Unity and Fragmentation in Modern Jewish History.* Ann Arbor, MI: UMI.

Mordecai M. Kaplan

Berkovits, Eliezer. 1974. *Major Themes in Modern Philosophies of Judaism*. New York: Ktav, ch. 5.

Borowitz, Eugene. 1983. *Choices in Modern Jewish Thought: A Partisan Guide*. New York: Behrman House, ch. 5.

Breslauer, S. Daniel. 1994. *Mordecai Kaplan's Thought in a Postmodern Age*. Atlanta, GA: Scholars Press.

Cohen, Jack. 1999. *Guides for an Age of Confusion: Studies in the Thinking of Abraham Y. Kook and Mordecai M. Kaplan*. New York: Fordham University Press.

Eisenstein, Ira. 1952. *Mordecai M. Kaplan: An Evaluation*. New York: Jewish Reconstructionist Foundation.

Gurock, Jeffrey S. 1997. *A Modern Heretic and a Traditional Community: Mordecai M. Kaplan, Orthodoxy, and American Judaism*. New York: Columbia University Press.

Kaplan, Mordecai M. 1934. *Judaism as a Civilization: Toward a Reconstruction of American Jewish Life*. New York: Macmillan. Republished 1994: Philadelphia: Jewish Publication Society.

_____. 1948. *The Future of the American Jew*. New York: Macmillan, 1948; New York: Reconstructionist Press, 1967.

_____. 1956. *Questions Jews Ask: Reconstructionist Answers*. New York: Reconstructionist Press.

_____. 1960. *The Greater Judaism in the Making: A Study of the Modern Evolution of Judaism*. New York: Reconstructionist Press.

Karp, Abraham. 1998. *Jewish Continuity in America: Creative Survival in a Free Society*. Tuscaloosa: University of Alabama Press.

Parzen, Herbert. 1964. *Architects of Conservative Judaism*. New York: Jonathan David.

Scult, Mel. 1993. *Judaism Faces the Twentieth Century: A Biography of Mordecai M. Kaplan*. Detroit: Wayne State University Press.

CHAPTER FOUR:
MID-TWENTIETH-CENTURY THEORISTS

Robert Gordis

Gordis, Robert. 1978. *Understanding Conservative Judaism*. New York: Rabbinical Assembly.

_____. 1986. *Judaic Ethics for a Lawless World*. New York: Jewish Theological Seminary of America.

_____. 1988. "The Ordination of Women." In *The Ordination of Women as Rabbis*, Simon Greenberg, ed. New York: Jewish Theological Seminary of America, pp. 47–68.

_____. 1990. *The Dynamics of Judaism: A Study in Jewish Law*. Bloomington, IN: Indiana University Press.

Jacob Agus

Agus, Jacob B. 1954. *Guideposts in Modern Judaism: An Analysis of Current Trends in Jewish Thought*. New York: Bloch.

_____. 1966. *The Vision and the Way: An Interpretation of Jewish Ethics*. New York: Ungar.

_____. 1997. *The Essential Agus: The Writings of Jacob B. Agus*. New York: New York University Press.

Dorff, Elliot N. 1997. "Jewish Law as Standards," in *American Rabbi: The Life and Thought of Jacob B. Agus*, Steven T. Katz, ed. New York: New York University Press, pp. 195–223; reprinted in an expanded form as "'Legislated Spiritual Disciplines': Jacob Agus' Philosophy of Jewish Law," in *Jewish Law Association Studies IX: The London 1996 Conference Volume*, E. A. Goldman, ed. Atlanta: Scholars Press, 1997, pp. 25–56.

Kaufman, William E. 1976. *Contemporary Jewish Philosophies*. New York: Reconstructionist Press and Behrman House, pp. 231–248.

See also the entries for chapter 8 in this volume to read about the responsa he wrote for the Conservative movement's Committee on Jewish Law and Standards.

Abraham Joshua Heschel

Berkovits, Eliezer. 1974. *Major Themes in Modern Philosophies of Judaism*. New York: Ktav, ch. 6.

Borowitz, Eugene. 1983. *Choices in Modern Jewish Thought: A Partisan Guide*. New York: Behrman House, ch. 8.

Dresner, Samuel. 2002. *Heschel, Hasidism, and Halakha*. New York: Fordham University Press.

Fierman, Morton C. 1990. *Leap of Action: Ideas in the Theology of Abraham Joshua Heschel*. Lanham, MD: University Press of America.

Hartman, David. 1999. *A Heart of Many Rooms: Celebrating the Many Voices within Judaism*. Woodstock, VT: Jewish Lights, ch. 9.

Heschel, Abraham Joshua. 1953. "Toward an Understanding of Halacha." *Yearbook of the Central Conference of American Rabbis* 63:386–409; reprinted in *Moral Grandeur and Spiritual Audacity: Abraham Joshua Heschel*, Susannah Heschel, ed. New York: Farrar, Straus, Giroux, 1996, pp. 127–145.

_____. 1955. *God in Search of Man: A Philosophy of Judaism*. New York: Farrar, Straus, and Cudahy.

_____. 1961. "The Individual Jew and His Obligations." *Conservative Judaism* 15 (Spring); reprinted in his *The Insecurity of Freedom: Essays on Human Existence*. Philadelphia: Jewish Publication Society, 1966, pp. 187–211.

_____. 2005. *Heavenly Torah as Refracted through the Generations*, Gordon Tucker trans. and commentator. New York: Continuum.

Hyman, James. 1998. "Meaningfulness, the Ineffable, and the Commandments." *Conservative Judaism* 50:2–3 (Winter/Spring 1998): 84–99.

Kaplan, Edward K. 1993. "Abraham Joshua Heschel." In *Interpreters of Judaism in the Late Twentieth Century*, Steven T. Katz, ed. Washington, D.C.: B'nai Brith Books, pp. 131–150.

_____. 1996. *Holiness in Words: Abraham Joshua Heschel's Poetics of Piety*. West Fulton, NY: State University of New York Press.

_____. 1998. *Abraham Joshua Heschel: Prophetic Witness*. New Haven, CT: Yale University Press.

Kasimow, Harold. 1979. *Divine-Human Encounter: A Study of Abraham Joshua Heschel*. Washington, D.C.: University Press of America.

Kaufman, William E. 1976. *Contemporary Jewish Philosophies.* New York: Reconstructionist Press and Behrman House, ch. 8.

Perlman, Lawrence. 1989. *Abraham Heschel's Idea of Revelation.* Atlanta, GA: Scholars Press.

_____. 2002. "As a Report About Revelation, the Bible Itself Is a Midrash." *Conservative Judaism* 55:1 (Fall): 30–37.

Scult, Mel. 2002. "Kaplan's Heschel: A View from the Kaplan Diary." *Conservative Judaism* 54:4 (Summer): 3–14.

Siegel, Seymour, ed. 1977. *Conservative Judaism and Jewish Law.* New York: Rabbinical Assembly.

Tucker, Gordon. 1998. "Heschel's *Torah min ha-shamayim:* Ancient Theology and Contemporary Autobiography." *Conservative Judaism* 50:2–3 (Winter/Spring): 48–55.

CHAPTER FIVE:
CONSERVATIVE THEORIES OF LAW SINCE 1970, PART I

Edward Feld

Feld, Edward. 2003. "A Divining Rod Has Two Branches: Choices for the Conservative Movement." *Conservative Judaism* 55:3 (Spring): 52–57.

Joel Roth

Roth, Joel. 1986. *The Halakhic Process: A Systematic Analysis.* New York: Jewish Theological Seminary of America.

_____. 1988. "On the Ordination of Women as Rabbis." In *The Ordination of Women as Rabbis,* Simon Greenberg, ed. New York: Jewish Theological Seminary of America, pp. 127–185.

_____. 1995. "Halakhic Responsibility." *Conservative Judaism* 47:3 (Spring): 24–27.

Tucker, Gordon. 1989. "God, the Good, and Halakhah." *Judaism* 38:3 (Summer): 365–376.

See also the entries for chapter 8 in this volume to read about some of the responsa Rabbi Roth wrote for the Conservative movement's Committee on Jewish Law and Standards.

Neil Gillman

Gillman, Neil. 1993. *Conservative Judaism: The New Century.* West Orange, NJ: Behrman House.

_____. 1994. "Authority and Parameters in Jewish Decision-Making." *The Reconstructionist* 50:2 (Fall): 73–79.

_____. 1996. "What Do American Jews Believe?—A Symposium." *Commentary* 102:2 (August): 39–40.

_____. 2002. "The Problems of Myth." *Sh'ma* 32/587 (January): 1–3.

Louis Jacobs

Dorff, Elliot N. 1993. "Louis Jacobs." In *Interpreters of Judaism in the Late Twentieth Century,* Steven T. Katz, ed. Washington, D.C.: B'nai Brith Books, pp. 167–188.

Gillman, Neil. 2003. "Underrated 20th Century Jewish Thinkers: Louis Jacobs." *Conservative Judaism* 55:4 (Summer): 58–60.

Jacobs, Louis. 1957. *We Have Reason to Believe*. London: Valentine, Mitchell.

_____. 1968. *Faith*. New York: Basic Books.

_____. 1975. *Theology in the Responsa*. London and Boston: Routledge & Kegan Paul.

_____. 1984. *A Tree of Life: Diversity, Flexibility, and Creativity in Jewish Law*. Oxford: Oxford University Press.

_____. 1984. *The Talmudic Argument*. Cambridge: Cambridge University Press.

_____. 1990. *God, Torah, Israel: Traditionalism without Fundamentalism*. Cincinnati: Hebrew Union College Press.

David M. Gordis

Gordis, David M. 2002. "Two Literary Talmudic Readings." In *History and Literature: New Readings of Jewish Texts in Honor of Arnold J. Band*. David C. Jacobson and William Cutter, eds. Providence, RI: Brown University Press (Brown Judaica Series #334), pp. 3–15.

CHAPTER SIX:
CONSERVATIVE THEORIES OF LAW SINCE 1970, PART II

Elliot N. Dorff

Dorff, Elliot N. 1973. "Towards a Legal Theory for the Conservative Movement," *Conservative Judaism* 27:3 (Spring): 65–77. "The Author Responds," Open Forum, *Conservative Judaism* 28:2 (Winter, 1974), 75–78.

_____. 1976. "Revelation." *Conservative Judaism* 31:1–2 (Fall–Winter): 58–69.

_____. 1977, 1996. *Conservative Judaism: Our Ancestors to Our Descendants*. New York: United Synagogue of America; second, revised edition: New York: United Synagogue of Conservative Judaism.

_____. 1977. "The Interaction of Jewish Law with Morality." *Judaism* 26:4 (Fall): 455–466.

_____. 1978. "Judaism as a Religious Legal System." *Hastings Law Journal* 29:6 (July): 1331–1360.

_____. 1979. "The Meaning of Covenant: A Contemporary Understanding." In *Issues in the Jewish-Christian Dialogue: Jewish Perspectives on Covenant, Mission and Witness*. Helga Croner and Leon Klenicki, eds. New York: Paulist Press, pp. 38–61.

_____. 1987. "Training Rabbis in the Land of the Free." In *The Seminary at 100*. Nina Beth Cardin and David Wolf Silverman, eds. New York: The Rabbinical Assembly and The Jewish Theological Seminary of America, pp. 11–28.

_____. 1987/1988. "The Effects of Science on Jewish Law." *Conservative Judaism* 40:2 (Winter): 52–60.

_____. 1988. "The Covenant: The Transcendent Thrust in Jewish Law." *The Jewish Law Annual* 7: 68–96. Reprinted in Dorff and Newman (1995), pp. 161–176.

_____. 1988. *A Living Tree: The Roots and Growth of Jewish Law* (with Arthur Rosett). Albany, NY: State University of New York Press, and New York, New York: The Jewish Theological Seminary of America.

_____. 1989. *Mitzvah Means Commandment*. New York: United Synagogue of America.

_____. 1992. *Knowing God: Jewish Journeys to the Unknowable*. Northvale, NJ: Jason Aronson Press, ch. 3.

_____. 1997. "Custom Drives Jewish Law on Women." *Conservative Judaism* 49:3 (Spring): 3–21. Response to critics: *Conservative Judaism* 51:1 (Fall 1998), pp. 66–73. Reprinted in *Gender Issues in Jewish Law: Essays and Responsa*, Walter Jacob and Moshe Zemer, eds. New York: Berghahn Books, 2001), pp. 82–106.

_____. 1998. "Jewish Law and Lore: The Case of Organ Transplantation." *The Jewish Law Annual* 12:65–114.

_____. 2002. *To Do the Right and the Good: A Jewish Approach to Modern Social Ethics*. Philadelphia: Jewish Publication Society, ch. 1 and Appendix.

_____. 2003. *Love Your Neighbor and Yourself: A Jewish Approach to Modern Personal Ethics*. Philadelphia: Jewish Publication Society, ch. 1 and Appendix.

_____ and Louis Newman, eds., 1995. *Contemporary Jewish Ethics and Morality: A Reader*. New York: Oxford University Press.

See also the entries for chapter 8 in this volume to read the responsa Rabbi Dorff wrote for the Conservative movement's Committee on Jewish Law and Standards.

Raymond Scheindlin

This is his first article on Jewish legal theory.

Alana Suskin

This is her first article on Jewish legal theory.

Gordon Tucker

Tucker, Gordon. 1993. "The Sayings of the Wise are like Goads: An Appreciation of the Works of Robert Cover." *Conservative Judaism* 45:3 (Spring): 17–39.

_____. 1993. "Homosexuality and Halakhic Judaism: A Conservative View." *Moment* 18:2 (June): 40–43.

_____. 1999. "Metaphysical Realism: Theoretical and Practical Considerations." *Conservative Judaism* 51:2 (Winter): 84–95.

_____ 2005. "D'rosh V'Kabbel Sakhar: Halakhic and Metahalakhic Arguments Concerning Judaism and Homosexuality." Unpublished responsum submitted to the Committee on Jewish Law and Standards.

See also the entries for chapter 8 in this volume to read the responsa Rabbi Tucker wrote for the Conservative movement's Committee on Jewish Law and Standards.

CHAPTER SEVEN:
SOME COMPARATIVE THEORIES TO THE RIGHT AND LEFT

Yeshayahu Leibowitz

Hartman, David. 1985. *A Living Covenant: The Innovative Spirit in Traditional Judaism*. New York: Free Press, pp. 10–15, 61–62, 124–126, 328–330.

_____. 1993. "Yeshayahu Leibowitz." In *Interpreters of Judaism in the Late Twentieth Century*, Steven T. Katz, ed. Washington, D.C.: B'nai Brith Books, pp. 189–204.

David Hartman

Ellenson, David Harry. 2004. *After Emancipation: Jewish Religious Responses to Modernity*. Cincinnati: Hebrew Union College Press, chs. 19 and 22.
Hartman, David. 1999. *A Heart of Many Rooms: Celebrating the Many Voices Within Judaism*. Woodstock, VT: Jewish Lights, Parts I and III.
Malino, Jonathan. 2004. *Judaism and Modernity: The Religious Philosophy of David Hartman*. Burlington, VT: Ashgate.
Sokol, Moshe. 1993. "David Hartman." In *Interpreters of Judaism in the Late Twentieth Century*, Steven T. Katz, ed. Washington, D.C.: B'nai Brith Books, pp. 91–112.

Reform Platform Statements

Borowitz, Eugene B. 1978. *Reform Judaism Today*. New York: Behrman House.
Meyer, Michael A. and W. Gunther Plaut. 2000. *The Reform Judaism Reader: North American Documents*. New York: UAHC Press.

Arthur Waskow

Bush, Lawrence. 1993. *Jews, Money, and Social Responsibility: Developing a "Torah of Money" for Contemporary Life*. Philadelphia: The Shefa Fund.
Waskow, Arthur. 1995. *Down-to-Earth Judaism: Food, Money, Sex, and the Rest of Life*. New York: W. Morrow.
_____. 1996. *Godwrestling—Round 2: Ancient Wisdom, Future Paths*. Woodstock, VT: Jewish Lights, esp. ch. 16.
_____, ed. 2000. *Torah of the Earth: Exploring 4,000 Years of Ecology in Jewish Thought*. Woodstock, VT: Jewish Lights, 2 vols., esp. 1:70–84 and 2:261–286, which are his own essays.

Arthur Green

Green, Arthur. 1992. *Seek My Face, Speak My Name: A Contemporary Jewish Theology*. Northvale, NJ: Jason Aronson.
_____. 1996. *Restoring the Aleph: Judaism for the Contemporary Seeker*. New York: Council for Initiatives in Jewish Education.
_____. 2003. *Ehyeh: A Kabbalah for Tomorrow*. Woodstock, VT: Jewish Lights.

Eugene Borowitz

Borowitz, Eugene. 1983. *Choices in Modern Jewish Thought: A Partisan Guide*. New York: Behrman House, chs. 11–12.
_____. 1984. *Liberal Judaism*. New York: UAHC Press.
_____. 1990. *Exploring Jewish Ethics: Papers on Covenant Responsibility*. Detroit: Wayne State University Press.
_____. 1991. *Renewing the Covenant: A Theology for the Postmodern Jew*. Philadelphia: Jewish Publication Society.
_____. 1999. *The Jewish Moral Virutes*. Philadelphia: Jewish Publication Society.

_____. 2002. *Studies in the Meaning of Judaism*. Philadelphia: Jewish Publication Society.

Ellenson, David and Lori Krafte-Jacobs. 1993. "Eugene Borowitz." In *Interpreters of Judaism in the Late Twentieth Century,* Steven T. Katz, ed. Washington, D.C.: B'nai Brith Books, pp. 17–40.

CHAPTER EIGHT:
SAMPLE ILLUSTRATIONS OF CONSERVATIVE
LEGAL THEORIES AT WORK

All responsa approved by the Committee on Jewish Law and Standards since 1980, and some before that date, can now be found on the Rabbinical Assembly website (www.rabbinicalassembly.org), under the title "Contemporary Halakhah." That portion of the website is open to members of the Rabbinical Assembly and non-members alike. In addition, many of the responsa adopted by the Committee have been published in book form:

1. *Proceedings of the Committee on Jewish Law and Standards of the Conservative Movement, 1927–1970,* David Golinkin, ed. (New York: Rabbinical Assembly, 1997), 3 vols.
2. *Proceedings of the Committee on Jewish Law and Standards of the Conservative Movement, 1980–1985,* no editor listed (New York: Rabbinical Assembly, 1988).
3. *Proceedings of the Committee on Jewish Law and Standards of the Conservative Movement, 1986–1990,* no editor listed (New York: Rabbinical Assembly, 2001).
4. *Responsa 1991–2000 of the Committee on Jewish Law and Standards of the Conservative Movement,* Kassel Abelson and David J. Fine, eds. (New York: Rabbinical Assembly, 2002).
5. David Golinkin, *An Index of Conservative Responsa and Practical Halakhic Studies, 1917–1990* (New York: Rabbinical Assembly, 1992).

In addition, The Rabbinical Assembly of Israel Law Committee *(Va'ad Halakhah)* has published to date six volumes of its responsa in Hebrew with English summaries. They can be procured from the Institute of Applied Halakhah at the Schechter Institute of Jewish Studies, POB 8600, Jerusalem 91083 and they are also available in Hebrew and English at www.responsafortoday.com.

NOTES

NOTES TO CHAPTER ONE

1. Elliot N. Dorff, "Traditional Judaism," *Conservative Judaism* 34:2 (November/December 1980), pp. 34–38.
2. See David Golinkin, ed., *Proceedings of the Committee on Jewish Law and Standards of the Conservative Movement 1927–1970* (New York: Rabbinical Assembly, 1997), Vol. III, pp. 1069–1084.
3. Elliot N. Dorff, *To Do the Right and the Good: A Jewish Approach to Modern Social Ethics* (Philadelphia: Jewish Publication Society, 2002), pp. 1–35.
4. The Commission on the Philosophy of Conservative Judaism, *Emet Ve-emunah: Statement of Principles of Conservative Judaism* (New York: Jewish Theological Seminary of America, Rabbinical Assembly, United Synagogue of America, Women's League for Conservative Judaism, Federation of Jewish Men's Clubs, 1988), p. 17.
5. *Conservative Judaism: Our Ancestors to Our Descendants* (New York: United Synagogue of Conservative Judaism, 1977; 2nd edition, 1996).
6. For a thorough discussion of the motives suggested by the Bible and the Rabbis, see my book, *Mitzvah Means Commandment* (New York: United Synagogue of America, 1989). For some medieval discussions of rationales for observing the commandments, see Saadiah Gaon, *Book of Doctrines and Beliefs,* chapter 3, and Maimonides, *Guide for the Perplexed,* part 3, chapters 25–49.
7. For more on the relationship between God, the law, and morality in the Bible and in rabbinic literature, see Elliot N. Dorff and Arthur Rosett, *A Living Tree: The Roots and Growth of Jewish Law* (Albany, NY: State University of New York Press, 1988), pp. 110–122, 249–257.
8. The Sifrei, both Talmuds, and Maimonides all maintain as a matter of biblical law that only men may serve as witnesses. For more on this, see my article, "Custom Drives Jewish Law on Women," *Conservative Judaism* 49:3 (Spring 1977), pp. 3–21; and Response to critics in *Conservative Judaism*

51:1 (Fall 1998), pp. 66–73; reprinted in *Gender Issues in Jewish Law: Essays and Responsa,* Walter Jacob and Moshe Zemer, eds. (New York: Berghahn Books, 2001), pp. 82–106. See also pp. 494–499 of this volume.

9. Elliot N. Dorff, *Mitzvah Means Commandment* (see note 6 above). For a shorter version of those ideas, see Elliot N. Dorff and Arthur Rosett, *A Living Tree: The Roots and Growth of Jewish Law* (see note 7 above), pp. 82–123 and 246–249.

NOTES TO CHAPTER TWO

1. This chapter draws much from my book, *Conservative Judaism: Our Ancestors to Our Descendants* (New York: United Synagogue of Conservative Judaism, 1977; 2nd edition, 1996), chapter 3, section C, pp. 69–100.

2. Other biblical passages that might give one this impression include those in which God directly rewards Israel for obeying the commandments or punishes Israel for disobeying them (e.g., Deut. 11:13–22, used as the second paragraph of the Shema; Lev. 26; Deut. 28) and those in which nature itself enforces the law (e.g., Lev. 20:22). Those certainly make it seem that Jewish law is immutable.

3. Others suggest a nice, alternative interpretation of the last words of this midrash, *"Nitzḥuni banai, nitzḥuni banai."* Instead of "My children have overcome Me, they have overcome Me," translate (on the basis of the root *netzaḥ*): "My children have given Me eternal life, they have given Me eternal life."

4. The Hebrew phrase *torah misinai* literally means "Torah from Sinai," although here—and often—it is translated "on Sinai." Professor Jose Faur, one of my professors of Talmud at the Jewish Theological Seminary of America, suggested another interpretation based on time rather than space: "Torah from [the time of] Sinai," i.e., beginning at Sinai and continuing through history.

5. Even though the direct meaning of the verse is that it will be to our merit as a people to obey God's law, the midrash takes "us" to mean "God and Israel," not just the people of Israel, and the word *tzedakah* ("righteousness") it takes to mean "benefit," which led to its later signification of "alms." Thus while Moses tells the Israelites to obey the Torah for their own merit before God, the midrash reinterprets the verse to mean that if the Israelites obey the Law, it will be a benefit to both the People Israel and to God.

NOTES TO CHAPTER THREE

1. M. Sotah 7:1; see B. Berakhot 13a, 15a, 40b; B. Megillah 17b; B. Shevuot 39a; Mishneh Torah, *Hilkhot Keriat Shema* 2:10; *Hilkhot Berakhot* 1:6; Shulḥan Arukh, *Oraḥ Ḥayim* 62:2, 101:4.

2. "Seminary Address 1915," in Mordecai Waxman, ed., *Tradition and Change: The Development of Conservative Judaism* (New York: The Burning Bush Press, 1958), p. 100.

3. "The Charter of the Seminary" (1902), in Waxman, ed., *Tradition and Change*, p. 102.

4. Hence the title of his essay, "Higher Criticism—Higher Anti-Semitism," in his *Seminary Addresses and Other Papers* (Cincinnati: Ark Publishing Company, 1915), pp. 35–40. One of the earliest and most well-known graduates of the Seminary shared that view; see Joseph H. Hertz, *Pentateuch and Haftorahs* (London: Soncino Press, 1936), pp. 198–200, 397–399, 403–406, 554–559, and 937–942.

5. Mordecai M. Kaplan, *The Meaning of God in Modern Jewish Religion* (New York: Behrman House, 1937 [reprinted by The Jewish Reconstructionist Press, 1947]), p. 59, and see pp. 59–63, 81–83, 90–91, and 96–103 for Kaplan's development of this theme of the Sabbath as a celebration of creativity and an impetus for us to be creative.

6. *The National Jewish Population Survey 2000–2001* (New York: United Jewish Communities, 2003), p. 7.

NOTES TO CHAPTER FOUR

1. Mordecai Waxman collected and translated some of the relevant essays by Frankel, Alexander Kohut, Israel Davidson, Schechter, Louis Ginzberg, Kaplan, and Gordis in his book *Tradition and Change: The Development of Conservative Judaism* (New York: The Burning Bush Press, 1958). Boaz Cohen's essay on this topic, "Towards a Philosophy of Jewish Law," was first published in 1949 and has been reprinted in Cohen's book, *Law and Tradition in Judaism* (New York: Ktav, 1959), pp. 1–38. Some of the early material (including the essay by Agus reprinted here) is reprinted along with some later essays in Seymour Siegel, ed., *Conservative Judaism and Jewish Law* (New York: Rabbinical Assembly, 1977). In February 1980, George Nudell, a JTS rabbinical student at the time, wrote an unpublished class paper entitled "The Clearing House: A History of the Committee on Jewish Law and Standards." It describes the vicissitudes of the Committee to that point, together with the arguments that produced those vicissitudes. The paper is available through the Rabbinical Assembly office (3080 Broadway, New York, NY 10027). Although Boaz Cohen (1899–1968) wrote many responsa in his capacities as secretary (1932–40) and then as chairman (1940–48) of the Committee on Jewish Law and then as chairman of the Joint Bet Din of the Seminary and the Rabbinical Assembly in the 1950s, his theoretical writings collected in the volume cited above, while clear and thoroughly documented, did not break new ground in Conservative legal theory and therefore are not included in this volume.

2. Jacob Agus, "Halakhah in the Conservative Movement," *Proceedings of*

the Rabbinical Assembly, vol. 37 (1975), p. 113. The entire essay appears on pp. 102–117.

3. See, for example, "The Code of Takkanot of Rabbenu Tam" in Louis Finkelstein, *Jewish Self-Government in the Middle Ages* (New York: Jewish Theological Seminary of America, 1924), pp. 179–91.

4. B. Berakhot 26b states that the Patriarchs established the practice of thrice-daily prayer.

5. Moses "instituted" *(hitkin)* the custom of the seven-day marrige feast and the seven days of mourning (Y. Ketubot 1:1 [25a])—that is, he sanctioned the old customs going back to Jacob (Gen. 29:27; 10:10; see also Judg. 14:12; I Sam. 31:13; Job 2:13). According to B. Bava Kamma 80b–81a, Joshua laid down *(hitnah)* ten stipulations on his entry into the Land of Israel governing the life of the Israelites there. Solomon instituted *(hitkin)* the laws of Sabbath boundaries *(eruvin)* and washing hands before meals (B. Eruvin 21b).

6. M. Gittin 4:2–7, 9. Hillel's *prozbul* is in 4:3; see also M. Sheviit 10:3.

7. B. Rosh Hashanah 31b.

8. See Menachem Elon, "Takkanot," *Encyclopedia Judaica* 15:712–728; the Chief Rabbinate's *takkanot* are described on pp. 727–728.

9. See Deuteronomy 21:15–17 for the law of primogeniture, and also Numbers 27:1–11, which prescribes that a man's estate will pass to his daughters only if there are no sons.

10. Jacob Agus, *Guideposts in Modern Judaism* (New York: Bloch Publishing Company, 1954), p. 279. Agus does not use the Passover liturgy to illustrate this point, as I do in the next several lines, but I think that it is in keeping with his meaning.

11. Ibid., pp. 301, 302.

12. Saadiah Gaon, *Book of Beliefs and Doctrines (Sefer Emunot Ve-de'ot),* Prolegomena, section 4.

13. Agus, *Guideposts in Modern Judaism (supra* n. 10), p. 280.

14. Ibid.

15. In a later passage (ibid., p. 301), Agus indicates why reason cannot be used exclusively to account for *any* area of life:

> The pole of reason or objectivity must be constantly replenished with subjective insights, if it is to keep from degenerating into a hollow mockery of itself. First, it must assimilate the subjective feeling of trust in reason itself. Second, it must operate with the subjective intuitive valuations of the sanctity of the human person, the validity of the goal of the Good or the validity of the moral law and the perception of beauty and harmony. Third, it renews itself and ascends to a higher level only thru *(sic)* periodic intuitive insights, that is, periodic reversions to the pole of subjectivity.

In religion, for Agus, revelation provides the pole of subjectivity, and hence with regard to religion he argues specifically for the need for revelation. As this passage indicates, though, Agus maintains that reason would need some such element of subjectivity in other areas of human experience as well for the reasons he mentions in this passage.

16. Ibid., p. 281. All citations in the next few paragraphs, in which I explain Agus's reasons for claiming that reason is not a sufficient ground for Jewish law, come from pp. 281–282 of *Guideposts*.

17. Ibid., pp. 282, 285, 288–289.

18. Ibid., pp. 323–325; reprinted in Seymour Siegel, ed., *Conservative Judaism and Jewish Law* (New York: Rabbinical Assembly, 1977), pp. 30–31.

19. Ibid.

20. *Guideposts*, p. 329; in Siegel, ibid., p. 35.

21. *Guideposts*, p. 322; in Siegel, ibid., p. 29.

22. *Guideposts*, pp. 332–333; in Siegel, ibid., p. 37.

23. *Guideposts*, pp. 333–335, 340–341; in Siegel, ibid., pp. 38–39, 42–43. Agus develops his point-field analysis of the meaning and existence of God in chapters four and five of *Guideposts*.

24. *Guideposts*, pp. 341–342; in Siegel, ibid., pp. 44–45.

25. *Guideposts*, pp. 295, 297.

26. Ibid., p. 298. See p. 292 for his statement on the need to preserve the law as an instrument of attaining morality and piety.

27. Ibid., p. 299.

28. Agus, "Halakhah" (*supra* n. 2), pp. 106–109. There Agus similarly objects to the "reductionism" of Orthodoxy and Reform in restricting Judaism to the Codes or the Prophets and argues instead for "a holistic approach" that uses both those sources as well as all others that have developed within the Jewish tradition and constantly weighs how they should be used in ways appropriate to our times.

29. Agus, *Guideposts* (*supra* n. 10), pp. 300, 303. Agus applies this analysis to *every* aspect of life, as the passage quoted in note 15 above indicates. The objectivity represented by reason is necessary for, and must be balanced by, the subjectivity proper to the particular area of life in question.

30. Ibid., p. 304.

31. Ibid., p. 309.

32. Ibid., pp. 311–312. I have embellished Agus's argument here, emphasizing the choice involved in the Orthodox interpretation of Jewish sources and adding the citation from B. Bava Batra 131a that a judge must decide according to what his own eyes see, but I think that this line of argumentation is very much in keeping with both the letter and the spirit of the arguments Agus himself made.

33. Ibid., p. 316.

34. See, for example, Elliot N. Dorff and Arthur Rosett, *A Living Tree: The Roots and Growth of Jewish Law* (Albany, NY: State University of New York Press, 1988), pp. 402–420.

35. Agus, *Guideposts* (*supra* n. 10), p. 317.

36. Ibid., p. 312.

37. Ibid., Part II, section 2; see also Jacob B. Agus, *The Jewish Quest: Essays on Basic Concepts of Jewish Theology* (New York: Ktav, 1983), pp. 43–86.

38. For a survey of the varying doctrines of revelation within Conservative Judaism, Agus's included, see Elliot N. Dorff, *Conservative Judaism: Our Ancestors to Our Descendants,* 2nd edition (New York: United Synagogue of Conservative Judaism, 1996), pp. 96–150.

39. Agus, "Halakhah" (*supra* n. 2), p. 110.

40. Agus, *Guideposts* (*supra* n. 10), p. 313.

41. Ibid.

42. Ibid, pp. 313–315.

43. Ibid., p. 316.

44. Ibid., pp. 317–318.

45. Most recently, Rabbi Ismar Schorsch, Chancellor of the Jewish Theological Seminary of America, speaking at the biennial convention of the United Synagogue of Conservative Judaism in Dallas, Texas in October 2003 called the "driving *teshuvah*" a "mistake." See Nacha Cattan, "Conservative Head Calls Sabbath-Driving Rule a 'Mistake,'" *The Jewish Forward* (November 7, 2003), pp. 9, 19.

46. Morris Adler, Jacob Agus, and Theodore Friedman, "A Responsum on the Sabbath," *Proceedings of the Rabbinical Assembly,* vol. 14 (1950), pp. 122–123, 130. Reprinted in Mordecai Waxman, ed., *Tradition and Change* (New York: The Burning Bush Press, 1958), 361–362, 368; and, in part, in Dorff, *Conservative Judaism* (*supra* n. 38), pp. 180–181.

47. Ibid., in *Proceedings,* pp. 124–128; in Waxman, pp. 362–366; in Dorff, pp. 181–182.

48. This description of Agus's 1961 reevaluation of the Sabbath responsum comes from his paper, "Reevaluation of the Responsum on the Sabbath," from which all the citations on pp. 152–154 (top) come. It is stored in the Rabbinical Assembly Archives as an unofficial paper submitted to the Committee on Jewish Law and Standards—that is, a paper on which the Committee did not vote. I want to thank Rabbi Gail Labovitz, Administrative Assistant of the Committee on Jewish Law and Standards in 1991–92, for making this paper and the one cited in the next endnote available to me.

49. Jacob B. Agus, "*Re Agunah,*" an undated and unofficial responsum in the Rabbinical Assembly Archives.

50. Jacob B. Agus, "The Mitzvah of Keruv," *Proceedings of the Committee on Jewish Law and Standards of the Conservative Movement, 1980–1985* (New York: Rabbinical Assembly, 1988), p. 147.

51. Agus, "Halakhah" (*supra* n. 2), p. 111. In none of these cases has the Conservative movement formally adopted a *takkanah*. Even in the one case that a rabbi wrote a responsum—namely, Rabbi Max Arzt's *teshuvah* about eating fish in restaurants (1940; see *Proceedings of the Rabbinical Assembly,* 1952, p. 49)—the *teshuvah* was written to justify what had by then become common practice among Conservative rabbis.

52. Ibid., pp. 111–113.

53. Ibid., pp. 115–116.

54. Gordon Tucker, "Final Report of the Commission for the Study of the Ordination of Women as Rabbis," in *The Ordination of Women as Rabbis: Studies and Responsa,* Simon Greenberg, ed. (New York: Jewish Theological Seminary, 1988), pp. 5–30, esp. 5–12.

55. My responsum, entitled "Jewish Norms for Sexual Behavior," was approved by eight of twenty-five members of the Committee on Jewish Law and Standards at its meeting on March 25, 1992; it is published in *Responsa 1991–2000 of the Committee on Jewish Law and Standards of the Conservative Movement,* Kassel Abelson and David Fine, eds. (New York: Rabbinical Assembly, 2002), pp. 696–711. The Rabbinical Assembly, meeting in convention in May 1992, passed a resolution directing its officers to establish such a commission that would report its findings to the Committee on Jewish Law and Standards within two years. See *Proceedings of the Rabbinical Assembly* vol. 54 (1992), pp. 317–318. The Commission produced an educational document on human sexuality (Elliot N. Dorff, *"This Is My Beloved, This Is My Friend": A Rabbinic Letter on Intimate Relations* [New York: Rabbinical Assembly, 1996]) and a report to the Committee on Jewish Law and Standards indicating the aspects of human sexuality which, in the opinion of the Commission, should be addressed anew or reconsidered by the Committee. It is currently doing that through its subcommittee on Marriage and Sexuality. Moreover, in December 2002 and January 2003, respectively, Judy Yudoff, president of the United Synagogue of Conservative Judaism, and Rabbi Reuven Hammer, president of the Rabbinical Assembly, asked the Committee on Jewish Law and Standards to revisit the whole issue, which it is, as of this writing, in the process of doing. In 1992, the Chancellor of the Jewish Theological Seminary and the President of the United Synagogue of Conservative Judaism both refused to get involved in the work of the Commission on Human Sexuality on the grounds that these legal matters should be decided solely by rabbis. Agus would forcefully disagree!

56. See Elliot N. Dorff, "Catholic/Jewish Dialogue: A Jewish Perspective on Vatican Documents," *Ecumenical Trends* (September 1988), pp. 116–120: reprinted in Abraham J. Karp, Louis Jacobs, and Chaim Zalman Dimitrovsky, eds., *Three Score and Ten: Essays in Honor of Rabbi Seymour J. Cohen* (Hoboken, NJ: Ktav, 1991), pp. 283–291. In addition to these documents, Pope John Paul II did more than any other pope in history in striving to achieve *rapprochement* with Jews and Judaism, visiting a synagogue in Rome (the first time that a pope has ever done that) and granting official Vatican recognition to the State of Israel; see Pope John Paul II, *Spiritual Pilgrimage: Texts on Jews and Judaism 1979–1995,* Eugene J. Fisher and Leon Klenicki, eds. (New York: Crossroad, 1995).

57. For a list of the conflicting texts in Heschel on the nature of revelation, see Dorff, *Conservative Judaism (supra* n. 38), p. 258, n. 43.

58. B. Pesaḥim 50b; B. Sotah 22b, 47a; B. Sanhedrin 105b; B. Horayot 10b; B. Arakhin 16b.

59. Abraham Joshua Heschel, *The Prophets* (Philadelphia: Jewish Publication Society, 1962), p. 9.

60. B. Berakhot 13a; B. Rosh Hashanah 28a; Shulḥan Arukh *Oraḥ Ḥayim* 60:4–5; 63:4; 98:1–2; 101:1.

NOTES TO CHAPTER FIVE

1. Edward Feld, *The Spirit of Renewal: Finding Faith after the Holocaust* (Woodstock, VT: Jewish Lights Publishing, 1994), pp. 166–167.

2. Edward Feld, "A Divining Rod Has Two Branches: Choices for the Conservative Movement," *Conservative Judaism* 55:3 (Spring 2003), p. 56.

3. Ibid., p. 57.

4. B. Berakhot 20a; B. Eruvin 100a; B. Yoma 74b; B. Yevamot 90b; etc. See Rashi to B. Berakhot 20a for an explanation of the principle.

5. Hans Kelsen, *General Theory of Law and State,* Anders Wedberg, trans. (Cambridge, MA: Harvard University Press, 1945), p. 115. See also Hans Kelsen, *Pure Theory of Law,* May Knight, trans. (Berkeley and Los Angeles: University of California Press, 1967), pp. 194ff.

6. This is my example, not Roth's.

7. See, for example, B. Berakhot 13a (with regard to saying the Shema); B. Eruvin 95b–96a (with regard to the use of phylacteries); B. Pesaḥim 114b (with regard to the need for two dippings at the seder); B. Rosh Hashanah 27a–29a (especially 28b, with regard to blowing the shofar); and see my discussion on *keva* and *kavanah* in prayer in my book, *Knowing God: Jewish Journeys to the Unknowable* (Northvale, NJ: Jason Aronson, 1992), pp. 177–191. Maimonides takes an extreme position: he rules that even non-Jews have a requirement of proper intention, and they have not fulfilled the seven duties of the Noahide Covenant unless they do so intentionally to fulfill a commandment of God as announced by Moses in the Torah (and not merely as acts their own reason requires); see Mishneh Torah, *Hilkhot Melakhim* 8:11. See also B. Shabbat 72b with regard to the related question of whether one needs to have intention in order to be held liable for violating a law. This latter question had yet a further development that even those who claimed that unintentional violation did not make one liable nevertheless held that one would be liable if one's violation of the law in doing an act was, though unintentional, an inevitable consequence of acting as one did (*pesik reisheh ve'al yamut,* "Can you cut off its [a chicken's] head and expect that it will not die?"); see B. Shabbat 75a, 103a, 111b, 117a, 120b, 133a, 143a; B. Sukkah 33b; B. Ketubot 6b; B. Bekhorot 25a.

8. Umberto Cassuto, *A Commentary on the Book of Exodus* (Jerusalem: Magnes Press [Hebrew University], 1967), pp. 260–264.

9. Menachem Elon, "Codification," *Encyclopedia Judaica* (Jerusalem: Keter, 1972), 5:642–643.

10. Umberto Cassuto has made this point with reference to biblical law codes, which, he says, "should not be regarded as a code of laws, or even as a number of codes, but only as separate instructions on given matters." See Umberto Cassuto, *Exodus* (*supra* n. 8), pp. 260–264. The Babylonian Talmud in Eruvin 27a and Kiddushin 34a expressly objects to treating the Mishnah's general rules as inviolable principles; moreover, in practice it recurrently interprets general principles announced in the Mishnah (with phrases like *zeh haklal*) not as generalizations at all but rather as additions of further specific cases. See Jacob Eliyahu Efrati, *Tekufat ha-Saboraim v'Sifrutah* (Petaḥ Tikvah: Agudat Benai Asher [New York and Jerusalem: Philip Feldheim, Inc. distributor], 1973 [Hebrew]), Part II, pp. 157–278, who points out that the Talmud interprets the phrase this way explicitly sixteen (or possibly eighteen) times among the eighty-five unrepeated instances in the Mishnah where this expression occurs. Efrati also claims that these discussions, limited to the Babylonian Talmud, are saboraic in origin (i.e., from 500–689 C.E.). (I want to thank my colleague at the University of Judaism, Dr. Elieser Slomovic, for this reference.) Sometimes this effort by the Babylonian Talmud to apply the Mishnah's announcement of a general rule to a specific case not yet covered by the Mishnah is specifically introduced by the phrase *zeh haklal le'atuyei mai*, "[When the Mishnah says] 'This is the general rule,' what [specific case] does it come to include?" That occurs eight times in the Talmud: B. Shabbat 103a; B. Eruvin 70b; B. Megillah 21a; B. Shevuot 37b; B. Avodah Zarah 73b; B. Ḥullin 41b, 54a; B. Niddah 57a. With regard to the genre of Jewish codes, its methodological strengths and weaknesses, and its origins in medieval systematics, see Elliot N. Dorff and Arthur Rosett, *A Living Tree: The Roots and Growth of Jewish Law* (Albany, NY: State University of New York Press, 1988), pp. 366–401.

11. Joel Roth, "On the Ordination of Women as Rabbis," in Simon Greenberg, ed., *The Ordination of Women as Rabbis: Studies and Responsa* (New York: The Jewish Theological Seminary of America, 1988), pp. 127–148 (demonstrating that women who take on all the commandments from which traditional Jewish law exempts them may count as part of a prayer quorum and serve as its leader in prayer), pp. 149–162 (that women may not serve as witnesses except by a court with sufficient authority to abrogate the biblical prohibition forbidding that), and p. 171 (urging that the Seminary faculty "openly and knowingly abrogate the prohibition against women serving as witnesses").

12. Ibid., p. 161. See also pp. 376–377 of his book, *The Halakhic Process: A Systemaic Analysis* (New York: Jewish Theological Seminary of America, 1986).

13. The Hanukkah story: I Maccabees, chapters 1–4. The talmudic story of Rabbi Yoḥanan ben Zakkai: B. Gittin 56a–b.

14. Martin Buber, *Two Types of Faith*, Norman P. Goldhawk, trans. (London: Routledge and Kegan Paul, 1951), esp. pp. 26–29, 170–174 (reprinted New York: Harper and Brothers, 1961), pp. 28–29 and the last few pages. Buber

also discusses this distinction in his *Eclipse of God: Studies in the Relation between Religion and Philosophy* (New York: Harper and Brothers, 1952), chapters 2–4, but he does not use the terms *pistis* and *emunah* there.

15. Lawrence Kotler-Berkowitz, Steven M. Cohen, Jonathon Ament, Vivian Klaff, Frank Mott, and Danyelle Peckerman-Neuman, *The National Jewish Population Survey 2000–2001* (New York: United Jewish Communities, 2003), pp. 7–8, 15–19 (available at www.ujc.org/njps).

16. Louis Jacobs, *A Tree of Life: Diversity, Flexibility, and Creativity in Jewish Law* (London: The Littman Library of Jewish Civilization, Oxford University Press, 1984), p. 239.

17. Louis Jacobs, *Faith* (New York: Basic Books, 1968), pp. 107–109. See also his book, *A Jewish Theology* (New York: Behrman House, 1973), chapter 14.

18. Jacobs, *A Tree of Life* (*supra* n. 16), pp. 239, 242.

19. Ibid., p. 242.

20. Ibid., p. 245.

21. Ibid., p. 246.

22. For a further discussion of Jacobs's approach to Judaism in general and Jewish law in particular, see my article, "Louis Jacobs," in *Interpreters of Judaism in the Late Twentieth Century*, Steven T. Katz, ed. (Washington, D.C.: B'nai Brith Books, 1993), pp. 167–188.

23. For further discussion of this topic, see chapter one and especially the appendix in my book, *Love Your Neighbor and Yourself: A Jewish Approach to Modern Personal Ethics* (Philadelphia: Jewish Publication Society, 2003), and see also appendix B in my book, *To Do the Right and the Good* (Philadelphia: Jewish Publication Society, 2002).

24. B. Yevamot 5b.

25. See Appendix B in my book, *To Do the Right and the Good* (*supra* n. 23) on the positive and negative interactions between law and morality, and see chapter one and the appendix in my book, *Love Your Neighbor and Yourself* (*supra* n. 23), for the ways in which religion can be both a negative and positive force in producing moral sensitivity and action and the ways in which law contributes to morality.

26. For a description of these moral theories, see my book, *Love Your Neighbor and Yourself* (*supra* n. 23), chapter one.

27. Aaron Mackler, "Cases and Principles in Jewish Bioethics: Toward a Holistic Model," in Elliot N. Dorff and Louis E. Newman, eds., *Contemporary Jewish Ethics and Morality: A Reader* (New York: Oxford University Press, 1995), pp. 177–193.

NOTES TO CHAPTER SIX

1. Depicting God as Groom and Israel as His bride was first suggested by the Prophet Hosea (2:4, 9, 18, 21–22). This imagery was also used by Isaiah (e.g., 54:5–8; 62:4–5), and later applied by Rabbi Akiva to the whole book

of Song of Songs (Avot D'Rabbi Natan, chapter 1). Hosea, of course, is complaining about Israel's adultery in going after foreign gods, but in doing so, he depicts God and the People Israel as husband and wife.

2. My earlier article (which I almost used for this volume), "Judaism as a Religious Legal System," *Hastings Law Journal* 29:6 (July, 1978), pp. 1331–1360, includes a more detailed description of the ways in which Jewish law is like a secular legal system and the ways in which it is distinctly religious.

3. David Ellenson, "How to Draw Guidance from a Heritage: Jewish Approaches to Mortal Choices," in *A Time to Be Born and a Time to Die: The Ethics of Choice*, Barry Kogan, ed. (New York: Aldine de Gruyter, 1990), pp. 219–232; reprinted in *Contemporary Jewish Ethics and Morality: A Reader*, Elliot N. Dorff and Louis E. Newman, eds. (New York: Oxford University Press, 1995), pp. 129–139. Eugene Borowitz, *Renewing the Covenant* (Philadelphia: Jewish Publication Society, 1990), esp. pp. 284–299, reprinted in Dorff and Newman, ibid., pp. 106–117.

4. While this appears in one way or another in many of the Rabbis' actual applications of the Torah, B. Bava Metzia 59b is probably the most graphic rabbinic assertion of their exclusive power. See discussion in chapter 2 above, pp. 36–38.

5. B. Berakhot 7a.

6. For more on the relationship between morality and God's law in biblical and rabbinic sources, see Elliot N. Dorff and Arthur Rosett, *A Living Tree: The Roots and Growth of Jewish Law* (Albany, NY: State University of New York Press and New York: Jewish Theological Seminary of America, 1988), pp. 110–123 and 249–257. For more on my own approach to the theological problem of evil, see my book, *Knowing God: Jewish Journeys to the Unknowable* (Northvale, NJ: Jason Aronson, 1992), chapter 5.

7. Louis E. Newman, "Ethics as Law, Law as Religion: Reflections on the Problem of Law and Ethics in Judaism," *Shofar* 9:1 (Fall 1990), pp. 13–31; reprinted in *Contemporary Jewish Ethics and Morality: A Reader* (*supra* n. 3), pp. 79–93.

8. For why I think that pluralism is warranted and even necessary, see my book, *To Do the Right and the Good: A Modern Approach to Social Ethics* (Philadelphia: Jewish Publication Society, 2002), chapters 2 and 3. For earlier articulations of my thoughts on pluralism, see my articles, "Pluralism," in *Frontiers of Jewish Thought*, Steven Katz, ed. (Washington, D.C.: B'nai Brith, 1992), pp. 213–234, and "Pluralism: Models for the Conservative Movement," *Conservative Judaism* 48:1 (Fall 1995), pp. 21–35.

9. Carol Gilligan, *In a Different Voice* (Cambridge, MA: Harvard University Press, 1982); Nel Noddings, *Caring: A Feminist Approach to Ethics and Moral Education* (Berkeley, CA: University of California Press, 1984); Deborah Tannen, *You Just Don't Understand: Women and Men in Conversation* (New York: Ballantine Books, 1990).

10. B. Berakhot 20b; B. Shabbat 31b; Mishneh Torah *Hilkhot Avodah Zarah*

(Laws of Idolatry) 12:3; Mishneh Torah *Hilkhot Shabbat* (Laws of the Sabbath) 3:5; Shulḥan Arukh. *Oraḥ Ḥayyim* 263:2, 271:2.

11. See Elliot N. Dorff, *Love Your Neighbor and Yourself: A Jewish Approach to Modern Personal Ethics* (Philadelphia: Jewish Publication Society, 2003), pp. 127–154.

12. Franz Rosenzweig, "The Builders," in *On Jewish Learning*, Nahum Glatzer, trans. (New York: Schocken, 1955), pp. 75–91.

13. *Rabbinical Assembly Proceedings 1985*, pp. 208–209.

14. For example, Genesis 6:5–8; Exodus 32:9–14; Numbers 14:11–20.

NOTES TO CHAPTER SEVEN

1. Elliot Dorff, *Conservative Judaism: Our Ancestors to Our Descendants* (New York: United Synagogue of Conservative Judaism, 1977; 2d revised edition, 1996), chapter 3, Section D.

2. Yeshayahu Leibowitz, *Judaism, Human Values, and the Jewish State* (Cambridge, MA: Harvard University Press, 1992), p. 16.

3. Ibid., pp. 14, 259.

4. Ibid., p. 31.

5. Ibid., p. 13. At the end of this quotation, Leibowitz is quoting the oft-repeated position of Rabbi Ḥanina in B. Kiddushin 31a; B. Bava Kamma 38a, 87a; and B. Avodah Zarah 3a.

6. Sifra 9:10 on Leviticus 20:26.

7. Leibowitz, *Judaism, Human Values, and the Jewish State* (*supra* n. 2), p. 11.

8. Ibid., p. 7.

9. Ibid., p. 8.

10. Ibid., p. 23.

11. Ibid.

12. For a detailed discussion of those, see my book, *Mitzvah Means Commandment* (New York: United Synagogue of America, 1989).

13. B. Menaḥot 29b.

14. Leibowitz, *Judaism, Human Values, and the Jewish State* (*supra* n. 2), p. 12.

15. B. Pesaḥim 50b; B. Sotah 22b, 47a; B. Sanhedrin 105b; B. Horayot 10b; B. Arakhin 16b.

16. Leibowitz, *Judaism, Human Values, and the Jewish State* (*supra* n. 2), p. 3.

17. Ibid., p. 4.

18. Ibid.

19. Ibid., p. 19.

20. Ibid. See Leviticus 19:18 for the commandment.

21. Ibid., p. 6.

22. Ibid., p. 11.

23. In my book, *Matters of Life and Death: A Jewish Approach to Modern Medical Ethics* (Philadelphia: Jewish Publication Society, 1998), p. 423, n. 30, I tell the first story I ever heard about Jewish law, one that I retell on p. 361, n. 29 of this volume.
24. Leibowitz, *Judaism, Human Values, and the Jewish State* (*supra* n. 2), p. 128.
25. Ibid, p. 129.
26. Ibid.
27. David Hartman, *A Living Covenant: The Innovative Spirit in Traditional Judaism* (New York: Free Press, 1985; reprinted by Woodstock, VT: Jewish Lights, 1997), p. 3.
28. Ibid.
29. Ibid., p. 4.
30. See Chapter 6, n. 1, above.
31. Hartman, *A Living Covenant* (*supra* n. 27), p. 5.
32. Ibid., pp. 4–5.
33. Ibid., pp. 8, 14–15.
34. Ibid., pp. 102–103.
35. Ibid., p. 105.
36. Ibid., pp. 14, 105, 107.
37. Ibid., p. 98.
38. Ibid., p. 96.
39. Ibid., p. 98.
40. Ibid., p. 99.
41. Ibid., p. 97.
42. Ibid., p. 96.
43. Ibid., p. 97.
44. Ibid., p. 18.
45. All of the platform statements of the Central Conference of American Rabbis can be accessed at www.ccarnet.org/platforms.
46. No author listed; this was the work of a commission chaired by Robert Gordis: *Emet Ve-emunah: Statement of Principles of Conservative Judaism* (New York: Jewish Theological Seminary of America, Rabbinical Assembly, United Synagogue of America, Women's League for Conservative Judaism, Federations of Jewish Men's Clubs, 1988), p. 23.
47. B. Kiddushin 40b.
48. *Emet Ve-emunah* (at note 46 above), p. 23.
49. Ibid., p. 25.
50. Joe Berkofsky, "Conservative Death Prophecy Draws Fire," *Jewish Telegraphic Agency*, March 5, 2004. Menitoff's essay appeared in the newsletter of the Central Conference of American Rabbis, which is available in print and online only to its members.
51. "Custom Drives Jewish Law on Women," *Conservative Judaism* 49:3 (Spring 1997), pp. 3–21. Response to critics: *Conservative Judaism* 51:1

(Fall 1998), pp. 66–73. Reprinted in *Gender Issues in Jewish Law: Essays and Responsa*, Walter Jacob and Moshe Zemer, eds. (New York: Berghahn Books, 2001), pp. 82–106.

52. Clifford Librach, "Does Conservative Judaism Have a Future?" *Commentary* 106:3 (September 1998), pp. 28–33. My response: Letter to the Editor, *Commentary* 107:1 (January 1999), pp. 3, 5, 6.

53. Ibid., p. 6.

54. See the Society's website at www.shj.org. It publishes a quarterly journal, *Humanistic Judaism,* and its website lists a number of books that explain its philosophy of Judaism.

55. Arthur Waskow, *Down-to-Earth Judaism: Food, Money, Sex, and the Rest of Life* (New York: William Morrow, 1995), p. 120.

56. Ibid., p. 122.

57. Ibid., p. 123.

58. Ibid. This is very much like the insight of Rabbi Harold M. Schulweis, in his essay, "Judaism: From Either/Or to Both/And," in *Contemporary Jewish Ethics and Morality: A Reader,* Elliot N. Dorff and Louis E. Newman, eds. (New York: Oxford University Press, 1995), pp. 25–37. Schulweis, though, maintains that that pluralistic approach was characteristic of the Rabbis of the Mishnah, Talmud, and Midrash, while Waskow seems to think that such an approach is an innovation needed to face the problems of today.

59. Ibid., p. 310.

60. Wade Clark Roof, *A Generation of Seekers: The Spiritual Journeys of the Baby Boom Generation* (San Francisco: HarperCollins, 1993).

61. Arthur Green, *Judaism for the Post-Modern Era* (Cincinnati: Hebrew Union College Press, 1995), p. 10.

62. Ibid.

63. Ibid., pp. 12–13.

64. Ibid., p. 13.

NOTES TO CHAPTER EIGHT

1. Morris Adler, Jacob Agus, and Theodore Friedman, "A Responsum on the Sabbath," in Mordecai Waxman, ed., *Tradition and Change: The Development of Conservative Judaism* (New York: Burning Bush Press, 1958), pp. 351–374; reprinted in substantial part in Elliot N. Dorff, *Conservative Judaism: Our Ancestors to Our Descendants* (New York: United Synagogue of Conservative Judaism, 1996), pp. 177–185; reprinted in its entirety in David Golinkin, ed., *Proceedings of the Committee on Jewish Law and Standards of the Conservative Movement, 1927–1970* (New York: Rabbinical Assembly, 1997), 3:1109–1134. This citation appears in Waxman, pp. 353–354; in Dorff, p. 178; in Golinkin, p. 1111.

2. In Waxman, p. 360; not in the selections in Dorff; in Golinkin, p. 1118.

3. In Waxman, p. 361; in Dorff, p. 180; in Golinkin, p. 1119.

4. In Waxman, pp. 360–361; in Dorff, pp. 179–180; in Golinkin, p. 1119.

5. In Waxman, p. 360; not in the selections in Dorff; in Golinkin, p. 1118.

6. In Waxman, pp. 370–371; in Dorff, p. 184; in Golinkin, p. 1129.

7. In Waxman, p. 362; in Dorff, p. 181; in Golinkin, p. 1121.

8. In Waxman, p. 363; not in the selections in Dorff; in Golinkin, p. 1122.

9. The principle of *tafasta merubbah lo tafasta* appears in B. Yoma 80a. The principle of *tov asarah tefaḥim ve'omed mimeah tefaḥim venofel* is in Avot D'Rabbi Natan 1:7.

10. Adler, Agus, and Friedman (*supra* n. 1): in Waxman, p. 365; not in the selections in Dorff; in Golinkin, p. 1124.

11. In Waxman, p. 360; in Dorff, p. 179; in Golinkin, p. 1119.

12. Jacob Agus, "Reevaluation of the Responsum on the Sabbath," an unofficial paper submitted to the CJLS and stored in the Rabbinical Assembly archives; quoted in my article on Agus's philosophy of law, "Jewish Law as Standards," in *American Rabbi: The Life and Thought of Jacob B. Agus,* Steven T. Katz, ed. (New York: New York University Press, 1997), p. 216.

13. Adler, Agus, and Friedman (*supra* n. 1); in Waxman, p. 364; in Dorff, p. 181; in Golinkin, p. 1122–1123.

14. Rabbi Moses Isserles, Responsa #21.

15. Gordon Tucker, "Final Report of the Commission for the Study of the Ordination of Women as Rabbis," in *The Ordination of Women as Rabbis: Studies and Responsa,* Simon Greenberg, ed. (New York: The Jewish Theological Seminary of America, 1988), p. 3.

16. Ibid., p. 10.

17. Ibid., p. 13.

18. Ibid., pp. 20–21 (italics in the original).

19. Ibid., p. 21.

20. Ibid.

21. Ibid.

22. Ibid., pp. 24–25.

23. Joel Roth, "On the Ordination of Women as Rabbis," in Greenberg, ed., *The Ordination of Women as Rabbis (supra* n. 15), p. 157.

24. Ibid., p. 171.

25. Ibid., p. 166.

26. Ibid., p. 171.

27. Ibid., p. 172.

28. See *Proceedings of the Committee on Jewish Law and Standards of the Conservative Movement 1980–1985* (New York: Rabbinical Assembly, 1988), p. 269.

29. *Summary Index of the Committee on Jewish Law and Standards* (New York: Rabbinical Assembly, 1998), p. 14:1.

30. Aaron Blumenthal, "The Status of Women in Jewish Law," *Conservative Judaism* 31:3 (Spring 1977), pp. 33–34. Reprinted in David R. Blumenthal, ed., *And Bring Them Closer to Torah: The Life and Works of Rabbi Aaron H. Blumenthal* (Hoboken, NJ: Ktav, 1986), p. 35.

31. M. Eduyot 1:12, 6:1, 8:5; M. Yevamot 16:7; B. Yevamot 116b.

32. *Encyclopedia Talmudit* (Hebrew), "*Ishah*," 2:252–253.

33. B. Ketubot 72a; B. Gittin 2b.

34. Shulḥan Arukh, *Ḥoshen Mishpat* 28; Rabbi Uziel's ruling is cited in Menachem Elon, *Jewish Law: History, Sources, Principles* (Philadelphia: Jewish Publication Society, 1994), p. 1602. The original material is in Warhaftig, *Osef Piskei Ha-Din*, pp. 137–138.

35. Myron Geller, "Woman Is Eligible to Testify," pp. 38–39 of the typescript.

36. Deuteronomy 23:3.

37. Aaron Mackler, "Women as Witnesses," p. 11 in the typescript. The citations from Faden and Beauchamp come from their book, *A History and Theory of Informed Consent* (New York: Oxford University Press, 1986), pp. 12, 18. Rabbi Mackler quotes Rabbi Spitzer's comments from a written communication with her on March 28, 2001, quoted with her permission.

38. Ibid., p. 13.

39. See note 30 above for the publication information for Rabbi Blumenthal's paper. Because they were all approved by the CJLS, the papers by Rabbis Spitz, Geller, and Grossman can all be found at www.rabbinicalassembly.org. Rabbi Mackler's paper can be procured from him directly at mackler@duq.edu.

40. Exodus 21:22–23; M. Ohalot 7:6. The most thorough treatment of abortion in Jewish law remains that of Rabbi David M. Feldman, *Abortion in Jewish Law* (New York: New York University Press, 1968); reprinted as *Marital Relations, Birth Control, and Abortion in Jewish Law* (New York: Schocken, 1973); and reprinted again, with some revisions, as *Birth Control in Jewish Law: Marital Relations, Contraception, and Abortion as Set Forth in the Classic Jewish Texts of Jewish Law* (Northvale, NJ: Jason Aronson, 1998). For the CJLS responsa on abortion, see *Proceedings of the Committee on Jewish Law and Standards of the Conservative Movement, 1980–1985* (New York: Rabbinical Assembly, 1988), pp. 3–40, which includes responsa by Kassel Abelson, David Feldman, Robert Gordis, Isaac Klein, and an official CJLS Statement on the Permissibility of Abortion written by Ben Zion Bokser and Kassel Abelson.

41. Debra Reed Blank, "Response to Miscarriage," in *Responsa of the Committee on Jewish Law and Standards of the Conservative Movement, 1991–2000*, Kassel Abelson and David Fine, eds. (New York: Rabbinical Assembly, 2001), p. 358. The full responsum is on pp. 357–363.

42. Ibid., p. 358.

43. Amy Eilberg, "Response to Miscarriage: A Dissent," p. 366, in *Responsa of the CJLS* (at note 41 above). The full dissent is on pp. 364–366.

44. Ibid., p. 364.

45. Ibid., p 365.

46. Ibid.

47. Ibid.

48. Ibid., p. 366.

49. In *Proceedings of the Committee on Jewish Law and Standards of the*

Conservative Movement, 1986–1990 (New York: Rabbinical Assembly, 2001): Avram Israel Reisner, "A Halakhic Ethic of Care for the Terminally Ill," pp. 13–64; Elliot N. Dorff, "A Jewish Approach to End-Stage Medical Care," pp. 65–126. In *Conservative Judaism* 43:3 (Spring 1991): Dorff, pp. 3–51; Reisner, pp. 52–89.

50. Avram Israel Reisner, "Mai Beinaihu? [What is the difference between them?]," *Conservative Judaism* 43:3 (Spring 1991), p. 91; *Proceedings of the Committee on Jewish Law and Standards of the Conservative Movement, 1986–1990* (New York: Rabbinical Assembly, 2001), p. 128.

51. Rabbi Friedman's responsum: *Proceedings of the Rabbinical Assembly 1953*, pp. 41–44. Rabbi Klein's responsum: *Summary Index of the Committee on Jewish Law and Standards*, p. 1:13. For the CJLS responsa on abortion, see note 40 above.

52. Rabbi Moses ben Naḥman (Naḥmanides), *The Holy Letter: A Study in Medieval Sexual Morality*, Seymour J. Cohen, ed. and trans. (New York: Ktav, 1976). Some scholars are not certain about the authorship of that letter, but it has been traditionally attributed to Naḥmanides. Similarly, there is a manual by Maimonides that gives advice to husbands as to how to stimulate and sustain an erection: *On Sexual Intercourse (Fi 'l-jima)*, Morris Gorlin, trans. (Brooklyn: Rambash Publishing Company, 1961). There is also a larger edition of that work, printed in the same book, which Gorlin thinks is spurious and is rather the work of another Jewish physician of the fourteenth century. In any case, that work additionally advises husbands on how to stimulate sexual interest in their wives and counsels women on how to maintain the health of their breasts. Rabbi Abraham ben David of Posquieres is commonly accepted as the author of *Ba'alei Ha-Nefesh* (Y. Kafah, ed., Jerusalem, 1964), which, in its first six chapters, is a code dealing with family law, but in the seventh chapter changes tone and audience and becomes an ethical tract that describes the moral norms and pious dispositions that enable a man to achieve self-control in sexual matters and to attain purity of heart and action in this part of life.

53. Orthodox rabbis, for example, are increasingly getting questions from unmarried couples who are living together about the necessity of *mikvah* and the like, and it is no longer a secret that family violence is at least as common among the Orthodox as it is among the other streams of Judaism. The Jewish Family Service of Los Angeles, for example, has a special program to combat family violence within the Orthodox community. The most scientific study of American sexual behavior indicates that Jews have more sexual partners between the ages of 18 and 44 than any other American religious group, including even the unchurched: Robert T. Michael, John H. Gagnon, Edward O. Laumann, and Gina Kolata, *Sex in America: A Definitive Survey* (Boston: Little, Brown, and Company, 1994), p. 103. This may well be because Jews tend to go to college and even graduate school in large numbers and therefore marry later, but, even so, this finding, as well as the phenomena mentioned above, clearly indicates that for

the observant as well as for those not so, the current situation among Jews with regard to sexuality and family relations is considerably different from the norms of Jewish law and well worth a fresh look as to how Judaism can inform our behavior, thought, and feelings in this area in our own day.

54. For example, Numbers 15:1, 17, 37.

55. Deuteronomy 31:12.

56. That parents must teach their children: Deuteronomy 6:7. The Rabbis (B. Kiddushin 30a) deduce that grandparents also have a duty to teach their grandchildren from Deuteronomy 4:9: "Take utmost care and watch yourselves scrupulously, so that you do not forget the things that you saw with your own eyes and so that they do not fade from your mind as long as you live. And make them known to your children and to your children's children." The establishment of schools by Rabbi Yehoshua ben Gamla: B. Bava Batra 21a. On this duty generally, see my book, *Love Your Neighbor and Yourself: A Jewish Approach to Modern Personal Ethics* (Philadelphia: Jewish Publication Society, 2003), pp. 143–150.

INDEX

End-notes, footnotes, preface, and all sources and citations are not indexed.

PERMISSIONS

I WOULD LIKE TO THANK the authors and/or publishers for permission to reprint the following articles:

1. Zacharias Frankel, "On Changes in Judaism," in *Tradition and Change: The Development of Conservative Judaism*, Mordecai Waxman, ed. (New York: Rabbinical Assembly, 1958), pp. 43–50.
2. Solomon Schechter, "Excerpts from the Seminary Addresses of Solomon Schechter," in *Tradition and Change: The Development of Conservative Judaism*, Mordecai Waxman, ed. (New York: Rabbinical Assembly, 1958), pp. 99–109.
3. Mordecai M. Kaplan, "Unity in Diversity in the Conservative Movement," in *Tradition and Change: The Development of Conservative Judaism*, Mordecai Waxman, ed. (New York: Rabbinical Assembly, 1958), pp. 211–228.
4. Robert Gordis, "Authority in Jewish Law," *Proceedings of the Rabbinical Assembly*, 41–44: 64–93; reprinted in Seymour Siegel, *Conservative Judaism and Jewish Law* (New York: Rabbinical Assembly, 1977), pp. 50–78.
5. Mordecai M. Kaplan, "Reply," in his *Questions Jews Ask: Reconstructionist Answers* (New York: Reconstructionist Press, 1956), pp. 264–276.
6. Abraham Joshua Heschel, "Toward an Understanding of Halachah," in Seymour Siegel, *Conservative Judaism and Jewish Law* (New York: Rabbinical Assembly, 1977), pp. 134–151.
7. Edward Feld, "Towards an Aggadic Judaism," *Conservative Judaism* 29:3 (Spring 1975), pp. 79–84.
8. Joel Roth, *The Halakhic Process: A Systemic Analysis* (New York: Jewish Theological Seminary of America, 1986), pp. 1–12; 231–234; 302–315; 375–377.
9. Neil Gillman, *Sacred Fragments: Recovering Theology for the Modern Jew* (Philadelphia: Jewish Publication Society, 1990), pp. 44–47; 54–60; 224; 228–236.
10. Louis Jacobs, *Beyond Reasonable Doubt* (London, England and Portland, Oregon: The Littman Library of Jewish Civilization, Vallentine Mitchell & Co., Inc., 1999), pp. 106–131.

.is Jacobs, *A Jewish Theology* (New York: Behrman House, 1973), pp. .24–232; 237–242 .

David M. Gordis, *Halacha as Process: The Jewish Path to the Good Life* (Los Angeles: University of Judaism, 1983), pp. 1–16.

13. Elliot N. Dorff, "Appendix: The Philosophical Foundations of My Approach to Bioethics," in his *Matters of Life and Death: A Jewish Approach to Modern Medical Ethics* (Philadelphia: Jewish Publication Society, 1998), pp. 395–417.

14. Alana Suskin, "A Feminist Theory of Halakhah," published for the first time in this volume.

15. Raymond P. Scheindlin, "The Inner Art of Prayer," published for the first time in this volume.

16. Gordon Tucker, "A Principled Defense of the Current Structure and Status of the Committee on Jewish Law and Standards," in *Responsa 1991–2000 of the Committee on Jewish Law and Standards of the Conservative Movement*, Kassel Abelson and David J. Fine, eds. (New York: Rabbinical Assembly, 2002), pp. 759–772.

17. Elliot N. Dorff, "Autonomy vs. Community: The Ongoing Reform/Conservative Difference," *Conservative Judaism* 48:2 (Winter 1996), pp. 64–68.

18. Eugene B. Borowitz, "The Reform Judaism of *Renewing the Covenant:* An Open Letter to Elliot Dorff," *Conservative Judaism* 50:1 (Fall 1997), pp. 61–65.

19. Elliot N. Dorff, "Matters of Degree and Kind: An Open Letter to Eugene Borowitz's Open Letter to Me," *Conservative Judaism* 50:1 (Fall 1997), pp. 66–71.